First published in the United Kingdom by Brookmark Publications 2009
A Division of Quayside Creative Limited
ISBN 978-0-9556733-4-4

1, The Quayside, Nantwich Marina, Chester Road,
Nantwich, Cheshire, CW5 8LB
Email: info@quaysidecreative.co.uk
Tel: 01270 610397

When They Were KINGS

The Crewe Speedway Story

Mark Potts, Tony Marks, Kev Tew & Andy Scoffin

- Introduction -

The Crewe speedway story evolved sometime in 1968 when Maurice Littlechild and Len Silver of Allied Presentations Limited (APL) tentatively enquired about the possibilities of bringing speedway to the South Cheshire area. APL were a group of established promoters with individual holdings at various tracks in the British Speedway Leagues, but were keen for further venues, especially in areas where speedway was not currently being staged. This made the town of Crewe a tempting prospect, as, since the demise of the Stoke Potters team at Sun Street, Hanley in 1963; the area was devoid of speedway. Littlechild set the wheels in motion by asking Ken Adams, a former Stoke rider and owner of a service station in Winterley, just a few miles from the town, to try and locate the old track in Crewe, where several pioneer dirt track meetings had been held in the very early days of the sport. It didn't take him long to find the old circuit and report back that it still existed. Without delay, Littlechild and Silver were on their way up from London and found themselves at the British Rail owned L.M.R. Sports Ground situated just off Earle Street in the town. Here they found a cricket pitch, surrounded by a cinder running track and a banked shale cycling track. After much debate, in a smoky room in the Crewe Arms Hotel, the directors of APL voted to go ahead with the project. Following an agreement with the railway authorities, a planning application was submitted along with a request to join Division II of the British League, which was soon accepted, but with one major drawback – they didn't yet have a stadium or a proper track to race on. So Littlechild approached New Zealander Colin Tucker, a master carpenter and builder by trade (who had ridden for Silver at Rayleigh and had won the 1968 "Stars Of Tomorrow" meeting at King's Lynn) to offer him the construction job. Tucker jumped at the opportunity and moved up to Crewe, taking residence in a caravan in what would become the riders car park. On January 14, planning application No. TP4315 (use of stadium for speedway racing), was enthusiastically given the green light at a meeting of the Crewe Town Council. Tucker had just four months to complete all the work, if Crewe were to compete in the 1969 campaign. APL stumped up around £10,000 for the project, with British Rail one of the first to help out by offering 2,000 railway sleepers for the safety and perimeter fencing. A sawmill in Betley milled them into sizes required for posts, rails and boards and Tucker then began the monumental task of constructing the fence and stadium facilities. Using five cwt. of nails, he first constructed the perimeter fence, and then used the smaller sleepers for the safety fence, which were spruced up with 420 gallons of red and white paint (red for the perimeter and white for the safety) to complete the job. Endless lorry loads of shale from Arbury Quarries (near Coventry) were delivered for the racing surface which was to be 470 yards in length, making it the biggest, fastest and scariest speedway track in Britain! Tucker worked 10-12 hours every day and slowly but surely the 8,000 capacity stadium began to take shape. Ken Adams was appointed general and team manager and Tucker the captain. Following a local competition, the team were christened "Crewe Kings," a more than appropriate name considering the new stadium was situated adjacent to King Street and one of the nearest public houses was the Kings Arms! Team colours were announced as red with a single white crown. By begging and borrowing, the essential equipment for the stadium and track arrived. The turnstiles were salvaged by Littlechild from the old Greenfield Stadium in Bradford (delivered by Rob Jackson, who lived in the city and would actually go on to ride for Crewe) and starting gate was supplied courtesy of APL director and Oxford promoter Danny Dunton. Incredibly in just sixteen weeks, the work was completed in time for the grand opening on May 19. What followed was a seven year story of highs and lows, thrills and spills, and many lasting memories for the sporting folk of this famous old railway town.

- Foreword -

I went to watch my very first speedway meeting at Wolverhampton in 1962 and have never been so excited and impressed with any sport in my life. I was hooked from the very first race and a new ambition in my young life began. From fan, to organising supporters to away matches, to track staff, and eventually I became a contracted speedway rider. Prior to the historic new venture at Earle Street, I had been mainly involved at my local Wolverhampton track, including a brief loan spell at Crayford. I decided on a move and signed for Leicester Lions whose promotion was part of the Allied Presentations group of tracks. Early in 1969 Leicester informed me I would be going out on loan to a new venture at Second Division Crewe. At this time my engines were being prepared by Scottish International Ken McKinlay and Crewe's first ever match was a challenge away at Middlesbrough. The bike set up and the awkward tight turns of Cleveland Park resulted in two heavy falls and only two points...oh – and a broken toe! I had surgery on my foot before the team met again for our first league match at Reading. Despite not being fully fit I won the first race and the team went on to give a good account of themselves, taking the much fancied "Racers" to a last heat decider. It did not help when I spoke to my partner Ian Bottomley (now married to my ex-wife) before the crucial final race, telling him I would take the Reading pair wide on the first turn, only to find out I was talking to Mick Bell – a Reading rider! We were covered in wet shale, race jackets were hard to see, and we didn't know each other that well! The first home meeting at Crewe was also the first time that most of the boys had seen the track – and what a track! Most riders had never seen such a huge raceway and without a doubt, most riders, including our own boys, did not have their bikes set up for such high speeds and race lines. I can remember the meeting so clearly. A massive crowd had turned out to see this spectacular sport at a track built around the British Rail cricket pitch! The match was a challenge against Rayleigh Rockets and we all gained valuable experience as the meeting unfolded. One Crewe rider stood out however – the Australian Geoff Curtis. From this meeting on, Crewe established a significant home advantage on the fast and often spectacular track. Team spirit was as important then as it is now and the boys always got together for a quick drink at the Borough Arms – where Geoff lodged, or the Kings Arms across the road. The teams and results over the following years are well covered by the writers of this book, but of course 1972 will always be remembered for our championship and cup double success, with a team that will go down in history. We all became friends, friends and team mates none of us will ever forget. There was individual success too for Phil Crump, so dominant in the league that magical season of 1972. The other members of the team played their part as well and I remember a vital and surprising 5-1 by Gary Moore and myself at Canterbury that helped us clinch a vital away win at a crucial stage of the season. The season ended happily for me with a 15 point maximum in the Chester Vase Individual end of season classic. This special season was set in stone, when in 2001 Crewe & Nantwich Borough Council invited some of the team to accept "The Sporting Roll of Honour Award" in recognition of that fabulous year when the Crewe speedway team really did become Kings. I became involved in the management side at Crewe in the last years of the club after being let down by a new promoter, who disappeared after a few meetings. Luckily Allied Presentations kept the club alive until attendances dropped to such an extent that the Kings had to close their doors. During the years at Crewe we sadly remember Geoff Curtis – who died after a bad fall riding in his native Australia. Geoff and I got on really well – he lent me his bike to race for Young England against Young Czechoslovakia, and we won (well almost he alone) the Best Pairs meeting at Middlesbrough. He left Crewe and eventually joined Reading before that fateful crash. I remember too Jack Millen, a giant of a character who was killed in a car accident, but the memories go on and on. Names like Dave Morton, the Collins boys, John Jackson, Peter Saunders, Peter Seaton, Rob Jackson, Barry Meeks, Paul O'Neil, Colin Tucker, Dai Evans, Don Beecroft and many more will all be mentioned with great affection and Phil Crump and his son Jason are still very much on the scene today. I have always thought that sport is so competitive, that it can be a stepping stone to success in any business – for me and many others that has been the case. After Crewe closed I joined Wolverhampton as General and Team Manager – signing seventeen-year-old Hans Nielsen in the process – later to become multi-World Champion. Today I run a coach tour business from the West Midlands and our interest remains as main team sponsors of Wolverhampton Speedway. So much research has gone into preparing this book that I hope it brings back a few sad but mainly happy memories of that golden age of speedway for the team based at Earle Street Stadium – the Crewe Kings.

Dave Parry

- A Night At The Races -

The L.M.R. Sports Ground played a very important part in my life as I was growing up. I went from standing on the terrace as a spectator during the speedway years, to becoming a member of the track staff alongside my father Norman, working on the pit gate fence, and finally racing a BriSCA Formula 1 during the stock car days. Crewe Speedway was; and still is; very special to me. As a kid I lived for my Monday night visit to Earle Street with my father. A short five minute walk from where we lived in Meredith Street would see us reach the turnstiles (William Street entrance in the early years, then Rainbow Street, once they were built on the town bend next to the bowling green), purchase a programme, then round to the pits, generally stopping to pick up a photo from the souvenir shop at the cricket pavilion. The sight of the riders resplendent in their leathers, boots, scarves and body colours, the sounds and smell exuding from those unsilenced exhaust pipes as the bikes were being warmed up was addictive. Approaching start time we would be stood in our usual position at the end of the back straight, awaiting the riders, track staff and Red Cross members to march out to the tones of *Entry of the Gladiators*. Following the introduction of the riders and practice starts, it was on with the racing. As the interval arrived it was round to the tea hut which was handily situated directly behind us for refreshments to lubricate my dry throat, after all those war cries orchestrated by the infamous "Cats Choir," then over to the start line to watch the second half races. A quick thumbs up to the rider going off gate four would generally prompt a wink or nod. I could almost reach over the boards and touch him. The one consequence of standing this close to the action was that you got covered in flying shale as the bikes roared from the tapes. Once the last race had been run, it was time to head for home, but not before stopping for a hamburger or hot dog from the lady with the red and white (suitable colour scheme) mini-van which was usually parked just outside the stadium in William Street.....happy days! I was fortunate to witness many of the sports great riders and characters grace the Earle Street bowl, non more so than "Crazy" Jack Millen, who I recall riding in pyjamas and body colour on back to front at one meeting! Some were at the twilight of their careers, and some were just starting out. Peter Collins and Michael Lee went on to win the world title. Sadly, Geoff Curtis, Gary Peterson, Tommy Jansson, Kevin Holden, Christer Sjösten, Vic Harding, Nigel Wasley, Roger Parker and Graham Banks (the latter two riding Grasstrack), lost their lives as a result of track crashes, whilst the likes of Graham Miles, Alan Wilkinson, Steve Weatherley and Joe Owen had their careers cut short due to serious injuries.

I sincerely hope you get as much pleasure from reading this book as I have from compiling it alongside Mark, Tony and Andy.

Kev Tew

- Acknowledgments -

We would like to thank the following for helping in the production of this book. *The Speedway Forum*, *Speedway Researcher*, Alan Corbett, Tom Jones, Brian Edge, Dave Fox of the *Crewe Chronicle*, Diane Dyer (Crewe Historical Society), Peterborough supporter Paul Hornsby, Steve Whitehouse, John Massey, Nick Hatton, Keith Halliwell, Norman Tew, Llew Roberts, Glyn Scarbrough, Steve Cook, Graham Tagg, Jules Hornbrook, Alan Heighway, Ken Burnett, John Somerville (Wright Wood Collection), Ian Charles Photography, Steve Brock, and to all riders, track staff and supporters who participated in the interviews, and sent in their memories and treasured photographs, especially Colin Tucker, whose assistance and enthusiasm was invaluable. Apologies to anyone we have missed out, who helped during the production of this book.

- Contents -

The following abbreviations are used in the meeting listings throughout the book:- **(F)** = Fell, **(X)** = Excluded, **(R)** = Engine Failure/Retirement, **(TR)** = Track Record, **(00.0)** = Awarded Race/No Time Available, **(+)** = Bonus Point(s), **(*)** = Guest/Stand-In Rider, ***(R/R)*** = Rider Replacement.

These abbreviations are used in the Rider Averages sections:- **M** = Matches, **R** = Races, **W** = Wins, **Pts** = Points, **BP** = Bonus Points, **Tot** = Total Points, **F** = Full Maximum, **P** = Paid Maximum, **CMA** = Calculated Match Average. Calculated Match Average is Total Points ÷ Rides x 4. Rider in **bold** indicates ever-present.

Please note that all facts and figures for this book have been acquired from the *Speedway Star*, official meeting programmes, and *The Crewe Chronicle* reports. However, on a number of occasions, some details published have been known to be incorrect. Every effort therefore has been made to record, what the authors consider, to be the correct facts and details. All averages for British League and Knock Out Cup matches, league tables and heat totals have been sourced from those published from the official British Speedway Promoters Association records compiler of the time, Bryan Seery.

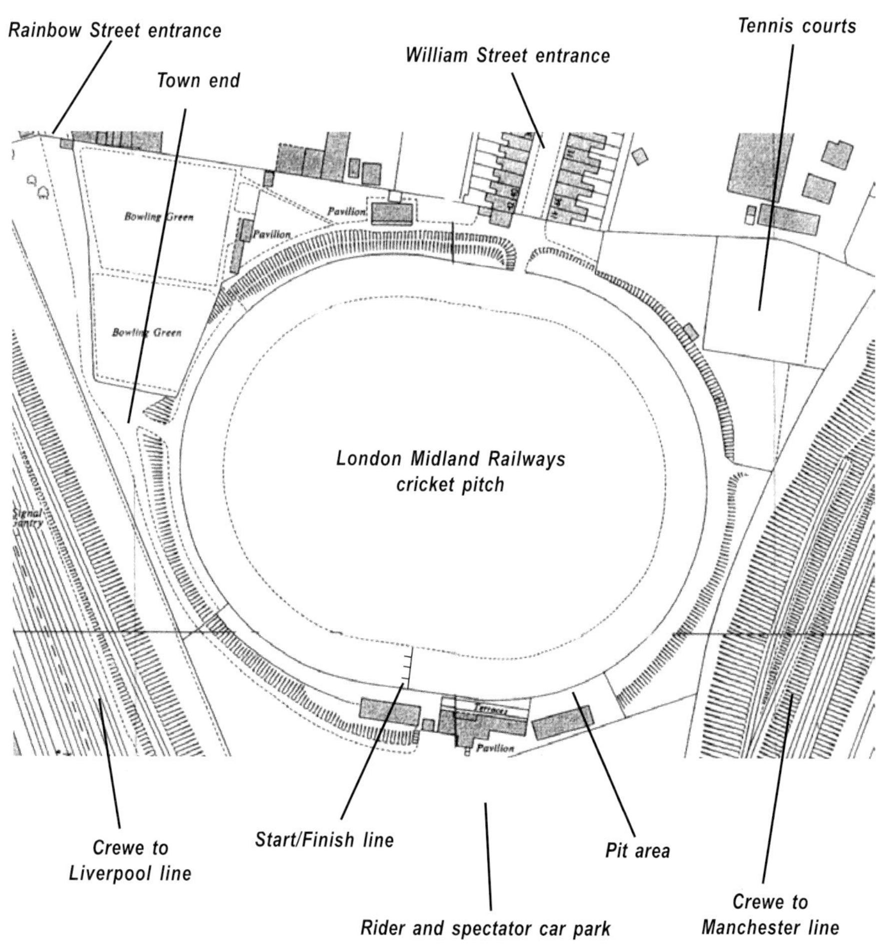

(ABOVE) Map of the L.M.R. Sports Ground (1961), located just off Earle Street, showing future speedway layout.

Colin Tucker, hard at work on the Earle Street safety fence.

The House That Tuck Built

-1969-

The House That Tuck Built

-1969-

The 1969 British Speedway League Division II season would see 16 teams competing. Belle Vue Colts* (defending league champions), Berwick, Canterbury (defending K.O. Cup champions), Crayford, Middlesbrough, Nelson, Plymouth, Rayleigh and Reading from the inaugural 1968 season were joined by Crewe, Doncaster, Eastbourne, Ipswich, King's Lynn Starlets,* Long Eaton and Rochester (who would be replaced by Romford after riding four away matches). Weymouth Eagles were the only non-starters from the previous campaign. The Crewe team meanwhile, had taken shape during the frantic months of track and stadium building. The most prominent signing was Australian international Geoff Curtis, who arrived at Earle Street fresh from helping his country to a 3-2 test series win over England in the 1968/69 season in Australia. Other signings were former Reading riders Pete Saunders and Ian Bottomley, and Bradford carpenter Rob Jackson, who had been noticed after his fine performance in the 1968 "Stars of Tomorrow" meeting at King's Lynn. Midlander Dave Parry, an ex-cycle speedway star, arrived on loan from Leicester, following a number of appearances for Crayford, with Halifax junior Glyn Blackburn and Oxford rider Peter Seaton making up the seven that would start the debut season. Home meetings were to be held on Monday evenings, originally starting at 7.15pm; admission would be 5/- for adults and 3/- for children, with a programme priced at 1/-. On May 1, some six weeks after the start of the speedway season, the Kings would compete in their first fixture. (*Reserve teams of Division I clubs Belle Vue Aces and the King's Lynn Stars.)

Meeting 1 - Thursday, May 1, 1969 - Challenge
Cleveland Park Stadium, Stockton Road, Middlesbrough
Track Length - 335 yards.

MIDDLESBROUGH TEESSIDERS.....52 CREWE KINGS.....26

Crewe's first meeting saw them comprehensively beaten by a Middlesbrough team, who had finished third in the previous year's Division II table, and were always going to be stern opposition. This proved to be the case as the Kings provided only two race winners (Saunders and Seaton) and one heat victory.

Heat 01	Leadbitter/Reading/**Bottomley/Tucker**	70.2	5 - 1	05 - 01
Heat 02	**Saunders**/Swales/Durham/**Jackson**	73.2	3 - 3	08 - 04
Heat 03	Lee/O'Neil/**Seaton/Curtis**	70.4	5 - 1	13 - 05
Heat 04	Mills/**Parry**/Durham/**Jackson**	72.8	4 - 2	17 - 07
Heat 05	Lee/O'Neil/**Tucker/Bottomley** (F)	70.6	5 - 1	22 - 08
Heat 06	Leadbitter/**Saunders**/Reading/**Parry**	72.0	4 - 2	26 - 10
Heat 07	**Seaton**/Durham/**Curtis**/Mills	74.0	**2 - 4**	28 - 14
Heat 08	Reading/**Bottomley/Saunders**/Swales	72.0	3 - 3	31 - 17
Heat 09	Lee/O'Neil/**Saunders/Parry**	72.4	5 - 1	36 - 18
Heat 10	Leadbitter/**Seaton/Curtis**/Reading	71.6	3 - 3	39 - 21
Heat 11	Mills/**Seaton/Bottomley**/Swales	71.2	3 - 3	42 - 24
Heat 12	O'Neil/Leadbitter/**Seaton/Parry**	71.4	5 - 1	47 - 25
Heat 13	Lee/Mills/**Curtis/Tucker**	70.6	5 - 1	52 - 26

MIDDLESBROUGH - Terry Lee 12, Tom Leadbitter 11 (+1), Paul O'Neil 9 (+3), Roger Mills 8 (+1), Pete Reading 6 (+1), Dave Durham 4 (+1), Tim Swales 2.
CREWE - Peter Seaton 9, Pete Saunders 7 (+1), Ian Bottomley 4 (+1), Geoff Curtis 3 (+1), Dave Parry 2, Colin Tucker 1, Rob Jackson 0.

Meeting 2 - Monday, May 12, 1969 - British League Division II
Reading Stadium, Oxford Road, Tilehurst, Reading
Track Length - 360 yards.

READING RACERS.....40 CREWE KINGS.....36

The Kings made their league bow on a rain sodden track against a team boasting a three match unbeaten record. Reading established an early advantage, but Crewe produced a stirring comeback which saw them draw level in the penultimate heat, thanks to a Curtis/Seaton maximum. However, the fightback was all in vain as a 5-1 for the Racers saw them maintain their perfect start to the season. The visitors provided six of the thirteen heat winners, with Dave Parry, becoming the first Kings rider to win a heat in the league.

Heat 01	**Parry**/Davies/Vernam/**Saunders**	78.0	3 - 3	03 - 03
Heat 02	Pratt/**R.Jackson**/Tabet (F)/**Blackburn** (F)	76.2	3 - 2	06 - 05
Heat 03	**Seaton**/Champion/Bell/**Bottomley**	76.0	3 - 3	09 - 08
Heat 04	A.Jackson/**Curtis**/Pratt (F)/**R.Jackson** (F)	76.0	3 - 2	12 - 10
Heat 05	Bell/**Parry**/Champion/**Saunders**	76.2	4 - 2	16 - 12
Heat 06	Davies/Vernam/**Curtis**/**Blackburn** (F)	79.2	5 - 1	21 - 13
Heat 07	A.Jackson/**Seaton**/**Bottomley**/Pratt	77.2	3 - 3	24 - 16
Heat 08	**Parry**/**Saunders**/Tabet/Davies (R)	78.0	**1 - 5**	25 - 21
Heat 09	**Curtis**/Champion/Bell/**Blackburn** (F)	77.0	3 - 3	28 - 24
Heat 10	**Bottomley**/Vernam/Davies/**Seaton**	77.2	3 - 3	31 - 27
Heat 11	A.Jackson/**Saunders**/**Parry**/Tabet	77.0	3 - 3	34 - 30
Heat 12	**Curtis**/**Seaton**/Vernam/Champion	78.0	**1 - 5**	35 - 35
Heat 13	A.Jackson/Bell/**Parry**/**Bottomley**	76.2	5 - 1	40 - 36

READING - Alan Jackson 12, Mick Bell 7 (+3), Dene Davies 6 (+1), Mike Vernam 6 (+2), Ian Champion 5, Phil Pratt 3, Bob Tabet 1.
CREWE - Dave Parry 10 (+1), Geoff Curtis 9, Peter Seaton 7 (+1), Ian Bottomley 4 (+1), Pete Saunders 4 (+1), Rob Jackson 2, Glyn Blackburn 0.

With the paint barely dry on the Earle Street safety fence, Crewe's first home fixture took place on Monday, May 19, with a challenge match against Len Silver's Rayleigh Rockets team. The opening programme notes saw Crewe promoter Maurice Littlechild give thanks to all who had contributed to the opening night and also explained the basic rules of speedway, in a feature called *'Maurie's Message.'*

'*Good evening everybody and welcome to Britain's newest and fastest Speedway. I know you will enjoy the racing not only this evening, but for many years to come, and it has been with a long future in mind that the promoting company, Allied Presentations Ltd. have invested heavily here in Crewe. We have a large number of people to thank and they are too numerous to mention here, but it would not be fitting to open our meeting without telling you of the immense co-operation we have received from all parties concerned. John Whitehouse and Val Purtwood of British Railways, our guests this evening, have been prime movers in the project and have helped us at every step. The same must be said for Sam Crawford, secretary of the L.M.R. Sports Club, whose ground this is; he and his members have been wholeheartedly behind us. Thank you to them all. Probably our biggest thanks must go to a lean and likeable young New Zealander, Colin Tucker. He has been responsible for the complete installation job and this includes the building of all the inner and outer fences, turnstile buildings, toilets, judges box, dressing rooms, roadways and of course the track and the electrical wiring. Every single nail and screw was put in with his own hands and he has literally worked night and day in atrocious weather to get finished in time. He is to be our team captain and he rides in the No.7 spot this evening, and to give you some idea of this man's dedication to our great sport, I should tell you that he opted to take part of his wages in the form of a new racing machine, and he will ride it tonight for the first time. Never have I ever wanted to see a man get to the top so much, for if any one deserved it, then that man is Colin Tucker. Give him a special cheer when he appears tonight folks for without him our opening meeting would probably have been in July! Another man who must receive my thanks is Ken Adams. Ken may be known to many of you already because he was skipper to the old Stoke Potters team for many years and was a great favourite there. Ken now owns a petrol filling station at Winterley, on the outskirts of the town and he has been responsible for much of the administration work. His long experience in the sport should make him one of the best team managers in the country. He writes elsewhere in this programme, and I have left it to him to tell you about the members of the team. To those of you who have never seen Speedway Racing before I should tell you briefly a few basic rules. The Second Division of the British League, of which Crewe is a member, has fifteen (other) teams and operates just like soccer with each team racing the others once home and once away.*

As in soccer the League points are awarded 2 for a win and 1 for a draw. Each match consists of thirteen races and two members from each team take part in each race. The winner of a race receives 3 points, the second 2 points and the third one point. So, as each race goes by the individual riders are earning points for the team, and naturally the winning team is that which scores the most points at the end of the thirteen heats. Each heat lasts for four laps and the play marshal shows the yellow flag to indicate to the riders that they have one lap left to go and the chequered flag for the finish. The riders numbered 6 and 7 in each team are the reserves and they may be used to replace any other riders during the match. In addition to this, if a team is 6 points behind then may use ***any*** *rider to replace another, this is called a "Tactical substitute." The announcer will give you as much information as possible to make your evening enjoyable. Finally a warm welcome to Frank Varey, the promoter of the 1st Division Sheffield track and a very famous pre-war rider. He is to officially open our track tonight and we asked him to do so because he once performed here as a rider way back in 1932 - thank you for coming Frank. Enough from me, let's enjoy the racing and look forward to our meeting next Monday when the Reading Racers provide the opposition, see you all then. Regards MAURIE.'*

Meeting 3 - Monday, May 19, 1969 - Challenge
L.M.R. Sports Ground, Earle Street, Crewe
Track Length - 470 yards.

CREWE KINGS.....33 RAYLEIGH ROCKETS.....45

The valiant efforts of Colin Tucker and the money pumped into the venture by APL seemed fully justified, when an estimated crowd of 6,000 turned up at Earle Street (including many ex-Stoke Potters fans), to witness Crewe's first ever home meeting. Rayleigh, who were currently second in the British League Division II table, won the first heat, courtesy of Mike Gardner and Barry Lee, with Dave Parry providing the first home points. Geoff Curtis won instant cult hero status with a flawless fifteen point maximum, but his efforts were still not enough to earn the home victory and Rayleigh secured the meeting with a maximum 5-1 in Heat 12. The first night had been a big success, but was soured somewhat during the second-half racing, when Curtis took a spill in the Rainbow Stakes, breaking a bone in his right foot and fracturing a rib. Ian Bottomley missed the home debut due to an injury sustained in a second-half appearance at Halifax the previous Saturday.

Heat	Riders	Time	Heat score	Match score
Heat 01	Gardner/**Parry**/Lee/**Saunders**	**77.0** (TR)	2 - 4	02 - 04
Heat 02	Wright/Maloney/**Blackburn**/**Tucker**	78.0	1 - 5	03 - 09
Heat 03	Brown/Etheridge/**Seaton**/**Jackson** (F)	**76.8** (TR)	1 - 5	04 - 14
Heat 04	**Curtis**/Stone/Maloney/**Blackburn**	**74.2** (TR)	3 - 3	07 - 17
Heat 05	Gardner/**Seaton**/Lee/**Jackson**	76.8	2 - 4	09 - 21
Heat 06	**Curtis**/Wright/**Parry**/Stone	**73.2** (TR)	**4 - 2**	13 - 23
Heat 07	**Curtis**/Brown/**Seaton**/Etheridge	75.0	**4 - 2**	17 - 25
Heat 08	**Saunders**/Lee/**Tucker**/Maloney	79.2	**4 - 2**	21 - 27
Heat 09	Stone/Wright/**Saunders**/**Seaton**	78.4	1 - 5	22 - 32
Heat 10	**Parry**/Brown/Etheridge/**Saunders**	77.8	3 - 3	25 - 35
Heat 11	**Curtis**/Gardner/**Tucker**/Lee (R)	75.0	**4 - 2**	29 - 37
Heat 12	Brown/Stone/**Parry**/**Jackson**	76.4	1 - 5	30 - 42
Heat 13	**Curtis**/Etheridge/Gardner/**Seaton**	75.0	3 - 3	33 - 45

CREWE - Geoff Curtis 15, Dave Parry 7, Pete Saunders 4, Peter Seaton 4, Colin Tucker 2, Glyn Blackburn 1, Rob Jackson 0.
RAYLEIGH - Dingle Brown 10, Mike Gardner 9 (+1), Terry Stone 7 (+1), Roger Wright 7 (+1), Laurie Etheridge 5 (+2), Barry Lee 4, Geoff Maloney 3 (+2).

Meeting 4 - Saturday, May 24, 1969 - British League Division II
Weir Stadium, Southend Arterial Road, Rayleigh
Track Length - 365 yards.

RAYLEIGH ROCKETS.....47 CREWE KINGS.....31

Rayleigh completed a double over Crewe in the space of five days, after winning this league encounter at Weir Stadium by sixteen points. With Geoff Curtis injured, the Kings brought in guest Paul O'Neil, who had ridden against Crewe in their fixture at Middlesbrough. The visitors matched the Rockets for the first four heats, but could not sustain their form and had fallen 10 points behind by Heat 9. Peter Seaton, who had performed well in an open meeting at Rayleigh the previous season, again showed his liking for the track, by top scoring with 13 points from his five starts and was the only winning Crewe rider on the night. Rockets star Mike Gardner registered a fine maximum.

Heat 01	Maloney/**Parry**/**Saunders**/Stone (X)	79.0	3 - 3	03 - 03
Heat 02	Wright/**Tucker**/**Blackburn**/Lee (F)	81.3	3 - 3	06 - 06
Heat 03	**Seaton**/Etheridge/Brown/**Bottomley**	77.8	3 - 3	09 - 09
Heat 04	Gardner/**Tucker**/**O'Neil**/Wright (R)	78.7	3 - 3	12 - 12
Heat 05	Brown/**Parry**/Etheridge/**Saunders**	81.6	4 - 2	16 - 14
Heat 06	Stone/Maloney/**O'Neil**/**Blackburn**	82.1	5 - 1	21 - 15
Heat 07	Gardner/**Seaton**/Wright/**Blackburn**	76.8	4 - 2	25 - 17
Heat 08	**Seaton**/Maloney/**Tucker**/Lee (F)	78.2	**2 - 4**	27 - 21
Heat 09	Brown/Etheridge/**O'Neil**/**Blackburn**	78.4	5 - 1	32 - 22
Heat 10	**Seaton**/Wright/**Parry**/Maloney	77.5	**2 - 4**	34 - 26
Heat 11	Gardner/Wright/**Parry**/**Saunders**	77.8	5 - 1	39 - 27
Heat 12	Etheridge/**Seaton**/**O'Neil**/Stone	78.2	3 - 3	42 - 30
Heat 13	Gardner/Brown/**Parry**/**Tucker**	77.2	5 - 1	47 - 31

RAYLEIGH - Mike Gardner 12, Dingle Brown 9 (+2), Laurie Etheridge 8 (+1), Roger Wright 8 (+1), Geoff Maloney 7 (+1), Terry Stone 3, Barry Lee 0.
CREWE - Peter Seaton 13, Dave Parry 7, Colin Tucker 5, Paul O'Neil* 4 (+2), Glyn Blackburn 1 (+1), Pete Saunders 1 (+1), Ian Bottomley 0.

Maurice Littlechild made an approach for Long Eaton rider Glyn Chandler, but when the deal fell through, signed New Zealander Paul O'Neil from Middlesbrough.

Meeting 5 - Monday, May 26, 1969 - Challenge
L.M.R. Sports Ground, Earle Street, Crewe
Track Length - 470 yards.

CREWE KINGS.....40 READING RACERS.....38

The two sides provided an exciting climax for the large Earle Street crowd. The Kings, on the back of four consecutive defeats, stormed into a commanding lead after Heat 7, but determined riding by the visitors saw them claw back the home advantage to within four points, going into the final two heats. An Ian Bottomley win in Heat 12 edged the Kings closer to their first win, which was finally achieved in the last heat when guest rider Terry Lee secured second place and the two points required. Paul O'Neil, deputising for Glyn Blackburn, won three of his four races, while Bottomley had two wins. Home rider Rob Jackson, loaned to Reading, scored two points.

Heat 01	**Parry**/Davies/**Saunders**/Vernam	77.8	**4 - 2**	04 - 02
Heat 02	**O'Neil**/R.Jackson/Tabet/**Tucker**	77.6	3 - 3	07 - 05
Heat 03	Bell/**Seaton**/**Bottomley**/Champion	79.0	3 - 3	10 - 08
Heat 04	**O'Neil**/A.Jackson/**Lee**/Tabet	77.0	**4 - 2**	14 - 10
Heat 05	Davies/**Bottomley**/**Seaton**/Vernam	75.3	3 - 3	17 - 13
Heat 06	A.Jackson/**Parry**/**Saunders**/R.Jackson	76.2	3 - 3	20 - 16
Heat 07	**O'Neil**/**Lee**/Champion/Bell	77.8	**5 - 1**	25 - 17
Heat 08	Davies/Tabet/**Saunders**/**Tucker**	73.8	1 - 5	26 - 22
Heat 09	**Bottomley**/A.Jackson/**Seaton**/R.Jackson	76.6	**4 - 2**	30 - 24
Heat 10	Champion/**Parry**/Bell/**Saunders**	74.0	2 - 4	32 - 28
Heat 11	Davies/**Lee**/**O'Neil**/Vernam	74.6	3 - 3	35 - 31
Heat 12	**Bottomley**/A.Jackson/Bell/**Parry**	77.2	3 - 3	38 - 34
Heat 13	Champion/**Lee**/Tabet/**Seaton**	77.4	2 - 4	40 - 38

CREWE - Paul O'Neil 10 (+1), Ian Bottomley 9 (+1), Terry Lee* 7 (+1), Dave Parry 7, Peter Seaton 4 (+1), Pete Saunders 3 (+1), Colin Tucker 0.
READING - Dene Davies 11, Alan Jackson 9, Ian Champion 7, Mick Bell 5 (+1), Bob Tabet 4 (+2), Rob Jackson* 2, Mike Vernam 0.

Meeting 6 - Thursday, May 29, 1969 - Challenge
Brooklands Sports Stadium, Brooklands Road, Mawneys, Romford
Track Length - 375 yards.

ROMFORD BOMBERS.....45 CREWE KINGS.....33

Following Rochester's move to Romford, Crewe became the opening night opponents at Brooklands Stadium, on a track laid in only nine days. The Kings kept pace with the home side in the early stages, until Bombers trio Ross Gilbertson, Phil Woodcock and Tony George powered them to victory. Ian Bottomley and Peter Seaton provided crumbs of comfort for the small band of travelling Crewe supporters, with the Kings providing a solitary heat win throughout the match.

Heat 01	Gilbertson/Wendon/**Saunders/Parry**	**71.9** (TR)	5 - 1	05 - 01
Heat 02	**Bottomley/Tucker**/Drew/Yeatman	75.8	**1 - 5**	06 - 06
Heat 03	Woodcock/**Seaton/O'Neil**/Benham	74.6	3 - 3	09 - 09
Heat 04	George/**Champion/Tucker**/Drew	72.2	3 - 3	12 - 12
Heat 05	Woodcock/**Saunders**/Benham/**Parry**	74.2	4 - 2	16 - 14
Heat 06	Gilbertson/**Champion/Bottomley**/Wendon	72.6	3 - 3	19 - 17
Heat 07	George/**Seaton/O'Neil**/Drew	74.4	3 - 3	22 - 20
Heat 08	Yeatman/Wendon/**Saunders/Tucker**	76.0	5 - 1	27 - 21
Heat 09	Woodcock/**Bottomley/Champion**/Benham (F)	72.4	3 - 3	30 - 24
Heat 10	Gilbertson/**O'Neil/Seaton**/Wendon	72.8	3 - 3	33 - 27
Heat 11	George/**Bottomley**/Yeatman/**Saunders**	73.6	4 - 2	37 - 29
Heat 12	Gilbertson/**Seaton/Champion**/Benham	73.0	3 - 3	40 - 32
Heat 13	Woodcock/George/**Bottomley/O'Neil**	73.0	5 - 1	45 - 33

ROMFORD - Ross Gilbertson 12, Phil Woodcock 12, Tony George 11 (+1), Frank Wendon 4 (+2), Chris Yeatman 4, Alan Benham 1, Judd Drew* 1.
CREWE - Ian Bottomley 9 (+1), Peter Seaton 7 (+1), Ian Champion* 6 (+2), Paul O'Neil 4 (+2), Pete Saunders 4, Colin Tucker 3 (+2), Dave Parry 0.

Meeting 7 - Monday, June 2, 1969 - British League Division II
L.M.R. Sports Ground, Earle Street, Crewe
Track Length - 470 yards.

CREWE KINGS.....42 MIDDLESBROUGH TEESSIDERS.....36

Crewe registered their first league win, after a thrilling last heat decider. After sharing the points in the first three heats, maximums in the next two gave the hosts some breathing space, but a Teessiders fight back, saw them trail by just two after Heat 10. However, in the falling rain, Crewe won two of the final three heats, to claim the two league points. Paul O'Neil top scored against his old team, with Geoff Curtis (back in the saddle after only a fortnight) and Ian Bottomley both returning double figure scores.

Heat 01	**O'Neil**/Leadbitter/Reading/**Saunders** (R)	78.2	3 - 3	03 - 03
Heat 02	**O'Neil**/Durham/Forrester/**Tucker** (R)	78.4	3 - 3	06 - 06
Heat 03	Lee/**Bottomley/Seaton**/Swales	78.4	3 - 3	09 - 09
Heat 04	**Curtis/O'Neil**/Forrester/Mills	76.2	**5 - 1**	14 - 10
Heat 05	**Bottomley/Seaton**/Leadbitter/Reading	76.0	**5 - 1**	19 - 11
Heat 06	Lee/Mills/**Parry/Tucker**	76.0	1 - 5	20 - 16
Heat 07	Lee/**Curtis/O'Neil**/Durham	75.8	3 - 3	23 - 19
Heat 08	**O'Neil/Tucker**/Reading/Forrester	77.8	**5 - 1**	28 - 20
Heat 09	Mills/**Bottomley**/Leadbitter/**Seaton**	76.0	2 - 4	30 - 24
Heat 10	Lee/Mills/**Parry/Tucker**	76.0	1 - 5	31 - 29
Heat 11	**Curtis**/Leadbitter/**Tucker**/Durham (F)	74.8	**4 - 2**	35 - 31
Heat 12	**Bottomley**/Lee/Mills/**Parry**	76.4	3 - 3	38 - 34
Heat 13	**Curtis**/Leadbitter/**Seaton**/Swales	75.8	**4 - 2**	42 - 36

CREWE - Paul O'Neil 12 (+2), Geoff Curtis 11, Ian Bottomley 10, Peter Seaton 4 (+2), Colin Tucker 3 (+1), Dave Parry 2, Pete Saunders 0.
MIDDLESBROUGH - Terry Lee 14, Roger Mills 8 (+3), Tom Leadbitter 8, Bruce Forrester 2 (+1), Pete Reading 2 (+1), Dave Durham 2, Tim Swales 0.

Meeting 8 - Wednesday, June 4, 1969 - British League Division II
Zoological Gardens, Hyde Road, West Gorton, Manchester
Track Length - 418 yards.

BELLE VUE COLTS.....57 CREWE KINGS.....21

Belle Vue welcomed Crewe to the famous Hyde Road stadium, and then gave them a severe thrashing. The current Division II Champions won all but two heats, and from Heat 5, recorded five consecutive maximums, to maintain their 100% home record and position at the top of the table. Geoff Curtis, battling back to fitness (and riding in a boot three times his normal size), was the only Crewe rider to make a fist of it on the dusty track and his wins in Heats 4 and 12 proved to be the only plus of the night for the visitors.

Heat	Riders	Time	Score	Total
Heat 01	Broadbelt/**Parry**/Moulin/**Seaton**	74.8	4 - 2	04 - 02
Heat 02	Owen/Bailey/**Tucker**/**Saunders**	74.2	5 - 1	09 - 03
Heat 03	Eyre/Moss/**O'Neil**/**Bottomley**	75.8	5 - 1	14 - 04
Heat 04	**Curtis**/Owen/**Tucker**/Waplington (F)	76.2	**2 - 4**	16 - 08
Heat 05	Eyre/Moss/**Seaton**/**Parry**	75.0	5 - 1	21 - 09
Heat 06	Broadbelt/Moulin/**Curtis**/**Saunders**	74.6	5 - 1	26 - 10
Heat 07	Owen/Waplington/**O'Neil**/**Bottomley**	75.6	5 - 1	31 - 11
Heat 08	Bailey/Moulin/**Seaton**/**Tucker**	76.2	5 - 1	36 - 12
Heat 09	Eyre/Moss/**Tucker**/**O'Neil**	76.4	5 - 1	41 - 13
Heat 10	Broadbelt/**Curtis**/Moulin/**Saunders**	74.4	4 - 2	45 - 15
Heat 11	Bailey/Waplington/**Seaton**/**Parry**	76.2	5 - 1	50 - 16
Heat 12	**Curtis**/Broadbelt/**Tucker**/Moss (F)	77.4	**2 - 4**	52 - 20
Heat 13	Eyre/Waplington/**Parry**/**Bottomley**	76.2	5 - 1	57 - 21

BELLE VUE - Ken Eyre 12, Eric Broadbelt 11, Chris Bailey 8 (+1), Taffy Owen 8, Ken Moss 6 (+3), Steve Waplington 6 (+3), Bill Moulin 6 (+2).
CREWE - Geoff Curtis 9, Colin Tucker 4, Dave Parry 3, Peter Seaton 3, Paul O'Neil 2, Ian Bottomley 0, Pete Saunders 0.

Meeting 9 - Thursday, June 5, 1969 - Challenge Trophy
Long Eaton Stadium, Station Road, Long Eaton
Track Length - 366 yards.

LONG EATON RANGERS.....54 CREWE KINGS.....23

Just one day after their thrashing at Hyde Road, Crewe endured another miserable away day, this time at the hands of Long Eaton. They lost Geoff Curtis once again with a foot injury gained in his first outing, but the match would be remembered for an unsavoury incident involving the Crewe skipper Colin Tucker and Roy Carter in Heat 6. Carter was originally excluded from the re-run, after Tucker had fallen heavily on the tote bend, but after a protest by Rangers manager Vic White, all four riders were called back to the gate, with the injured Tucker replaced by Dave Parry. As the riders approached the tapes, Tucker ran onto the track, switched off Carter's fuel, and launched into an argument with the home rider. Track officials intervened to separate the pair. Home rider Gil Farmer stepped in for the absent Pete Saunders.

Heat	Riders	Time	Score	Total
Heat 01	Carter/**Parry**/**Farmer**/Penniket (F)	73.6	3 - 3	03 - 03
Heat 02	**O'Neil**/Adaway/**Tucker**/Shakespeare	73.6	**2 - 4**	05 - 07
Heat 03	Gay/Lomas/**Seaton**/**Bottomley**	73.8	5 - 1	10 - 08
Heat 04	Shakespeare/Wrathall/**Tucker**/**Curtis** (R)	73.8	5 - 1	15 - 09
Heat 05	Lomas/Gay/**Parry**/**Farmer**	73.4	5 - 1	20 - 10
Heat 06	Penniket/Carter/**Seaton**/**Parry**	71.4	5 - 1	25 - 11
Heat 07	**O'Neil**/Wrathall/Shakespeare/**Seaton**	72.4	3 - 3	28 - 14
Heat 08	Carter/**O'Neil**/Adaway/**Farmer**	72.2	4 - 2	32 - 16
Heat 09	**O'Neil**/Lomas/**Bottomley** (R)/Gay (X)	73.2	**2 - 3**	34 - 19
Heat 10	Penniket/Carter/**Seaton**/**Bottomley**	72.2	5 - 1	39 - 20
Heat 11	Wrathall/Adaway/**Tucker**/**Parry**	73.2	5 - 1	44 - 21
Heat 12	Penniket/Gay/**Seaton**/**O'Neil**	73.0	5 - 1	49 - 22
Heat 13	Lomas/Wrathall/**Bottomley**/**Tucker**	74.8	5 - 1	54 - 23

(ABOVE) The British Rail owned L.M.R. Sports Ground, in January 1969, just prior to work commencing on it's conversion into a speedway venue.

(ABOVE) The running track and banked cycle track, separated by a narrow grass strip, facing towards the town centre.

(ABOVE) Just four months later, and the stadium nearing completion. Colin Tucker tries out the newly laid track, with the tower of Christ Church in the distance. Only he and Geoff Curtis had ridden the circuit before the opening fixture. (BELOW) The final touches before the grand opening on May 19. An electrician wires up a stop light, while the safety fence receives a first coat of paint on the pits bend.

(ABOVE) The Kings pose at Tilehurst, before their opening league fixture with Reading. The team that day was (from left to right) Geoff Curtis, Ian Bottomley, Dave Parry, Peter Seaton, Glyn Blackburn, Pete Saunders and Rob Jackson.

(ABOVE) Glyn Blackburn hits the front at Reading during Heat 2. Rob Jackson is seen in third place. The Kings eventually lost the match 40-36.

(ABOVE) Opening night against Rayleigh. Dave Parry and Mike Gardner lead out the teams, followed by Pete Saunders, sporting his trademark white boots, with Barry Lee.

(ABOVE) Glyn Blackburn (outside), Roger Wright, Colin Tucker and Geoff Maloney blast from the tapes in Heat 2 of the match. The official crowd figure was 6,000, but was probably far higher, after the gates were opened to avoid turnstile congestion.

LONG EATON - Roy Carter 10 (+2), Tony Lomas 10 (+1), Peter Wrathall 9 (+2), Geoff Penniket 9, Pete Gay 7 (+2), Pat Adaway 5 (+1), Malcolm Shakespeare 4 (+1).
CREWE - Paul O'Neil 11, Peter Seaton 4, Dave Parry 3, Colin Tucker 3, Gil Farmer* 1 (+1), Ian Bottomley 1, Geoff Curtis 0.

The meeting with Long Eaton was originally to have been a two-legged encounter for the Challenge Trophy (as advertised on the front of the Long Eaton programme), but no second leg took place. Despite heavy defeats in their two previous matches, promoter Maurice Littlechild was pleased with Crewe's early progress. He was interviewed in early June by Dick Bott of the *Speedway Star & News* about why the Crewe track was so exciting and he commented: *"Things are really popping at the British Rail circuit. The way things are going, we'll make this place the Belle Vue of the Potteries. British Rail are so pleased with the interest shown by the public, that they're planning to build a £45,000 clubhouse. And I'll tell you why we are getting big crowds.....because we've got guys going round this dust bowl at 65mph that's why. And because it's a big round track that lets guys dive under each other and pass and re-pass and keeps the fans on the tips of their toe-nails."*

Meeting 10 - Monday, June 9, 1969 - Knock Out Cup, First Round
L.M.R. Sports Ground, Earle Street, Crewe
Track Length - 470 yards.

CREWE KINGS.....49 DONCASTER STALLIONS.....29

Home advantage was enough to see Crewe safely through to the quarter-finals of the K.O. Cup. Colin Tucker top scored with eleven points, in the Kings' best overall performance to date. Geoff Curtis scored five in his first two rides, but lost a chain while leading on the last lap of his next race. Doncaster though were not happy with events on and off the track, and protested bitterly against the inclusion of Crewe's three overseas riders (Curtis, O'Neil and Tucker), which contravened league rules. There were also lengthy delays during the night whilst the dusty track was hosed down, and when the starting gate failed near the end of the meeting.

Heat	Riders	Time	Heat score	Match score
Heat 01	**O'Neil**/Shearer/Bridgett/**Bottomley**	76.8	3 - 3	03 - 03
Heat 02	**Tucker**/Ulph/**Saunders**/Devonport (R)	75.8	**4 - 2**	07 - 05
Heat 03	**Parry**/Hawkes/**Seaton**/Timms	75.0	**4 - 2**	11 - 07
Heat 04	**Curtis**/Baugh/**Saunders**/Devonport (R)	74.8	**4 - 2**	15 - 09
Heat 05	**Parry**/Shearer/**Seaton**/Bridgett (F)	75.0	**4 - 2**	19 - 11
Heat 06	**O'Neil**/**Bottomley**/Baugh/Ulph	73.8	**5 - 1**	24 - 12
Heat 07	Shearer/**Curtis**/**Saunders**/Hawkes (F)	74.8	3 - 3	27 - 15
Heat 08	**Tucker**/Timms/Bridgett/**Saunders**	75.0	3 - 3	30 - 18
Heat 09	Baugh/**Seaton**/Ulph/**Parry**	75.2	2 - 4	32 - 22
Heat 10	**Bottomley**/**O'Neil**/Timms/Ulph (R)	74.8	**5 - 1**	37 - 23
Heat 11	Shearer/**Tucker**/Ulph/**Curtis** (R)	74.8	2 - 4	39 - 27
Heat 12	**Parry**/**Bottomley**/Baugh/Bridgett	74.6	**5 - 1**	44 - 28
Heat 13	**Tucker**/**Seaton**/Timms/Shearer (R)	75.0	**5 - 1**	49 - 29

CREWE – Colin Tucker 11, Dave Parry 9, Paul O'Neil 8 (+1), Ian Bottomley 7 (+2), Peter Seaton 6 (+1), Geoff Curtis 5, Pete Saunders 3 (+1).
DONCASTER – Terry Shearer 10, Dave Baugh 7, Derek Timms 4, Stuart Ulph 4, Alan Bridgett 2 (+2), Guy Hawkes 2, George Devonport 0.

After the meeting, parking problems surrounding the stadium saw the office swamped with calls of complaint. All supporters were advised to use the stadium car park for future meetings.

Meeting 11 - Monday, June 16, 1969 - British League Division II
L.M.R. Sports Ground, Earle Street, Crewe
Track Length - 470 yards.

CREWE KINGS.....52 IPSWICH WITCHES.....26

Ipswich endured a torrid evening at Earle Street, providing only one heat winner all night. Geoff Curtis secured a four ride maximum and also shattered his own track record in Heat 7.

Dave Parry was an impressive winner in Heat 9, when coming from last place and Colin Tucker dropped only one point from three rides. The under-strength Witches never looked comfortable in the wet conditions, although Ron Bagley and John Harrhy did well collecting nineteen of their total points haul.

Heat 01	**O'Neil**/**Bottomley**/Bagley/Spittles	74.4	**5 - 1**	05 - 01
Heat 02	**Tucker**/**Saunders**/Coomber/Wasden	75.6	**5 - 1**	10 - 02
Heat 03	**Parry**/Harrhy/**Seaton**/Baker	74.8	**4 - 2**	14 - 04
Heat 04	**Curtis**/Bagley/**Saunders**/Wasden	74.6	**4 - 2**	18 - 06
Heat 05	Harrhy/**Parry**/**Seaton**/Spittles	78.0	3 - 3	21 - 09
Heat 06	**Bottomley**/Bagley/**O'Neil**/Coomber	74.6	**4 - 2**	25 - 11
Heat 07	**Curtis**/Baker/**Saunders**/Harrhy	**72.8** (TR)	**4 - 2**	29 - 13
Heat 08	**Tucker**/Harrhy/Spittles/**O'Neil** (R)	73.8	3 - 3	32 - 16
Heat 09	**Parry**/Bagley/**Seaton**/Coomber	74.0	**4 - 2**	36 - 18
Heat 10	**O'Neil**/Harrhy/Baker/**Bottomley** (F)	74.0	3 - 3	39 - 21
Heat 11	**Curtis**/**Tucker**/Bagley/Baker	73.4	**5 - 1**	44 - 22
Heat 12	**Bottomley**/Bagley/**Parry**/Harrhy	74.8	**4 - 2**	48 - 24
Heat 13	**Curtis**/Baker/**Seaton**/Coomber	73.4	**4 - 2**	52 - 26

CREWE – Geoff Curtis 12, Dave Parry 9, Ian Bottomley 8 (+1), Colin Tucker 8 (+1), Paul O'Neil 7, Pete Saunders 4 (+1), Peter Seaton 4 (+1).
IPSWICH – Ron Bagley 10, John Harrhy 9, Ernie Baker 5 (+1), Ted Spittles 1 (+1), Mike Coomber 1, Dennis Wasden 0, *Pete Bailey (R/R).*

Meeting 12 - Friday, June 20, 1969 - British League Division II
Plymouth Sports Stadium, Pennycross, Plymouth
Track Length - 413 yards.

PLYMOUTH DEVILS.....49 CREWE KINGS.....28

The away day blues continued at lowly Plymouth when the Kings again endured a heavy defeat. Colin Sanders excelled for the home team with a maximum, while Geoff Curtis again proved to be Crewe's most consistent performer, scoring twelve from five starts. Peter Seaton was injured in a Heat 3 fall, preventing him from taking any further part in the match. Unfortunately Paul O'Neil arrived too late to participate.

Heat 01	Sanders/Coles/**Wallace**/**Parry**	81.0	5 - 1	05 - 01
Heat 02	Hammond/**Bottomley**/Smith/**Saunders** (F)	83.4	4 - 2	09 - 03
Heat 03	Roynon/**Tucker**/Marks/**Seaton** (X)	79.8	4 - 2	13 - 05
Heat 04	**Curtis**/Whitaker/Hammond/**Bottomley**	82.8	3 - 3	16 - 08
Heat 05	Marks/Roynon/**Wallace**/**Parry**	83.0	5 - 1	21 - 09
Heat 06	Sanders/**Curtis**/Coles/**Saunders**	81.8	4 - 2	25 - 11
Heat 07	Hammond/Whitaker/**Tucker**/**Bottomley**	83.8	5 - 1	30 - 12
Heat 08	**Bottomley**/Coles/Smith/**Wallace**	83.6	3 - 3	33 - 15
Heat 09	**Curtis**/Roynon/Marks/**Saunders**	81.2	3 - 3	36 - 18
Heat 10	Sanders/**Tucker**/Coles/**Bottomley** (F)	82.8	4 - 2	40 - 20
Heat 11	**Curtis**/Whitaker/Smith/**Wallace** (R)	83.0	3 - 3	43 - 23
Heat 12	Sanders/**Tucker**/**Curtis**/Marks	81.2	3 - 3	46 - 26
Heat 13	Whitaker/**Parry**/Roynon (F)/**Tucker** (X)	83.8	3 - 2	49 - 28

PLYMOUTH - Colin Sanders 12, Dave Whitaker 9 (+1), John Hammond 7 (+1), Chris Roynon 7 (+1), Bob Coles 6 (+1), Keith Marks 5 (+1), Tony Smith 3 (+2).
CREWE - Geoff Curtis 12 (+1), Colin Tucker 7, Ian Bottomley 5, Dave Parry 2, Stuart Wallace* 2, Pete Saunders 0, Peter Seaton 0.

Meeting 13 - Monday, June 23, 1969 - British League Division II
L.M.R. Sports Ground, Earle Street, Crewe
Track Length - 470 yards.

CREWE KINGS.....48 CANTERBURY CRUSADERS.....30

The Kings' comprehensive win didn't impress Crusaders promoter Johnnie Hoskins, who wagered a £50 bet with Crewe boss Maurice Littlechild that his current cup holders would avenge this defeat in their forthcoming K.O. Cup tie. Paul O'Neil showed why Crewe had missed him so much at Plymouth with a maximum, and there was a nine point haul from Geoff Curtis, with the only blot on his night occurring in Heat 4 when he snapped a chain. Glyn Blackburn, drafted in for the injured Peter Seaton, scored in each of his rides. Not surprisingly, Canterbury's Peter Murray - top of the Division II averages - was the pick of the visiting riders.

Heat 01	**O'Neil**/Vale/**Parry**/Miles	74.0	**4 - 2**	04 - 02
Heat 02	**Bottomley**/**Saunders**/Crowhurst/Percy	74.2	**5 - 1**	09 - 03
Heat 03	**Blackburn**/**Tucker**/Piddock/Hibben	73.8	**5 - 1**	14 - 04
Heat 04	Murray/**Saunders**/Percy/**Curtis** (R)	74.4	2 - 4	16 - 08
Heat 05	Vale/Miles/**Blackburn**/**Tucker** (R)	74.0	1 - 5	17 - 13
Heat 06	**O'Neil**/**Parry**/Crowhurst/Murray (R)	75.6	**5 - 1**	22 - 14
Heat 07	**Curtis**/**Saunders**/Hibben/Piddock	73.0	**5 - 1**	27 - 15
Heat 08	**O'Neil**/**Bottomley**/Miles/Percy	74.0	**5 - 1**	32 - 16
Heat 09	Murray/Vale/**Blackburn**/**Tucker**	75.0	1 - 5	33 - 21
Heat 10	**O'Neil**/Piddock/**Parry**/Hibben	73.6	**4 - 2**	37 - 23
Heat 11	**Curtis**/Vale/**Bottomley**/Miles	73.8	**4 - 2**	41 - 25
Heat 12	**Tucker**/Murray/Piddock/**Parry**	74.6	3 - 3	44 - 28
Heat 13	**Curtis**/Murray/**Blackburn**/Vale (R)	75.0	**4 - 2**	48 - 30

CREWE - Paul O'Neil 12, Geoff Curtis 9, Pete Saunders 6 (+2), Ian Bottomley 6 (+1), Glyn Blackburn 6, Colin Tucker 5 (+1), Dave Parry 4 (+1).
CANTERBURY - Peter Murray 10, Ken Vale 9 (+1), Martyn Piddock 4 (+1), Graham Miles 3 (+1), Jim Crowhurst 2, John Hibben 1, Dave Percy 1.

Meeting 14 - Monday, June 30, 1969 - British League Division II
L.M.R. Sports Ground, Earle Street, Crewe
Track Length - 470 yards.

CREWE KINGS.....53 ROMFORD BOMBERS.....25

Geoff Curtis smashed the Earle Street track record during the home romp against the highly rated Bombers. Bolstered by a new engine, the Aussie recorded a time of 71.8 in Heat 4, beating Romford star Ross Gilbertson in the process. The visitors found Crewe in irresistible form and did not manage a single heat advantage, recording only one race win, courtesy of Phil Woodcock. Curtis and Paul O'Neil secured maximums with Colin Tucker and Glyn Blackburn also chipping in sixteen points, as the Kings registered their biggest home league win to date.

Heat 01	**O'Neil**/Gilbertson/**Parry**/Wendon (R)	73.4	**4 - 2**	04 - 02
Heat 02	**Blackburn**/**Saunders**/Benham/Yeatman	76.6	**5 - 1**	09 - 03
Heat 03	**Tucker**/Woodcock/Foote/**Bottomley** (R)	74.6	3 - 3	12 - 06
Heat 04	**Curtis**/Gilbertson/**Saunders**/Benham	**71.8** (TR)	**4 - 2**	16 - 08
Heat 05	Woodcock/**Tucker**/**Blackburn**/Wendon	72.0	3 - 3	19 - 11
Heat 06	**O'Neil**/Gilbertson/**Parry**/Yeatman (F)	73.2	**4 - 2**	23 - 13
Heat 07	**Curtis**/Woodcock/Foote/**Saunders**	72.4	3 - 3	26 - 16
Heat 08	**O'Neil**/Gilbertson/**Blackburn**/Benham	74.2	**4 - 2**	30 - 18
Heat 09	**Bottomley**/Woodcock/**Tucker**/Gilbertson (F)	73.4	**4 - 2**	34 - 20
Heat 10	**O'Neil**/Woodcock/**Parry**/Foote	73.4	**4 - 2**	38 - 22
Heat 11	**Curtis**/**Blackburn**/Foote/Wendon	73.8	**5 - 1**	43 - 23
Heat 12	**Tucker**/**Parry**/Gilbertson/Woodcock (R)	73.6	**5 - 1**	48 - 24
Heat 13	**Curtis**/**Bottomley**/Benham/Foote (R)	73.2	**5 - 1**	53 - 25

CREWE - Geoff Curtis 12, Paul O'Neil 12, Colin Tucker 9, Glyn Blackburn 7 (+2), Ian Bottomley 5 (+1), Dave Parry 5 (+1), Pete Saunders 3 (+1).
ROMFORD - Phil Woodcock 11, Ross Gilbertson 9, Brian Foote 3 (+2), Charlie Benham 2, Frank Wendon 0, Chris Yeatman 0, *Tony George (R/R)*.

Towards the end of June, the Crewe Speedway Supporters Club was officially formed with 125 fans enrolling almost immediately. Keith Standring was appointed secretary, and had the responsibility of organising activities for club members, including social nights and coach trips to away venues.

Meeting 15 - Friday, July 4, 1969 - British League Division II
Shielfield Park, Tweedmouth, Berwick-upon-Tweed
Track Length - 440 yards.

BERWICK BANDITS.....43 CREWE KINGS.....35

Crewe made the long trip up to Berwick, but not even twenty-four points and five race wins from Geoff Curtis and Paul O'Neil could provide them with that first elusive away win. The Bandits, already beaten five times on their own track, started the better, and it wasn't until Heat 8 that Crewe secured a heat advantage, thanks to a Curtis and O'Neil maximum. The match however, would be remembered for a spectacular crash in Heat 8, which saw Grieves Davidson, Ken Omand and O'Neil all take a tumble. Davidson would later be taken to hospital suffering from neck injuries. Curtis's points haul from the past few meetings saw him climb to second in the Division II averages.

Heat 01	Hall/**O'Neil**/**Parry**/Omand	80.2	3 - 3	03 - 03
Heat 02	Davidson/Nichol/**Blackburn**/**Bruce** (R)	83.4	5 - 1	08 - 04
Heat 03	Williams/**Bottomley**/Black/**Tucker**	82.0	4 - 2	12 - 06
Heat 04	**Curtis**/Robinson/Nichol/**Blackburn**	81.4	3 - 3	15 - 09
Heat 05	**O'Neil**/Williams/Black/**Parry**	81.8	3 - 3	18 - 12
Heat 06	Hall/**Bottomley**/**Curtis**/Omand (R)	81.2	3 - 3	21 - 15
Heat 07	Davidson/Robinson/**Tucker**/**Bottomley**	82.6	5 - 1	26 - 16
Heat 08	**Curtis**/**O'Neil**/Omand/Davidson (X)	80.0	**1 - 5**	27 - 21
Heat 09	**Curtis**/Black/**Bruce**/Williams (R)	79.2	**2 - 4**	29 - 25
Heat 10	Hall/Omand/**Blackburn**/**Bottomley**	81.6	5 - 1	34 - 26
Heat 11	Robinson/**O'Neil**/**Parry**/Nichol	80.6	3 - 3	37 - 29
Heat 12	**Curtis**/Hall/**Bottomley**/Williams	80.0	**2 - 4**	39 - 33
Heat 13	Robinson/**O'Neil**/Black/**Parry**	80.8	4 - 2	43 - 35

BERWICK - Mark Hall 11, Maury Robinson 10 (+1), Grieves Davidson 6, Brian Black 5 (+1), Roy Williams 5, Alex Nichol 3 (+2), Ken Omand 3 (+1).
CREWE - Geoff Curtis 13 (+1), Paul O'Neil 11 (+1), Ian Bottomley 5, Dave Parry 2 (+2), Glyn Blackburn 2, Malcolm Bruce* 1, Colin Tucker 1.

Meeting 16 - Sunday, July 6, 1969 - British League Division II
Arlington Raceway, Arlington Road, Hailsham, Eastbourne
Track Length - 342 yards.

EASTBOURNE EAGLES.....11 CREWE KINGS.....13

Heavy rainfall an hour before the start of the meeting put the fixture in doubt. Dave Jessup added to his growing reputation by winning the first heat, but when rain began to fall again with only four heats completed, the meeting was abandoned by referee George Allen. Buckinghamshire grass tracker Barry Meeks made his Crewe debut.

Heat 01	Jessup/**Saunders**/Cook/**Parry**	71.0	4 - 2	04 - 02
Heat 02	**Saunders**/**Meeks**/Hay/Boughtflower (F)	82.0	**1 - 5**	05 - 07
Heat 03	Golden/Sims/**Tucker**/**Bottomley** (R)	82.0	5 - 1	10 - 08
Heat 04	**Meeks**/**Curtis**/Trott/Boughtflower (F)	89.0	**1 - 5**	11 - 13

(Abandoned after four heats due to rain - result does not stand.)

EASTBOURNE - Alby Golden 3, Dave Jessup 3, Laurie Sims 2 (+1), Derek Cook 1, Garry Hay 1, Reg Trott 1, Ray Boughtflower 0.
CREWE - Barry Meeks 5 (+1), Pete Saunders 5, Geoff Curtis 2 (+1), Colin Tucker 1, Ian Bottomley 0, Dave Parry 0.

For the next league match, the Kings faced Len Silver's Rayleigh, with Maurice Littlechild confident that Crewe would get their revenge for their opening home defeat. He would comment: *"Already Len is boasting what his Rockets are going to do and his riders are following suit.*

Forget about your victory on May 19. You caught us on the hop then. You were fully match fit and had just recorded two away wins on the previous two days. This time you will find that our boys have settled down. They know their own track now and it will be a different kettle of fish this time." Rayleigh though had not been out of the top three in the league all season and had recently won at Eastbourne in the K.O. Cup, so were arriving in confident mood. However, with their star rider, Mike Gardner now with Cradley Heath, Crewe too were confident of extending their unbeaten home league record.

Meeting 17 - Monday, July 7, 1969 - British League Division II
L.M.R. Sports Ground, Earle Street, Crewe
Track Length - 470 yards.

CREWE KINGS.....43 RAYLEIGH ROCKETS.....35

Paul O'Neil and Geoff Curtis remained unbeaten for the second home fixture in a row (O'Neil's third consecutive Earle Street maximum), with Colin Tucker, Glyn Blackburn and Ian Bottomley also winning heats. Crewe gained their revenge over the Essex outfit, although the visitors, operating rider replacement for Laurie Etheridge, led after four heats. The meeting however, was not without mishap for the hosts. Tucker retired in two heats - one with broken handlebars and another due to engine failure and Pete Saunders pulled up in his opening ride after losing his goggles. Dave Parry was another to suffer when he lost a chain in Heat 12, which could have caused a nasty injury after wrapping around his leg. During the second-half, Crewe reserve Blackburn hit the boards and broke his right wrist, while Tucker damaged his kneecap competing for the Count Bartelli Trophy.

Heat 01	**O'Neil**/Maloney/Wright/**Parry**	72.4	3 - 3	03 - 03
Heat 02	**Blackburn**/Stone/Newman/**Saunders** (R)	76.0	3 - 3	06 - 06
Heat 03	Brown/Maloney/**Bottomley**/**Tucker** (R)	74.0	1 - 5	07 - 11
Heat 04	**Curtis**/Stone/**Saunders**/Mackay	72.2	**4 - 2**	11 - 13
Heat 05	**Tucker**/**Bottomley**/Wright/Maloney	00.0	**5 - 1**	16 - 14
Heat 06	**O'Neil**/**Parry**/Mackay/Newman	72.0	**5 - 1**	21 - 15
Heat 07	**Curtis**/Wright/Brown/**Saunders**	73.8	3 - 3	24 - 18
Heat 08	**O'Neil**/Maloney/Stone/**Blackburn** (F)	72.6	3 - 3	27 - 21
Heat 09	**Bottomley**/Newman/Brown/**Tucker** (R)	77.4	3 - 3	30 - 24
Heat 10	**O'Neil**/Maloney/**Parry**/Stone	73.2	**4 - 2**	34 - 26
Heat 11	**Curtis**/Wright/Maloney/**Blackburn**	73.0	3 - 3	37 - 29
Heat 12	Stone/**Tucker**/Brown/**Parry** (R)	75.6	2 - 4	39 - 33
Heat 13	**Curtis**/Wright/**Bottomley**/Brown	73.0	**4 - 2**	43 - 35

CREWE - Geoff Curtis 12, Paul O'Neil 12, Ian Bottomley 7 (+1), Colin Tucker 5, Dave Parry 3 (+1), Glyn Blackburn 3, Pete Saunders 1.
RAYLEIGH - Geoff Maloney 9 (+2), Terry Stone 8 (+1), Roger Wright 8 (+1), Dingle Brown 6 (+2), Bob Newman 3 (+1), Malcolm Mackay 1, *Laurie Etheridge (R/R).*

Meeting 18 - Thursday, July 10, 1969 - British League Division II
Brooklands Sports Stadium, Brooklands Road, Mawneys, Romford
Track Length - 375 yards.

ROMFORD BOMBERS.....40 CREWE KINGS.....38

The Kings took part in a terrific meeting against unbeaten-at-home Romford, but just failed in their attempt to bring the two points back to Cheshire. Missing Paul O'Neil with illness, they had to fully utilise their reserves and by Heat 11, could only field one rider. Even so, with Ian Bottomley recording his first British League maximum, Geoff Curtis and Pete Saunders contributing seventeen points, Crewe went into the final heat of the match with a narrow two point lead, but a home maximum had the Bombers crowd in raptures after a brilliant team ride by Ross Gilbertson and Phil Woodcock. Romford had maintained their home record, even though the Kings had provided nine of the thirteen race winners! The list of walking wounded grew when Bottomley broke his arm in a Heat 12 pile up, but picked himself up to win the re-run! Dave Parry dislocated a shoulder in the last.

Heat 01	**Saunders**/B.Curtis/**Parry**/Wendon (R)	77.8	**2 - 4**	02 - 04
Heat 02	**Saunders**/Foote/Schofield/**Meeks**	76.0	3 - 3	05 - 07
Heat 03	**Bottomley**/Woodcock/**Tucker**/Benham	74.0	**2 - 4**	07 - 11
Heat 04	**G.Curtis**/Gilbertson/Foote/**Meeks**	74.8	3 - 3	10 - 14
Heat 05	Woodcock/**Meeks**/**Parry**/Benham (F)	76.0	3 - 3	13 - 17
Heat 06	Wendon/Woodcock/**Meeks**/**Saunders** (F)	76.8	5 - 1	18 - 18
Heat 07	**Bottomley**/Foote/Gilbertson/**Tucker**	77.0	3 - 3	21 - 21
Heat 08	**Saunders**/Wendon/**Meeks**/Schofield (F)	78.8	**2 - 4**	23 - 25
Heat 09	**G.Curtis**/Woodcock/Foote/**Saunders** (F)	75.0	3 - 3	26 - 28
Heat 10	**Bottomley**/Gilbertson/Wendon/**Tucker** (F)	77.0	3 - 3	29 - 31
Heat 11	Foote/Gilbertson/**Parry** (3 riders only)	76.0	5 - 1	34 - 32
Heat 12	**Bottomley**/**G.Curtis**/Wendon/Schofield	77.6	**1 - 5**	35 - 37
Heat 13	Woodcock/Gilbertson/**Tucker**/**Parry** (X)	78.0	5 - 1	40 - 38

ROMFORD - Phil Woodcock 12 (+1), Ross Gilbertson 9 (+3), Brian Foote 9 (+2), Frank Wendon 7 (+1), Brian Curtis 2, Roland Schofield 1 (+1), Charlie Benham 0, *Tony George (R/R).*
CREWE - Ian Bottomley 12, Pete Saunders 9, Geoff Curtis 8 (+1), Barry Meeks 4, Dave Parry 3 (+1), Colin Tucker 2.

For a track in its infancy, it was a proud moment when news reached the Crewe camp that Earle Street had been chosen to stage a test series match between Young England and the highly gifted Young Czechoslovakian team.

Meeting 19 - Monday, July 14, 1969 - Knock Out Cup, Second Round
L.M.R. Sports Ground, Earle Street, Crewe
Track Length - 470 yards.

CREWE KINGS.....44 CANTERBURY CRUSADERS.....33

Johnnie Hoskins lost his £50 bet and hold of the K.O. Cup. The Crusaders started the night minus heat-leader Peter Murray, who had been recalled by his parent club Wimbledon. Ken Vale showed his liking for the track when amassing fifteen points from six outings, but Crewe produced a more solid all-round display, with four different heat winners during the quarter-final tie. Geoff Curtis won one heat after suffering a puncture on the final bend of the last lap and there was a good home debut for Barry Meeks, who contributed seven points from his four rides.

Heat 01	**O'Neil**/**Parry**/Vale/Hibben	73.8	**5 - 1**	05 - 01
Heat 02	**Saunders**/**Meeks**/Thomas/Brice	77.0	**5 - 1**	10 - 02
Heat 03	**Tucker**/Piddock/Miles/**Jackson** (F)	76.6	3 - 3	13 - 05
Heat 04	Vale/Thomas/**Saunders**/**Curtis** (R)	76.0	1 - 5	14 - 10
Heat 05	Piddock/**Meeks**/**Tucker**/Hibben	75.8	3 - 3	17 - 13
Heat 06	Vale/**Saunders**/**Parry**/Brice (R)	76.2	3 - 3	20 - 16
Heat 07	**Curtis**/Piddock/Miles/**Saunders**	75.8	3 - 3	23 - 19
Heat 08	**O'Neil**/**Meeks**/Thomas/Hibben	77.6	**5 - 1**	28 - 20
Heat 09	Vale/**Tucker**/Piddock/**Jackson**	75.0	2 - 4	30 - 24
Heat 10	**O'Neil**/**Parry**/Miles/Piddock	73.0	**5 - 1**	35 - 25
Heat 11	**Curtis**/Miles/**Meeks**/Hibben	72.8	**4 - 2**	39 - 27
Heat 12	Vale/**Tucker**/**Parry** (R)/Thomas (F)	76.8	2 - 3	41 - 30
Heat 13	**Curtis**/Vale/Hibben/**Meeks** (R)	73.6	3 - 3	44 - 33

CREWE - Geoff Curtis 9, Paul O'Neil 9, Colin Tucker 8 (+1), Barry Meeks 7 (+2), Pete Saunders 6, Dave Parry 5 (+3), Rob Jackson 0.
CANTERBURY - Ken Vale 15, Martyn Piddock 8, Graham Miles 5 (+2), Barry Thomas 4 (+1), John Hibben 1 (+1), Neville Brice 0, *Peter Murray (R/R).*

The Crewe management announced that the new track floodlights (with the lighting poles already in place) would soon be operational.

Meeting 20 - Wednesday, July 16, 1969 - British League Division II
Crayford & Bexley Heath Stadium, London Road, Crayford
Track Length - 300 yards.

CRAYFORD HIGHWAYMEN.....44 CREWE KINGS.....34

The Kings suffered mechanical faults and bad luck throughout, and it cost them dear. In Heat 1, former Crayford rider Dave Parry was left at the gate and in the next, Kings newcomer Freddie Sweet's bike choked out. Heat 3 saw Crewe skipper Colin Tucker fall entering the final straight, and Sweet's meeting got even worse, retiring in Heat 6, and then excluded in Heat 9. Despite this, Crewe put up a real fight on the tight 300 yard London Road circuit, with Geoff Curtis, Paul O'Neil and Barry Meeks, scoring twenty-eight points between them. Home skipper Geoff Ambrose (who resided in Betley, just a few miles from the Crewe track), had mechanical problems while warming his machine up prior to the start of the meeting, and his rides had to be taken by reserves. For Mick Steel, this proved a stroke of good fortune as he began a remarkable sequence of four successive rides, which all resulted in victories. He then sat out Heat 6, before riding in the next, completing a remarkable fifteen point maximum.

Heat 01	Harrison/**O'Neil**/Clark/**Parry**	76.2	4 - 2	04 - 02
Heat 02	Steel/**Meeks**/Drew/**Sweet** (R)	75.0	4 - 2	08 - 04
Heat 03	Steel/**Saunders**/Armstrong/**Tucker** (R)	72.9	4 - 2	12 - 06
Heat 04	Steel/**Meeks**/**Curtis**/Childs (R)	72.7	3 - 3	15 - 09
Heat 05	Steel/**O'Neil**/**Parry**/Armstrong (R)	73.1	3 - 3	18 - 12
Heat 06	**Curtis**/Harrison/Clark/**Sweet** (R)	73.7	3 - 3	21 - 15
Heat 07	Steel/Childs/**Saunders**/**Tucker**	73.5	5 - 1	26 - 16
Heat 08	**Curtis**/Harrison/**Meeks**/Drew	72.5	**2 - 4**	28 - 20
Heat 09	**Meeks**/Armstrong/Drew/**Sweet** (X)	73.0	3 - 3	31 - 23
Heat 10	Harrison/Clark/**O'Neil**/**Saunders** (F)	73.4	5 - 1	36 - 24
Heat 11	Childs/**O'Neil**/**Parry**/Drew	73.4	3 - 3	39 - 27
Heat 12	Clark/**Curtis**/**Meeks**/Drew	73.0	3 - 3	42 - 30
Heat 13	**O'Neil**/Childs/**Tucker**/Armstrong	73.5	**2 - 4**	44 - 34

CRAYFORD - Mick Steel 15, Chris Harrison 10, Colin Clark 7 (+2), Tony Childs 7 (+1), Tony Armstrong 3, Judd Drew 2 (+1).
CREWE - Paul O'Neil 10, Geoff Curtis 9 (+1), Barry Meeks 9 (+1), Pete Saunders 3, Dave Parry 2 (+2), Colin Tucker 1, Freddie Sweet 0.

Meeting 21 - Monday, July 21, 1969 - British League Division II
L.M.R. Sports Ground, Earle Street, Crewe
Track Length - 470 yards.

CREWE KINGS.....34 BELLE VUE COLTS.....44

Crewe's ultimate test, a home league encounter with runaway leaders Belle Vue, was dogged by a spate of mechanical problems which would eventually see their proud home league record relinquished. The Kings led after Heat 1, but from then on it was a tale of what might have been. Dave Parry, leading Heat 2, had to drop out, and in the next, Paul O'Neil's bike packed up on the final lap while well ahead. Parry suffered the misfortune of another retirement in Heat 4, with O'Neil again failing to finish in the next. Geoff Curtis and Parry restored some home pride in Heat 7 with a 5-1, but the gremlins struck again in the ninth, with Curtis ahead going into the last lap. Maximums in the final two heats gave the score some respectability.

Heat 01	**O'Neil**/Broadbelt/**Saunders**/Moss	73.8	**4 - 2**	04 - 02
Heat 02	Bailey/Moulin/**Meeks**/**Parry** (R)	75.4	1 - 5	05 - 07
Heat 03	Owen/**Tucker**/Eyre/**O'Neil** (R)	76.2	2 - 4	07 - 11
Heat 04	Waplington/**Curtis**/Moulin/**Parry** (R)	75.2	2 - 4	09 - 15
Heat 05	Moss/Broadbelt/**Tucker**/**O'Neil**	75.0	1 - 5	10 - 20
Heat 06	Moulin/Bailey/**O'Neil**/**Saunders**	75.0	1 - 5	11 - 25
Heat 07	**Curtis**/**Parry**/Owen/Eyre	73.8	**5 - 1**	16 - 26
Heat 08	Moulin/Moss/**Saunders**/**Parry**	75.4	1 - 5	17 - 31
Heat 09	Waplington/Bailey/**Tucker**/**Curtis** (R)	74.6	1 - 5	18 - 36
Heat 10	**O'Neil**/Bailey/Owen/**Saunders**	73.4	3 - 3	21 - 39
Heat 11	**Curtis**/Broadbelt/Moulin/**Meeks**	74.8	3 - 3	24 - 42
Heat 12	**O'Neil**/**Tucker**/Eyre/Waplington (F)	74.6	**5 - 1**	29 - 43
Heat 13	**Curtis**/**Parry**/Broadbelt/Owen	74.8	**5 - 1**	34 - 44

CREWE - Geoff Curtis 11, Paul O'Neil 10, Colin Tucker 6 (+1), Dave Parry 4 (+2), Pete Saunders 2, Barry Meeks 1, *Ian Bottomley (R/R).*
BELLE VUE - Bill Moulin 10 (+2), Chris Bailey 9 (+2), Eric Broadbelt 7 (+1), Steve Waplington 6, Ken Moss 5 (+1), Taffy Owen 5 (+1), Ken Eyre 2.

Following the home reversal, Maurice Littlechild organised a complete overhaul of all the Crewe machinery and attempted to purchase a new Czech Jawa-Eso machine from Prague, to be delivered in time for the home clash with Plymouth. It was also announced that Peter Seaton, injured since a fall at Plymouth on June 20, had been transferred to King's Lynn Starlets. On July 28, the Crewe v Long Eaton K.O. Cup Semi-Final tie was postponed due to heavy rain.

Meeting 22 - Thursday, July 31, 1969 - British League Division II
Long Eaton Stadium, Station Road, Long Eaton
Track Length - 366 yards.

LONG EATON RANGERS.....47 CREWE KINGS.....31

Colin Tucker was again a man at war at Station Road, this time clashing with home rider Gil Farmer. During Heat 12, with the pair battling for third spot, Tucker was forced off his bike with the referee excluding Farmer, and awarding the point to Tucker. However, not content with the decision, the Crewe skipper stormed into the home pits and confronted Farmer, before being restrained. Curtis and O'Neil again recorded double figure scores.

Heat 01	Lomas/Shakespeare/**O'Neil**/**Saunders**	73.4	5 - 1	05 - 01
Heat 02	Hornby/Farmer/**Meeks**/**Tucker**	74.0	5 - 1	10 - 02
Heat 03	Wrathall/Carter/**Parry**/**Bottomley** (F)	72.2	5 - 1	15 - 03
Heat 04	Penniket/**Curtis**/**Meeks**/Farmer	72.8	3 - 3	18 - 06
Heat 05	Wrathall/**O'Neil**/**Saunders**/Carter (F)	73.6	3 - 3	21 - 09
Heat 06	Lomas/Shakespeare/**Curtis**/**Meeks**	74.0	5 - 1	26 - 10
Heat 07	Penniket/**Parry**/Farmer/**Bottomley**	73.0	4 - 2	30 - 12
Heat 08	Shakespeare/**O'Neil**/**Curtis**/Hornby	73.4	3 - 3	33 - 15
Heat 09	**Curtis**/Wrathall/**Tucker**/Carter	73.0	**2 - 4**	35 - 19
Heat 10	Lomas/Shakespeare/**Parry**/**Bottomley**	74.0	5 - 1	40 - 20
Heat 11	Penniket/**O'Neil**/**Saunders**/Hornby	73.8	3 - 3	43 - 23
Heat 12	**Curtis**/Lomas/**Tucker**/Farmer (X)	72.8	**2 - 4**	45 - 27
Heat 13	**O'Neil**/Wrathall/**Parry**/Penniket	72.8	**2 - 4**	47 - 31

LONG EATON - Tony Lomas 11, Peter Wrathall 10, Malcolm Shakespeare 9 (+3), Geoff Penniket 9, Gil Farmer 3 (+1), Bernie Hornby 3, Roy Carter 2 (+1).
CREWE - Geoff Curtis 10 (+1), Paul O'Neil 10, Dave Parry 5, Pete Saunders 2 (+2), Barry Meeks 2 (+1), Colin Tucker 2, Ian Bottomley 0.

Meeting 23 - Sunday, August 3, 1969 - British League Division II
King's Lynn Stadium, Saddlebow Road, King's Lynn
Track Length - 400 yards.

KING'S LYNN STARLETS.....29 CREWE KINGS.....48

The Kings finally broke their away day duck by comfortably defeating an injury-hit King's Lynn team, who did not register a single heat advantage. All the Kings riders scored steadily, and for the second match in a row, Crewe suffered no mechanical problems, much to their relief. Despite the heavy defeat, Starlets captain Ian Turner turned in an impressive display, contributing nearly half of his team's total.

Heat 01	**O'Neil**/Featherstone/**Saunders** (X)/Osborne (R)	75.8	**2 - 3**	02 - 03
Heat 02	**Tucker**/Ingamells/**Meeks**/Osborne (R)	76.6	**2 - 4**	04 - 07
Heat 03	Turner/**Bottomley**/**Parry**/Peasland (F)	75.6	3 - 3	07 - 10
Heat 04	Turner/**Curtis**/**Meeks**/Ingamells	74.2	3 - 3	10 - 13
Heat 05	Price/**Saunders**/**O'Neil**/Peasland	78.0	3 - 3	13 - 16
Heat 06	**Tucker**/Price/Featherstone/**Curtis** (X)	76.6	3 - 3	16 - 19
Heat 07	Turner/**Parry**/**Bottomley**/Ingamells	74.6	3 - 3	19 - 22
Heat 08	**Saunders**/**Meeks**/Featherstone/Osborne	77.4	**1 - 5**	20 - 27

Heat 09	**Curtis**/Price/**Tucker**/Turner (R)	76.2	**2 - 4**	22 - 31
Heat 10	**Parry**/**Bottomley**/Price/Featherstone	76.0	**1 - 5**	23 - 36
Heat 11	**Saunders**/Turner/**Tucker**/Osborne	76.2	**2 - 4**	25 - 40
Heat 12	**Bottomley**/**Curtis**/Peasland/Price (F)	77.0	**1 - 5**	26 - 45
Heat 13	Turner/**O'Neil**/**Parry**/Ingamells	75.0	3 - 3	29 - 48

KING'S LYNN - Ian Turner 14, Arthur Price 8, Tony Featherstone 4 (+1), John Ingamells 2, Tony Peasland 1, Russell Osborne 0, *Graham Edmonds (R/R).*
CREWE - Ian Bottomley 8 (+2), Pete Saunders 8, Colin Tucker 8, Dave Parry 7 (+2), Geoff Curtis 7 (+1), Paul O'Neil 6 (+1), Barry Meeks 4 (+2).

Meeting 24 - Monday, August 4, 1969 - British League Division II
L.M.R. Sports Ground, Earle Street, Crewe
Track Length - 470 yards.

CREWE KINGS.....61 PLYMOUTH DEVILS.....17

A day after their first away victory, the Kings hammered an under-strength Plymouth side. They dropped just four points throughout the night, recording their biggest ever win, which also turned out to be Plymouth's worst ever reversal, in a meeting that produced a bonus point in every heat. The hosts recorded eleven maximums and provided all race winners, with Plymouth's extra points coming when Colin Tucker suffered a puncture in Heat 4, and Paul O'Neil doing likewise in Heat 6 when leading. Geoff Curtis was unbeaten and twice came within a whisker of his own track record. Ian Bottomley and Pete Saunders both recorded their best scores at Earle Street and Dave Parry produced a bonus point each time out.

Heat 01	**Saunders**/**O'Neil**/Coles/Sanders	75.4	**5 - 1**	05 - 01
Heat 02	**Tucker**/**Meeks**/Hammond/Facey	75.2	**5 - 1**	10 - 02
Heat 03	**Bottomley**/**Parry**/Sanders/Marks (R)	75.0	**5 - 1**	15 - 03
Heat 04	**Curtis**/Whitaker/Facey/**Tucker** (R)	72.0	3 - 3	18 - 06
Heat 05	**Bottomley**/**Parry**/Coles/Sanders	74.6	**5 - 1**	23 - 07
Heat 06	**Saunders**/Whitaker/Hammond/**O'Neil** (R)	74.2	3 - 3	26 - 10
Heat 07	**Curtis**/**Tucker**/Whitaker/Marks	72.0	**5 - 1**	31 - 11
Heat 08	**Meeks**/**Saunders**/Coles/Facey	74.6	**5 - 1**	36 - 12
Heat 09	**Bottomley**/**Parry**/Whitaker/Hammond	74.2	**5 - 1**	41 - 13
Heat 10	**O'Neil**/**Saunders**/Coles/Marks	74.0	**5 - 1**	46 - 14
Heat 11	**Curtis**/**Meeks**/Coles/Sanders	72.2	**5 - 1**	51 - 15
Heat 12	**O'Neil**/**Parry**/Whitaker/Facey	74.6	**5 - 1**	56 - 16
Heat 13	**Curtis**/**Bottomley**/Sanders/Hammond	72.8	**5 - 1**	61 - 17

CREWE - Geoff Curtis 12, Ian Bottomley 11 (+1), Pete Saunders 10 (+2), Dave Parry 8 (+4), Paul O'Neil 8 (+1), Barry Meeks 7 (+2), Colin Tucker 5 (+1).
PLYMOUTH - Dave Whitaker 7, Bob Coles 5, John Hammond 2 (+1), Colin Sanders 2, Clark Facey 1 (+1), Keith Marks 0, *Chris Roynon (R/R).*

On August 7, the *Crewe Chronicle*, reported that the Kings had won their fight to retain the services of their three colonial riders. Basic regulations stipulated that in Division II, a maximum of two colonials per team could be used, but with Crewe being a new team, they were given special management dispensation, in view of being unable to obtain the services of Long Eaton's Glyn Chandler, who did not take up the option of a transfer to the club. This had caused several opponents to lodge protests with the Speedway Control Board, but the Kings were allowed to carry on by a majority vote, although the ruling would only apply for this season. Further good news was received when Ian Bottomley and Dave Parry were included in the twenty-eight man Young England squad for the forthcoming test series with Young Czechoslovakia. On August 7, the Crewe pairing of Geoff Curtis and Dave Parry won the Teesside Best Pairs Trophy at Middlesbrough, but only following a three-man run-off, after the pair finished on 18 points alongside Terry Lee & Dave Durham of Middlesbrough and Mick Bell & Dene Davies of Reading. Curtis represented Crewe and led from start to finish. Things got even better for him just two days later when he won the Berwick Festival Trophy, where he smashed the Shielfield track record by 1.8 seconds, recording a time of

77.2 in Heat 1. Bottomley also competed in the event, suffering a spectacular crash on the third lap of Heat 3.

Meeting 25 - Monday, August 11, 1969 - British League Division II
L.M.R. Sports Ground, Earle Street, Crewe
Track Length - 470 yards.

CREWE KINGS.....57 EASTBOURNE EAGLES.....21

Eastbourne came to Crewe in confident mood, with former Division I veterans Alby Golden and Reg Trott in their starting line-up. The pair did manage sixteen points from twelve rides, but it was never going to be enough to cause the upset that the Eagles had hoped for. Young Dave Jessup scored four points, but three of the four remaining Eastbourne riders failed to trouble the score chart. The final heat produced the best race of the night, when a fantastic duel between Geoff Curtis and Ian Bottomley (who were both chasing maximums), saw the Aussie just edge home.

Heat 01	**O'Neil**/Trott/Jessup/**Meeks**	73.8	3 - 3	03 - 03
Heat 02	**Tucker**/**Saunders**/Cook/Platt	77.5	**5 - 1**	08 - 04
Heat 03	**Bottomley**/Golden/**Parry**/Sims	74.4	**4 - 2**	12 - 06
Heat 04	**Curtis**/Trott/**Tucker**/Platt	73.4	**4 - 2**	16 - 08
Heat 05	**Bottomley**/Golden/Jessup/**Parry** (R)	75.4	3 - 3	19 - 11
Heat 06	**Meeks**/**Tucker**/Trott/Cook (R)	75.5	**5 - 1**	24 - 12
Heat 07	**Curtis**/Golden/**Tucker**/Sims	73.2	**4 - 2**	28 - 14
Heat 08	**Meeks**/**Saunders**/Golden/Boughtflower	75.0	**5 - 1**	33 - 15
Heat 09	**Bottomley**/**Parry**/Trott/Cook	75.7	**5 - 1**	38 - 16
Heat 10	**O'Neil**/Golden/**Meeks**/Sims	74.8	**4 - 2**	42 - 18
Heat 11	**Curtis**/**Saunders**/Jessup/Trott	73.7	**5 - 1**	47 - 19
Heat 12	**O'Neil**/**Parry**/Golden/Trott	74.8	**5 - 1**	52 - 20
Heat 13	**Curtis**/**Bottomley**/Jessup/Sims	74.5	**5 - 1**	57 - 21

CREWE - Geoff Curtis 12, Ian Bottomley 11 (+1), Paul O'Neil 9, Colin Tucker 7 (+1), Barry Meeks 7, Pete Saunders 6 (+3), Dave Parry 5 (+2).
EASTBOURNE - Alby Golden 10, Reg Trott 6, Dave Jessup 4 (+2), Derek Cook 1, Ray Boughtflower 0, Cec Platt 0, Laurie Sims 0, *Hugh Saunders (R/R).*

Meeting 26 - Monday, August 18, 1969 - Division II International, Third Test
L.M.R. Sports Ground, Earle Street, Crewe
Track Length - 470 yards.

YOUNG ENGLAND.....54 YOUNG CZECHOSLOVAKIA.....54

Ian Bottomley captained Young England on his home track, with Dave Parry also featuring as first reserve, in the momentous occasion of Earle Street's first ever international. The meeting proved to be the best so far at Crewe, but would prove a personal disaster for Bottomley. In his first race he crashed into the safety fence while trying to pass Miroslav Verner, ending up with a broken bone in his hand. Parry won his first race, but suffered mechanical problems in his next two. Local rider Geoff Ambrose scored ten points.

Heat 01	Ledecky/Leadbitter/Stancl/Bottomley	74.2	2 - 4	02 - 04
Heat 02	Prusa/Lee/Lid/Broadbelt	76.2	2 - 4	04 - 08
Heat 03	Verner/Ambrose/Bailey/Majstr	75.0	3 - 3	07 - 11
Heat 04	Broadbelt/Ledecky/Stancl/Lee	75.0	3 - 3	10 - 14
Heat 05	Bailey/Ambrose/Prusa/Lid	73.0	5 - 1	15 - 15
Heat 06	Verner/Leadbitter/Majstr/Bottomley (F)	76.0	2 - 4	17 - 19
Heat 07	Bailey/Ledecky/Ambrose/Stancl	73.8	4 - 2	21 - 21
Heat 08	Parry/Prusa/Leadbitter/Klokocka	74.0	4 - 2	25 - 23
Heat 09	Verner/Lee/Majstr/Mills	75.0	2 - 4	27 - 27
Heat 10	Stancl/Leadbitter/Ledecky/Parry	75.2	2 - 4	29 - 31
Heat 11	Prusa/Lee/Mills/Lid	74.8	3 - 3	32 - 34
Heat 12	Bailey/Verner/Ambrose/Majstr	73.8	4 - 2	36 - 36
Heat 13	Stancl/Lee/Mills/Ledecky	75.0	3 - 3	39 - 39

Heat 14	Prusa/Ambrose/Bailey/Klokocka	73.4	3 - 3	42 - 42
Heat 15	Verner/Leadbitter/Majstr/Parry	73.8	2 - 4	44 - 46
Heat 16	Bailey/Ambrose/Ledecky/Stancl	74.8	5 - 1	49 - 47
Heat 17	Prusa/Leadbitter/Mills/Lid	74.0	3 - 3	52 - 50
Heat 18	Verner/Lee/Majstr/Mills	73.0	2 - 4	54 - 54

YOUNG ENGLAND - Chris Bailey 14 (+2), Tom Leadbitter 11, Geoff Ambrose 10 (+2), Terry Lee 10, Roger Mills (Reserve) 3 (+3), Eric Broadbelt 3, Dave Parry (Reserve) 3, Ian Bottomley 0. Team Manager: Ken Adams.
YOUNG CZECHOSLOVAKIA - Miroslav Verner 17, Karel Prusa 15, Frantisek Ledecky 9, Jiri Stancl 8 (+1), Zdenek Majstr 4, Josef Lid 1, Jan Klokocka (Reserve) 0. Team Manager: Pavel Kacer.

During the short interval, the new floodlights were switched on. At a cost of £3,500, they would now enable the season to be extended until the end of October, with future meetings now commencing at 7.30pm.

Meeting 27 - Saturday, August 23, 1969 - British League Division II
Seed Hill Stadium, Carr Road, Nelson
Track Length - 300 yards.

NELSON ADMIRALS.....41 CREWE KINGS.....37

Crewe took part in a meeting that contained ten re-runs, with the tapes broken on no fewer than seven occasions (three times by Paul O'Neil and twice by Geoff Curtis). The Kings did in fact produce eight heat winners during the narrow reversal, but could not turn the majority into a winning margin after sharing the points on six occasions. Dave Parry top scored for the Kings with ten from his five starts.

Heat 01	**O'Neil**/Schofield/Riley/**Meeks** (X)	61.4	3 - 3	03 - 03
Heat 02	**Saunders**/Sheldrick/Lee/**Blackburn** (X)	61.6	3 - 3	06 - 06
Heat 03	**Parry**/Thompson/Harrison/**Tucker**	62.6	3 - 3	09 - 09
Heat 04	Knapkin/**Curtis**/Sheldrick/**Saunders** (X)	61.0	4 - 2	13 - 11
Heat 05	Thompson/**Saunders**/**Meeks**/Harrison	61.8	3 - 3	16 - 14
Heat 06	Schofield/Riley/**Saunders**/**Blackburn**	62.4	5 - 1	21 - 15
Heat 07	Knapkin/**Curtis**/Sheldrick/**Parry**	61.0	4 - 2	25 - 17
Heat 08	**O'Neil**/Lee/Riley/**Meeks**	62.2	3 - 3	28 - 20
Heat 09	**Parry**/**Saunders**/Harrison/Thompson	62.0	**1 - 5**	29 - 25
Heat 10	**Parry**/Schofield/Riley/**Tucker** (R)	62.2	3 - 3	32 - 28
Heat 11	**Meeks**/Lee/**Blackburn**/Knapkin (R)	63.4	**2 - 4**	34 - 32
Heat 12	Harrison/Sheldrick/**Curtis**/**Tucker**	62.6	5 - 1	39 - 33
Heat 13	**O'Neil**/Knapkin/**Parry**/Thompson	60.6	**2 - 4**	41 - 37

NELSON - Alan Knapkin 8, Dave Schofield 7, Sid Sheldrick 6 (+1), Stuart Riley 5 (+4), Chris Harrison* 5 (+1), Jack Lee 5 (+1), Peter Thompson 5.
CREWE - Dave Parry 10, Paul O'Neil 9, Pete Saunders 8 (+1), Geoff Curtis 5, Barry Meeks 4 (+1), Glyn Blackburn 1, Colin Tucker 0.

Geoff Curtis, top of the Kings averages at the cut-off date of August 23, would be Crewe's representative in the forthcoming Division II Riders Championship at Hackney on September 26. He also received news that he had been chosen to skipper the Young Australasia side for the five match series against Young Britain.

Meeting 28 - Monday, August 25, 1969 - British League Division II
L.M.R. Sports Ground, Earle Street, Crewe
Track Length - 470 yards.

CREWE KINGS.....56 KING'S LYNN STARLETS.....21

A first league double was achieved by Crewe when they easily overcame a poor King's Lynn team, with all thirteen heats once again won by the home side. Barry Meeks, Dave Parry and Pete Saunders all secured paid maximums. Former rider Peter Seaton failed to score on his return to Earle Street.

Heat 01	**Meeks**/Price/Osborne/**O'Neil** (R)	76.8	3 - 3	03 - 03
Heat 02	**Tucker**/Ingamells/**Blackburn**/Seaton	72.2	**4 - 2**	07 - 05
Heat 03	**Parry/Saunders**/Featherstone/Turner	75.8	**5 - 1**	12 - 06
Heat 04	**Curtis/Tucker**/Ingamells/Turner	73.8	**5 - 1**	17 - 07
Heat 05	**Saunders/Parry**/Price/Osborne	75.0	**5 - 1**	22 - 08
Heat 06	**Meeks/O'Neil**/Price/Seaton	76.4	**5 - 1**	27 - 09
Heat 07	**Tucker**/Ingamells/Featherstone/**Curtis** (R)	75.0	3 - 3	30 - 12
Heat 08	**Meeks/Blackburn**/Osborne/Ingamells (F)	76.4	**5 - 1**	35 - 13
Heat 09	**Parry/Saunders**/Featherstone/Seaton (R)	75.8	**5 - 1**	40 - 14
Heat 10	**O'Neil/Meeks**/Turner/Ingamells	75.0	**5 - 1**	45 - 15
Heat 11	**Curtis**/Price/Osborne/**Blackburn** (R)	74.0	3 - 3	48 - 18
Heat 12	**Parry**/Turner/**O'Neil** (R)/Price (R)	75.8	**3 - 2**	51 - 20
Heat 13	**Curtis/Saunders**/Turner/Featherstone (R)	73.8	**5 - 1**	56 - 21

CREWE - Barry Meeks 11 (+1), Dave Parry 11 (+1), Pete Saunders 9 (+3), Geoff Curtis 9, Colin Tucker 8 (+1), Paul O'Neil 5 (+1), Glyn Blackburn 3 (+1).
KING'S LYNN - Arthur Price 6, John Ingamells 5, Ian Turner 4, Russell Osborne 3 (+2), Tony Featherstone 3 (+1), Peter Seaton 0, *Graham Edmonds (R/R).*

Meeting 29 - Friday, August 29, 1969 - British League Division II
Ipswich Stadium, Foxhall Road, Foxhall Heath, Ipswich
Track Length - 328 yards.

IPSWICH WITCHES.....42 CREWE KINGS.....36

The Witches took the points but Geoff Curtis the plaudits. He scored a brilliant six ride maximum, exactly half of Crewe's total. The Kings should have picked up their second away league victory of the season, but with Ian Bottomley still injured and Paul O'Neil suffering an off day, only Barry Meeks and Pete Saunders managed any real back up for the rampant Aussie. Ipswich meanwhile scored solidly throughout, with John Harrhy their star rider of the night.

Heat 01	Spittles/**Meeks**/Bailey/**O'Neil** (R)	72.4	4 - 2	04 - 02
Heat 02	**Saunders**/Slee/Aldridge/**Tucker** (X)	73.6	3 - 3	07 - 05
Heat 03	**Curtis**/Baker/Bagley/**Parry**	71.6	3 - 3	10 - 08
Heat 04	**Curtis**/Harrhy/**Tucker**/Slee	71.8	**2 - 4**	12 - 12
Heat 05	Baker/Bagley/**Meeks/O'Neil** (R)	73.0	5 - 1	17 - 13
Heat 06	**Curtis**/Bailey/Spittles/**Saunders** (F)	72.0	3 - 3	20 - 16
Heat 07	Harrhy/**Parry/Saunders**/Slee	72.8	3 - 3	23 - 19
Heat 08	Bailey/**Meeks**/Aldridge/**Tucker**	73.8	4 - 2	27 - 21
Heat 09	**Curtis/Saunders**/Bagley/Baker	73.4	**1 - 5**	28 - 26
Heat 10	Bailey/**Meeks**/Spittles/**Parry**	75.2	4 - 2	32 - 28
Heat 11	Harrhy/Aldridge/**Meeks/O'Neil**	73.8	5 - 1	37 - 29
Heat 12	**Curtis**/Bagley/**Saunders**/Spittles	73.4	**2 - 4**	39 - 33
Heat 13	**Curtis**/Harrhy/Baker/**Tucker**	71.8	3 - 3	42 - 36

IPSWICH - John Harrhy 10, Pete Bailey 9, Ron Bagley 6 (+2), Ernie Baker 6 (+1), Ted Spittles 5 (+1), Bernie Aldridge 4 (+2), Neville Slee 2.
CREWE - Geoff Curtis 18, Barry Meeks 8, Pete Saunders 7 (+2), Dave Parry 2, Colin Tucker 1, Paul O'Neil 0, *Ian Bottomley (R/R).*

Meeting 30 - Sunday, August 31, 1969 - British League Division II
Arlington Raceway, Arlington Road, Hailsham, Eastbourne
Track Length - 342 yards.

EASTBOURNE EAGLES.....43 CREWE KINGS.....34

Eastbourne won a closely fought contest, securing victory in the last heat. The match, part of a double header (the Eagles earlier defeated Plymouth 47-30), had been rained off on July 6 with Crewe ahead, but this time the home side remained unbeaten in the first seven heats and never relinquished their lead.

Heat 01	Jessup/**O'Neil**/Platt (F)/**Meeks** (F)	69.4	3 - 2	03 - 02
Heat 02	Boughtflower/**Tucker/Blackburn**/Smith	71.2	3 - 3	06 - 05

Heat 03	Golden/**Saunders**/Sims/**Parry**	68.8	4 - 2	10 - 07
Heat 04	**Curtis**/Trott/Smith/**Blackburn**	67.6	3 - 3	13 - 10
Heat 05	Golden/**Meeks**/Sims/**O'Neil**	68.8	4 - 2	17 - 12
Heat 06	Platt/**Tucker**/**Curtis**/Jessup (F)	70.4	3 - 3	20 - 15
Heat 07	Trott/**Parry**/Boughtflower/**Saunders** (F)	67.8	4 - 2	24 - 17
Heat 08	**Meeks**/**Saunders**/Boughtflower/Platt	69.0	**1 - 5**	25 - 22
Heat 09	Golden/**Curtis**/Sims/**Tucker**	68.8	4 - 2	29 - 24
Heat 10	Jessup/**Parry**/Platt/**Saunders**	69.8	4 - 2	33 - 26
Heat 11	Trott/**Meeks**/Boughtflower/**O'Neil**	67.2	4 - 2	37 - 28
Heat 12	**Curtis**/**Meeks**/Jessup/Sims	69.0	**1 - 5**	38 - 33
Heat 13	Trott/Golden/**Parry**/**O'Neil** (F)	68.6	5 - 1	43 - 34

EASTBOURNE - Alby Golden 11 (+1), Reg Trott 11, Dave Jessup 7, Ray Boughtflower 6, Ces Platt 4, Laurie Sims 3, Tony Smith 1 (+1).
CREWE - Geoff Curtis 9 (+1), Barry Meeks 9 (+1), Dave Parry 5, Pete Saunders 4 (+1), Colin Tucker 4, Paul O'Neil 2, Glyn Blackburn 1 (+1).

Meeting 31 - Monday, September 1, 1969 - British League Division II
L.M.R. Sports Ground, Earle Street, Crewe
Track Length - 470 yards.

CREWE KINGS.....62 READING RACERS.....16

Home riders extended their run of consecutive race wins at Earle Street to 56, after Reading lost every race and heat of this one-sided contest. The high flying Racers, who had already won five times on their travels, were simply blown away by the Kings, who came within a point of Belle Vue Colts' record Division II scoreline of 63-15 against Weymouth in 1968. Paul O'Neil, riding on new machinery, put his recent troubles behind him, dropping only one point, which was to fellow team-mate Barry Meeks in Heat 6. Dave Parry weighed in with a paid twelve points from four rides in Crewe's biggest victory, which was also Reading's worst ever reversal.

Heat 01	**O'Neil**/**Meeks**/Bell/Tabet	72.0	**5 - 1**	05 - 01
Heat 02	**Tucker**/**Saunders**/Leigh/Pratt	76.6	**5 - 1**	10 - 02
Heat 03	**Parry**/**Bottomley**/Vernam/Davies (R)	75.2	**5 - 1**	15 - 03
Heat 04	**Curtis**/**Saunders**/May/Leigh	74.4	**5 - 1**	20 - 04
Heat 05	**Parry**/Bell/**Bottomley**/Tabet	75.4	**4 - 2**	24 - 06
Heat 06	**Meeks**/**O'Neil**/May/Pratt	75.0	**5 - 1**	29 - 07
Heat 07	**Curtis**/**Saunders**/Davies/Vernam	74.6	**5 - 1**	34 - 08
Heat 08	**Tucker**/Bell/**Meeks**/May	76.0	**4 - 2**	38 - 10
Heat 09	**Bottomley**/**Parry**/May/Pratt	76.8	**5 - 1**	43 - 11
Heat 10	**O'Neil**/**Meeks**/Vernam/Davies	75.2	**5 - 1**	48 - 12
Heat 11	**Tucker**/**Curtis**/Bell/Tabet	76.4	**5 - 1**	53 - 13
Heat 12	**O'Neil**/**Parry**/May/Davies	74.8	**5 - 1**	58 - 14
Heat 13	**Curtis**/Bell/**Bottomley**/Vernam	74.2	**4 - 2**	62 - 16

CREWE - Geoff Curtis 11 (+1), Paul O'Neil 11 (+1), Dave Parry 10 (+2), Colin Tucker 9, Barry Meeks 8 (+2), Ian Bottomley 7 (+1), Pete Saunders 6 (+3).
READING - Mick Bell 8, Dickie May 4, Mike Vernam 2, Dene Davies 1, Bernie Leigh 1, Phil Pratt 0, Bob Tabet 0.

Meeting 32 - Thursday, September 4, 1969 - British League Division II
Cleveland Park Stadium, Stockton Road, Middlesbrough
Track Length - 335 yards.

MIDDLESBROUGH TEESSIDERS.....48 CREWE KINGS.....30

Another small circuit proved Crewe's undoing, but this time they had no complaints, with only Geoff Curtis showing any real form. Paul O'Neil performed admirably on his old track, but the Teessiders proved too strong for the Kings to mount any serious challenge for the points. Pete Saunders and Ian Bottomley had falls first time out and failed to score a point throughout the meeting. Tom Leadbitter top scored for the home side, dropping his only point to Curtis.

Heat 01	Leadbitter/**O'Neil**/Reading/**Meeks**	72.2	4 - 2	04 - 02
Heat 02	Swales/**Tucker**/Forrester/**Saunders** (X)	74.6	4 - 2	08 - 04
Heat 03	Lee/Durham/**Parry**/**Bottomley** (F)	72.2	5 - 1	13 - 05
Heat 04	**Curtis**/**Tucker**/Swales/Mills (R)	72.6	**1 - 5**	14 - 10
Heat 05	Lee/Durham/**Meeks**/**O'Neil**	72.0	5 - 1	19 - 11
Heat 06	**Curtis**/Leadbitter/Reading/**Saunders**	72.4	3 - 3	22 - 14
Heat 07	**Curtis**/Swales/Mills/**Bottomley**	72.6	3 - 3	25 - 17
Heat 08	Forrester/**Meeks**/Reading/**Tucker**	73.4	4 - 2	29 - 19
Heat 09	Durham/**O'Neil**/Lee/**Curtis**	73.4	4 - 2	33 - 21
Heat 10	Leadbitter/**Meeks**/Reading/**Parry**	73.6	4 - 2	37 - 23
Heat 11	Forrester/**O'Neil**/Swales/**Meeks** (F)	74.4	4 - 2	41 - 25
Heat 12	Leadbitter/**Curtis**/Durham/**Bottomley**	73.2	4 - 2	45 - 27
Heat 13	Lee/**Parry**/**O'Neil**/Forrester	74.0	3 - 3	48 - 30

MIDDLESBROUGH - Tom Leadbitter 11, Terry Lee 10, Dave Durham 8 (+2), Bruce Forrester 7, Tim Swales 7, Pete Reading 4 (+1), Roger Mills 1 (+1).
CREWE - Geoff Curtis 11, Paul O'Neil 7 (+1), Barry Meeks 5, Colin Tucker 4 (+1), Dave Parry 3, Ian Bottomley 0, Pete Saunders 0.

On September 5, the three Crewe colonials featured for Young Australasia, who lost 48-59 to Young Britain in the first test at Berwick, in front of 4,000 fans. Geoff Curtis scored 8, Paul O'Neil 5, with Colin Tucker failing to register a point.

Meeting 33 - Monday, September 8, 1969 - Knock Out Cup, Semi-Final
L.M.R. Sports Ground, Earle Street, Crewe
Track Length - 470 yards.

CREWE KINGS.....58 LONG EATON RANGERS.....20

The Kings progressed to the final of the K.O. Cup after a resounding victory over hapless Long Eaton. Colin Tucker, continuing his good form, shared a dead heat (Crewe's first) with Geoff Curtis in the final heat, preventing the latter from recording another maximum. Glyn Chandler, who had been previously linked with a move to Earle Street, endured a wretched night, failing to score in each of his three rides. Ian Bottomley, Barry Meeks and Dave Parry all returned good scores.

Heat 01	**O'Neil**/**Meeks**/Penniket/Gay	73.2	**5 - 1**	05 - 01
Heat 02	**Parry**/**Tucker**/Farmer/Hornby (F)	74.4	**5 - 1**	10 - 02
Heat 03	**Bottomley**/Farmer/Wrathall/**Saunders** (R)	75.8	3 - 3	13 - 05
Heat 04	**Curtis**/Shakespeare/Hornby/**Parry** (R)	73.8	3 - 3	16 - 08
Heat 05	**Bottomley**/Penniket/Wrathall/**Saunders**	75.8	3 - 3	19 - 11
Heat 06	**Tucker**/**Meeks**/Shakespeare/Penniket (R)	75.0	**5 - 1**	24 - 12
Heat 07	**Curtis**/**Parry**/Wrathall/Chandler (R)	73.4	**5 - 1**	29 - 13
Heat 08	**Tucker**/**Meeks**/Shakespeare/Hornby (F)	75.6	**5 - 1**	34 - 14
Heat 09	**Bottomley**/**Saunders**/Farmer/Shakespeare (R)	75.6	**5 - 1**	39 - 15
Heat 10	**O'Neil**/**Meeks**/Wrathall/Chandler (F)	74.8	**5 - 1**	44 - 16
Heat 11	**Curtis**/**Tucker**/Gay/Penniket	74.4	**5 - 1**	49 - 17
Heat 12	**Parry**/Wrathall/**Saunders**/Shakespeare	75.2	**4 - 2**	53 - 19
Heat 13	**Curtis** & **Tucker**/Penniket/Chandler	75.0	**5 - 1**	58 - 20

CREWE - Colin Tucker 12½ (+2½), Geoff Curtis 11½ (+½), Ian Bottomley 9, Barry Meeks 8 (+4), Dave Parry 8 (+1), Paul O'Neil 6, Pete Saunders 3 (+1).
LONG EATON - Peter Wrathall 6 (+2), Gil Farmer 4, Geoff Penniket 4, Malcolm Shakespeare 4, Bernie Hornby 1 (+1), Pete Gay 1, Glyn Chandler 0.

Belle Vue Colts would be Crewe's opponents in the K.O. Cup final, with the first leg at Earle Street, after Belle Vue won the toss. On September 9, Paul O'Neil top scored for Young Australasia, who lost the second test 42-66 at Nelson. Geoff Curtis contributed 11 points, with Geoff Ambrose scoring 17 from his six rides for the Brits. The following night, the Young Lions again defeated the colonials, this time at Crayford. Ambrose, on his home track, scored 7, with Curtis and O'Neil finishing with 6 apiece.

(ABOVE) The Kings mid-season. (Left to right) Ken Adams (team manager), Paul O'Neil, Dave Parry, Pete Saunders, Geoff Curtis, Ian Bottomley, Colin Tucker (on bike), Barry Meeks and promoter Maurice Littlechild. (BELOW) Crewe skipper Colin Tucker warming up for the clash with Romford on June 30.

(ABOVE) Geoff Curtis receives the Berwick Festival Trophy, which he won on August 9.
(BELOW) Young Britain v Young Australasia at Shielfield Park, Berwick in the first test on September 5. Young Britain won the match 59-48. Among the colonials were Geoff Curtis, Paul O'Neil and Colin Tucker.

(ABOVE) Barry Meeks and Alby Golden battle for the lead at Eastbourne on Sunday, August 31. (BELOW) Meeks at Earle Street. Like many riders, he had progressed to speedway from grass-tracking.

Meeting 34 - Friday, September 12, 1969 - British League Division II
Canterbury City Football Ground, Kingsmead Road, Canterbury
Track Length - 390 yards.

CANTERBURY CRUSADERS.....45 CREWE KINGS.....33

Martyn Piddock recorded a maximum to help Canterbury to a comfortable victory. Paul O'Neil didn't help the Crewe cause by arriving fifty minutes late, after being delayed in the London traffic. Reserve Dave Parry replaced him in Heat 1 and then went on to win Heat 2. This would be the only away race win until the tenth, by which time the tie was as good as over. Pete Saunders scored in each of his rides, as did Geoff Curtis, who secured four second places.

Heat	Riders	Time	Score	Total
Heat 01	Murray/Hibben/**Parry**/**Meeks**	82.8	5 - 1	05 - 01
Heat 02	**Parry**/Banks/Kite/**Tucker**	83.8	3 - 3	08 - 04
Heat 03	Thomas/Brice/**Saunders**/**Bottomley**	79.4	5 - 1	13 - 05
Heat 04	Piddock/**Curtis**/**Tucker**/Kite	79.4	3 - 3	16 - 08
Heat 05	Thomas/**Curtis**/**Meeks**/Brice	80.2	3 - 3	19 - 11
Heat 06	Murray/**Curtis**/Hibben/**Parry**	78.4	4 - 2	23 - 13
Heat 07	Piddock/**Saunders**/**Bottomley**/Kite	80.0	3 - 3	26 - 16
Heat 08	Banks/Hibben/**Meeks**/**Tucker**	82.0	5 - 1	31 - 17
Heat 09	Thomas/**Curtis**/**Parry**/Brice	80.0	3 - 3	34 - 20
Heat 10	**Saunders**/**Bottomley**/Hibben/Murray (R)	84.0	**1 - 5**	35 - 25
Heat 11	Piddock/**Meeks**/Banks/**O'Neil**	80.4	4 - 2	39 - 27
Heat 12	Murray/**Saunders**/**Bottomley**/Banks	79.0	3 - 3	42 - 30
Heat 13	Piddock/**O'Neil**/**Saunders**/Thomas (F)	81.0	3 - 3	45 - 33

CANTERBURY - Martyn Piddock 12, Peter Murray 9, Barry Thomas 9, John Hibben 6 (+2), Graham Banks 6, Neville Brice 2 (+1), Alan Kite 1 (+1).
CREWE - Pete Saunders 9 (+1), Geoff Curtis 8, Dave Parry 5 (+1), Ian Bottomley 4 (+3), Barry Meeks 4 (+1), Paul O'Neil 2, Colin Tucker 1 (+1).

On Sunday, September 14, at Doncaster, Crewe's league fixture (part of a double header with Romford) was postponed due to a waterlogged track.

Meeting 35 - Monday, September 15, 1969 - British League Division II
L.M.R. Sports Ground, Earle Street, Crewe
Track Length - 470 yards.

CREWE KINGS.....51 BERWICK BANDITS.....26

The scoreline suggested another home stroll, but the Bandits provided spirited opposition and Peter Kelly became the first away rider to win a race in league competition, since Belle Vue's visit on July 21, ending a run of 71 consecutive home victories. The visitors in fact provided four race winners, with heat leader Mark Hall pulling in an impressive 11 points, and this, nursing a leg injury. Paul O'Neil was the fastest King on the night, recording 73.2 in Heat 12 and he dropped just a solitary point from four rides.

Heat	Riders	Time	Score	Total
Heat 01	**Meeks**/**O'Neil**/Hall/Williams	73.8	**5 - 1**	05 - 01
Heat 02	**Parry**/**Tucker**/Paterson/Nicol	74.2	**5 - 1**	10 - 02
Heat 03	Kelly/**Saunders**/**Bottomley** (X)/Black (X)	79.0	2 - 3	12 - 05
Heat 04	**Curtis**/Robinson/**Parry**/Nicol	74.0	**4 - 2**	16 - 07
Heat 05	Hall/**Saunders**/Williams/**Bottomley**	74.4	2 - 4	18 - 11
Heat 06	**O'Neil**/Hall/**Meeks**/Robinson	73.6	**4 - 2**	22 - 13
Heat 07	**Parry**/**Curtis**/Black/Kelly	74.8	**5 - 1**	27 - 14
Heat 08	**Meeks**/**Tucker**/Williams/Robinson (R)	74.2	**5 - 1**	32 - 15
Heat 09	Robinson/**Saunders**/**Bottomley**/Paterson	73.8	3 - 3	35 - 18
Heat 10	**O'Neil**/**Meeks**/Williams/Black	74.8	**5 - 1**	40 - 19
Heat 11	Hall/**Curtis**/**Tucker**/Williams	74.6	3 - 3	43 - 22
Heat 12	**O'Neil**/Robinson/**Saunders**/Nicol	73.2	**4 - 2**	47 - 24
Heat 13	**Curtis**/Hall/**Bottomley**/Black	73.4	**4 - 2**	51 - 26

CREWE - Paul O'Neil 11 (+1), Geoff Curtis 10 (+1), Barry Meeks 9 (+1), Dave Parry 7, Pete Saunders 7, Colin Tucker 5 (+3), Ian Bottomley 2 (+1).

BERWICK - Mark Hall 11, Maury Robinson 7, Peter Kelly 3, Roy Williams 3, Brian Black 1, Ian Paterson 1, Alex Nicol 0.

Crewe underwent extensive training in the build-up to the K.O. Cup Final first leg, in the hope of taking a big lead to Manchester. The day before the Earle Street clash, Geoff Curtis and Paul O'Neil rode for Young Australasia in the fourth test at Eastbourne. Curtis scored 10 and O'Neil 3 in the 38-69 defeat.

Meeting 36 - Monday, September 22, 1969 - Knock Out Cup, Final, First Leg
L.M.R. Sports Ground, Earle Street, Crewe
Track Length - 470 yards.

CREWE KINGS.....42 BELLE VUE COLTS.....36

The Kings gained revenge over the newly crowned Division II champions for their first home league reversal of the season, but the margin of victory made Belle Vue favourites to lift the cup. The whole meeting was a fantastic advert for Division II, and although Crewe were never behind in the tie, the result was only decided in the final heat of the night. The drama unfolded as early as Heat 2, when Dave Parry collided with Mike Hiftle and was forced to pull up on the last lap with a dislocated shoulder. Colin Tucker won the heat from Hiftle by half a wheel. Paul O'Neil also had a frustrating meeting, winning two races and failing to score in his other two - firstly due to mechanical trouble, and then after colliding with Barry Meeks. Ken Moss and Chris Bailey were the top scorers for the Colts.

Heat 01	**O'Neil**/Moss/**Meeks**/Broadbelt	74.2	**4 - 2**	04 - 02
Heat 02	**Tucker**/Hiftle/Owen/**Parry** (R)	74.4	3 - 3	07 - 05
Heat 03	**Bottomley**/Bailey/**Saunders**/Broadbelt	75.2	**4 - 2**	11 - 07
Heat 04	**Curtis**/Hiftle/**Tucker**/Waplington	74.6	**4 - 2**	15 - 09
Heat 05	Broadbelt/Moss/**Bottomley**/**Saunders**	75.2	1 - 5	16 - 14
Heat 06	Waplington/**Meeks**/Owen/**O'Neil** (R)	74.8	2 - 4	18 - 18
Heat 07	**Curtis**/Moss/Bailey/**Parry**	74.4	3 - 3	21 - 21
Heat 08	**Meeks**/**Tucker**/Moss/Hiftle	73.8	**5 - 1**	26 - 22
Heat 09	**Bottomley**/Owen/Waplington/**Saunders**	75.0	3 - 3	29 - 25
Heat 10	Bailey/**Meeks**/Waplington/**O'Neil**	74.2	2 - 4	31 - 29
Heat 11	Moss/**Tucker**/**Curtis**/Broadbelt	75.0	3 - 3	34 - 32
Heat 12	**O'Neil**/Bailey/**Tucker**/Waplington	74.2	**4 - 2**	38 - 34
Heat 13	**Curtis**/Bailey/**Bottomley**/Hiftle	74.2	**4 - 2**	42 - 36

CREWE - Geoff Curtis 10 (+1), Colin Tucker 9 (+1), Ian Bottomley 8, Barry Meeks 8, Paul O'Neil 6, Pete Saunders 1, Dave Parry 0.
BELLE VUE - Chris Bailey 10 (+1), Ken Moss 10 (+1), Steve Waplington 5 (+1), Taffy Owen 4 (+1), Mike Hiftle 4, Eric Broadbelt 3, *Ken Eyre (R/R).*

Meeting 37 - Wednesday, September 24, 1969 - Knock Out Cup, Final, Second Leg
Zoological Gardens, Hyde Road, West Gorton, Manchester
Track Length - 418 yards.

BELLE VUE COLTS.....55 CREWE KINGS.....23

(Belle Vue won on aggregate 91 - 65)

The six point lead held by the Kings from the first leg, had been wiped out by Heat 2 of the return at Hyde Road, in front of the Colts' biggest crowd of the season. Crewe didn't win a single heat and provided only three race winners, which proved scant consolation for the large gathering of Crewe fans (around fourteen coachloads) who had made the trip to Manchester. Paul O'Neil and Geoff Curtis did their utmost to gain some respectability, but the rest of the side contributed only five points between them.

Heat 01	Broadbelt/**O'Neil**/Moss/**Meeks**	75.2	4 - 2	04 - 02
Heat 02	Hiftle/Owen/**Parry**/**Tucker** (X)	76.2	5 - 1	09 - 03
Heat 03	Hiftle/Bailey/**Saunders**/**Bottomley**	77.2	5 - 1	14 - 04
Heat 04	**Curtis**/Hiftle/Owen/**Tucker**	74.6	3 - 3	17 - 07
Heat 05	Bailey/Waplington/**Parry**/**O'Neil**	76.2	5 - 1	22 - 08

Heat 06	Moss/Broadbelt/**Curtis/Meeks**	76.0	5 - 1	27 - 09
Heat 07	Hiftle/**O'Neil**/Waplington/**Bottomley**	75.6	4 - 2	31 - 11
Heat 08	**Curtis**/Moss/Owen/**Meeks**	75.8	3 - 3	34 - 14
Heat 09	Broadbelt/Bailey/**Tucker/Curtis** (R)	76.2	5 - 1	39 - 15
Heat 10	Broadbelt/Moss/**Bottomley/Saunders**	75.8	5 - 1	44 - 16
Heat 11	**O'Neil**/Waplington/Owen/**Meeks**	76.2	3 - 3	47 - 19
Heat 12	Broadbelt/**Curtis**/Bailey/**Bottomley**	76.2	4 - 2	51 - 21
Heat 13	Bailey/**O'Neil**/Waplington/**Bottomley**	75.4	4 - 2	55 - 23

BELLE VUE - Eric Broadbelt 14 (+1), Chris Bailey 11 (+2), Mike Hiftle 11, Ken Moss 8 (+1), Steve Waplington 6 (+1), Taffy Owen 5 (+4), *Ken Eyre (R/R).*
CREWE - Geoff Curtis 9, Paul O'Neil 9, Dave Parry 2, Ian Bottomley 1, Pete Saunders 1, Colin Tucker 1, Barry Meeks 0.

There was more despair during the second-half, when Geoff Curtis was struck by Barry Meeks after falling in his path, in an unfortunate accident. Although it looked serious, the tough Aussie walked unaided from the first aid room, with bad bruising, which made him extremely doubtful for the Division II Riders Championship at Hackney, two nights later. On September 25, Paul O'Neil starred for Young Australasia in their 57-51 final test victory over the Young Brits at Ipswich, scoring 14 points. Curtis missed the match due to his Hyde Road spill.

Friday, September 26, 1969 - British League Division II Riders Championship
Hackney Wick Stadium, Waterden Road, London
Track Length - 345 yards.

WINNER.....GEOFF AMBROSE

Geoff Curtis failed in his bid to become the Division II Riders Champion after scoring just six points in front of a crowd approaching 10,000. Still not fully-fit, he managed two wins, but was excluded for breaking the tapes twice and retired from another heat with mechanical problems. Meeting reserve Paul O'Neil took five rides and finished with six points. Geoff Ambrose won the title, with Mick Bell (Reading) second and Ross Gilbertson (Romford), third, following a run-off.

Heat 01	Trott/Lee/Sanders/Brown	70.0
Heat 02	Gilbertson/Bell/Woodcock/Devonport	68.6
Heat 03	Murray/Spittles/Turner/O'Neil	69.2
Heat 04	Robinson/Ambrose/Wrathall (F)/Broadbelt (X)	69.4
Heat 05	Ambrose/Woodcock/Schofield/Lee (X)	68.6
Heat 06	Gilbertson/Murray/Sanders/O'Neil (R)	69.0
Heat 07	Bell/Robinson/Trott/Spittles	69.8
Heat 08	**Curtis**/Turner/Wrathall/Brown	72.0
Heat 09	Gilbertson/Wrathall/Woodcock/Spittles	69.0
Heat 10	Robinson/O'Neil/Sanders/Turner (R)	70.4
Heat 11	Woodcock/Trott/Schofield/**Curtis**	70.0
Heat 12	Ambrose/Bell/Murray/Brown	69.4
Heat 13	Bell/O'Neil/Piddock/Turner	69.6
Heat 14	Ambrose/Sanders/Spittles/**Curtis**	70.2
Heat 15	Murray/Trott/Wrathall/Woodcock (R)	69.6
Heat 16	Piddock/Gilbertson/Robinson/Schofield	68.6
Heat 17	**Curtis**/Robinson/Piddock/Murray (R)	70.2
Heat 18	Bell/Schofield/Wrathall/Sanders	69.4
Heat 19	Ambrose/Gilbertson/Trott/Turner	69.0
Heat 20	Piddock/O'Neil/Spittles/Brown	70.2
R/O for 2nd	Bell/Gilbertson	68.6

Geoff Ambrose *(Crayford)* 14, Mick Bell *(Reading)* 13, Ross Gilbertson *(Romford)* 13, Maury Robinson *(Berwick)* 11, Peter Murray *(Canterbury)* 9, Reg Trott *(Eastbourne)* 9, Geoff Curtis *(Crewe)* 6, Peter Wrathall *(Long Eaton)* 5, Colin Sanders *(Plymouth)* 5, Ted Spittles *(Ipswich)* 4, Dave Schofield *(Nelson)* 4, Ian Turner *(King's Lynn II)* 3, Terry Lee *(Teesside)* 2, Eric Broadbelt *(Belle Vue II)* 0, Dingle Brown *(Rayleigh)* 0, George Devonport *(Crayford)* 0. Meeting Reserves: Martyn Piddock *(Canterbury)* 8, Phil Woodcock *(Romford)* 7, Paul O'Neil *(Crewe)* 6.

Meeting 38 - Sunday, September 28, 1969 - British League Division II
Doncaster Greyhound Stadium, York Road, Doncaster
Track Length - 350 yards.

DONCASTER STALLIONS.....47 CREWE KINGS.....31

A double header saw the Stallions lose to Reading 36-42 in the first match, but beat Crewe in the second. The Doncaster track, labelled the worst in the league, could not be blamed for Crewe's poor performance and again the Kings were beset with problems throughout their final away fixture of the season. Barry Meeks was injured in a Heat 1 spill and took no further part in the meeting. Pete Saunders fell in the third, and Dave Parry was excluded in Heat 9 for tape-breaking.

Heat 01	Shearer/**O'Neil**/**Meeks**/Bridgett	74.6	3 - 3	03 - 03
Heat 02	Ulph/**Parry**/Wyer/**Tucker**	76.8	4 - 2	07 - 05
Heat 03	Baugh/Timms/**Bottomley**/**Saunders** (F)	73.2	5 - 1	12 - 06
Heat 04	**Curtis**/Hawkins/**Parry**/Wyer (X)	76.0	**2 - 4**	14 - 10
Heat 05	Timms/**O'Neil**/**Parry**/Baugh (X)	76.0	3 - 3	17 - 13
Heat 06	**Curtis**/Shearer/Bridgett/**Tucker**	74.2	3 - 3	20 - 16
Heat 07	Hawkins/Wyer/**Saunders**/**Bottomley**	74.4	5 - 1	25 - 17
Heat 08	**Parry**/Ulph/Bridgett/**Tucker**	76.6	3 - 3	28 - 20
Heat 09	Timms/**Curtis**/Wyer/**Tucker**	76.2	4 - 2	32 - 22
Heat 10	Shearer/Ulph/**Saunders**/**Bottomley**	76.8	5 - 1	37 - 23
Heat 11	**O'Neil**/Ulph/**Parry**/Hawkins	75.0	**2 - 4**	39 - 27
Heat 12	Shearer/**Curtis**/Wyer/**Bottomley**	76.0	4 - 2	43 - 29
Heat 13	Hawkins/**O'Neil**/Timms/**Saunders**	75.4	4 - 2	47 - 31

DONCASTER - Terry Shearer 11, Derek Timms 9 (+1), Stuart Ulph 9 (+1), Chris Hawkins 8, Doug Wyer 5 (+1), Dave Baugh 3, Alan Bridgett 2 (+2).
CREWE - Geoff Curtis 10, Paul O'Neil 9, Dave Parry 8 (+1), Pete Saunders 2, Barry Meeks 1 (+1), Ian Bottomley 1, Colin Tucker 0.

Meeting 39 - Monday, September 29, 1969 - British League Division II
L.M.R. Sports Ground, Earle Street, Crewe
Track Length - 470 yards.

CREWE KINGS.....53 CRAYFORD HIGHWAYMEN.....24

Even without the injured Geoff Curtis, Crewe were still too strong for a Crayford team that included the newly crowned Division II Riders Champion Geoff Ambrose. The winning margin would have been even greater but for a rare occurrence in the final heat, when Ian Bottomley retired on lap one and Colin Tucker did likewise a circuit later, leaving the Crayford pair of Archie Wilkinson and Colin Clark to coast home for a 5-0 win. Paul O'Neil registered a brilliant 15 point maximum, but the fastest home rider of the night was Bottomley, who twice went under the 74 second mark. Ambrose had a somewhat disappointing meeting and won just once, contributing only five to the Highwaymen's total. He did though feature in the race of the night in Heat 7, when a fantastic duel with Bottomley, saw the home rider pass him round the boards on the last lap.

Heat 01	**O'Neil**/**Meeks**/Wilkinson/Harrison	74.4	**5 - 1**	05 - 01
Heat 02	**Saunders**/**Tucker**/Clark/Drew	77.0	**5 - 1**	10 - 02
Heat 03	Ambrose/**Parry**/Drew/**Bottomley** (R)	74.0	2 - 4	12 - 06
Heat 04	**O'Neil**/**Saunders**/Childs/Clark	74.8	**5 - 1**	17 - 07
Heat 05	**Bottomley**/**Parry**/Wilkinson/Harrison	73.8	**5 - 1**	22 - 08
Heat 06	**O'Neil**/**Meeks**/Childs/Clark	74.2	**5 - 1**	27 - 09
Heat 07	**Bottomley**/Ambrose/**Saunders**/Armstrong	73.4	**4 - 2**	31 - 11
Heat 08	**Tucker**/Wilkinson/**Meeks**/Ambrose (R)	76.0	**4 - 2**	35 - 13
Heat 09	**Bottomley**/**Parry**/Childs/Clark	74.0	**5 - 1**	40 - 14
Heat 10	**O'Neil**/**Meeks**/Childs/Armstrong (R)	74.8	**5 - 1**	45 - 15
Heat 11	**Tucker**/Harrison/**Saunders**/Wilkinson (F)	75.8	**4 - 2**	49 - 17
Heat 12	**O'Neil**/Childs/**Parry**/Clark	75.0	**4 - 2**	53 - 19
Heat 13	Wilkinson/Clark/**Tucker** (R)/**Bottomley** (R)	78.0	0 - 5	53 - 24

CREWE - Paul O'Neil 15, Ian Bottomley 9, Colin Tucker 8 (+1), Barry Meeks 7 (+3), Dave Parry 7 (+2), Pete Saunders 7 (+1), *Geoff Curtis (R/R).*
CRAYFORD - Archie Wilkinson 7, Tony Childs 6, Geoff Ambrose 5, Colin Clark 3 (+1), Chris Harrison 2, Judd Drew 1, Tony Armstrong 0.

Meeting 40 - Monday, October 6, 1969 - British League Division II
L.M.R. Sports Ground, Earle Street, Crewe
Track Length - 470 yards.

CREWE KINGS.....54 NELSON ADMIRALS.....24

Geoff Ambrose made a second visit to Earle Street in the space of a week, riding as one of the two guests for the depleted Admirals. This time he enjoyed his night, scoring half of the visiting total, winning his first three rides. Paul O'Neil was again the top Crewe scorer with a four ride maximum.

Heat	Riders	Time	Heat score	Match score
Heat 01	**O'Neil**/Owen/**Tucker**/Riley	74.6	**4 - 2**	04 - 02
Heat 02	**Bottomley**/**Saunders**/Thompson/Lee	75.6	**5 - 1**	09 - 03
Heat 03	Ambrose/**Meeks**/Owen/**Parry**	74.6	2 - 4	11 - 07
Heat 04	**Curtis**/**Saunders**/Lee/Evans (R)	76.0	**5 - 1**	16 - 08
Heat 05	Ambrose/**Meeks**/**Parry**/Owen (R)	74.0	3 - 3	19 - 11
Heat 06	**O'Neil**/**Tucker**/Evans/Thompson	73.8	**5 - 1**	24 - 12
Heat 07	Ambrose/**Saunders**/Evans/**Curtis** (R)	75.0	2 - 4	26 - 16
Heat 08	**Tucker**/**Bottomley**/Owen/Riley (R)	75.2	**5 - 1**	31 - 17
Heat 09	**Meeks**/Evans/**Parry**/Thompson	74.6	**4 - 2**	35 - 19
Heat 10	**O'Neil**/Ambrose/**Tucker**/Evans	73.4	**4 - 2**	39 - 21
Heat 11	**Curtis**/**Bottomley**/Owen/Riley	74.8	**5 - 1**	44 - 22
Heat 12	**O'Neil**/**Parry**/Evans/Lee	75.0	**5 - 1**	49 - 23
Heat 13	**Curtis**/**Meeks**/Ambrose/Owen	73.8	**5 - 1**	54 - 24

CREWE - Paul O'Neil 12, Barry Meeks 9 (+1), Geoff Curtis 9, Ian Bottomley 7 (+2), Colin Tucker 7 (+1), Pete Saunders 6 (+2), Dave Parry 4 (+2).
NELSON - Geoff Ambrose* 12, Dai Evans 5, Taffy Owen* 5, Jack Lee 1, Peter Thompson 1, Stuart Riley 0, *Murray Burt (R/R).*

Meeting 41 - Monday, October 13, 1969 - British League Division II
L.M.R. Sports Ground, Earle Street, Crewe
Track Length - 470 yards.

CREWE KINGS.....56 DONCASTER STALLIONS.....22

Thirteen heat winners and ten heat wins saw Crewe gain a handsome win over an under-strength Doncaster outfit - a result which raised hopes of a top half finish in the league table. Ian Bottomley, demoted to reserve, reacted positively with three wins from three rides, including a victory over team mate Geoff Curtis, which was the only point dropped by the Aussie ace.

Heat	Riders	Time	Heat score	Match score
Heat 01	**O'Neil**/Evans/**Tucker**/Bridgett	74.4	**4 - 2**	04 - 02
Heat 02	**Bottomley**/Ulph/**Saunders**/Devonport (X)	74.0	**4 - 2**	08 - 04
Heat 03	**Meeks**/**Parry**/Hawkins/Timms	74.2	**5 - 1**	13 - 05
Heat 04	**Curtis**/Ulph/Wyer/**Saunders**	75.0	3 - 3	16 - 08
Heat 05	**Meeks**/**Parry**/Bridgett/Evans	74.0	**5 - 1**	21 - 09
Heat 06	**Tucker**/**O'Neil**/Wyer/Devonport (R)	75.6	**5 - 1**	26 - 10
Heat 07	**Curtis**/Evans/**Saunders**/Hawkins	74.8	**4 - 2**	30 - 12
Heat 08	**Bottomley**/Ulph/Bridgett/**Tucker**	74.0	3 - 3	33 - 15
Heat 09	**Parry**/**Meeks**/Devonport/Wyer (R)	74.6	**5 - 1**	38 - 16
Heat 10	**O'Neil**/**Tucker**/Timms/Hawkins	75.2	**5 - 1**	43 - 17
Heat 11	**Bottomley**/**Curtis**/Evans/Bridgett	73.8	**5 - 1**	48 - 18
Heat 12	**Parry**/Ulph/Wyer/**O'Neil**	74.8	3 - 3	51 - 21
Heat 13	**Curtis**/**Meeks**/Ulph/Evans	73.8	**5 - 1**	56 - 22

CREWE - Geoff Curtis 11 (+1), Barry Meeks 10 (+2), Dave Parry 10 (+2), Ian Bottomley 9, Paul O'Neil 8 (+1), Colin Tucker 6 (+1), Pete Saunders 2.

DONCASTER - Stuart Ulph 9, Dai Evans* 5, Doug Wyer 3 (+2), Alan Bridgett 2 (+1), George Devonport 1, Chris Hawkins 1, Derek Timms 1.

On October 15, at the Coppenhall Club in Crewe, the Speedway Supporters Club held a buffet dance. Police Chief Superintendent H. O. Kenworthy was guest of honour and presented a canteen of cutlery to Geoff Curtis and Paul O'Neil for topping the Crewe score charts in the K.O. Cup Final. Curtis also received the Supporters Club Trophy.

Meeting 42 - Monday, October 20, 1969 - British League Division II
L.M.R. Sports Ground, Earle Street, Crewe
Track Length - 470 yards.

CREWE KINGS.....32 LONG EATON RANGERS.....10

Fog caused endless problems in Crewe's final home league meeting of the season, and eventually caused the abandonment of the match. At the end of Heat 5 the fog descended, and although it cleared enough to allow a further two heats, ACU referee Jack Greene came down from the commentary box to check the visibility and decided that conditions were too dangerous to continue and called off the meeting.

Heat 01	**O'Neil/Bottomley**/Wrathall/Carter (F)	73.0	**5 - 1**	05 - 01
Heat 02	**Saunders/Tucker**/Gay/Chandler	76.4	**5 - 1**	10 - 02
Heat 03	**Parry/Meeks**/Penniket/Farmer (F)	75.0	**5 - 1**	15 - 03
Heat 04	**Curtis**/Wrathall/**Saunders**/Gay	75.0	**4 - 2**	19 - 05
Heat 05	**Meeks**/Penniket/Farmer/**Parry** (R)	76.2	3 - 3	22 - 08
Heat 06	**O'Neil/Bottomley**/Wrathall/Chandler	76.4	**5 - 1**	27 - 09
Heat 07	**Curtis/Saunders**/Penniket/Farmer	76.0	**5 - 1**	32 - 10

(Abandoned after seven heats due to fog - result stands.)

CREWE - Pete Saunders 6 (+1), Geoff Curtis 6, Paul O'Neil 6, Barry Meeks 5 (+1), Ian Bottomley 4 (+2), Dave Parry 3, Colin Tucker 2 (+1).
LONG EATON - Geoff Penniket 4, Peter Wrathall 4, Gil Farmer 1 (+1), Pete Gay 1, Roy Carter 0, Glyn Chandler 0, *Malcolm Shakespeare (R/R)*.

Meeting 43 - Monday, October 27, 1969 - Cheshire Open Championship
L.M.R. Sports Ground, Earle Street, Crewe
Track Length - 470 yards.

WINNER.....GEOFF CURTIS

A star-studded Division II field competed in front of a 7,000 crowd for the Cheshire Open Championship in the final meeting of the season at Earle Street, but it was home riders who dominated the show. Geoff Curtis capped off a terrific season by snatching the British Rail Trophy, but was pressurised all the way by Ian Bottomley, Colin Tucker and Barry Meeks.

Heat 01	Curtis/Parry/Vale/Turner	74.6
Heat 02	Tucker/Meeks/Ambrose/Harrhy (R)	74.6
Heat 03	Murray/Saunders/Price/O'Neil (R)	75.8
Heat 04	Bottomley/Hall/Broadbelt/Moss	74.4
Heat 05	Tucker/Hall/Price/Turner (R)	74.0
Heat 06	Bottomley/Ambrose/Parry/Saunders	73.6
Heat 07	Curtis/O'Neil/Moss/Jackson	74.8
Heat 08	Meeks/Vale/Broadbelt/Murray	73.8
Heat 09	O'Neil/Turner/Ambrose/Broadbelt (R)	74.8
Heat 10	Moss/Murray/Tucker/Parry	74.8
Heat 11	Curtis/Meeks/Bottomley (R)/Price (F)	73.8
Heat 12	Vale/Hall/Palmer/Saunders	75.8
Heat 13	Bottomley/Murray/Jackson/Turner	74.6
Heat 14	Parry/Meeks/O'Neil/Hall	74.8
Heat 15	Tucker/Curtis/Broadbelt/Saunders	75.2
Heat 16	Ambrose/Moss/Vale/Price	73.6
Heat 17	Moss/Meeks/Saunders/Turner (R)	74.6

Heat 18	Parry/Broadbelt/Palmer/Price	75.4
Heat 19	Ambrose/Curtis/Murray/Hall	73.8
Heat 20	Bottomley/Tucker/Vale/O'Neil	74.6

Geoff Curtis 13, Ian Bottomley 12, Colin Tucker 12, Barry Meeks 11, Geoff Ambrose 10, Dave Parry 9, Ken Moss 9, Ken Vale 8, Peter Murray 8, Paul O'Neil 6, Mark Hall 6, Eric Broadbelt 5, Pete Saunders 3, Ian Turner 2, Arthur Price 2, John Harrhy 0. Meeting Reserves: Alan Palmer 2, Rob Jackson 1. *(Turner replaced Terry Lee).*

So the first season of speedway in Crewe had been a resounding success. The team had finished a very respectable seventh in the league table, reached the final of the K.O. Cup and Geoff Curtis had finished the campaign fifth in the Division II averages. They had only been beaten once at home, with just 28 league races out of 189 won by a visiting rider, although their away form was the joint second worst in the division. Crowds had also been good, averaging around 4,400. Work commenced almost immediately after the final meeting, on improving spectator facilities. Colin Tucker began the construction of covered accommodation for around 2,500 supporters, which would stretch along the whole of the back straight and take in both bends. On November 12, Ken Adams held the first of his Wednesday afternoon training sessions. The attendees would include local rider Charlie Scarbrough, Keith Teasdale and seventeen-year-old Chester youngster John Jackson, who had impressed the Crewe management during several second-half appearances at the back end of the season.

- 1969 Season Summary -

				Wins to Crewe	
Date	**Opponents/Meeting**	**Res**	**Score**	**Race**	**Heat**
Thu, May 1	Middlesbrough (Ch)	L	26 - 52	2	1
Mon, May 12	Reading (BL)	L	36 - 40	6	2
Mon, May 19	**Rayleigh (Ch)**	L	33 - 45	7	4
Sat, May 24	Rayleigh (BL)	L	31 - 47	3	2
Mon, May 26	**Reading (Ch)**	W	40 - 38	6	4
Thu, May 29	Romford (Ch)	L	33 - 45	1	1
Mon, June 2	**Middlesbrough (BL)**	W	42 - 36	8	5
Wed, June 4	Belle Vue (BL)	L	21 - 57	2	2
Thu, June 5	Long Eaton (CH)	L	23 - 54	3	2
Mon, June 9	**Doncaster (KOC 1)**	W	49 - 29	10	8
Mon, June 16	**Ipswich (BL)**	W	52 - 26	12	10
Fri, June 20	Plymouth (BL)	L	28 - 49	4	0
Mon, June 23	**Canterbury (BL)**	W	48 - 30	10	9
Mon, June 30	**Romford (BL)**	W	53 - 25	12	10
Fri, July 4	Berwick (BL)	L	35 - 43	5	3
Sun, July 6	Eastbourne (BL)	A	13 - 11	-	-
Mon, July 7	**Rayleigh (BL)**	W	43 - 35	11	5
Thu, July 10	Romford (BL)	L	38 - 40	9	4
Mon, July 14	**Canterbury (KOC 2)**	W	44 - 33	8	5
Wed, July 16	Crayford (BL)	L	34 - 44	4	2
Mon, July 21	**Belle Vue (BL)**	L	34 - 44	6	4
Thu, July 31	Long Eaton (BL)	L	31 - 47	3	3
Sun, August 3	King's Lynn (BL)	W	48 - 29	8	7
Mon, August 4	**Plymouth (BL)**	W	61 - 17	13	11
Mon, August 11	**Eastbourne (BL)**	W	57 - 21	13	11
Mon, August 18	**Y. Eng. v Y. Czech. (Int)**	-	54 - 54	-	-
Sat, August 23	Nelson (BL)	L	37 - 41	8	3
Mon, August 25	**King's Lynn (BL)**	W	56 - 21	13	10
Fri, August 29	Ipswich (BL)	L	36 - 42	7	3
Sun, August 31	Eastbourne (BL)	L	34 - 43	3	2

Mon, September 1	**Reading (BL)**	W	62 - 16	13	13
Thu, September 4	Middlesbrough (BL)	L	30 - 48	3	1
Mon, September 8	**Long Eaton (KOC S/F)**	W	58 - 20	13	10
Fri, September 12	Canterbury (BL)	L	33 - 45	2	1
Mon, September 15	**Berwick (BL)**	W	51 - 26	9	9
Mon, September 22	**Belle Vue (KOC F)**	W	42 - 36	9	6
Wed, September 24	Belle Vue (KOC F)	L	23 - 55	3	0
Sun, September 28	Doncaster (BL)	L	31 - 47	4	2
Mon, September 29	**Crayford (BL)**	W	53 - 24	11	11
Mon, October 6	**Nelson (BL)**	W	54 - 24	10	10
Mon, October 13	**Doncaster (BL)**	W	56 - 22	13	10
Mon, October 20	**Long Eaton (BL)**	W	32 - 10	7	6
Mon, October 27	**Cheshire Open Ch. (Ind)**	Geoff Curtis		-	-

- British League Division II Final Table -

		Home					Away					
	M	W	D	L	F	A	W	D	L	F	A	Pts
1. Belle Vue (1)	30	14	0	1	785	380	9	1	5	609	558	47
2. Reading (8)	30	13	1	1	678	481	6	0	9	543	622	39
3. Romford	30	11	0	4	649	517	8	1	6	573	592	39
4. Crayford (6)	30	15	0	0	730	434	4	0	11	544½	621½	38
5. Rayleigh (5)	30	12	1	2	671	495	4	1	10	540	625	34
6. Canterbury (7)	30	13	2	0	695	471	2	0	13	529	634	32
7. Crewe	**30**	**14**	**0**	**1**	**754**	**377**	**1**	**0**	**14**	**503**	**662**	**30**
8. Eastbourne	30	13	0	2	651½	505½	1	2	12	483	680	30
9. Middlesbrough (3)..	30	10	1	4	661	509	4	0	11	493	674	29
10. Long Eaton	30	11	0	4	622	539	3	1	11	475½	651½	29
11. Ipswich	30	12	0	3	625	539	1	1	13	491	672	27
12. Doncaster	30	9	0	6	602	558	3	0	12	463	700	24
13. Nelson (2)	30	10	2	3	604½	560½	1	0	14	459	704	24
14. Berwick (10)	30	10	0	5	630½	528½	1	1	13	484½	676½	23
15. Plymouth (4)	30	9	0	6	629	534	0	0	15	371	783	18
16. King's Lynn	30	6	1	8	576	582	2	0	13	449	708	17

(Figures in brackets indicate finishing position in 1968. Romford rode their first 4 away matches as Rochester, following planning problems with their proposed City Way Stadium home, before gaining approval to move into Brooklands Sports Stadium, Romford. Nelson rode their home fixture against Canterbury at Kingsmead Stadium.)

- Crewe Rider Averages -

(League and Knock Out Cup only)

	M	R	W	Pts	BP	Tot	F	P	CMA
Geoff Curtis	33	135	88½	329½	11½	341	6	3	10.104
Paul O'Neil	32	123	63	260	13	273	5	2	8.878
Barry Meeks	24	92	17	147	27	174	0	3	7.565
Ian Bottomley	28	103	34	161	20	181	1	2	7.029
Dave Parry	35	132	25	189	34	223	0	4	6.758
Colin Tucker	34	123	26½	174½	20½	195	0	1	6.341
Pete Saunders	34	119	14	146	30	176	0	2	5.916
Also rode									
Peter Seaton	7	26	4	37	5	42	0	0	6.462
Glyn Blackburn	9	28	3	24	5	29	0	0	4.143
Rob Jackson	2	4	0	2	0	2	0	0	2.000
Freddie Sweet	1	3	0	0	0	0	0	0	0.000
Substitutes									
Malcolm Bruce	1	2	0	1	0	1	0	0	2.000
Stuart Wallace	1	4	0	2	0	2	0	0	2.000

- League Heat Scores -

	Home	Away	Total
5 - 1 heat win to Crewe	87	13	100
4 - 2 heat win to Crewe	46	23	69
3 - 2 heat win to Crewe	1	1	2
3 - 3 drawn heat	34	71	105
2 - 3 heat win to Opponents	1	4	5
2 - 4 heat win to Opponents	9	39	48
1 - 5 heat win to Opponents	10	44	54
0 - 5 heat win to Opponents	1	0	1

- Team Honours -

Knock Out Cup Runners-Up.

- Individual/Pairs Honours -

Teesside Best Pairs (Middlesbrough)
1. Geoff Curtis & Dave Parry 2. Terry Lee & Dave Durham 3. Mick Bell & Dene Davies.

Berwick Festival Trophy (Berwick)
1. Geoff Curtis 2. Steve Waplington 3. Bill Moulin.

Cheshire Open Championship (Crewe)
1. Geoff Curtis 2. Ian Bottomley 3. Colin Tucker.

(ABOVE) Geoff Curtis, who won over 65% of his league and cup rides in 1969.

(ABOVE) Geoff Curtis and Barry Meeks, August 1969, with the puppies of stray dog "Sandy" who came to live with Colin Tucker. (BELOW) "Tuck" warms up his bike in the pits.

(ABOVE) Action from Crewe's second home match versus Reading on May 26. (Wright Wood Collection, courtesy of John Somerville.)

(ABOVE LEFT) New Zealander Paul O'Neil, whose first season at Crewe yielded five full maximums. (ABOVE RIGHT) Dave Parry, the only ever-present in the Kings squad.

The Record Breakers -1970-

The Record Breakers
-1970-

Seventeen teams came to the tapes for the 1970 campaign, including all from the previous season, with the exception of Plymouth, who reverted to an open licence. Two newcomers were Peterborough, who took over the Plymouth licence, and Workington, whose application was accepted just prior to commencement. Middlesbrough became Teesside, and Doncaster were also subject to a name change, becoming the "Dragons." Belle Vue Colts, champions of the past two seasons, moved fourteen miles up the road to Rochdale, with Nelson switching mid-season to Bradford, and King's Lynn Starlets, doing likewise to nearby Boston. On the Crewe front, John Jackson was a new addition to the squad, and on February 2, Australian Warren Hawkins left Sydney on the *S.S. Ellino*, bound for Earle Street. Hawkins was the Sydney Showground's leading handicap rider, and the Kings were alerted by the fact that he had a ten-yard greater handicap than Geoff Curtis, and was keen to try his luck in England following relaxation of the maximum colonial rule. Curtis meanwhile remained undecided on his future, but on the eve of the season, dropped the bombshell all Crewe fans had been dreading – that he was signing for Division I outfit Newcastle. On his departure Maurice Littlechild would comment: *"We tried every possible avenue to allow Geoff to stay with Crewe and still give him the opportunity of his desired Division One rides, but at the crunch there was nothing we could do."* Another rider to leave would be Pete Saunders, who found the travelling up from his Watford home just too much of a burden. He signed for Peterborough, joining another former Crewe rider Peter Seaton. Admission was raised to 6/- for adults, but remained at 3/- for children. Programmes were again priced 1/-.

Meeting 1 - Friday, March 27, 1970 - Players No. 6 Trophy, First Leg
L.M.R. Sports Ground, Earle Street, Crewe
Track Length - 470 yards.

CREWE KINGS.....44 ROCHDALE HORNETS.....33

A large Good Friday crowd braved the freezing conditions and witnessed the track record broken twice. In the opening race, Paul O'Neil lowered the mark to 71.0, only for Barry Meeks to smash it four heats later with a time of 70.4. Team new boy John Jackson won his first race (after a re-run), although Crewe's other new signing, Warren Hawkins, had a less than memorable debut, scoring only three from four rides, after falling twice on the pits bend.

Heat	Riders	Time	Score	Total
Heat 01	**O'Neil**/Waplington/Owen/**Parry**	**71.0** (TR)	3 - 3	03 - 03
Heat 02	**Jackson**/Whittaker/**Tucker**/Richardson (X)	72.0	**4 - 2**	07 - 05
Heat 03	**Meeks/Hawkins**/Broadbelt/Moss	71.4	**5 - 1**	12 - 06
Heat 04	**Bottomley**/Bailey/**Tucker**/Richardson	73.2	**4 - 2**	16 - 08
Heat 05	**Meeks**/Waplington/**Hawkins**/Owen	**70.4** (TR)	**4 - 2**	20 - 10
Heat 06	**O'Neil/Parry**/Whittaker/Bailey	72.6	**5 - 1**	25 - 11
Heat 07	Broadbelt/Moss/**Bottomley/Tucker** (R)	71.8	1 - 5	26 - 16
Heat 08	Waplington/**Parry/Jackson**/Broadbelt	71.8	3 - 3	29 - 19
Heat 09	**Meeks**/Whittaker/Moss (R)/**Hawkins** (X)	72.6	**3 - 2**	32 - 21
Heat 10	Moss/Broadbelt/**Parry/O'Neil** (R)	72.4	1 - 5	33 - 26
Heat 11	**Bottomley**/Waplington/**Jackson**/Owen	73.0	**4 - 2**	37 - 28
Heat 12	Bailey/**O'Neil**/Broadbelt/**Hawkins** (F)	73.2	2 - 4	39 - 32
Heat 13	**Bottomley/Meeks**/Moss/Waplington (F)	72.2	**5 - 1**	44 - 33

CREWE - Barry Meeks 11 (+1), Ian Bottomley 10, Paul O'Neil 8, John Jackson 5 (+1), Dave Parry 5 (+1), Warren Hawkins 3 (+1), Colin Tucker 2.
ROCHDALE - Steve Waplington 9, Eric Broadbelt 7 (+1), Ken Moss 6 (+1), Chris Bailey 5, Phil Whittaker 5, Taffy Owen 1 (+1), Gerry Richardson 0.

Barry Meeks' blistering time in Heat 5 was later credited by the *Guinness Book Of Records* as being the fastest recorded speed on a British speedway track (an average of 54.62mph).

Meeting 2 - Sunday, March 29, 1970 - Players No. 6 Trophy, Second Leg
Athletic Grounds, Milnrow Road, Rochdale
Track Length - 427 yards.

ROCHDALE HORNETS.....46 CREWE KINGS.....32

(Rochdale won on aggregate 79 - 76)

Seven coachloads of Crewe supporters made the Easter Sunday trip to the Athletic Grounds and were part of a re-opening day crowd of 6,000 to witness Rochdale's first home fixture since 1930, when they competed in the Northern League. The Kings, with an eleven point advantage from the first leg, still led the tie after Heat 12, but the Hornets won the final heat to snatch the silverware. Both teams complained after the meeting about the poor state of the track.

Heat	Riders	Time	Score	Total
Heat 01	**O'Neil**/Moss/**Parry**/Broadbelt (F)	**81.0** (TR)	**2 - 4**	02 - 04
Heat 02	Richardson/Whittaker/**Jackson**/**Tucker**	86.8	5 - 1	07 - 05
Heat 03	Owen/Bailey/**Meeks**/**Hawkins**	85.6	5 - 1	12 - 06
Heat 04	**Bottomley**/Whittaker/**Jackson**/Waplington (F)	85.0	**2 - 4**	14 - 10
Heat 05	**O'Neil**/Owen/**Parry**/Bailey	83.6	**2 - 4**	16 - 14
Heat 06	Moss/**Bottomley**/**Tucker**/Broadbelt	86.6	3 - 3	19 - 17
Heat 07	Waplington/**Meeks**/**Jackson**/Richardson	87.4	3 - 3	22 - 20
Heat 08	Moss/Whittaker/**Jackson**/**Tucker**	87.0	5 - 1	27 - 21
Heat 09	**O'Neil**/Owen/Bailey/**Bottomley**	83.8	3 - 3	30 - 24
Heat 10	Broadbelt/Moss/**Hawkins**/**Meeks**	83.6	5 - 1	35 - 25
Heat 11	**O'Neil**/Waplington/Whittaker/**Parry** (R)	86.2	3 - 3	38 - 28
Heat 12	Owen/**Meeks**/**Bottomley**/Broadbelt	84.4	3 - 3	41 - 31
Heat 13	Bailey/Waplington/**O'Neil**/**Bottomley**	81.2	5 - 1	46 - 32

ROCHDALE - Ken Moss 10 (+1), Taffy Owen 10, Phil Whittaker 7 (+3), Steve Waplington 7 (+1), Chris Bailey 6 (+2), Eric Broadbelt 3, Gerry Richardson 3.
CREWE - Paul O'Neil 13, Ian Bottomley 6 (+1), Barry Meeks 5, John Jackson 4 (+1), Dave Parry 2, Colin Tucker 1 (+1), Warren Hawkins 1.

Meeting 3 - Sunday, April 5, 1970 - Yorkshire/Cheshire Challenge
Doncaster Greyhound Stadium, York Road, Doncaster
Track Length - 350 yards.

DONCASTER DRAGONS.....41 CREWE KINGS.....37

Gordon McGregor led the Dragons to a four point victory with a faultless maximum. Paul O'Neil and Barry Meeks led the away challenge with a combined total of twenty five points, and despite steady rainfall throughout the meeting, the heat times actually got faster on the much improved York Road track.

Heat	Riders	Time	Score	Total
Heat 01	McGregor/**O'Neil**/**Jackson**/Haslinger	74.8	3 - 3	03 - 03
Heat 02	Wilson/**Tucker**/**Jay**/Holmes (F)	76.4	3 - 3	06 - 06
Heat 03	**Meeks**/Wasden/Emms/**Hawkins**	74.4	3 - 3	09 - 09
Heat 04	Harrison/Wilson/**Jay**/**Bottomley** (R)	76.0	5 - 1	14 - 10
Heat 05	**O'Neil**/Emms/Wasden/**Jackson** (R)	74.0	3 - 3	17 - 13
Heat 06	McGregor/**Bottomley**/Haslinger/**Tucker**	73.4	4 - 2	21 - 15
Heat 07	**O'Neil**/Harrison/**Meeks**/Wilson	73.0	**2 - 4**	23 - 19
Heat 08	Holmes/Haslinger/**Jay**/**Jackson** (R)	75.0	5 - 1	28 - 20
Heat 09	**Meeks**/Emms/Wasden/**Jay**	74.0	3 - 3	31 - 23
Heat 10	McGregor/**Meeks**/**Hawkins**/Haslinger	72.4	3 - 3	34 - 26
Heat 11	**O'Neil**/**Jackson**/Harrison/Holmes (X)	72.6	**1 - 5**	35 - 31
Heat 12	McGregor/**Meeks**/**Bottomley**/Wasden	71.8	3 - 3	38 - 34
Heat 13	**O'Neil**/Emms/Harrison/**Hawkins** (F)	72.6	3 - 3	41 - 37

DONCASTER - Gordon McGregor 12, Cliff Emms 7 (+1), Chris Harrison 7 (+1), Ian Wilson 5 (+1), Dennis Wasden 4 (+2), Hec Haslinger 3 (+1), Mike Holmes 3.
CREWE - Paul O'Neil 14, Barry Meeks 11, John Jackson 3 (+2), Ian Bottomley 3 (+1), Stuart Jay* 3 (+1), Colin Tucker 2, Warren Hawkins 1 (+1).

Meeting 4 - Monday, April 6, 1970 - British League Division II
L.M.R. Sports Ground, Earle Street, Crewe
Track Length - 470 yards.

CREWE KINGS.....49 RAYLEIGH ROCKETS.....27

The Kings could not have made a worst start to their league campaign, with a first heat 5-0 reversal. Firstly Paul O'Neil was excluded for breaking the tapes, then in the re-run, John Jackson dropped out with mechanical problems and O'Neil's replacement, Rob Jackson, took a fall. However, the home side were soon comfortably ahead with Rockets skipper Geoff Maloney the only one to show a credible return. Barry Meeks won all four of his rides and O'Neil the three he started. The threat of rain throughout the day had a significant affect on the evening's attendance.

Heat 01	Maloney/Champion/**J.Jackson** (R)/**R.Jackson** (F)	79.6	0 - 5	00 - 05
Heat 02	**Tucker**/**J.Jackson**/Moore/Guilfoyle (F)	77.0	**5 - 1**	05 - 06
Heat 03	**Meeks**/Brown/**Hawkins** (R)/Stone (X)	72.6	**3 - 2**	08 - 08
Heat 04	**Bottomley**/**Tucker**/Moore/A.Jackson	74.0	**5 - 1**	13 - 09
Heat 05	**Meeks**/**Hawkins**/Maloney/Champion	73.4	**5 - 1**	18 - 10
Heat 06	**O'Neil**/A.Jackson/Moore/**R.Jackson**	74.0	3 - 3	21 - 13
Heat 07	**Bottomley**/Brown/**Tucker**/Moore	74.0	**4 - 2**	25 - 15
Heat 08	**R.Jackson**/Maloney/Stone/**J.Jackson**	74.6	3 - 3	28 - 18
Heat 09	**Meeks**/**Hawkins**/Moore/A.Jackson	73.2	**5 - 1**	33 - 19
Heat 10	**O'Neil**/**R.Jackson**/Stone/Brown (R)	73.4	**5 - 1**	38 - 20
Heat 11	Maloney/**Bottomley**/Champion/**J.Jackson** (R)	73.0	2 - 4	40 - 24
Heat 12	**O'Neil**/**Hawkins**/Champion/Brown	73.4	**5 - 1**	45 - 25
Heat 13	**Meeks**/Maloney/**Bottomley**/Stone	73.0	**4 - 2**	49 - 27

CREWE - Barry Meeks 12, Ian Bottomley 9, Paul O'Neil 9, Warren Hawkins 6 (+3), Colin Tucker 6 (+1), Rob Jackson 5 (+1), John Jackson 2 (+1).
RAYLEIGH - Geoff Maloney 11, Ian Champion 4 (+1), Gary Moore 4 (+1), Dingle Brown 4, Terry Stone 2 (+1), Alan Jackson 2, Laurie Guilfoyle 0.

Meeting 5 - Monday, April 13, 1970 - Cheshire/Notts Trophy, First Leg
L.M.R. Sports Ground, Earle Street, Crewe.
Track Length - 470 yards.

CREWE KINGS.....49 LONG EATON RANGERS.....28

Colin Tucker replaced Warren Hawkins in two heats and took full advantage to record his best Earle Street score. Hawkins collided with the boards in his opening ride and was stretchered off with a damaged ankle. He bravely returned two heats later only to aggravate the injury, and a trip to hospital revealed it to be broken. Crewe eventually won the first leg by 21 points, despite the valiant efforts of Long Eaton's new signing Ken Vale.

Heat 01	**J.Jackson**/Shakespeare/**O'Neil** (R)/Carter (F)	71.6	**3 - 2**	03 - 02
Heat 02	**Tucker**/Gay/**R.Jackson**/Bouchard	75.2	**4 - 2**	07 - 04
Heat 03	Vale/**Meeks**/Farmer/**Hawkins** (X)	76.4	2 - 4	09 - 08
Heat 04	**Tucker**/Leadbitter/**Bottomley**/Bouchard	77.2	**4 - 2**	13 - 10
Heat 05	**Meeks**/**Hawkins**/Carter/Gay	77.4	**5 - 1**	18 - 11
Heat 06	**O'Neil**/**J.Jackson**/Leadbitter/Gay	77.4	**5 - 1**	23 - 12
Heat 07	Vale/**Tucker**/**Bottomley**/Farmer	77.0	3 - 3	26 - 15
Heat 08	**J.Jackson**/Leadbitter/Carter/**R.Jackson** (F)	00.0	3 - 3	29 - 18
Heat 09	**Tucker**/**Meeks**/Leadbitter/Gay	78.0	**5 - 1**	34 - 19
Heat 10	**O'Neil**/Vale/**J.Jackson**/Farmer (R)	77.0	**4 - 2**	38 - 21
Heat 11	Vale/**Bottomley**/Carter/**R.Jackson**	78.2	2 - 4	40 - 25
Heat 12	**Tucker**/Leadbitter/**O'Neil**/Gay	77.6	**4 - 2**	44 - 27
Heat 13	**Bottomley**/**Meeks**/Carter/Vale	77.0	**5 - 1**	49 - 28

CREWE - Colin Tucker 14, Barry Meeks 9 (+2), John Jackson 9 (+1), Ian Bottomley 7 (+1), Paul O'Neil 7, Warren Hawkins 2 (+1), Rob Jackson 1.
LONG EATON - Ken Vale 11, Tom Leadbitter* 8, Roy Carter 4 (+1), Pete Gay 2, Malcolm Shakespeare 2, Gil Farmer 1, Geoff Bouchard 0.

Meeting 6 - Thursday, April 16, 1970 - Cheshire/Notts Trophy, Second Leg
Long Eaton Stadium, Station Road, Long Eaton
Track Length - 366 yards.

LONG EATON RANGERS.....47 CREWE KINGS.....31

(Crewe won on aggregate 80 - 75)

Crewe secured the Cheshire/Notts Trophy in an incident packed second leg. Mechanical problems and falls plagued the home side throughout their first home fixture of the season. Both sides used guests on the night, with Rochdale's Steve Waplington replacing Peter Wrathall for Long Eaton and Dene Davies of Reading coming in for Warren Hawkins. Crewe's Rob Jackson fell in the first heat and withdrew from the meeting. Malcolm Shakespeare recorded an impressive maximum for the Rangers.

Heat 01	Shakespeare/**O'Neil**/Carter/**R.Jackson** (X)	72.8	4 - 2	04 - 02
Heat 02	Gay/Bouchard/**J.Jackson/Tucker**	74.8	5 - 1	09 - 03
Heat 03	Vale/**Meeks/Davies**/Farmer	75.0	3 - 3	12 - 06
Heat 04	Gay/Waplington/**J.Jackson/Bottomley** (F)	75.2	5 - 1	17 - 07
Heat 05	Vale/**Meeks**/Farmer/**O'Neil**	74.8	4 - 2	21 - 09
Heat 06	Shakespeare/**Bottomley/Tucker**/Carter (F)	75.0	3 - 3	24 - 12
Heat 07	**Davies**/Waplington/Gay/**Meeks**	75.8	3 - 3	27 - 15
Heat 08	**O'Neil**/Carter/**J.Jackson**/Bouchard	76.0	**2 - 4**	29 - 19
Heat 09	Vale/**Tucker/Bottomley**/Farmer (F)	78.0	3 - 3	32 - 22
Heat 10	Shakespeare/**Davies/J.Jackson**/Carter (F)	75.6	3 - 3	35 - 25
Heat 11	Waplington/Bouchard/**O'Neil/Davies**	73.0	5 - 1	40 - 26
Heat 12	Shakespeare/Farmer/**Meeks/Tucker**	75.4	5 - 1	45 - 27
Heat 13	**Meeks**/Waplington/**O'Neil**/Vale	75.0	**2 - 4**	47 - 31

LONG EATON - Malcolm Shakespeare 12, Steve Waplington* 9 (+1), Ken Vale 9, Pete Gay 7 (+1), Geoff Bouchard 4 (+2), Gil Farmer 3 (+1), Roy Carter 3.
CREWE - Barry Meeks 8, Paul O'Neil 7, Dene Davies* 6 (+1), John Jackson 4 (+1), Ian Bottomley 3 (+1), Colin Tucker 3 (+1), Rob Jackson 0.

Meeting 7 - Monday, April 20, 1970 - Knock Out Cup, First Round
L.M.R. Sports Ground, Earle Street, Crewe
Track Length - 470 yards.

CREWE KINGS.....49 NELSON ADMIRALS.....29

Home advantage again saw the Kings progress to the next round of the K.O. Cup, with a solid performance by their injury hit side. Colin Tucker, complete with new engine, and Barry Meeks spearheaded the home victory, which was virtually assured by the end of Heat 5, after opening up a fourteen point lead. Nelson's Gary Peterson was pick of the visiting riders.

Heat 01	**O'Neil/Tucker**/Knapkin/Schofield (R)	75.0	**5 - 1**	05 - 01
Heat 02	**J.Jackson/R.Jackson**/Thompson/Sheldrick	76.2	**5 - 1**	10 - 02
Heat 03	**Meeks**/Peterson/Bridgett/**Blackburn**	75.2	3 - 3	13 - 05
Heat 04	**Bottomley**/Wells/**R.Jackson**/Thompson	77.0	**4 - 2**	17 - 07
Heat 05	**Meeks/Blackburn**/Knapkin/Schofield	77.8	**5 - 1**	22 - 08
Heat 06	**Tucker**/Peterson/Wells/**O'Neil** (R)	76.0	3 - 3	25 - 11
Heat 07	Peterson/**Bottomley**/Bridgett/**R.Jackson**	78.2	2 - 4	27 - 15
Heat 08	**Tucker/J.Jackson**/Thompson/Knapkin	78.8	**5 - 1**	32 - 16
Heat 09	**Meeks**/Wells/**Blackburn**/Sheldrick	79.8	**4 - 2**	36 - 18
Heat 10	Peterson/**O'Neil/Tucker**/Bridgett	77.6	3 - 3	39 - 21
Heat 11	Knapkin/**J.Jackson/Bottomley**/Schofield (R)	78.0	3 - 3	42 - 24
Heat 12	**O'Neil/Blackburn**/Bridgett/Schofield (R)	77.6	**5 - 1**	47 - 25
Heat 13	Peterson/**Bottomley**/Knapkin/**Meeks**	77.2	2 - 4	49 - 29

CREWE - Colin Tucker 9 (+2), Barry Meeks 9, Ian Bottomley 8 (+1), Paul O'Neil 8, John Jackson 7 (+1), Glyn Blackburn 5 (+2), Rob Jackson 3 (+1).
NELSON - Gary Peterson 13, Alan Knapkin 6, Alf Wells 5 (+1), Alan Bridgett 3 (+1), Peter Thompson 2, Dave Schofield 0, Sid Sheldrick 0.

Meeting 8 - Monday, April 27, 1970 - Challenge
L.M.R. Sports Ground, Earle Street, Crewe
Track Length - 470 yards.

CREWE KINGS.....40 STARS OF THE LEAGUE.....38

Treacherous conditions on a rain-soaked Earle Street track made for a tremendous speedway contest, which was only decided after a home maximum in the final heat. Race of the night was Heat 7, with a matter of inches separating Ian Bottomley, John Jackson and Chris Bailey as they crossed the finishing line. As the rain continued to fall, heat times inevitably increased and by Heat 10, a time of 83.8 was recorded - nearly fourteen seconds outside the track record.

Heat 01	**O'Neil**/Broadbelt/Maloney/**Tucker**	74.8	3 - 3	03 - 03
Heat 02	Ross/**J.Jackson**/**R.Jackson**/Poyser	77.0	3 - 3	06 - 06
Heat 03	**Meeks**/Bailey/Harrhy/**Blackburn**	75.8	3 - 3	09 - 09
Heat 04	**Bottomley**/Leadbitter/Poyser/**R.Jackson** (F)	76.4	3 - 3	12 - 12
Heat 05	Maloney/Broadbelt/**J.Jackson**/**Blackburn**	75.2	1 - 5	13 - 17
Heat 06	**O'Neil**/Leadbitter/Ross/**Tucker** (R)	75.6	3 - 3	16 - 20
Heat 07	**Bottomley**/**J.Jackson**/Bailey/Harrhy (R)	76.0	**5 - 1**	21 - 21
Heat 08	Maloney/**Tucker**/**J.Jackson**/Poyser	79.0	3 - 3	24 - 24
Heat 09	Leadbitter/Ross/**Meeks**/**Blackburn**	81.0	1 - 5	25 - 29
Heat 10	**Tucker**/**O'Neil**/Bailey/Ross	83.8	**5 - 1**	30 - 30
Heat 11	Maloney/**Bottomley**/**J.Jackson**/Broadbelt	79.0	3 - 3	33 - 33
Heat 12	Bailey/**O'Neil**/Leadbitter/**Blackburn**	82.2	2 - 4	35 - 37
Heat 13	**Meeks**/**Bottomley**/Broadbelt/Ross	80.0	**5 - 1**	40 - 38

CREWE - Ian Bottomley 10 (+1), Paul O'Neil 10 (+1), John Jackson 7 (+3), Barry Meeks 7, Colin Tucker 5, Rob Jackson 1 (+1), Glyn Blackburn 0.
STARS OF THE LEAGUE - Geoff Maloney *(Rayleigh)* 10 (+1), Tom Leadbitter *(Teesside)* 8, Chris Bailey *(Rochdale)* 7, Andy Ross *(Peterborough)* 6 (+2), Eric Broadbelt *(Rochdale)* 5 (+1), John Harrhy *(Ipswich)* 1 (+1), John Poyser *(Peterborough)* 1 (+1).

Meeting 9 - Monday, May 4, 1970 - British League Division II
L.M.R. Sports Ground, Earle Street, Crewe
Track Length - 470 yards.

CREWE KINGS.....52 IPSWICH WITCHES.....26

Ipswich suffered their second successive 52-26 league reversal at Earle Street and again did not record a heat advantage. They did manage a share of the points on five occasions, but only John "Tiger" Louis with nine points looked comfortable on the vast Crewe bowl. Ian Bottomley scored a brilliant maximum and was well-supported by Paul O'Neil and Barry Meeks, although the latter damaged ribs in a fall during the second-half.

Heat 01	**O'Neil**/**Tucker**/Bailey/Spittles	75.4	**5 - 1**	05 - 01
Heat 02	**J.Jackson**/**R.Jackson**/Pepper/Slee	77.4	**5 - 1**	10 - 02
Heat 03	**Meeks**/Bagley/Louis/**Blackburn**	78.0	3 - 3	13 - 05
Heat 04	**Bottomley**/Harrhy/**R.Jackson**/Pepper	76.2	**4 - 2**	17 - 07
Heat 05	**Meeks**/**Blackburn**/Bailey/Spittles	76.2	**5 - 1**	22 - 08
Heat 06	**Tucker**/Harrhy/**O'Neil**/Slee	76.0	**4 - 2**	26 - 10
Heat 07	**Bottomley**/Louis/**J.Jackson**/Bagley	75.4	**4 - 2**	30 - 12
Heat 08	**Tucker**/Bailey/Pepper/**R.Jackson** (R)	77.6	3 - 3	33 - 15
Heat 09	Louis/**Meeks**/**Blackburn**/Harrhy	77.0	3 - 3	36 - 18
Heat 10	**O'Neil**/Louis/Bagley/**Tucker**	75.0	3 - 3	39 - 21
Heat 11	**Bottomley**/**J.Jackson**/Bagley/Pepper	76.0	**5 - 1**	44 - 22
Heat 12	**O'Neil**/Harrhy/Louis/**Blackburn**	75.0	3 - 3	47 - 25
Heat 13	**Bottomley**/**Meeks**/Bagley/Bailey	75.8	**5 - 1**	52 - 26

CREWE - Ian Bottomley 12, Barry Meeks 10 (+1), Paul O'Neil 10, Colin Tucker 8 (+1), John Jackson 6 (+1), Glyn Blackburn 3 (+2), Rob Jackson 3 (+1).
IPSWICH - John Louis 9 (+2), John Harrhy 6, Ron Bagley 5 (+1), Pete Bailey 4, Stan Pepper 2 (+1), Neville Slee 0. Ted Spittles 0.

Towards the latter stages of the match, an incident occurred that would see Colin Tucker leave the club. The relationship between Tucker and fellow New Zealander Paul O'Neil had soured as the season progressed, and things came to a head in the Congleton Final during the second-half when O'Neil broke the tapes, but escaped exclusion by the referee. Tucker refused to take part in the re-run, which was won by his rival. Following the race, the pair scuffled in the pits and had to be separated by fellow riders and officials. Despite everything he had done for the Crewe cause, Tucker was asked to leave the club. To make up the shortfall, Maurice Littlechild moved swiftly to sign the experienced Nelson rider Dai Evans.

Meeting 10 - Thursday, May 7, 1970 - British League Division II
Ipswich Stadium, Foxhall Road, Foxhall Heath, Ipswich
Track Length - 328 yards.

IPSWICH WITCHES.....48 CREWE KINGS.....30

Crewe's inability to replicate their home form on the road was typified here, when just three days after thrashing the Witches on their own track, they were easily beaten at Foxhall Heath. This time they did have an excuse, as their depleted side were missing the injured Ian Bottomley, Dave Parry and Warren Hawkins. Paul O'Neil scored a dozen points and John Jackson, labelled the most exciting newcomer of the season by the *Speedway Star & News*, returned a respectable nine.

Heat 01	**O'Neil**/Bailey/**Evans**/Noy	75.0	**2 - 4**	02 - 04
Heat 02	**J.Jackson**/Slee/**R.Jackson**/Pepper	74.8	**2 - 4**	04 - 08
Heat 03	Louis/Bagley/**Meeks**/**Blackburn**	73.2	5 - 1	09 - 09
Heat 04	Harrhy/Slee/**Osborn**/**R.Jackson**	74.8	5 - 1	14 - 10
Heat 05	Louis/Bagley/**Evans**/**O'Neil**	72.8	5 - 1	19 - 11
Heat 06	Bailey/**J.Jackson**/Noy/**Osborn** (F)	73.6	4 - 2	23 - 13
Heat 07	Harrhy/Slee/**Blackburn**/**Meeks** (F)	75.8	5 - 1	28 - 14
Heat 08	**O'Neil**/Bailey/**J.Jackson**/Pepper	72.6	**2 - 4**	30 - 18
Heat 09	Louis/Bagley/**J.Jackson**/**Meeks**	72.6	5 - 1	35 - 19
Heat 10	Bailey/**Meeks**/Slee/**Blackburn**	73.0	4 - 2	39 - 21
Heat 11	**O'Neil**/Harrhy/Pepper/**Evans**	73.2	3 - 3	42 - 24
Heat 12	Bagley/**J.Jackson**/**Meeks**/Noy	73.6	3 - 3	45 - 27
Heat 13	**O'Neil**/Louis/Harrhy/**Blackburn** (F)	73.6	3 - 3	48 - 30

IPSWICH - John Louis 11, Pete Bailey 10, Ron Bagley 9 (+3), John Harrhy 9 (+1), Neville Slee 7 (+2), Stan Pepper 1 (+1), Clive Noy 1.
CREWE - Paul O'Neil 12, John Jackson 9, Barry Meeks 4 (+1), Dai Evans 2, Glyn Blackburn 1, Rob Jackson 1, Brian Osborn* 1.

Meeting 11 - Saturday, May 9, 1970 - British League Division II
Rayleigh Weir Stadium, Southend Arterial Road, Rayleigh
Track Length - 365 yards.

RAYLEIGH ROCKETS.....39 CREWE KINGS.....39

The Kings ended their seven match sequence of away league defeats, but could not quite manage to bring both points back to South Cheshire. In a last heat cliff-hanger, Paul O'Neil won and John Jackson battled his way through the field to help earn Crewe's first league draw. O'Neil recorded another maximum in a meeting that witnessed ten falls in the first five heats. Crewe were indebted to Rayleigh junior Allan Emmett, who was loaned for the night and scored a valuable four points.

Heat 01	**O'Neil**/**Evans**/Champion/Maloney (F)	79.3	**1 - 5**	01 - 05
Heat 02	**J.Jackson**/Moore/Hall/**R.Jackson**	79.4	3 - 3	04 - 08
Heat 03	Stone/**Meeks**/A.Jackson/**Blackburn**	79.8	4 - 2	08 - 10
Heat 04	**J.Jackson**/**Emmett**/Hall/Clark (F)	78.3	**1 - 5**	09 - 15
Heat 05	**O'Neil**/Stone/**Evans**/A.Jackson (F)	78.0	**2 - 4**	11 - 19
Heat 06	Champion/Maloney/**Emmett**/**J.Jackson**	76.0	5 - 1	16 - 20
Heat 07	Moore/**Meeks**/Hall/**Blackburn**	77.2	4 - 2	20 - 22
Heat 08	**Evans**/Champion/Moore/**R.Jackson**	77.6	3 - 3	23 - 25

Heat 09	A. Jackson/**J.Jackson**/Stone/**Emmett**	76.0	4 - 2	27 - 27
Heat 10	Maloney/**Meeks**/Champion/**Blackburn** (F)	74.7	4 - 2	31 - 29
Heat 11	**O'Neil**/Moore/**Evans**/Hall	76.1	**2 - 4**	33 - 33
Heat 12	Maloney/Stone/**Emmett**/**Meeks** (F)	72.6	5 - 1	38 - 34
Heat 13	**O'Neil**/**J.Jackson**/Moore/A.Jackson	74.6	**1 - 5**	39 - 39

RAYLEIGH - Gary Moore 9 (+1), Geoff Maloney 8 (+1), Terry Stone 8 (+1), Ian Champion 7, Alan Jackson 4, Tony Hall 3 (+1), Colin Clark 0.
CREWE - Paul O'Neil 12, John Jackson 10 (+1), Dai Evans 7 (+1), Barry Meeks 6, Allan Emmett* 4 (+1), Glyn Blackburn 0, Rob Jackson 0.

Meeting 12 - Monday, May 11, 1970 - British League Division II
L.M.R. Sports Ground, Earle Street, Crewe
Track Length - 470 yards.

CREWE KINGS.....49 DONCASTER DRAGONS.....29

Despite a spirited performance by Aussie Hec Haslinger, the new look Dragons were never in the hunt for the points, although they did succeed in preventing the home side from breaking the fifty points barrier for a second successive week. Haslinger was the only Doncaster rider to win a heat, as Paul O'Neil and Barry Meeks stole the show with maximums - O'Neil's second in successive matches.

Heat 01	**O'Neil**/McGregor/Haslinger/**Evans** (R)	76.2	3 - 3	03 - 03
Heat 02	**J.Jackson**/Lee/Wasden/**R.Jackson** (R)	75.8	3 - 3	06 - 06
Heat 03	**Meeks**/**Blackburn**/Emms/Roynon	76.8	**5 - 1**	11 - 07
Heat 04	**Bottomley**/**J.Jackson**/Lee/Harrison	77.0	**5 - 1**	16 - 08
Heat 05	**Meeks**/Haslinger/McGregor/**Blackburn**	74.8	3 - 3	19 - 11
Heat 06	**O'Neil**/Haslinger/**Evans**/Wasden	76.2	**4 - 2**	23 - 13
Heat 07	**J.Jackson**/Roynon/Emms/**Bottomley** (R)	81.0	3 - 3	26 - 16
Heat 08	Haslinger/**Evans**/Lee/**R.Jackson**	77.0	2 - 4	28 - 20
Heat 09	**Meeks**/**Blackburn**/Lee/Wasden (R)	77.4	**5 - 1**	33 - 21
Heat 10	**O'Neil**/**Evans**/Roynon/Emms	76.0	**5 - 1**	38 - 22
Heat 11	Haslinger/McGregor/**R.Jackson**/**Bottomley** (R)	76.8	1 - 5	39 - 27
Heat 12	**O'Neil**/**Blackburn**/Harrison/Roynon (R)	75.8	**5 - 1**	44 - 28
Heat 13	**Meeks**/**J.Jackson**/McGregor/Emms	76.2	**5 - 1**	49 - 29

CREWE - Barry Meeks 12, Paul O'Neil 12, John Jackson 10 (+2), Glyn Blackburn 6 (+3), Dai Evans 5 (+1), Ian Bottomley 3, Rob Jackson 1.
DONCASTER - Hec Haslinger 11 (+1), Gordon McGregor 6 (+2), Jack Lee 5, Chris Roynon 3, Cliff Emms 2 (+1), Dennis Wasden 1 (+1), Chris Harrison 1.

Meeting 13 - Monday, May 18, 1970 - Revenge Challenge
L.M.R. Sports Ground, Earle Street, Crewe
Track Length - 470 yards.

CREWE KINGS.....39 ROCHDALE HORNETS.....37

Dry and dusty track conditions contributed to a thrill-a-minute challenge match, where four of the first six heats were re-run after riders had fallen. The result rested on the final heat with Barry Meeks and Glyn Blackburn not disappointing the home faithful, after conjuring up a 4-2 victory. Twice in the match only two riders finished the race, and in Heat 10, Dai Evans fell but remounted to earn a valuable point, as Hornets Steve Waplington had already crashed out.

Heat 01	**O'Neil**/Broadbelt/**Evans**/Moss (F)	75.2	**4 - 2**	04 - 02
Heat 02	Wilkinson/Tyrer/**R.Jackson** (R)/**Blackburn** (X)	77.8	0 - 5	04 - 07
Heat 03	**Meeks**/**J.Jackson**/Waplington/Wilkinson (F)	77.4	**5 - 1**	09 - 08
Heat 04	**Blackburn**/Wilkinson/**Mills**/Bailey	77.0	**4 - 2**	13 - 10
Heat 05	**J.Jackson**/Broadbelt/**Meeks**/Moss	75.0	**4 - 2**	17 - 12
Heat 06	Bailey/**Evans**/**O'Neil** (R)/Wilkinson (X)	76.0	2 - 3	19 - 15
Heat 07	Waplington/**Blackburn**/**Mills**/Owen	76.2	3 - 3	22 - 18
Heat 08	Moss/**R.Jackson**/Wilkinson/**Evans**	76.4	2 - 4	24 - 22
Heat 09	**J.Jackson**/Bailey/**Meeks**/Wilkinson (R)	75.0	**4 - 2**	28 - 24

Heat 10	Owen/**O'Neil**/**Evans**/Waplington (F)	76.0	3 - 3	31 - 27
Heat 11	Moss/Broadbelt/**Blackburn**/**Mills**	75.8	1 - 5	32 - 32
Heat 12	**O'Neil**/Owen/Bailey/**J.Jackson**	75.0	3 - 3	35 - 35
Heat 13	**Meeks**/Waplington/**Blackburn**/Broadbelt	76.0	**4 - 2**	39 - 37

CREWE - John Jackson 8 (+1), Barry Meeks 8, Paul O'Neil 8, Glyn Blackburn 7, Dai Evans 4 (+1), Roger Mills* 2 (+1), Rob Jackson 2.
ROCHDALE - Chris Bailey 6 (+1), Eric Broadbelt 6 (+1), Ken Moss 6, Steve Waplington 6, Alan Wilkinson 6, Taffy Owen 5, Paul Tyrer 2 (+1).

Meeting 14 - Thursday, May 21, 1970 - British League Division II
Cleveland Park Stadium, Stockton Road, Middlesbrough
Track Length - 335 yards.

TEESSIDE TEESSIDERS.....38 CREWE KINGS.....39

A controversial decision in another exciting last heat decider saw the Kings leave the Cleveland Park Stadium with both points but with few friends. With the Teessiders holding a three-point lead going into Heat 13, home riders Roger Mills and Bob Jameson faced Paul O'Neil and John Jackson, requiring just two points to secure victory. Mills however, broke the tapes and was excluded, but then re-instated following a confrontation with referee R. G. Owen. This prompted Maurice Littlechild, amidst a chorus of boos, to call his riders back to the pits. The official did himself no favours by changing his decision yet again. The Kings raced to a 5-1, winning the meeting by a single point.

Heat 01	**O'Neil**/Reading/Leadbitter/**Evans**	73.2	3 - 3	03 - 03
Heat 02	Knock/Moore/**Mulligan**/**Blackburn** (X)	76.0	5 - 1	08 - 04
Heat 03	**Jackson**/**Meeks**/Jameson/Durham (F)	73.6	**1 - 5**	09 - 09
Heat 04	**O'Neil**/Moore/Mills (R)/**Mulligan** (F)	75.2	**2 - 3**	11 - 12
Heat 05	Jameson/**O'Neil**/**Evans**/Knock	73.0	3 - 3	14 - 15
Heat 06	**Jackson**/Leadbitter/Reading/**Mulligan** (F)	72.6	3 - 3	17 - 18
Heat 07	Mills/**Meeks**/**Jackson**/Moore	70.8	3 - 3	20 - 21
Heat 08	Reading/**Evans**/Knock/**Mulligan**	73.6	4 - 2	24 - 23
Heat 09	**Meeks**/Jameson/Durham/**Mulligan**	72.8	3 - 3	27 - 26
Heat 10	Leadbitter/**Jackson**/Reading/**Meeks**	72.4	4 - 2	31 - 28
Heat 11	Mills/**O'Neil**/**Evans**/Knock	72.2	3 - 3	34 - 31
Heat 12	Leadbitter/**Meeks**/**Evans**/Durham	73.2	3 - 3	37 - 34
Heat 13	**Jackson**/**O'Neil**/Moore/Jameson (F)	72.8	**1 - 5**	38 - 39

TEESSIDE - Tom Leadbitter 9 (+1), Pete Reading 7 (+1), Bob Jameson 6, Roger Mills 6, Mick Moore 5 (+1), John Knock 4, Dave Durham 1 (+1).
CREWE - John Jackson 12 (+1), Paul O'Neil 12 (+1), Barry Meeks 9 (+1), Dai Evans 5 (+3), John Mulligan 1, Glyn Blackburn 0, *Ian Bottomley (R/R)*.

Meeting 15 - Friday, May 22, 1970 - Challenge
Derwent Park Stadium, Workington
Track Length - 398 yards.

WORKINGTON COMETS.....55 CREWE KINGS.....23

Crewe made the long trip to Derwent Park and were duly hammered. The Comets, backed by a large and vociferous crowd, were brilliantly led by Mackay, Wilson and Penniket. The Kings won just two races, courtesy of O'Neil and Jackson, with the Kiwi posting the fastest time of the night in the first heat, which Jackson equalled six heats later. Crewe officials and riders later complained about the depth of shale on the track.

Heat 01	**O'Neil**/Wilson/**Evans**/Sansom	79.8	**2 - 4**	02 - 04
Heat 02	Valentine/Lonsdale/**Blackburn**/**Mulligan**	82.4	5 - 1	07 - 05
Heat 03	Blythe/Mackay/**Meeks**/**Jackson**	82.2	5 - 1	12 - 06
Heat 04	Penniket/Valentine/**Blackburn**/**Jameson**	80.6	5 - 1	17 - 07
Heat 05	Mackay/Blythe/**O'Neil**/**Evans**	81.2	5 - 1	22 - 08
Heat 06	Wilson/Sansom/**Blackburn**/**Jameson**	82.8	5 - 1	27 - 09
Heat 07	**Jackson**/Valentine/Penniket/**Meeks**	79.8	3 - 3	30 - 12

Heat 08	Wilson/**Evans**/**Mulligan** (3 riders only)	82.4	3 - 3	33 - 15
Heat 09	Mackay/Blythe/**Jameson**/**Blackburn**	82.2	5 - 1	38 - 16
Heat 10	Sansom/**Jackson**/Wilson/**Meeks**	80.0	4 - 2	42 - 18
Heat 11	Penniket/**Jackson**/Lonsdale/**O'Neil**	80.6	4 - 2	46 - 20
Heat 12	Sansom/**Jameson**/Blythe/**Meeks**	81.0	4 - 2	50 - 22
Heat 13	Mackay/Penniket/**Jackson**/**O'Neil** (X)	81.6	5 - 1	55 - 23

WORKINGTON - Malcolm Mackay 11 (+1), Geoff Penniket 9 (+2), Reg Wilson 9, Chris Blythe 8 (+2), Lou Sansom 8 (+1), Bob Valentine 7 (+1), Vic Lonsdale 3 (+1).
CREWE - John Jackson 8, Paul O'Neil 4, Glyn Blackburn 3, Dai Evans 3, Bob Jameson* 3, John Mulligan 1 (+1), Barry Meeks 1.

Following a journey of 325 miles, and with only twenty-four hours to prepare, the Kings embarked on a trip to Eastbourne - another 500 mile trek to and from their South Cheshire base.

Meeting 16 - Sunday, May 24, 1970 - British League Division II
Arlington Raceway, Arlington Road, Hailsham, Eastbourne
Track Length - 342 yards.

EASTBOURNE EAGLES.....58 CREWE KINGS.....20

An under-strength and tired looking Crewe team endured their biggest ever defeat when they received a real thumping by title-chasing Eastbourne, who recorded five maximums from the opening six heats. Dai Evans and John Jackson provided seventeen of Crewe's meagre total, and for the first time in their short history, the Kings failed to produce a race winner. Home riders Trott and Cook both scored maximums and Dave Jessup posted a paid one. Crewe No.8 John Mulligan was lucky to escape uninjured when he flew over the top of his handlebars on the third bend during his only outing in Heat 12.

Heat 01	Jessup/Woolford/**Evans**/**O'Neil**	00.0	5 - 1	05 - 01
Heat 02	Kennett/Sims/**Blackburn**/**Cousins**	00.0	5 - 1	10 - 02
Heat 03	Cook/**Jackson**/Golden/**Meeks**	00.0	4 - 2	14 - 04
Heat 04	Trott/Kennett/**O'Neil**/**Cousins**	00.0	5 - 1	19 - 05
Heat 05	Cook/Golden/**Evans**/**O'Neil**	00.0	5 - 1	24 - 06
Heat 06	Jessup/Woolford/**Jackson**/**Blackburn**	00.0	5 - 1	29 - 07
Heat 07	Trott/**Jackson**/Kennett/**Meeks**	00.0	4 - 2	33 - 09
Heat 08	Sims/**Evans**/Woolford/**Cousins**	00.0	4 - 2	37 - 11
Heat 09	Cook/**Jackson**/Golden/**Evans**	00.0	4 - 2	41 - 13
Heat 10	Jessup/Woolford/**Jackson**/**Blackburn**	00.0	5 - 1	46 - 14
Heat 11	Trott/**Evans**/Sims/**O'Neil**	00.0	4 - 2	50 - 16
Heat 12	Cook/Jessup/**Evans**/**Mulligan**	00.0	5 - 1	55 - 17
Heat 13	Trott/**Jackson**/**Cousins**/Golden	00.0	3 - 3	58 - 20

EASTBOURNE - Derek Cook 12, Reg Trott 12, Dave Jessup 11 (+1), Mac Woolford 7 (+3), Dave Kennett 6 (+1), Laurie Sims 6 (+1), Alby Golden 4 (+1).
CREWE - John Jackson 10, Dai Evans 7, Ray Cousins 1 (+1), Glyn Blackburn 1, Paul O'Neil 1, Barry Meeks 0, John Mulligan 0, *Ian Bottomley (R/R)*.

Meeting 17 - Monday, May 25, 1970 - British League Division II
L.M.R. Sports Ground, Earle Street, Crewe
Track Length - 470 yards.

CREWE KINGS.....47 READING RACERS.....31

When Reading last visited Earle Street, they suffered their worst ever defeat, so this result was undoubtedly an improvement, even though Crewe were still minus the services of Ian Bottomley, Dave Parry and Warren Hawkins, and feeling the effects of marathon treks to Workington and Eastbourne. Paul O'Neil was back to his best following two poor returns on the road, with John Jackson continuing his excellent start to the season, notching up double figures, and also providing the highlight of the night, when coming from the back to win Heat 7. For the Racers, Dene Davies pushed his machine 400 yards for a point in Heat 3 and Mike Vernam won Heat 13 in the fastest time of the night.

Heat 01	**O'Neil**/Vernam/Leigh/**Evans**	77.8	3 - 3	03 - 03
Heat 02	**R.Jackson**/Whitaker/Hammond/**Blackburn**	79.8	3 - 3	06 - 06
Heat 03	Young/**J.Jackson**/Davies/**Meeks** (R)	77.4	2 - 4	08 - 10
Heat 04	**O'Neil**/**Blackburn**/Hammond/May	77.4	**5 - 1**	13 - 11
Heat 05	Vernam/**J.Jackson**/**Meeks**/Leigh	76.2	3 - 3	16 - 14
Heat 06	**O'Neil**/May/**Evans**/Whitaker (R)	75.4	**4 - 2**	20 - 16
Heat 07	**J.Jackson**/Young/Hammond/**Blackburn**	76.0	3 - 3	23 - 19
Heat 08	**Evans**/**R.Jackson**/Hammond/Leigh	76.4	**5 - 1**	28 - 20
Heat 09	**Meeks**/**J.Jackson**/Whitaker/May	74.8	**5 - 1**	33 - 21
Heat 10	**O'Neil**/Young/**Evans**/Davies	74.6	**4 - 2**	37 - 23
Heat 11	**Meeks**/Vernam/**R.Jackson**/Whitaker	74.0	**4 - 2**	41 - 25
Heat 12	**O'Neil**/Young/**J.Jackson**/Davies	74.8	**4 - 2**	45 - 27
Heat 13	Vernam/**Meeks**/Young/**Evans**	73.8	2 - 4	47 - 31

CREWE - Paul O'Neil 15, John Jackson 10 (+1), Barry Meeks 9 (+1), Rob Jackson 6 (+1), Dai Evans 5, Glyn Blackburn 2 (+1), *Ian Bottomley (R/R).*
READING - Mike Vernam 10, Bob Young 10, John Hammond 4 (+2), Dave Whitaker 3, Dickie May 2, Bernie Leigh 1 (+1), Dene Davies 1.

It was reported that local personality Paul Vincent aimed to walk 75 miles (300 laps) around the Earle Street circuit, to warm up for a charity John O'Groats to Land's End walk later in the year.

Meeting 18 - Monday, June 1, 1970 - British League Division II
L.M.R. Sports Ground, Earle Street, Crewe
Track Length - 470 yards.

CREWE KINGS.....53 KING'S LYNN STARLETS.....25

The Starlets, now mainly represented by home grown riders graduated from their weekend training schools, had started the season with a run of impressive results, but were brought back down to earth with a considerable bump, as Crewe romped to their biggest win of the season. With Ian Bottomley still side-lined with a rib injury, Paul O'Neil took advantage of the extra ride to score his second successive fifteen point maximum. Barry Meeks also got in on the act with a paid one, as King's Lynn left Earle Street without a single heat advantage or race win.

Heat 01	**O'Neil**/Edmonds/**Evans**/Featherstone	73.8	**4 - 2**	04 - 02
Heat 02	**R.Jackson**/Bywater/Ingamells/**Blackburn**	77.0	3 - 3	07 - 05
Heat 03	**J.Jackson**/**Meeks**/Price/Osborne	74.2	**5 - 1**	12 - 06
Heat 04	**O'Neil**/Turner/**Blackburn**/Bywater	72.6	**4 - 2**	16 - 08
Heat 05	**Meeks**/**J.Jackson**/Edmonds/Featherstone (R)	74.0	**5 - 1**	21 - 09
Heat 06	**O'Neil**/Turner/**Evans**/Ingamells (R)	73.8	**4 - 2**	25 - 11
Heat 07	**J.Jackson**/**Blackburn**/Price/Osborne	74.8	**5 - 1**	30 - 12
Heat 08	**Evans**/**R.Jackson**/Bywater/Turner (R)	75.4	**5 - 1**	35 - 13
Heat 09	**Meeks**/Turner/Bywater/**J.Jackson** (R)	73.8	3 - 3	38 - 16
Heat 10	**O'Neil**/Price/Osborne/**Evans** (R)	73.6	3 - 3	41 - 19
Heat 11	**Meeks**/Edmonds/Featherstone/**R.Jackson**	74.6	3 - 3	44 - 22
Heat 12	**O'Neil**/**J.Jackson**/Turner/Price	73.0	**5 - 1**	49 - 23
Heat 13	**Meeks**/Edmonds/**Evans**/Osborne	73.4	**4 - 2**	53 - 25

CREWE - Paul O'Neil 15, Barry Meeks 14 (+1), John Jackson 10 (+2), Dai Evans 6, Rob Jackson 5 (+1), Glyn Blackburn 3 (+1), *Ian Bottomley (R/R).*
KING'S LYNN - Graham Edmonds 7, Ian Turner 7, Jack Bywater 4 (+1), Arthur Price 4, Tony Featherstone 1 (+1), John Ingamells 1 (+1), Russell Osborne 1 (+1).

Meeting 19 - Wednesday, June 3, 1970 - British League Division II
King's Lynn Stadium, Saddlebow Road, King's Lynn
Track Length - 400 yards.

KING'S LYNN STARLETS.....47 CREWE KINGS.....31

Just 48 hours after beating the Starlets by twenty-eight points, Crewe once again succumbed to inferior opposition riding their own track – a trend that would have to be quickly reversed if they were to be taken as serious title contenders. Ian Turner proved unbeatable all night and

Jack Bywater just failed in Heat 8 to secure his first maximum. Paul O'Neil was again the pick of the Crewe riders, benefiting from riding the track the previous week as Oxford's No.8.

Heat 01	Bywater/**O'Neil**/Edmonds/**Evans**	75.4	4 - 2	04 - 02
Heat 02	Featherstone/Ingamells/**Blackburn**/**Cousins** (R)	76.6	5 - 1	09 - 03
Heat 03	**Jackson**/Price/**Meeks**/Osborne	75.0	**2 - 4**	11 - 07
Heat 04	Turner/Featherstone/**Cousins**/**Bottomley**	74.8	5 - 1	16 - 08
Heat 05	**O'Neil**/**Evans**/Price/Osborne	75.0	**1 - 5**	17 - 13
Heat 06	Bywater/Edmonds/**Blackburn**/**Bottomley**	77.0	5 - 1	22 - 14
Heat 07	Turner/Featherstone/**Meeks**/**Jackson**	73.6	5 - 1	27 - 15
Heat 08	**O'Neil**/Bywater/**Evans**/Ingamells (F)	76.0	**2 - 4**	29 - 19
Heat 09	Price/Featherstone/**Blackburn**/**Cousins** (F)	77.4	5 - 1	34 - 20
Heat 10	Bywater/**Meeks**/**Jackson**/Edmonds	78.2	3 - 3	37 - 23
Heat 11	Turner/**O'Neil**/**Evans**/Featherstone	74.2	3 - 3	40 - 26
Heat 12	Edmonds/**Meeks**/**Bottomley**/Osborne (X)	76.0	3 - 3	43 - 29
Heat 13	Turner/**Jackson**/Price/**O'Neil** (X)	75.0	4 - 2	47 - 31

KING'S LYNN - Ian Turner 12, Jack Bywater 11, Tony Featherstone 9 (+3), Arthur Price 7, Graham Edmonds 6 (+1), John Ingamells 2 (+1), Russell Osborne 0.
CREWE - Paul O'Neil 10, John Jackson 6 (+1), Barry Meeks 6, Dai Evans 4 (+2), Glyn Blackburn 3, Ian Bottomley 1 (+1), Ray Cousins 1.

Meeting 20 - Saturday, June 6, 1970 - Knock Out Cup, Second Round
Canterbury City Football Ground, Kingsmead Road, Canterbury
Track Length - 390 yards.

CANTERBURY CRUSADERS.....52 CREWE KINGS.....26

Johnnie Hoskins'men kept alive their hopes of a league and cup double by easily brushing aside the Kings, who had been initially boosted by the return from injury of Ian Bottomley and Warren Hawkins, even though neither were fully race fit. Paul O'Neil scored exactly half of the Crewe total and was the only visiting race winner. Barry Meeks meanwhile, had a nasty scare while competing in the Castle Wall Trophy during the second-half. He collided with home rider Graham Miles on the last bend, sending him crashing into the safety fence and into the crowd. Fortunately he escaped with only rib injuries.

Heat 01	Banks/**O'Neil**/Rennison/**Evans** (X)	79.6	4 - 2	04 - 02
Heat 02	Kite/**Blackburn**/**Hawkins**/Rennison (R)	82.0	3 - 3	07 - 05
Heat 03	Miles/Thomas/**Meeks**/**Jackson**	79.2	5 - 1	12 - 06
Heat 04	Smith/Rennison/**Hawkins**/**Bottomley**	78.8	5 - 1	17 - 07
Heat 05	**O'Neil**/Miles/**Evans**/Thomas (R)	79.8	**2 - 4**	19 - 11
Heat 06	Banks/Crowson/**Bottomley**/**Blackburn**	79.0	5 - 1	24 - 12
Heat 07	Smith/Rennison/**Jackson**/**Meeks**	79.8	5 - 1	29 - 13
Heat 08	**O'Neil**/Kite/**Evans**/Banks	79.2	**2 - 4**	31 - 17
Heat 09	Thomas/Miles/**Hawkins**/**Bottomley**	78.6	5 - 1	36 - 18
Heat 10	Banks/Crowson/**Jackson**/**Meeks**	79.2	5 - 1	41 - 19
Heat 11	Smith/**O'Neil**/**Evans**/Kite	78.8	3 - 3	44 - 22
Heat 12	Miles/Crowson/**Meeks**/**Bottomley**	81.0	5 - 1	49 - 23
Heat 13	**O'Neil**/Thomas/Smith/**Jackson**	78.6	3 - 3	52 - 26

CANTERBURY - Graham Miles 10 (+1), Graeme Smith 10 (+1), Graham Banks 9, Barry Thomas 7 (+1), Barry Crowson 6 (+3), Jake Rennison 5 (+2), Alan Kite 5.
CREWE - Paul O'Neil 13, Dai Evans 3 (+1), Warren Hawkins 3 (+1), Glyn Blackburn 2, John Jackson 2, Barry Meeks 2, Ian Bottomley 1.

Meeting 21 - Monday, June 8, 1970 - British League Division II
L.M.R. Sports Ground, Earle Street, Crewe
Track Length - 470 yards.

CREWE KINGS.....52 LONG EATON RANGERS.....26

Long Eaton remained in the hunt after seven heats, but when they lost guests Gary Peterson and former Crewe captain Colin Tucker due to wrecked engines, their hopes of an upset disappeared under a blitz of home maximums. Paul O'Neil's home purple patch continued with his third successive maximum, and things got even better for him when he became the first King to claim the Silver Helmet, after holder Malcolm Shakespeare had to forfeit the title through injury. Barry Meeks bravely rode with ribs in plaster.

Heat 01	**O'Neil**/Peterson/Farmer/**Evans**	73.2	3 - 3	03 - 03
Heat 02	**Hawkins**/**Blackburn**/Bass/Carter	73.2	**5 - 1**	08 - 04
Heat 03	**Meeks**/Vale/Bouchard/**Jackson**	73.4	3 - 3	11 - 07
Heat 04	Tucker/**Blackburn**/**Bottomley**/Bass	73.6	3 - 3	14 - 10
Heat 05	Peterson/**Meeks**/**Jackson**/Farmer	73.6	3 - 3	17 - 13
Heat 06	**O'Neil**/Tucker/**Evans**/Carter	74.4	**4 - 2**	21 - 15
Heat 07	Vale/**Bottomley**/**Blackburn**/Peterson (R)	74.8	3 - 3	24 - 18
Heat 08	**Evans**/**Hawkins**/Tucker/Bass (X)	76.8	**5 - 1**	29 - 19
Heat 09	**Meeks**/**Jackson**/Carter/Vale (R)	73.0	**5 - 1**	34 - 20
Heat 10	**O'Neil**/**Evans**/Vale/Bouchard	74.8	**5 - 1**	39 - 21
Heat 11	**Bottomley**/Bouchard/Farmer/**Hawkins** (R)	76.0	3 - 3	42 - 24
Heat 12	**O'Neil**/**Jackson**/Vale/Tucker	74.4	**5 - 1**	47 - 25
Heat 13	**Meeks**/**Bottomley**/Farmer/Bouchard	74.2	**5 - 1**	52 - 26

CREWE - Paul O'Neil 12, Barry Meeks 11, Ian Bottomley 8 (+2), Dai Evans 6 (+1), John Jackson 5 (+3), Glyn Blackburn 5 (+2), Warren Hawkins 5 (+1).
LONG EATON - Ken Vale 7, Colin Tucker* 6, Gary Peterson* 5, Gil Farmer 3 (+2), Geoff Bouchard 3 (+1), Steve Bass 1, Roy Carter 1.

Meeting 22 - Monday, June 15, 1970 - British League Division II
L.M.R. Sports Ground, Earle Street, Crewe
Track Length - 470 yards.

CREWE KINGS.....58 PETERBOROUGH PANTHERS.....20

Despite having former Crewe riders Peter Seaton and Pete Saunders in their ranks, the Panthers still lost twelve of the thirteen heats. Only Andy Ross, with four second places, looked comfortable for the visitors. Ian Bottomley, now back to full fitness, was unbeaten in a solid Kings display. During the second-half, Paul O'Neil, who impressed the spectating Denmark and Wolverhampton star Ole Olsen, defended his Silver Helmet title with an easy win over Ross.

Heat 01	**Evans**/**O'Neil**/Greer/Seaton	73.8	**5 - 1**	05 - 01
Heat 02	**Blackburn**/**Hawkins**/Stayte/Hughes	74.2	**5 - 1**	10 - 02
Heat 03	**Jackson**/Saunders/**Meeks**/Davies	74.0	**4 - 2**	14 - 04
Heat 04	**Bottomley**/Ross/**Blackburn**/Stayte	74.2	**4 - 2**	18 - 06
Heat 05	**Meeks**/**Jackson**/Saunders/Greer	73.8	**5 - 1**	23 - 07
Heat 06	**O'Neil**/Ross/**Evans**/Hughes (F)	73.0	**4 - 2**	27 - 09
Heat 07	**Bottomley**/Davies/**Blackburn**/Saunders	73.0	**4 - 2**	31 - 11
Heat 08	**Hawkins**/**Evans**/Greer/Stayte	74.2	**5 - 1**	36 - 12
Heat 09	**Jackson**/Ross/Hughes/**Meeks**	74.0	3 - 3	39 - 15
Heat 10	**O'Neil**/**Evans**/Davies/Saunders	73.2	**5 - 1**	44 - 16
Heat 11	**Bottomley**/**Hawkins**/Greer/Seaton (R)	74.4	**5 - 1**	49 - 17
Heat 12	**O'Neil**/Ross/**Jackson**/Saunders	72.2	**4 - 2**	53 - 19
Heat 13	**Bottomley**/**Meeks**/Greer/Hughes	73.6	**5 - 1**	58 - 20

CREWE - Ian Bottomley 12, Paul O'Neil 11 (+1), John Jackson 9 (+1), Dai Evans 8 (+2), Warren Hawkins 7 (+2), Barry Meeks 6 (+1), Glyn Blackburn 5.
PETERBOROUGH - Andy Ross 8, Richard Greer 4, Brian Davies 3, Pete Saunders 3, Joe Hughes 1 (+1), John Stayte 1, Peter Seaton 0.

News was released that Maurice Littlechild was contemplating a reduction to the Earle Street track, in an effort to encourage more exciting and evenly contested racing, which would also hopefully improve Crewe's dismal results away from home. On June 20, Nelson rode in their final home meeting, inflicting a 56-22 defeat on Peterborough, before transferring to Bradford.

Meeting 23 - Monday, June 22, 1970 - British League Division II
L.M.R. Sports Ground, Earle Street, Crewe
Track Length - 470 yards.

CREWE KINGS.....56 BERWICK BANDITS.....22

Paul O'Neil maintained his tremendous form around Earle Street with a fourth maximum in five meetings, extending his run without defeat to a visiting rider to 23. Barry Meeks and Glyn Blackburn both returned good scores, and reserve Warren Hawkins won each of his three starts. Rob Jackson guested for the Bandits and top scored for them with six points. To cap off another great night, O'Neil again defended his Silver Helmet title, easily beating Alan Paynter.

Heat 01	**O'Neil**/**Evans**/Robinson/Omand	73.2	**5 - 1**	05 - 01
Heat 02	**Hawkins**/**Blackburn**/Brady/Paynter	73.2	**5 - 1**	10 - 02
Heat 03	**Meeks**/**J.Jackson**/R.Jackson/Baldock (R)	72.8	**5 - 1**	15 - 03
Heat 04	**Blackburn**/**Bottomley**/Paynter/Williams	74.4	**5 - 1**	20 - 04
Heat 05	**Meeks**/Robinson/Omand/**J.Jackson** (R)	74.2	3 - 3	23 - 07
Heat 06	**O'Neil**/**Evans**/Brady/Williams	74.0	**5 - 1**	28 - 08
Heat 07	**Blackburn**/R.Jackson/Baldock/**Bottomley** (R)	75.0	3 - 3	31 - 11
Heat 08	**Hawkins**/Paynter/Omand/**Evans** (R)	76.2	3 - 3	34 - 14
Heat 09	**J.Jackson**/Williams/**Meeks**/Brady	74.0	**4 - 2**	38 - 16
Heat 10	**O'Neil**/R.Jackson/Baldock/**Evans**	74.4	3 - 3	41 - 19
Heat 11	**Hawkins**/**Bottomley**/Omand/Robinson (R)	74.2	**5 - 1**	46 - 20
Heat 12	**O'Neil**/**J.Jackson**/R.Jackson/Williams	73.8	**5 - 1**	51 - 21
Heat 13	**Meeks**/**Bottomley**/Paynter/Baldock	74.0	**5 - 1**	56 - 22

CREWE - Paul O'Neil 12, Barry Meeks 10, Warren Hawkins 9, Glyn Blackburn 8 (+1), John Jackson 7 (+2), Ian Bottomley 6 (+3), Dai Evans 4 (+2).
BERWICK - Rob Jackson* 6, Alan Paynter 4, Ken Omand 3 (+2), Maury Robinson 3, Peter Baldock 2 (+2), Alistair Brady 2, Roy Williams 2.

Newcomers Bradford Northern made their home bow in front of over 10,000 spectators at Odsal Stadium, defeating Eastbourne 44-34.

Meeting 24 - Monday, June 29, 1970 - British League Division II
L.M.R. Sports Ground, Earle Street, Crewe
Track Length - 470 yards.

CREWE KINGS.....47 CANTERBURY CRUSADERS.....31

Canterbury suffered only their second league defeat of the season, but made the Kings fight all the way for the points. In Heat 12 Paul O'Neil defeated Graeme Smith, who was top of the league's averages, in what would be the fastest time of the night and a rehearsal for their Silver Helmet clash - also won by the home ace. Dai Evans provided the biggest cheer of the night in Heat 4 when he fought out a thriller with Smith. The Canterbury star led from the first lap and looked set for victory, until the Welshman pipped him by a wheel on the line.

Heat 01	Crowson/**Blackburn**/Banks/**O'Neil** (R)	75.8	2 - 4	02 - 04
Heat 02	**Hawkins**/**Evans**/Rennison/Kite	74.8	**5 - 1**	07 - 05
Heat 03	**Meeks**/**Jackson**/Miles/Thomas	74.0	**5 - 1**	12 - 06
Heat 04	**Evans**/Smith/Rennison/**Bottomley**	74.0	3 - 3	15 - 09
Heat 05	**Meeks**/**Jackson**/Crowson/Banks	73.8	**5 - 1**	20 - 10
Heat 06	**O'Neil**/Smith/Rennison/**Blackburn**	73.4	3 - 3	23 - 13
Heat 07	Miles/**Evans**/Thomas/**Bottomley** (R)	75.8	2 - 4	25 - 17
Heat 08	**Hawkins**/**Blackburn**/Banks/Kite	74.6	**5 - 1**	30 - 18
Heat 09	Smith/**Jackson**/**Meeks**/Rennison	73.8	3 - 3	33 - 21
Heat 10	**O'Neil**/Miles/**Blackburn**/Thomas	74.4	**4 - 2**	37 - 23
Heat 11	Smith/**Hawkins**/Crowson/**Bottomley**	74.0	2 - 4	39 - 27
Heat 12	**O'Neil**/Smith/**Jackson**/Thomas	72.4	**4 - 2**	43 - 29
Heat 13	**Bottomley**/Crowson/**Meeks**/Miles	73.6	**4 - 2**	47 - 31

CREWE - Paul O'Neil 9, Barry Meeks 8 (+1), Warren Hawkins 8, John Jackson 7 (+2), Dai Evans 7 (+1), Glyn Blackburn 5 (+1), Ian Bottomley 3.
CANTERBURY - Graeme Smith 12, Barry Crowson 7, Graham Miles 6, Jake Rennison 3 (+2), Graham Banks 2, Barry Thomas 1, Alan Kite 0.

Meeting 25 - Wednesday, July 1, 1970 - Challenge
Victoria Park Stadium, Newtongrange
Track Length - 430 yards.

NEWTONGRANGE SAINTS.....40 CREWE KINGS.....37

With Colin Tucker in their line-up, the Saints, operating on an open licence, defeated the Kings, despite a Paul O'Neil maximum. The match was a keenly-contested affair, until a Maury Robinson/Colin Tucker maximum ended Crewe's hopes of victory. Robinson beat O'Neil in the Rider of the Night final after the Crewe rider took a fall.

Heat	Riders	Time	Score	Total
Heat 01	**O'Neil**/Robinson/**Blackburn**/Gallacher (F)	81.8	**2 - 4**	02 - 04
Heat 02	Nicol/**Evans**/Mackie/**Morris** (F)	83.0	4 - 2	06 - 06
Heat 03	Murray/**Jackson**/**Meeks**/Tucker	81.0	3 - 3	09 - 09
Heat 04	Nicol/Brady/**Bottomley**/**Morris** (F)	83.6	5 - 1	14 - 10
Heat 05	**O'Neil**/Tucker/Murray/**Blackburn**	81.8	3 - 3	17 - 13
Heat 06	Robinson/**Evans**/Gallacher/**Bottomley**	81.0	4 - 2	21 - 15
Heat 07	**Jackson**/**Meeks**/Brady/Nicol	82.8	**1 - 5**	22 - 20
Heat 08	Mackie/**Blackburn**/Gallacher (F)/**Morris** (R)	89.2	3 - 2	25 - 22
Heat 09	**Evans**/Murray/Tucker/**Bottomley**	82.0	3 - 3	28 - 25
Heat 10	Robinson/**Jackson**/**Meeks**/Nicol	81.0	3 - 3	31 - 28
Heat 11	**O'Neil**/Brady/Mackie/**Blackburn**	82.8	3 - 3	34 - 31
Heat 12	Robinson/Tucker/**Meeks**/**Bottomley** (R)	83.0	5 - 1	39 - 32
Heat 13	**O'Neil**/**Jackson**/Murray/Brady	81.4	**1 - 5**	40 - 37

NEWTONGRANGE - Maury Robinson 11, Brian Murray 7 (+1), Alex Nicol 6, Colin Tucker 5 (+2), Alistair Brady 5 (+1), Alan Mackie 5 (+1), Jimmy Gallacher 1.
CREWE - Paul O'Neil 12, John Jackson 9 (+1), Dai Evans 7, Barry Meeks 5 (+3), Glyn Blackburn 3, Ian Bottomley 1, Brian Morris* 0.

The following night, Paul O'Neil was again in the wars when competing in the Suffolk Open Championship at Reading. During the meeting he suffered a bad fall and was taken to hospital with back injuries.

Meeting 26 - Friday, July 3, 1970 - Challenge
Plymouth Sports Stadium, Pennycross, Plymouth
Track Length - 413 yards.

PLYMOUTH DEVILS.....46 CREWE KINGS.....32

For the second time in three days, the Kings were turned over by a team operating on an open licence. In front of a crowd of around 1,000, the under-strength Crewe side put in a poor performance. Guest Tony Childs, John Jackson and Barry Meeks scored all but four of the final total.

Heat	Riders	Time	Score	Total
Heat 01	**Childs**/Hammond/Sanders/**Moore**	80.0	3 - 3	03 - 03
Heat 02	Dennis/**Mulligan**/**Hawkins**/Facey (R)	80.4	3 - 3	06 - 06
Heat 03	O'Connor/Roynon/**Meeks**/**Evans**	77.0	5 - 1	11 - 07
Heat 04	**Jackson**/Sanders/**Mulligan**/Facey (F)	79.0	**2 - 4**	13 - 11
Heat 05	O'Connor/**Childs**/Roynon/**Moore**	78.2	4 - 2	17 - 13
Heat 06	Hammond/Sanders/**Jackson**/**Hawkins**	79.0	5 - 1	22 - 14
Heat 07	**Meeks**/O'Connor/Facey/**Evans**	79.0	3 - 3	25 - 17
Heat 08	**Childs**/Dennis/Facey/**Mulligan**	80.0	3 - 3	28 - 20
Heat 09	Roynon/**Jackson**/O'Connor/**Hawkins** (R)	78.8	4 - 2	32 - 22
Heat 10	**Meeks**/Hammond/Sanders/**Evans**	78.2	3 - 3	35 - 25
Heat 11	Roynon/**Jackson**/Dennis/**Childs** (R)	80.2	4 - 2	39 - 27
Heat 12	Sanders/**Jackson**/**Meeks**/O'Connor (R)	79.0	3 - 3	42 - 30
Heat 13	Hammond/**Childs**/Roynon/**Evans**	79.4	4 - 2	46 - 32

(ABOVE) Chester youngster John Jackson, who was handed a team place following some impressive displays in the Wednesday afternoon winter training schools. (BELOW) Another new signing was Aussie Warren Hawkins (left), seen here sharing a joke with Ian Bottomley.

(ABOVE) The frozen looking Crewe line-up for the first away fixture of the season at Rochdale on March 29. (Left to right) John Jackson, Colin Tucker, Barry Meeks, Warren Hawkins, Ian Bottomley, Dave Parry, Paul O'Neil and team manager Ken Adams. (Wright Wood Collection, courtesy of John Somerville.)

(ABOVE) Colin Tucker during happier times at Earle Street.

(ABOVE) Veteran Dai Evans, who joined the club from Nelson, just after the start of the season. (BELOW) Action from the Crewe v Peterborough match on June 15.

PLYMOUTH - Chris Roynon 10 (+1), John Hammond 10, Colin Sanders 9 (+3), Dave O'Connor 9, Danny Dennis 6, Colin Facey 2 (+2), *Bob Coles (R/R).*
CREWE - Tony Childs* 10, John Jackson 10, Barry Meeks 8 (+1), John Mulligan 3, Warren Hawkins 1 (+1), Dai Evans 0, Chris Moore 0.

Meeting 27 - Sunday, July 5, 1970 - Four Team Tournament, First Leg
Athletic Grounds, Milnrow Road, Rochdale
Track Length - 427 yards.

ROCHDALE HORNETS.....32 TEESSIDE TEESSIDERS.....26
CREWE KINGS.....20 BERWICK BANDITS.....18

A welcome change from the normal league and cup format saw the Kings partake in their first Four Team Tournament. The opening leg was held at Rochdale, and as expected, home riders excelled early on in the meeting, but surprisingly did not win any of the final seven heats. Paul O'Neil ended the afternoon as Crewe's only winner, taking the chequered flag in Heat 12 and 14.

			R	T	C	B
Heat 01	Broadbelt/Paynter/**Hawkins**/Jameson	78.8	3	0	1	2
Heat 02	Bailey/Robinson/Leadbitter/**Meeks**	80.0	3	1	0	2
Heat 03	Owen/**O'Neil**/Omand/Mills	79.4	3	0	2	1
Heat 04	Durham/**Jackson**/Tyrer/Williams	80.0	1	3	2	0
Heat 05	Broadbelt/Mills/Robinson/**Jackson**	79.0	3	2	0	1
Heat 06	Bailey/Durham/**O'Neil**/Paynter	80.6	3	2	1	0
Heat 07	Williams/**Meeks**/Jameson/Owen (R)	82.4	0	1	2	3
Heat 08	Leadbitter/Tyrer/Omand/**Hawkins**	80.8	2	3	0	1
Heat 09	Broadbelt/**Meeks**/Durham/Omand (F)	82.0	3	1	2	0
Heat 10	Mills/Bailey/**Evans**/Williams	80.2	2	3	1	0
Heat 11	Leadbitter/Owen/**Jackson**/Paynter	82.4	2	3	1	0
Heat 12	**O'Neil**/Tyrer/Robinson/Jameson	80.4	2	0	3	1
Heat 13	Jameson/Bailey/**Jackson**/Omand	79.2	2	3	1	0
Heat 14	**O'Neil**/Williams/Leadbitter/Broadbelt (R)	80.6	0	1	3	2
Heat 15	Robinson/Owen/**Hawkins**/Durham	81.8	2	0	1	3
Heat 16	Mills/Paynter/Tyrer/**Meeks**	81.0	1	3	0	2

ROCHDALE - Chris Bailey 10, Eric Broadbelt 9, Taffy Owen 7, Paul Tyrer 6.
TEESSIDE - Tom Leadbitter 8, Roger Mills 8, Dave Durham 6, Bob Jameson 4.
CREWE - Paul O'Neil 9, John Jackson 4, Barry Meeks 4, Warren Hawkins 2, Dai Evans (Reserve) 1.
BERWICK - Maury Robinson 7, Roy Williams 5, Alan Paynter 4, Ken Omand 2.

Meeting 28 - Monday, July 6, 1970 - Challenge
L.M.R. Sports Ground, Earle Street, Crewe
Track Length - 470 yards.

CREWE KINGS.....48 WORKINGTON COMETS.....30

The Cumbrians made their first visit to Earle Street, and despite a catalogue of mechanical problems, did not disgrace themselves during the eighteen-point defeat. Comets drafted in Bradford's Gary Peterson to deputise for the injured Lou Sansom, and he was the star of the night, with only Ian Bottomley preventing him from recording a five ride maximum, by just edging him out in a scintillating final heat. Dave Parry made a return to the team after a long lay-off and was placed in each of his rides.

Heat 01	Peterson/**Parry**/**O'Neil**/Wilson	73.8	3 - 3	03 - 03
Heat 02	**Hawkins**/**Evans**/Lonsdale/Blythe (F)	75.2	**5 - 1**	08 - 04
Heat 03	**Jackson**/**Meeks**/Mackay/Valentine	75.6	**5 - 1**	13 - 05
Heat 04	**Evans**/Penniket/**Bottomley**/Lonsdale (R)	74.0	**4 - 2**	17 - 07
Heat 05	Peterson/**Meeks**/**Jackson**/Wilson	72.8	3 - 3	20 - 10
Heat 06	**O'Neil**/Penniket/**Parry**/Blythe (R)	73.4	**4 - 2**	24 - 12
Heat 07	**Bottomley**/Valentine/**Evans**/Mackay	73.4	**4 - 2**	28 - 14
Heat 08	**Parry**/Penniket/Lonsdale/**Hawkins** (R)	75.2	3 - 3	31 - 17
Heat 09	Peterson/**Meeks**/**Jackson**/Penniket (R)	72.6	3 - 3	34 - 20
Heat 10	**O'Neil**/Valentine/**Parry**/Mackay (R)	73.0	**4 - 2**	38 - 22

Heat 11	Peterson/**Bottomley**/**Hawkins**/Wilson	74.0	3 - 3	41 - 25
Heat 12	Valentine/**Jackson**/**O'Neil**/Penniket	73.8	3 - 3	44 - 28
Heat 13	**Bottomley**/Peterson/**Meeks**/Mackay	74.0	**4 - 2**	48 - 30

CREWE - Ian Bottomley 9, Paul O'Neil 8 (+2), John Jackson 7 (+2), Barry Meeks 7 (+1), Dave Parry 7, Dai Evans 6 (+1), Warren Hawkins 4 (+1).
WORKINGTON - Gary Peterson* 14, Bob Valentine 7, Geoff Penniket 6, Vic Lonsdale 2 (+1), Malcolm Mackay 1, Chris Blythe 0, Reg Wilson 0.

Meeting 29 - Monday, July 13, 1970 - British League Division II
L.M.R. Sports Ground, Earle Street, Crewe
Track Length - 470 yards.

CREWE KINGS.....47 ROCHDALE HORNETS.....31

The Kings closed in on the all-time Division II home league victories record after winning their 19th straight meeting, setting a new mark among the current teams. It was also appropriate that they did it against their biggest rivals, who under the guise of the Belle Vue Colts, had so far been the only team to win in the league at Earle Street, and also held the record of 21 matches. Paul O'Neil once again went through the card unbeaten. Taffy Owen was the best of the Hornets, but was no match for O'Neil in their Silver Helmet clash.

Heat 01	**O'Neil**/Broadbelt/Tyrer/**Hawkins** (F)	72.8	3 - 3	03 - 03
Heat 02	Moss/**Bottomley**/**Evans**/Waplington	74.0	3 - 3	06 - 06
Heat 03	**Jackson**/Owen/**Meeks**/Wilkinson	73.2	**4 - 2**	10 - 08
Heat 04	**Evans**/Moss/**Parry**/Bailey	73.8	**4 - 2**	14 - 10
Heat 05	**Meeks**/**Jackson**/Broadbelt/Tyrer (R)	74.0	**5 - 1**	19 - 11
Heat 06	**O'Neil**/Bailey/Waplington/**Hawkins**	74.2	3 - 3	22 - 14
Heat 07	Owen/**Parry**/Wilkinson/**Evans** (R)	73.6	2 - 4	24 - 18
Heat 08	Owen/**Hawkins**/**Evans**/Moss (R)	73.6	3 - 3	27 - 21
Heat 09	Bailey/**Jackson**/**Meeks**/Waplington	73.4	3 - 3	30 - 24
Heat 10	**O'Neil**/Owen/**Evans**/Wilkinson	73.4	**4 - 2**	34 - 26
Heat 11	Bailey/**Parry**/**Bottomley**/Broadbelt	74.2	3 - 3	37 - 29
Heat 12	**O'Neil**/**Jackson**/Owen/Bailey	72.6	**5 - 1**	42 - 30
Heat 13	**Parry**/**Meeks**/Broadbelt/Wilkinson	74.0	**5 - 1**	47 - 31

CREWE - Paul O'Neil 12, John Jackson 9 (+2), Dave Parry 8, Barry Meeks 7 (+2), Dai Evans 6 (+2), Ian Bottomley 3 (+1), Warren Hawkins 2.
ROCHDALE - Taffy Owen 11, Chris Bailey 8, Ken Moss 5, Eric Broadbelt 4, Paul Tyrer 1 (+1), Steve Waplington 1 (+1), Alan Wilkinson 1.

The added attraction of sidecar racing during the second-half ensured Crewe's biggest crowd of the season. Among the spectators were World Champion Ivan Mauger and England captain Nigel Boocock. Following Dave Parry's inclusion in the team, Glyn Blackburn left the club following a dispute over his demotion. On July 15, Paul O'Neil scored nine and finished equal fifth in the Northern Riders Trophy at Odsal, won by home rider Gary Peterson.

Meeting 30 - Thursday, July 16, 1970 - Four Team Tournament, Second Leg
Cleveland Park Stadium, Stockton Road, Middlesbrough
Track Length - 335 yards.

ROCHDALE HORNETS.....32 TEESSIDE TEESSIDERS.....24
CREWE KINGS.....22 BERWICK BANDITS.....18

(Scores after two legs - Rochdale 64, Teesside 50, Crewe 42, Berwick 36)

Teesside's hopes of reducing Rochdale's advantage from the first leg were thwarted after the Hornets won this leg too. John Jackson top-scored for Crewe with three wins.

			R	T	C	B
Heat 01	Leadbitter/Paynter/Tyrer/**Meeks**	72.4	1	3	0	2
Heat 02	Robinson/Broadbelt/**O'Neil**/Whaley	72.0	2	0	1	3
Heat 03	Bailey/**Evans**/Meldrum/Forrester	76.0	3	0	2	1
Heat 04	Jameson/Williams/Owen/**Jackson**	73.2	1	3	0	2

Heat 05.... Robinson/Owen/**Evans**/Leadbitter	72.0	2	0	1	3
Heat 06.... **Jackson**/Bailey/Mills/Paynter	72.4	2	1	3	0
Heat 07.... Broadbelt/Forrester/Williams/**Meeks**	72.2	3	2	0	1
Heat 08.... Jameson/**O'Neil**/Tyrer/Meldrum	72.8	1	3	2	0
Heat 09.... **Jackson**/Broadbelt/Leadbitter/Meldrum	70.4	2	1	3	0
Heat 10.... Mills/**Evans**/Williams/Tyrer	72.2	0	3	2	1
Heat 11.... Owen/Forrester/**O'Neil**/Paynter	71.6	3	2	1	0
Heat 12.... Robinson/Bailey/Whaley/**Meeks**	72.2	2	1	0	3
Heat 13.... Owen/Mills/**Meeks**/Meldrum	71.4	3	2	1	0
Heat 14.... **O'Neil**/Bailey/Leadbitter/Williams	71.6	2	1	3	0
Heat 15.... **Jackson**/Wilkinson/Robinson/Forrester	72.8	2	0	3	1
Heat 16.... Broadbelt/Jameson/Paynter/**Evans**	71.8	3	2	0	1

ROCHDALE - Eric Broadbelt 10, Chris Bailey 9, Taffy Owen 9, Paul Tyrer 2, Alan Wilkinson (Reserve) 2.
TEESSIDE - Bob Jameson 8, Roger Mills 6, Tom Leadbitter 5, Bruce Forrester 4, Brian Whaley (Reserve) 1.
CREWE - John Jackson 9, Paul O'Neil 7, Dai Evans 5, Barry Meeks 1.
BERWICK - Maury Robinson 10, Roy Williams 4, Alan Paynter 3, Andy Meldrum 1.

Meeting 31 - Saturday, July 18, 1970 - Four Team Tournament, Third Leg
Shielfield Park, Tweedmouth, Berwick-upon-Tweed
Track Length - 440 yards.

TEESSIDE TEESSIDERS.....39 ROCHDALE HORNETS.....27 CREWE KINGS.....17 BERWICK BANDITS.....13

(Scores after three legs - Rochdale 91, Teesside 89, Crewe 59, Berwick 49)

This proved to be a disastrous home leg for the Bandits when they finished last. Tom Leadbitter and Bob Jameson were unbeaten for the Teessiders as they stormed back into contention, trailing by only two points on aggregate, with the final leg at Crewe remaining.

		T	R	C	B
Heat 01..... **Jackson**/Robinson/Owen/Swales	78.2	0	1	3	2
Heat 02..... Mills/Broadbelt/**Meeks**/Omand	78.4	3	2	1	0
Heat 03..... Leadbitter/Bailey/Williams/**Evans**	80.4	3	2	0	1
Heat 04..... Jameson/Paynter/**O'Neil**/Tyrer	80.6	3	0	1	2
Heat 05..... Jameson/Wilkinson/**Meeks**/Meldrum	80.8	3	2	1	0
Heat 06..... Leadbitter/**Jackson**/Tyrer/Omand	79.0	3	1	2	0
Heat 07..... Owen/**O'Neil**/Mills/Williams	80.2	1	3	2	0
Heat 08..... Broadbelt/Swales/**Evans**/Paynter	79.0	2	3	1	0
Heat 09..... Robinson/Mills/Tyrer/**Evans**	78.8	2	1	0	3
Heat 10..... Swales/Bailey/**O'Neil**/Omand (F)	78.2	3	2	1	0
Heat 11..... Jameson/Broadbelt/Williams/**Jackson** (F)	80.0	3	2	0	1
Heat 12..... Leadbitter/Owen/**Meeks**/Paynter	79.8	3	2	1	0
Heat 13..... Jameson/Owen/Omand/**Evans**	80.4	3	2	0	1
Heat 14..... Leadbitter/Robinson/Broadbelt/**O'Neil**	79.8	3	1	0	2
Heat 15..... Wilkinson/Swales/**Meeks**/Williams	81.0	2	3	1	0
Heat 16..... **Jackson**/Mills/Paynter/Bailey (X)	79.8	2	0	3	1

TEESSIDE - Bob Jameson 12, Tom Leadbitter 12, Roger Mills 8, Tim Swales 7.
ROCHDALE - Eric Broadbelt 8, Taffy Owen 8, Alan Wilkinson (Reserve) 5, Chris Bailey 4, Paul Tyrer 2.
CREWE - John Jackson 8, Barry Meeks 4, Paul O'Neil 4, Dai Evans 1.
BERWICK - Maury Robinson 7, Alan Paynter 3, Roy Williams 2, Ken Omand 1, Andy Meldrum (Reserve) 0.

Meeting 32 - Sunday, July 19, 1970 - British League Division II
Doncaster Greyhound Stadium, York Road, Doncaster
Track Length - 350 yards.

DONCASTER DRAGONS.....42 CREWE KINGS.....35

Crewe's first away league fixture since June 3, proved to be a great day for Doncaster's George Major. He not only recorded a maximum, but also broke the track record in Heat 9, which he then equalled in the final heat. To cap off a terrific meeting, he took the Silver Helmet off Paul O'Neil, when the Crewe rider fell after hitting the safety fence, sustaining a bad knee injury.

Heat 01	Roynon/Wilson/**O'Neil** (R)/**Hawkins** (X)	71.4	5 - 0	05 - 00
Heat 02	Wasden/Emms/**Bottomley/Evans**	73.2	5 - 1	10 - 01
Heat 03	Major/**Jackson/Meeks**/Haslinger	69.8	3 - 3	13 - 04
Heat 04	**Evans**/Harrison/Emms/**Bottomley**	72.0	3 - 3	16 - 07
Heat 05	Major/Haslinger/**Hawkins/O'Neil**	70.0	5 - 1	21 - 08
Heat 06	Roynon/**Evans/Parry**/Wilson	71.4	3 - 3	24 - 11
Heat 07	**Jackson**/Emms/Harrison/**Meeks**	**69.2** (=TR)	3 - 3	27 - 14
Heat 08	**Jackson/O'Neil**/Wilson/Wasden	70.0	**1 - 5**	28 - 19
Heat 09	Major/**Parry/Evans**/Haslinger	**69.0** (TR)	3 - 3	31 - 22
Heat 10	**Jackson**/Roynon/**Meeks**/Wilson	69.8	**2 - 4**	33 - 26
Heat 11	**O'Neil/Evans**/Harrison/Wasden (R)	72.0	**1 - 5**	34 - 31
Heat 12	Roynon/Haslinger/**Evans/Parry**	71.6	5 - 1	39 - 32
Heat 13	Major/**Jackson/O'Neil**/Emms	**69.0** (=TR)	3 - 3	42 - 35

DONCASTER - George Major 12, Chris Roynon 11, Cliff Emms 5 (+2), Hec Haslinger 4 (+2), Chris Harrison 4 (+1), Ian Wilson 3 (+1), Dennis Wasden 3.
CREWE - John Jackson 13, Dai Evans 9 (+2), Paul O'Neil 6 (+2), Dave Parry 3 (+1), Barry Meeks 2 (+1), Ian Bottomley 1, Warren Hawkins 1.

Meeting 33 - Monday, July 20, 1970 - Four Team Tournament, Fourth Leg
L.M.R. Sports Ground, Earle Street, Crewe
Track Length - 470 yards.

CREWE KINGS.....39 ROCHDALE HORNETS.....32
TEESSIDE TEESSIDERS.....16 BERWICK BANDITS.....9

(Final aggregate scores - Rochdale 123, Teesside 105, Crewe 98, Berwick 58)

Rochdale won the tournament with a solid performance at Earle Street, even though home riders won ten of sixteen heats, with Barry Meeks and John Jackson each dropping only a single point. Taffy Owen was the only unbeaten rider on the night as Berwick finished last in all four legs.

			C	R	T	B
Heat 01	**Bottomley**/Moss/Paynter/Jameson (R)	74.0	3	2	0	1
Heat 02	**Meeks**/Leadbitter/Robinson/Bailey	73.4	3	0	2	1
Heat 03	Owen/**Parry**/Mills/Omand	73.0	2	3	1	0
Heat 04	**Jackson**/Wilkinson/Forrester/Brady	74.2	3	2	1	0
Heat 05	**Jackson**/Robinson/Moss/Mills	73.0	3	1	0	2
Heat 06	Bailey/Paynter/**Evans**/Forrester	74.0	1	3	0	2
Heat 07	Owen/**Meeks**/Swales/Brady	72.8	2	3	1	0
Heat 08	Leadbitter/**Bottomley**/Wilkinson/Omand	73.6	2	1	3	0
Heat 09	**Meeks**/Moss/Omand/Forrester	73.6	3	2	0	1
Heat 10	**Bottomley**/Bailey/Mills/Brady (R)	73.8	3	2	1	0
Heat 11	Owen/**Jackson**/Leadbitter/Paynter	72.8	2	3	1	0
Heat 12	**Parry**/Wilkinson/Robinson/Swales	74.0	3	2	0	1
Heat 13	**Jackson**/Bailey/Swales/Omand	72.4	3	2	1	0
Heat 14	**Parry**/Leadbitter/Moss/Brady (R)	73.2	3	1	2	0
Heat 15	Owen/Forrester/Robinson/**Bottomley** (R)	73.0	0	3	2	1
Heat 16	**Meeks**/Wilkinson/Mills/Paynter	73.0	3	2	1	0

CREWE - John Jackson 11, Barry Meeks 11, Ian Bottomley 8, Dave Parry (Reserve) 8, Dai Evans 1.
ROCHDALE - Taffy Owen 12, Chris Bailey 7, Alan Wilkinson 7, Ken Moss 6.
TEESSIDE - Tom Leadbitter 8, Bruce Forrester 3, Roger Mills 3, Tim Swales (Reserve) 2, Bob Jameson 0.
BERWICK - Maury Robinson 5, Alan Paynter 3, Ken Omand 1, Alistair Brady 0.

Meeting 34 - Monday, July 27, 1970 - Chester Vase Handicap
L.M.R. Sports Ground, Earle Street, Crewe
Track Length - 470 yards.

WINNER.....JOHN JACKSON

Rain marred the Chester Vase Handicap meeting and made for treacherous conditions. The competition was to include six riders starting off a twenty yard handicap. Unfortunately, this was reduced to five owing to Paul O'Neil's absence through injury. Gary Peterson arrived late and missed his first ride, but was the first handicapper to win a race in Heat 8. However, it was Crewe youngster John Jackson who won the meeting after dropping just two points. Chris Bailey worked hard to finish second after failing to score in his opening ride. Ian Bottomley was also in contention after winning his first three, but mechanical failure in his remaining outings cost him his chance. Colin Tucker also rode well on his former track, winning two races.

Heat 01	Tucker/Moore/Evans/Bailey	75.0
Heat 02	Bottomley/Turner/Parry/Smith	73.4
Heat 03	Meeks/Leadbitter/Mulligan/R.Jackson (R)	74.0
Heat 04	J.Jackson/Owen/Hawkins/Valentine	72.8
Heat 05	Bailey/J.Jackson/Turner/Meeks	73.2
Heat 06	Valentine/Smith/Moore/R.Jackson	73.8
Heat 07	Bottomley/Tucker/Hawkins/Leadbitter	74.8
Heat 08	Peterson/Owen/Evans/Parry	76.0
Heat 09	Bailey/Smith/Owen/Leadbitter (R)	76.2
Heat 10	Peterson/Turner/Moore/Hawkins	76.0
Heat 11	Meeks/Valentine/Tucker/Parry	76.4
Heat 12	Bottomley/J.Jackson/Evans/R.Jackson	77.8
Heat 13	Bailey/Valentine/Peterson/Bottomley (R)	76.6
Heat 14	J.Jackson/Moore/Leadbitter/Parry (R)	78.8
Heat 15	Tucker/Owen/R.Jackson/Turner	81.2
Heat 16	Smith/Hawkins/Meeks/Evans (F)	00.0
Heat 17	Bailey/Parry/Hawkins/R.Jackson	79.0
Heat 18	Owen/Meeks/Moore/Bottomley	80.4
Heat 19	J.Jackson/Smith/Peterson/Tucker (R)	79.0
Heat 20	Valentine/Leadbitter/Evans/Turner (R)	81.2

John Jackson 13, Chris Bailey 12, Bob Valentine 10, Taffy Owen 10, Colin Tucker 9, Graeme Smith 9, Ian Bottomley 9, Barry Meeks 9, Gary Peterson 8, Gary Moore 7, Ian Turner 5, Tom Leadbitter 5, Warren Hawkins 5, Dai Evans 4, Dave Parry 3, Rob Jackson 1. Meeting Reserve: John Mulligan 1. *(Tucker replaced Paul O'Neil and R.Jackson replaced Arthur Price - Turner, Smith, Leadbitter, Peterson and Owen started 20 yards behind start gate.)*

Meeting 35 - Wednesday, July 29, 1970 - British League Division II
Odsal Stadium, Rooley Avenue, Bradford
Track Length - 385 yards.

BRADFORD NORTHERN.....55 CREWE KINGS.....23

Since their move from Nelson, Bradford had hammered all who had visited, and when Crewe came calling, they too were given the same treatment. Gary Peterson scored a maximum with Dave Schofield and Alf Wells securing paid ones. Dai Evans, riding in a reserve berth, showed his liking for the track, by top scoring for the Kings and Bob Jameson of Teesside, deputising for the injured Paul O'Neil, scored in each of his rides. During Heat 2, home rider Peter Thompson unfortunately broke an ankle.

Heat 01	Knapkin/Sheldrick/**Jameson**/**Hawkins**	72.4	5 - 1	05 - 01
Heat 02	**Evans**/Bridgett/**Bottomley**/Thompson	76.2	**2 - 4**	07 - 05
Heat 03	Wells/Schofield/**Parry**/**Meeks**	75.4	5 - 1	12 - 06
Heat 04	Peterson/Bridgett/**Jackson**/**Bottomley**	73.4	5 - 1	17 - 07
Heat 05	Wells/Schofield/**Jameson**/**Hawkins**	75.2	5 - 1	22 - 08
Heat 06	Knapkin/**Evans**/Sheldrick/**Jackson**	72.4	4 - 2	26 - 10
Heat 07	Peterson/**Meeks**/Bridgett/**Parry**	73.4	4 - 2	30 - 12
Heat 08	Sheldrick/**Jameson**/**Evans**/Bridgett	74.0	3 - 3	33 - 15
Heat 09	Wells/Schofield/**Evans**/**Jackson**	75.4	5 - 1	38 - 16
Heat 10	Knapkin/Sheldrick/**Meeks**/**Parry**	73.8	5 - 1	43 - 17
Heat 11	Peterson/**Evans**/**Jameson**/Bridgett	74.4	3 - 3	46 - 20
Heat 12	Schofield/**Evans**/Knapkin/**Meeks**	76.8	4 - 2	50 - 22
Heat 13	Peterson/Wells/**Jameson**/**Meeks**	74.6	5 - 1	55 - 23

BRADFORD - Gary Peterson 12, Alf Wells 11 (+1), Alan Knapkin 10, Dave Schofield 9 (+3), Sid Sheldrick 8 (+2), Alan Bridgett 5 (+1), Peter Thompson 0.

CREWE - Dai Evans 11 (+1), Bob Jameson* 6 (+1), Barry Meeks 3, Ian Bottomley 1, John Jackson 1, Dave Parry 1, Warren Hawkins 0.

Meeting 36 - Friday, July 31, 1970 - British League Division II
L.M.R. Sports Ground, Earle Street, Crewe.
Track Length - 470 yards.

CREWE KINGS.....43 BRADFORD NORTHERN.....35

Crewe made amends for their Odsal slaughter by completing twelve months without a home league defeat, after narrowly beating a determined Bradford outfit. The Friday night clash, the best of the season so far at Earle Street, was marred by a sickening crash during Heat 9. Gary Peterson and Dave Parry collided on the second bend of the last lap, with both bikes smashing into the boards. Peterson came off worst, swallowing his tongue, and was taken to hospital with head injuries. John Harrhy of Ipswich guested for Paul O'Neil, and home rider Rob Jackson, replaced Alf Wells for the visitors.

Heat	Result	Time	Score	Total
Heat 01	**Hawkins**/Knapkin/Sheldrick/**Harrhy**	75.4	3 - 3	03 - 03
Heat 02	**Evans**/Bridgett/**Bottomley**/Adlington	74.2	**4 - 2**	07 - 05
Heat 03	**Meeks**/**Parry**/R.Jackson/Schofield	74.4	**5 - 1**	12 - 06
Heat 04	Peterson/**J.Jackson**/Adlington/**Evans**	72.8	2 - 4	14 - 10
Heat 05	**Parry**/Knapkin/**Meeks**/Sheldrick	74.0	**4 - 2**	18 - 12
Heat 06	Peterson/**Harrhy**/**Hawkins**/Bridgett	73.4	3 - 3	21 - 15
Heat 07	**J.Jackson**/**Evans**/Schofield/R.Jackson	73.4	**5 - 1**	26 - 16
Heat 08	Peterson/Sheldrick/**Bottomley**/**Hawkins**	73.0	1 - 5	27 - 21
Heat 09	**Parry**/**Meeks**/Bridgett/Peterson (X)	00.0	**5 - 1**	32 - 22
Heat 10	Knapkin/**Hawkins**/**Harrhy**/Schofield (R)	73.2	3 - 3	35 - 25
Heat 11	Knapkin/Sheldrick/**Bottomley**/**J.Jackson** (R)	73.4	1 - 5	36 - 30
Heat 12	**Evans**/Sheldrick/**Harrhy**/Adlington	75.0	**4 - 2**	40 - 32
Heat 13	Knapkin/**J.Jackson**/**Meeks**/Adlington	73.0	3 - 3	43 - 35

CREWE - Dai Evans 8 (+1), Dave Parry 8 (+1), Barry Meeks 7 (+2), John Jackson 7, Warren Hawkins 6 (+1), John Harrhy* 4 (+1), Ian Bottomley 3.
BRADFORD - Alan Knapkin 13, Gary Peterson 9, Sid Sheldrick 7 (+3), Alan Bridgett 3, Robin Adlington 1, Rob Jackson* 1, Dave Schofield 1.

During the Heat 9 crash, two spectators (Graham Wood and Philip Taylor) were also hurt when hit by one of the bikes, after standing too close to the safety fence. Supporters were warned by Maurice Littlechild in the next home programme to remain well clear of the fence when racing was in progress.

Meeting 37 - Monday, August 3, 1970 - British League Division II
Reading Greyhound Stadium, Oxford Road, Tilehurst, Reading
Track Length - 360 yards.

READING RACERS.....49 CREWE KINGS.....29

Already without Dave Parry and Paul O'Neil, Crewe almost lost the services of Dai Evans following an incident in Heat 3, when injuring his foot. Most of the Kings riders struggled to cope with the tight bends of Tilehurst, and only guest Ross Gilbertson mastered the track for the visitors, scoring twelve from five outings.

Heat	Result	Time	Score	Total
Heat 01	Vernam/**Gilbertson**/Hammond/**Hawkins**	72.0	4 - 2	04 - 02
Heat 02	Leigh/Platt/**Mulligan**/**Bottomley**	74.2	5 - 1	09 - 03
Heat 03	Young/Davies/**Meeks**/**Evans**	74.4	5 - 1	14 - 04
Heat 04	May/Leigh/**Jackson**/**Bottomley**	73.2	5 - 1	19 - 05
Heat 05	**Gilbertson**/Young/Davies/**Hawkins**	73.8	3 - 3	22 - 08
Heat 06	Vernam/**Jackson**/**Meeks**/Hammond	73.0	3 - 3	25 - 11
Heat 07	Leigh/**Meeks**/Platt/**Evans**	74.4	4 - 2	29 - 13
Heat 08	**Gilbertson**/Hammond/**Hawkins**/Platt	73.4	**2 - 4**	31 - 17
Heat 09	**Jackson**/Davies/Young/**Mulligan**	74.2	3 - 3	34 - 20
Heat 10	Vernam/Leigh/**Jackson**/**Meeks**	73.2	5 - 1	39 - 21

Heat 11	May/**Gilbertson**/**Hawkins**/Platt	72.2	3 - 3	42 - 24
Heat 12	Vernam/**Jackson**/Davies/**Meeks**	73.6	4 - 2	46 - 26
Heat 13	May/**Gilbertson**/**Evans**/Young	72.8	3 - 3	49 - 29

READING - Mike Vernam 12, Bernie Leigh 10 (+2), Dickie May 9, Dene Davies 6 (+2), Bob Young 6 (+1), Ces Platt 3 (+1), John Hammond 3.
CREWE - Ross Gilbertson* 12, John Jackson 9, Barry Meeks 4 (+1), Warren Hawkins 2 (+1), Dai Evans 1 (+1), John Mulligan 1, Ian Bottomley 0.

Meeting 38 - Monday, August 10, 1970 - Division II International, Club Challenge
L.M.R. Sports Ground, Earle Street, Crewe
Track Length - 470 yards.

CREWE KINGS.....48 YOUNG CZECHOSLOVAKIA.....59

It took a full national team to finally win a meeting at Earle Street, although the Kings (the only club side to be awarded a match with the tourists) gave them a massive scare, as Young England had lost two of the opening three tests by 16 and 28 points. The Crewe effort therefore had to be applauded, as with three heats remaining, they trailed by just a point. Paul O'Neil, back from injury, rode well for his fourteen points and was well-supported by Ian Bottomley. Cousins Vaclav and Miroslav Verner, plus Jiri Stancl topped the Czech score chart, notching eight wins between them.

Heat 01	**O'Neil**/**Hawkins**/Majstr/Stancl (F)	74.4	**5 - 1**	05 - 01
Heat 02	V.Verner/Spinka/**J.Jackson**/**Bottomley** (R)	74.0	1 - 5	06 - 06
Heat 03	M.Verner/**Evans**/**Meeks**/Klokocka	72.4	3 - 3	09 - 09
Heat 04	**Bottomley**/Novotny/Lid (R)/**R.Jackson** (R)	74.8	**3 - 2**	12 - 11
Heat 05	**O'Neil**/Spinka/V.Verner/**Hawkins**	72.0	3 - 3	15 - 14
Heat 06	M.Verner/**Parry**/**J.Jackson**/Klokocka	72.2	3 - 3	18 - 17
Heat 07	Stancl/Majstr/**Meeks**/**Evans**	73.0	1 - 5	19 - 22
Heat 08	M.Verner/**O'Neil**/Lid/**Hawkins** (R)	72.2	2 - 4	21 - 26
Heat 09	V.Verner/**Meeks**/**Bottomley**/Spinka	73.8	3 - 3	24 - 29
Heat 10	**J.Jackson**/**Parry**/Stancl/Majstr	72.0	**5 - 1**	29 - 30
Heat 11	**O'Neil**/V.Verner/**Parry**/Novotny	72.2	**4 - 2**	33 - 32
Heat 12	M.Verner/Stancl/**Evans**/**J.Jackson**	73.0	1 - 5	34 - 37
Heat 13	Majstr/**Meeks**/**Hawkins**/Spinka	73.4	3 - 3	37 - 40
Heat 14	**Bottomley**/Lid/Novotny/**R.Jackson**	74.0	3 - 3	40 - 43
Heat 15	**O'Neil**/Stancl/**Bottomley**/M.Verner	72.4	**4 - 2**	44 - 45
Heat 16	Majstr/Spinka/**Evans**/**J.Jackson**	74.2	1 - 5	45 - 50
Heat 17	Lid/V.Verner/**Meeks**/**Hawkins**	75.0	1 - 5	46 - 55
Heat 18	Stancl/**Bottomley**/V.Verner/**O'Neil** (R)	74.0	2 - 4	48 - 59

CREWE - Paul O'Neil 14, Ian Bottomley 10 (+1), Barry Meeks 7 (+1), John Jackson 5 (+1), Dave Parry 5 (+1), Dai Evans 4, Warren Hawkins 3 (+2), Rob Jackson 0. Team Manager: Ken Adams.
YOUNG CZECHOSLOVAKIA - Vaclav Verner 12 (+2), Miroslav Verner 12, Jiri Stancl 11 (+1), Zdenek Majstr 9 (+1), Milan Spinka 6 (+2), Josef Lid 6, Zbynek Novotny 3 (+1), Jan Klokocka 0. Team Manager: Pavel Kacer.

Meeting 39 - Monday, August 17, 1970 - British League Division II
L.M.R. Sports Ground, Earle Street, Crewe
Track Length - 470 yards.

CREWE KINGS.....54 CRAYFORD HIGHWAYMEN.....24

Crayford, minus the talents of Geoff Ambrose, now with Division I outfit Wolverhampton, were comprehensively beaten by a Kings side who all registered a race win. Only on two occasions did a home rider fail to score - Paul O'Neil in Heat 10 and John Jackson in the next - both due to retirements. It was only the efforts of guest Taffy Owen of Rochdale, who scored exactly half of the visiting total, that prevented an even bigger thrashing.

Heat 01	**O'Neil**/Owen/**Parry**/Steel	73.8	**4 - 2**	04 - 02
Heat 02	**Bottomley**/Armstrong/**Hawkins**/Clark	74.8	**4 - 2**	08 - 04

Heat 03	**Meeks**/**Evans**/Devonport/Timms	74.0	**5 - 1**	13 - 05
Heat 04	**Hawkins**/**Jackson**/Childs/Clark	74.8	**5 - 1**	18 - 06
Heat 05	**Evans**/Owen/**Meeks**/Steel	74.4	**4 - 2**	22 - 08
Heat 06	**O'Neil**/**Parry**/Childs/Armstrong	73.6	**5 - 1**	27 - 09
Heat 07	**Jackson**/**Hawkins**/Timms/Devonport	74.0	**5 - 1**	32 - 10
Heat 08	Owen/**Bottomley**/**Parry**/Steel	74.8	3 - 3	35 - 13
Heat 09	**Meeks**/**Evans**/Childs/Armstrong	73.8	**5 - 1**	40 - 14
Heat 10	**Parry**/Timms/Clark/**O'Neil** (R)	75.8	3 - 3	43 - 17
Heat 11	Owen/**Bottomley**/Childs/**Jackson** (R)	75.6	2 - 4	45 - 21
Heat 12	**O'Neil**/**Evans**/Timms/Childs	74.0	**5 - 1**	50 - 22
Heat 13	**Meeks**/Owen/**Jackson**/Devonport	73.8	**4 - 2**	54 - 24

CREWE - Barry Meeks 10, Dai Evans 9 (+3), Paul O'Neil 9, Dave Parry 7 (+2), Ian Bottomley 7, Warren Hawkins 6 (+1), John Jackson 6 (+1).
CRAYFORD - Taffy Owen* 12, Tony Childs 4, Derek Timms 4, Tony Armstrong 2, Colin Clark 1 (+1), George Devonport 1, Mick Steel 0.

On August 22, three Crewe riders were invited to take part in a second half mini-match at Coventry's Brandon Stadium, following the Bees league match against Glasgow Tigers.

COVENTRY 'B'.....16 CREWE KINGS.....8

Heat 01	Harrhy/**O'Neil**/Emms/**Jackson**	70.0	4 - 2	04 - 02
Heat 02	Bailey/**Jackson**/Emms/**Meeks**	70.4	4 - 2	08 - 04
Heat 03	Harrhy/Bailey/**O'Neil**/**Meeks**	70.6	5 - 1	13 - 05
Heat 04	**O'Neil**/Harrhy/Bailey/**Jackson** (R)	70.4	3 - 3	16 - 08

COVENTRY 'B' - John Harrhy 8, Pete Bailey 6, Cliff Emms 2.
CREWE - Paul O'Neil 6, John Jackson 2, Barry Meeks 0.

Meeting 40 - Monday, August 24, 1970 - British League Division II
L.M.R. Sports Ground, Earle Street, Crewe
Track Length - 470 yards.

CREWE KINGS.....53 ROMFORD BOMBERS.....24

Romford used ex-Division I rider Des Lukehurst without official approval, but his inclusion did little to change the result. Crewe could not have had an easier match to break the successive home league wins record, and although Lukehurst did top score for the Bombers, his efforts were overshadowed by Barry Meeks' maximum. The penultimate heat ended in spectacular style when Lukehurst's rear tyre blew on the back straight of the final lap, sending him crashing into Paul O'Neil. With Dai Evans already out of the race, Tony George was the only finisher, although O'Neil was awarded second place by the referee. Ian Bottomley picked up a paid maximum from reserve.

Heat 01	**O'Neil**/**Parry**/Gilbertson/Sanders	74.0	**5 - 1**	05 - 01
Heat 02	**Bottomley**/**Hawkins**/Holden/George (R)	74.4	**5 - 1**	10 - 02
Heat 03	**Meeks**/Lukehurst/**Evans**/Foote	73.6	**4 - 2**	14 - 04
Heat 04	**Hawkins**/Lukehurst/Holden/**Jackson** (R)	74.2	3 - 3	17 - 07
Heat 05	**Meeks**/Gilbertson/Sanders/**Evans** (R)	74.0	3 - 3	20 - 10
Heat 06	**O'Neil**/**Parry**/Holden/Benham	74.2	**5 - 1**	25 - 11
Heat 07	**Bottomley**/Lukehurst/**Hawkins**/Foote	74.4	**4 - 2**	29 - 13
Heat 08	**Bottomley**/**Parry**/Sanders/Holden	74.6	**5 - 1**	34 - 14
Heat 09	**Meeks**/**Evans**/Gilbertson/Sanders	73.8	**5 - 1**	39 - 15
Heat 10	Lukehurst/**Parry**/Foote/**O'Neil** (R)	74.8	2 - 4	41 - 19
Heat 11	**Jackson**/**Bottomley**/Holden/Gilbertson	75.0	**5 - 1**	46 - 20
Heat 12	George/**O'Neil**/Lukehurst (X)/**Evans** (R)	81.8	2 - 3	48 - 23
Heat 13	**Meeks**/**Jackson**/Gilbertson/Foote (F)	73.8	**5 - 1**	53 - 24

CREWE - Barry Meeks 12, Ian Bottomley 11 (+1), Dave Parry 8 (+3), Paul O'Neil 8, Warren Hawkins 6 (+1), John Jackson 5 (+1), Dai Evans 3 (+1).
ROMFORD - Des Lukehurst 9, Ross Gilbertson 5, Kevin Holden 4 (+1), Tony George 3, Colin Sanders 2 (+1), Brian Foote 1, Charlie Benham 0, *Phil Woodcock R/R.*

Three Crewe riders took part in the opening Young Britain and Young Australasia test at Teesside on August 27. John Jackson netted 12 for the Brits, with Paul O'Neil and Warren Hawkins scoring one each for the colonials in their 64-44 defeat.

Meeting 41 - Monday, August 31, 1970 - Division II International, Second Test
L.M.R. Sports Ground, Earle Street, Crewe
Track Length - 470 yards.

YOUNG BRITAIN.....55 YOUNG AUSTRALASIA.....53

Young Britain won a fantastic speedway contest to open up a 2-0 lead in the series, despite the heroic efforts of Crewe's Paul O'Neil (riding with 15 stitches in his left leg sustained while guesting for Canterbury at Rochdale the previous afternoon), who scored a magnificent 18 point maximum. He was superbly supported by Gary Peterson and Bob Valentine, with the trio netting 49 of the Australasian total. Both sides were evenly matched throughout the contest with thirteen drawn heats. Young Britain, with home riders Barry Meeks, Dave Parry and John Jackson in their line-up, were never in front until victory was secured in the last heat, despite colonial riders winning fourteen races! Bradford's Alan Knapkin was the match winner, recording the fastest time of the night. Crewe's Warren Hawkins also rode in the meeting, scoring two points.

Heat 01	Peterson/Hawkins/Jessup/May	74.2	1 - 5	01 - 05
Heat 02	O'Neil/Jackson/Knapkin/Haslinger	74.0	3 - 3	04 - 08
Heat 03	Valentine/Meeks/Mackay/Leadbitter	75.0	2 - 4	06 - 12
Heat 04	Peterson/Knapkin/Jackson/Hawkins	75.0	3 - 3	09 - 15
Heat 05	O'Neil/Meeks/Parry/Haslinger	74.8	3 - 3	12 - 18
Heat 06	Valentine/Jessup/May/Mackay	77.0	3 - 3	15 - 21
Heat 07	Peterson/Meeks/Leadbitter/Hawkins	73.8	3 - 3	18 - 24
Heat 08	O'Neil/Jessup/May/Sansom	75.0	3 - 3	21 - 27
Heat 09	Knapkin/Valentine/Mackay/Jackson (F)	00.0	3 - 3	24 - 30
Heat 10	Peterson/Wilkinson/Jessup/Hawkins	77.4	3 - 3	27 - 33
Heat 11	O'Neil/Jackson/Knapkin/Davies	76.8	3 - 3	30 - 36
Heat 12	Meeks/Valentine/Wilkinson/Mackay	76.4	4 - 2	34 - 38
Heat 13	Knapkin/Jackson/Peterson/Hawkins (R)	74.8	5 - 1	39 - 39
Heat 14	O'Neil/Parry/Meeks/Haslinger	75.2	3 - 3	42 - 42
Heat 15	Valentine/Wilkinson/Jessup/Mackay	74.6	3 - 3	45 - 45
Heat 16	Peterson/Leadbitter/Meeks/Sansom	74.0	3 - 3	48 - 48
Heat 17	O'Neil/Jessup/Wilkinson/Davies	75.0	3 - 3	51 - 51
Heat 18	Knapkin/Valentine/Jackson/Mackay	73.6	4 - 2	55 - 53

YOUNG BRITAIN - Alan Knapkin 13 (+2), Barry Meeks 11 (+2), Dave Jessup 9 (+2), John Jackson 8 (+2), Alan Wilkinson (Reserve) 6 (+1), Tom Leadbitter 3 (+1), Dave Parry (Reserve) 3 (+1), Dickie May 2 (+2). Team Manager: Maurice Littlechild.

YOUNG AUSTRALASIA - Paul O'Neil 18, Gary Peterson 16, Bob Valentine 15, Warren Hawkins 2 (+1), Malcolm Mackay 2 (+1), Dene Davies (Reserve) 0, Hec Haslinger 0, Lou Sansom (Reserve) 0. Team Manager: Bob Jameson.

Meeting 42 - Wednesday, September 2, 1970 - British League Division II
Crayford and Bexley Heath Stadium, London Road, Crayford
Track Length - 265 yards.

CRAYFORD HIGHWAYMEN.....47 CREWE KINGS.....31

Even though the Kings were without the services of John Jackson (competing in the Junior Championship), and Paul O'Neil through injury, they still put up a spirited performance, and only a late flurry of maximums sealed victory for the Highwaymen. Peter Seaton, guesting for his former club, top scored for the visitors with eight from four rides.

Heat 01	**Seaton**/Foote/**Parry**/Steel	62.5	**2 - 4**	02 - 04
Heat 02	Drew/**Hawkins**/**Bottomley**/Armstrong	65.3	3 - 3	05 - 07
Heat 03	Timms/**Meeks**/**Evans**/Clark	62.7	3 - 3	08 - 10
Heat 04	Childs/Drew/**Bottomley**/**Mulligan**	62.9	5 - 1	13 - 11

(ABOVE) Sidecars made their debut at Earle Street on July 13. They proved to be a popular second half attraction whenever they were booked to appear. (BELOW) Dave Parry (left) and Gary Peterson receive attention following a nasty pile up during the Crewe v Bradford match on July 31.

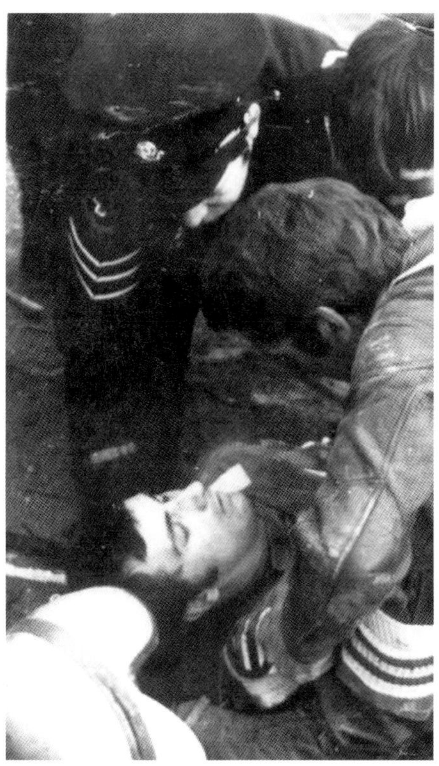

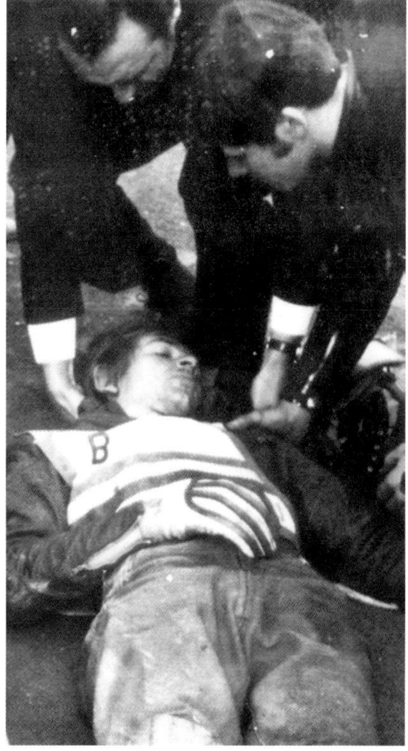

(ABOVE) Warren Hawkins (left) and Paul O'Neil on parade prior to doing battle with the Czechoslovakian touring side. (BELOW) The souvenir pennant presented to each rider (courtesy of John Jackson).

(ABOVE) The Speedway Supporters Club float in the Crewe Carnival procession. (BELOW) Skipper Barry Meeks poses with Crewe Speedway Queen Gail Parry - wife of Dave.

Heat 05.............	Timms/**Seaton**/**Parry**/Clark	62.3	3 - 3	16 - 14
Heat 06.............	Foote/**Hawkins**/Steel/**Mulligan** (R)	62.3	4 - 2	20 - 16
Heat 07.............	**Evans**/Childs/**Meeks**/Drew	62.5	**2 - 4**	22 - 20
Heat 08.............	Steel/**Parry**/**Bottomley**/Armstrong	63.5	3 - 3	25 - 23
Heat 09.............	Timms/**Hawkins**/Drew/**Bottomley** (R)	62.2	4 - 2	29 - 25
Heat 10.............	Foote/Steel/**Evans**/**Meeks**	61.9	5 - 1	34 - 26
Heat 11.............	**Seaton**/Childs/Armstrong/**Parry** (R)	63.4	3 - 3	37 - 29
Heat 12.............	Clark/Foote/**Evans**/**Seaton** (R)	63.0	5 - 1	42 - 30
Heat 13.............	Timms/Childs/**Hawkins**/**Evans**	63.1	5 - 1	47 - 31

CRAYFORD - Derek Timms 12, Brian Foote* 10 (+1), Tony Childs 9 (+1), Judd Drew 6 (+1), Mick Steel 6 (+1), Colin Clark 3, Tony Armstrong 1 (+1).
CREWE - Peter Seaton* 8, Warren Hawkins 7, Dai Evans 6 (+1), Dave Parry 4 (+1), Ian Bottomley 3 (+2), Barry Meeks 3, John Mulligan 0.

John Jackson was the highest placed Division II rider in the Junior Championship of the British Isles at Swindon, finishing joint-fourth with eleven points from his five starts.

Meeting 43 - Thursday, September 3, 1970 - British League Division II
Long Eaton Stadium, Station Road, Long Eaton
Track Length - 366 yards.

LONG EATON RANGERS.....43 CREWE KINGS.....35

Even though John Jackson returned to top score, and was backed up with a double figure return from Dai Evans, the Kings still fell short of a Rangers team tasting league victory for the first time since June 25. Malcolm Shakespeare led the home charge going through the card undefeated.

Heat 01.............	Shakespeare/**Jackson**/Carter/**Parry**	71.4	4 - 2	04 - 02
Heat 02.............	Wrathall/**Hawkins**/Bass/**Bottomley**	74.8	4 - 2	08 - 04
Heat 03.............	**Meeks**/Farmer/**Evans**/Bouchard	74.2	**2 - 4**	10 - 08
Heat 04.............	**Jackson**/Vale/Wrathall/**Bottomley**	71.2	3 - 3	13 - 11
Heat 05.............	Bouchard/**Meeks**/Farmer/**Parry**	73.4	4 - 2	17 - 13
Heat 06.............	Shakespeare/**Jackson**/Carter/**Hawkins**	71.8	4 - 2	21 - 15
Heat 07.............	Bass/**Evans**/**Meeks**/Vale	73.4	3 - 3	24 - 18
Heat 08.............	Carter/**Parry**/Bass/**Bottomley**	73.8	4 - 2	28 - 20
Heat 09.............	**Jackson**/Farmer/Bouchard/**Hawkins**	71.4	3 - 3	31 - 23
Heat 10.............	Shakespeare/**Evans**/Carter/**Meeks**	71.8	4 - 2	35 - 25
Heat 11.............	**Evans**/Vale/Bass/**Parry**	72.8	3 - 3	38 - 28
Heat 12.............	Shakespeare/**Jackson**/Bouchard/**Hawkins**	71.6	4 - 2	42 - 30
Heat 13.............	**Jackson**/**Evans**/Farmer/Vale	72.2	**1 - 5**	43 - 35

LONG EATON - Malcolm Shakespeare 12, Steve Bass 6 (+1), Roy Carter 6, Gil Farmer 6, Geoff Bouchard 5 (+1), Peter Wrathall 4 (+1), Ken Vale 4.
CREWE - John Jackson 15, Dai Evans 10 (+1), Barry Meeks 6 (+1), Warren Hawkins 2, Dave Parry 2, Ian Bottomley 0, *Paul O'Neil (R/R)*.

As expected, Paul O'Neil was confirmed as Crewe's representative in the Division II Riders Championship at Hackney, on September 25.

Meeting 44 - Friday, September 4, 1970 - British League Division II
Derwent Park Stadium, Workington
Track Length - 398 yards.

WORKINGTON COMETS.....51 CREWE KINGS.....27

Crewe's punishing schedule of three away meetings in as many days finally caught up with them at Derwent Park, when they were well beaten by a much-improved Workington team. Dai Evans and John Jackson did their best to make the score respectable, but only Evans tasted victory all night. Mackay, Valentine and Sansom all scored paid maximums for the Comets. As a result, the Kings dropped to seventh in the league table.

Heat 01	Valentine/**Jackson**/Wilson/**Parry**	76.0	4 - 2	04 - 02
Heat 02	Kumeta/**Bottomley**/**Hawkins**/Blythe (X)	80.0	3 - 3	07 - 05
Heat 03	Mackay/Sansom/**Evans**/**Meeks**	77.8	5 - 1	12 - 06
Heat 04	Blythe/**Jackson**/Penniket/**Bottomley**	78.8	4 - 2	16 - 08
Heat 05	Sansom/Mackay/**Meeks**/**Parry**	78.2	5 - 1	21 - 09
Heat 06	Valentine/**Jackson**/Wilson/**Hawkins**	77.0	4 - 2	25 - 11
Heat 07	**Evans**/Penniket/**Meeks**/Blythe (X)	79.8	**2 - 4**	27 - 15
Heat 08	Wilson/**Evans**/**Jackson**/Kumeta	78.0	3 - 3	30 - 18
Heat 09	Mackay/Sansom/**Jackson**/**Hawkins**	78.4	5 - 1	35 - 19
Heat 10	Wilson/Valentine/**Evans**/**Meeks**	77.6	5 - 1	40 - 20
Heat 11	**Evans**/Penniket/**Parry**/Kumeta	79.6	**2 - 4**	42 - 24
Heat 12	Sansom/Valentine/**Meeks**/**Jackson** (R)	79.6	5 - 1	47 - 25
Heat 13	Mackay/**Evans**/Penniket/**Parry** (F)	77.6	4 - 2	51 - 27

WORKINGTON - Malcolm Mackay 11 (+1), Lou Sansom 10 (+2), Bob Valentine 10 (+2), Reg Wilson 8, Geoff Penniket 6, Chris Blythe 3, Dave Kumeta 3.
CREWE - Dai Evans 12, John Jackson 8 (+1), Barry Meeks 3, Ian Bottomley 2, Warren Hawkins 1 (+1), Dave Parry 1, *Paul O'Neil (R/R).*

Meeting 45 - Monday, September 7, 1970 - County Challenge
L.M.R. Sports Ground, Earle Street, Crewe.
Track Length - 470 yards.

CREWE KINGS.....50 DONCASTER DRAGONS.....27

The home side rested Ian Bottomley and Dave Parry, but were still too strong for the Dragons. Juniors Barrie Smitherman and Vince Mann made their debuts and neither were overawed by the occasion. Warren Hawkins registered his biggest points haul of the season.

Heat 01	**Hawkins**/Emms/**Moore**/Wilson	76.0	**4 - 2**	04 - 02
Heat 02	**Hawkins**/Corradine/**Mann**/Wasden	75.6	**4 - 2**	08 - 04
Heat 03	**Meeks**/Major/Haslinger/**Evans**	75.4	3 - 3	11 - 07
Heat 04	**Jackson**/**Hawkins**/Corradine/Harrison (R)	75.8	**5 - 1**	16 - 08
Heat 05	**Meeks**/**Evans**/Wilson/Emms	75.0	**5 - 1**	21 - 09
Heat 06	**Moore**/**Smitherman**/Harrison/Wasden (R)	78.2	**5 - 1**	26 - 10
Heat 07	**Jackson**/Haslinger/**Hawkins**/Major (R)	75.0	**4 - 2**	30 - 12
Heat 08	Corradine/**Smitherman**/Wilson/**Mann** (F)	77.8	2 - 4	32 - 16
Heat 09	**Meeks**/**Evans**/Wasden/Harrison (R)	75.8	**5 - 1**	37 - 17
Heat 10	**Hawkins**/Haslinger/Major/**Moore** (X)	74.8	3 - 3	40 - 20
Heat 11	Emms/Wilson/**Jackson** (R) (3 riders only)	78.0	0 - 5	40 - 25
Heat 12	**Evans**/**Moore**/Major/Corradine	75.2	**5 - 1**	45 - 26
Heat 13	**Jackson**/**Meeks**/Haslinger/Emms	74.6	**5 - 1**	50 - 27

CREWE - Warren Hawkins 12 (+1), Barry Meeks 11 (+1), John Jackson 9, Dai Evans 7 (+2), Gary Moore* 6 (+1), Barrie Smitherman 4 (+1), Vince Mann 1.
DONCASTER - Hec Haslinger 6 (+1), Malcolm Corradine 6, Cliff Emms 5, George Major 4 (+1), Ian Wilson 4 (+1), Chris Harrison 1, Dennis Wasden 1.

During the second half, sixteen-year-old grass-tracker Peter Collins, who was introduced to the club by John Jackson, caused quite a stir when winning two races on Jackson's bike, which had Maurice Littlechild talking about offering him a contract for the following season. On September 9, Dai Evans, Barry Meeks and John Jackson all took part in the Odsal Trophy at Bradford. Evans finished 7th with 9, and Meeks 12th with 6. Jackson fell in his opening ride and withdrew from the meeting. Rumours meanwhile persisted over the proposed reduction of the Earle Street track (reported in the *Speedway Star* to be around 90 yards). The alteration would require moving the safety fence on both straights and also reducing the banking on both bends. This of course was subject to agreement with the L.M.R. cricket club and British Rail.

Meeting 46 - Thursday, September 10, 1970 - British League Division II
Brooklands Sports Stadium, Brooklands Road, Mawneys, Romford
Track Length - 375 yards.

ROMFORD BOMBERS.....48 CREWE KINGS.....30

Crewe's threadbare squad, now minus John Jackson following his Odsal spill the previous night, put in a lacklustre performance in cold and windy conditions. Even the guest appearance of Eastbourne whizzkid Dave Jessup, who tasted victory in four of his five rides, could not inspire the Kings, as they failed to record a single heat advantage. Phil Woodcock starred for the Bombers with maximum points.

Heat 01	Woodcock/Holden/**Parry**/**Jessup** (R)	69.4	5 - 1	05 - 01
Heat 02	Foote/**Hawkins**/Benham/**Bottomley**	73.6	4 - 2	09 - 03
Heat 03	Lukehurst/**Evans**/**Meeks**/Sanders	73.0	3 - 3	12 - 06
Heat 04	**Jessup**/Foote/Gilbertson/**Bottomley**	70.2	3 - 3	15 - 09
Heat 05	Lukehurst/**Hawkins**/Sanders/**Parry**	71.6	4 - 2	19 - 11
Heat 06	Woodcock/**Evans**/Holden/**Hawkins**	70.2	4 - 2	23 - 13
Heat 07	Gilbertson/Foote/**Evans**/**Meeks**	72.2	5 - 1	28 - 14
Heat 08	**Parry**/Holden/Benham/**Hawkins**	74.0	3 - 3	31 - 17
Heat 09	**Jessup**/Lukehurst/Sanders/**Parry**	70.8	3 - 3	34 - 20
Heat 10	Woodcock/**Evans**/**Meeks**/Holden	70.8	3 - 3	37 - 23
Heat 11	**Jessup**/Gilbertson/Benham/**Parry**	71.0	3 - 3	40 - 26
Heat 12	Woodcock/Sanders/**Meeks**/**Percy**	71.6	5 - 1	45 - 27
Heat 13	**Jessup**/Gilbertson/Benham/**Evans**	71.0	3 - 3	48 - 30

ROMFORD - Phil Woodcock 12, Ross Gilbertson 8 (+1), Des Lukehurst 8, Brian Foote 7 (+1), Kevin Holden 5 (+1), Charlie Benham 4 (+3), Colin Sanders 4 (+2).
CREWE - Dave Jessup* 12, Dai Evans 7, Warren Hawkins 4, Dave Parry 4, Barry Meeks 3 (+2), Ian Bottomley 0, Dave Percy* 0, *John Jackson (R/R)*.

On September 12, Paul O'Neil rode for Young Australasia in their 59-49 third test defeat to Young Britain at Berwick. Still clearly unfit, he failed to score, finishing last in Heat 1, then retired in Heat 4. Warren Hawkins also appeared scoring two points.

Meeting 47 - Sunday, September 13, 1970 - Challenge Cup
Boston Sports Stadium, New Hammond Beck Road, Boston
Track Length - 380 yards.

BOSTON BARRACUDAS.....42 CREWE KINGS.....36

Heavy afternoon rain put this challenge match in doubt, so it was no surprise that only a few hundred hardy souls turned up to witness a keenly fought contest and a brilliant 15 point maximum by John Jackson. Guest Gary Moore was the only other heat winner for the Kings.

Heat 01	**Moore**/Featherstone/**Parry**/Slee	70.8	**2 - 4**	02 - 04
Heat 02	Bywater/**Hawkins**/**Bottomley**/Osborn	70.2	3 - 3	05 - 07
Heat 03	Price/Osborne/**Meeks**/**Evans**	70.0	5 - 1	10 - 08
Heat 04	**Jackson**/Ingamells/Osborn/**Bottomley**	72.6	3 - 3	13 - 11
Heat 05	Osborne/Price/**Parry**/**Moore**	70.0	5 - 1	18 - 12
Heat 06	**Jackson**/Slee/**Hawkins**/Featherstone (X)	00.0	**2 - 4**	20 - 16
Heat 07	Bywater/Ingamells/**Meeks**/**Evans**	70.4	5 - 1	25 - 17
Heat 08	**Jackson**/**Parry**/Osborn/Bywater	70.0	**1 - 5**	26 - 22
Heat 09	**Jackson**/Osborne/Price/**Hawkins**	70.6	3 - 3	29 - 25
Heat 10	Bywater/**Meeks**/**Evans**/Slee	72.0	3 - 3	32 - 28
Heat 11	**Moore**/Ingamells/Bywater/**Hawkins**	72.0	3 - 3	35 - 31
Heat 12	**Jackson**/Osborne/**Meeks**/Slee	71.2	**2 - 4**	37 - 35
Heat 13	Ingamells/Price/**Moore**/**Evans** (R)	71.0	5 - 1	42 - 36

BOSTON - Jack Bywater 10 (+1), John Ingamells 9 (+1), Russell Osborne 9 (+1), Arthur Price 8 (+3), Brian Osborn 2 (+1), Tony Featherstone 2, Neville Slee 2.
CREWE - John Jackson 15, Gary Moore* 7, Barry Meeks 5, Dave Parry 4 (+1), Warren Hawkins 3, Ian Bottomley 1 (+1), Dai Evans 1 (+1).

Meeting 48 - Monday, September 14, 1970 - Best Pairs Championship
L.M.R. Sports Ground, Earle Street, Crewe
Track Length - 470 yards.

WINNERS.....BOB VALENTINE & DAI EVANS

Workington's Bob Valentine and home favourite Dai Evans, won the Best Pairs Championship by a single point from Kings skipper Barry Meeks and Teesside's "Tiger" Tom Leadbitter, dropping their only points to Paul O'Neil in the opening heat, with the Kiwi going through the programme undefeated.

Heat 01	O'Neil/Valentine/Evans/Hawkins	76.4
Heat 02	Meeks/Leadbitter/Moore/Parry	76.0
Heat 03	Moss/Wilkinson/Jackson/Bottomley	76.2
Heat 04	O'Neil/Hawkins/Owen/Jameson	74.8
Heat 05	Valentine/Evans/Leadbitter/Meeks	75.0
Heat 06	Parry/Bottomley/Moore/Jackson (R)	76.0
Heat 07	Wilkinson/Owen/Moss/Jameson	75.4
Heat 08	O'Neil/Leadbitter/Meeks/Mulligan (F)	74.8
Heat 09	Evans/Valentine/Moore/Parry	75.6
Heat 10	Bottomley/Jameson/Jackson/Owen (R)	76.2
Heat 11	O'Neil/Wilkinson/Moss/Mulligan (F)	74.6
Heat 12	Valentine/Bottomley/Evans/Jackson	75.6
Heat 13	Leadbitter/Meeks/Wilkinson/Moss (R)	76.4
Heat 14	Owen/Moore/Jameson/Parry	76.4
Heat 15	O'Neil/Jackson/Bottomley/Hawkins	75.6
Heat 16	Wilkinson/Valentine/Evans (3 riders only)	76.0
Heat 17	Leadbitter/Meeks/Jameson/Owen	75.6
Heat 18	O'Neil/Hawkins/Parry/Moore	75.6
Heat 19	Valentine/Evans/Owen/Jameson	76.2
Heat 20	Leadbitter/Meeks/Bottomley/Jackson (R)	76.4
Heat 21	Wilkinson/Moore/Parry (3 riders only)	76.8

Bob Valentine (15) & Dai Evans (10) 25, Tom Leadbitter (14) & Barry Meeks (10) 24, Paul O'Neil (18) & Warren Hawkins (4) 22, Alan Wilkinson (14) & Ken Moss (5) 19, Ian Bottomley (9) & John Jackson (4) 13, Gary Moore (7) & Dave Parry (5) 12, Taffy Owen (7) & Bob Jameson (4) 11. Meeting Reserve: John Mulligan 0. *(Moore replaced Alan Knapkin, Wilkinson replaced Eric Broadbelt and Owen replaced Gary Peterson.)*

Meeting 49 - Thursday, September 17, 1970 - British League Division II
Canterbury City Football Ground, Kingsmead Road, Canterbury
Track Length - 390 yards.

CANTERBURY CRUSADERS.....50 CREWE KINGS.....28

Dave Parry, Warren Hawkins and Paul O'Neil did Crewe no favours by arriving late, causing a 30 minute delay in proceedings, and each copped a £3 fine for their troubles. Barry Meeks posed further problems for the Kings by not arriving at all! With little time to prepare, Crewe found themselves 23-7 down after only five heats and never recovered. John Jackson and O'Neil were the pick of the visiting side with two race wins apiece.

Heat 01	Crowson/**O'Neil**/Banks/**Bottomley**	80.4	4 - 2	04 - 02
Heat 02	Hubbard/Kite/**Parry** (3 riders only)	81.0	5 - 1	09 - 03
Heat 03	Thomas/Rennison/**Parry**/**Evans** (F)	81.4	5 - 1	14 - 04
Heat 04	Smith/**Hawkins**/Hubbard/**Jackson**	80.2	4 - 2	18 - 06
Heat 05	Thomas/Rennison/**O'Neil**/**Bottomley**	78.6	5 - 1	23 - 07
Heat 06	**Jackson**/Banks/Crowson/**Hawkins**	78.8	3 - 3	26 - 10
Heat 07	Hubbard/**Jackson**/**Evans**/Smith	79.2	3 - 3	29 - 13
Heat 08	Banks/**Parry**/Kite/**Bottomley**	80.0	4 - 2	33 - 15
Heat 09	Thomas/**Jackson**/Rennison/**Hawkins**	78.6	4 - 2	37 - 17
Heat 10	**O'Neil**/Banks/Crowson/**Evans**	80.6	3 - 3	40 - 20
Heat 11	**O'Neil**/Kite/Smith/**Bottomley**	81.0	3 - 3	43 - 23
Heat 12	**Jackson**/Crowson/**Evans**/Rennison	79.2	**2 - 4**	45 - 27
Heat 13	Hubbard/Thomas/**Parry**/**Evans** (R)	76.8	5 - 1	50 - 28

CANTERBURY - Barry Thomas 11 (+1), Ted Hubbard 10, Graham Banks 8, Barry Crowson 7 (+2), Jake Rennison 5 (+2), Alan Kite 5 (+1), Dave Smith 4 (+1).
CREWE - John Jackson 10, Paul O'Neil 9, Dave Parry 5, Dai Evans 2 (+1), Warren Hawkins 2, Ian Bottomley 0.

Meeting 50 - Sunday, September 20, 1970 - British League Division II
Athletic Grounds, Milnrow Road, Rochdale
Track Length - 427 yards.

ROCHDALE HORNETS.....41 CREWE KINGS.....37

The Hornets came within a whisker of losing their proud home record in an exciting Sunday afternoon clash. Without the services of Chris Bailey and Eric Broadbelt, Rochdale were heavily reliant on Steve Waplington and Alan Wilkinson. Neither let the home fans down, scoring solidly throughout, and teaming up in the all-important last heat decider to ensure victory. Paul O'Neil, back to his best, topped the Crewe chart, with John Jackson just missing out on a maximum, courtesy of Waplington in Heat 4.

Heat 01	**O'Neil**/Tyrer/Goad/**Bottomley**	77.8	3 - 3	03 - 03
Heat 02	Richardson/Goad/**Parry**/**Mulligan** (X)	81.0	5 - 1	08 - 04
Heat 03	Wilkinson/**Meeks**/Moss/**Evans**	78.4	4 - 2	12 - 06
Heat 04	Waplington/**Jackson**/**Parry**/Richardson (F)	78.0	3 - 3	15 - 09
Heat 05	**O'Neil**/Wilkinson/**Bottomley**/Richardson	78.4	**2 - 4**	17 - 13
Heat 06	**Jackson**/Tyrer/Moss/**Mulligan**	77.8	3 - 3	20 - 16
Heat 07	Waplington/Richardson/**Evans**/**Meeks**	79.8	5 - 1	25 - 17
Heat 08	**O'Neil**/Moss/**Bottomley**/Goad	78.8	**2 - 4**	27 - 21
Heat 09	**Jackson**/**Parry**/Wilkinson/Waplington (F)	79.0	**1 - 5**	28 - 26
Heat 10	Moss/**Evans**/**Parry**/Tyrer	79.4	3 - 3	31 - 29
Heat 11	Waplington/**O'Neil**/**Bottomley**/Richardson (F)	80.0	3 - 3	34 - 32
Heat 12	**Jackson**/Wilkinson/Tyrer/**Meeks**	77.6	3 - 3	37 - 35
Heat 13	Wilkinson/**O'Neil**/Waplington/**Mulligan**	78.8	4 - 2	41 - 37

ROCHDALE - Alan Wilkinson 11, Steve Waplington 10, Ken Moss 7 (+1), Gerry Richardson 5 (+1), Paul Tyrer 5 (+1), Colin Goad 3 (+2), *Chris Bailey (R/R).*
CREWE - Paul O'Neil 13, John Jackson 11, Dave Parry 5 (+3), Ian Bottomley 3 (+1), Dai Evans 3, Barry Meeks 2, John Mulligan 0.

On the same day, Warren Hawkins scored three for Young Australasia in their 74-34 fourth test hammering at Eastbourne.

Meeting 51 - Monday, September 21, 1970 - British League Division II
L.M.R. Sports Ground, Earle Street, Crewe
Track Length - 470 yards.

CREWE KINGS.....46 TEESSIDE TEESSIDERS.....32

The Kings ended a sequence of six successive league defeats (their worst run to date), which also ensured a first double of the season. Teesside captain Tom Leadbitter coped admirably on the fast Crewe track and prevented Barry Meeks from securing a possible maximum in the final heat, after the latter fell while contesting second place.

Heat 01	Leadbitter/**O'Neil**/Jameson/**Bottomley**	76.0	2 - 4	02 - 04
Heat 02	**Parry**/**Hawkins**/Durham/Reading	75.4	**5 - 1**	07 - 05
Heat 03	**Meeks**/Swales/**Evans**/Forrester (F)	75.2	4 - 2	11 - 07
Heat 04	**Jackson**/**Hawkins**/Mills/Durham	74.6	**5 - 1**	16 - 08
Heat 05	**Meeks**/Leadbitter/Jameson/**Evans** (R)	75.0	3 - 3	19 - 11
Heat 06	**O'Neil**/Mills/Reading/**Bottomley** (R)	74.2	3 - 3	22 - 14
Heat 07	Leadbitter/Swales/**Hawkins**/**Jackson** (R)	75.0	1 - 5	23 - 19
Heat 08	**Parry**/Jameson/**Bottomley**/Durham	74.8	**4 - 2**	27 - 21
Heat 09	**Meeks**/**Evans**/Mills/Swales	75.4	**5 - 1**	32 - 22
Heat 10	**Bottomley**/**O'Neil**/Swales/Forrester	75.0	**5 - 1**	37 - 23
Heat 11	Leadbitter/**Hawkins**/Jameson/**Jackson** (R)	74.8	2 - 4	39 - 27
Heat 12	**O'Neil**/Swales/**Evans**/Mills	74.2	**4 - 2**	43 - 29
Heat 13	**Jackson**/Leadbitter/Reading/**Meeks** (F)	75.0	3 - 3	46 - 32

CREWE - Paul O'Neil 10 (+1), Barry Meeks 9, Warren Hawkins 7 (+2), John Jackson 6, Dave Parry 6, Dai Evans 4 (+1), Ian Bottomley 4.

TEESSIDE - Tom Leadbitter 13, Tim Swales 7 (+1), Bob Jameson 5 (+1), Roger Mills 4, Pete Reading 2, Dave Durham 1, Bruce Forrester 0.

Meeting 52 - Wednesday, September 23, 1970 - British League Division II
East of England Showground, Alwalton, Peterborough
Track Length - 380 yards.

PETERBOROUGH PANTHERS.....42 CREWE KINGS.....36

Arguably Peterborough's best home meeting of the season provided tense excitement and thrills from the very start. Crewe were desperately unlucky to lose, with John Jackson's machine failing twice when handily placed. Warren Hawkins also lost a guaranteed third place during Heat 11, when a flat tyre slowed him down only yards from the line.

Heat 01	Ross/**O'Neil**/Saunders/**Hawkins**	71.2	4 - 2	04 - 02
Heat 02	**Bottomley**/Hill/**Parry**/Johnson	74.6	**2 - 4**	06 - 06
Heat 03	Seaton/**Evans**/**Meeks**/Hughes	74.2	3 - 3	09 - 09
Heat 04	**Jackson**/Greer/**Bottomley**/Johnson (R)	72.6	**2 - 4**	11 - 13
Heat 05	**O'Neil**/Seaton/**Hawkins**/Hughes (R)	72.8	**2 - 4**	13 - 17
Heat 06	Ross/**Bottomley**/Saunders/**Jackson** (R)	72.6	4 - 2	17 - 19
Heat 07	Greer/**Meeks**/Hill/**Evans** (R)	71.8	4 - 2	21 - 21
Heat 08	Saunders/**Hawkins**/**Bottomley**/Hill	73.4	3 - 3	24 - 24
Heat 09	**Jackson**/Seaton/Hughes/**Parry**	72.8	3 - 3	27 - 27
Heat 10	Ross/Saunders/**Evans**/**Meeks**	73.6	5 - 1	32 - 28
Heat 11	Greer/**O'Neil**/Hill/**Hawkins** (R)	72.4	4 - 2	36 - 30
Heat 12	Ross/**Meeks**/Hughes/**Jackson** (R)	72.6	4 - 2	40 - 32
Heat 13	**Evans**/Greer/**Bottomley**/Seaton	71.4	**2 - 4**	42 - 36

PETERBOROUGH - Andy Ross 12, Richard Greer 10, Pete Saunders 7, Peter Seaton 7, Mervyn Hill 4, Joe Hughes 2 (+1), Pat Johnson 0.
CREWE - Ian Bottomley 8 (+1), Paul O'Neil 7, Dai Evans 6, John Jackson 6, Barry Meeks 5 (+1), Warren Hawkins 3, Dave Parry 1.

Friday, September 25, 1970 - British League Division II Riders Championship
Hackney Wick Stadium, Waterden Road, London
Track Length - 345 yards.

Winner.....DAVE JESSUP

Title favourite Dave Jessup (Eastbourne) emerged as the winner of the Division II Riders Championship. Paul O'Neil finished a disappointing 8th with 8 points, but the New Zealander however, had the satisfaction of denying the champion of his maximum in the final heat.

Heat 01	Jessup/Crowson/Ross/Harrhy (F)	69.2
Heat 02	Leadbitter/Price/May/Robinson (X)	71.5
Heat 03	Broadbelt/Peterson/Childs/**O'Neil**	68.9
Heat 04	Gilbertson/Valentine/McGregor/Maloney	69.5
Heat 05	Harrhy/Price/Childs/Gilbertson (R)	70.9
Heat 06	Peterson/Leadbitter/Maloney/Ross	68.3
Heat 07	Crowson/Valentine/**O'Neil**/Robinson	68.3
Heat 08	Jessup/May/Broadbelt/McGregor	68.1
Heat 09	Leadbitter/Harrhy/**O'Neil**/McGregor	69.7
Heat 10	Valentine/Broadbelt/Ross/Price	68.2
Heat 11	Crowson/May/Maloney/Childs (R)	69.0
Heat 12	Jessup/Gilbertson/Peterson/Robinson	68.3
Heat 13	Harrhy/Broadbelt/Maloney/Robinson	70.9
Heat 14	**O'Neil**/Gilbertson/Ross/May (R)	69.4
Heat 15	Peterson/Crowson/Price/McGregor (R)	69.7
Heat 16	Jessup/Valentine/Leadbitter/Childs	69.1
Heat 17	Peterson/May/Harrhy/Valentine	70.1
Heat 18	Robinson/Ross/Childs/Vale	72.3
Heat 19	Broadbelt/Crowson/Leadbitter/Gilbertson	68.6

Heat 20	**O'Neil**/Jessup/Maloney/Price	69.9
R/O for 2nd	Crowson/Peterson	68.9

Dave Jessup *(Eastbourne)* 14, Barry Crowson *(Canterbury)* 12, Gary Peterson *(Bradford)* 12, Eric Broadbelt *(Rochdale)* 11, Tom Leadbitter *(Teesside)* 10, John Harrhy *(Ipswich)* 9, Bob Valentine *(Workington)* 9, Paul O'Neil *(Crewe)* 8, Ross Gilbertson *(Romford)* 7, Richard May *(Reading)* 7, Arthur Price *(Boston)* 5, Andy Ross *(Peterborough)* 5, Geoff Maloney *(Rayleigh)* 4, Maury Robinson *(Berwick)* 3, Tony Childs *(Crayford)* 3, Gordon McGregor *(Doncaster)* 1. Meeting Reserves: Ken Vale *(Long Eaton)* 0, Alan Knapkin *(Bradford)* Did not ride.

The following night, Ipswich became the new holders of the Division II K.O. Cup defeating Berwick 82-74 on aggregate. Paul O'Neil and Warren Hawkins represented Young Australasia in the final test at Canterbury, which they won 62-45 to prevent the whitewash. O'Neil top scored with fourteen points, Hawkins contributing five.

Meeting 53 - Monday, September 28, 1970 - British League Division II
L.M.R. Sports Ground, Earle Street, Crewe
Track Length - 470 yards.

CREWE KINGS.....53 EASTBOURNE EAGLES.....25

Eastbourne's title aspirations were dealt a real body blow when they suffered a heavy Earle Street defeat. Already under-strength, the Eagles were further weakened by the withdrawal of Dave Jessup, who had arrived at the track during the afternoon, but was then whisked away to compete for parent club Wembley at Exeter. Alan Wilkinson (Rochdale) guested for the visitors and scored 14 of their meagre total.

Heat 01	**Hawkins**/**O'Neil**/Wilkinson/Sims	72.2	**5 - 1**	05 - 01
Heat 02	**Bottomley**/D.Kennett/Pratt/**Parry**	75.8	3 - 3	08 - 04
Heat 03	**Meeks**/**Evans**/Trott/G.Kennett	75.0	**5 - 1**	13 - 05
Heat 04	**Jackson**/**Bottomley**/D.Kennett/Pratt	74.8	**5 - 1**	18 - 06
Heat 05	Wilkinson/**Meeks**/**Evans**/Sims	74.6	3 - 3	21 - 09
Heat 06	**O'Neil**/Wilkinson/**Hawkins**/D.Kennett (R)	74.6	**4 - 2**	25 - 11
Heat 07	**Bottomley**/Trott/**Parry**/G.Kennett	74.4	**4 - 2**	29 - 13
Heat 08	Wilkinson/**Parry**/Sims/**Hawkins** (R)	74.4	2 - 4	31 - 17
Heat 09	**Meeks**/**Evans**/D.Kennett/Trott (R)	74.8	**5 - 1**	36 - 18
Heat 10	**O'Neil**/**Hawkins**/G.Kennett/Trott	75.0	**5 - 1**	41 - 19
Heat 11	Wilkinson/**Jackson**/**Parry**/D.Kennett	74.4	3 - 3	44 - 22
Heat 12	**O'Neil**/**Evans**/G.Kennett/Trott	74.6	**5 - 1**	49 - 23
Heat 13	**Jackson**/Wilkinson/**Meeks**/G.Kennett	74.4	**4 - 2**	53 - 25

CREWE - Paul O'Neil 11 (+1), Barry Meeks 9, Ian Bottomley 8 (+1), John Jackson 8, Dai Evans 7 (+4), Warren Hawkins 6 (+1), Dave Parry 4 (+1).
EASTBOURNE - Alan Wilkinson* 14, Dave Kennett 4, Reg Trott 3, Gordon Kennett 2, Phil Pratt 1 (+1), Laurie Sims 1, *Derek Cook (R/R)*.

Meeting 54 - Monday, October 5, 1970 - British League Division II
L.M.R. Sports Ground, Earle Street, Crewe
Track Length - 470 yards.

CREWE KINGS.....41 WORKINGTON COMETS.....37

The Comets, easily the most improved team in the division, promised to take home the points, and very nearly carried off their boast. The Kings needing the win to complete an unblemished home league record had six different race winners on the night, but still had to rely on Warren Hawkins and John Jackson to earn a draw in the final heat to take the match. Hawkins produced some thrilling rides and won a fantastic duel with Taffy Owen in Heat 11. Bob Valentine and Owen both scored twelve apiece in what was Crewe's 25th consecutive home league win.

Heat 01	**Parry**/Valentine/**O'Neil**/Kumeta	74.2	**4 - 2**	04 - 02
Heat 02	**Bottomley**/Blythe/Sansom/**Hawkins** (R)	78.0	3 - 3	07 - 05

Heat 03 .... **Meeks**/**Evans**/Mackay/Penniket (R) 74.8 **5 - 1** 12 - 06
Heat 04 .... **Jackson**/Owen/Blythe/**Bottomley** 76.0 3 - 3 15 - 09
Heat 05 .... Valentine/**Evans**/Kumeta/**Meeks** 74.8 2 - 4 17 - 13
Heat 06 .... **O'Neil**/Owen/**Parry**/Sansom 74.4 **4 - 2** 21 - 15
Heat 07 .... Mackay/**Jackson**/**Bottomley**/Blythe 76.6 3 - 3 24 - 18
Heat 08 .... Valentine/**Hawkins**/**Parry**/Kumeta 74.4 3 - 3 27 - 21
Heat 09 .... Owen/**Evans**/Blythe/**Meeks** (R) 75.0 2 - 4 29 - 25
Heat 10 .... **O'Neil**/Mackay/**Parry**/Penniket 74.2 **4 - 2** 33 - 27
Heat 11 .... **Hawkins**/Owen/Valentine/**Jackson** 74.8 3 - 3 36 - 30
Heat 12 .... Owen/**O'Neil**/Mackay/**Evans** 74.4 2 - 4 38 - 34
Heat 13 .... Valentine/**Hawkins**/**Jackson**/Blythe 75.0 3 - 3 41 - 37

CREWE - Paul O'Neil 9, Warren Hawkins 7, Dai Evans 6 (+1), John Jackson 6 (+1), Dave Parry 6 (+1), Ian Bottomley 4 (+1), Barry Meeks 3.
WORKINGTON - Bob Valentine 12 (+1), Taffy Owen 12, Malcolm Mackay 7, Chris Blythe 4 (+1), Lou Sansom 1 (+1), Dave Kumeta 1, Geoff Penniket 0.

Meeting 55 - Wednesday, October 7, 1970 - Top Dogs Trophy, First Leg
Odsal Stadium, Rooley Avenue, Bradford
Track Length - 385 yards.

BRADFORD NORTHERN.....46 CREWE KINGS.....31

Northern riders Peterson, Schofield and Knapkin masterminded Bradford's fifteen point first leg advantage, although the Kings stayed in touch with some determined riding from reserve Warren Hawkins, who was finally finding his feet in his first season in British speedway. However, the tie was marred by a bad crash in Heat 5, when Crewe's John Mulligan hit the fence coming out of the second bend. He was thrown into the air and collided with a floodlight stanchion, suffering serious head injuries.

Heat 01 .... Knapkin/Adlington/**O'Neil** (R)/**Mulligan** (R) 72.8 5 - 0 05 - 00
Heat 02 .... **Hawkins**/**Bottomley**/Fitzgerald/Bridgett (F) 74.6 **1 - 5** 06 - 05
Heat 03 .... Peterson/Schofield/**Evans**/**Meeks** 75.0 5 - 1 11 - 06
Heat 04 .... Wells/**Hawkins**/Fitzgerald/**Jackson** 74.4 4 - 2 15 - 08
Heat 05 .... Peterson/Schofield/**O'Neil**/**Mulligan** (F) 75.0 5 - 1 20 - 09
Heat 06 .... Knapkin/**Hawkins**/Adlington/**Bottomley** (X) 74.2 4 - 2 24 - 11
Heat 07 .... Wells/**Meeks**/**Evans**/Fitzgerald 74.4 3 - 3 27 - 14
Heat 08 .... **Bottomley**/Adlington/**Hawkins**/Fitzgerald (R) 75.0 **2 - 4** 29 - 18
Heat 09 .... Schofield/Peterson/**Hawkins**/**Bottomley** 76.2 5 - 1 34 - 19
Heat 10 .... Knapkin/**Meeks**/Adlington/**Evans** (R) 74.2 4 - 2 38 - 21
Heat 11 .... **O'Neil**/**Hawkins**/Fitzgerald/Wells (X) 76.2 **1 - 5** 39 - 26
Heat 12 .... Knapkin/**Meeks**/Schofield/**Jackson** (R) 74.4 4 - 2 43 - 28
Heat 13 .... Peterson/**O'Neil**/**Evans**/Fitzgerald 72.4 3 - 3 46 - 31

BRADFORD - Alan Knapkin 12, Gary Peterson 11 (+1), Dave Schofield 8 (+2), Robin Adlington 6 (+1), Alf Wells 6, Barry Fitzgerald 3, Alan Bridgett 0.
CREWE - Warren Hawkins 11 (+1), Barry Meeks 6, Paul O'Neil 6, Ian Bottomley 5 (+1), Dai Evans 3 (+2), John Jackson 0, John Mulligan 0.

John Jackson won the Graham's Handicap Trophy at Workington on October 9, beating home rider Bob Valentine by one point.

Meeting 56 - Saturday, October 10, 1970 - British League Division II
Shielfield Park, Tweedmouth, Berwick-upon-Tweed
Track Length - 440 yards.

BERWICK BANDITS.....43 CREWE KINGS.....35

Bottom-of-the-league Berwick won their fourth successive match thanks to a Doug Wyer maximum and a fine return by veteran Maury Robinson. Once again Paul O'Neil was the pick of the Crewe side, riding in their final league match of the campaign. The victory helped the Bandits to climb off the foot of the table.

Heat 01	**O'Neil**/Robinson/Milloy/**Parry** (R)	79.2	3 - 3	03 - 03
Heat 02	Paynter/**Hawkins**/**Bottomley**/Omand (R)	81.0	3 - 3	06 - 06
Heat 03	Wyer/**Meeks**/Kelly/**Evans** (R)	81.2	4 - 2	10 - 08
Heat 04	Robinson/**Jackson**/**Hawkins**/Paynter	80.8	3 - 3	13 - 11
Heat 05	Wyer/**O'Neil**/Kelly/**Hawkins**	79.6	4 - 2	17 - 13
Heat 06	**Jackson**/Robinson/**Bottomley**/Milloy (R)	79.8	**2 - 4**	19 - 17
Heat 07	Wyer/Paynter/**Evans**/**Meeks**	81.0	5 - 1	24 - 18
Heat 08	**O'Neil**/**Jackson**/Omand/Milloy (X)	80.2	**1 - 5**	25 - 23
Heat 09	Wyer/Kelly/**Jackson**/**Bottomley**	80.0	5 - 1	30 - 24
Heat 10	**Meeks**/Robinson/Milloy/**Hawkins**	80.2	3 - 3	33 - 27
Heat 11	**O'Neil**/**Parry**/Brady/Omand (R)	80.6	**1 - 5**	34 - 32
Heat 12	Robinson/Kelly/**Meeks**/**Jackson**	80.6	5 - 1	39 - 33
Heat 13	Wyer/**O'Neil**/Paynter/**Evans**	80.8	4 - 2	43 - 35

BERWICK - Doug Wyer 15, Maury Robinson 12, Peter Kelly 6 (+2), Alan Paynter 6 (+1), Lex Milloy 2 (+2), Alistair Brady 1, Ken Omand 1, *Roy Williams (R/R)*.
CREWE - Paul O'Neil 13, John Jackson 8 (+1), Barry Meeks 6, Warren Hawkins 3 (+1), Ian Bottomley 2 (+1), Dave Parry 2 (+1), Dai Evans 1.

Meeting 57 - Sunday, October 11, 1970 - Border Trophy, First Leg
Athletic Grounds, Milnrow Road, Rochdale
Track Length - 427 yards.

ROCHDALE HORNETS.....44 CREWE KINGS.....34

After Crewe's heroic attempt in the league match at the Athletic Grounds, they were invited to take part in a two-legged challenge for the Border Trophy, and again put up a decent show. Broadbelt, Wilkinson and Moss performed well for the home side, with John Jackson doing likewise for the Kings.

Heat 01	Broadbelt/**O'Neil**/**Hawkins**/Gardner	76.8	3 - 3	03 - 03
Heat 02	Moss/**Bottomley**/Tyrer/**Hawkins** (F)	79.0	4 - 2	07 - 05
Heat 03	Wilkinson/**Meeks**/Richardson/**Evans**	79.0	4 - 2	11 - 07
Heat 04	**Jackson**/Moss/**Bottomley**/Waplington (R)	77.8	**2 - 4**	13 - 11
Heat 05	Wilkinson/Broadbelt/**O'Neil**/**Bottomley** (F)	77.6	5 - 1	18 - 12
Heat 06	Broadbelt/**Jackson**/**Hawkins**/Gardner	77.4	3 - 3	21 - 15
Heat 07	**Evans**/Moss/**Meeks**/Waplington	79.6	**2 - 4**	23 - 19
Heat 08	Moss/**Parry**/**Bottomley**/Tyrer	79.2	3 - 3	26 - 22
Heat 09	**Jackson**/Wilkinson/Richardson/**Hawkins** (F)	77.2	3 - 3	29 - 25
Heat 10	Broadbelt/**Evans**/Gardner/**Meeks**	77.4	4 - 2	33 - 27
Heat 11	Waplington/**Jackson**/Moss/**O'Neil**	79.0	4 - 2	37 - 29
Heat 12	Broadbelt/Wilkinson/**Jackson**/**Meeks**	79.6	5 - 1	42 - 30
Heat 13	**O'Neil**/Wilkinson/**Evans**/Waplington	79.8	**2 - 4**	44 - 34

ROCHDALE - Eric Broadbelt 14 (+1), Alan Wilkinson 12 (+1), Ken Moss 11, Steve Waplington 3, Gerry Richardson 2 (+1), Robbie Gardner 1, Paul Tyrer 1, *Chris Bailey (R/R)*.
CREWE - John Jackson 11, Dai Evans 6, Paul O'Neil 6, Ian Bottomley 4 (+1), Barry Meeks 3, Warren Hawkins 2 (+2), Dave Parry 2.

Meeting 58 - Monday, October 12, 1970 - Top Dogs Trophy, Second Leg
L.M.R. Sports Ground, Earle Street, Crewe
Track Length - 470 yards.

CREWE KINGS.....46 BRADFORD NORTHERN.....32

(Bradford won on aggregate 78 - 77)

Trailing by fifteen points from the first leg, Crewe made a terrific attempt to claw back the deficit, only to fall agonisingly short. By Heat 6, they were just five in arrears, but Northern shared the points in the next six heats to snatch the trophy. Gary Peterson showed his class with a five ride maximum as Bradford provided nine race winners - the most by any visiting league team to date. Crewe were not helped by their recent glut of fixtures, which had taken its toll on man and machinery, with only four bikes and the track spare available between them.

Heat 01	**O'Neil**/**Parry**/Knapkin/Lee	75.2	**5 - 1**	05 - 01
Heat 02	Adlington/**Bottomley**/Fitzgerald/**Hawkins**	77.4	2 - 4	07 - 05
Heat 03	Peterson/**Meeks**/**Evans**/Schofield	75.0	3 - 3	10 - 08
Heat 04	**Jackson**/**Hawkins**/Wells/Fitzgerald	75.0	**5 - 1**	15 - 09
Heat 05	Knapkin/**Evans**/**Meeks**/Adlington (R)	73.8	3 - 3	18 - 12
Heat 06	**Parry**/**O'Neil**/Adlington/Wells (R)	76.0	**5 - 1**	23 - 13
Heat 07	Peterson/**Hawkins**/**Jackson**/Schofield	75.0	3 - 3	26 - 16
Heat 08	Knapkin/**Parry**/**Bottomley**/Lee	73.8	3 - 3	29 - 19
Heat 09	Peterson/**Hawkins**/**Meeks**/Adlington	74.8	3 - 3	32 - 22
Heat 10	Peterson/**O'Neil**/**Parry**/Schofield	74.6	3 - 3	35 - 25
Heat 11	Knapkin/**Jackson**/**Bottomley**/Lee	75.0	3 - 3	38 - 28
Heat 12	Peterson/**O'Neil**/**Evans**/Adlington	75.6	3 - 3	41 - 31
Heat 13	**Jackson**/**Hawkins**/Schofield/Adlington	76.0	**5 - 1**	46 - 32

CREWE - John Jackson 9 (+1), Paul O'Neil 9 (+1), Warren Hawkins 8 (+2), Dave Parry 8 (+2), Ian Bottomley 4 (+2), Dai Evans 4 (+2), Barry Meeks 4 (+2),
BRADFORD - Gary Peterson 15, Alan Knapkin 10, Robin Adlington 4, Barry Fitzgerald 1, Dave Schofield 1, Alf Wells 1, Jack Lee 0.

Canterbury took a massive step towards the league title on October 14, with a stunning 58-20 win at Crayford. They were confirmed champions three days later, after Rayleigh had beaten Rochdale 43-35. Crewe suffered their first postponement of the season on October 19, when the second leg of their Border Trophy clash with Rochdale was called off shortly before the 7.30pm start time. Maurice Littlechild addressed the 1,500 crowd and gave them the choice of staging the match the following week or go ahead with the scheduled season finale – the Supporters Trophy. The fans, eager to see some silverware in the trophy cabinet, voted unanimously for the Rochdale clash.

Meeting 59 - Monday, October 26, 1970 - Border Trophy, Second Leg
L.M.R. Sports Ground, Earle Street, Crewe
Track Length - 470 yards.

CREWE KINGS.....45 ROCHDALE HORNETS.....32

(Crewe won on aggregate 79 - 76)

The fans vote for re-staging this match was fully justified when the Kings beat their rivals by three points on aggregate to win the Border Trophy. The Hornets looked well beaten when 36-17 down after nine heats, but a determined fight back saw them needing a maximum in the final heat to snatch the trophy. Alan Wilkinson, who had dropped just a point, teamed up with skipper Eric Broadbelt and faced Barry Meeks and John Jackson in a great final heat of a long season, but it was skipper Meeks who crossed the finishing line first, much to the delight of the home crowd. One stand out statistic of the night was the time recorded in Heat 2. Ian Bottomley, coaxing home Warren Hawkins on a groggy machine, won the race in a time of 110.8!

Heat 01	**O'Neil**/Broadbelt/**Parry**/Richardson	74.2	**4 - 2**	04 - 02
Heat 02	**Bottomley**/**Hawkins**/Moss (F)/Tyrer (R)	110.8	**5 - 0**	09 - 02
Heat 03	Wilkinson/**Hawkins**/Moss/**Evans** (R)	74.4	2 - 4	11 - 06
Heat 04	**Jackson**/**Hawkins**/Moss/Waplington (R)	74.4	**5 - 1**	16 - 07
Heat 05	**Meeks**/Broadbelt/**Evans**/Richardson (F)	74.6	**4 - 2**	20 - 09
Heat 06	**O'Neil**/**Parry**/Moss/Waplington	74.2	**5 - 1**	25 - 10
Heat 07	Wilkinson/**Jackson**/**Bottomley**/Gardner	74.0	3 - 3	28 - 13
Heat 08	**Bottomley**/**Parry**/Richardson/Moss (R)	75.0	**5 - 1**	33 - 14
Heat 09	Wilkinson/**Meeks**/**Evans**/Richardson	76.8	3 - 3	36 - 17
Heat 10	Broadbelt/Wilkinson/**O'Neil**/**Parry**	76.2	1 - 5	37 - 22
Heat 11	Moss/**Jackson**/Broadbelt/**Bottomley**	75.8	2 - 4	39 - 26
Heat 12	Wilkinson/**Evans**/**O'Neil**/Richardson	75.0	3 - 3	42 - 29
Heat 13	**Meeks**/Wilkinson/Broadbelt/**Jackson**	74.6	3 - 3	45 - 32

CREWE - Paul O'Neil 8 (+1), Barry Meeks 8, Ian Bottomley 7 (+1), John Jackson 7, Warren Hawkins 6 (+2), Dave Parry 5 (+2), Dai Evans 4 (+1).
ROCHDALE - Alan Wilkinson 16 (+1), Eric Broadbelt 9 (+1), Ken Moss 6, Gerry Richardson 1, Robbie Gardner 0, Paul Tyrer 0, Steve Waplington 0. *Chris Bailey (R/R).*

Although Crewe had again finished in the top half of the league table, another dismal away record prevented a serious tilt at the title. Record breakers at home, only the Young Czechs had won a meeting at Earle Street, and this only after a titanic struggle. Crowd figures were slightly down on the 1969 figure, but were still far better than their footballing neighbours at Gresty Road. Plans were at an advanced stage as the season drew to a close for the track size to be reduced by approximately 40 yards, and work on the project began towards the end of the year. On the riding side, it was predicted youngster Peter Collins could be the next big thing at Earle Street, although it was highly likely that Paul O'Neil (who finished 5th in the Division II averages), would be making the step up to Division I, with Halifax favourites for his signature, following a number of appearances for the Dukes during the latter stages of the season.

- 1970 Season Summary -

Date	Opponents/Meeting	Res	Score	Wins to Crewe Race	Wins to Crewe Heat
Fri, March 27	**Rochdale (Ch)**	W	44 - 33	9	8
Sun, March 29	Rochdale (Ch)	L	32 - 46	5	3
Sun, April 5	Doncaster (Ch)	L	37 - 41	6	2
Mon, April 6	**Rayleigh (BL)**	W	49 - 27	11	9
Mon, April 13	**Long Eaton (Ch)**	W	49 - 28	10	9
Thu, April 16	Long Eaton (Ch)	L	31 - 47	3	2
Mon, April 20	**Nelson (KOC 1)**	W	49 - 29	9	7
Mon, April 27	**Stars of the League (Ch)**	W	40 - 38	7	3
Mon, May 4	**Ipswich (BL)**	W	52 - 26	12	8
Thu, May 7	Ipswich (BL)	L	30 - 48	5	3
Sat, May 9	Rayleigh (BL)	D	39 - 39	7	5
Mon, May 11	**Doncaster (BL)**	W	49 - 29	11	7
Mon, May 18	**Rochdale (Ch)**	W	39 - 37	7	6
Thu, May 21	Teesside (BL)	W	39 - 38	6	3
Fri, May 22	Workington (Ch)	L	23 - 55	2	1
Sun, May 24	Eastbourne (BL)	L	20 - 58	0	0
Mon, May 25	**Reading (BL)**	W	47 - 31	10	7
Mon, June 1	**King's Lynn (BL)**	W	53 - 25	13	9
Wed, June 3	King's Lynn (BL)	L	31 - 47	3	3
Sat, June 6	Canterbury (KOC 2)	L	26 - 52	3	2
Mon, June 8	**Long Eaton (BL)**	W	52 - 26	10	7
Mon, June 15	**Peterborough (BL)**	W	58 - 20	13	12
Mon, June 22	**Berwick (BL)**	W	56 - 22	13	9
Mon, June 29	**Canterbury (BL)**	W	47 - 31	9	7
Wed, July 1	Newtongrange (Ch)	L	37 - 40	6	3
Fri, July 3	Plymouth (Ch)	L	32 - 46	5	1
Sun, July 5	Roc/Ber/Tee (4TT)	L	Crewe 20	2	-
Mon, July 6	**Workington (Ch)**	W	48 - 30	8	7
Mon, July 13	**Rochdale (BL)**	W	47 - 31	8	6
Thu, July 16	Tee/Ber/Roc (4TT)	L	Crewe 22	4	-
Sat, July 18	Ber/Roc/Tee (4TT)	L	Crewe 17	2	-
Sun, July 19	Doncaster (BL)	L	35 - 42	5	3
Mon, July 20	**Roc/Ber/Tee (4TT)**	W	Crewe 39	10	-
Mon, July 27	**Chester Vase H'cap. (Ind)**	John Jackson		-	-
Wed, July 29	Bradford (BL)	L	23 - 55	1	1
Fri, July 31	**Bradford (BL)**	W	43 - 35	7	6
Mon, August 3	Reading (BL)	L	29 - 49	3	1
Mon, August 10	**Young Czech. (Ch)**	L	48 - 59	7	5
Mon, August 17	**Crayford (BL)**	W	54 - 24	11	10
Mon, August 24	**Romford (BL)**	W	53 - 24	11	9

Mon, August 31	**Y. Bri. v Y. Aus. (Int)**	-	55 - 53	-	-
Wed, September 2	Crayford (BL)	L	31 - 47	3	2
Thu, September 3	Long Eaton (BL)	L	35 - 43	5	2
Fri, September 4	Workington (BL)	L	27 - 51	2	2
Mon, September 7	**Doncaster (Ch)**	W	50 - 27	11	9
Thu, September 10	Romford (BL)	L	30 - 48	5	0
Sun, September 13	Boston (Ch)	L	36 - 42	7	4
Mon, September 14	**Best Pairs Ch.**	Bob Valentine & Dai Evans			-
Thu, September 17	Canterbury (BL)	L	28 - 50	4	1
Sun, September 20	Rochdale (BL)	L	37 - 41	6	3
Mon, September 21	**Teesside (BL)**	W	46 - 32	10	6
Wed, September 23	Peterborough (BL)	L	36 - 42	5	4
Mon, September 28	**Eastbourne (BL)**	W	53 - 25	10	9
Mon, October 5	**Workington (BL)**	W	41 - 37	7	4
Wed, October 7	Bradford (Ch)	L	31 - 46	3	3
Sat, October 10	Berwick (BL)	L	35 - 43	5	3
Sun, October 11	Rochdale (Ch)	L	34 - 44	4	3
Mon, October 12	**Bradford (Ch)**	W	46 - 32	4	4
Mon, October 26	**Rochdale (Ch)**	W	45 - 32	7	6

- British League Division II Final Table -

		Home					Away					
	M	W	D	L	F	A	W	D	L	F	A	Pts
1. Canterbury	32	16	0	0	774	472	7	1	8	610	636	47
2. Eastbourne	32	16	0	0	788	458	6	1	9	576½	667½	45
3. Rochdale	32	16	0	0	842	395	5	2	9	618	625	44
4. Bradford	32	16	0	0	826	418	2	1	13	529	716	37
5. Teesside	32	15	0	1	752	492	3	0	13	552	694	36
6. Ipswich	32	13	2	1	717	529	4	0	12	537	707	36
7. Crewe	**32**	**16**	**0**	**0**	**800**	**445**	**1**	**1**	**14**	**505**	**741**	**35**
8. Romford	32	12	0	4	702½	541½	5	1	10	551	690	35
9. Reading	32	14	0	2	723	521	3	0	13	555½	690½	34
10. Peterborough	32	13	1	2	681	567	1	1	14	510	734	30
11. Workington	32	12	0	4	690	555	1	1	14	555	681	27
12. Rayleigh	32	12	1	3	666	577	1	0	15	489½	752½	27
13. Boston	32	10	1	5	658½	585½	2	1	13	485½	756½	26
14. Crayford	32	11	1	4	682	561	0	0	16	471	777	23
15. Doncaster	32	8	1	7	621½	616½	3	0	13	502	745	23
16. Berwick	32	10	0	6	661	584	0	0	16	428	816	20
17. Long Eaton	32	8	3	5	613½	631½	0	0	16	474	769	19

(Nelson moved to Bradford after 8 matches. King's Lynn Starlets moved to Boston after 21 matches.)

- Crewe Rider Averages -

(League and Knock Out Cup only)

	M	R	W	Pts	BP	Tot	F	P	CMA
Paul O'Neil	27	118	77	280	6	286	7	2	9.695
John Jackson	32	139	41	250	26	276	0	1	7.942
Barry Meeks	33	134	46	221	18	239	3	1	7.134
Dai Evans	31	135	17	181	33	214	0	1	6.341
Warren Hawkins.	23	78	12	103	16	119	0	0	6.103
Ian Bottomley	28	94	23	123	16	139	2	1	5.915
Dave Parry	17	63	8	75	14	89	0	0	5.651
Glyn Blackburn	15	47	3	49	13	62	0	0	5.277
				Also rode					
Colin Tucker	3	11	5	23	4	27	0	0	9.818

Rob Jackson	8	23	3	24	5	29	0	0	5.043
Ray Cousins	2	7	0	2	1	3	0	0	1.714
John Mulligan	5	13	0	2	0	2	0	0	0.615
Substitutes									
Ross Gilbertson	1	5	2	12	0	12	0	0	9.600
Dave Jessup	1	6	4	12	0	12	0	0	8.000
Peter Seaton	1	4	2	8	0	8	0	0	8.000
Bob Jameson	1	5	0	6	1	7	0	0	5.600
Allan Emmett	1	4	0	4	1	5	0	0	5.000
John Harrhy	1	4	0	4	1	5	0	0	5.000
Brian Osborn	1	2	0	1	0	1	0	0	2.000
Dave Percy	1	1	0	0	0	0	0	0	0.000

- League Heat Scores -

	Home	Away	Total
5 - 1 heat win to Crewe	80	12	92
4 - 2 heat win to Crewe	45	23	68
3 - 2 heat win to Crewe	1	1	2
3 - 3 drawn heat	59	64	123
2 - 3 heat win to Opponents	1	0	1
2 - 4 heat win to Opponents	17	51	68
1 - 5 heat win to Opponents	4	56	60
0 - 5 heat win to Opponents	1	1	2

- Team Honours -

Cheshire/Notts Trophy Winners.
Border Trophy Winners.

- Individual/Pairs Honours -

Chester Vase Handicap (Crewe)
1. John Jackson 2. Chris Bailey 3. Bob Valentine.

Best Pairs (Crewe)
1. Bob Valentine & Dai Evans 2. Barry Meeks & Tom Leadbitter, 3. Paul O'Neil & Warren Hawkins.

Graham's Handicap Trophy (Workington)
1. John Jackson 2. Bob Valentine 3. Taffy Owen.

(ABOVE) Paul O'Neil, who topped the Kings averages.

(ABOVE) Ian Bottomley leads "The White Knight" Graeme Smith, (riding the boards) and team mate Barry Crowson during the Crewe v Canterbury clash. Note the supporters taking cover from the flying shale, a hazard of spectating on the Earle Street bends!

(ABOVE) Crewe Best Pairs winners Bob "Bluey" Valentine and Dai Evans receive their tankards from Maurice Littlechild.

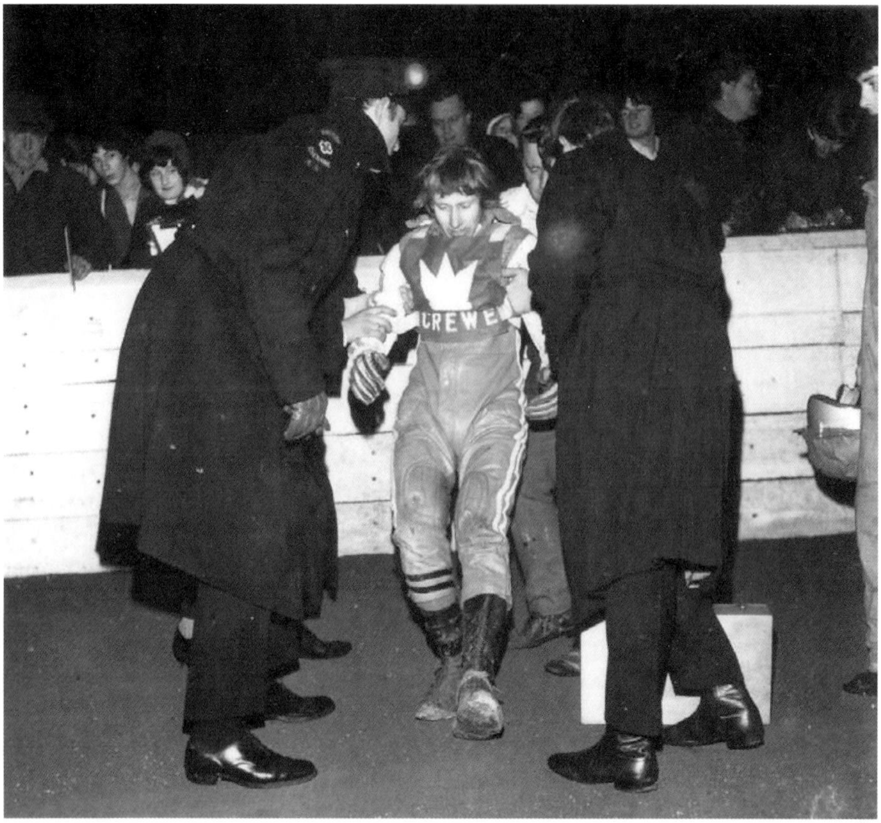

(ABOVE) John Jackson being helped to his feet by first aid men following a rare fall at Earle Street. (BELOW LEFT) John "Mad" Mulligan, who's season ended with a nasty track crash at Bradford on October 7. (BELOW RIGHT) Glyn Blackburn, who made 19 appearances, before leaving the club mid-season.

The King From Mildura -1971-

The King From Mildura
-1971-

Major changes in Division II saw one side move up a division, two drop out, and three new additions. Reading surprised many by taking over the vacant Division I licence, which had become available following the closure of Newcastle. It was the end of the road for Crayford who withdrew in early March, and for Doncaster, whose management gained approval to relocate south to re-open Perry Barr, Birmingham. Hull and Sunderland completed the seventeen team line-up for the new campaign. The Knock Out Cup competition, sponsored for the first time by the *Speedway Express* magazine, received a much-needed revamp, and gone was the lottery of the draw, with all ties held on a home and away basis, as a trial in Division II. Crewe received a bye in the first round, and drew Berwick in the second. Earle Street was also afforded the honour of staging not one, but two international meetings, with the talented Young Czechs returning for a third year, plus a visit from Young Sweden. For the second year in a row, the club lost their star rider on the eve of the season, when Paul O'Neil signed a first division contract with Halifax. Originally it was hoped that the Kiwi would link up with the Dukes at reserve, thus allowing him to stay with the Kings, but when fellow countryman Colin McKee remained in New Zealand, he was drafted into the main body of the team. Crewe's team-building plans received two further set-backs, when firstly Warren Hawkins announced that he would not be returning to England for a second season, and then teenage prospect Peter Collins rejected Maurice Littlechild's offer of a contract, choosing to concentrate on his studies - only to sign for boyhood heroes Belle Vue. The Kings promoter was obviously upset at missing out on one of speedway's hottest talents, especially when he was loaned out to Belle Vue's sister track Rochdale, who just happened to be Crewe's biggest rivals. Littlechild was also unhappy with Aces and Hornets boss Dent Oliver for "poaching" his protégé and would comment: *"I have always held the Belle Vue management in the highest esteem, for over the years they have done considerable good for the sport. But when they start taking the credit for having discovered Peter Collins, my blood just boils."* On a positive note, Barry Meeks moved to the area after buying a garage in Warmingham, dispelling rumours that he was about to move to a team nearer his Oxfordshire home. Popular Aussie Gary Moore joined the ranks from Rayleigh, after a number of guest appearances for the Kings at the back end of the previous season. Spectator facilities were further improved over the winter months, but the most notable change was to the Earle Street circuit, reduced by approximately 40 yards, in the hope of producing more evenly-contested matches. Admission was set at 35p for adults and 15p for children and senior citizens, with programmes priced at 5p. Good Friday was once again the date chosen for Crewe's opening fixture of the new season.

Meeting 1 - Friday, April 9, 1971 - Top Dogs Trophy, First Leg
L.M.R. Sports Ground, Earle Street, Crewe
Track Length - 430 yards.

CREWE KINGS.....31 BRADFORD NORTHERN.....47

Crewe made a disastrous start to their third campaign, losing their first meeting at Earle Street to a Division II outfit since July 21, 1969. Short of match practice and weakened by the departure of Paul O'Neil, the Kings looked virtual strangers on their radically altered track. A strong Northern side, who had won each of their opening four meetings, looked confident from the off, ending with six heat wins to Crewe's two. Dave Parry top scored for the hosts, but Gary Moore had a home debut to forget, failing to register a point from his three starts.

Heat 01	**Meeks**/Wells/Sheldrick/**Evans** (F)	**78.0** (TR)	3 - 3	03 - 03
Heat 02	Bridgett/Adlington/**Smitherman**/**Bottomley** (F)	81.0	1 - 5	04 - 08
Heat 03	**Parry**/Baugh/Schofield/**Moore** (R)	**77.4** (TR)	3 - 3	07 - 11
Heat 04	Knapkin/**Bottomley**/**Jackson**/Adlington	77.6	3 - 3	10 - 14
Heat 05	**Parry**/Sheldrick/Wells/**Moore**	78.0	3 - 3	13 - 17
Heat 06	Knapkin/Bridgett/**Meeks**/**Evans**	77.6	1 - 5	14 - 22
Heat 07	**Bottomley**/Schofield/**Jackson**/Baugh	77.2	**4 - 2**	18 - 24
Heat 08	**Parry**/**Evans**/Adlington/Sheldrick (R)	78.8	**5 - 1**	23 - 25
Heat 09	Knapkin/Bridgett/**Parry**/**Moore**	**77.0** (TR)	1 - 5	24 - 30

Heat 10	**Meeks**/Baugh/Schofield/**Bottomley** (F)	76.4	3 - 3	27 - 33
Heat 11	Sheldrick/Wells/**Smitherman**/**Jackson** (R)	80.4	1 - 5	28 - 38
Heat 12	Schofield/Knapkin/**Meeks**/**Bottomley**	77.8	1 - 5	29 - 43
Heat 13	Baugh/**Parry**/Bridgett/**Jackson**	78.0	2 - 4	31 - 47

CREWE - Dave Parry 12, Barry Meeks 8, Ian Bottomley 5, Dai Evans 2 (+1), John Jackson 2 (+1), Barrie Smitherman 2, Gary Moore 0.
BRADFORD - Alan Knapkin 11 (+1), Alan Bridgett 8 (+2), Dave Schofield 7 (+2), Dave Baugh 7, Sid Sheldrick 6 (+1), Alf Wells 5 (+2), Robin Adlington 3 (+1).

Meeting 2 - Wednesday, April 14, 1971 - Top Dogs Trophy, Second Leg
Odsal Stadium, Rooley Avenue, Bradford
Track Length - 380 yards.

BRADFORD NORTHERN.....50 CREWE KINGS.....27

(Bradford won on aggregate 97 - 58)

A long and hard season was predicted for the Kings after their comprehensive defeat on aggregate in the Top Dogs Trophy. Crewe riders won just three races, which included a Heat 5 victory for Sunderland guest Jack Millen, replacing Dai Evans who was suffering with flu. Ian Bottomley though did restore some pride, when he was the surprise winner of the second half Rider of the Night final, after defeating the home trio of Knapkin, Wells and Baugh.

Heat 01	Baugh/**Millen**/Sheldrick/**Meeks**	74.8	4 - 2	04 - 02
Heat 02	Bridgett/**Bottomley**/**Smitherman**/Adlington (F)	75.4	3 - 3	07 - 05
Heat 03	Schofield/Wells/**Moore**/**Parry**	77.4	5 - 1	12 - 06
Heat 04	Knapkin/Bridgett/**Jackson**/**Smitherman**	73.8	5 - 1	17 - 07
Heat 05	**Millen**/Schofield/Wells/**Meeks**	74.4	3 - 3	20 - 10
Heat 06	**Jackson**/Baugh/Sheldrick/**Bottomley** (F)	72.6	3 - 3	23 - 13
Heat 07	Knapkin/Bridgett/**Millen**/**Moore**	73.4	5 - 1	28 - 14
Heat 08	**Parry**/Sheldrick/Adlington (F)/**Millen** (X)	73.0	**2 - 3**	30 - 17
Heat 09	Wells/**Bottomley**/Schofield/**Jackson**	73.4	4 - 2	34 - 19
Heat 10	Baugh/**Parry**/Sheldrick/**Moore**	73.6	4 - 2	38 - 21
Heat 11	Knapkin/**Meeks**/**Bottomley**/Adlington	72.8	3 - 3	41 - 24
Heat 12	Baugh/**Bottomley**/Schofield/**Parry**	72.4	4 - 2	45 - 26
Heat 13	Bridgett/Knapkin/**Meeks**/**Jackson** (F)	74.2	5 - 1	50 - 27

BRADFORD - Alan Knapkin 11 (+1), Dave Baugh 11, Alan Bridgett 10 (+2), Dave Schofield 7, Alf Wells 6 (+2), Sid Sheldrick 5 (+1), Robin Adlington 0.
CREWE - Ian Bottomley 7 (+1), Jack Millen* 6, Dave Parry 5, John Jackson 4, Barry Meeks 3, Barrie Smitherman 1 (+1), Gary Moore 1.

Meeting 3 - Friday, April 16, 1971 - Border Trophy, First Leg
Athletic Grounds, Milnrow Road, Rochdale
Track Length - 427 yards.

ROCHDALE HORNETS.....47 CREWE KINGS.....31

Peter Collins scored a paid fifteen point maximum in his first competitive meeting, to further infuriate the Crewe management, still bitter over his defection to Belle Vue and the Hornets. Rochdale further angered the Kings camp when they refused permission for Bradford's Alan Knapkin to stand in for flu-victim Dai Evans. During the meeting the visitors were down to only four working machines on a freezing cold evening. Home reserve Paul Callaghan was unlucky to break a collar-bone in a spill second time out.

Heat 01	Wilkinson/**Meeks**/Goad/**Moore** (F)	78.2	4 - 2	04 - 02
Heat 02	Collins/**Beecroft**/**Bottomley**/Callaghan	79.0	3 - 3	07 - 05
Heat 03	**Parry**/**Meeks**/Richardson/Gardner	80.6	**1 - 5**	08 - 10
Heat 04	Collins/Tyrer/**Jackson**/**Beecroft**	77.2	5 - 1	13 - 11
Heat 05	**Meeks**/**Moore**/Gardner/Richardson (F)	81.2	**1 - 5**	14 - 16
Heat 06	Wilkinson/Goad/**Beecroft**/**Jackson** (R)	79.2	5 - 1	19 - 17
Heat 07	Tyrer/Collins/**Bottomley**/**Parry** (X)	77.4	5 - 1	24 - 18
Heat 08	**Parry**/Goad/**Moore**/Callaghan (X)	80.4	**2 - 4**	26 - 22

Heat 09	Collins/**Jackson**/Gardner/**Bottomley**	79.0	4 - 2	30 - 24
Heat 10	Wilkinson/Goad/**Beecroft/Parry**	79.0	5 - 1	35 - 25
Heat 11	Tyrer/Collins/**Meeks/Moore**	78.0	5 - 1	40 - 26
Heat 12	Wilkinson/**Jackson/Parry**/Gardner (F)	80.0	3 - 3	43 - 29
Heat 13	Tyrer/**Meeks**/Richardson/**Jackson**	78.6	4 - 2	47 - 31

ROCHDALE - Peter Collins 13 (+2), Alan Wilkinson 12, Paul Tyrer 11 (+1), Colin Goad 7 (+2), Robbie Gardner 2, Gerry Richardson 2, Paul Callaghan 0.
CREWE - Barry Meeks 10 (+1), Dave Parry 7 (+1), John Jackson 5, Don Beecroft 4, Gary Moore 3 (+1), Ian Bottomley 2 (+1).

Meeting 4 - Saturday, April 17, 1971 - British League Division II
Canterbury City Football Ground, Kingsmead Road, Canterbury
Track Length - 390 yards.

CANTERBURY CRUSADERS.....48 CREWE KINGS.....30

Don Beecroft, Gary Moore and junior Barrie Smitherman, made their Crewe league debuts, in the opening match of the campaign, but all struggled against the reigning champions. Graham Banks recorded a full house for the Crusaders, with John Jackson the pick of the Kings, with three race wins and eleven points.

Heat 01	Banks/**Meeks**/Tabet/**Beecroft**	78.0	4 - 2	04 - 02
Heat 02	Hubbard/**Bottomley**/Barkaway/**Smitherman**	79.8	4 - 2	08 - 04
Heat 03	Hammond/**Moore**/D.Smith/**Smitherman**	81.0	4 - 2	12 - 06
Heat 04	**Jackson**/G.Smith/Barkaway/**Bottomley**	80.0	3 - 3	15 - 09
Heat 05	Hammond/**Parry/Meeks**/D.Smith	79.2	3 - 3	18 - 12
Heat 06	Banks/**Jackson/Bottomley**/Tabet	78.0	3 - 3	21 - 15
Heat 07	Barkaway/**Parry**/G.Smith/**Moore**	80.4	4 - 2	25 - 17
Heat 08	Hubbard/Tabet/**Meeks/Beecroft**	78.9	5 - 1	30 - 18
Heat 09	**Jackson**/D.Smith/Hammond/**Bottomley**	79.0	3 - 3	33 - 21
Heat 10	Banks/**Parry**/Tabet/**Moore**	78.8	4 - 2	37 - 23
Heat 11	**Jackson/Meeks**/G.Smith/Hubbard (F)	79.0	**1 - 5**	38 - 28
Heat 12	Banks/Hubbard/**Parry/Jackson** (R)	78.1	5 - 1	43 - 29
Heat 13	G.Smith/Hammond/**Meeks/Moore**	80.0	5 - 1	48 - 30

CANTERBURY - Graham Banks 12, John Hammond 9 (+2), Ted Hubbard 8 (+1), Graeme Smith 7, Mike Barkaway 5 (+1), Bob Tabet 4 (+1), Dave Smith 3.
CREWE - John Jackson 11, Barry Meeks 7 (+2), Dave Parry 7, Ian Bottomley 3 (+1), Gary Moore 2, Don Beecroft 0, Barrie Smitherman 0.

On Sunday, April 18, nineteen-year-old Phil Crump, a welder by trade from Mildura,Victoria, flew over to England to try his luck at Earle Street, in the hope of securing a contract. The young Aussie had been recommended to Maurice Littlechild as *"a rider with great potential"* by veteran Neil Street, after watching him ride in Australia. Littlechild was also in the hunt for former Belle Vue rider Norman Nevitt, residing in the Haslington area, but with two First Division tracks also eyeing developments, it was highly unlikely that the move would come to fruition.

Meeting 5 - Monday, April 19, 1971 - Sherwood Trophy, First Leg
L.M.R. Sports Ground, Earle Street, Crewe
Track Length - 430 yards.

CREWE KINGS.....48 LONG EATON RANGERS.....30

The Kings ended a four match losing streak with an eighteen point victory over Long Eaton. John Jackson continued his bright start to the season with a maximum and skipper Barry Meeks chipped in with three wins and a second. Reserves Ian Bottomley and Don Beecroft offered good support, contributing thirteen points between them.

Heat 01	**Meeks**/Shakespeare/**Moore**/Farmer	79.2	**4 - 2**	04 - 02
Heat 02	**Bottomley/Beecroft**/Wrathall/Bass	79.4	**5 - 1**	09 - 03
Heat 03	Bouchard/**Parry/Evans**/Wakefield	79.6	3 - 3	12 - 06
Heat 04	**Jackson/Bottomley**/Wrathall/Mills	80.0	**5 - 1**	17 - 07

Heat 05	Shakespeare/Bouchard/**Evans**/**Parry**	79.6	1 - 5	18 - 12
Heat 06	**Meeks**/Shakespeare/Wrathall/**Moore**	77.2	3 - 3	21 - 15
Heat 07	**Jackson**/**Bottomley**/Bouchard/Wakefield	**77.0** (=TR)	**5 - 1**	26 - 16
Heat 08	**Beecroft**/Bass/**Moore**/Farmer (R)	82.4	**4 - 2**	30 - 18
Heat 09	**Parry**/Wrathall/**Evans**/Farmer	78.4	**4 - 2**	34 - 20
Heat 10	Bouchard/**Meeks**/Wakefield/**Moore**	79.4	2 - 4	36 - 24
Heat 11	**Jackson**/Shakespeare/**Beecroft**/Farmer (X)	77.2	**4 - 2**	40 - 26
Heat 12	**Meeks**/**Evans**/Wrathall/Bass	77.4	**5 - 1**	45 - 27
Heat 13	**Jackson**/Bouchard/Shakespeare/**Parry**	77.2	3 - 3	48 - 30

CREWE - John Jackson 12, Barry Meeks 11, Ian Bottomley 7 (+2), Don Beecroft 6 (+1), Dai Evans 5 (+2), Dave Parry 5, Gary Moore 2.
LONG EATON - Geoff Bouchard 11 (+1), Malcolm Shakespeare 10 (+1), Peter Wrathall 6 (+1), Steve Bass 2, Ken Wakefield 1, Gil Farmer 0, Roger Mills 0.

New arrival Phil Crump rode in a "Vultures Race" prior to the Long Eaton match, in the hope of securing the No.7 spot, but lost out to Don Beecroft. However, during the second-half, he did enough to warrant inclusion for the trip to Hull.

Meeting 6 - Wednesday, April 21, 1971 - Challenge
Boulevard Stadium, Airlie Street, Kingston-upon-Hull
Track Length - 415 yards.

HULL VIKINGS.....46 CREWE KINGS.....32

Former skipper Colin Tucker would have enjoyed this hard fought victory over his former employers. The Kings held a two-point lead after Heat 6, but a determined Hull fightback saw the final seven races won by a home rider. Phil Crump, replacing Dave Parry in the number 5 berth, won his very first race in Crewe colours, and went on to finish with a credible five points from four outings.

Heat 01	Childs/**Meeks**/**Moore**/Baldock (R)	80.2	3 - 3	03 - 03
Heat 02	**Bottomley**/Admundson/**Beecroft**/Wasden	80.0	**2 - 4**	05 - 07
Heat 03	**Crump**/**Evans**/Tucker/Devonport (F)	81.0	**1 - 5**	06 - 12
Heat 04	Amundson/Wilson/**Jackson**/**Bottomley** (F)	80.2	5 - 1	11 - 13
Heat 05	Tucker/**Meeks**/Devonport/**Moore**	80.2	4 - 2	15 - 15
Heat 06	**Jackson**/Childs/**Bottomley**/Baldock	79.0	**2 - 4**	17 - 19
Heat 07	Wilson/Amundson/**Evans**/**Crump**	79.4	5 - 1	22 - 20
Heat 08	Amundson/**Moore**/**Beecroft**/Wasden (R)	82.4	3 - 3	25 - 23
Heat 09	Tucker/**Jackson**/Devonport/**Bottomley**	79.4	4 - 2	29 - 25
Heat 10	Childs/**Crump**/**Evans**/Baldock	79.0	3 - 3	32 - 28
Heat 11	Wilson/Amundson/**Meeks**/**Moore**	82.0	5 - 1	37 - 29
Heat 12	Childs/Tucker/**Jackson**/**Crump**	80.0	5 - 1	42 - 30
Heat 13	Wilson/**Meeks**/Devonport/**Evans** (F)	79.8	4 - 2	46 - 32

HULL - Robin Amundson 12 (+2), Reg Wilson 11 (+1), Tony Childs 11, Colin Tucker 9 (+1), George Devonport 3, Pete Baldock 0, Dennis Wasden 0.
CREWE - John Jackson 7, Barry Meeks 7, Phil Crump 5, Dai Evans 4 (+2), Ian Bottomley 4, Gary Moore 3 (+1), Don Beecroft 2 (+1).

Meeting 7 - Thursday, April 22, 1971 - Sherwood Trophy, Second Leg
Long Eaton Stadium, Station Road, Long Eaton
Track Length - 366 yards.

LONG EATON RANGERS.....53 CREWE KINGS.....24

(Long Eaton won on aggregate 83 - 72)

Barry Meeks arrived just seconds before the first heat, then crashed out of the meeting with a badly bruised leg following a fall in Heat 5. Phil Crump became the next Crewe casualty three heats later, cartwheeling into the safety fence, with his bike landing on top of him, badly bruising a foot. Long Eaton were far too strong on a deep and bumpy track, with home debutant Roger Mills and Malcolm Shakespeare scoring maximums, and Geoff Bouchard picking up a paid one.

(ABOVE) All change at Earle Street. The home straight safety fence and infield being moved inwards, to reduce the track length by almost 40 yards. (BELOW) Riders and management pose for the camera during a pre-season practice session. They are (from left to right) Dave Parry, John Jackson, Dai Evans, Barry Meeks, Ian Bottomley, new signing Gary Moore, Halifax bound Paul O'Neil, Maurice Littlechild and Ken Adams.

(ABOVE) Ian Bottomley (far left) entertains Gary Moore, team manager Norman Russell (aka Tom Norman), Barry Meeks, Don Beecroft, John Jackson, Barrie Smitherman, Dave Parry and guest Jack Millen, prior to the second leg of the Top Dogs Trophy meeting at Bradford on April 14.

(LEFT) Aussie Don Beecroft, who appeared in several of Crewe's opening meetings.

(BELOW) "The King from Mildura" Phil Crump, at the start of what would be a glittering career.

Heat 01	Shakespeare/Wrathall/**Meeks**/**Moore**	70.4	5 - 1	05 - 01
Heat 02	**Crump**/Farmer/Bass/**Bottomley**	73.8	3 - 3	08 - 04
Heat 03	Bouchard/**Evans**/**Parry**/Scott	74.2	3 - 3	11 - 07
Heat 04	Mills/**Crump**/**Jackson**/Farmer	72.8	3 - 3	14 - 10
Heat 05	Bouchard/Scott/**Moore**/**Meeks** (F)	75.6	5 - 1	19 - 11
Heat 06	Shakespeare/**Jackson**/Wrathall/**Bottomley**	72.8	4 - 2	23 - 13
Heat 07	Mills/Farmer/**Parry**/**Evans** (R)	75.0	5 - 1	28 - 14
Heat 08	**Jackson**/Wrathall/Bass (X)/**Crump** (X)	74.2	**2 - 3**	30 - 17
Heat 09	Bouchard/**Jackson**/**Beecroft**/Scott (F)	75.2	3 - 3	33 - 20
Heat 10	Shakespeare/Wrathall/**Parry**/**Evans**	74.6	5 - 1	38 - 21
Heat 11	Mills/Bass/**Parry**/**Moore**	74.8	5 - 1	43 - 22
Heat 12	Shakespeare/Bouchard/**Jackson**/**Parry**	74.2	5 - 1	48 - 23
Heat 13	Mills/Scott/**Beecroft**/**Evans**	74.8	5 - 1	53 - 24

LONG EATON - Roger Mills 12, Malcolm Shakespeare 12, Geoff Bouchard 11 (+1), Peter Wrathall 7 (+2), Gerry Scott 4 (+2), Gil Farmer 4 (+1), Steve Bass 3 (+2).
CREWE - John Jackson 9 (+1), Phil Crump 5, Dave Parry 4 (+1), Don Beecroft 2 (+1), Dai Evans 2, Barry Meeks 1, Gary Moore 1, Ian Bottomley 0.

Meeting 8 - Sunday, April 25, 1971 - British League Division II
Boston Sports Stadium, New Hammond Beck Road, Boston
Track Length - 380 yards.

BOSTON BARRACUDAS.....53 CREWE KINGS.....25

On a freezing cold day, Crewe did little to warm the home supporters with another poor away performance. Arthur Price was the man who could do no wrong, recording a maximum and twice equalling his own track record. Phil Crump won his opening race for the third meeting in a row and ended up the top scoring King. John Jackson and Jim Ryman were involved in a nasty crash in the second-half Scratch Final and were both stretchered off.

Heat 01	Price/Bywater/**Meeks**/**Bottomley**	**66.8** (=TR)	5 - 1	05 - 01
Heat 02	**Crump**/Glover/Cross/**Moore** (R)	68.2	3 - 3	08 - 04
Heat 03	Ryman/Featherstone/**Parry**/**Evans** (R)	69.2	5 - 1	13 - 05
Heat 04	Glover/**Jackson**/**Moore**/Osborne (R)	68.0	3 - 3	16 - 08
Heat 05	Ryman/Featherstone/**Bottomley**/**Meeks**	68.8	5 - 1	21 - 09
Heat 06	Price/**Crump**/Bywater/**Jackson**	67.4	4 - 2	25 - 11
Heat 07	Glover/Osborne/**Crump**/**Parry**	68.2	5 - 1	30 - 12
Heat 08	**Jackson**/Bywater/Cross/**Bottomley**	69.8	3 - 3	33 - 15
Heat 09	**Crump**/**Jackson**/Featherstone/Ryman	68.2	**1 - 5**	34 - 20
Heat 10	Price/**Evans**/Bywater/**Parry**	**66.8** (=TR)	4 - 2	38 - 22
Heat 11	Cross/Osborne/**Meeks**/**Crump**	69.2	5 - 1	43 - 23
Heat 12	Price/Featherstone/**Jackson**/**Moore** (R)	67.8	5 - 1	48 - 24
Heat 13	Osborne/Ryman/**Evans**/**Meeks**	68.8	5 - 1	53 - 25

BOSTON - Arthur Price 12, Jim Ryman 8 (+1), Carl Glover 8, Tony Featherstone 7 (+3), Russell Osborne 7 (+2), Jack Bywater 6 (+1), Vic Cross 5 (+2).
CREWE - Phil Crump 9, John Jackson 8 (+1), Dai Evans 3, Barry Meeks 2, Gary Moore 1 (+1), Ian Bottomley 1, Dave Parry 1.

Meeting 9 - Monday, April 26, 1971 - Border Trophy, Second Leg
L.M.R. Sports Ground, Earle Street, Crewe
Track Length - 430 yards.

CREWE KINGS.....39 ROCHDALE HORNETS.....39

(Rochdale won on aggregate 86 - 70)

The track record was broken on three occasions during an evenly-contested meeting. Paul Tyrer recorded a time of 76.8 in Heat 4, which was beaten one race later by team-mate Alan Wilkinson. John Jackson then reclaimed it in Heat 7 with a time of 76.2. The Kings failed to make up any of Rochdale's first leg advantage, but the meeting was a great see-saw encounter for the Earle Street faithful. Gary Moore enjoyed his best return to date in Crewe colours, finishing as joint-top scorer with Dai Evans. Wilkinson showed his liking for the new track by registering a well-earned maximum.

Heat 01	Wilkinson/Goad/**Meeks**/**Crump**	77.2	1 - 5	01 - 05
Heat 02	**Moore**/Richardson/Drury/**Bottomley**	79.0	3 - 3	04 - 08
Heat 03	**Evans**/Moss/**Parry**/Drury	77.4	**4 - 2**	08 - 10
Heat 04	Tyrer/**Jackson**/**Bottomley**/Richardson	**76.8** (TR)	3 - 3	11 - 13
Heat 05	Wilkinson/**Evans**/**Moore**/Goad	**76.6** (TR)	3 - 3	14 - 16
Heat 06	Tyrer/**Crump**/Drury/**Meeks** (R)	77.2	2 - 4	16 - 20
Heat 07	**Jackson**/Moss/**Bottomley**/Gardner	**76.2** (TR)	**4 - 2**	20 - 22
Heat 08	**Crump**/**Moore**/Drury/Goad	79.0	**5 - 1**	25 - 23
Heat 09	**Evans**/Tyrer/**Parry**/Richardson	77.8	**4 - 2**	29 - 25
Heat 10	Moss/**Meeks**/**Crump**/Gardner	79.0	3 - 3	32 - 28
Heat 11	Wilkinson/**Jackson**/**Moore**/Goad	76.4	3 - 3	35 - 31
Heat 12	Tyrer/Moss/**Evans**/**Meeks**	77.8	1 - 5	36 - 36
Heat 13	Wilkinson/**Moore**/**Jackson**/Drury	76.8	3 - 3	39 - 39

CREWE - Gary Moore 9 (+3), Dai Evans 9, John Jackson 8 (+1), Phil Crump 6 (+1), Barry Meeks 3, Ian Bottomley 2 (+1), Dave Parry 2.
ROCHDALE - Alan Wilkinson 12, Paul Tyrer 11, Ken Moss 9 (+1), Graham Drury 3 (+1), Colin Goad 2 (+1), Gerry Richardson 2, Robbie Gardner 0.

Meeting 10 - Monday, May 3, 1971 - British League Division II
L.M.R. Sports Ground, Earle Street, Crewe
Track Length - 430 yards.

CREWE KINGS.....56 PETERBOROUGH PANTHERS.....22

The Kings won their opening home league match with ease, as only Andy Ross tasted victory for the sorry looking Panthers. Dave Parry and Ian Bottomley reacted positively to the news that their places in the team were in jeopardy, by scoring seventeen points between them. Crewe old boy Pete Saunders failed to score in his two outings.

Heat 01	**Meeks**/Ross/**Bottomley**/Hughes	79.0	**4 - 2**	04 - 02
Heat 02	**Moore**/**Crump**/Clark/Saunders	79.4	**5 - 1**	09 - 03
Heat 03	**Parry**/Carter/**Evans**/Ross	78.6	**4 - 2**	13 - 05
Heat 04	**Jackson**/Clark/Greer/**Crump** (R)	79.4	3 - 3	16 - 08
Heat 05	**Evans**/**Parry**/Ross/Hughes	78.6	**5 - 1**	21 - 09
Heat 06	**Bottomley**/**Meeks**/Greer/Saunders	77.8	**5 - 1**	26 - 10
Heat 07	**Jackson**/Carter/Greer/**Crump**	77.6	3 - 3	29 - 13
Heat 08	**Moore**/**Bottomley**/Clark/Hughes	78.0	**5 - 1**	34 - 14
Heat 09	**Parry**/**Evans**/Greer/Carter	77.8	**5 - 1**	39 - 15
Heat 10	**Meeks**/**Bottomley**/Carter/Stayte	77.2	**5 - 1**	44 - 16
Heat 11	Ross/**Jackson**/**Moore**/Clark	78.4	3 - 3	47 - 19
Heat 12	**Evans**/**Meeks**/Greer/Stayte	79.2	**5 - 1**	52 - 20
Heat 13	**Jackson**/Ross/**Parry**/Carter	77.6	**4 - 2**	56 - 22

CREWE - John Jackson 11, Barry Meeks 10 (+2), Dai Evans 9 (+1), Dave Parry 9 (+1), Ian Bottomley 8 (+2), Gary Moore 7 (+1), Phil Crump 2 (+1).
PETERBOROUGH - Andy Ross 8, Richard Greer 5 (+2), Roy Carter 5, Brian Clark 4, Joe Hughes 0, Pete Saunders 0, John Stayte 0, *Peter Seaton (R/R).*

Maurice Littlechild announced plans for Crewe to operate a squad system, with each line-up selected from nine or ten riders on a "horses for courses" basis, in an attempt to improve a dismal away record.

Meeting 11 - Thursday, May 6, 1971 - British League Division II
Cleveland Park Stadium, Stockton Road, Middlesbrough
Track Length - 335 yards.

TEESSIDE TEESSIDERS.....42 CREWE KINGS.....35

Crewe staged a magnificent fightback after trailing by eleven points, but just ran out of steam at the end of this highly competitive meeting. John Jackson led the Kings revival by winning Heats 4, 8 and 9, which left his side trailing by a single point. However, the Teessiders gained revenge for last year's controversial home defeat by winning three of the last four heats.

Heat 01	Durham/Forrester/**Bottomley**/**Meeks**	74.2	5 - 1	05 - 01
Heat 02	Tony Swales/Reading/**Moore** (F)/**Crump** (X)	75.0	5 - 0	10 - 01
Heat 03	Tim Swales/**Evans**/Davies/**Parry**	74.0	4 - 2	14 - 03
Heat 04	**Jackson**/**Crump**/Jameson/Tony Swales	72.8	**1 - 5**	15 - 08
Heat 05	Tim Swales/**Meeks**/**Bottomley**/Davies	73.6	3 - 3	18 - 11
Heat 06	Forrester/**Jackson**/Durham/**Moore**	72.8	4 - 2	22 - 13
Heat 07	**Evans**/Jameson/**Parry**/Tony Swales	73.0	**2 - 4**	24 - 17
Heat 08	**Jackson**/**Crump**/Durham/Reading	72.6	**1 - 5**	25 - 22
Heat 09	**Jackson**/Tim Swales/**Crump**/Davies	71.6	**2 - 4**	27 - 26
Heat 10	Forrester/**Evans**/Durham/**Parry**	73.8	4 - 2	31 - 28
Heat 11	Jameson/**Bottomley**/Tony Swales/**Meeks** (F)	75.0	4 - 2	35 - 30
Heat 12	Forrester/**Crump**/Davies/**Jackson**	73.2	4 - 2	39 - 32
Heat 13	Tim Swales/**Evans**/**Meeks**/Jameson (R)	74.0	3 - 3	42 - 35

TEESSIDE - Bruce Forrester 11 (+1), Tim Swales 11, Dave Durham 6, Bob Jameson 6, Tony Swales 4, Pete Reading 2 (+1), Dene Davies 2.
CREWE - John Jackson 11, Dai Evans 9, Phil Crump 7 (+2), Ian Bottomley 4 (+1), Barry Meeks 3 (+1), Dave Parry 1, Gary Moore 0.

New Zealander Jack Millen was added to the Kings squad in an effort to strengthen the middle order. He had requested a transfer from sister track Sunderland, due to his dislike of the tight Boldon circuit.

Meeting 12 - Sunday, May 9, 1971 - British League Division II
Arlington Raceway, Arlington Road, Hailsham, Eastbourne
Track Length - 342 yards.

EASTBOURNE EAGLES.....54 CREWE KINGS.....23

Early season title favourites Eastbourne turned in another impressive Arlington display, as Crewe's poor away form returned. The Eagles gained ten heat advantages and had the league points in the bag by the end of Heat 9. The small travelling band of Kings supporters had little to cheer, apart from John Jackson's two race wins and new signing Jack Millen's Heat 11 victory over hot prospect Gordon Kennett. Barry Meeks, Gary Moore and Don Beecroft all failed to get on the score sheet.

Heat 01	Sims/Johns/**Millen**/**Meeks**	66.8	5 - 1	05 - 01
Heat 02	D.Kennett/**Crump**/Woolford/**Moore**	66.8	4 - 2	09 - 03
Heat 03	Trott/Ballard/**Evans**/**Beecroft**	67.6	5 - 1	14 - 04
Heat 04	G.Kennett/**Jackson**/D.Kennett/**Crump**	65.8	4 - 2	18 - 06
Heat 05	Ballard/Trott/**Millen**/**Meeks**	65.8	5 - 1	23 - 07
Heat 06	Sims/**Jackson**/Johns/**Moore**	67.4	4 - 2	27 - 09
Heat 07	**Jackson**/D.Kennett/**Evans**/G.Kennett	66.8	**2 - 4**	29 - 13
Heat 08	Johns/Woolford/**Millen**/**Crump**	67.4	5 - 1	34 - 14
Heat 09	Ballard/Trott/**Jackson**/**Moore**	67.2	5 - 1	39 - 15
Heat 10	Johns/Sims/**Evans**/**Beecroft**	66.8	5 - 1	44 - 16
Heat 11	**Millen**/G.Kennett/**Evans** (R)/Woolford (F)	67.8	**2 - 3**	46 - 19
Heat 12	**Jackson**/Ballard/Sims/**Crump**	65.8	3 - 3	49 - 22
Heat 13	G.Kennett/Trott/**Evans**/**Millen**	66.8	5 - 1	54 - 23

EASTBOURNE - Malcolm Ballard 10 (+1), Reg Trott 9 (+3), Laurie Sims 9 (+2), Roger Johns 9 (+1), Gordon Kennett 8, Dave Kennett 6, Mac Woolford 3 (+1).
CREWE - John Jackson 11, Jack Millen 6, Dai Evans 4, Phil Crump 2, Don Beecroft 0, Barry Meeks 0, Gary Moore 0.

The journey back from Eastbourne saw the team finally arrive back in Crewe at around 6.00am on Monday morning, after their coach ran out of diesel coming off the M6. The weary riders had little time to prepare for their home meeting with Workington the same evening.

Meeting 13 - Monday, May 10, 1971 - British League Division II
L.M.R. Sports Ground, Earle Street, Crewe
Track Length - 430 yards.

CREWE KINGS.....39 WORKINGTON COMETS.....39

Crewe's record run of 26 consecutive Division II victories at Earle Street came to an end, when Workington fought back from the brink of defeat to snatch the unlikeliest of draws. After nine heats the Kings led by ten, but hadn't bargained on Welshman Taffy Owen winning three of the last four heats to complete a perfect five ride maximum. Dave Kumeta, a Crewe second-halfer during the previous two seasons, used his track knowledge to help the Cumbrians cause, scoring ten valuable points.

Heat 01	Owen/Hornby/**Meeks**/**Bottomley**	77.0	1 - 5	01 - 05
Heat 02	**Crump**/**Moore**/Blythe/Penniket	77.2	**5 - 1**	06 - 06
Heat 03	**Parry**/Kumeta/**Evans**/Sansom	78.2	**4 - 2**	10 - 08
Heat 04	**Jackson**/**Moore**/Blythe/Mackay (F)	77.0	**5 - 1**	15 - 09
Heat 05	Owen/**Evans**/Hornby/**Parry**	77.8	2 - 4	17 - 13
Heat 06	Mackay/**Bottomley**/Penniket/**Meeks**	79.4	2 - 4	19 - 17
Heat 07	**Jackson**/Kumeta/Sansom/**Moore**	78.2	3 - 3	22 - 20
Heat 08	**Crump**/**Bottomley**/Blythe/Hornby (X)	78.8	**5 - 1**	27 - 21
Heat 09	**Evans**/**Parry**/Mackay/Penniket (R)	77.8	**5 - 1**	32 - 22
Heat 10	Owen/Kumeta/**Bottomley**/**Meeks**	77.4	1 - 5	33 - 27
Heat 11	Owen/**Crump**/**Jackson**/Hornby	77.6	3 - 3	36 - 30
Heat 12	Kumeta/Mackay/**Meeks**/**Evans**	78.0	1 - 5	37 - 35
Heat 13	Owen/**Parry**/Kumeta/**Jackson**	77.4	2 - 4	39 - 39

CREWE - Phil Crump 8, John Jackson 7 (+1), Dave Parry 7 (+1), Dai Evans 6, Ian Bottomley 5 (+1), Gary Moore 4 (+2), Barry Meeks 2.
WORKINGTON - Taffy Owen 15, Dave Kumeta 10 (+1), Malcolm Mackay 6 (+1), Bernie Hornby 3 (+1), Chris Blythe 3, Lou Sansom 1 (+1), Geoff Penniket 1.

Meeting 14 - Monday, May 17, 1971 - British League Division II
L.M.R. Sports Ground, Earle Street, Crewe
Track Length - 430 yards.

CREWE KINGS.....49 RAYLEIGH ROCKETS.....29

All seven home riders won at least one outing against an injury-ravaged Rayleigh. Already operating rider replacement for the sidelined Alan Jackson, the Rockets then lost heat leader Geoff Maloney in a three man pile up in Heat 1, for which Phil Crump was excluded from the re-run. The visitors managed a share of the points in six heats, but only Hugh Saunders managed a race win, equalling the track record in Heat 10, which was replicated by Dave Parry in the last. Visiting reserve Nigel Rackett deserved praise, scoring in each of his permitted rides. Dai Evans was the pick of the Kings, winning three of his four starts.

Heat 01	**Meeks**/Saunders/Rackett/**Crump** (X)	77.8	3 - 3	03 - 03
Heat 02	**Moore**/Rackett/Emmett/**Crump**	77.8	3 - 3	06 - 06
Heat 03	**Evans**/Brown/**Parry**/Saunders	78.2	**4 - 2**	10 - 08
Heat 04	**Moore**/**Jackson**/Emmett/Young	77.4	**5 - 1**	15 - 09
Heat 05	**Evans**/Brown/Saunders/**Parry**	79.2	3 - 3	18 - 12
Heat 06	**Bottomley**/Rackett/**Meeks**/Young	78.0	**4 - 2**	22 - 14
Heat 07	**Jackson**/Saunders/Brown/**Moore**	77.8	3 - 3	25 - 17
Heat 08	**Crump**/**Bottomley**/Beecroft/Emmett	77.6	**5 - 1**	30 - 18
Heat 09	**Parry**/Rackett/**Evans**/Young	77.0	**4 - 2**	34 - 20
Heat 10	Saunders/**Meeks**/**Bottomley**/Brown	**76.2** (=TR)	3 - 3	37 - 23
Heat 11	**Crump**/Rackett/**Jackson**/Emmett	77.0	**4 - 2**	41 - 25
Heat 12	**Evans**/Saunders/Young/**Meeks**	77.6	3 - 3	44 - 28
Heat 13	**Parry**/**Jackson**/Rackett/Brown	**76.2** (=TR)	**5 - 1**	49 - 29

CREWE - Dai Evans 10, John Jackson 8 (+2), Dave Parry 7, Ian Bottomley 6 (+2), Phil Crump 6, Barry Meeks 6, Gary Moore 6.
RAYLEIGH - Nigel Rackett 10 (+1), Hugh Saunders 10 (+1), Dingle Brown 5 (+1), Allan Emmett 2 (+1), Bob Young 1 (+1), Don Beecroft* 1, Geoff Maloney 0, *Alan Jackson (R/R).*

Following the meeting, Ian Bottomley ended his time at the club by announcing his retirement from the sport, to concentrate on his haulage business, leaving Dave Parry as the only surviving member of the original side.

Meeting 15 - Friday, May 21, 1971 - British League Division II
Athletic Grounds, Milnrow Road, Rochdale
Track Length - 427 yards.

ROCHDALE HORNETS.....41 CREWE KINGS.....37

Rochdale's proud home record remained intact - but only just - as Crewe threw away a six point lead with just four heats remaining. Alan Wilkinson and Peter Collins provided a maximum in Heat 10 to start the comeback, and the same pair repeated the scoreline two races later, to leave the Hornets requiring only a draw for victory. Phil Crump beat Collins in his first three rides, much to the satisfaction of Maurice Littlechild.

Heat 01	Wilkinson/**Meeks**/Goad/**Millen**	77.6	4 - 2	04 - 02
Heat 02	**Crump**/Collins/Drury/**Moore**	77.0	3 - 3	07 - 05
Heat 03	**Evans**/Moss/**Parry**/Johnson	78.8	**2 - 4**	09 - 09
Heat 04	**Crump**/Collins/**Jackson**/Tyrer (R)	77.2	**2 - 4**	11 - 13
Heat 05	**Millen**/Moss/**Meeks**/Johnson	80.0	**2 - 4**	13 - 17
Heat 06	Wilkinson/**Jackson**/**Moore**/Goad	78.0	3 - 3	16 - 20
Heat 07	**Evans**/Tyrer/Collins/**Parry**	79.2	3 - 3	19 - 23
Heat 08	**Crump**/Collins/**Millen**/Drury	78.0	**2 - 4**	21 - 27
Heat 09	Wilkinson/**Jackson**/**Moore**/Moss	79.0	3 - 3	24 - 30
Heat 10	Wilkinson/Collins/**Crump**/**Evans**	78.8	5 - 1	29 - 31
Heat 11	**Millen**/Tyrer/Drury/**Meeks**	80.2	3 - 3	32 - 34
Heat 12	Collins/Wilkinson/**Jackson**/**Crump**	78.4	5 - 1	37 - 35
Heat 13	Tyrer/**Evans**/Moss/**Meeks**	79.0	4 - 2	41 - 37

ROCHDALE - Alan Wilkinson 14 (+1), Peter Collins 12 (+2), Paul Tyrer 7, Ken Moss 5, Graham Drury 2 (+2), Colin Goad 1, Clive Johnson 0.
CREWE - Phil Crump 10, Dai Evans 8, Jack Millen 7, John Jackson 6, Barry Meeks 3, Gary Moore 2 (+2), Dave Parry 1.

Meeting 16 - Monday, May 24, 1971 - British League Division II
L.M.R. Sports Ground, Earle Street, Crewe
Track Length - 430 yards.

CREWE KINGS.....46 IPSWICH WITCHES.....32

A crowd of over 2,000 braved a wet and stormy night to witness racing in appalling conditions. The late arrival of Ron Bagley reduced the K.O. Cup holders to six men, but John Louis made up the shortfall with three heat wins and thirteen points. Phil Crump, elevated from reserve, returned his best figures to date, winning a trio of races by a street. Fellow countryman Gary Moore also thrived in the conditions, but Jack Millen had a mixed debut, failing to score in the match, due to a combination of tape breaking and machinery troubles, which he rectified for the second-half, winning his heat and finishing second in the final.

Heat 01	**Crump**/Davey/Noy/**Millen**	80.0	3 - 3	03 - 03
Heat 02	**Moore**/**Meeks**/Noy/Garrod	82.0	**5 - 1**	08 - 04
Heat 03	**Parry**/**Evans**/Spittles/Bailey	79.8	**5 - 1**	13 - 05
Heat 04	**Jackson**/Louis/**Moore**/Garrod	80.2	**4 - 2**	17 - 07
Heat 05	Davey/Bailey/**Evans**/**Parry**	80.8	1 - 5	18 - 12
Heat 06	**Crump**/Louis/**Meeks**/Noy	79.0	**4 - 2**	22 - 14
Heat 07	**Jackson**/**Moore**/Spittles/Bailey	82.2	**5 - 1**	27 - 15
Heat 08	Davey/**Meeks**/Garrod/**Millen** (R)	81.2	2 - 4	29 - 19
Heat 09	Louis/**Evans**/Noy/**Parry**	82.0	2 - 4	31 - 23
Heat 10	**Crump**/**Moore**/Bailey/Spittles	81.8	**5 - 1**	36 - 24
Heat 11	Louis/**Jackson**/Davey/**Meeks**	81.6	2 - 4	38 - 28
Heat 12	Louis/**Crump**/**Evans**/Noy	81.8	3 - 3	41 - 31
Heat 13	**Moore**/**Jackson**/Bailey/Davey	83.0	**5 - 1**	46 - 32

CREWE - Gary Moore 11 (+2), Phil Crump 11, John Jackson 10 (+1), Dai Evans 6 (+2), Barry Meeks 5 (+1), Dave Parry 3, Jack Millen 0.
IPSWICH - John Louis 13, Tony Davey 9, Pete Bailey 4 (+1), Clive Noy 3 (+1), Ted Spittles 2, Rex Garrod 1.

Meeting 17 - Monday, May 31, 1971 - West Midlands Trophy, First Leg
L.M.R. Sports Ground, Earle Street, Crewe
Track Length - 430 yards.

CREWE KINGS.....56 BIRMINGHAM BRUMMIES.....22

The Brummies were blitzed in their debut appearance at Earle Street and failed to provide a single race winner in the first leg of the West Midlands Trophy. Dai Evans and Jack Millen both recorded maximums, with Millen earning special praise for his fast gating. Race of the night was Heat 6, when Phil Crump came from the back to overhaul Ian Wilson on the final bend. Skipper Barry Meeks boosted his average with a paid twelve.

Heat 01	**Crump**/Corradine/**Moore**/Wilkinson (F)	80.2	**4 - 2**	04 - 02
Heat 02	**Millen**/**Meeks**/Harrison/Emms	78.8	**5 - 1**	09 - 03
Heat 03	**Evans**/Wilson/Major/**Parry**	79.8	3 - 3	12 - 06
Heat 04	**Millen**/**Jackson**/Haslinger/Harrison	78.8	**5 - 1**	17 - 07
Heat 05	**Evans**/**Parry**/Wilkinson/Corradine	78.2	**5 - 1**	22 - 08
Heat 06	**Crump**/Wilson/**Moore**/Haslinger	79.0	**4 - 2**	26 - 10
Heat 07	**Millen**/**Meeks**/Wilson/Major (X)	78.2	**5 - 1**	31 - 11
Heat 08	**Meeks**/**Moore**/Corradine/Wilkinson	78.0	**5 - 1**	36 - 12
Heat 09	**Evans**/Haslinger/**Parry**/Emms	77.6	**4 - 2**	40 - 14
Heat 10	**Moore**/**Crump**/Major/Wilson	78.8	**5 - 1**	45 - 15
Heat 11	**Meeks**/Wilkinson/Corradine/**Jackson** (F)	77.8	3 - 3	48 - 18
Heat 12	**Evans**/Major/Haslinger/**Crump** (R)	79.0	3 - 3	51 - 21
Heat 13	**Millen**/**Jackson**/Wilson/Wilkinson	77.8	**5 - 1**	56 - 22

CREWE - Dai Evans 12, Jack Millen 12, Barry Meeks 10 (+2), Phil Crump 8 (+1), Gary Moore 7 (+1), John Jackson 4 (+2), Dave Parry 3 (+1).
BIRMINGHAM - Ian Wilson 6, Malcolm Corradine 4 (+1), Hec Haslinger 4 (+1), George Major 4 (+1), Archie Wilkinson 3, Chris Harrison 1, Cliff Emms 0.

During the second-half, Crewe youngster Barrie Smitherman fell and broke his leg, but thanks to the quick reactions of brother Gerald, following close behind, a far more serious accident was prevented, when he laid down his machine.

Meeting 18 - Tuesday, June 1, 1971 - West Midlands Trophy, Second Leg
Perry Barr Greyhound Stadium, Regina Drive, Walsall Road, Birmingham
Track Length - 350 yards.

BIRMINGHAM BRUMMIES.....44 CREWE KINGS.....34

(Crewe won on aggregate 90 - 66)

Birmingham won their first meeting of the season on the new bumpy Perry Barr track, but could not prevent the silverware heading back up the M6. Brummies skipper George Major won each time out in an exciting match, where overtaking occurred in ten of the thirteen heats. Dai Evans again top scored for the Kings, with five second places.

Heat 01	Wilkinson/**Moore**/**Crump**/Corradine	70.0	3 - 3	03 - 03
Heat 02	Harrison/Emms/**Meeks**/**Millen**	69.0	5 - 1	08 - 04
Heat 03	Major/**Evans**/**Parry**/Wilson (F)	68.3	3 - 3	11 - 07
Heat 04	Emms/**Jackson**/**Meeks**/Haslinger	69.2	3 - 3	14 - 10
Heat 05	Major/**Crump**/**Moore**/Wilson	68.2	3 - 3	17 - 13
Heat 06	Corradine/Wilkinson/**Jackson**/**Millen**	69.5	5 - 1	22 - 14
Heat 07	Emms/**Evans**/Haslinger/**Parry**	69.6	4 - 2	26 - 16
Heat 08	Corradine/**Moore**/Harrison/**Meeks**	68.3	4 - 2	30 - 18
Heat 09	Major/**Evans**/**Jackson**/Wilson	68.0	3 - 3	33 - 21
Heat 10	**Jackson**/**Evans**/Wilkinson/Corradine	68.0	**1 - 5**	34 - 26
Heat 11	Harrison/**Moore**/**Crump**/Haslinger	69.0	3 - 3	37 - 29
Heat 12	Harrison/**Meeks**/**Parry**/Wilkinson	68.5	3 - 3	40 - 32
Heat 13	Major/**Evans**/Haslinger/**Crump**	68.0	4 - 2	44 - 34

BIRMINGHAM - George Major 12, Chris Harrison 10, Cliff Emms 8 (+1), Archie Wilkinson 6 (+1), Malcolm Corradine 6, Hec Haslinger 2, Ian Wilson 0.
CREWE - Dai Evans 10 (+1), John Jackson 7 (+1), Gary Moore 7 (+1), Phil Crump 4 (+2), Barry Meeks 4 (+1), Dave Parry 2 (+2), Jack Millen 0.

Meeting 19 - Wednesday, June 2, 1971 - British League Division II
Odsal Stadium, Rooley Avenue, Bradford
Track Length - 380 yards.

BRADFORD NORTHERN.....54 CREWE KINGS.....24

This was to be another away meeting that was over long before the end, when the Kings were simply blown aside by the hosts. The nearest a Crewe rider got to actually winning a race was in Heat 2, when Jack Millen made an error on the last bend, gifting the race to Peter Thompson.

Heat 01	Baugh/Bridgett/**Crump**/**Moore** (F)	72.2	5 - 1	05 - 01
Heat 02	Thompson/**Millen**/**Meeks**/Adlington (X)	74.4	3 - 3	08 - 04
Heat 03	Wells/**Evans**/Schofield/**Parry**	71.8	4 - 2	12 - 06
Heat 04	Knapkin/**Millen**/Thompson/**Jackson**	71.2	4 - 2	16 - 08
Heat 05	Schofield/Wells/**Crump**/**Moore** (R)	71.6	5 - 1	21 - 09
Heat 06	Baugh/**Millen**/Bridgett/**Jackson**	72.4	4 - 2	25 - 11
Heat 07	Knapkin/**Evans**/**Parry**/Thompson	71.8	3 - 3	28 - 14
Heat 08	Bridgett/**Meeks**/Adlington/**Moore**	73.8	4 - 2	32 - 16
Heat 09	Wells/Schofield/**Evans**/**Millen** (R)	70.6	5 - 1	37 - 17
Heat 10	Baugh/Bridgett/**Parry**/**Evans**	72.8	5 - 1	42 - 18
Heat 11	Knapkin/**Meeks**/**Crump**/Adlington (F)	71.6	3 - 3	45 - 21
Heat 12	Schofield/**Millen**/Baugh/**Parry**	71.4	4 - 2	49 - 23
Heat 13	Wells/Knapkin/**Evans**/**Crump**	71.2	5 - 1	54 - 24

BRADFORD - Alan Knapkin 11 (+1), Alf Wells 11 (+1), Dave Baugh 10, Dave Schofield 9 (+1), Alan Bridgett 8 (+2), Peter Thompson 4, Robin Adlington 1.
CREWE - Jack Millen 8, Dai Evans 6, Barry Meeks 5 (+1), Phil Crump 3 (+1), Dave Parry 2 (+1), John Jackson 0, Gary Moore 0.

Meeting 20 - Monday, June 7, 1971 - Speedway Express Knock Out Cup, Second Round, First Leg
L.M.R. Sports Ground, Earle Street, Crewe
Track Length - 430 yards.

CREWE KINGS.....54 BERWICK BANDITS.....24

Maurice Littlechild ordered his riders to take a thirty point lead to Shielfield Park and they followed his orders to the letter. Last season's beaten cup finalists were sixteen points down after only four races as the home side reeled off successive maximums. John Jackson was back to his best with four wins, and in Heat 4 he set a new track record which he equalled three races later. Phil Crump dropped his only point to partner Gary Moore in the opening race of the night.

Heat 01	**Moore**/**Crump**/Brady/Robinson	76.4	**5 - 1**	05 - 01
Heat 02	**Millen**/**Meeks**/Campbell/Kelly (F)	77.8	**5 - 1**	10 - 02
Heat 03	**Evans**/**Parry**/Paynter/Meldrum	78.0	**5 - 1**	15 - 03
Heat 04	**Jackson**/**Millen**/Kelly/Wyer (X)	**75.8** (TR)	**5 - 1**	20 - 04
Heat 05	Robinson/**Evans**/Brady/**Parry**	77.6	2 - 4	22 - 08
Heat 06	**Crump**/**Moore**/Kelly/Wyer (R)	77.2	**5 - 1**	27 - 09
Heat 07	**Jackson**/**Millen**/Paynter/Meldrum	**75.8** (=TR)	**5 - 1**	32 - 10
Heat 08	Robinson/**Meeks**/**Moore**/Brady	76.8	3 - 3	35 - 13
Heat 09	Wyer/**Evans**/**Parry**/Campbell	77.2	3 - 3	38 - 16
Heat 10	**Crump**/Paynter/Meldrum/**Moore** (R)	77.2	3 - 3	41 - 19
Heat 11	**Jackson**/Wyer/**Meeks**/Robinson	77.0	**4 - 2**	45 - 21
Heat 12	**Crump**/**Evans**/Meldrum/Wyer	76.4	**5 - 1**	50 - 22
Heat 13	**Jackson**/Robinson/**Parry**/Paynter	76.6	**4 - 2**	54 - 24

CREWE - John Jackson 12, Phil Crump 11 (+1), Dai Evans 9 (+1), Jack Millen 7 (+2), Gary Moore 6 (+2), Barry Meeks 5 (+1), Dave Parry 4 (+2).
BERWICK - Maury Robinson 8, Doug Wyer 5, Alan Paynter 4, Andy Meldrum 2 (+1), Alistair Brady 2, Peter Kelly 2, Bobby Campbell 1.

Meeting 21 - Saturday, June 12, 1971 - Speedway Express Knock Out Cup, Second Round, Second Leg
Shielfield Park, Tweedmouth, Berwick-upon-Tweed
Track Length - 440 yards.

BERWICK BANDITS.....50 CREWE KINGS.....28

(Crewe won on aggregate 82 - 74)

An almighty row broke out delaying the start of the meeting, over Crewe's inclusion of John Jackson, who was not programmed to ride as he had been holidaying in the Isle of Man watching the T.T. Races. However, following a journey by air and road, he arrived at Shielfield Park, but Berwick refused to ride if he was allowed to take the place of Dave Parry, who had not made the journey due to mechanical problems. Referee, E. S. Chapman, was called in, and ruled in favour of the home side, so Crewe were forced to move Don Beecroft up to the No.3 spot in place of Parry and track inexperienced Berwick youngster Mick Beaton at reserve. On a bitterly cold evening, the Bandits just failed to make up their first leg deficit. Doug Wyer was in top form on a recently re-laid racing surface, equalling Geoff Curtis's 1969 track record in Heat 5, which he then beat four races later. He completed his maximum in the final heat, when holding off Phil Crump. Dai Evans and Crump did enough to see the Kings into the quarter-finals, with Evans rounding off the evening by taking the Rider of the Night final.

Heat 01	Brady/**Moore**/**Crump**/Robinson	78.2	3 - 3	03 - 03
Heat 02	Campbell/**Meeks**/Kelly/**Beaton**	78.6	4 - 2	07 - 05
Heat 03	Wyer/**Evans**/**Millen**/Paynter (R)	80.2	3 - 3	10 - 08
Heat 04	Meldrum/Kelly/**Meeks**/**Beecroft**	78.4	5 - 1	15 - 09
Heat 05	Wyer/**Crump**/Paynter/**Moore**	**77.2** (=TR)	4 - 2	19 - 11
Heat 06	Brady/Robinson/**Beaton**/**Beecroft** (R)	78.8	5 - 1	24 - 12
Heat 07	**Evans**/Meldrum/**Millen**/Kelly	78.2	**2 - 4**	26 - 16
Heat 08	Campbell/Brady/**Meeks**/**Moore** (R)	79.2	5 - 1	31 - 17
Heat 09	Wyer/**Moore**/**Crump**/Paynter (R)	**76.8** (TR)	3 - 3	34 - 20
Heat 10	Robinson/**Evans**/Brady/**Millen**	78.2	4 - 2	38 - 22
Heat 11	**Crump**/Meldrum/Campbell/**Moore**	79.4	3 - 3	41 - 25
Heat 12	Robinson/**Evans**/Kelly/**Millen**	78.2	4 - 2	45 - 27
Heat 13	Wyer/Meldrum/**Crump**/**Evans** (R)	79.0	5 - 1	50 - 28

BERWICK - Doug Wyer 12, Alistair Brady 9 (+1), Andy Meldrum 9 (+1), Maury Robinson 8 (+1), Bobby Campbell 7 (+1), Peter Kelly 4 (+1), Alan Paynter 1.
CREWE - Dai Evans 9, Phil Crump 8 (+2), Barry Meeks 4, Gary Moore 4, Jack Millen 2 (+1), Mick Beaton* 1, Don Beecroft 0.

Meeting 22 - Monday, June 14, 1971 - British League Division II
L.M.R. Sports Ground, Earle Street, Crewe
Track Length - 430 yards.

CREWE KINGS.....46 HULL VIKINGS.....32

The track record was broken three times during a remarkable night of speedway at Earle Street. Barry Meeks equalled the week old record in Heat 2, before Dai Evans set a new mark three races later. Phil Crump then matched this in Heat 6, but the fast times were not just reserved for the home riders, as Reg Wilson got in on the act, knocking 0.4 seconds off in the next. Meeks then regained it in Heat 11, which was equalled by Evans in the penultimate heat. In all, John Jackson's previous best was either matched or bettered on ten occasions. The Vikings, already missing George Devonport, then lost former King Colin Tucker, following a nasty collision with Jack Millen in Heat 3, which left the visitors down to five fit riders, which was too much of an handicap, despite the heroic efforts of Wilson and Tony Childs.

Heat 01	**Crump**/Childs/**Moore**/Wasden	76.4	**4 - 2**	04 - 02
Heat 02	**Meeks**/Amundson/Baldock/**Parry** (X)	**75.8** (=TR)	3 - 3	07 - 05
Heat 03	Childs/**Evans**/Amundson/**Millen** (X)	76.8	2 - 4	09 - 09
Heat 04	**Jackson**/Wilson/**Parry**/Baldock	76.0	**4 - 2**	13 - 11
Heat 05	**Evans**/Childs/Wasden/**Millen** (F)	**75.6** (TR)	3 - 3	16 - 14
Heat 06	**Crump**/Wilson/**Moore**/Amundson	**75.6** (=TR)	**4 - 2**	20 - 16
Heat 07	Wilson/**Jackson**/**Parry**/Baldock	**75.2** (TR)	3 - 3	23 - 19
Heat 08	**Meeks**/**Moore**/Wasden/Baldock (R)	75.6	**5 - 1**	28 - 20
Heat 09	Wilson/**Evans**/**Millen**/Childs	75.4	3 - 3	31 - 23
Heat 10	Wilson/**Moore**/Amundson/**Crump** (R)	75.6	2 - 4	33 - 27

Heat 11	**Meeks/Jackson**/Childs/Wasden	**75.0** (TR)	**5 - 1**	38 - 28
Heat 12	**Evans/Crump**/Wilson/Baldock	**75.0** (=TR)	**5 - 1**	43 - 29
Heat 13	Childs/**Jackson/Millen**/Wasden	75.8	3 - 3	46 - 32

CREWE - Dai Evans 10, John Jackson 9 (+1), Barry Meeks 9, Phil Crump 8 (+1), Gary Moore 6 (+1), Jack Millen 2 (+2), Dave Parry 2 (+1).
HULL - Reg Wilson 14, Tony Childs 11, Robin Amundson 4, Dennis Wasden 2 (+1), Pete Baldock 1 (+1), Colin Tucker 0, *George Devonport (R/R)*.

Meeting 23 - Thursday, June 17, 1971 - British League Division II
Brooklands Sports Stadium, Brooklands Road, Mawneys, Romford
Track Length - 375 yards.

ROMFORD BOMBERS.....48 CREWE KINGS.....30

A good all-round Romford performance, where a paid six was the lowest score, was enough to see off Crewe. Phil Crump and John Jackson did their utmost to salvage something from the match, but their efforts came too late to have any effect. Heat 8 saw Bomber Terry Shearer shown the chequered flag after completing only three laps. He then broke the tapes in the re-run and was replaced by Charlie Benham, who team rode Mike Sampson to a 5-1, much to the annoyance of Maurice Littlechild, who was unimpressed with the latter's erratic riding style. Luckless Dave Parry suffered more injury heartache, breaking a collar-bone in an awkward fall during Heat 9, a race that John Jackson was almost forced out of too, when a stray helmet colour got caught up in his handlebars!

Heat 01	Saunders/**Crump/Moore**/Sampson (F)	71.8	3 - 3	03 - 03
Heat 02	Shearer/Benham/**Meeks/Parry**	71.2	5 - 1	08 - 04
Heat 03	Foote/Sanders/**Millen/Evans** (F)	72.0	5 - 1	13 - 05
Heat 04	**Jackson**/Benham/Vernam/**Meeks**	70.8	3 - 3	16 - 08
Heat 05	**Crump**/Sanders/**Moore**/Foote (X)	71.0	**2 - 4**	18 - 12
Heat 06	Sampson/Saunders/**Parry/Jackson** (F)	73.4	5 - 1	23 - 13
Heat 07	Vernam/**Evans**/Benham/**Millen**	72.0	4 - 2	27 - 15
Heat 08	Benham/Sampson/**Crump/Moore**	71.8	5 - 1	32 - 16
Heat 09	Sanders/Foote/**Jackson/Parry** (X)	71.8	5 - 1	37 - 17
Heat 10	**Jackson**/Saunders/Sampson/**Evans** (R)	70.6	3 - 3	40 - 20
Heat 11	Shearer/**Crump**/Vernam/**Moore**	71.6	4 - 2	44 - 22
Heat 12	**Jackson**/Saunders/Sanders/**Millen**	71.2	3 - 3	47 - 25
Heat 13	**Crump/Evans**/Vernam/Foote (R)	71.2	**1 - 5**	48 - 30

ROMFORD - Hugh Saunders 9 (+1), Colin Sanders 8 (+2), Charlie Benham 8 (+1), Mike Sampson 6 (+2), Mike Vernam 6 (+1), Terry Shearer 6, Brian Foote 5 (+1).
CREWE - Phil Crump 11, John Jackson 10, Dai Evans 4 (+1), Gary Moore 2 (+1), Barry Meeks 1, Jack Millen 1, Dave Parry 1.

Meeting 24 - Sunday, June 20, 1971 - Lincs/Cheshire Trophy, First Leg
Boston Sports Stadium, New Hammond Beck Road, Boston
Track Length - 380 yards.

BOSTON BARRACUDAS.....39½ CREWE KINGS.....38½

Crewe came within a whisker of taking a lead back to Earle Street, but were denied victory in the final heat when Phil Crump, certain of third place aboard Gary Moore's bike (his own being damaged earlier), was forced to pull up due to a loose carburettor, allowing Jim Ryman through to take the all-important point. The opening race of the night saw Moore and Vic Cross dead-heat for second place, but it was left to ex-King's Lynn rider Graham Edmonds, guesting for the injured Dave Parry, to provide Crewe's top score.

Heat 01	Price/Cross & **Moore/Crump** (F)	67.2	4½ -1½	04½ - 01½
Heat 02	**Meeks/Edmonds**/Featherstone/Osborne	67.8	**1 - 5**	05½ - 06½
Heat 03	**Evans**/Bywater/Ryman/**Millen**	67.6	3 - 3	08½ - 09½
Heat 04	**Jackson**/Glover/Featherstone/**Meeks**	66.8	3 - 3	11½ - 12½
Heat 05	Bywater/**Crump**/Featherstone/**Edmonds**	66.8	4 - 2	15½ - 14½
Heat 06	Price/**Edmonds/Jackson**/Cross	68.0	3 - 3	18½ - 17½

Heat 07 .... **Millen**/Featherstone/Glover/**Evans** (F)	68.6	3 - 3	21½ - 20½
Heat 08 .... **Edmonds**/**Meeks**/Cross/Osborne	68.0	**1 - 5**	22½ - 25½
Heat 09 .... Bywater/Ryman/**Edmonds**/**Jackson**	67.2	5 - 1	27½ - 26½
Heat 10 .... Price/**Millen**/**Evans**/Featherstone	67.8	3 - 3	30½ - 29½
Heat 11 .... Glover/**Meeks**/Osborne/**Crump** (R)	67.8	4 - 2	34½ - 31½
Heat 12 .... **Jackson**/**Millen**/Price/Bywater	68.0	**1 - 5**	35½ - 36½
Heat 13 .... Glover/**Evans**/Ryman/**Crump** (R)	66.2	4 - 2	39½ - 38½

BOSTON - Arthur Price 10, Carl Glover 9 (+1), Jack Bywater 8, Tony Featherstone 5 (+1), Jim Ryman 4 (+2), Vic Cross 2½, Russell Osborne 1.
CREWE - Graham Edmonds* 8 (+1), John Jackson 7 (+1), Barry Meeks 7 (+1), Jack Millen 7 (+1), Dai Evans 6 (+1), Phil Crump 2, Gary Moore 1½.

Crewe's injury woes continued when Don Beecroft fell and broke a wrist in a second-half spin. In the next round of the K.O. Cup, the Kings were drawn against Bradford, with the first leg scheduled for Earle Street.

Meeting 25 - Monday, June 21, 1971 - Division II International, Fourth Test
L.M.R. Sports Ground, Earle Street, Crewe
Track Length - 430 yards.

YOUNG ENGLAND.....60 YOUNG SWEDEN.....48

Young England, captained for the night by John Jackson, defeated their Swedish counterparts to win the series with a match to spare. The sparse crowd were treated to some exciting racing on a track made tricky by early evening rain. Alan Wilkinson and John Louis were the main scorers for the young Lions, with Crewe's Barry Meeks contributing ten points. Tommy Jansson top scored for the tourists, as he had done in the previous two tests.

Heat 01 .... Louis/Bergqvist/Jackson/Claesson	76.8	4 - 2	04 - 02
Heat 02 .... Jansson/Wilkinson/Knapkin/Karlsson	78.8	3 - 3	07 - 05
Heat 03 .... Meeks/Sjösten/Andersson/Bouchard (F)	78.4	3 - 3	10 - 08
Heat 04 .... Wilkinson/Knapkin/Bergqvist/Salomonsson	77.0	5 - 1	15 - 09
Heat 05 .... Karlsson/Jansson/Meeks/Bouchard	80.4	1 - 5	16 - 14
Heat 06 .... Louis/Jackson/Andersson/Sjösten	80.0	5 - 1	21 - 15
Heat 07 .... Salomonsson/Bergqvist/Tyrer/Meeks (F)	79.8	1 - 5	22 - 20
Heat 08 .... Louis/Jansson/Karlsson/Jackson (R)	79.2	3 - 3	25 - 23
Heat 09 .... Wilkinson/Knapkin/Sjösten/Andersson	77.4	5 - 1	30 - 24
Heat 10 .... Jackson/Salomonsson/Bergqvist/Louis (X)	79.6	3 - 3	33 - 27
Heat 11 .... Wilkinson/Jansson/Karlsson/Knapkin	78.0	3 - 3	36 - 30
Heat 12 .... Sjösten/Meeks/Andersson/Bouchard	80.0	2 - 4	38 - 34
Heat 13 .... Wilkinson/Knapkin/Bergqvist/Salomonsson	83.0	5 - 1	43 - 35
Heat 14 .... Meeks/Tyrer/Jansson/Karlsson	79.2	5 - 1	48 - 36
Heat 15 .... Louis/Sjösten/Andersson/Price	82.2	3 - 3	51 - 39
Heat 16 .... Bergqvist/Tyrer/Meeks/Salomonsson	80.4	3 - 3	54 - 42
Heat 17 .... Louis/Jansson/Karlsson/Jackson	80.8	3 - 3	57 - 45
Heat 18 .... Wilkinson/Sjösten/Andersson/Knapkin	80.0	3 - 3	60 - 48

YOUNG ENGLAND - Alan Wilkinson 17, John Louis 15, Barry Meeks 10 (+1), Alan Knapkin 7 (+4), John Jackson 6 (+1), Paul Tyrer (Reserve) 5 (+1), Geoff Bouchard 0, Arthur Price (Reserve) 0. Team Manager: Ken Adams. *(Price replaced Dave Parry.)*
YOUNG SWEDEN - Tommy Jansson 12 (+1), Tommy Bergqvist 10 (+2), Christer Sjösten 10, Hakan Karlsson 6 (+3), Lars-Åke Andersson 5 (+3), Stefan Salomonsson (Reserve) 5, Karl-Erik Claesson 0. Team Manager: Christer Bergström. *(Sjösten replaced Terje Henriksson.)*

Meeting 26 - Monday, June 28, 1971 - Lincs/Cheshire Trophy, Second Leg
L.M.R. Sports Ground, Earle Street, Crewe
Track Length - 430 yards.

CREWE KINGS.....49 BOSTON BARRACUDAS.....29

(Crewe won on aggregate 87½ - 68½)

The scoreline in the return leg of the Lincs/Cheshire Trophy somewhat flattered the home side and it wasn't until after Heat 12 that they secured the silverware. Phil Crump, continuing the impressive start to his debut season, registered a first full maximum, and twice came within a whisker of the track record. Former Crayford and Nelson rider Stuart Riley replaced Dave Parry, but failed to score in either of his two rides.

Heat 01	**Crump**/Price/**Moore**/Bywater	76.0	**4 - 2**	04 - 02
Heat 02	**Meeks**/Cross/Featherstone/**Riley**	77.2	3 - 3	07 - 05
Heat 03	**Millen**/Osborne/**Evans**/Ryman	76.6	**4 - 2**	11 - 07
Heat 04	**Jackson**/Glover/Featherstone/**Riley**	75.8	3 - 3	14 - 10
Heat 05	Price/**Evans**/**Millen**/Bywater	75.4	3 - 3	17 - 13
Heat 06	**Crump**/Glover/**Moore**/Cross	75.4	**4 - 2**	21 - 15
Heat 07	**Meeks**/Ryman/**Jackson**/Osborne	75.6	**4 - 2**	25 - 17
Heat 08	Price/**Meeks**/Featherstone/**Moore**	76.0	2 - 4	27 - 21
Heat 09	**Evans**/Glover/**Millen**/Featherstone	76.2	**4 - 2**	31 - 23
Heat 10	**Crump**/Glover/**Moore**/Ryman (R)	75.4	**4 - 2**	35 - 25
Heat 11	**Meeks**/Price/**Jackson**/Cross	75.6	**4 - 2**	39 - 27
Heat 12	**Crump**/**Evans**/Ryman/Glover (R)	75.8	**5 - 1**	44 - 28
Heat 13	**Jackson**/**Millen**/Price/Osborne	75.8	**5 - 1**	49 - 29

CREWE - Phil Crump 12, Barry Meeks 11, Dai Evans 8 (+1), John Jackson 8, Jack Millen 7 (+2), Gary Moore 3, Stuart Riley 0.
BOSTON - Arthur Price 11, Carl Glover 8, Tony Featherstone 3 (+2), Jim Ryman 3, Vic Cross 2, Russell Osborne 2, Jack Bywater 0.

Phil Crump made his First Division debut at Belle Vue on July 3. Riding for visitors Newport, he scored two third places from four outings. The following afternoon, Rayleigh blew the Division II title chase wide open with a 40-36 win at Eastbourne.

Meeting 27 - Monday, July 5, 1971 - Four Team Tournament, First Leg
L.M.R. Sports Ground, Earle Street, Crewe
Track Length - 430 yards.

CREWE KINGS.....42 BOSTON BARRACUDAS.....23
ROCHDALE HORNETS.....16 BRADFORD NORTHERN.....14

The track record of 75.0 seconds was bettered in each of the first ten heats on a memorable night at the South Cheshire circuit. The opening race saw John Jackson lower the mark to 74.2, which was beaten by Peter Collins four heats later. Phil Crump equalled this in the seventh, with Collins repeating it in Heat 10! Crewe strolled to victory, scoring 42 out of a possible 48 points, winning thirteen heats - with Collins taking the other three for Rochdale. Gary Moore created his own bit of history by riding for different teams in successive races. He went out for Boston in Heat 15 as a replacement for Carl Glover, who had pulled out after a mishap in the pits, then rode for the Kings in the final heat after Barry Meeks was excluded for breaking the tapes. Crump was again in magical form, securing his second home maximum in a row.

			C	Bo	R	Br
Heat 01	**Jackson**/Glover/Schofield/Tyrer	**74.2** (TR)	3	2	0	1
Heat 02	**Evans**/Featherstone/Drury/Adlington	74.8	3	2	1	0
Heat 03	**Crump**/Price/Collins/Baugh	74.4	3	2	1	0
Heat 04	**Meeks**/Knapkin/Ryman/Moss	74.8	3	1	0	2
Heat 05	Collins/**Jackson**/Adlington/Ryman	**74.0** (TR)	2	0	3	1
Heat 06	**Evans**/Price/Moss/Schofield (R)	74.6	3	2	1	0
Heat 07	**Crump**/Knapkin/Tyrer/Featherstone	**74.0** (=TR)	3	0	1	2
Heat 08	**Meeks**/Glover/Baugh/Drury	74.6	3	2	0	1
Heat 09	**Jackson**/Featherstone/Baugh/Gardner	74.4	3	2	0	1
Heat 10	Collins/Knapkin/Glover/**Evans**	**74.0** (=TR)	0	1	3	2
Heat 11	**Crump**/Drury/Schofield (R)/Ryman (R)	75.4	3	0	2	0
Heat 12	**Meeks**/Adlington/Price/Tyrer	75.4	3	1	0	2
Heat 13	**Evans**/Ryman/Baugh/Tyrer (X)	75.6	3	2	0	1
Heat 14	**Jackson**/Price/Drury/Knapkin (R)	74.8	3	2	1	0
Heat 15	**Crump**/Moore/Adlington/Moss	74.2	3	2	0	1
Heat 16	Collins/Featherstone/**Moore**/Dewhurst (R)	75.0	1	2	3	0

CREWE - Phil Crump 12, John Jackson 11, Dai Evans 9, Barry Meeks 9, Gary Moore (Reserve) 1.
BOSTON - Arthur Price 7, Tony Featherstone 6, Carl Glover 5, Jim Ryman 3, Gary Moore* (Reserve) 2.
ROCHDALE - Peter Collins 10, Graham Drury 4, Ken Moss 1, Paul Tyrer 1, Robbie Gardner (Reserve) 0.
BRADFORD - Alan Knapkin 6, Robin Adlington 4, Dave Baugh 3, Dave Schofield 1, Stan Dewhurst (Reserve) 0.

Meeting 28 - Wednesday, July 7, 1971 - Four Team Tournament, Second Leg
Odsal Stadium, Rooley Avenue, Bradford
Track Length - 380 yards.

CREWE KINGS.....31 BRADFORD NORTHERN.....30
BOSTON BARRACUDAS.....17 ROCHDALE HORNETS.....17

(Scores after two legs – Crewe 73, Bradford 44, Boston 40, Rochdale 33)

A superb effort from the Crewe quartet saw them pull off a shock victory, which made them firm favourites to win the competition. Dai Evans demonstrated his liking for the big banked Odsal track, winning the last three of his four outings.

		C	Br	Bo	R
Heat 01..... **Millen**/Ryman/Gardner/Wells (F)	72.8	3	0	2	1
Heat 02..... Schofield/Price/**Evans**/Collins	72.2	1	3	2	0
Heat 03..... **Crump**/Knapkin/Drury/Bywater	71.2	3	2	0	1
Heat 04..... Tyrer/**Meeks**/Baugh/Glover	72.0	2	1	0	3
Heat 05..... **Crump**/Wells/Tyrer/Price	71.0	3	2	0	1
Heat 06..... Drury/**Meeks**/Ryman/Schofield	72.8	2	0	1	3
Heat 07..... Collins/Knapkin/Glover/**Millen**	71.2	0	2	1	3
Heat 08..... **Evans**/Baugh/Gardner/Bywater	72.2	3	2	0	1
Heat 09..... Wells/**Meeks**/Bywater/Collins	72.4	2	3	1	0
Heat 10..... Glover/**Crump**/Adlington/Gardner	73.0	2	1	3	0
Heat 11..... **Evans**/Knapkin/Ryman/Tyrer	72.4	3	2	1	0
Heat 12..... **Millen**/Baugh/Price/Drury	71.8	3	2	1	0
Heat 13..... Adlington/Moore/**Millen** (F)/Tyrer (F)	72.2	0	3	2	0
Heat 14..... **Evans**/Wells/Drury/Glover	71.8	3	2	0	1
Heat 15..... Adlington/Price/**Meeks**/Gardner	70.6	1	3	2	0
Heat 16..... Collins/Baugh/Ryman/**Crump**	71.2	0	2	1	3

CREWE - Dai Evans 10, Phil Crump 8, Barry Meeks 7, Jack Millen 6.
BRADFORD - Robin Adlington (Reserve) 7, Dave Baugh 7, Alf Wells 7, Alan Knapkin 6, Dave Schofield 3.
BOSTON - Arthur Price 5, Jim Ryman 5, Carl Glover 4, Gary Moore* (Reserve) 2, Jack Bywater 1.
ROCHDALE - Peter Collins 6, Graham Drury 5, Paul Tyrer 4, Robbie Gardner 2.

Meeting 29 - Friday, July 9, 1971 - Four Team Tournament, Third Leg
Athletic Grounds, Milnrow Road, Rochdale
Track Length - 427 yards.

ROCHDALE HORNETS.....30 BOSTON BARRACUDAS.....20
CREWE KINGS.....19 BRADFORD NORTHERN.....15

(Scores after three legs - Crewe 92, Rochdale 63, Boston 60, Bradford 59)

The third leg of the tournament came to a dramatic halt after the conclusion of Heat 14, when it was discovered that no track doctor was present. This only became apparent after Bradford's Alf Wells fell heavily and was stretchered off with head injuries. As there were only two races remaining, the result was allowed to stand. Crewe recovered well after failing to score in four of the first five heats.

		R	Bo	C	Br
Heat 01..... **Crump**/Glover/Tyrer/Dewhurst	78.0	1	2	3	0
Heat 02..... Wells/Price/Drury/**Evans**	78.6	1	2	0	3
Heat 03..... Collins/Ryman/Knapkin/**Millen**	77.6	3	2	0	1
Heat 04..... Moss/Adlington/Cross/**Jackson**	79.2	3	1	0	2
Heat 05..... Tyrer/Price/Knapkin/**Jackson**	80.0	3	2	0	1
Heat 06..... **Millen**/Drury/Glover/Adlington	80.2	2	1	3	0
Heat 07..... Collins/**Evans**/Ryman/Dewhurst	78.0	3	1	2	0
Heat 08..... **Crump**/Wells/Moss/Cross	78.2	1	0	3	2
Heat 09..... Tyrer/**Evans**/Adlington/Cross	79.6	3	0	2	1
Heat 10..... Knapkin/Ryman/Drury/**Crump** (R)	79.2	1	2	0	3

Heat 11	Collins/Wells/**Meeks**/Glover (R)	78.2	3	0	1	2
Heat 12	Moss/Price/**Millen**/Dewhurst	80.6	3	2	1	0
Heat 13	**Meeks**/Cross/Drury/Dewhurst	80.4	1	2	3	0
Heat 14	Ryman/Tyrer/**Millen**/Wells (X)	79.4	2	3	1	0

(Abandoned after fourteen heats due to the absence of the track doctor.)

ROCHDALE - Peter Collins 9, Paul Tyrer 9, Ken Moss 7, Graham Drury 5.
BOSTON - Jim Ryman 8, Arthur Price 6, Vic Cross 3, Carl Glover 3.
CREWE - Phil Crump 6, Jack Millen 5, Dai Evans 4, Barry Meeks (Reserve) 4, John Jackson 0.
BRADFORD - Alf Wells 7, Alan Knapkin 5, Robin Adlington 3, Stan Dewhurst 0.

Meeting 30 - Monday, July 12, 1971 - British League Division II
L.M.R. Sports Ground, Earle Street, Crewe
Track Length - 430 yards.

CREWE KINGS.....54 EASTBOURNE EAGLES.....24

Championship favourites Eastbourne endured their biggest hiding of the campaign, as Crewe's fortunes showed signs of improvement. John Jackson scored a superb maximum, but the star of the night was Phil Crump, who twice broke the track record with some cavalier riding. In Heat 10 he lowered it to 73.8, then went out two heats later, clipping a full second off it. Rapidly becoming one of the league's hottest properties, Crump recorded a paid maximum to add to his recent impressive scores. Gary Moore, Dai Evans and Jack Millen all returned good figures in a match where the poor Eagles failed to register a single heat advantage.

Heat 01	**Moore**/**Crump**/Ballard/Woolford	77.6	**5 - 1**	05 - 01
Heat 02	**Millen**/Johns/Trott/**Riley**	77.2	3 - 3	08 - 04
Heat 03	**Evans**/McNeil/D.Kennett/**Meeks** (R)	78.8	3 - 3	11 - 07
Heat 04	**Jackson**/Trott/G.Kennett/**Riley**	75.0	3 - 3	14 - 10
Heat 05	Woolford/**Meeks**/**Evans**/Ballard	77.2	3 - 3	17 - 13
Heat 06	**Crump**/**Moore**/G.Kennett/Johns	74.6	**5 - 1**	22 - 14
Heat 07	**Jackson**/McNeil/**Riley**/D.Kennett (R)	75.4	**4 - 2**	26 - 16
Heat 08	**Moore**/**Millen**/Woolford/Trott	76.8	**5 - 1**	31 - 17
Heat 09	**Evans**/G.Kennett/**Meeks**/Johns	76.4	**4 - 2**	35 - 19
Heat 10	**Crump**/McNeil/**Moore**/G.Kennett	**73.8** (TR)	**4 - 2**	39 - 21
Heat 11	**Jackson**/**Millen**/Ballard/Woolford	74.8	**5 - 1**	44 - 22
Heat 12	**Crump**/**Meeks**/G.Kennett/McNeil	**72.8** (TR)	**5 - 1**	49 - 23
Heat 13	**Jackson**/**Evans**/Ballard/D.Kennett	75.2	**5 - 1**	54 - 24

CREWE - John Jackson 12, Phil Crump 11 (+1), Dai Evans 9 (+2), Gary Moore 9 (+1), Jack Millen 7 (+2), Barry Meeks 5 (+1), Stuart Riley 1.
EASTBOURNE - Bobby McNeil 6, Gordon Kennett 5 (+1), Mac Woolford 4, Reg Trott 3 (+1), Malcolm Ballard 3, Roger Johns 2, Dave Kennett 1 (+1).

On July 14, John Jackson took part in the Junior Championship of the British Isles at Swindon. He started well winning Heat 1, but scored only two points more, to finish equal 11th with Peter Collins. The event was won by King's Lynn's Ian Turner who won each of his five races. On the same night, Bradford went to the top of the league following their 46-32 home win over Romford, and Eastbourne's 37-41 reversal at Hull.

Meeting 31 - Friday, July 16, 1971 - British League Division II
Derwent Park Stadium, Workington
Track Length - 398 yards.

WORKINGTON COMETS.....53 CREWE KINGS.....25

Phil Crump and Jack Millen took the chequered flag in the first two heats, but Mackay, Owen and Sansom powered the Comets to an impressive victory. John Jackson, who had previously performed well at Derwent Park, was blighted with mechanical problems throughout the meeting, managing just three (paid four) points.

Heat 01	**Crump**/Owen/Amundson/**Moore**	75.8	3 - 3	03 - 03
Heat 02	**Millen**/Vale/Blythe/**Riley**	78.6	3 - 3	06 - 06

Heat 03	Kumeta/Sansom/**Evans**/**Meeks**	77.8	5 - 1	11 - 07
Heat 04	Mackay/Vale/**Millen**/**Jackson** (R)	77.8	5 - 1	16 - 08
Heat 05	Sansom/Kumeta/**Crump**/**Moore**	75.6	5 - 1	21 - 09
Heat 06	Owen/Amundson/**Riley**/**Jackson**	77.6	5 - 1	26 - 10
Heat 07	Mackay/**Evans**/Vale/**Meeks**	76.4	4 - 2	30 - 12
Heat 08	**Crump**/**Millen**/Amundson/Blythe	76.4	**1 - 5**	31 - 17
Heat 09	Sansom/**Evans**/**Jackson**/Kumeta	77.6	3 - 3	34 - 20
Heat 10	Owen/Amundson/**Meeks**/**Evans**	79.0	5 - 1	39 - 21
Heat 11	Mackay/Blythe/**Millen**/**Crump**	77.4	5 - 1	44 - 22
Heat 12	Owen/**Jackson**/Kumeta/**Evans**	77.6	4 - 2	48 - 24
Heat 13	Mackay/Sansom/**Crump**/**Meeks**	77.8	5 - 1	53 - 25

WORKINGTON - Malcolm Mackay 12, Taffy Owen 11, Lou Sansom 10 (+2), Kym Amundson 6 (+3), Dave Kumeta 6 (+1), Ken Vale 5 (+1), Chris Blythe 3 (+2).
CREWE - Phil Crump 8, Jack Millen 7 (+1), Dai Evans 5, John Jackson 3 (+1), Barry Meeks 1, Stuart Riley 1, Gary Moore 0.

Meeting 32 - Monday, July 19, 1971 - Speedway Express Knock Out Cup, Third Round, First Leg
L.M.R. Sports Ground, Earle Street, Crewe
Track Length - 430 yards.

CREWE KINGS.....47 BRADFORD NORTHERN.....31

The Kings won this first leg against the league leaders, but the overall tie remained evenly poised. Alan Knapkin scored over half of Bradford's total, and dropped his only points to Phil Crump. Dave Parry, returning from a broken collar-bone, won his first race, heading home partner Gary Moore in Heat 2. John Jackson was withdrawn from his final two rides due to a leg infection.

Heat 01	**Crump**/Knapkin/**Millen**/Murray	75.2	**4 - 2**	04 - 02
Heat 02	**Parry**/**Moore**/Sheldrick/Dewhurst	77.6	**5 - 1**	09 - 03
Heat 03	Knapkin/**Evans**/**Meeks**/Adlington	74.2	3 - 3	12 - 06
Heat 04	**Jackson**/Baugh/**Parry**/Dewhurst	75.4	**4 - 2**	16 - 08
Heat 05	Knapkin/**Evans**/Murray/**Meeks**	00.0	2 - 4	18 - 12
Heat 06	**Crump**/**Millen**/Baugh/Sheldrick (R)	73.4	**5 - 1**	23 - 13
Heat 07	Knapkin/**Jackson**/Adlington/**Parry**	74.2	2 - 4	25 - 17
Heat 08	**Millen**/**Moore**/Murray/Adlington	76.2	**5 - 1**	30 - 18
Heat 09	**Evans**/**Meeks**/Baugh/Sheldrick	76.0	**5 - 1**	35 - 19
Heat 10	**Crump**/Knapkin/**Millen**/Dewhurst	73.2	**4 - 2**	39 - 21
Heat 11	Adlington/**Moore**/**Parry**/Murray	76.2	3 - 3	42 - 24
Heat 12	Knapkin/**Crump**/Baugh/**Meeks**	74.4	2 - 4	44 - 28
Heat 13	**Evans**/Adlington/Murray/**Moore**	76.4	3 - 3	47 - 31

CREWE - Phil Crump 11, Dai Evans 10, Jack Millen 7 (+1), Gary Moore 6 (+2), Dave Parry 5 (+1), John Jackson 5, Barry Meeks 3 (+2).
BRADFORD - Alan Knapkin 16, Robin Adlington 6, Dave Baugh 5, Brian Murray 3 (+1), Sid Sheldrick 1, Stan Dewhurst 0, *Alf Wells (R/R)*.

Meeting 33 - Wednesday, July 21, 1971 - British League Division II
Boulevard Stadium, Airlie Street, Kingston-upon-Hull
Track Length - 415 yards.

HULL VIKINGS.....47 CREWE KINGS.....31

The Vikings, with Colin Tucker and out-of-retirement Ian Bottomley in their starting line-up, won comfortably enough thanks to Tony Childs' five ride maximum and fourteen points from Reg Wilson. The Kings, 10-2 down after two heats, never recovered, with only Phil Crump looking at ease on the difficult Boulevard circuit. The defeat left Crewe second from the bottom in the league table with only Sunderland below them.

Heat 01	Childs/Tucker/**Crump**/**Moore**	76.6	5 - 1	05 - 01
Heat 02	Bottomley/Wasden/**Millen**/**Parry**	79.2	5 - 1	10 - 02
Heat 03	Wilson/**Meeks**/**Evans**/Amundson (X)	79.8	3 - 3	13 - 05
Heat 04	Childs/**Jackson**/Wasden/**Millen**	77.0	4 - 2	17 - 07
Heat 05	**Crump**/Wilson/Bottomley/**Moore**	77.4	3 - 3	20 - 10

Heat 06	Childs/Tucker/**Jackson/Parry**	78.8	5 - 1	25 - 11
Heat 07	Wilson/**Evans**/Wasden/**Meeks**	77.8	4 - 2	29 - 13
Heat 08	Tucker/**Moore/Millen**/Bottomley	82.2	3 - 3	32 - 16
Heat 09	Wilson/**Jackson/Crump**/Wasden	77.2	3 - 3	35 - 19
Heat 10	Childs/**Evans**/Tucker/**Meeks**	77.8	4 - 2	39 - 21
Heat 11	**Crump/Moore**/Tucker/Bottomley (F)	78.0	**1 - 5**	40 - 26
Heat 12	Childs/**Evans**/Wasden/**Jackson**	77.4	4 - 2	44 - 28
Heat 13	Wilson/**Crump/Evans**/Bottomley	76.8	3 - 3	47 - 31

HULL - Tony Childs 15, Reg Wilson 14, Colin Tucker 9 (+2), Dennis Wasden 5 (+1), Ian Bottomley 4 (+1), Robin Amundson 0, *George Devonport (R/R).*
CREWE - Phil Crump 10 (+1), Dai Evans 8 (+2), John Jackson 5, Gary Moore 4 (+1), Jack Millen 2 (+1), Barry Meeks 2, Dave Parry 0.

Meeting 34 - Sunday, July 25, 1971 - Four Team Tournament, Fourth Leg
Boston Sports Stadium, New Hammond Beck Road, Boston
Track Length - 380 yards.

BOSTON BARRACUDAS.....26 CREWE KINGS.....24
BRADFORD NORTHERN.....23 ROCHDALE HORNETS.....22

(Final aggregate scores - Crewe 116, Boston 86, Rochdale 85, Bradford 82)

A fantastic closely fought four way contest was eventually won by Boston, but the tournament honours went to Crewe, taking victory by a massive thirty point margin. Jack Millen and Phil Crump won two heats each.

			Bo	C	Br	R
Heat 01	Price/**Millen**/Adlington/Tyrer	66.8	3	2	1	0
Heat 02	Knapkin/Glover/Wilkinson/**Evans** (X)	68.2	2	0	3	1
Heat 03	**Crump**/Ryman/Moss/Sheldrick	68.2	2	3	0	1
Heat 04	Featherstone/Drury/**Jackson**/Murray	71.2	3	1	0	2
Heat 05	Wilkinson/Price/**Jackson**/Sheldrick	68.8	2	1	0	3
Heat 06	**Crump**/Murray/Tyrer/Glover	68.2	0	3	2	1
Heat 07	Bywater/**Evans**/Adlington/Ryman	68.8	0	2	1	3
Heat 08	Knapkin/Featherstone/**Millen**/Drury	67.8	2	1	3	0
Heat 09	Price/**Evans**/Murray/Drury	66.4	3	2	1	0
Heat 10	**Millen**/Glover/Moss/Sheldrick	67.8	2	3	0	1
Heat 11	Tyrer/Knapkin/Ryman/**Jackson**	67.2	1	0	2	3
Heat 12	Featherstone/Adlington/Wilkinson (X)/**Crump** (X)	00.0	3	0	2	0
Heat 13	Adlington/Drury/Glover/**Jackson**	67.8	1	0	3	2
Heat 14	Knapkin/Price/**Crump**/Moss	66.4	2	1	3	0
Heat 15	**Millen**/Bywater/Murray/Osborne (R)	68.8	0	3	1	2
Heat 16	Tyrer/**Evans**/Sheldrick/Featherstone	67.6	0	2	1	3

BOSTON - Arthur Price 10, Tony Featherstone 8, Carl Glover 5, Jim Ryman 3, Russell Osborne (Reserve) 0.
CREWE - Jack Millen 9, Phil Crump 7, Dai Evans 6, John Jackson 2.
BRADFORD - Alan Knapkin 11, Robin Adlington 7, Brian Murray 4, Sid Sheldrick 1.
ROCHDALE - Paul Tyrer 7, Jack Bywater* (Reserve) 5, Graham Drury 4, Alan Wilkinson 4, Ken Moss 2.

The Long Eaton weather hoodoo struck again for the third time on July 26, when torrential rain washed out the league clash at Earle Street - Crewe's first cancellation of the season.

Meeting 35 - Wednesday, July 28, 1971 - Speedway Express Knock Out Cup, Third Round, Second Leg
Odsal Stadium, Rooley Avenue, Bradford
Track Length - 380 yards.

BRADFORD NORTHERN.....46 CREWE KINGS.....32

(Crewe won on aggregate 79 - 77)

Crewe upset the odds and the large home contingent with a gutsy performance, in one of the most exciting meetings of the season so far at Odsal. After Heat 7, Bradford had pulled back fourteen of their first leg deficit, but the Kings recorded a valuable maximum in the next heat, when skipper Barry Meeks led home Phil Crump. The whole outcome depended on the twenty-sixth and final heat, with Northern requiring a maximum to progress and a 4-2 to tie, but Crump stormed to victory, sparking wild celebrations in the Crewe camp.

Heat 01	Baugh/**Crump**/Adlington/**Moore**	71.6	4 - 2	04 - 02
Heat 02	**Meeks**/Sheldrick/Bridgett/**Parry**	72.8	3 - 3	07 - 05
Heat 03	Knapkin/**Millen**/Murray/**Evans**	71.4	4 - 2	11 - 07
Heat 04	Baugh/**Jackson**/Sheldrick/**Meeks**	72.6	4 - 2	15 - 09
Heat 05	Knapkin/**Crump**/**Moore**/Murray	71.0	3 - 3	18 - 12
Heat 06	Baugh/Adlington/**Jackson**/**Parry**	73.0	5 - 1	23 - 13
Heat 07	Bridgett/Knapkin/**Meeks**/**Evans**	72.2	5 - 1	28 - 14
Heat 08	**Meeks**/**Crump**/Sheldrick/Adlington (F)	72.4	**1 - 5**	29 - 19
Heat 09	Knapkin/**Evans**/Murray/**Jackson**	71.4	4 - 2	33 - 21
Heat 10	Baugh/**Evans**/**Meeks**/Adlington (X)	71.2	3 - 3	36 - 24
Heat 11	Adlington/**Crump**/Bridgett/**Jackson**	71.4	4 - 2	40 - 26
Heat 12	Baugh/**Jackson**/**Evans**/Murray (R)	71.6	3 - 3	43 - 29
Heat 13	**Crump**/Knapkin/Bridgett/**Millen**	71.4	3 - 3	46 - 32

BRADFORD - Dave Baugh 15, Alan Knapkin 13 (+1), Alan Bridgett 6 (+2), Robin Adlington 6 (+1), Sid Sheldrick 4, Brian Murray 2, *Alf Wells (R/R).*
CREWE - Phil Crump 11 (+1), Barry Meeks 8 (+1), Dai Evans 5 (+1), John Jackson 5, Jack Millen 2, Gary Moore 1 (+1), Dave Parry 0.

Meeting 36 - Thursday, July 29, 1971 - British League Division II
Long Eaton Stadium, Station Road, Long Eaton
Track Length - 366 yards.

LONG EATON RANGERS.....50 CREWE KINGS.....27

The Crewe away day blues continued at Station Road, although mechanical failures did add to the severity of the scoreline. Dai Evans oiled a plug, Gary Moore snapped a throttle cable, and John Jackson suffered a magneto fault, as only Phil Crump escaped the gremlins, scoring 12 from his five rides. Stuart Riley, originally pencilled in to replace flu victim Jack Millen, did not arrive until the second-half, and was replaced by Crewe second halfer Charlie Scarbrough, who had turned up for an after meeting spin.

Heat 01	Shakespeare/**Crump**/Champion/**Moore** (R)	71.8	4 - 2	04 - 02
Heat 02	Whittaker/**Parry**/**Meeks**/Jarvis	75.8	3 - 3	07 - 05
Heat 03	Bouchard/Farmer/**Parry**/**Evans** (F)	73.2	5 - 1	12 - 06
Heat 04	Mills/**Jackson**/**Meeks**/Whittaker (F)	74.8	3 - 3	15 - 09
Heat 05	**Crump**/Bouchard/Farmer/**Moore** (R)	72.4	3 - 3	18 - 12
Heat 06	Champion/Shakespeare/**Parry**/**Jackson**	74.8	5 - 1	23 - 13
Heat 07	Mills/Whittaker/**Evans** (R)/**Scarbrough** (F)	72.2	5 - 0	28 - 13
Heat 08	**Crump**/Champion/Jarvis/**Meeks**	74.6	3 - 3	31 - 16
Heat 09	Bouchard/Farmer/**Parry**/**Jackson** (R)	75.6	5 - 1	36 - 17
Heat 10	Shakespeare/Champion/**Scarbrough**/**Evans** (F)	74.4	5 - 1	41 - 18
Heat 11	Mills/**Crump**/**Moore**/Jarvis	72.2	3 - 3	44 - 21
Heat 12	**Evans**/Farmer/**Moore**/Shakespeare (F)	76.6	**2 - 4**	46 - 25
Heat 13	Bouchard/**Crump**/Mills/**Evans**	74.4	4 - 2	50 - 27

LONG EATON - Geoff Bouchard 11, Roger Mills 10, Ian Champion 8 (+1), Malcolm Shakespeare 8 (+1), Gil Farmer 7 (+3), Phil Whittaker 5 (+1), Peter Jarvis 1 (+1).
CREWE - Phil Crump 12, Dave Parry 5, Dai Evans 3, Barry Meeks 2 (+2), Gary Moore 2 (+1), John Jackson 2, Charlie Scarbrough 1.

Meeting 37 - Monday, August 2, 1971 - British League Division II
L.M.R. Sports Ground, Earle Street, Crewe
Track Length - 430 yards.

CREWE KINGS.....50 BOSTON BARRACUDAS.....28

Crewe's heat leader trio were responsible for the rout of title contenders Boston. Dai Evans stole the show with an impeccable maximum and lowered the track record to 72.6, which he then equalled in the final heat. The visitors did make a fist of it during the early stages of the match, until Crewe stepped up a gear to win all but one of the remaining eight heats.

Heat	Riders	Time	Heat score	Match score
Heat 01	Price/**Crump**/Featherstone/**Moore** (R)	73.4	2 - 4	02 - 04
Heat 02	**Meeks**/**Parry**/Bywater/Bales (R)	75.4	**5 - 1**	07 - 05
Heat 03	**Evans**/Ryman/Osborne/**Millen** (R)	74.0	3 - 3	10 - 08
Heat 04	Glover/**Jackson**/Bywater/**Parry**	73.8	2 - 4	12 - 12
Heat 05	**Evans**/Price/Featherstone/**Millen** (R)	73.0	3 - 3	15 - 15
Heat 06	**Crump**/**Moore**/Glover/Bales	73.2	**5 - 1**	20 - 16
Heat 07	**Jackson**/**Meeks**/Osborne/Ryman	73.2	**5 - 1**	25 - 17
Heat 08	Price/**Moore**/Featherstone/**Meeks**	74.6	2 - 4	27 - 21
Heat 09	**Evans**/**Millen**/Bywater/Glover	**72.6** (TR)	**5 - 1**	32 - 22
Heat 10	**Crump**/Ryman/**Moore**/Osborne	72.8	**4 - 2**	36 - 24
Heat 11	**Jackson**/Price/**Meeks**/Featherstone	74.4	**4 - 2**	40 - 26
Heat 12	**Crump**/**Millen**/Glover/Bywater	73.2	**5 - 1**	45 - 27
Heat 13	**Evans**/**Jackson**/Ryman/Price (F)	**72.6** (=TR)	**5 - 1**	50 - 28

CREWE - Dai Evans 12, Phil Crump 11, John Jackson 10 (+1), Barry Meeks 6 (+1), Gary Moore 5 (+1), Jack Millen 4 (+2), Dave Parry 2 (+1).
BOSTON - Arthur Price 10, Carl Glover 5, Jim Ryman 5, Tony Featherstone 3 (+1), Jack Bywater 3, Russell Osborne 2 (+1), Ray Bales 0.

Following the second-half racing, famous high dive artist Stanley Lindbergh performed his party piece of diving off an 80 foot tower (blindfolded and on fire), into a tank of water just six feet deep! Crewe were drawn against arch rivals Rochdale in the semi-finals of the K.O. Cup, with the first leg at Earle Street on August 16.

Meeting 38 - Monday, August 9, 1971 - Division II International, Second Test
L.M.R. Sports Ground, Earle Street, Crewe
Track Length - 430 yards.

YOUNG ENGLAND.....54 YOUNG CZECHOSLOVAKIA.....54

For the second time in three seasons at Earle Street, the talented Young Czechs forced a draw with their English counterparts, after snatching a 5-1 in the last heat. Captain John Louis and Peter Collins were the two main scorers for the Lions, in one of the best ever contests seen at the track. John Jackson scored in all but one of his rides, but reserve Barry Meeks trailed home last in his only outing in Heat 10. The all-action leg trailing style of Pavel Mares saw him finish as top scorer for the tourists with three wins and three second places.

Heat	Riders	Time	Heat score	Match score
Heat 01	Mares/Jackson/Collins/V.Verner	76.2	3 - 3	03 - 03
Heat 02	Glover/Stancl/Wilson/Spinka	76.6	4 - 2	07 - 05
Heat 03	Majstr/Louis/M.Verner/Knapkin	74.8	2 - 4	09 - 09
Heat 04	Mares/Wilson/V.Verner/Glover	75.4	2 - 4	11 - 13
Heat 05	Louis/Knapkin/Stancl/Spinka	76.4	5 - 1	16 - 14
Heat 06	Majstr/Collins/M.Verner/Jackson	74.0	2 - 4	18 - 18
Heat 07	Louis/Mares/Knapkin/Volf	74.8	4 - 2	22 - 20
Heat 08	Collins/Stancl/Jackson/Busta (R)	74.4	4 - 2	26 - 22
Heat 09	Majstr/M.Verner/Wilson/Glover	74.6	1 - 5	27 - 27
Heat 10	Collins/Mares/V.Verner/Meeks	74.4	3 - 3	30 - 30
Heat 11	Spinka/Glover/Wilson/Stancl (R)	76.8	3 - 3	33 - 33
Heat 12	Majstr/Knapkin/Louis/M.Verner	75.0	3 - 3	36 - 36
Heat 13	Mares/Glover/V.Verner/Wilson	75.4	2 - 4	38 - 40
Heat 14	Louis/Stancl/Knapkin/Spinka	74.4	4 - 2	42 - 42
Heat 15	M.Verner/Collins/Jackson/Majstr (R)	75.6	3 - 3	45 - 45
Heat 16	Louis/Mares/Knapkin/V.Verner (R)	75.2	4 - 2	49 - 47
Heat 17	Collins/Stancl/Jackson/Spinka (R)	76.0	4 - 2	53 - 49
Heat 18	M.Verner/Majstr/Wilson/Glover	76.2	1 - 5	54 - 54

YOUNG ENGLAND - John Louis 15 (+1), Peter Collins 14 (+1), Alan Knapkin 7 (+1), Carl Glover 7, Reg Wilson 6 (+1), John Jackson 5 (+1), Barry Meeks (Reserve) 0. Team Manager: Ken Adams. *(Collins replaced Alan Wilkinson.)*
YOUNG CZECHOSLOVAKIA - Pavel Mares 15, Zdenek Majstr 14 (+1), Miroslav Verner 10 (+1), Jiri Stancl 9, Vaclav Verner 3 (+1), Milan Spinka 3, Pavel Busta (Reserve) 0, Jaroslav Volf (Reserve) 0. Team Manager: Jaroslav Bartosek.

Meeting 39 - Friday, August 13, 1971 - British League Division II
East of England Showground, Alwalton, Peterborough
Track Length - 380 yards.

PETERBOROUGH PANTHERS.....47 CREWE KINGS.....30

A saturated track made for slow times, but once again, the result did not truly reflect Crewe's endeavours. John Jackson won his first three races, and looked certain for a fourth, until his engine cut out on the last bend of Heat 9. In a desperate attempt to gain at least a point, he tried pushing his bike to the finish line, but was passed by the other riders. Phil Crump had mixed fortunes. He was excluded after hitting the boards in the first heat, but recovered sufficiently to record wins in each of the final three heats. Former King Pete Saunders contributed nine to the Panthers total.

Heat 01	Davis/**Millen**/**Crump** (X)/Carter (X)	78.2	3 - 2	03 - 02
Heat 02	Clark/Saunders/**Parry**/**Moore**	78.4	5 - 1	08 - 03
Heat 03	Hughes/Stayte/**Meeks**/**Evans** (R)	76.6	5 - 1	13 - 04
Heat 04	**Jackson**/Greer/Saunders/**Parry**	74.8	3 - 3	16 - 07
Heat 05	Hughes/**Crump**/Stayte/**Millen**	74.2	4 - 2	20 - 09
Heat 06	**Jackson**/Davis/**Moore**/Carter	73.4	**2 - 4**	22 - 13
Heat 07	Saunders/Greer/**Meeks**/**Evans** (R)	75.4	5 - 1	27 - 14
Heat 08	**Jackson**/Clark/**Millen**/Davis	74.2	**2 - 4**	29 - 18
Heat 09	Hughes/Stayte/**Parry**/**Jackson** (R)	73.8	5 - 1	34 - 19
Heat 10	Saunders/**Evans**/Davis/**Meeks**	74.8	4 - 2	38 - 21
Heat 11	**Crump**/Greer/Clark/**Evans**	73.4	3 - 3	41 - 24
Heat 12	**Crump**/Clark/Stayte/**Moore**	74.6	3 - 3	44 - 27
Heat 13	**Crump**/Hughes/Greer/**Meeks**	73.8	3 - 3	47 - 30

PETERBOROUGH - Joe Hughes 11, Pete Saunders 9 (+2), Brian Clark 8 (+1), Richard Greer 7 (+2), John Stayte 6 (+3), John Davis 6, Roy Carter 0.
CREWE - Phil Crump 11, John Jackson 9, Jack Millen 3, Dai Evans 2, Barry Meeks 2, Dave Parry 2, Gary Moore 1.

Meeting 40 - Monday, August 16, 1971 - Speedway Express Knock Out Cup, Semi-Final, First Leg
L.M.R. Sports Ground, Earle Street, Crewe
Track Length - 430 yards.

CREWE KINGS.....49 ROCHDALE HORNETS.....29

An excellent thirteen points from Peter Collins could not prevent the Kings from racking up a healthy twenty point first leg advantage. He won on three occasions, but lost out to Jack Millen in Heat 6 and Phil Crump in the penultimate heat. Rochdale boss Dent Oliver complained bitterly that the track had been over-watered and resembled a "skating rink," as both Ian Hindle and Terry Kelly fell during the course of the match.

Heat 01	**Millen**/**Crump**/Moss/Hindle (F)	75.6	**5 - 1**	05 - 01
Heat 02	**Moore**/Kelly/**Parry**/Gardner	78.4	**4 - 2**	09 - 03
Heat 03	**Evans**/**Moore**/Tyrer/Drury (X)	78.6	**5 - 1**	14 - 04
Heat 04	Collins/**Jackson**/Kelly/**Parry**	75.6	2 - 4	16 - 08
Heat 05	**Evans**/**Moore**/Moss/Hindle (F)	77.2	**5 - 1**	21 - 09
Heat 06	**Millen**/Collins/**Crump**/Gardner	74.8	**4 - 2**	25 - 11
Heat 07	**Jackson**/Drury/**Parry**/Kelly (F)	76.2	**4 - 2**	29 - 13
Heat 08	Tyrer/**Millen**/Kelly/**Moore** (F)	77.4	2 - 4	31 - 17
Heat 09	Collins/**Evans**/**Meeks**/Drury	74.8	3 - 3	34 - 20
Heat 10	**Crump**/Tyrer/**Parry**/Drury	76.2	**4 - 2**	38 - 22
Heat 11	Collins/**Jackson**/**Moore**/Kelly	75.4	3 - 3	41 - 25
Heat 12	**Crump**/Collins/Tyrer/**Meeks**	75.2	3 - 3	44 - 28
Heat 13	**Jackson**/**Evans**/Drury/Moss	75.6	**5 - 1**	49 - 29

CREWE - Dai Evans 10 (+1), John Jackson 10, Phil Crump 9 (+1), Gary Moore 8 (+3), Jack Millen 8, Dave Parry 3, Barry Meeks 1 (+1).
ROCHDALE - Peter Collins 13, Paul Tyrer 7 (+1), Terry Kelly 4, Graham Drury 3, Ken Moss 2, Robbie Gardner 0, Ian Hindle 0.

Meeting 41 - Saturday, August 21, 1971 - British League Division II
Rayleigh Weir Stadium, Southend Arterial Road, Rayleigh
Track Length - 365 yards.

RAYLEIGH ROCKETS.....38 CREWE KINGS.....39

If ever Crewe were going to break their away league duck, then it was here at injury ravaged Rayleigh, who were minus Geoff Maloney, Dingle Brown, Alan Jackson, Nigel Rackett and Hugh Saunders. However, despite having to track novices Dave Slatford and Mike Weston, the Rockets led by seven points going into Heat 11. Crewe then introduced John Jackson as a tactical substitute which changed the course of the meeting as he led home Phil Crump in the fastest time of the night. Jackson and Dai Evans then teamed up for a 4-2 to reduce the Rockets lead to just one, with Crump and Barry Meeks replicating the score in the final heat to win the match, thus ending Rayleigh's faint title hopes and Crewe's 24 league match losing run on the road.

Heat	Riders	Time	Score	Total
Heat 01	**Crump**/Young/Slatford (F)/**Millen** (R)	76.8	**2 - 3**	02 - 03
Heat 02	Beech/**Parry**/Stone/**Moore**	75.2	4 - 2	06 - 05
Heat 03	Emmett/**Meeks**/Weston/**Evans** (F)	74.6	4 - 2	10 - 07
Heat 04	Young/**Jackson**/Stone/**Parry**	73.8	4 - 2	14 - 09
Heat 05	**Crump**/Emmett/**Millen**/Weston	73.6	**2 - 4**	16 - 13
Heat 06	**Jackson**/Stone/**Moore**/Slatford	74.2	**2 - 4**	18 - 17
Heat 07	Young/Stone/**Evans**/**Meeks**	75.4	5 - 1	23 - 18
Heat 08	Emmett/**Moore**/**Parry**/Beech (F)	73.4	3 - 3	26 - 21
Heat 09	**Jackson**/Emmett/Stone/**Moore**	70.6	3 - 3	29 - 24
Heat 10	Beech/**Meeks**/Slatford/**Evans** (R)	73.2	4 - 2	33 - 26
Heat 11	**Jackson**/**Crump**/Young/Beech	69.6	**1 - 5**	34 - 31
Heat 12	**Jackson**/Emmett/**Evans**/Slatford	71.0	**2 - 4**	36 - 35
Heat 13	**Crump**/Young/**Meeks**/Beech (F)	72.0	**2 - 4**	38 - 39

RAYLEIGH - Allan Emmett 12, Bob Young 11, Terry Stone 7 (+2), Tiger Beech 6, Dave Slatford 1, Mike Weston 1, *Alan Jackson (R/R)*.
CREWE - John Jackson 14, Phil Crump 11 (+1), Barry Meeks 5, Dave Parry 3 (+1), Gary Moore 3, Dai Evans 2, Jack Millen 1.

Meeting 42 - Monday, August 23, 1971 - British League Division II
L.M.R. Sports Ground, Earle Street, Crewe
Track Length - 430 yards.

CREWE KINGS.....55 CANTERBURY CRUSADERS.....23

Four Crewe riders recorded double figure scores as the Kings enjoyed an easy win over the sorry looking champions. Dai Evans led the way with a maximum, as three of the visitors failed to register a single point. Ted Hubbard was the only Canterbury rider to win a heat, which he achieved in the reserves race. A faulty start gate led to Evans receiving a facial cut when the tapes failed to go up, resulting in two races being started off the green light.

Heat	Riders	Time	Score	Total
Heat 01	**Crump**/**Millen**/Gilbertson/Kennett	76.2	**5 - 1**	05 - 01
Heat 02	Hubbard/**Meeks**/**Parry**/Pratt (R)	78.8	3 - 3	08 - 04
Heat 03	**Evans**/Banks/**Moore**/Tabet (R)	76.8	**4 - 2**	12 - 06
Heat 04	**Jackson**/**Parry**/Hubbard/Smith (R)	75.8	**5 - 1**	17 - 07
Heat 05	**Evans**/Gilbertson/Banks/**Moore**	75.8	3 - 3	20 - 10
Heat 06	**Crump**/**Millen**/Hubbard/Smith	76.2	**5 - 1**	25 - 11
Heat 07	**Jackson**/**Parry**/Banks/Tabet (R)	76.2	**5 - 1**	30 - 12
Heat 08	**Millen**/**Meeks**/Gilbertson/Pratt	76.8	**5 - 1**	35 - 13
Heat 09	**Evans**/Hubbard/Smith/**Moore**	76.2	3 - 3	38 - 16
Heat 10	**Millen**/**Crump**/Banks/Tabet	76.2	**5 - 1**	43 - 17
Heat 11	**Jackson**/Smith/Gilbertson/**Meeks**	76.0	3 - 3	46 - 20
Heat 12	**Crump**/Banks/**Moore**/Smith	77.0	**4 - 2**	50 - 22
Heat 13	**Evans**/**Jackson**/Hubbard/Gilbertson (R)	75.4	**5 - 1**	55 - 23

CREWE - Dai Evans 12, Phil Crump 11 (+1), John Jackson 11 (+1), Jack Millen 10 (+2), Dave Parry 5 (+3), Barry Meeks 4 (+1), Gary Moore 2.
CANTERBURY - Ted Hubbard 8, Graham Banks 7 (+1), Ross Gilbertson 5 (+1), Graeme Smith 3 (+1), Barney Kennett 0, Phil Pratt 0, Bob Tabet 0, *Dave Piddock (R/R)*.

(ABOVE) The Crewe team at Earle Street. (BELOW) Jack Millen takes the inside line against the Birmingham Brummies.

(ABOVE) The teams marching out on parade at Odsal, although Dai Evans, Phil Crump and Gary Moore seem pre-occupied with one of the pretty Bradford cheerleaders!
(BELOW) The one and only Charlie Scarbrough, who made his only two appearances for the club during the season.

(ABOVE) Mayor of Crewe, Councillor Sydney Bayman, presents John Jackson with his commemorative pennant, on the occasion of the Young England v Young Czechs second test match at Earle Street on August 9.

(ABOVE) The tapes go up at the start of Heat 1. From the inside are John Jackson, Vaclav Verner, Peter Collins and Pavel Mares.

(ABOVE) Jack "The Villain" Millen. He would ride just two league matches for Sunderland at the start of the season, before arriving at Earle Street. His no-nonense style and madcap antics would soon establish him as one of the league's biggest draws.

Towards the end of August, John Jackson signed a loan agreement with First Division Oxford, but Crewe would still have first call on his services. Meanwhile sixteen-year-old Mancunian Dave Morton was creating quite a stir in the Kings camp with some impressive second-half rides, and was predicted to make a team appearance before the season's end.

Meeting 43 - Saturday, August 28, 1971 - British League Division II
Shielfield Park, Tweedmouth, Berwick-upon-Tweed
Track Length - 440 yards.

BERWICK BANDITS.....56 CREWE KINGS.....21

Berwick gave Crewe another thumping to maintain their 100% home record, after roaring into a big lead - winning five of the first six heats by the maximum score. Dai Evans and Dave Parry contributed thirteen to the Kings' meagre total, but Phil Crump and John Jackson struggled for points, especially the latter, who was mounted on a troublesome new ESO machine.

Heat	Riders	Time	Score	Total
Heat 01	Brady/Robinson/**Millen/Crump**	79.2	5 - 1	05 - 01
Heat 02	**Parry**/G.Beaton/**Meeks**/J.Beaton	81.4	**2 - 4**	07 - 05
Heat 03	Campbell/Meldrum/**Evans/Moore**	79.4	5 - 1	12 - 06
Heat 04	Wyer/J.Beaton/**Meeks/Jackson**	79.4	5 - 1	17 - 07
Heat 05	Campbell/Meldrum/**Crump/Millen**	79.2	5 - 1	22 - 08
Heat 06	Brady/Robinson/**Parry/Jackson** (R)	80.8	5 - 1	27 - 09
Heat 07	Wyer/**Evans**/J.Beaton/**Moore**	78.6	4 - 2	31 - 11
Heat 08	Brady/G.Beaton/**Millen/Meeks**	80.4	5 - 1	36 - 12
Heat 09	Meldrum/**Parry**/Campbell (F)/**Jackson** (R)	78.8	3 - 2	39 - 14
Heat 10	Robinson/**Evans**/Brady/**Parry**	78.8	4 - 2	43 - 16
Heat 11	Wyer/**Crump**/G.Beaton/**Millen**	78.8	4 - 2	47 - 18
Heat 12	Robinson/**Evans**/Campbell/**Crump**	78.8	4 - 2	51 - 20
Heat 13	Wyer/Meldrum/**Crump/Evans** (R)	78.2	5 - 1	56 - 21

BERWICK - Doug Wyer 12, Maury Robinson 10 (+2), Alistair Brady 10, Andy Meldrum 9 (+3), Bobby Campbell 7, George Beaton 5 (+1), Jim Beaton 3 (+1).
CREWE - Dai Evans 7, Dave Parry 6, Phil Crump 4, Barry Meeks 2, Jack Millen 2, John Jackson 0, Gary Moore 0.

Phil Crump was confirmed as Crewe's representative for the Division II Riders Championship at Hackney on October 2.

Meeting 44 - Monday, August 30, 1971 - British League Division II
L.M.R. Sports Ground, Earle Street, Crewe
Track Length - 430 yards.

CREWE KINGS.....62 BIRMINGHAM BRUMMIES.....16

Twelve maximum scores culminated in Crewe equalling their biggest home league win, set in 1969 against Reading. It was a disastrous first league visit to Earle Street for the West Midlanders, and even their solitary success in Heat 4 had an element of luck about it, when an engine failure caused leader John Jackson to drop out after he had zipped past George Major. All seven Kings won at least one race, with a paid eight the lowest score.

Heat	Riders	Time	Score	Total
Heat 01	**Millen/Crump**/Shearer/Wilkinson	75.0	**5 - 1**	05 - 01
Heat 02	**Moore/Meeks**/Wilson/Haslinger	77.2	**5 - 1**	10 - 02
Heat 03	**Parry/Evans**/Corradine/Harrison	77.4	**5 - 1**	15 - 03
Heat 04	Major/**Moore**/Wilson/**Jackson** (R)	77.8	2 - 4	17 - 07
Heat 05	**Evans/Parry**/Shearer/Wilkinson	77.2	**5 - 1**	22 - 08
Heat 06	**Crump/Millen**/Haslinger/Major (R)	76.8	**5 - 1**	27 - 09
Heat 07	**Jackson/Moore**/Corradine/Harrison	76.0	**5 - 1**	32 - 10
Heat 08	**Millen/Meeks**/Wilson/Wilkinson	78.2	**5 - 1**	37 - 11
Heat 09	**Parry/Evans**/Major/Haslinger	77.0	**5 - 1**	42 - 12
Heat 10	**Millen/Crump**/Corradine/Wilson (R)	77.2	**5 - 1**	47 - 13
Heat 11	**Meeks/Jackson**/Shearer/Wilkinson	77.8	**5 - 1**	52 - 14
Heat 12	**Parry/Crump**/Major/Corradine	77.2	**5 - 1**	57 - 15
Heat 13	**Jackson/Evans**/Shearer/Harrison	77.8	**5 - 1**	62 - 16

CREWE - Jack Millen 11 (+1), Dave Parry 11 (+1), Phil Crump 9 (+3), Dai Evans 9 (+3), John Jackson 8 (+1), Barry Meeks 7 (+2), Gary Moore 7 (+1).
BIRMINGHAM - George Major 5, Terry Shearer 4, Malcolm Corradine 3, Ian Wilson 3, Hec Haslinger 1, Chris Harrison 0, Archie Wilkinson 0.

Meeting 45 - Tuesday, August 31, 1971 - British League Division II
Perry Barr Greyhound Stadium, Regina Drive, Walsall Road, Birmingham
Track Length - 350 yards.

BIRMINGHAM BRUMMIES.....50 CREWE KINGS.....28

In an incredible swing of some 68 points, Birmingham gained handsome revenge just twenty-four hours after their thumping at Crewe. Phil Crump won three of his five rides and was the only away rider to offer any real resistance. He rounded off the meeting by winning the second half Champion of the Evening final.

Heat 01	**Crump**/Wilkinson/Shearer/**Millen**	65.6	3 - 3	03 - 03
Heat 02	**Moore**/Haslinger/**Meeks**/Emms (X)	68.7	**2 - 4**	05 - 07
Heat 03	Harrison/Corradine/**Evans**/**Parry**	66.5	5 - 1	10 - 08
Heat 04	Major/Haslinger/**Meeks**/**Jackson**	66.5	5 - 1	15 - 09
Heat 05	Harrison/**Moore**/Corradine/**Crump** (X)	67.2	4 - 2	19 - 11
Heat 06	Shearer/Wilkinson/**Jackson**/**Moore**	66.1	5 - 1	24 - 12
Heat 07	Major/**Evans**/Haslinger/**Parry**	66.8	4 - 2	28 - 14
Heat 08	Wilkinson/**Millen**/Emms/**Meeks**	66.7	4 - 2	32 - 16
Heat 09	Corradine/Harrison/**Jackson**/**Moore**	67.2	5 - 1	37 - 17
Heat 10	Shearer/Wilkinson/**Millen**/**Evans** (F)	66.6	5 - 1	42 - 18
Heat 11	Major/**Crump**/**Millen**/Emms	65.6	3 - 3	45 - 21
Heat 12	**Crump**/Shearer/**Evans**/Harrison	67.2	**2 - 4**	47 - 25
Heat 13	**Crump**/Major/Corradine/**Jackson**	65.8	3 - 3	50 - 28

BIRMINGHAM - George Major 11, Archie Wilkinson 9 (+2), Terry Shearer 9 (+1), Chris Harrison 8 (+1), Malcolm Corradine 7 (+2), Hec Haslinger 5 (+1), Cliff Emms 1.
CREWE - Phil Crump 11, Gary Moore 5, Jack Millen 4 (+1), Dai Evans 4, John Jackson 2, Barry Meeks 2, Dave Parry 0.

On September 3, the Rochdale versus Crewe K.O. Cup semi-final second leg was postponed due to rain, much to the relief of the Rochdale management, who would have been without Peter Collins and Ian Hindle (both riding for parent club Belle Vue at Glasgow) and Graham Drury, who was out injured. Due to a fixture backlog, the Hornets were hoping to switch the match to Belle Vue's Hyde Road, but Crewe refused the request and attempted to claim the match by default. Holders Ipswich awaited the winners after beating Workington. Meanwhile, Crewe skipper Barry Meeks announced he was standing down as soon as a replacement could be found, so he could concentrate on his garage business in Warmingham. On a brighter note, Phil Crump was chosen to represent Young Australasia in their forthcoming test series with Young England.

Meetings 46 & 47 - Monday, September 6, 1971 - British League Division II (Double Header)
L.M.R. Sports Ground, Earle Street, Crewe
Track Length - 430 yards.

CREWE KINGS.....48 BERWICK BANDITS.....30

Followed by

CREWE KINGS.....61 SUNDERLAND STARS.....17

Crewe collected four valuable league points from their first home double header. Jack Millen suffered a blown engine in his opening ride, but won two heats on borrowed machinery, before standing down for the Sunderland clash. This allowed junior Ray Hassall to make his debut, and the youngster didn't let the side down, scoring in each of his four rides. Phil Crump and Dai Evans were unbeaten by an opponent throughout both matches, with Crump securing his first home league maximum against a sorry looking Stars outfit.

Heat 01	**Crump**/Brady/Robinson/**Millen** (R)	76.6	3 - 3	03 - 03
Heat 02	**Meeks**/**Moore**/J.Beaton/G.Beaton	77.4	**5 - 1**	08 - 04

Heat 03	**Parry**/**Evans**/Meldrum/Campbell	77.2	**5 - 1**	13 - 05
Heat 04	Wyer/**Moore**/G.Beaton/**Jackson** (R)	78.0	2 - 4	15 - 09
Heat 05	**Evans**/Robinson/Brady/**Parry**	77.6	3 - 3	18 - 12
Heat 06	**Crump**/Wyer/**Moore**/J.Beaton	76.0	**4 - 2**	22 - 14
Heat 07	**Jackson**/Campbell/Meldrum/**Moore**	76.6	3 - 3	25 - 17
Heat 08	**Millen**/Brady/**Meeks**/G.Beaton	77.2	**4 - 2**	29 - 19
Heat 09	**Evans**/Wyer/Robinson/**Parry**	76.8	3 - 3	32 - 22
Heat 10	**Millen**/**Crump**/Meldrum/Campbell	75.8	**5 - 1**	37 - 23
Heat 11	Robinson/**Jackson**/**Meeks**/Brady	77.2	3 - 3	40 - 26
Heat 12	**Crump**/Wyer/Meldrum/**Parry**	75.6	3 - 3	43 - 29
Heat 13	**Evans**/**Jackson**/Campbell/J.Beaton	76.0	**5 - 1**	48 - 30

CREWE - Phil Crump 11 (+1), Dai Evans 11 (+1), John Jackson 7 (+1), Jack Millen 6, Barry Meeks 5 (+1), Gary Moore 5 (+1), Dave Parry 3.
BERWICK - Doug Wyer 9, Maury Robinson 7 (+2), Alistair Brady 5 (+1), Andy Meldrum 4 (+2), Bobby Campbell 3, George Beaton 1, Jim Beaton 1.

Heat 01	**Crump**/Dent/**Hassall**/Mackie	75.8	**4 - 2**	04 - 02
Heat 02	**Moore**/**Meeks**/Knock/Richardson	78.0	**5 - 1**	09 - 03
Heat 03	**Evans**/**Parry**/Barclay/Gatenby	78.2	**5 - 1**	14 - 04
Heat 04	**Jackson**/**Moore**/Knock/Wrathall (F)	77.8	**5 - 1**	19 - 05
Heat 05	**Evans**/Mackie/Dent/**Parry** (R)	79.0	3 - 3	22 - 08
Heat 06	**Crump**/**Hassall**/Wrathall/Richardson	76.2	**5 - 1**	27 - 09
Heat 07	**Jackson**/**Moore**/Barclay/Gatenby	77.8	**5 - 1**	32 - 10
Heat 08	**Meeks**/Mackie/**Hassall**/Knock	78.2	**4 - 2**	36 - 12
Heat 09	**Evans**/**Parry**/Mackie/Wrathall (R)	78.6	**5 - 1**	41 - 13
Heat 10	**Crump**/**Hassall**/Barclay/Gatenby	77.0	**5 - 1**	46 - 14
Heat 11	**Jackson**/**Meeks**/Mackie/Dent	77.4	**5 - 1**	51 - 15
Heat 12	**Crump**/**Parry**/Gatenby/Barclay	78.0	**5 - 1**	56 - 16
Heat 13	**Jackson**/**Evans**/Dent/Gatenby (R)	77.2	**5 - 1**	61 - 17

CREWE - Phil Crump 12, John Jackson 12, Dai Evans 11 (+1), Barry Meeks 7 (+2), Gary Moore 7 (+2), Dave Parry 6 (+3), Ray Hassall 6 (+2).
SUNDERLAND - Alan Mackie 6, Russ Dent 4 (+1), George Barclay 3, John Knock 2, Dave Gatenby 1, Peter Wrathall 1, Gerry Richardson 0.

Phil Crump faced John Jackson in the first test match between Young England and Young Australasia at Peterborough on September 10. The Anzacs lost a feisty affair 55-53, with Crump scoring 15 and Jackson 5.

Meeting 48 - Sunday, September 12, 1971 - British League Division II
Sunderland Greyhound Stadium, Newcastle Road, East Boldon
Track Length - 310 yards.

SUNDERLAND STARS.....40 CREWE KINGS.....38

Phil Crump's maximum had the home fans applauding, but it still didn't deliver Crewe's second away league win of the season against bottom-of-the-table Sunderland. Crump and Jack Millen (on his return to Boldon) gave the Kings the perfect start, and they led up to the end of Heat 9. But in a superb speedway encounter, the Wearsiders fought back with a brace of 5-1's and secured the match with a share of the points in the final heat. Crewe youngster Dave Morton made his league debut and picked up a point in each of his three rides.

Heat 01	**Crump**/**Millen**/Dent/Mackie	67.2	**1 - 5**	01 - 05
Heat 02	Richardson/**Moore**/**Meeks**/Gatenby (F)	72.0	3 - 3	04 - 08
Heat 03	Barclay/**Evans**/Lynch/**Parry**	69.8	4 - 2	08 - 10
Heat 04	Wrathall/**Meeks**/**Morton**/Richardson (F)	70.6	3 - 3	11 - 13
Heat 05	**Crump**/**Millen**/Lynch/Barclay	68.2	**1 - 5**	12 - 18
Heat 06	Dent/**Moore**/**Morton**/Mackie (F)	69.4	3 - 3	15 - 21
Heat 07	**Evans**/Dent/Wrathall/**Parry**	68.8	3 - 3	18 - 24
Heat 08	**Millen**/Wrathall/Mackie/**Meeks**	69.0	3 - 3	21 - 27
Heat 09	Barclay/Lynch/**Morton**/**Moore** (F)	69.8	5 - 1	26 - 28
Heat 10	Dent/Mackie/**Evans**/**Parry**	68.4	5 - 1	31 - 29

Heat 11	**Crump**/Wrathall/**Millen**/Gatenby	69.2	**2 - 4**	33 - 33
Heat 12	Dent/**Moore**/Lynch/**Evans** (X)	70.0	4 - 2	37 - 35
Heat 13	**Crump**/Barclay/Wrathall/**Moore**	67.6	3 - 3	40 - 38

SUNDERLAND - Russ Dent 12, Peter Wrathall 9 (+2), George Barclay 8, John Lynch 5 (+1), Alan Mackie 3 (+2), Gerry Richardson 3, Dave Gatenby 0.
CREWE - Phil Crump 12, Jack Millen 8 (+2), Dai Evans 6, Gary Moore 6, Dave Morton 3 (+2), Barry Meeks 3 (+1), Dave Parry 0.

Meeting 49 - Monday, September 13, 1971 - British League Division II
L.M.R. Sports Ground, Earle Street, Crewe
Track Length - 430 yards.

CREWE KINGS.....43 BRADFORD NORTHERN.....35

Table toppers Bradford came to town intent on avenging their K.O. Cup elimination, but despite thirteen point returns by Knapkin and Adlington, they still left empty-handed, thanks mainly to a Phil Crump maximum and strong back up from Dai Evans and John Jackson. The meeting went to a last heat decider, with Northern requiring a maximum to draw, but all their hopes soon evaporated after Evans and Jackson powered away from the gate to easily take the win and match points.

Heat 01	**Crump**/**Millen**/Baugh/Chessell	75.0	**5 - 1**	05 - 01
Heat 02	**Meeks**/Adlington/**Moore**/Sheldrick	77.2	**4 - 2**	09 - 03
Heat 03	Knapkin/**Evans**/**Parry**/Fielding	77.6	3 - 3	12 - 06
Heat 04	**Jackson**/Adlington/**Moore**/Baugh	76.0	**4 - 2**	16 - 08
Heat 05	**Evans**/Knapkin/Chessell/**Parry**	75.8	3 - 3	19 - 11
Heat 06	**Crump**/Adlington/Sheldrick/**Millen** (R)	75.6	3 - 3	22 - 14
Heat 07	Knapkin/**Jackson**/**Moore**/Chessell	75.8	3 - 3	25 - 17
Heat 08	Knapkin/Adlington/**Meeks**/**Millen** (R)	76.8	1 - 5	26 - 22
Heat 09	**Evans**/Baugh/Sheldrick/**Parry**	75.8	3 - 3	29 - 25
Heat 10	**Crump**/Adlington/Knapkin/**Moore**	74.8	3 - 3	32 - 28
Heat 11	Adlington/**Jackson**/Chessell/**Meeks**	75.8	2 - 4	34 - 32
Heat 12	**Crump**/Baugh/**Moore**/Fielding	75.0	**4 - 2**	38 - 34
Heat 13	**Evans**/**Jackson**/Knapkin/Chessell	75.2	**5 - 1**	43 - 35

CREWE - Phil Crump 12, Dai Evans 11, John Jackson 9 (+1), Gary Moore 4 (+1), Barry Meeks 4, Jack Millen 2 (+1), Dave Parry 1 (+1).
BRADFORD - Robin Adlington 13 (+1), Alan Knapkin 13 (+1), Dave Baugh 5, Sid Sheldrick 2 (+2), Rod Chessell 2 (+1), Mick Fielding 0, *Alf Wells (R/R).*

Two days later Phil Crump inspired Young Australasia to a 68-40 second test victory at Bradford's Odsal Stadium. After falling in his first outing, he won his next five. Barry Meeks scored five for the Lions.

Meeting 50 - Monday, September 20, 1971 - British League Division II
L.M.R. Sports Ground, Earle Street, Crewe
Track Length - 430 yards.

CREWE KINGS.....54 ROMFORD BOMBERS.....24

Maximums from John Jackson and Phil Crump helped the Kings record another big home win. Romford, missing big track specialist Bob Coles (out with a broken foot), relied heavily on Brian Foote, and he didn't let them down, scoring ten from his six starts. Jackson however, was the most impressive home rider, leading from the gate on each occasion, and recording the fastest time of the night in Heat 11. Jack Millen was excluded in Heat 10 for unfair riding, which cost him a second place.

Heat 01	**Crump**/**Millen**/Holden/Davies	77.2	**5 - 1**	05 - 01
Heat 02	**Moore**/**Parry**/Spittles/Gills	80.0	**5 - 1**	10 - 02
Heat 03	**Evans**/**Meeks**/Foote/Benham	78.6	**5 - 1**	15 - 03
Heat 04	**Jackson**/Stevens/**Moore**/Spittles	76.2	**4 - 2**	19 - 05
Heat 05	Foote/Holden/**Evans**/**Meeks**	77.4	1 - 5	20 - 10

Heat 06	**Crump**/**Millen**/Gills/Stevens (R)	75.8	**5 - 1**	25 - 11
Heat 07	**Jackson**/Foote/**Moore**/Benham	76.0	**4 - 2**	29 - 13
Heat 08	**Moore**/**Millen**/Foote/Holden (R)	77.2	**5 - 1**	34 - 14
Heat 09	**Evans**/Stevens/Gills/**Meeks**	77.0	3 - 3	37 - 17
Heat 10	**Crump**/Foote/Holden/**Millen** (X)	76.2	3 - 3	40 - 20
Heat 11	**Jackson**/Holden/**Parry**/Gills	75.6	**4 - 2**	44 - 22
Heat 12	**Crump**/**Meeks**/Benham/Stevens (R)	77.2	**5 - 1**	49 - 23
Heat 13	**Jackson**/**Evans**/Foote/Holden	75.8	**5 - 1**	54 - 24

CREWE - Phil Crump 12, John Jackson 12, Dai Evans 9 (+1), Gary Moore 8, Jack Millen 6 (+3), Barry Meeks 4 (+2), Dave Parry 3 (+1).
ROMFORD - Brian Foote 10, Kevin Holden 6 (+2), Stan Stevens 4, Ian Gills 2 (+1), Charlie Benham 1, Ted Spittles 1, Dene Davies 0, *Bob Coles (R/R)*.

Crewe's Anzac pair of Millen and Crump rode for Young Australasia at Canterbury on September 25, in the final test match 43-65 defeat to the Young Lions. Millen scored ten, but Crump was plagued with engine problems throughout the meeting, and managed just five. In the league title race, Eastbourne took a massive step towards the championship, with a comfortable 54-23 win over Long Eaton. Rochdale finally conceded defeat in their attempt to re-stage their rained off K.O. Cup semi-final, thus handing the Kings a place in the final - their second appearance in three seasons.

Meetings 51 & 52 - Monday, September 27, 1971 - British League Division II (Double Header)
L.M.R. Sports Ground, Earle Street, Crewe
Track Length - 430 yards.

CREWE KINGS.....53 TEESSIDE TEESSIDERS.....25

Followed by

CREWE KINGS.....55 LONG EATON RANGERS.....19

A second double header at Earle Street saw Crewe safely into the top half of the league table, despite motor problems for John Jackson against Teesside, and Phil Crump in the next. In match one, Crump put in another faultless display to record his fifth consecutive league maximum, and in the next, Jack Millen took over Crump's mantle to record his own full house, with Barry Meeks dropping only one point - and that to Dave Parry. Crump had a nightmare against the Rangers, completing just one of four rides, ending a run of 21 straight victories when retiring in the opening heat.

Heat 01	**Crump**/Forrester/**Meeks**/Tony Swales	76.8	**4 - 2**	04 - 02
Heat 02	**Parry**/Durham/**G.Moore**/M.Moore	77.0	**4 - 2**	08 - 04
Heat 03	**Jackson**/**Evans**/Lee/Aufrett	76.2	**5 - 1**	13 - 05
Heat 04	**G.Moore**/**Millen**/Tim Swales/M.Moore	79.0	**5 - 1**	18 - 06
Heat 05	**Evans**/Forrester/**Jackson**/Tony Swales	76.4	**4 - 2**	22 - 08
Heat 06	**Crump**/Tim Swales/**Meeks**/Durham	76.4	**4 - 2**	26 - 10
Heat 07	**Millen**/Lee/**G.Moore**/Aufrett	78.4	**4 - 2**	30 - 12
Heat 08	Forrester/**Parry**/**Meeks**/M.Moore	78.2	3 - 3	33 - 15
Heat 09	**Evans**/Durham/**Parry**/Tim Swales	77.8	**4 - 2**	37 - 17
Heat 10	**Crump**/**Meeks**/Lee/Aufrett	76.8	**5 - 1**	42 - 18
Heat 11	**Parry**/Forrester/Tony Swales/**Millen** (R)	78.6	3 - 3	45 - 21
Heat 12	**Crump**/Tim Swales/Lee/**G.Moore**	77.2	3 - 3	48 - 24
Heat 13	**Evans**/**Millen**/Durham/Forrester (X)	77.8	**5 - 1**	53 - 25

CREWE - Phil Crump 12, Dai Evans 11 (+1), Dave Parry 9, Jack Millen 7 (+2), Barry Meeks 5 (+2), Gary Moore 5, John Jackson 4.
TEESSIDE - Bruce Forrester 9, Terry Lee 5 (+1), Dave Durham 5, Tim Swales 5, Tony Swales 1 (+1), Frank Aufrett 0, Mick Moore 0.

Heat 01	**Meeks**/Champion/Shakespeare (R)/**Crump** (R)	79.4	**3 - 2**	03 - 02
Heat 02	**Parry**/**Moore**/Champion/Jarvis	78.8	**5 - 1**	08 - 03
Heat 03	**Evans**/**Jackson**/Bouchard/Bass	77.2	**5 - 1**	13 - 04
Heat 04	**Millen**/**Moore**/Champion/Mills (R)	78.0	**5 - 1**	18 - 05
Heat 05	**Evans**/**Jackson**/Bouchard/Whittaker	79.4	**5 - 1**	23 - 06

Heat 06	**Meeks**/Mills/Jarvis/**Crump** (R)	80.0	3 - 3	26 - 09
Heat 07	**Millen**/Shakespeare/**Moore**/Bouchard	78.2	**4 - 2**	30 - 11
Heat 08	**Parry**/**Meeks**/Whittaker/Champion	80.0	**5 - 1**	35 - 12
Heat 09	**Evans**/**Jackson**/Mills/Jarvis (F)	79.2	**5 - 1**	40 - 13
Heat 10	**Meeks**/**Crump**/Bass/Bouchard (R)	81.0	**5 - 1**	45 - 14
Heat 11	**Millen**/Shakespeare/Whittaker/**Parry**	77.6	3 - 3	48 - 17
Heat 12	**Jackson**/Shakespeare (X)/**Crump** (R)/Bouchard (R)	79.2	**3 - 0**	51 - 17
Heat 13	**Millen**/Shakespeare/**Evans**/Bass	78.8	**4 - 2**	55 - 19

CREWE - Jack Millen 12, Barry Meeks 11 (+1), Dai Evans 10, John Jackson 9 (+3), Dave Parry 6, Gary Moore 5 (+2), Phil Crump 2 (+1).
LONG EATON - Malcolm Shakespeare 6, Ian Champion 4, Roger Mills 3, Phil Whittaker 2 (+1), Geoff Bouchard 2, Peter Jarvis 1 (+1), Steve Bass 1.

Meeting 53 - Thursday, September 30, 1971 - British League Division II
Ipswich Stadium, Foxhall Road, Foxhall Heath, Ipswich
Track Length - 328 yards.

IPSWICH WITCHES.....45 CREWE KINGS.....32

Crewe's final away league match of the season was a dress rehearsal for the upcoming K.O. Cup final, and produced a meeting fit for the final itself. Phil Crump beat home hero John Louis on two occasions, but fell in his last outing, spoiling a five-ride maximum. Louis though had his revenge when beating the Aussie in their Silver Helmet match race.

Heat 01	**Crump**/Louis/**Moore**/Noy	68.4	**2 - 4**	02 - 04
Heat 02	Prinsloo/**Moore**/**Meeks**/Pepper	71.4	3 - 3	05 - 07
Heat 03	Davey/**Jackson**/**Evans**/Howgego	67.8	3 - 3	08 - 10
Heat 04	Prinsloo/**Meeks**/Bailey (R)/**Millen** (X)	70.0	3 - 2	11 - 12
Heat 05	**Crump**/Davey/Howgego/**Morton**	67.4	3 - 3	14 - 15
Heat 06	Louis/Noy/**Millen**/**Moore**	67.6	5 - 1	19 - 16
Heat 07	**Jackson**/**Evans**/Bailey/Prinsloo (F)	69.0	**1 - 5**	20 - 21
Heat 08	Prinsloo/Noy/**Meeks**/**Morton**	71.2	5 - 1	25 - 22
Heat 09	Davey/Howgego/**Moore**/**Millen** (R)	68.2	5 - 1	30 - 23
Heat 10	**Crump**/Louis/**Jackson**/Noy	68.0	**2 - 4**	32 - 27
Heat 11	**Crump**/Prinsloo/Bailey/**Moore**	68.0	3 - 3	35 - 30
Heat 12	Louis/Howgego/**Evans**/**Millen**	69.0	5 - 1	40 - 31
Heat 13	Davey/Bailey/**Jackson**/**Crump** (F)	67.8	5 - 1	45 - 32

IPSWICH - Tony Davey 11, Peter Prinsloo 11, John Louis 10, Ted Howgego 5 (+3), Pete Bailey 4 (+2), Clive Noy 4 (+2), Stan Pepper 0.
CREWE - Phil Crump 12, John Jackson 7, Dai Evans 4 (+2), Barry Meeks 4 (+1), Gary Moore 4, Jack Millen 1, Dave Morton 0.

Eastbourne were crowned league champions on October 1, following a narrow 39-38 victory at Peterborough, after nearest rivals Bradford lost heavily at Rochdale.

Saturday, October 2, 1971 - British League Division II Riders Championship
Hackney Wick Stadium, Waterden Road, London
Track Length - 345 yards.

WINNER.....JOHN LOUIS

Favourite John Louis continued his rich vein of form, winning the Division II Riders Championship, dropping only one point in the process. Phil Crump and Rochdale's Peter Collins finished joint-fourth with eleven points.

Heat 01	Louis/Shakespeare/**Crump**/Holden	66.2
Heat 02	Gilbertson/Baugh/Forrester/Wyer	66.8
Heat 03	Saunders/Major/Wilson (R)/Ballard (R)	68.0
Heat 04	Price/Mackay/Dent/Collins (X)	69.0
Heat 05	Shakespeare/Wilson/Dent/Baugh	67.4
Heat 06	Louis/Price/Major/Forrester	67.4
Heat 07	Saunders/Collins/**Crump**/Gilbertson (R)	66.0

Heat 08	Wyer/Holden/Ballard/Mackay (F)	68.6
Heat 09	Shakespeare/Saunders/Mackay/Forrester	67.8
Heat 10	Collins/Louis/Baugh/Ballard (R)	66.6
Heat 11	**Crump**/Wyer/Wilson (F)/Price (X)	69.0
Heat 12	Dent/Major/Gilbertson/Holden (F)	68.4
Heat 13	Shakespeare/Price/Gilbertson/Greer	68.0
Heat 14	Louis/Saunders/Dent/Wyer	68.2
Heat 15	**Crump**/Major/Baugh/Mackay	68.4
Heat 16	Collins/Wilson/Forrester/Holden	68.0
Heat 17	Collins/Shakespeare/Major/Wyer	66.8
Heat 18	Louis/Wilson/Mackay/Gilbertson	68.0
Heat 19	**Crump**/Mills/Forrester/Dent	67.8
Heat 20	Price/Saunders/Baugh/Holden	69.0

John Louis *(Ipswich)* 14, Malcolm Shakespeare *(Long Eaton)* 13, Hugh Saunders *(Rayleigh)* 12, Peter Collins *(Rochdale)* 11, Phil Crump *(Crewe)* 11, Arthur Price *(Boston)* 10, George Major *(Birmingham)* 8, Reg Wilson *(Hull)* 6, Russ Dent *(Sunderland)* 6, Dave Baugh *(Bradford)* 5, Ross Gilbertson *(Canterbury)* 5, Doug Wyer *(Berwick)* 5, Malcolm Mackay *(Workington)* 4, Bruce Forrester *(Teesside)* 3, Kevin Holden *(Romford)* 2, Malcolm Ballard *(Eastbourne)* 1. Meeting Reserves: Roger Mills *(Long Eaton)* 2, Richard Greer (*Peterborough)* 0. *(Baugh replaced Alan Knapkin).*

Many Crewe fans who had travelled down by train to support Phil Crump, received quite a surprise to find Dave Parry on dining car duties. Parry, who was employed by British Rail, served out the refreshments before changing out of his uniform into civvies and continuing his journey with the fans to Hackney.

Meeting 54 - Monday, October 4, 1971 - British League Division II
L.M.R. Sports Ground, Earle Street, Crewe.
Track Length - 430 yards

CREWE KINGS.....55 ROCHDALE HORNETS.....23

The Kings completed another home league season without defeat, after easily beating Rochdale, who tracked a much changed side. Minus heat leaders Peter Collins and Paul Tyrer (touring Russia with Belle Vue), they drafted in former Hornet Taffy Owen (Workington) and Carl Glover (Boston), who scored more than their team-mates put together. As a warm-up for the pending K.O. Cup ties, Phil Crump registered another maximum and for a second successive home match, Crewe riders won every heat. Dave Parry was also in sparkling form, winning each of his three outings. Heat 12 was cut short after Paul Callaghan ploughed into the boards.

Heat 01	**Crump**/Owen/**Meeks**/Moss	75.0	**4 - 2**	04 - 02
Heat 02	**Parry**/**Moore**/Gardner/Goad	77.2	**5 - 1**	09 - 03
Heat 03	**Jackson**/Gardner/Callaghan/**Evans** (R)	75.2	3 - 3	12 - 06
Heat 04	**Millen**/Glover/**Moore**/Gardner	76.6	**4 - 2**	16 - 08
Heat 05	**Jackson**/**Evans**/Moss/Owen	75.6	**5 - 1**	21 - 09
Heat 06	**Crump**/Glover/Goad/**Meeks**	75.0	3 - 3	24 - 12
Heat 07	**Moore**/Owen/**Millen**/Lyons	77.0	**4 - 2**	28 - 14
Heat 08	**Parry**/Moss/**Meeks**/Gardner	77.6	**4 - 2**	32 - 16
Heat 09	**Jackson**/**Evans**/Glover/Goad	75.6	**5 - 1**	37 - 17
Heat 10	**Crump**/**Meeks**/Callaghan/Lyons	75.4	**5 - 1**	42 - 18
Heat 11	**Parry**/**Millen**/Owen/Goad	77.2	**5 - 1**	47 - 19
Heat 12	**Crump**/**Jackson**/Glover/Callaghan (F)	00.0	**5 - 1**	52 - 20
Heat 13	**Evans**/Owen/Gardner/**Millen** (R)	76.8	3 - 3	55 - 23

CREWE - Phil Crump 12, John Jackson 11 (+1), Dave Parry 9, Dai Evans 7 (+2), Jack Millen 6 (+1), Gary Moore 6 (+1), Barry Meeks 4 (+1).
ROCHDALE - Taffy Owen* 7, Carl Glover* 6, Robbie Gardner 4 (+1), Ken Moss 3, Paul Callaghan 2 (+1), Colin Goad 1 (+1), Geoff Lyons 0.

Dai Evans was a surprise winner of the Bradford Open Championship at Odsal on October 6. Superb gating throughout the meeting saw him unbeaten, with Phil Crump finishing runner-up with Berwick's Doug Wyer third.

Meeting 55 - Friday, October 8, 1971 - Challenge
Derwent Park Stadium, Workington
Track Length - 398 yards.

WORKINGTON COMETS.....38 CREWE KINGS.....40

Guest Reg Wilson (Hull), Dave Morton and Charlie Scarbrough came into the shorthanded Crewe side for this challenge, and finished on the winning side in a rare away win. Torrential rain halfway through the match somewhat spoiled the night's entertainment and added almost ten seconds to the average heat time.

Heat 01	**Crump**/Amundson/Owen/**Scarbrough**	77.2	3 - 3	03 - 03
Heat 02	Kumeta/Watson/**Morton**/**Moore**	79.4	5 - 1	08 - 04
Heat 03	Sansom/**Evans**/Vale/**Millen**	75.8	4 - 2	12 - 06
Heat 04	Mackay/**Moore**/Kumeta/**Morton**	77.2	4 - 2	16 - 08
Heat 05	**Crump**/Vale/**Scarbrough**/Sansom	77.2	**2 - 4**	18 - 12
Heat 06	**Wilson**/Owen/**Moore**/Amundson	76.8	**2 - 4**	20 - 16
Heat 07	**Evans**/**Millen**/Mackay/Kumeta	77.2	**1 - 5**	21 - 21
Heat 08	Watson/**Morton**/**Scarbrough**/Amundson (X)	85.8	3 - 3	24 - 24
Heat 09	**Moore**/Sansom/Vale/**Wilson** (F)	86.8	3 - 3	27 - 27
Heat 10	**Millen**/Kumeta/**Evans**/Owen	86.2	**2 - 4**	29 - 31
Heat 11	Watson/Mackay/**Moore**/**Crump** (R)	87.6	5 - 1	34 - 32
Heat 12	**Evans**/**Wilson**/Owen/Vale	84.2	**1 - 5**	35 - 37
Heat 13	**Crump**/Sanson/Mackay/**Millen**	83.2	3 - 3	38 - 40

WORKINGTON - Steve Watson 8 (+1), Malcolm Mackay 7 (+2), Lou Sansom 7, Dave Kumeta 6, Taffy Owen 4 (+1), Ken Vale 4 (+1), Kym Amundson 2.
CREWE - Phil Crump 9, Dai Evans 9, Gary Moore 7, Jack Millen 5 (+1), Reg Wilson* 5 (+1), Dave Morton 3, Charlie Scarbrough 2 (+1).

Meeting 56 - Monday, October 11, 1971 - Speedway Express Knock Out Cup, Final, First Leg
L.M.R. Sports Ground, Earle Street, Crewe
Track Length - 430 yards.

CREWE KINGS.....41 IPSWICH WITCHES.....37

The Kings effectively handed the trophy to Ipswich following a rain-effected first leg. John Louis was the Witches hero, dropping just one point in five rides, and was well supported by Tony Davey and reserve Peter Prinsloo, who racked up four seconds and a third. Phil Crump ended the night on a high, stripping Louis of the Silver Helmet - ending a superb run of 21 consecutive defences by the Ipswich man.

Heat 01	Louis/**Crump**/Noy/**Meeks**	76.8	2 - 4	02 - 04
Heat 02	**Moore**/Prinsloo/**Parry**/Watkins (F)	80.4	**4 - 2**	06 - 06
Heat 03	Davey/**Millen**/**Evans**/Howgego	78.6	3 - 3	09 - 09
Heat 04	**Jackson**/Prinsloo/**Moore**/Bailey	78.4	**4 - 2**	13 - 11
Heat 05	Louis/**Millen**/**Evans**/Noy	77.6	3 - 3	16 - 14
Heat 06	**Crump**/**Meeks**/Prinsloo/Bailey	77.6	**5 - 1**	21 - 15
Heat 07	Davey/Louis/**Jackson**/**Moore**	77.4	1 - 5	22 - 20
Heat 08	**Parry**/Prinsloo/**Meeks**/Noy	83.8	**4 - 2**	26 - 22
Heat 09	**Evans**/Bailey/**Millen**/Watkins	82.0	**4 - 2**	30 - 24
Heat 10	Davey/**Crump**/**Meeks**/Howgego	78.0	3 - 3	33 - 27
Heat 11	Louis/Prinsloo/**Moore**/**Jackson**	82.2	1 - 5	34 - 32
Heat 12	**Crump**/Davey/**Millen**/Bailey	80.0	**4 - 2**	38 - 34
Heat 13	Louis/**Jackson**/**Evans**/Howgego	80.6	3 - 3	41 - 37

CREWE - Phil Crump 10, Dai Evans 6 (+3), John Jackson 6, Jack Millen 6, Gary Moore 5, Barry Meeks 4 (+2), Dave Parry 4.
IPSWICH - John Louis 14 (+1), Tony Davey 11, Peter Prinsloo 9 (+1), Pete Bailey 2, Clive Noy 1, Ted Howgego 0, Ray Watkins 0.

Arrangements were made for the majority of the Crewe team and supporters to travel down to Ipswich on a “special” train for the second leg. The fare for the trip was £2.25.

Meeting 57 - Thursday, October 14, 1971 - Speedway Express Knock Out Cup, Final, Second Leg
Ipswich Stadium, Foxhall Road, Foxhall Heath, Ipswich
Track Length - 328 yards.

IPSWICH WITCHES.....55 CREWE KINGS.....23

(Ipswich won on aggregate 92 - 64)

As expected, Ipswich won the K.O. Cup for the second successive season, with John Louis and Tony Davey going through the card unbeaten. Reserve Peter Prinsloo once again excelled, contributing nine points to the winning total. The home side cancelled out Crewe's slender lead after the first heat, but in truth, nothing went right for the Kings, with Dave Parry and John Jackson suffering falls and Jack Millen clouting the safety fence in Heat 3, resulting in him taking no further part in proceedings. Phil Crump added to Crewe's woes by losing a chain while leading Heat 7, but did have the last laugh over arch-rival John Louis, retaining the Silver Helmet after Louis suffered an engine failure on the last lap. Maurice Littlechild was magnanimous in defeat and admitted: *"There was no living with the Witches tonight."*

Heat 01	Louis/Noy/**Meeks**/**Crump** (X)	76.0	5 - 1	05 - 01
Heat 02	Prinsloo/Watkins/**Moore**/**Parry**	74.4	5 - 1	10 - 02
Heat 03	Davey/**Evans**/Howgego/**Millen** (X)	72.0	4 - 2	14 - 04
Heat 04	Bailey/**Jackson**/Prinsloo/**Parry**	72.4	4 - 2	18 - 06
Heat 05	Davey/**Crump**/Howgego/**Meeks**	70.6	4 - 2	22 - 08
Heat 06	Louis/**Jackson**/Noy/**Moore**	70.2	4 - 2	26 - 10
Heat 07	**Evans**/Prinsloo/Bailey/**Crump** (R)	72.4	3 - 3	29 - 13
Heat 08	Prinsloo/Noy/**Meeks**/**Parry** (F)	71.8	5 - 1	34 - 14
Heat 09	Davey/**Jackson**/Howgego/**Moore**	72.2	4 - 2	38 - 16
Heat 10	Louis/Noy/**Evans**/**Meeks**	72.4	5 - 1	43 - 17
Heat 11	**Crump**/Bailey/**Jackson**/Watkins	70.2	**2 - 4**	45 - 21
Heat 12	Louis/Howgego/**Evans**/**Jackson** (F)	69.0	5 - 1	50 - 22
Heat 13	Davey/Bailey/**Crump**/**Moore**	69.8	5 - 1	55 - 23

IPSWICH - Tony Davey 12, John Louis 12, Peter Prinsloo 9, Pete Bailey 8 (+2), Clive Noy 7 (+3), Ted Howgego 5 (+1), Ray Watkins 2 (+1).
CREWE - Dai Evans 7, John Jackson 7, Phil Crump 6, Barry Meeks 2, Gary Moore 1, Jack Millen 0, Dave Parry 0.

Crewe's proposed challenge match with Workington was washed out on October 18, and with the Chester Vase meeting scheduled for the following week, would not be re-arranged.

Meeting 58 - Monday, October 25, 1971 - Chester Vase
L.M.R. Sports Ground, Earle Street, Crewe
Track Length - 430 yards.

WINNER.....PHIL CRUMP

Phil Crump rounded off a magnificent debut season by winning the Chester Vase with a faultless display of riding. Peter Collins proved to be Crump's main rival, starting the competition with four straight wins, before a fall in Heat 17 while attempting an overtake, cost him the trophy. Last year's winner John Jackson was the next highest placed Crewe rider, finishing in fifth position.

Heat 01	Crump/Mills/Saunders/Meeks	75.6
Heat 02	Price/Moore/Evans/Tyrer	76.4
Heat 03	Collins/Millen/Foote/Jackson (F)	73.8
Heat 04	Wilson/Louis/Holden/Owen	75.4
Heat 05	Crump/Millen/Wilson/Morton	75.2
Heat 06	Collins/Meeks/Holden/Moore	73.8
Heat 07	Louis/Jackson/Tyrer/Mills (R)	75.8
Heat 08	Owen/Price/Foote/Saunders	75.0
Heat 09	Crump/Jackson/Moore/Owen	76.6
Heat 10	Louis/Meeks/Foote/Hassall	76.4
Heat 11	Price/Millen/Holden/Morton	77.0
Heat 12	Collins/Tyrer/Saunders/Hassall	74.8

Heat 13	Crump/Holden/Tyrer/Foote	76.0
Heat 14	Jackson/Price/Wilson/Meeks	75.6
Heat 15	Collins/Owen/Morton/Hassall	75.0
Heat 16	Louis/Millen/Saunders/Moore	76.6
Heat 17	Crump/Louis/Price/Collins (F)	75.0
Heat 18	Tyrer/Owen/Meeks/Millen	76.2
Heat 19	Wilson/Moore/Morton/Foote	77.2
Heat 20	Saunders/Jackson/Holden/Hassall	76.2

Phil Crump 15, John Louis 13, Peter Collins 12, Arthur Price 11, John Jackson 9, Reg Wilson 8, Jack Millen 8, Paul Tyrer 7, Taffy Owen 7, Kevin Holden 6, Hugh Saunders 6, Barry Meeks 5, Gary Moore 5, Brian Foote 3, Roger Mills 2, Dai Evans 1. Meeting Reserves: Dave Morton 2, Ray Hassall 0.

The Chester Vase brought the curtain down on another Earle Street campaign. The end of season dance was held on November 6 at nearby Gorsty Hall, and was again a well-attended affair.

So it had happened once again. Crewe finished seventh in the league for a third successive season, due mainly to an impressive home record; but managed only one league victory on their travels, again preventing any challenge for honours. Champions Eastbourne won seven away fixtures, as had Canterbury the previous season, so the Crewe management knew exactly what was required if they were to be taken as serious contenders. As in previous seasons, a new hero had emerged, and once again was of Australasian origin. Young Phil Crump started quietly and relatively unnoticed in his first few meetings, but as his confidence grew, so did his scores, and at the conclusion, he topped the Kings averages. First Divison promoters were again hovering to take away the club's best assets. Crump had already proved himself in the higher grade, after appearances for Hackney, King's Lynn, Wolverhampton and Oxford. His return to Crewe however, would depend on him dodging the Australian Army draft. Another man in demand was John Jackson, who too had ridden in the First Division for Cradley Heath and Oxford. To be successful in 1972, the Kings would need to retain their heat leaders, strengthen their lower order - and more crucially - start winning away from home!

- 1971 Season Summary -

				Wins to Crewe	
Date	**Opponents/Meeting**	**Res**	**Score**	**Race**	**Heat**
Fri, April 9	**Bradford (Ch)**	L	31 - 47	6	2
Wed, April 14	Bradford (Ch)	L	27 - 50	3	1
Fri, April 16	Rochdale (Ch)	L	31 - 47	3	3
Sat, April 17	Canterbury (BL)	L	30 - 48	3	1
Mon, April 19	**Long Eaton (Ch)**	W	48 - 30	10	8
Wed, April 21	Hull (Ch)	L	32 - 46	3	3
Thu, April 22	Long Eaton (Ch)	L	24 - 53	2	1
Sun, April 25	Boston (BL)	L	25 - 53	3	1
Mon, April 26	**Rochdale (Ch)**	D	39 - 39	5	4
Mon, May 3	**Peterborough (BL)**	W	56 - 22	12	10
Thu, May 6	Teesside (BL)	L	35 - 42	4	4
Sun, May 9	Eastbourne (BL)	L	23 - 54	3	2
Mon, May 10	**Workington (BL)**	D	39 - 39	6	5
Mon, May 17	**Rayleigh (BL)**	W	49 - 29	12	7
Fri, May 21	Rochdale (BL)	L	37 - 41	7	4
Mon, May 24	**Ipswich (BL)**	W	46 - 32	8	7
Mon, May 31	**Birmingham (Ch)**	W	56 - 22	13	10
Tue, June 1	Birmingham (Ch)	L	34 - 44	1	1
Wed, June 2	Bradford (BL)	L	24 - 54	0	0
Mon, June 7	**Berwick (KOC R2)**	W	54 - 24	10	9
Sat, June 12	Berwick (KOC R2)	L	28 - 50	2	1
Mon, June 14	**Hull (BL)**	W	46 - 32	8	6
Thu, June 17	Romford (BL)	L	30 - 48	5	2

Sun, June 20	Boston (Ch)	L	38½ - 39½	6	3
Mon, June 21	**Y. Eng. v Y. Swe. (Int)**	-	60 - 48	-	-
Mon, June 28	**Boston (Ch)**	W	49 - 29	11	9
Mon, July 5	**Roc/Bra/Bos (4TT)**	W	Crewe 42	13	-
Wed, July 7	Bra/Bos/Roc (4TT)	W	Crewe 31	7	-
Fri, July 9	Roc/Bos/Bra (4TT)	L	Crewe 19	4	-
Mon, July 12	**Eastbourne (BL)**	W	54 - 24	12	9
Fri, July 16	Workington (BL)	L	25 - 53	3	1
Mon, July 19	**Bradford (KOC R3)**	W	47 - 31	8	7
Wed, July 21	Hull (BL)	L	31 - 47	2	1
Sun, July 25	Bos/Roc/Bra (4TT)	L	Crewe 24	4	-
Wed, July 28	Bradford (KOC R3)	L	32 - 46	3	1
Thu, July 29	Long Eaton (BL)	L	27 - 50	3	1
Mon, August 2	**Boston (BL)**	W	50 - 28	10	8
Mon, August 9	**Y. Eng. v Y. Czech. (Int)**	-	54 - 54	-	-
Fri, August 13	Peterborough (BL)	L	30 - 47	6	2
Mon, August 16	**Rochdale (KOC S/F)**	W	49 - 29	9	8
Sat, August 21	Rayleigh (BL)	W	39 - 38	7	6
Mon, August 23	**Canterbury (BL)**	W	55 - 23	12	9
Sat, August 28	Berwick (BL)	L	21 - 56	1	1
Mon, August 30	**Birmingham (BL)**	W	62 - 16	12	12
Tue, August 31	Birmingham (BL)	L	28 - 50	4	2
Mon, September 6	**Berwick (BL)**	W	48 - 30	11	6
Mon, September 6	**Sunderland (BL)**	W	61 - 17	13	12
Sun, September 12	Sunderland (BL)	L	38 - 40	6	3
Mon, September 13	**Bradford (BL)**	W	43 - 35	9	5
Mon, September 20	**Romford (BL)**	W	54 - 24	12	10
Mon, September 27	**Teesside (BL)**	W	53 - 25	12	10
Mon, September 27	**Long Eaton (BL)**	W	55 - 19	13	11
Thu, September 30	Ipswich (BL)	L	32 - 45	5	3
Mon, October 4	**Rochdale (BL)**	W	55 - 23	13	10
Fri, October 8	Workington (Ch)	W	40 - 38	8	5
Mon, October 11	**Ipswich (KOC F)**	W	41 - 37	6	6
Thu, October 14	Ipswich (KOC F)	L	23 - 55	2	1
Mon, October 25	**Chester Vase (Ind)**	Phil Crump		-	-

- British League Division II Final Table -

		Home					Away					
	M	W	D	L	F	A	W	D	L	F	A	Pts
1. Eastbourne	32	15	0	1	800	438	7	3	6	594	649	47
2. Bradford	32	16	0	0	778	468	5	1	10	592	651	43
3. Ipswich	32	14	1	1	746	495	6	2	8	599	646	43
4. Boston	32	15	0	1	744	503	3	3	10	568	670	39
5. Rayleigh	32	12	2	2	688	555	6	0	10	589	654	38
6. Hull	32	12	2	2	703	542	4	0	12	589	657	34
7. Crewe	**32**	**15**	**1**	**0**	**826**	**418**	**1**	**0**	**15**	**475**	**766**	**33**
8. Berwick	32	16	0	0	784½	461½	0	0	16	500	747	32
9. Rochdale	32	14	0	2	700	544	2	0	14	477	767	32
10. Long Eaton	32	13	2	1	690	555	0	1	15	505	735	29
11. Birmingham	32	13	1	2	704	541	0	2	14	477	771	29
12. Romford	32	12	0	4	700	542	1	0	15	522½	721½	26
13. Teesside	32	12	0	4	707½	536½	1	0	15	483½	762½	26
14. Canterbury	32	12	2	2	702	543	0	0	16	458	789	26
15. Workington	32	11	0	5	701	547	1	1	14	533	703	25
16. Peterborough	32	11	1	4	691	553	0	0	16	482	764	23
17. Sunderland	32	9	1	6	635	600	0	0	16	398	847	19

- Crewe Rider Averages -

(League and Knock Out Cup only)

	M	R	W	Pts	BP	Tot	F	P	CMA
Phil Crump	38	164	85	349	19	368	6	6	8.976
John Jackson	37	149	63	294	16	310	4	3	8.322
Dai Evans	38	160	50	284	25	309	2	4	7.725
Jack Millen	31	109	23	155	25	180	1	2	6.606
Barry Meeks	39	138	16	165	32	197	0	2	5.710
Gary Moore	39	143	18	160	30	190	0	0	5.315
Dave Parry	34	112	20	128	18	146	0	1	5.214
				Also rode					
Ray Hassall	1	4	0	6	2	8	0	0	8.000
Ian Bottomley	6	21	2	27	7	34	0	0	6.476
Dave Morton	2	6	0	3	2	5	0	0	3.333
Charlie Scarbrough	1	2	0	1	0	1	0	0	2.000
Stuart Riley	2	5	0	2	0	2	0	0	1.600
Don Beecroft	3	6	0	0	0	0	0	0	0.000
Barrie Smitherman	1	2	0	0	0	0	0	0	0.000
				Substitute					
Mick Beaton	1	2	0	1	0	1	0	0	2.000

- League Heat Scores -

	Home	Away	Total
5 - 1 heat win to Crewe	93	11	104
3 - 0 heat win to Crewe	1	0	1
4 - 2 heat win to Crewe	42	21	63
3 - 2 heat win to Crewe	1	2	3
3 - 3 drawn heat	51	54	105
2 - 3 heat win to Opponents	0	3	3
2 - 4 heat win to Opponents	14	47	61
1 - 5 heat win to Opponents	6	68	74
0 - 5 heat win to Opponents	0	2	2

- Team Honours -

Speedway Express Knock Out Cup Runners-Up.
West Midlands Trophy Winners.
Lincs/Cheshire Trophy Winners.
Four Team Tournament Winners.

- Individual/Pairs Honours -

Teesside Open Championship (Teesside)
1. Tim Swales 2. Alan Knapkin, 3. John Jackson.

John Peel Best Pairs (Workington)
1. Chris Blythe & Bernie Hornby 2. John Jackson & Dai Evans 3. Malcolm Mackay & Kym Amundson.

Stadium Silver Helmet (Teesside)
1. Bruce Forrester 2. Phil Crump 3. Dave Durham.

Bradford Open Championship (Bradford)
1. Dai Evans 2. Phil Crump 3. Doug Wyer.

Midland Junior Riders Championship (Wolverhampton)
1. Dave Baugh 2. George Major 3. John Jackson.

Chester Vase (Crewe)
1. Phil Crump 2. John Louis 3. Peter Collins.

Crewe No.1 Phil Crump.

(ABOVE) Newly crowned World Champion Ole Olsen congratulates the top three in the Bradford Open Championship. Winner Dai Evans, is flanked by runner-up Phil Crump, and Berwick's Doug Wyer. (BELOW) The Kings with their runners-up tankards and medals after the K.O. Cup Final defeat at Ipswich.

(ABOVE) Young Dave Morton on opposite lock, a style which would earn him a regular team spot in 1972. (BELOW) Barry Meeks, an ever-present in league and K.O. Cup competition.

TEESSIDE
RAYLEIGH
READING
CREWE
PETERBOROUGH
SUNDERLAND

Date 18 Sept 71

TEAM/RIDER'S NAME Dave Morton

TEESSIDE SPEEDWAY, Stockton Road, Middlesbrough *Tel.* 47381—Markfield 2841
RAYLEIGH SPEEDWAY, Rayleigh Weir, Essex *Tel.* 5498—Romford 60065
READING SPEEDWAY, Oxford Road, Tilehurst *Tel.* 27151—Henley-on-Thames 3709
CREWE SPEEDWAY, Earle Street, Crewe *Tel.* 56806—Waltham Cross 28338
PETERBOROUGH SPEEDWAY, Showground, Peterborough *Tel.* 5868—Chesham 5353
SUNDERLAND SPEEDWAY

ALLIED PRESENTATIONS LTD.
Registered Office :
HACKNEY WICK STADIUM, Waterden Road, London E.15
Telephone 01-985-9810 — 01-985-9822

DATE OF MEETING				13 Sept				
RIDER/TRACK	Sunderland			Crewe				
MATCH STARTS ...	3 2.25							
MATCH POINTS ...	3							
BONUS POINTS ...	2							
TOTAL POINTS ...	5 5-00							
MATCH RACE ...								
S/H STARTS ...	1 .75			2 1.50				
S/H POINTS ...	—			0				
TRAVEL EXPENSES ...	5.00			1.00				
GUARANTEES ...								
GROSS TOTAL ...	10.75			2.50				
FUEL OIL ...								
INSURANCE ...	- 60			(2) 30				
SPARES ...								
ADVANCES ...								
DEDUCTIONS TOTAL	- 60			30				
NETT TOTAL ...	10-15			2.20				

ENCLOSED PLEASE FIND CHEQUE £ 12 : 35

(ABOVE) One of Dave Morton's early pay sheets, which includes his league debut at Sunderland on September 12, and second half rides at Crewe the following night. The pay rates were 75p a start, £1 a point, with 15p per start deducted for insurance. (BELOW LEFT) Barrie Smitherman, one of three family members from Shropshire, who rode together at Earle Street.

(ABOVE) Former Crayford and Nelson rider Stuart Riley, who appeared in two matches during the campaign.

When They Were Kings -1972-

When They Were Kings
-1972-

The usual pre-season merry-go-round saw newcomers Scunthorpe replace Knock Out Cup holders Ipswich, who took over the vacant Division I licence from West Ham, after the Londoners were forced to close when the Custom House stadium was sold for re-development. Romford moved in on a temporary basis (to become the West Ham Bombers) after eviction from their Brooklands home. Crewe gained Cheshire rivals, with the Rochdale licence and assets being purchased by Ellesmere Port. Colin Tucker once again performed minor miracles by completing the Thornton Road track in only five weeks. Applications from Barrow and Chesterton were turned down, the latter denied due to Crewe's strong objections that the area could not support two speedway teams. Barrow were granted an open licence. The K.O. Cup draw saw the Kings paired with Ellesmere Port in the only round one tie, and for the first time since the league's formation, Division II riders were allowed to compete in the preliminary qualifying rounds of the World Championship. On the Crewe team front, Barry Meeks, who had operated a Saturday morning training school at Earle Street during the close season, was transferred to Bradford, with Dai Evans appointed captain. But the surprise move was Jack Millen's shock return to Sunderland, who claimed, much to Maurice Littlechild's anger, that the Kiwi had only been on a season loan. Dave Morton and Ray Hassall were expected to fill the vacancies, but big things were predicted for another Aussie whom Phil Crump had recommended. Melbourne's Garry Flood was keen to try his hand on the British tracks, but as a highly skilled dirt rider, was also looking to secure a contract with a British scrambles machine factory. The best news for the Crewe faithful however, was that Crump had escaped the Army draft and was returning to Earle Street, although sister Division I track King's Lynn were also hopeful of his signature. Crump was a wanted man after twice riding for Australia in their test series with Great Britain down under. Ipswich tried in vain to tempt the Crewe camp with an offer of £1,000 for his services. The Kings gave pre-season trials to Aussies John Robinson and Cam Taylor, but neither were signed. Admission rose to 40p for adults and 20p for children and programmes from 5p to 8p. All was set therefore, for Crewe's fourth season in Division II, which would begin with a challenge match at Workington.

Meeting 1 - Friday, March 17, 1972 - Challenge, First Leg
Derwent Park Stadium, Workington
Track Length - 398 yards.

WORKINGTON COMETS.....43 CREWE KINGS.....35

With Phil Crump not due back in the country until March 23, the Kings opened their campaign with a makeshift team which included guests Jim Ryman (Boston) and Jack Millen (now Sunderland). In a rousing challenge match, Crewe produced eight heat winners, despite a catalogue of retirements, exclusions and falls. Comets new signing from Bradford, Dave Schofield, broke an ankle in his third outing after a tussle with Millen, who was excluded from the re-run.

Heat 01	**Morton**/Amundson/**Evans**/Owen (R)	80.8	**2 - 4**	02 - 04
Heat 02	Watson/Kumeta/**Moore**/**Millen**	81.0	5 - 1	07 - 05
Heat 03	**Ryman**/Schofield/Sansom/**Hassall**	80.6	3 - 3	10 - 08
Heat 04	**Jackson**/**Millen**/Mackay/Kumeta	78.2	**1 - 5**	11 - 13
Heat 05	Schofield/Sansom/**Evans**/**Morton** (R)	80.2	5 - 1	16 - 14
Heat 06	Owen/**Jackson**/Amundson/**Moore**	78.0	4 - 2	20 - 16
Heat 07	**Ryman**/Mackay/Kumeta/**Hassall** (R)	79.2	3 - 3	23 - 19
Heat 08	**Millen**/Amundson/Watson/**Morton** (R)	79.2	3 - 3	26 - 22
Heat 09	**Jackson**/Sansom/Watson/**Millen** (X)	78.6	3 - 3	29 - 25
Heat 10	Amundson/Owen/**Ryman**/**Moore** (R)	79.0	5 - 1	34 - 26
Heat 11	**Jackson**/Mackay/**Evans**/Watson	78.2	**2 - 4**	36 - 30
Heat 12	**Ryman**/Owen/Kumeta/**Jackson**	80.0	3 - 3	39 - 33
Heat 13	Mackay/**Evans**/Sansom/**Hassall** (F)	00.0	4 - 2	43 - 35

WORKINGTON - Kym Amundson 8, Malcolm Mackay 8, Taffy Owen 7 (+1), Lou Sansom 6 (+2), Steve Watson 5 (+2), Dave Schofield 5, Dave Kumeta 4 (+3).
CREWE - John Jackson 11, Jim Ryman* 10, Jack Millen* 5 (+1), Dai Evans 5, Dave Morton 3, Gary Moore 1, Ray Hassall 0.

Heavy mid-afternoon rain on March 31, left the Earle Street track unfit for racing, so the traditional Good Friday opening fixture against Bradford in the Top Dogs Trophy was postponed.

Meeting 2 - Tuesday, April 4, 1972 - British League Division II
Perry Barr Greyhound Stadium, Regina Drive, Walsall Road, Birmingham
Track Length - 350 yards.

BIRMINGHAM BRUMMIES.....43 CREWE KINGS.....35

Bad weather again threatened to spoil Crewe's first league match of the season, but thankfully the rain held off and the Perry Barr crowd were treated to some fine racing. The Brummies held a ten point lead after Heat 9, but a Kings fight back ensured the match went to the last heat. Phil Crump fell in his first outing, but won three of his remaining four rides and successfully defended his Silver Helmet title against Pete Bailey. Newcomer Garry Flood made his debut and secured four third places.

Heat	Riders	Time	Score	Total
Heat 01	Shearer/**Evans**/**Morton**/Wilkinson	71.8	3 - 3	03 - 03
Heat 02	Corradine/**Moore**/**Flood**/Browning (F)	66.0	3 - 3	06 - 06
Heat 03	Bailey/Gardner/**Parry**/**Crump** (F)	67.8	5 - 1	11 - 07
Heat 04	Major/Corradine/**Flood**/**Jackson**	66.0	5 - 1	16 - 08
Heat 05	Bailey/**Morton**/**Evans**/Gardner	66.4	3 - 3	19 - 11
Heat 06	**Jackson**/Shearer/**Moore**/Wilkinson	68.4	**2 - 4**	21 - 15
Heat 07	Major/**Crump**/**Parry**/Corradine	66.6	3 - 3	24 - 18
Heat 08	Browning/Wilkinson/**Flood**/**Morton**	67.4	5 - 1	29 - 19
Heat 09	**Crump**/Bailey/Gardner/**Moore**	66.4	3 - 3	32 - 22
Heat 10	**Crump**/Shearer/**Flood**/Wilkinson	68.0	**2 - 4**	34 - 26
Heat 11	Browning/**Morton**/**Evans**/Major	68.0	3 - 3	37 - 29
Heat 12	**Crump**/**Jackson**/Gardner/Shearer (F)	66.4	**1 - 5**	38 - 34
Heat 13	Major/Bailey/**Evans**/**Parry**	66.8	5 - 1	43 - 35

BIRMINGHAM - Pete Bailey 10 (+1), George Major 9, Terry Shearer 7, Arthur Browning 6, Malcolm Corradine 5 (+1), Mike Gardner 4 (+2), Archie Wilkinson 2 (+1).
CREWE - Phil Crump 11, Dai Evans 5 (+2), John Jackson 5 (+1), Dave Morton 5 (+1), Garry Flood 4 (+1), Gary Moore 3, Dave Parry 2 (+1).

Meeting 3 - Wednesday, April 5, 1972 - Top Dogs Trophy, First Leg
Odsal Stadium, Rooley Avenue, Bradford
Track Length - 380 yards.

BRADFORD NORTHERN.....42 CREWE KINGS.....36

Bradford's Alf Wells was suspended, for once again failing to turn up for another early season fixture, so second-halfer Mick Fairbairn was drafted in. It proved to be a shrewd move as he registered a paid eleven in the home side's six point first leg victory, achieved after seven of the first eight heats were drawn. Phil Crump, Dai Evans and Garry Flood all recorded heat wins for the visitors. Former King Barry Meeks had a miserable night scoring only a solitary point.

Heat	Riders	Time	Score	Total
Heat 01	Knapkin/**Evans**/**Morton**/Meeks (F)	72.6	3 - 3	03 - 03
Heat 02	Sheldrick/**Moore**/**Flood**/Roynon (X)	73.0	3 - 3	06 - 06
Heat 03	**Crump**/Adlington/Fairbairn/**Parry**	70.6	3 - 3	09 - 09
Heat 04	**Flood**/Baugh/Sheldrick/**Moore**	72.2	3 - 3	12 - 12
Heat 05	Fairbairn/**Morton**/**Evans**/Adlington (R)	74.6	3 - 3	15 - 15
Heat 06	Knapkin/**Jackson**/Meeks/**Moore** (F)	71.2	4 - 2	19 - 17
Heat 07	**Crump**/Baugh/Sheldrick/**Parry**	70.6	3 - 3	22 - 20
Heat 08	**Flood**/Sheldrick/Roynon/**Morton** (F)	72.4	3 - 3	25 - 23
Heat 09	Adlington/Fairbairn/**Moore**/**Jackson**	73.2	5 - 1	30 - 24
Heat 10	**Crump**/Knapkin/**Flood**/Meeks	69.8	**2 - 4**	32 - 28

Heat 11 .... **Evans**/Baugh/**Morton**/Roynon	73.0	**2 - 4**	34 - 32
Heat 12 .... Fairbairn/Knapkin/**Jackson**/**Crump** (X)	75.8	5 - 1	39 - 33
Heat 13 .... **Crump**/Baugh/Sheldrick/**Evans**	70.8	3 - 3	42 - 36

BRADFORD - Alan Knapkin 10 (+1), Mick Fairbairn 9 (+2), Sid Sheldrick 8 (+3), Dave Baugh 8, Robin Adlington 5, Chris Roynon 1 (+1), Barry Meeks 1.
CREWE - Phil Crump 12, Garry Flood 8 (+1), Dai Evans 6 (+1), Dave Morton 4 (+1), John Jackson 3, Gary Moore 3, Dave Parry 0.

Maurice Littlechild was quick to sing the praises of Garry Flood and was convinced he had again struck colonial gold: *"A real fighter. Tremendous throttle control and technique, rather like Phil Crump. Surprised me the way he tackled Birmingham recently, which is rather a tight circuit. Most Aussies are lost for a while - can't turn on our tracks. Garry managed beautifully. He's going to be a good 'un."* Indeed, such was Littlechild's confidence; he predicted that Flood would make the Australian test team before the season's end!

Meeting 4 - Monday, April 10, 1972 - Challenge, Second Leg
L.M.R. Sports Ground, Earle Street, Crewe
Track Length - 430 yards.

CREWE KINGS.....40 WORKINGTON COMETS.....38

(Workington won on aggregate 81 - 75)

The heavens opened during Heat 1 of Crewe's curtain raiser and poured for the rest of the meeting. The Kings stormed into a 21-9 lead after five heats, but their performance deteriorated as track conditions worsened, and only a Crump/Jackson maximum in the final race ensured a winning start at home, although the Comets did win on aggregate. The second-half was postponed due to the racing surface becoming waterlogged.

Heat 01 .... Owen/**Morton**/**Evans**/Amundson	74.8	3 - 3	03 - 03
Heat 02 .... **Moore**/Kumeta/**Parry**/Davies	77.2	**4 - 2**	07 - 05
Heat 03 .... **Crump**/**Flood**/Sansom/Watson (F)	77.4	**5 - 1**	12 - 06
Heat 04 .... **Jackson**/**Moore**/Mackay/Davies	75.0	**5 - 1**	17 - 07
Heat 05 .... **Crump**/Owen/**Flood**/Amundson (R)	76.6	**4 - 2**	21 - 09
Heat 06 .... Kumeta/Mackay/**Evans**/**Morton**	78.8	1 - 5	22 - 14
Heat 07 .... Sansom/**Jackson**/**Moore**/Watson	80.2	3 - 3	25 - 17
Heat 08 .... Owen/Kumeta/**Moore**/**Parry**	80.0	1 - 5	26 - 22
Heat 09 .... **Crump**/Mackay/**Flood**/Kumeta (R)	79.2	**4 - 2**	30 - 24
Heat 10 .... Sansom/**Moore**/**Evans**/Watson	81.8	3 - 3	33 - 27
Heat 11 .... Owen/Sansom/**Jackson**/**Parry**	85.0	1 - 5	34 - 32
Heat 12 .... Mackay/Sansom/**Evans**/**Flood** (R)	83.6	1 - 5	35 - 37
Heat 13 .... **Crump**/**Jackson**/Owen/Watson	80.2	**5 - 1**	40 - 38

CREWE - Phil Crump 12, Gary Moore 9 (+2), John Jackson 8 (+1), Dai Evans 4 (+2), Garry Flood 4 (+1), Dave Morton 2, Dave Parry 1.
WORKINGTON - Taffy Owen 12, Lou Sansom 11 (+2), Malcolm Mackay 8 (+1), Dave Kumeta 7 (+1), Kym Amundson 0, Lindsay Davies 0, Steve Watson 0.

Dai Evans failed in his attempt to reach the next stage of the World Championship, scoring seven points at Canterbury on April 15. Rayleigh's Bob Young won after a run-off.

Meeting 5 - Monday, April 17, 1972 - Sherwood Trophy, First Leg
L.M.R. Sports Ground, Earle Street, Crewe
Track Length - 430 yards.

CREWE KINGS.....54 LONG EATON RANGERS.....24

John Jackson clipped 1.2 seconds off the Earle Street track record after gating superbly in Heat 4, and then went inside the old mark three races later. Phil Crump and Dai Evans recorded maximums as Crewe built up a healthy thirty point first leg advantage to take to Station Road.

Heat 01 .... **Crump**/Bouchard/**Morton**/Harrison	74.0	**4 - 2**	04 - 02
Heat 02 .... Champion/**Moore**/**Parry**/Jarvis	76.2	3 - 3	07 - 05

Heat 03	**Evans**/**Flood**/Bass/Farmer	76.2	**5 - 1**	12 - 06
Heat 04	**Jackson**/Mills/**Moore**/Jarvis	**71.4** (TR)	**4 - 2**	16 - 08
Heat 05	**Evans**/**Flood**/Harrison/Bouchard	75.2	**5 - 1**	21 - 09
Heat 06	**Crump**/Mills/Champion/**Morton** (R)	74.6	3 - 3	24 - 12
Heat 07	**Jackson**/**Moore**/Bass/Farmer	72.2	**5 - 1**	29 - 13
Heat 08	**Moore**/Bouchard/**Parry**/Harrison	75.8	**4 - 2**	33 - 15
Heat 09	**Evans**/Mills/**Flood**/Champion	74.4	**4 - 2**	37 - 17
Heat 10	**Crump**/**Parry**/Farmer/Bass (R)	74.8	**5 - 1**	42 - 18
Heat 11	**Jackson**/Harrison/Bouchard/**Parry**	73.2	3 - 3	45 - 21
Heat 12	**Crump**/Mills/**Flood**/Champion	74.6	**4 - 2**	49 - 23
Heat 13	**Evans**/**Jackson**/Bass/Bouchard	73.6	**5 - 1**	54 - 24

CREWE - Phil Crump 12, Dai Evans 12, John Jackson 11 (+1), Gary Moore 8 (+1), Garry Flood 6 (+2), Dave Parry 4 (+2), Dave Morton 1.
LONG EATON - Roger Mills 8, Geoff Bouchard 5 (+1), Ian Champion 4 (+1), Steve Bass 3, Chris Harrison 3, Gil Farmer 1, Peter Jarvis 0.

Meeting 6 - Thursday, April 20, 1972 - Sherwood Trophy, Second Leg
Long Eaton Stadium, Station Road, Long Eaton
Track Length - 366 yards.

LONG EATON RANGERS.....40 CREWE KINGS.....38

(Crewe won on aggregate 92 - 64)

Despite riding with a badly swollen left knee, Phil Crump recorded a faultless maximum (his third in a row). John Jackson and Dave Parry were the other Crewe heat winners, in the narrow two-point defeat, which secured the Sherwood Trophy by twenty-eight points on aggregate.

Heat 01	**Crump**/Bouchard/Harrison/**Hassall**	71.6	3 - 3	03 - 03
Heat 02	**Parry**/Jarvis/Champion/**Moore**	77.2	3 - 3	06 - 06
Heat 03	Bass/**Flood**/**Evans**/Farmer (F)	76.6	3 - 3	09 - 09
Heat 04	**Jackson**/Mills/Champion/**Parry**	73.8	3 - 3	12 - 12
Heat 05	**Crump**/Farmer/Bass/**Hassall**	73.6	3 - 3	15 - 15
Heat 06	Bouchard/**Moore**/Harrison/**Jackson** (R)	73.2	4 - 2	19 - 17
Heat 07	Mills/**Flood**/**Evans**/Champion	73.6	3 - 3	22 - 20
Heat 08	Jarvis/Harrison/**Parry**/**Hassall**	77.8	5 - 1	27 - 21
Heat 09	Farmer/Bass/**Moore**/**Jackson** (R)	75.4	5 - 1	32 - 22
Heat 10	Bouchard/**Evans**/**Flood**/Harrison	73.8	3 - 3	35 - 25
Heat 11	**Crump**/Jarvis/**Jackson**/Mills (R)	74.0	**2 - 4**	37 - 29
Heat 12	**Crump**/Bouchard/**Evans**/Farmer	74.4	**2 - 4**	39 - 33
Heat 13	**Crump**/**Flood**/Bass/Mills (R)	74.0	**1 - 5**	40 - 38

LONG EATON - Geoff Bouchard 10, Steve Bass 7 (+2), Peter Jarvis 7, Gil Farmer 5, Roger Mills 5, Chris Harrison 4 (+2), Ian Champion 2 (+2).
CREWE - Phil Crump 15, Garry Flood 7 (+2), Dai Evans 5 (+2), John Jackson 4, Dave Parry 4, Gary Moore 3, Ray Hassall 0.

The following night Phil Crump progressed from the World Championship Qualifying Round, finishing second to Rayleigh's Geoff Maloney at Peterborough, after securing thirteen points. John Jackson however, was not so fortunate, suffering with motor troubles all night, scoring only two points. Crump celebrated his qualification by signing for King's Lynn, but would still continue to ride for Crewe until the end of the season.

Meeting 7 - Monday, April 24, 1972 - British League Division II
L.M.R. Sports Ground, Earle Street, Crewe
Track Length - 430 yards.

CREWE KINGS.....37 PETERBOROUGH PANTHERS.....41

In terms of shock results, this was one of the biggest, as Peterborough ended a long run of away defeats and Crewe's proud record of 41 unbeaten home league matches. The Panthers became the first club to win in league competition around Earle Street since Belle Vue Colts in July 1969, and this on the back of previous visits, where they had been hammered by more than thirty-four points. Ray Hassall won a pre-match "Vultures Race" to earn a place in the side,

(ABOVE) Crewe new-boy Garry Flood.

(ABOVE) The young Aussie practicing a start.

(ABOVE) The Kings of '72, sporting new body colours. (Left to right) Dave Morton, John Jackson, Dave Parry, Gary Moore, Dai Evans, Les Moore (mechanic), Phil Crump and Garry Flood.

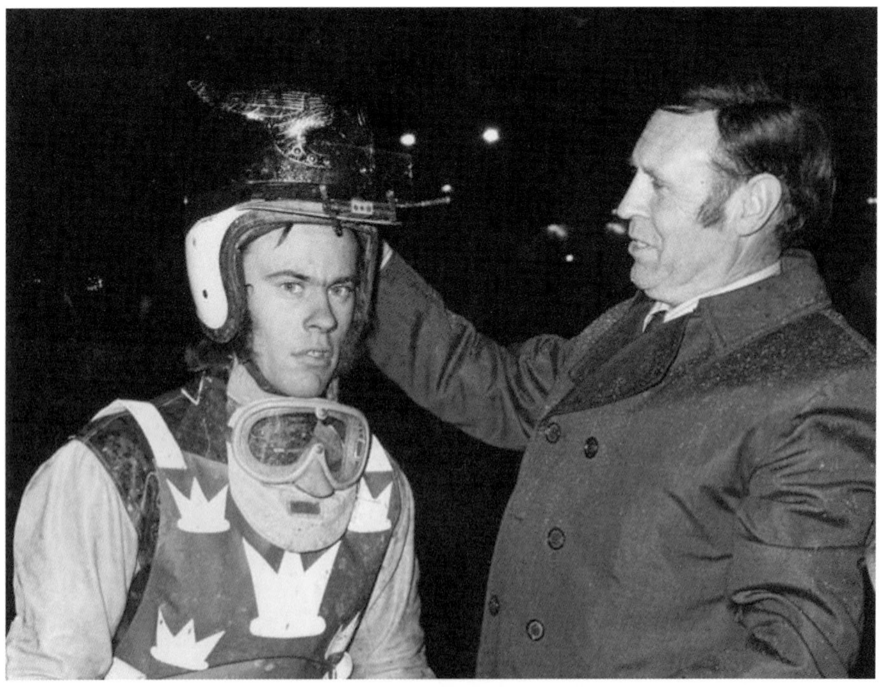

(ABOVE) Maurice Littlechild presents Phil Crump with the Silver Helmet, which he won at Birmingham on April 4.

but failed to score. The Kings led by six points after seven heats, but the visitors hit back with maximum points in the next two, which swung the meeting in their favour. John Jackson and Dave Morton once again struggled on troublesome machinery. To complete a miserable night for the home support, Phil Crump lost his Silver Helmet to Richard Greer after finishing the race with a flat tyre.

Heat 01	**Crump**/Harrhy/Noy/**Morton** (R)	75.4	3 - 3	03 - 03
Heat 02	Davis/**Moore**/Clark/**Hassall**	76.6	2 - 4	05 - 07
Heat 03	**Flood**/**Evans**/Carter/Witt	75.4	**5 - 1**	10 - 08
Heat 04	Davis/Greer/**Moore**/**Jackson**	76.6	1 - 5	11 - 13
Heat 05	**Flood**/**Evans**/Harrhy/Noy	75.2	**5 - 1**	16 - 14
Heat 06	**Crump**/Greer/Clark/**Morton**	74.6	3 - 3	19 - 17
Heat 07	**Jackson**/**Moore**/Carter/Witt	74.4	**5 - 1**	24 - 18
Heat 08	Davis/Noy/**Morton**/**Hassall**	76.4	1 - 5	25 - 23
Heat 09	Greer/Clark/**Evans**/**Flood** (R)	74.2	1 - 5	26 - 28
Heat 10	**Crump**/Davis/Carter/**Moore**	74.6	3 - 3	29 - 31
Heat 11	Harrhy/**Jackson**/Noy/**Hassall**	75.0	2 - 4	31 - 35
Heat 12	**Crump**/Greer/**Flood**/Carter	74.0	**4 - 2**	35 - 37
Heat 13	Harrhy/**Evans**/Davis/**Jackson**	74.0	2 - 4	37 - 41

CREWE - Phil Crump 12, Dai Evans 7 (+2), Garry Flood 7, Gary Moore 5 (+1), John Jackson 5, Dave Morton 1, Ray Hassall 0.
PETERBOROUGH - John Davis 12, Richard Greer 9 (+1), John Harrhy 9, Brian Clark 4 (+2), Clive Noy 4 (+2), Roy Carter 3 (+1), Alan Witt 0.

Meeting 8 - Monday, May 1, 1972 - Speedway Express Knock Out Cup, First Round, First Leg
L.M.R. Sports Ground, Earle Street, Crewe
Track Length - 430 yards.

CREWE KINGS.....49 ELLESMERE PORT GUNNERS.....29

Garry Flood showed his potential as a future heat leader when top scoring in the Cheshire derby. Riding at reserve, he was given extra rides after skipper Dai Evans blew his engine in Heat 3, and was only denied a five ride maximum by John Jackson in Heat 11, who completed his own full house in the last race of the match. The Gunners led by four after three heats, but then Crewe stepped up a gear, finishing with a twenty point lead to take to Thornton Road. Phil Crump recorded his fifth maximum in succession.

Heat 01	**Crump**/Goad/Tyrer/**Morton**	72.4	3 - 3	03 - 03
Heat 02	**Flood**/Blythe/Kelly/**Moore** (R)	73.6	3 - 3	06 - 06
Heat 03	Callaghan/Blythe/**Parry**/**Evans** (R)	75.4	1 - 5	07 - 11
Heat 04	**Jackson**/**Moore**/Drury/Kelly	72.6	**5 - 1**	12 - 12
Heat 05	**Flood**/**Parry**/Tyrer/Goad	74.6	**5 - 1**	17 - 13
Heat 06	**Crump**/Drury/**Morton**/Blythe	72.8	**4 - 2**	21 - 15
Heat 07	**Jackson**/**Moore**/Callaghan/Gardner	72.8	**5 - 1**	26 - 16
Heat 08	**Flood**/Tyrer/Goad/**Moore** (R)	73.4	3 - 3	29 - 19
Heat 09	**Flood**/Drury/Blythe/**Parry**	75.2	3 - 3	32 - 22
Heat 10	**Crump**/Callaghan/**Moore**/Gardner	73.0	**4 - 2**	36 - 24
Heat 11	**Jackson**/**Flood**/Tyrer/Goad (R)	73.2	**5 - 1**	41 - 25
Heat 12	**Crump**/**Parry**/Drury/Callaghan	75.0	**5 - 1**	46 - 26
Heat 13	**Jackson**/Tyrer/Drury/**Evans**	72.6	3 - 3	49 - 29

CREWE - Garry Flood 14 (+1), Phil Crump 12, John Jackson 12, Gary Moore 5 (+2), Dave Parry 5 (+2), Dave Morton 1, Dai Evans 0.
ELLESMERE PORT - Graham Drury 7 (+1), Paul Tyrer 7 (+1), Paul Callaghan 6, Chris Blythe 5 (+2), Colin Goad 3 (+1), Terry Kelly 1 (+1), Robbie Gardner 0, *Ken Moss (R/R).*

West Ham (formerly Romford) management announced that they were to close due to the impending demolition of the Custom House stadium.

Meeting 9 - Tuesday, May 2, 1972 - Speedway Express Knock Out Cup, First Round, Second Leg
Ellesmere Port Stadium, Thornton Road, Ellesmere Port
Track Length - 423 yards.

ELLESMERE PORT GUNNERS.....33 CREWE KINGS.....45

(Crewe won on aggregate 94 - 62)

Crewe produced a power-house display to comfortably progress in the K.O. Cup. John Jackson was the most impressive King, lowering the track record in his first ride, and then just for good measure, knocked a further 0.2 seconds off in Heat 9. Phil Crump, Garry Flood and Dai Evans provided solid back-up, with eleven of the thirteen heats won by a visiting rider.

Heat 01	**Crump**/Goad/**Morton**/Tyrer	78.0	**2 - 4**	02 - 04
Heat 02	**Flood**/Blythe/**Moore**/Kelly (F)	79.8	**2 - 4**	04 - 08
Heat 03	Blythe/**Evans**/**Parry**/Tyrer (F)	78.4	3 - 3	07 - 11
Heat 04	**Jackson**/Drury/Blythe/**Flood**	**76.2** (TR)	3 - 3	10 - 14
Heat 05	**Crump**/**Flood**/Gardner/Callaghan	77.0	**1 - 5**	11 - 19
Heat 06	**Jackson**/Goad/**Moore**/Tyrer (R)	76.4	**2 - 4**	13 - 23
Heat 07	**Evans**/Drury/Blythe/**Parry**	78.2	3 - 3	16 - 26
Heat 08	**Flood**/Drury/Goad/**Moore**	77.4	3 - 3	19 - 29
Heat 09	**Jackson**/Tyrer/Gardner/**Moore**	**76.0** (TR)	3 - 3	22 - 32
Heat 10	Tyrer/**Evans**/Goad/**Parry**	77.6	4 - 2	26 - 34
Heat 11	**Crump**/Drury/**Flood**/Kelly (F)	77.4	**2 - 4**	28 - 38
Heat 12	**Jackson**/Tyrer/**Evans**/Blythe	76.8	**2 - 4**	30 - 42
Heat 13	**Crump**/Goad/Drury/**Moore**	77.6	3 - 3	33 - 45

ELLESMERE PORT - Graham Drury 9 (+1), Colin Goad 8 (+1), Chris Blythe 7 (+2), Paul Tyrer 7, Robbie Gardner 2 (+1), Paul Callaghan 0, Terry Kelly 0. *Ken Moss (R/R).*
CREWE - Phil Crump 12, John Jackson 12, Garry Flood 9 (+1), Dai Evans 8, Gary Moore 2, Dave Parry 1 (+1), Dave Morton 1.

On May 8, the Crewe v Sunderland league meeting was postponed due to a waterlogged track.

Meeting 10 - Friday, May 12, 1972 - British League Division II
East of England Showground, Alwalton, Peterborough
Track Length - 380 yards.

PETERBOROUGH PANTHERS.....45 CREWE KINGS.....33

The Panthers completed an early season double, which left Crewe still pointless in the league table. Phil Crump recorded his seventh straight maximum and broke the Alwalton track record when powering home in Heat 1. Garry Flood won three heats in a row, as visiting riders were successful in nine of the thirteen heats. John Jackson recorded a solitary win in Heat 4, but the rest of the side mustered only two points between them.

Heat 01	**Crump**/Harrhy/Clark/**Moore**	**69.2** (TR)	3 - 3	03 - 03
Heat 02	Noy/Witt/**Morton**/**Flood** (F)	71.2	5 - 1	08 - 04
Heat 03	Carter/Davis/**Parry**/**Evans**	69.4	5 - 1	13 - 05
Heat 04	**Jackson**/Noy/Greer/**Flood**	70.4	3 - 3	16 - 08
Heat 05	**Crump**/Carter/Davis/**Moore**	72.0	3 - 3	19 - 11
Heat 06	Harrhy/**Jackson**/Clark/**Morton**	75.4	4 - 2	23 - 13
Heat 07	**Crump**/Noy/Greer/**Evans**	71.8	3 - 3	26 - 16
Heat 08	**Flood**/Witt/Clark/**Jackson** (R)	72.4	3 - 3	29 - 19
Heat 09	**Flood**/Carter/Davis/**Evans**	71.6	3 - 3	32 - 22
Heat 10	**Flood**/Harrhy/Noy/**Evans**	72.4	3 - 3	35 - 25
Heat 11	**Crump**/Greer/Witt/**Moore**	70.4	3 - 3	38 - 28
Heat 12	Harrhy/**Flood**/Carter/**Jackson**	71.6	4 - 2	42 - 30
Heat 13	**Crump**/Greer/Davis/**Morton**	70.6	3 - 3	45 - 33

PETERBOROUGH - John Harrhy 10, Clive Noy 8 (+1), Roy Carter 8, Richard Greer 6 (+2), John Davis 5 (+4), Alan Witt 5 (+2), Brian Clark 3 (+2).
CREWE - Phil Crump 15, Garry Flood 11, John Jackson 5, Dave Morton 1, Dave Parry 1, Dai Evans 0, Gary Moore 0.

Meeting 11 - Monday, May 15, 1972 - British League Division II
L.M.R. Sports Ground, Earle Street, Crewe
Track Length - 430 yards.

CREWE KINGS.....49 BRADFORD NORTHERN.....29

It was fourth time lucky for the Kings as they finally kick-started their assault on the league crown. Northern skipper Alan Knapkin won three of his five outings, and was the only visitor to win a race, recording the quickest time of the match in Heat 9. He also defeated Phil Crump in Heat 12, to deny him another maximum, ending a sequence of 40 straight wins by the Aussie ace. Crewe's heat leader trio each recorded double figures, with John Jackson unbeaten and Garry Flood chipping in with a paid eleven. Barry Meeks scored four on his return to Earle Street.

Heat 01	**Crump**/Baugh/**Moore**/Bridgett	74.8	**4 - 2**	04 - 02
Heat 02	**Flood**/Meeks/**Morton**/Dewhurst	74.4	**4 - 2**	08 - 04
Heat 03	**Evans**/Adlington/Sheldrick/**Parry**	75.0	3 - 3	11 - 07
Heat 04	**Jackson**/Knapkin/Meeks/**Morton**	73.8	3 - 3	14 - 10
Heat 05	**Evans**/Baugh/**Parry**/Bridgett	75.2	**4 - 2**	18 - 12
Heat 06	**Crump**/Knapkin/**Moore**/Meeks	75.8	**4 - 2**	22 - 14
Heat 07	**Jackson**/**Morton**/Adlington/Sheldrick	75.0	**5 - 1**	27 - 15
Heat 08	Knapkin/**Flood**/Baugh/**Moore** (R)	74.0	2 - 4	29 - 19
Heat 09	Knapkin/**Evans**/Meeks/**Parry**	73.4	2 - 4	31 - 23
Heat 10	**Crump**/**Flood**/Adlington/Sheldrick	74.4	**5 - 1**	36 - 24
Heat 11	**Jackson**/**Flood**/Baugh/Dewhurst	74.0	**5 - 1**	41 - 25
Heat 12	Knapkin/**Crump**/**Parry**/Meeks	73.6	3 - 3	44 - 28
Heat 13	**Jackson**/**Evans**/Baugh/Dewhurst	74.0	**5 - 1**	49 - 29

CREWE - John Jackson 12, Phil Crump 11, Dai Evans 10 (+1), Garry Flood 9 (+2), Dave Morton 3 (+1), Dave Parry 2 (+1), Gary Moore 2.
BRADFORD - Alan Knapkin 13, Dave Baugh 7, Barry Meeks 4 (+1), Robin Adlington 4, Sid Sheldrick 1 (+1), Alan Bridgett 0, Stan Dewhurst 0.

Phil Crump rose to second in the Division II averages with a 10.89 CMA. On May 17, he won the Northumberland Open Championship at open licence track Ashington with a five ride maximum, setting a new track record of 74.0 in the process.

Meeting 12 - Saturday, May 20, 1972 - British League Division II
Rayleigh Weir Stadium, Southend Arterial Road, Rayleigh
Track Length - 365 yards.

RAYLEIGH ROCKETS.....40 CREWE KINGS.....38

A see-saw thriller at the Weir Stadium saw the Kings up by six points after five races, only for the Rockets to fight back to lead by ten at the end of Heat 10. Two away 5-1's then cut the advantage to just two, thus forcing a last heat decider for a third successive season. Phil Crump won the final three heats to complete yet another full-house, but his efforts were all in vain in the last, as Garry Flood failed to pass either Bob Young or Allan Emmett.

Heat 01	**Crump**/Maloney/Brown/**Parry**	69.6	3 - 3	03 - 03
Heat 02	Rackett/**Morton**/Stone/**Moore**	72.2	4 - 2	07 - 05
Heat 03	**Flood**/**Evans**/Young/Beech	70.8	**1 - 5**	08 - 10
Heat 04	**Jackson**/Emmett/**Moore**/Stone	70.4	**2 - 4**	10 - 14
Heat 05	**Crump**/Young/**Parry**/Beech (R)	69.6	**2 - 4**	12 - 18
Heat 06	Brown/Maloney/**Jackson**/**Morton**	71.0	5 - 1	17 - 19
Heat 07	Emmett/Rackett/**Evans**/**Flood**	70.0	5 - 1	22 - 20
Heat 08	Brown/**Moore**/Rackett/**Parry**	71.6	4 - 2	26 - 22
Heat 09	Young/**Morton**/Beech/**Moore**	70.2	4 - 2	30 - 24
Heat 10	Maloney/Brown/**Evans**/**Morton**	70.6	5 - 1	35 - 25
Heat 11	**Crump**/**Flood**/Emmett/Rackett (F)	70.6	**1 - 5**	36 - 30
Heat 12	**Crump**/**Evans**/Beech/Maloney (F)	69.4	**1 - 5**	37 - 35
Heat 13	**Crump**/Young/Emmett/**Flood**	69.4	3 - 3	40 - 38

RAYLEIGH - Dingle Brown 9 (+2), Bob Young 8, Allan Emmett 7 (+1), Geoff Maloney 7 (+1), Nigel Rackett 6 (+1), Tiger Beech 2, Terry Stone 1.
CREWE - Phil Crump 15, Dai Evans 6 (+2), Garry Flood 5 (+1), John Jackson 4, Dave Morton 4, Gary Moore 3, Dave Parry 1.

Champions Eastbourne led the table with fifteen points from thirteen meetings. Peterborough were second, with six wins from seven, which included three away victories. Crewe remained bottom despite their first victory, but did have matches in hand on their rivals. The Kings proposed meeting with the Young Czechs, scheduled for August 21, was called off when the tourists pulled out of their scheduled nine match tour due to domestic reasons. The Crewe management also failed in their bid to stage an "extra" Division II international between England and Australasia.

Meeting 13 - Sunday, May 21, 1972 - British League Division II
Sunderland Greyhound Stadium, Newcastle Road, East Boldon
Track Length - 310 yards.

SUNDERLAND STARS.....34 CREWE KINGS.....43

Classy Crewe strolled to victory at Sunderland, despite Jack Millen's valiant efforts against his old team, and only a 5-0 last heat gift saved the Stars from an even bigger drubbing. Phil Crump stated his intent early on when equalling the Boldon track record, but for once couldn't cap his performance with a maximum, due to a retirement in the final heat. There were also good returns for John Jackson and Garry Flood, but Dave Parry's indifferent start to the season continued with just a single point from three rides.

Heat 01	**Crump**/Dent/**Parry**/Wrathall (X)	**65.0** (=TR)	**2 - 4**	02 - 04
Heat 02	Gatenby/**Moore**/**Morton**/Wells	68.8	3 - 3	05 - 07
Heat 03	**Flood**/Millen/**Evans**/Barclay (X)	66.4	**2 - 4**	07 - 11
Heat 04	**Jackson**/Smith/Gatenby/**Moore**	66.2	3 - 3	10 - 14
Heat 05	**Crump**/Millen/Barclay/**Parry**	65.4	3 - 3	13 - 17
Heat 06	**Jackson**/Wrathall/Dent/**Morton**	66.8	3 - 3	16 - 20
Heat 07	**Flood**/**Evans**/Smith/Wells	71.2	**1 - 5**	17 - 25
Heat 08	Gatenby/**Morton**/Wrathall/**Moore**	70.0	4 - 2	21 - 27
Heat 09	Millen/**Jackson**/**Morton**/Barclay	66.6	3 - 3	24 - 30
Heat 10	**Flood**/**Evans**/Dent/Millen	68.0	**1 - 5**	25 - 35
Heat 11	**Crump**/Smith/Gatenby/**Parry**	66.0	3 - 3	28 - 38
Heat 12	**Jackson**/**Evans**/Dent/Barclay	66.2	**1 - 5**	29 - 43
Heat 13	Millen/Smith/**Flood** (F)/**Crump** (R)	67.4	5 - 0	34 - 43

SUNDERLAND - Jack Millen 10, Dave Gatenby 8 (+2), Graeme Smith 7 (+1), Russ Dent 5 (+1), Peter Wrathall 3, George Barclay 1 (+1), Jim Wells 0.
CREWE - John Jackson 11, Phil Crump 9, Garry Flood 9, Dai Evans 7 (+3), Dave Morton 4 (+2), Gary Moore 2, Dave Parry 1.

Meeting 14 - Monday, May 22, 1972 - British League Division II
L.M.R. Sports Ground, Earle Street, Crewe
Track Length - 430 yards.

CREWE KINGS.....51 WEST HAM BOMBERS.....27

The Bombers were shot down in flames by an early barrage of home maximums, which saw the Kings 27-9 up after six heats. Phil Crump and Garry Flood both finished with paid elevens, but John Jackson upstaged both with a third consecutive Earle Street maximum, which was achieved in the final heat when he forced his way through to overhaul the visitors top-scorer Brian Foote.

Heat 01	**Crump**/Holden/Stevens/**Parry**	75.0	3 - 3	03 - 03
Heat 02	**Moore**/**Morton**/Lanham/Benham	77.0	**5 - 1**	08 - 04
Heat 03	**Flood**/Sampson/**Evans**/Foote	75.2	**4 - 2**	12 - 06
Heat 04	**Jackson**/**Morton**/Coles/Lanham	73.0	**5 - 1**	17 - 07
Heat 05	**Evans**/**Flood**/Holden/Stevens	75.8	**5 - 1**	22 - 08
Heat 06	**Crump**/**Parry**/Lanham/Coles	77.0	**5 - 1**	27 - 09
Heat 07	**Jackson**/Foote/Sampson/**Morton**	73.8	3 - 3	30 - 12
Heat 08	Stevens/**Parry**/Lanham/**Moore** (R)	76.6	2 - 4	32 - 16
Heat 09	**Flood**/**Evans**/Coles/Benham	75.2	**5 - 1**	37 - 17
Heat 10	**Crump**/Foote/Sampson/**Parry**	76.2	3 - 3	40 - 20
Heat 11	**Jackson**/Stevens/**Morton**/Lanham	75.0	**4 - 2**	44 - 22

Heat 12 .... Foote/**Flood**/**Crump**/Coles	75.6	3 - 3	47 - 25
Heat 13 .... **Jackson**/Foote/**Evans**/Sampson	75.4	**4 - 2**	51 - 27

CREWE - John Jackson 12, Phil Crump 10 (+1), Garry Flood 10 (+1), Dai Evans 7 (+1), Dave Morton 5 (+2), Dave Parry 4 (+1), Gary Moore 3.
WEST HAM - Brian Foote 9, Stan Stevens 6 (+1), Mike Sampson 4 (+2), Kevin Holden 3, Mike Lanham 3, Bob Coles 2, Charlie Benham 0.

Phil Crump's impressive run of big scores shot him to the top of the Division II averages. On May 24, he scored a fifteen point maximum to win the Hull Open Championship, earning himself a new set of leathers, presented to him by Pat Phoenix ("Elsie Tanner" of Coronation Street fame). Next night he began his quest to reach the semi-finals in the British zone of the World Championship at Sheffield, where he finished a credible 9th. On May 27, he arrived at Swindon for his next round, but due to a communication error, should have been riding at Coventry! Fortunately he was allowed to compete as a replacement for the injured Sandor Levai, and gave himself a great chance of qualifying when finishing third with twelve points.

Meeting 15 - Monday, May 29, 1972 - British League Division II
L.M.R. Sports Ground, Earle Street, Crewe
Track Length - 430 yards.

CREWE KINGS.....61 BIRMINGHAM BRUMMIES.....17

The only consolation for Birmingham was that they improved upon their 62-16 trouncing of the previous season! Backed by a large following, the Brummies, without the services of Arthur Browning, who was honouring a scrambling engagement arranged prior to him signing for the club, and with Malcolm Corradine nursing three broken bones in his foot, lost every heat - nine by the maximum score. John Jackson and Phil Crump went through the card undefeated as five different Crewe riders recorded wins, including a first league triumph for Dave Morton. Dai Evans provided an abject lesson in the skills of team riding, following his partner home in each of his rides.

Heat 01 .... **Crump**/**Morton**/Emms/Bailey	74.0	**5 - 1**	05 - 01
Heat 02 .... **Parry**/Gardner/**Moore**/Hines	75.8	**4 - 2**	09 - 03
Heat 03 .... **Flood**/**Evans**/Shearer/Major	73.6	**5 - 1**	14 - 04
Heat 04 .... **Jackson**/**Parry**/Hines/Corradine	72.6	**5 - 1**	19 - 05
Heat 05 .... **Flood**/**Evans**/Bailey/Emms	74.8	**5 - 1**	24 - 06
Heat 06 .... **Crump**/**Morton**/Hines/Corradine	73.8	**5 - 1**	29 - 07
Heat 07 .... **Jackson**/**Parry**/Major/Shearer	73.0	**5 - 1**	34 - 08
Heat 08 .... **Morton**/Gardner/**Moore**/Emms	75.2	**4 - 2**	38 - 10
Heat 09 .... **Flood**/**Evans**/Bailey/Corradine	74.6	**5 - 1**	43 - 11
Heat 10 .... **Crump**/Major/**Morton**/Shearer	74.0	**4 - 2**	47 - 13
Heat 11 .... **Jackson**/**Moore**/Emms/Bailey	72.0	**5 - 1**	52 - 14
Heat 12 .... **Crump**/Shearer/**Flood**/Major	74.8	**4 - 2**	56 - 16
Heat 13 .... **Jackson**/**Evans**/Bailey/Gardner	72.6	**5 - 1**	61 - 17

CREWE - Phil Crump 12, John Jackson 12, Garry Flood 10, Dai Evans 8 (+4), Dave Morton 8 (+2), Dave Parry 7 (+2), Gary Moore 4 (+1).
BIRMINGHAM - Mike Gardner 4, Pete Bailey 3, George Major 3, Terry Shearer 3, Cliff Emms 2, Mick Hines 2, Malcolm Corradine 0.

Events in Division II saw Colin Tucker hang up his leathers and take over the team manager's job at Hull. Barrow (an interest of Ivan Mauger), who had been operating on an open licence, stepped in to take over the remaining fixtures of the now homeless West Ham. On June 1, Phil Crump won the Teesside Open Championship, and the next night at Glasgow, finished in joint third place, gaining the ten points required to qualify for the semi-final of the World Championship (British zone), becoming the first lower league rider to achieve this for twenty-one years. To complete a hectic schedule twenty-four hours later, he scored a brilliant fifteen point maximum for King's Lynn in their 59-19 defeat of Newport. Back at Crewe, American Freddie Ortiz arrived after paying his own fare from California, in the hope of breaking into the Kings squad, unaware of the ruling precluding non-colonial foreign riders from competing in the Second Division!

Meeting 16 - Sunday, June 4, 1972 - Speedway Express Knock Out Cup, Second Round, First Leg
Quibell Park Stadium, Brumby Wood Lane, Scunthorpe
Track Length - 440 yards.

SCUNTHORPE SAINTS.....19 CREWE KINGS.....59

The Kings fantastic run of form continued on a slick Quibell Park track, with a massive forty point first leg win - the biggest away victory by a British speedway team at any level of competition. Cheered on by over 500 travelling supporters, Crewe recorded nine 5-1's and provided all thirteen race winners. Phil Crump recorded yet another maximum.

Heat 01	**Crump**/**Morton**/Bowerman/Maxted	80.2	**1 - 5**	01 - 05
Heat 02	**Parry**/**Moore**/Osborn/Haynes	83.0	**1 - 5**	02 - 10
Heat 03	**Flood**/Bellham/**Evans**/Wilson	82.2	**2 - 4**	04 - 14
Heat 04	**Jackson**/**Moore**/Haynes/Bass	80.6	**1 - 5**	05 - 19
Heat 05	**Crump**/**Morton**/Bellham/Wilson	83.0	**1 - 5**	06 - 24
Heat 06	**Jackson**/**Parry**/Maxted/Bowerman	82.6	**1 - 5**	07 - 29
Heat 07	**Flood**/**Evans**/Haynes/Bass (R)	83.4	**1 - 5**	08 - 34
Heat 08	**Morton**/Bellham/Maxted/**Moore** (F)	84.0	3 - 3	11 - 37
Heat 09	**Jackson**/**Parry**/Haynes/Bellham	82.0	**1 - 5**	12 - 42
Heat 10	**Flood**/**Evans**/Bowerman/Maxted	84.4	**1 - 5**	13 - 47
Heat 11	**Crump**/Osborn/**Morton**/Haynes	83.4	**2 - 4**	15 - 51
Heat 12	**Evans**/Wilson/Maxted/**Jackson** (R)	83.6	3 - 3	18 - 54
Heat 13	**Crump**/**Flood**/Haynes/Bass	84.6	**1 - 5**	19 - 59

SCUNTHORPE - Alan Bellham 5, Rod Haynes 4, Brian Maxted 3 (+2), Brian Osborn 3, John Bowerman 2, Ian Wilson 2, Phil Bass 0.
CREWE - Phil Crump 12, Garry Flood 11 (+1), John Jackson 9, Dai Evans 8 (+2), Dave Morton 8 (+2), Dave Parry 7 (+2), Gary Moore 4 (+2).

Crewe's victory was deemed bigger than Wembley's 63-21 victory at West Ham in August 1952, which was achieved over 14 heats.

Meeting 17 - Monday, June 5, 1972 - Speedway Express Knock Out Cup, Second Round, Second Leg
L.M.R. Sports Ground, Earle Street, Crewe
Track Length - 430 yards.

CREWE KINGS.....59 SCUNTHORPE SAINTS.....19

(Crewe won on aggregate 118 - 38)

The records were sent tumbling again, as Crewe smashed the previous best K.O. Cup aggregate score by 32 points, held by Ipswich after their 48 point advantage against Peterborough in 1971. Poor Scunthorpe once again failed to win a single heat, which saw Crewe's unbeaten run stretch to 44 races. Phil Crump and John Jackson completed maximums, with paid ones for Garry Flood, Dave Morton and skipper Dai Evans, who for a second home meeting in a row, picked up a bonus in each of his rides.

Heat 01	**Crump**/**Morton**/Maxted/Bowerman	77.4	**5 - 1**	05 - 01
Heat 02	Osborn/**Moore**/**Parry**/Haynes	77.8	3 - 3	08 - 04
Heat 03	**Flood**/**Evans**/Bass/Bellham	77.0	**5 - 1**	13 - 05
Heat 04	**Jackson**/Wilson/**Parry**/Haynes	77.6	**4 - 2**	17 - 07
Heat 05	**Flood**/**Evans**/Maxted/Osborn	76.2	**5 - 1**	22 - 08
Heat 06	**Crump**/**Morton**/Osborn/Wilson	76.4	**5 - 1**	27 - 09
Heat 07	**Jackson**/Bass/**Parry**/Bellham	75.0	**4 - 2**	31 - 11
Heat 08	**Morton**/Bass/**Moore**/Bowerman	75.0	**4 - 2**	35 - 13
Heat 09	**Flood**/**Evans**/Osborn/Haynes	76.2	**5 - 1**	40 - 14
Heat 10	**Crump**/**Morton**/Bowerman/Bass (R)	75.0	**5 - 1**	45 - 15
Heat 11	**Jackson**/Maxted/**Moore**/Bellham	74.4	**4 - 2**	49 - 17
Heat 12	**Crump**/**Flood**/Bass/Wilson	74.0	**5 - 1**	54 - 18
Heat 13	**Jackson**/**Evans**/Maxted/Bellham	75.4	**5 - 1**	59 - 19

CREWE - Phil Crump 12, John Jackson 12, Garry Flood 11 (+1), Dave Morton 9 (+3), Dai Evans 8 (+4), Gary Moore 4, Dave Parry 3 (+1).
SCUNTHORPE - Phil Bass 6, Brian Maxted 5, Brian Osborn 5, Ian Wilson 2, John Bowerman 1, Alan Bellham 0, Rod Haynes 0.

On June 6, Phil Crump won the Cheshire Open Championship at Ellesmere Port, again without forfeiting a race. John Jackson also competed, finishing joint fourth.

Meeting 18 - Monday, June 12, 1972 - British League Division II
L.M.R. Sports Ground, Earle Street, Crewe
Track Length - 430 yards.

CREWE KINGS.....44 ELLESMERE PORT GUNNERS.....34

The Kings won the first league encounter against their Cheshire neighbours, but had to fight tooth and nail to secure the two points. John Jackson registered his sixth successive Earle Street maximum and there was another good showing from the improving Dave Morton. Phil Crump won his first two rides, but a puncture in Heat 10 robbed him of another perfect home score.

Heat	Riders	Time	Score	Total
Heat 01	**Crump**/**Morton**/Goad/Tyrer	74.2	**5 - 1**	05 - 01
Heat 02	Blythe/**Parry**/Callaghan/**Moore**	74.8	2 - 4	07 - 05
Heat 03	**Flood**/Blythe/**Evans**/Francis	75.4	**4 - 2**	11 - 07
Heat 04	**Jackson**/Blythe/Drury/**Parry**	73.8	3 - 3	14 - 10
Heat 05	Goad/**Flood**/Tyrer/**Evans**	75.4	2 - 4	16 - 14
Heat 06	**Crump**/**Morton**/Drury/Blythe	75.0	**5 - 1**	21 - 15
Heat 07	**Jackson**/Francis/**Parry**/Callaghan	74.2	**4 - 2**	25 - 17
Heat 08	**Morton**/Blythe/Goad/**Moore**	75.0	3 - 3	28 - 20
Heat 09	Goad/**Evans**/Drury/**Flood** (R)	76.2	2 - 4	30 - 24
Heat 10	Callaghan/**Morton**/Francis/**Crump** (R)	75.4	2 - 4	32 - 28
Heat 11	**Jackson**/Tyrer/**Moore**/Goad	74.4	**4 - 2**	36 - 30
Heat 12	**Crump**/Drury/Francis/**Flood**	75.0	3 - 3	39 - 33
Heat 13	**Jackson**/**Evans**/Tyrer/Drury	74.8	**5 - 1**	44 - 34

CREWE - John Jackson 12, Dave Morton 9 (+2), Phil Crump 9, Dai Evans 5 (+1), Garry Flood 5, Dave Parry 3, Gary Moore 1.
ELLESMERE PORT - Chris Blythe 9, Colin Goad 8 (+1), Graham Drury 5 (+1), Cyril Francis 4 (+1), Paul Callaghan 4, Paul Tyrer 4.

Phil Crump added the Bradford Olympiad to his growing number of individual titles on June 14 after another highly impressive performance. He was still top of the Division II averages, with John Jackson up to seventh, following his own run of big scores.

Meeting 19 - Thursday, June 15, 1972 - British League Division II
Long Eaton Stadium, Station Road, Long Eaton
Track Length - 366 yards.

LONG EATON RANGERS.....31 CREWE KINGS.....47

Crewe went sixth in the table following their second away league win, achieved against a depleted Long Eaton side, minus the services of heat leaders Joe Hughes (broken wrist) and Geoff Bouchard (dislocated finger). John Jackson was Crewe's most consistent performer, winning all four outings, and was well-supported by Garry Flood and Dave Morton. For once Phil Crump failed to shine, suffering with an engine misfire, but did give a glimpse of his abilities recording a time of 70.4 in Heat 11 - over 2.4 seconds quicker than any other rider on the night.

Heat	Riders	Time	Score	Total
Heat 01	Bass/**Morton**/Harrison/**Crump** (R)	74.6	4 - 2	04 - 02
Heat 02	**Moore**/**Parry**/Whittaker/Jarvis (R)	77.2	**1 - 5**	05 - 07
Heat 03	**Flood**/Bass/Edwards/**Evans**	74.6	3 - 3	08 - 10
Heat 04	**Jackson**/Mills/**Moore**/Whittaker	74.0	**2 - 4**	10 - 14
Heat 05	**Crump**/**Morton**/Edwards/Mills (X)	73.2	**1 - 5**	11 - 19
Heat 06	**Jackson**/Bass/Harrison/**Parry**	73.2	3 - 3	14 - 22
Heat 07	Mills/**Evans**/Whittaker/**Flood** (R)	74.4	4 - 2	18 - 24

Heat 08 .... Bass/**Morton**/Harrison/**Moore** (F)	74.6	4 - 2	22 - 26
Heat 09 .... **Jackson**/**Parry**/Harrison/Whittaker	74.4	**1 - 5**	23 - 31
Heat 10 .... **Flood**/Mills/**Evans**/Bass	72.8	**2 - 4**	25 - 35
Heat 11 .... **Crump**/Mills/**Morton**/Jarvis	70.4	**2 - 4**	27 - 39
Heat 12 .... **Jackson**/**Evans**/Whittaker/Edwards	72.8	**1 - 5**	28 - 44
Heat 13 .... **Flood**/Mills/Jarvis/**Crump** (R)	73.4	3 - 3	31 - 47

LONG EATON - Roger Mills 11, Steve Bass 10, Chris Harrison 4 (+1), Phil Whittaker 3, Martin Edwards 2 (+1), Peter Jarvis 1 (+1), *Joe Hughes (R/R)*.
CREWE - John Jackson 12, Garry Flood 9, Dave Morton 7 (+1), Phil Crump 6, Dai Evans 5 (+1), Dave Parry 4 (+2), Gary Moore 4.

The race for the title saw Peterborough become new favourites, after hammering Eastbourne 52-25 at Alwalton on June 16. The victory put the Panthers just one point behind the leaders with five matches in hand.

Meeting 20 - Monday, June 19, 1972 - British League Division II
L.M.R. Sports Ground, Earle Street, Crewe
Track Length - 430 yards.

CREWE KINGS.....59 EASTBOURNE EAGLES.....19

Eastbourne suffered their second drubbing in the space of four days, as the Kings spelt out a title warning to their rivals. Crewe slammed home seven successive 5-1's, before they dropped their first points in the next, when Gary Moore fell after hitting the fence coming off the pits bend. Dave Morton emerged as the winner after just pipping Roger Johns virtually on the line. John Jackson and Phil Crump were hardly tested in their four outings, with Morton and Dai Evans both scoring paid maximums - Evans once again guiding his partner home in each of his rides.

Heat 01 .... **Crump**/**Morton**/McNeil/Johns	73.8	**5 - 1**	05 - 01
Heat 02 .... **Parry**/**Moore**/Bruce/Geer (R)	75.8	**5 - 1**	10 - 02
Heat 03 .... **Flood**/**Evans**/Ballard/Trott	75.0	**5 - 1**	15 - 03
Heat 04 .... **Jackson**/**Parry**/Kennett/Geer	75.0	**5 - 1**	20 - 04
Heat 05 .... **Flood**/**Evans**/McNeil/Johns	75.2	**5 - 1**	25 - 05
Heat 06 .... **Crump**/**Morton**/Kennett/Bruce	74.2	**5 - 1**	30 - 06
Heat 07 .... **Jackson**/**Parry**/Ballard/Trott	73.0	**5 - 1**	35 - 07
Heat 08 .... **Morton**/Johns/McNeil/**Moore** (F)	75.8	3 - 3	38 - 10
Heat 09 .... **Flood**/**Evans**/Kennett/Bruce	74.6	**5 - 1**	43 - 11
Heat 10 .... **Crump**/**Morton**/Johns/Ballard	74.2	**5 - 1**	48 - 12
Heat 11 .... **Jackson**/Johns/McNeil/**Moore** (F)	73.2	3 - 3	51 - 15
Heat 12 .... **Crump**/Ballard/Kennett/**Flood**	74.8	3 - 3	54 - 18
Heat 13 .... **Jackson**/**Evans**/McNeil/Kennett	74.6	**5 - 1**	59 - 19

CREWE - Phil Crump 12, John Jackson 12, Dave Morton 9 (+3), Garry Flood 9, Dai Evans 8 (+4), Dave Parry 7 (+2), Gary Moore 2 (+1).
EASTBOURNE - Bobby McNeil 5 (+2), Roger Johns 5, Gordon Kennett 4 (+1), Malcolm Ballard 4, Simon Bruce 1, Trevor Geer 0, Reg Trott 0.

Eastbourne manager Dave Lanning didn't pull any punches with his post match comments, lambasting the Earle Street track: *"Crewe have a completely ridiculous home advantage on their 'Wall of Death' circuit."* On June 20, Phil Crump failed in his bid to reach the final of the World Championship (British zone), finishing with just four points in the semi-final at Leicester. His attempts were not helped by a fall in his opening ride.

Meeting 21 - Wednesday, June 21, 1972 - British League Division II
Odsal Stadium, Rooley Avenue, Bradford
Track Length - 380 yards.

BRADFORD NORTHERN.....34 CREWE KINGS.....40

Past criticisms that the Kings could only ride their own track were firmly dispelled here, when they won a pulsating meeting by six points - Northern's biggest home league defeat. Already without injured skipper Alan Knapkin, they suffered a further setback when Alf Wells sustained a wrist injury in Heat 3, preventing him taking any further part in the match. In a bizarre final heat, Phil Crump was the only finisher, after Barry Meeks was left at the gate, Robin Adlington lost a chain and Garry Flood fell.

Heat 01	**Crump**/Baugh/Wells/**Morton**	71.4	3 - 3	03 - 03
Heat 02	**Parry**/Meeks/Sheldrick/**Moore**	72.8	3 - 3	06 - 06
Heat 03	**Flood**/**Evans**/Bridgett/Wells (F)	74.0	**1 - 5**	07 - 11
Heat 04	**Jackson**/Sheldrick/Adlington (F)/**Moore** (R)	73.2	**2 - 3**	09 - 14
Heat 05	**Crump**/Meeks/Bridgett/**Morton** (R)	72.6	3 - 3	12 - 17
Heat 06	Adlington/Baugh/**Jackson**/**Parry**	74.2	5 - 1	17 - 18
Heat 07	Adlington/**Evans**/**Flood**/Sheldrick (X)	74.0	3 - 3	20 - 21
Heat 08	Baugh/**Parry**/Meeks/**Morton**	74.2	4 - 2	24 - 23
Heat 09	**Jackson**/Bridgett/**Parry**/Sheldrick	71.2	**2 - 4**	26 - 27
Heat 10	**Evans**/Meeks/**Flood**/Baugh (R)	77.0	**2 - 4**	28 - 31
Heat 11	**Crump**/Adlington/**Morton**/Meeks	72.0	**2 - 4**	30 - 35
Heat 12	Baugh/**Jackson**/Bridgett/**Evans**	73.4	4 - 2	34 - 37
Heat 13	**Crump**/Adlington (R)/**Flood** (F)/Meeks(R)	00.0	**0 - 3**	34 - 40

BRADFORD - Dave Baugh 10 (+1), Robin Adlington 8, Barry Meeks 7, Alan Bridgett 5 (+1), Sid Sheldrick 3 (+1), Alf Wells 1 (+1), *Alan Knapkin (R/R).*
CREWE - Phil Crump 12, John Jackson 9, Dai Evans 7 (+1), Dave Parry 6, Garry Flood 5 (+1), Dave Morton 1, Gary Moore 0.

On June 24, Crewe's new junior team the "Princes" took part in a four heat challenge match against their King's Lynn counterparts at Saddlebow Road, following the Stars clash with Exeter.

KING'S LYNN JUNIOR STARS.....13 CREWE PRINCES.....11

Programmed King's Lynn riders - Peter Taylor, John Gosling, David Gagen.
Programmed Crewe riders - Ray Hassall, Reg Brassington, Barry Booth.
(No other details available.)

The following afternoon John Jackson rode for England in the opening Division II International against Sweden at Workington, scoring eleven in their 55-52 win.

Meeting 22 - Monday, June 26, 1972 - British League Division II
L.M.R. Sports Ground, Earle Street, Crewe
Track Length - 430 yards.

CREWE KINGS.....51 TEESSIDE TEESSIDERS.....27

John Jackson recorded an eighth successive Earle Street maximum as Crewe dared to dream of a possible league and cup double. Phil Crump made light work of his four rides, and skipper Dai Evans scored double figures. Ray Hassall came in for the injured Garry Flood and was placed in each of his outings. Roger Wright and Dave Durham provided spirited opposition, but the best the Teessiders could muster were a share of the points in five heats.

Heat 01	**Crump**/**Morton**/Durham/Tim Swales	73.0	**5 - 1**	05 - 01
Heat 02	**G.Moore**/**Parry**/M.Moore/Reading	78.8	**5 - 1**	10 - 02
Heat 03	**Evans**/Wright/**Hassall**/Tony Swales	77.6	**4 - 2**	14 - 04
Heat 04	**Jackson**/Auffret/M.Moore/**Parry** (R)	75.6	3 - 3	17 - 07
Heat 05	Durham/**Evans**/**Hassall**/Tim Swales	76.4	3 - 3	20 - 10
Heat 06	**Crump**/**Morton**/Auffret/Reading	74.4	**5 - 1**	25 - 11
Heat 07	**Jackson**/Wright/Durham/**G.Moore**	74.8	3 - 3	28 - 14
Heat 08	**Morton**/Wright/**G.Moore**/Tim Swales	76.2	**4 - 2**	32 - 16
Heat 09	**Evans**/Auffret/**Hassall**/Reading	76.8	**4 - 2**	36 - 18
Heat 10	**Crump**/Wright/Tony Swales/**Morton** (R)	75.4	3 - 3	39 - 21
Heat 11	**Jackson**/Durham/Reading/**G.Moore**	74.2	3 - 3	42 - 24
Heat 12	**Crump**/Wright/**Hassall**/Auffret	74.0	**4 - 2**	46 - 26
Heat 13	**Jackson**/**Evans**/Durham/Tony Swales	74.8	**5 - 1**	51 - 27

CREWE - Phil Crump 12, John Jackson 12, Dai Evans 10 (+1), Dave Morton 7 (+2), Ray Hassall 4 (+1), Gary Moore 4, Dave Parry 2 (+1).

TEESSIDE - Roger Wright 10, Dave Durham 8 (+1), Frank Auffret 5, Mick Moore 2 (+1), Pete Reading 1 (+1), Tony Swales 1 (+1), Tim Swales 0.

John Jackson (programmed as Johnson!) won the Cumberland Open Championship at Workington with a faultless display, but the Crewe camp received bad news regarding Phil Crump. It was confirmed that he had broken his scaphoid bone in his right wrist and was told to rest for a month to allow the injury to mend. However, with Ivan Mauger already riding with an identical injury, Crump commented: *"If he can carry on riding, so can I."* Concerns meanwhile grew over the health of promoter Maurice Littlechild, who was unable to attend the home match with Sunderland - the first fixture he had missed at Earle Street.

Meeting 23 - Monday, July 3, 1972 - Speedway Express Knock Out Cup, Third Round, First Leg
L.M.R. Sports Ground, Earle Street, Crewe
Track Length - 430 yards.

CREWE KINGS.....53 SUNDERLAND STARS.....25

Despite a series of early mishaps, Crewe still built up a healthy twenty-eight point quarter-final first leg lead. Dave Morton was excluded from the opening heat, with Garry Flood falling on the last lap of Heat 5, while well ahead of former King Jack Millen. John Jackson picked up an exclusion for tape breaking in the seventh.

Heat 01	**Crump**/Gatenby/Wrathall/**Morton** (X)	78.6	3 - 3	03 - 03
Heat 02	Wells/**Moore**/**Parry**/Gatenby	80.2	3 - 3	06 - 06
Heat 03	**Flood**/Millen/**Evans**/Barclay	76.0	**4 - 2**	10 - 08
Heat 04	**Jackson**/**Parry**/Smith/Gatenby	75.8	**5 - 1**	15 - 09
Heat 05	Millen/**Evans**/Dent/**Flood** (F)	76.8	2 - 4	17 - 13
Heat 06	**Morton**/**Crump**/Smith/Wells	74.8	**5 - 1**	22 - 14
Heat 07	**Moore**/**Parry**/Barclay/Millen (R)	79.8	**5 - 1**	27 - 15
Heat 08	**Morton**/Wells/**Moore**/Wrathall	76.6	**4 - 2**	31 - 17
Heat 09	**Flood**/**Evans**/Wells/Smith	76.0	**5 - 1**	36 - 18
Heat 10	**Crump**/**Morton**/Millen/Barclay	74.8	**5 - 1**	41 - 19
Heat 11	**Jackson**/Wells/Wrathall/**Moore**	74.4	3 - 3	44 - 22
Heat 12	**Crump**/Millen/**Flood**/Smith	75.4	**4 - 2**	48 - 24
Heat 13	**Jackson**/**Evans**/Wells/Wrathall	74.8	**5 - 1**	53 - 25

CREWE - Phil Crump 11 (+1), John Jackson 9, Dave Morton 8 (+1), Dai Evans 7 (+2), Garry Flood 7, Gary Moore 6, Dave Parry 5 (+3).
SUNDERLAND - Jim Wells 9, Jack Millen 8, Peter Wrathall 2 (+2), Dave Gatenby 2, Graeme Smith 2, George Barclay 1, Russ Dent 1.

During the second-half, Crewe's junior side took on the youngsters of Wolverhampton, and were easily winning the match, until rain caused the cancellation of the final two heats.

CREWE PRINCES.....14 WOLVERHAMPTON WOLF CUBS.....4

Heat 01	**Hassall**/**Booth**/Teale/Wasley	77.6	**5 - 1**	05 - 01
Heat 02	**Nicholas**/**Brassington**/Freegard/Scarbrough	57.2	**5 - 1**	10 - 02
Heat 03	**Nicholas**/Teale/**Brassington**/Wasley	60.0	**4 - 2**	14 - 04

(Abandoned after three heats. Heats 2 and 3 were run over three laps.)

CREWE - Peter Nicholas 6, Reg Brassington 3, Ray Hassall 3, Barry Booth 2.
WOLVERHAMPTON - Ian Teale 3, Tony Freegard 1, Charlie Scarbrough* 0, Nigel Wasley 0.

On July 4, Phil Crump (15) and Dave Parry (11) finished runners-up to home duo Colin Goad and Ian Gills in the Handicap Best Pairs at Ellesmere Port. Two days later promoter Maurice Littlechild, the main founder and driving force of the Kings, passed away in Waltham Abbey War Memorial Hospital, aged just 52. He had undergone a serious operation in January and had been suffering with poor health for some time.

Meeting 24 - Friday, July 7, 1972 - Speedway Express Knock Out Cup, Third Round, Second Leg
Sunderland Greyhound Stadium, Newcastle Road, East Boldon
Track Length - 310 yards.

SUNDERLAND STARS.....42 CREWE KINGS.....36

(Crewe won on aggregate 89 - 67)

With a black cloud hovering over the camp, the Kings went into the second leg minus Phil Crump, who was on international duty at Hackney. Utilising the rider replacement rule, John Jackson responded in some style with a brilliant seventeen point return, with only Jack Millen denying him his maximum in the final heat. The overall result was never in doubt, especially once Crewe led the match after five races. Dave Gatenby rode well for the Wearsiders, securing four victories from five outings. This defeat though ended the Kings' eleven match winning run.

Heat 01	**Jackson**/Dent/Barclay/**Morton**	65.4	3 - 3	03 - 03
Heat 02	Gatenby/**Moore**/**Parry**/Wells (X)	67.8	3 - 3	06 - 06
Heat 03	**Jackson**/Millen/Wrathall/**Flood** (X)	65.6	3 - 3	09 - 09
Heat 04	Gatenby/**Evans**/**Moore**/Smith	66.8	3 - 3	12 - 12
Heat 05	**Jackson**/Millen/**Morton**/Wrathall	**65.0** (=TR)	**2 - 4**	14 - 16
Heat 06	Barclay/**Evans**/Dent/**Parry**	66.0	4 - 2	18 - 18
Heat 07	Gatenby/Smith/**Flood**/**Morton** (F)	66.4	5 - 1	23 - 19
Heat 08	Barclay/**Moore**/Wells/**Morton** (F)	66.4	4 - 2	27 - 21
Heat 09	Gatenby/Millen/**Evans**/**Moore**	68.0	5 - 1	32 - 22
Heat 10	**Jackson**/Dent/Barclay/**Flood** (F)	65.6	3 - 3	35 - 25
Heat 11	**Jackson**/Smith/**Evans**/Wells	66.8	**2 - 4**	37 - 29
Heat 12	**Flood**/Dent/**Evans**/Gatenby (R)	66.4	**2 - 4**	39 - 33
Heat 13	Millen/**Jackson**/**Flood**/Smith	66.2	3 - 3	42 - 36

SUNDERLAND - Dave Gatenby 12, Jack Millen 9 (+1), George Barclay 8 (+2), Russ Dent 7, Graeme Smith 4 (+1), Peter Wrathall 1 (+1), Jim Wells 1.
CREWE - John Jackson 17, Dai Evans 7, Garry Flood 5 (+1), Gary Moore 5 (+1), Dave Parry 1 (+1), Dave Morton 1, *Phil Crump (R/R).*

Phil Crump endured a wasted journey down to Hackney, as the Australia versus Sweden Inter-Nations Championship match was washed-out after three heats. Following the death of Maurice Littlechild, team manager Ken Adams was promoted to general manager, with his job going to Dai Evans's mechanic and brother-in-law Les Moore, who had previously taken charge of the team away from home.

Meeting 25 - Monday, July 10, 1972 - British League Division II
L.M.R. Sports Ground, Earle Street, Crewe
Track Length - 430 yards.

CREWE KINGS.....61 SCUNTHORPE SAINTS.....17

Crewe won their ninth league match in a row after hammering bottom of the table Scunthorpe for a third time this season. After losing both cup legs 59-19, the Saints knew another hiding was on the cards when they found themselves 29-7 down after only six heats. John Jackson left Earle Street with yet another full house in the bag, and Phil Crump, Dave Morton, Garry Flood and Dai Evans all remained unbeaten by an opponent. Scunthorpe's top scorer was Phil Bass with seven points from six outings, but three of the visitors found the fast Crewe bowl a little too daunting and failed to score, including Crewe junior Reg Brassington, who stepped in at No.8 for the short-handed Saints. Morton provided the best moment of the night when coming from last to win Heat 8. A second-half sidecar handicap event helped to swell the attendance.

Heat 01	**Crump**/**Morton**/Watkins/Brassington	74.6	**5 - 1**	05 - 01
Heat 02	**Parry**/**Moore**/Underwood/Wilson	77.0	**5 - 1**	10 - 02
Heat 03	**Evans**/**Flood**/Kelly/Haynes	76.0	**5 - 1**	15 - 03
Heat 04	**Jackson**/Bass/**Parry**/Wilson (R)	75.4	**4 - 2**	19 - 05
Heat 05	**Flood**/**Evans**/Kelly/Watkins	76.0	**5 - 1**	24 - 06
Heat 06	**Crump**/**Morton**/Bass/Underwood	74.6	**5 - 1**	29 - 07
Heat 07	**Jackson**/Bass/Kelly/**Parry** (R)	74.8	3 - 3	32 - 10
Heat 08	**Morton**/Underwood/**Moore**/Watkins	76.6	**4 - 2**	36 - 12
Heat 09	**Flood**/**Evans**/Underwood/Bass (F)	77.4	**5 - 1**	41 - 13
Heat 10	**Morton**/**Crump**/Kelly/Haynes	74.2	**5 - 1**	46 - 14

Heat 11 .... **Jackson**/**Moore**/Bass/Watkins	74.8	**5 - 1**	51 - 15
Heat 12 .... **Crump**/**Flood**/Bass/Underwood	74.0	**5 - 1**	56 - 16
Heat 13 .... **Jackson**/**Evans**/Kelly/Watkins (R)	75.0	**5 - 1**	61 - 17

CREWE - John Jackson 12, Phil Crump 11 (+1), Garry Flood 10 (+2), Dave Morton 10 (+2), Dai Evans 9 (+3), Gary Moore 5 (+2), Dave Parry 4.
SCUNTHORPE - Phil Bass 7, Terry Kelly 5 (+1), Doug Underwood 4, Ray Watkins 1, Reg Brassington* 0, Rod Haynes 0, Ian Wilson 0, *Brian Maxted (R/R).*

Crewe's title hopes received an unexpected boost following Peterborough's shock 42-36 defeat at Ellesmere Port. The injury ravaged Panthers lost the services of Clive Noy and John Davis, who were both involved in crashes that required hospital treatment.

Meeting 26 - Wednesday, July 12, 1972 - British League Division II
Boulevard Stadium, Airlie Street, Kingston-upon-Hull
Track Length - 415 yards.

HULL VIKINGS.....41 CREWE KINGS.....36

Following Peterborough's defeat, it was vital that the Kings maintained their terrific run at the Boulevard, but it was the Vikings who pillaged the points from a thrilling encounter. Crewe started well with two 4-2's, as Phil Crump captured the track record in the opening race, but lost Garry Flood after a fall in the first attempt at running Heat 3. The sides were evenly matched throughout, which culminated in a last heat decider. Crump had to go it alone as both reserves had taken their permitted rides, but unfortunately he was forced to retire. Nicky Allott, son of former Sheffield rider Guy, was a late replacement for the injured Dai Evans.

Heat 01 .... **Crump**/Childs/**Morton**/Loakes	**73.4** (TR)	**2 - 4**	02 - 04
Heat 02 .... **Parry**/Boston/**Moore**/Hornby	75.0	**2 - 4**	04 - 08
Heat 03 .... Amundson/Boston/**Allott**/**Flood** (X)	76.0	5 - 1	09 - 09
Heat 04 .... **Jackson**/Mills/Boston/**Moore**	75.2	3 - 3	12 - 12
Heat 05 .... **Crump**/Amundson/**Morton**/Hornby	74.2	**2 - 4**	14 - 16
Heat 06 .... **Jackson**/Childs/Loakes/**Parry**	74.8	3 - 3	17 - 19
Heat 07 .... Boston/**Parry**/Mills/**Allott**	76.4	4 - 2	21 - 21
Heat 08 .... **Morton**/Loakes/**Moore**/Hornby	75.0	**2 - 4**	23 - 25
Heat 09 .... Amundson/Boston/**Moore**/**Parry**	75.6	5 - 1	28 - 26
Heat 10 .... Loakes/Childs/**Parry**/**Moore**	75.6	5 - 1	33 - 27
Heat 11 .... **Crump**/**Morton**/Mills/Hornby	75.4	**1 - 5**	34 - 32
Heat 12 .... **Jackson**/Childs/**Allott** (3 riders only)	74.4	**2 - 4**	36 - 36
Heat 13 .... Mills/Amundson/**Crump** (R) (3 riders only)	77.6	5 - 0	41 - 36

HULL - Pete Boston 10 (+3), Robin Amundson 10 (+1), Tony Childs 8 (+1), Dave Mills 7, Brian Loakes 6 (+1), Bernie Hornby 0.
CREWE - Phil Crump 9, John Jackson 9, Dave Morton 7 (+1), Dave Parry 6, Gary Moore 3, Nicky Allott* 2, Garry Flood 0.

On the same day, Maurice Littlechild's funeral was held at High Beech Church, before he was laid to rest in Upshire churchyard. Hundreds attended including Ken Adams, who represented Crewe. On July 15, John Jackson and Dave Morton finished first and second in the Division II riders only Shaytona at Halifax, scoring fourteen and thirteen respectively. Morton clocked 66.6 in Heat 4, which was only two-fifths of a second outside the fastest time recorded by a Division I rider at the Yorkshire track this season. Their prizes included five new rear tyres!

Meeting 27 - Monday, July 17, 1972 - British League Division II
L.M.R. Sports Ground, Earle Street, Crewe
Track Length - 430 yards.

CREWE KINGS.....56 LONG EATON RANGERS.....22

Reserve Dave Parry produced a first class display, and put his return to form down to a new pair of black leathers! Once again the Kings dominated, providing all the race winners, even though they only had one starter in Heats 10 and 13. John Jackson lost his first race at Earle

Street since Peterborough's visit on April 24, ending an incredible run of 40 successive league and cup heat wins. Phil Crump scored his first home maximum for three matches and Gary Moore showed improvement with a paid ten, following some disappointing early season scores. Heat 3 saw Dai Evans stretchered off with a back injury, after colliding with the machine of Steve Bass, who had fallen in front of him. Dave Morton was also in the wars, damaging a finger in a Heat 8 fall, and missed both the re-run and scheduled ride in Heat 10. Crewe junior Reg Brassington stood in at reserve for the Rangers, scoring five points.

Heat 01	**Crump**/**Morton**/Bouchard/Emms	76.6	**5 - 1**	05 - 01
Heat 02	**Parry**/Brassington/**Moore**/Whittaker	78.0	**4 - 2**	09 - 03
Heat 03	**Parry**/**Flood**/Hughes/Bass (X)	76.8	**5 - 1**	14 - 04
Heat 04	**Jackson**/**Parry**/Mills/Whittaker	75.2	**5 - 1**	19 - 05
Heat 05	**Moore**/Bouchard/Emms/**Flood** (R)	78.2	3 - 3	22 - 08
Heat 06	**Crump**/**Morton**/Brassington/Mills (R)	75.6	**5 - 1**	27 - 09
Heat 07	**Parry**/**Jackson**/Bass/Hughes	75.6	**5 - 1**	32 - 10
Heat 08	**Moore**/**Parry**/Bouchard/Emms	77.2	**5 - 1**	37 - 11
Heat 09	**Flood**/Brassington/Whittaker/**Moore**	77.6	3 - 3	40 - 14
Heat 10	**Crump**/Hughes/Bass (3 riders only)	75.2	3 - 3	43 - 17
Heat 11	**Jackson**/**Moore**/Emms/Bouchard	75.4	**5 - 1**	48 - 18
Heat 12	**Crump**/**Flood**/Hughes/Whittaker	75.4	**5 - 1**	53 - 19
Heat 13	**Jackson**/Bouchard/Bass (3 riders only)	75.0	3 - 3	56 - 22

CREWE - Dave Parry 13 (+2), Phil Crump 12, John Jackson 11 (+1), Gary Moore 9 (+1), Garry Flood 7 (+2), Dave Morton 4 (+2), Dai Evans 0.
LONG EATON - Geoff Bouchard 6, Reg Brassington* 5, Joe Hughes 4, Steve Bass 3 (+2), Cliff Emms 2 (+1), Phil Whittaker 1 (+1), Roger Mills 1.

As a mark of respect, a "white" programme cover was printed in honour of Maurice Littlechild. Among the tributes inside was one from skipper Dai Evans. *'None of the team ever realised just how ill Maury was. But that was Maury. He only ever considered himself after he had thought about everyone else. It was that kind of devotion which made him the finest guvnor in the business. With half-a-dozen or so tracks behind me before Maury gave me a chance at Crewe, I reckon I know a bit about speedway promoters. The younger lads in the team were only just beginning to know Maury, but like me will never forget him. We shall remember him always, especially in the forthcoming Knock-Out Cup matches, for we all know just how much he set his heart on our winning that trophy this year. We'll try hard not to let him down. The boys in the team join me, and thousands more, in sending their deepest sympathies to Mrs Littlechild, sons Alan and Terry and daughters Irene and Pamela.'*

Meeting 28 - Thursday, July 20, 1972 - British League Division II
Cleveland Park Stadium, Stockton Road, Middlesbrough
Track Length - 335 yards.

TEESSIDE TEESSIDERS.....37 CREWE KINGS.....40

Teesside lost their proud unbeaten home record to a Crewe team who simply refused to be beaten. No more than three points separated the sides during the match, and going into the last heat, the hosts led by a single point. Frank Auffret and Dave Durham faced Phil Crump and Garry Flood in the decider, but it was Crump who streaked away from the tapes, closely followed by his partner, and despite the best efforts of the home duo to get past, they held firm to win another valuable two points.

Heat 01	**Crump**/Reading/**Morton**/Tim Swales	73.0	**2 - 4**	02 - 04
Heat 02	M.Moore/**G.Moore**/**Parry**/Tony Swales	76.6	3 - 3	05 - 07
Heat 03	**Flood**/Reading/Auffret (X)/**Brassington** (X)	72.6	**2 - 3**	07 - 10
Heat 04	Durham/**Jackson**/M.Moore/**G.Moore**	72.0	4 - 2	11 - 12
Heat 05	Auffret/**Crump**/Durham/**Morton**	71.8	4 - 2	15 - 14
Heat 06	**Jackson**/Tim Swales/Reading/**Parry**	71.6	3 - 3	18 - 17
Heat 07	**Flood**/Durham/M.Moore/**Brassington**	71.8	3 - 3	21 - 20
Heat 08	Tony Swales/**Parry**/**G.Moore**/Reading	72.6	3 - 3	24 - 23
Heat 09	Auffret/**Jackson**/M.Moore/**Parry**	70.2	4 - 2	28 - 25

Heat 10	**Flood**/Tim Swales/**Brassington**/Reading (X)	72.0	**2 - 4**	30 - 29
Heat 11	**Crump**/Durham/Tony Swales/**Parry**	71.0	3 - 3	33 - 32
Heat 12	**Jackson**/Auffrett/Tim Swales/**G.Moore**	70.0	3 - 3	36 - 35
Heat 13	**Crump**/**Flood**/Auffret/Durham	70.8	**1 - 5**	37 - 40

TEESSIDE - Frank Auffret 9, Dave Durham 8, Mick Moore 6 (+1), Pete Reading 5 (+1), Tim Swales 5 (+1), Tony Swales 4 (+1), *Bruce Forrester (R/R).*
CREWE - Garry Flood 11 (+1), Phil Crump 11, John Jackson 10, Gary Moore 3 (+1), Dave Parry 3 (+1), Reg Brassington 1, Dave Morton 1.

Meeting 29 - Monday, July 24, 1972 - British League Division II
L.M.R. Sports Ground, Earle Street, Crewe
Track Length - 430 yards

CREWE KINGS.....58 CANTERBURY CRUSADERS.....19

Both sides went into the meeting under strength, and by the end of the night, another three riders had been sidelined. Kings junior Ray Hassall and Canterbury's Ted Hubbard were first race casualties following a sickening opening lap pile-up. Hubbard lost control while attempting to pass Phil Crump entering the back straight, bringing down Hassall in the process. Both were taken to hospital, with Hubbard detained overnight with head injuries and the Crewe youngster suffering from a suspected broken collar-bone. The Crusaders then lost reserve Brian "Barney" Kennett following another nasty crash in Heat 4. As for the match, Crewe didn't concede a heat, with maximums for Crump and John Jackson. Peter Nicholas had an unforgettable Kings debut, finishing with a brilliant paid twelve maximum.

Heat 01	**Crump**/Banks/**Parry** (X)/Hubbard (X)	72.6	**3 - 2**	03 - 02
Heat 02	**Moore**/Kennett/**Parry**/Benham	75.6	**4 - 2**	07 - 04
Heat 03	**Flood**/**Nicholas**/Hughes/Piddock	75.0	**5 - 1**	12 - 05
Heat 04	**Jackson**/**Parry**/Banks/Kennett (F)	74.2	**5 - 1**	17 - 06
Heat 05	**Flood**/**Nicholas**/Hughes/Silk	75.0	**5 - 1**	22 - 07
Heat 06	**Crump**/Banks/**Moore**/Benham	74.8	**4 - 2**	26 - 09
Heat 07	**Jackson**/**Parry**/Hughes/Piddock (R)	74.4	**5 - 1**	31 - 10
Heat 08	**Parry**/**Moore**/Benham/Piddock	76.0	**5 - 1**	36 - 11
Heat 09	**Flood**/**Nicholas**/Banks/Benham	76.2	**5 - 1**	41 - 12
Heat 10	**Crump**/Hughes/**Moore**/Piddock	73.8	**4 - 2**	45 - 14
Heat 11	**Jackson**/Benham/**Moore**/Silk	73.6	**4 - 2**	49 - 16
Heat 12	**Crump**/Banks/**Flood**/Piddock	73.0	**4 - 2**	53 - 18
Heat 13	**Jackson**/**Nicholas**/Hughes/Silk	74.0	**5 - 1**	58 - 19

CREWE - Phil Crump 12, John Jackson 12, Garry Flood 10, Peter Nicholas 8 (+4), Dave Parry 8 (+2), Gary Moore 8 (+1), Ray Hassall 0.
CANTERBURY - Graham Banks 8, Bob Hughes 6, Charlie Benham 3, Barney Kennett 2, Ted Hubbard 0, Dave Piddock 0, Ian Silk 0, *Ross Gilbertson (R/R).*

On July 22, Phil Crump scored two points for Australia in their 30-48 loss to England in the Inter-Nations Tournament at Halifax.

Meeting 30 - Tuesday, July 25, 1972 - British League Division II
Ellesmere Port Stadium, Thornton Road, Ellesmere Port
Track Length - 423 yards.

ELLESMERE PORT GUNNERS.....38 CREWE KINGS.....40

The Gunners had already beaten title chasing Peterborough and Rayleigh in their previous two home league meetings and were keen to add Crewe to their collection of high flyers. Nine heats were shared in a terrific Thornton Road encounter, where eleven of the thirteen heats were won by a visiting rider. Ellesmere Port held a two-point lead with two heats to go, but a brace of 4-2's for the Kings saw them squeeze home. The reliable pair of Phil Crump and John Jackson remained unbeaten, with Garry Flood and Gary Moore also contributing to the hard fought victory. Crewe juniors Barry Booth and Peter Nicholas deputised for the injured Dai Evans and Dave Morton. The victory put the Kings top of the league for the very first time in their short history.

Heat 01	**Crump**/Tyrer/Blythe/**Booth**	76.2	3 - 3	03 - 03
Heat 02	**Moore**/Francis/Gills/**Parry** (R)	79.4	3 - 3	06 - 06
Heat 03	**Flood**/Drury/Gardner/**Nicholas**	78.2	3 - 3	09 - 09
Heat 04	**Jackson**/Francis/Goad/**Moore** (R)	77.8	3 - 3	12 - 12
Heat 05	**Crump**/Gardner/**Booth**/Drury	77.6	**2 - 4**	14 - 16
Heat 06	**Jackson**/Tyrer/Blythe/**Parry**	76.6	3 - 3	17 - 19
Heat 07	**Flood**/Francis/Goad/**Nicholas** (F)	78.8	3 - 3	20 - 22
Heat 08	Gills/Blythe/**Moore**/**Booth**	80 0	5 - 1	25 - 23
Heat 09	**Jackson**/Gardner/Drury/**Parry**	78.2	3 - 3	28 - 26
Heat 10	Tyrer/**Flood**/**Moore**/Blythe (F)	79.0	3 - 3	31 - 29
Heat 11	**Crump**/Goad/Gills/**Booth**	78.2	3 - 3	34 - 32
Heat 12	**Jackson**/Tyrer/**Moore**/Drury	78.2	**2 - 4**	36 - 36
Heat 13	**Crump**/Goad/**Flood**/Gardner	78.0	**2 - 4**	38 - 40

ELLESMERE PORT - Paul Tyrer 9, Colin Goad 6 (+2), Cyril Francis 6, Ian Gills 5 (+2), Robbie Gardner 5 (+1), Chris Blythe 4 (+3), Graham Drury 3 (+1).
CREWE - Phil Crump 12, John Jackson 12, Garry Flood 9, Gary Moore 6 (+1), Barry Booth 1, Peter Nicholas 0, Dave Parry 0.

On July 28, the Crewe Princes rode in a junior challenge match at Monmore Green, following the Wolves derby with Cradley. Nicky Allott was pick of the Crewe youngsters.

WOLVERHAMPTON WOLF CUBS.....17 CREWE PRINCES.....13

Heat 01	**Booth**/**Allott**/Anderson/Wasley (X)	70.4	**1 - 5**	01 - 05
Heat 02	Freegard/Teale/**Brassington**/**Nicholas** (F)	71.2	5 - 1	06 - 06
Heat 03	**Allott**/Freegard/Teale/**Booth**	70.4	3 - 3	09 - 09
Heat 04	Owen/Wasley/**Brassington**/**Nicholas**	71.2	5 - 1	14 - 10
Heat 05	Freegard/**Allott**/**Nicholas**/Wasley	70.8	3 - 3	17 - 13

WOLVERHAMPTON - Tony Freegard 8, Terry Owen 3, Ian Teale 3, Nigel Wasley 2, Keith Anderson 1.
CREWE - Nicky Allott 7, Barry Booth 3, Reg Brassington 2, Peter Nicholas 1.

Meeting 31 - Sunday, July 30, 1972 - Speedway Express Knock Out Cup, Semi-Final, First Leg
Arlington Raceway, Arlington Road, Hailsham, Eastbourne
Track Length - 342 yards.

EASTBOURNE EAGLES.....44 CREWE KINGS.....34

The league's top two clashed in the first leg of the K.O. Cup semi-final, but it was Crewe who took the giant step towards the final, after holding the Eagles to a ten point lead. Eastbourne's Malcolm Ballard and Phil Crump provided some scintillating racing for the large Arlington crowd, although the meeting was marred somewhat by Crewe's refusal to allow a dusty track to be watered, resulting in much of the action taking place in a cloud of dust. Skipper Dai Evans returned to the Kings line-up after his injury lay-off. Eagles promoter Dave Lanning commented after the match: *"The most spirited display we've had from a visiting team for a long time."*

Heat 01	Ballard/**Crump**/Cook/**Booth**	64.4	4 - 2	04 - 02
Heat 02	Geer/Gachet/**Moore**/**Parry**	67.2	5 - 1	09 - 03
Heat 03	**Flood**/McNeil/**Evans**/Johns (X)	65.8	**2 - 4**	11 - 07
Heat 04	**Jackson**/Kennett/**Moore**/Geer	64.2	**2 - 4**	13 - 11
Heat 05	**Crump**/McNeil/Johns/**Parry**	64.6	3 - 3	16 - 14
Heat 06	**Jackson**/Ballard/**Moore**/Cook	64.6	**2 - 4**	18 - 18
Heat 07	Kennett/**Flood**/Geer/**Evans**	65.0	4 - 2	22 - 20
Heat 08	Gachet/Cook/**Booth**/**Moore** (X)	67.6	5 - 1	27 - 21
Heat 09	**Crump**/Johns/McNeil/**Jackson** (X)	65.8	3 - 3	30 - 24
Heat 10	Ballard/**Moore**/Cook/**Flood** (R)	66.2	4 - 2	34 - 26
Heat 11	**Crump**/Kennett/**Flood**/Gachet	66.0	**2 - 4**	36 - 30
Heat 12	Ballard/Johns/**Jackson**/**Moore** (F)	65.8	5 - 1	41 - 31
Heat 13	**Crump**/Kennett/McNeil/**Flood**	66.4	3 - 3	44 - 34

EASTBOURNE - Malcolm Ballard 11, Gordon Kennett 9, Bobby McNeil 6 (+2), Roger Johns 5 (+2), Paul Gachet 5 (+1), Derek Cook 4 (+1), Trevor Geer 4.
CREWE - Phil Crump 14, John Jackson 7, Garry Flood 6, Gary Moore 5, Barry Booth 1, Dai Evans 1, Dave Parry 0.

Meeting 32 - Monday, July 31, 1972 - Speedway Express Knock Out Cup, Semi-Final, Second Leg
L.M.R. Sports Ground, Earle Street, Crewe
Track Length - 430 yards.

CREWE KINGS.....47 EASTBOURNE EAGLES.....31

(Crewe won on aggregate 81 - 75)

Crewe reached the K.O. Cup final for the third time in four seasons, after a nail biter at Earle Street. Eastbourne arrived determined to avenge their humiliating 59-19 league reversal, and by the end of Heat 5, still led by four on aggregate. The home cause was not helped by mechanical gremlins throughout the night, which in turn affected the scoring of Gary Moore, Garry Flood and Dave Parry. However, John Jackson and Phil Crump steered clear of the motor problems and received valuable support from Dave Morton (returning from injury), and Parry. At the death, the Eagles required a maximum to force a replay, but Jackson and Dai Evans kept their nerve to see Crewe home. A fault with the starting gate saw Heats 2-4 started off the red stop light.

Heat 01	**Crump**/**Morton**/Ballard/Cook	74.0	**5 - 1**	05 - 01
Heat 02	**Parry**/Geer/Gachet/**Moore** (R)	77.8	3 - 3	08 - 04
Heat 03	**Flood**/McNeil/**Evans**/Johns	76.2	**4 - 2**	12 - 06
Heat 04	**Jackson**/**Parry**/Kennett/Gachet	74.0	**5 - 1**	17 - 07
Heat 05	McNeil/Ballard/**Evans**/**Flood** (R)	75.4	1 - 5	18 - 12
Heat 06	**Crump**/**Morton**/Kennett/Geer	74.2	**5 - 1**	23 - 13
Heat 07	**Jackson**/McNeil/**Parry**/Johns	74.0	**4 - 2**	27 - 15
Heat 08	**Morton**/Ballard/**Moore**/Cook (R)	75.4	**4 - 2**	31 - 17
Heat 09	Kennett/**Flood**/Geer/**Parry** (R)	75.8	2 - 4	33 - 21
Heat 10	**Crump**/McNeil/Kennett/**Morton** (F)	74.6	3 - 3	36 - 24
Heat 11	**Jackson**/Ballard/**Parry**/Cook	75.2	**4 - 2**	40 - 26
Heat 12	**Crump**/McNeil/Kennett/**Flood**	75.4	3 - 3	43 - 29
Heat 13	**Jackson**/Ballard/**Evans**/Geer	75.0	**4 - 2**	47 - 31

CREWE - Phil Crump 12, John Jackson 12, Dave Morton 7 (+2), Dave Parry 7 (+1), Garry Flood 5, Dai Evans 3, Gary Moore 1.
EASTBOURNE - Bobby McNeil 11, Malcolm Ballard 9 (+1), Gordon Kennett 7 (+2), Trevor Geer 3, Paul Gachet 1 (+1), Derek Cook 0, Roger Johns 0.

On the same night, the first leg of the other semi-final between Birmingham and Peterborough was rained off. On August 4, the Panthers entertained Birmingham, in what was now the first leg, and won 43-35. Two days later, Crewe's away league fixture at Boston was called off at 6.00pm due to a waterlogged track.

Meeting 33 - Monday, August 7, 1972 - British League Division II
L.M.R. Sports Ground, Earle Street, Crewe
Track Length - 430 yards.

CREWE KINGS.....54 BOSTON BARRACUDAS.....24

Not even a power cut could halt Crewe's charge for the title. The starting gate, track lights, floodlights and sound system were all put out of action after the conclusion of Heat 7. Following a fifteen minute delay, it was decided to start and control the remaining heats using flags, with helpers and marshals stationed around the centre green. Fortunately the match was completed before darkness fell. Four Crewe riders finished with paid twelve points, including the resurgent Dave Parry, who beat both Phil Crump and John Jackson during the night.

Heat 01	**Crump**/**Morton**/Featherstone/Price	72.2	**5 - 1**	05 - 01
Heat 02	**Parry**/Cross/Bales/**Moore** (R)	74.4	3 - 3	08 - 04
Heat 03	**Flood**/Featherstone/**Evans**/Osborne	74.6	**4 - 2**	12 - 06
Heat 04	**Jackson**/**Parry**/Cross/Bales	72.8	**5 - 1**	17 - 07
Heat 05	**Flood**/Featherstone/**Evans**/Price	73.8	**4 - 2**	21 - 09
Heat 06	**Parry**/**Crump**/Glover/Cross	74.0	**5 - 1**	26 - 10
Heat 07	**Parry**/**Jackson**/Osborne/Glover	74.4	**5 - 1**	31 - 11
Heat 08	Featherstone/**Moore**/Bales/**Parry**	00.0	2 - 4	33 - 15
Heat 09	**Flood**/Glover/**Evans**/Cross	00.0	**4 - 2**	37 - 17

(ABOVE) Dave Parry and John Jackson about to do battle against Bradford in the Top Dogs Trophy. (BELOW) Heat 1 gets underway in Crewe's record-breaking K.O. Cup victory at Scunthorpe. The riders are Dave Morton (outside), John Bowerman, Phil Crump and Brian Maxted. Note the travelling support in the background.

(ABOVE) Maurice Littlechild, who was one of the most popular promoters in British Speedway. After serving in the R.A.F.V.R. during World War Two, he became team manager at Ipswich in 1960. After a short spell at Norwich, he opened King's Lynn. His death on July 6, was mourned all over the country.

(ABOVE) Dai Evans and Jack Millen in action at Sunderland.

Heat 10 .... **Crump**/Bales/Osborne/**Morton** (R)	00.0	3 - 3	40 - 20
Heat 11 .... **Jackson**/Price/**Moore**/Featherstone	00.0	**4 - 2**	44 - 22
Heat 12 .... **Crump**/**Flood**/Glover/Osborne	00.0	**5 - 1**	49 - 23
Heat 13 .... **Jackson**/**Evans**/Price/Featherstone	00.0	**5 - 1**	54 - 24

(No times after Heat 7 due to mains electricity failure.)

CREWE - Phil Crump 11 (+1), Garry Flood 11 (+1), John Jackson 11 (+1), Dave Parry 11 (+1), Dai Evans 5 (+1), Gary Moore 3, Dave Morton 2 (+1).
BOSTON - Tony Featherstone 8, Ray Bales 4 (+1), Carl Glover 4, Vic Cross 3, Arthur Price 3, Russell Osborne 2 (+1), *Jim Ryman (R/R).*

Following the win, Phil Crump and John Jackson occupied the top two positions in the Division II averages. On the same night, Peterborough raced at bottom of the table Scunthorpe, and with one heat remaining led the tie 38-34. But in a dramatic finale, Panthers Roy Carter broke a rocker-arm, putting him out of the race, and then Ted Howgego's bike stopped 500 yards from the line. His attempt to push the bike to the finish to claim the all-important point failed when he was timed-out just six feet from the line. The 5-0 win handed the Saints the unlikeliest 39-38 victory.

Meeting 34 - Sunday, August 13, 1972 - British League Division II
Boston Sports Stadium, New Hammond Beck Road, Boston
Track Length - 380 yards.

BOSTON BARRACUDAS.....47 CREWE KINGS.....31

This was always going to be a tough test for the Kings. Boston, unbeaten at home, and with title aspirations themselves, started this double header meeting by hammering Canterbury 55-22, then restricted Crewe to a single heat advantage during a comfortable sixteen point win. Phil Crump scored fourteen, but lost a rare opening ride to Arthur Price. He would however, get his revenge in Heat 6, easily beating the Barracudas star by nearly half a lap.

Heat 01 .... Price/**Crump**/Featherstone/**Morton** (F)	75.6	4 - 2	04 - 02
Heat 02 .... Bales/**Moore**/Cross/**Parry** (R)	75.8	4 - 2	08 - 04
Heat 03 .... Price/**Flood**/Osborne/**Evans**	75.1	4 - 2	12 - 06
Heat 04 .... **Jackson**/Glover/Cross/**Moore**	74.5	3 - 3	15 - 09
Heat 05 .... **Crump**/Osborne/Bales/**Morton**	75.6	3 - 3	18 - 12
Heat 06 .... **Crump**/Price/Featherstone/**Jackson**	74.9	3 - 3	21 - 15
Heat 07 .... **Evans**/Glover/**Flood**/Cross	74.8	**2 - 4**	23 - 19
Heat 08 .... Featherstone/**Morton**/Bales/**Moore**	76.2	4 - 2	27 - 21
Heat 09 .... Osborne/Glover/**Jackson**/**Moore**	75.4	5 - 1	32 - 22
Heat 10 .... Price/Featherstone/**Flood**/**Evans** (X)	74.5	5 - 1	37 - 23
Heat 11 .... **Crump**/Glover/Bales/**Parry** (R)	74.5	3 - 3	40 - 26
Heat 12 .... Price/**Evans**/Davies/**Jackson**	73.8	4 - 2	44 - 28
Heat 13 .... **Crump**/Osborne/Glover/**Flood**	74.7	3 - 3	47 - 31

BOSTON - Arthur Price 14, Carl Glover 9 (+2), Russell Osborne 8, Tony Featherstone 7 (+2), Ray Bales 6 (+2), Vic Cross 2 (+1), Lindsay Davies 1, *Jim Ryman (R/R).*
CREWE - Phil Crump 14, Dai Evans 5, Garry Flood 4, John Jackson 4, Gary Moore 2, Dave Morton 2, Dave Parry 0.

Meeting 35 - Monday, August 14, 1972 - British League Division II
L.M.R. Sports Ground, Earle Street, Crewe
Track Length - 430 yards.

CREWE KINGS.....45 BERWICK BANDITS.....33

Berwick became only the third team to top thirty points in the league at Earle Street this season, as the Kings were again plagued by mechanical troubles throughout the evening. Phil Crump and John Jackson were again undefeated, but Dave Morton had a night to forget. He fell in Heat 1 on a heavily watered track, and then again in Heat 8, which resulted in a broken arm after being hit by an opponent's machine. At this point Crewe led by four, but ground out three more heat victories to win the tie by a rather flattering twelve point margin.

Heat 01	**Crump**/D.Templeton/Jones/**Morton** (F)	75.6	3 - 3	03 - 03
Heat 02	**Parry**/Davies/D.Jackson/**Moore** (R)	76.2	3 - 3	06 - 06
Heat 03	**Flood**/**Evans**/Meldrum/W.Templeton	77.2	**5 - 1**	11 - 07
Heat 04	**J.Jackson**/Gallacher/D.Jackson/**Parry** (R)	75.0	3 - 3	14 - 10
Heat 05	**Flood**/D.Templeton/**Evans**/Jones	76.2	**4 - 2**	18 - 12
Heat 06	**Crump**/Gallacher/Davies/**Parry**	74.2	3 - 3	21 - 15
Heat 07	**J.Jackson**/W.Templeton/Meldrum/**Moore**	75.0	3 - 3	24 - 18
Heat 08	Gallacher/**Moore**/Davies/**Morton** (X)	77.2	2 - 4	26 - 22
Heat 09	**Evans**/Gallacher/**Flood**/Davies	75.2	**4 - 2**	30 - 24
Heat 10	**Crump**/Meldrum/W.Templeton/**Parry**	74.0	3 - 3	33 - 27
Heat 11	**J.Jackson**/Meldrum/**Moore**/D.Templeton	75.8	**4 - 2**	37 - 29
Heat 12	**Crump**/Meldrum/Gallacher/**Flood**	73.2	3 - 3	40 - 32
Heat 13	**J.Jackson**/**Evans**/W.Templeton/D.Templeton	75.0	**5 - 1**	45 - 33

CREWE - Phil Crump 12, John Jackson 12, Dai Evans 8 (+2), Garry Flood 7, Gary Moore 3, Dave Parry 3, Dave Morton 0.
BERWICK - Jimmy Gallacher 10 (+1), Andy Meldrum 8 (+1), Geoff Davies 4 (+1), Willie Templeton 4 (+1), Doug Templeton 4, Dennis Jackson 2 (+2), Graham Jones 1 (+1).

Peterborough lost the second leg of the K.O. Cup semi-final 42-36 at Perry Barr, but went through 79-77 on aggregate. On August 17, Phil Crump captained Australasia to a 55-51 win over England in the opening Division II test at Teesside. He lopped 1.2 seconds off the track record in Heat 1 on his way to claiming eighteen points. John Jackson scored eight, but Garry Flood failed to get off the mark. Two nights later at Rayleigh, the colonials won the second test 56-52, to take the series with one match remaining. Crump scored fifteen and Flood three, with the former falling heavily in Heat 16, badly bruising a wrist.

Meeting 36 - Sunday, August 20, 1972 - British League Division II
Quibell Park Stadium, Brumby Wood Lane, Scunthorpe
Track Length - 440 yards.

SCUNTHORPE SAINTS.....30 CREWE KINGS.....48

Reg Brassington came into the Kings side in place of Dave Morton, as the visitors easily overcame the injury-hit Scunthorpe side, who suffered their heaviest home league defeat to date. Phil Crump recorded a perfect score and received excellent support from Garry Flood, who dropped his only point in the final heat. The Saints had no answer to the powerful Kings outfit and managed just a solitary 4-2 heat win, which incredibly turned out to be their only advantage during 52 heats ridden against Crewe this season.

Heat 01	**Crump**/Watkins/**Brassington**/Ryan	**78.0** (TR)	**2 - 4**	02 - 04
Heat 02	Bowerman/**Moore**/**Parry**/Garrod (R)	81.1	3 - 3	05 - 07
Heat 03	**Flood**/**Evans**/Underwood/Wilson	81.4	**1 - 5**	06 - 12
Heat 04	**Jackson**/Garrod/**Moore**/Bass	81.1	**2 - 4**	08 - 16
Heat 05	**Crump**/Wilson/Underwood/**Brassington**	81.2	3 - 3	11 - 19
Heat 06	**Jackson**/Watkins/Bowerman/**Parry**	81.2	3 - 3	14 - 22
Heat 07	**Flood**/Bass/**Evans**/Garrod	83.1	**2 - 4**	16 - 26
Heat 08	**Moore**/Watkins/Bowerman/**Brassington**	83.4	3 - 3	19 - 29
Heat 09	Underwood/**Jackson**/Garrod/**Parry**	82.0	4 - 2	23 - 31
Heat 10	**Flood**/**Evans**/Watkins/Ryan	84.2	**1 - 5**	24 - 36
Heat 11	**Crump**/Bass/**Moore**/Bowerman	81.3	**2 - 4**	26 - 40
Heat 12	Underwood/**Jackson**/**Evans**/Watkins	82.4	3 - 3	29 - 43
Heat 13	**Crump**/**Flood**/Bass/Ryan	85.6	**1 - 5**	30 - 48

SCUNTHORPE - Doug Underwood 8 (+1), Ray Watkins 7, John Bowerman, 5 (+2), Phil Bass 5, Rex Garrod 3, Ian Wilson 2, Mike Ryan 0.
CREWE - Phil Crump 12, Garry Flood 11 (+1), John Jackson 10, Gary Moore 7, Dai Evans 6 (+3), Dave Parry 1 (+1), Reg Brassington 1.

Following the afternoon meeting, Crump, Flood and Jackson made the short trip to Boston to take part in the final England v Australasia test. Crump again scored eighteen points, one more than his former Crewe comrade Jack Millen, as the Anzacs wrapped up a 3-0 series win.

Reserve John Jackson scored five for the Lions. On the same day, Boston did their own title chances no harm with a 41-37 win at Peterborough.

Meeting 37 - Monday, August 21, 1972 - Top Dogs Trophy, Second Leg
L.M.R. Sports Ground, Earle Street, Crewe
Track Length - 430 yards.

CREWE KINGS.....57 BRADFORD NORTHERN.....21

(Crewe won on aggregate 93 - 63)

The long delayed home leg of the Top Dogs Trophy (originally rained off on March 31), finally took place, with Bradford's slender six point first leg lead never going to be enough to retain the trophy. The best Northern could do on the night was to share the points in three heats, as all home riders contributed to the big win. Peter Nicholas picked up a hard earned point after falling in Heat 6. He scrambled to his feet and pushed his machine 200 yards to the line. Barry Booth, another promising Kings youngster, was drafted into the Bradford side, until late arrival Mick Fairbairn turned up.

Heat 01	**Crump**/Bridgett/Baugh/**Nicholas**	75.0	3 - 3	03 - 03
Heat 02	**Moore**/**Parry**/Booth/Fielding	78.6	**5 - 1**	08 - 04
Heat 03	Knapkin/**Flood**/**Evans**/Sheldrick	77.4	3 - 3	11 - 07
Heat 04	**Parry**/**Jackson**/Adlington/Fielding	76.0	**5 - 1**	16 - 08
Heat 05	**Flood**/**Evans**/Baugh/Bridgett	75.8	**5 - 1**	21 - 09
Heat 06	**Crump**/Adlington/**Nicholas**/Booth (R)	73.6	**4 - 2**	25 - 11
Heat 07	**Parry**/**Jackson**/Knapkin/Sheldrick	75.4	**5 - 1**	30 - 12
Heat 08	**Moore**/**Nicholas**/Bridgett/Fielding	77.4	**5 - 1**	35 - 13
Heat 09	**Evans**/**Flood**/Adlington/Fairbairn	75.8	**5 - 1**	40 - 14
Heat 10	**Crump**/Knapkin/**Nicholas**/Sheldrick	74.6	**4 - 2**	44 - 16
Heat 11	**Jackson**/**Moore**/Bridgett/Baugh (R)	74.6	**5 - 1**	49 - 17
Heat 12	**Crump**/Knapkin/Adlington/**Flood** (R)	75.0	3 - 3	52 - 20
Heat 13	**Jackson**/**Evans**/Fairbairn/Bridgett	75.4	**5 - 1**	57 - 21

CREWE - Phil Crump 12, John Jackson 10 (+2), Dai Evans 8 (+3), Gary Moore 8 (+1), Dave Parry 8 (+1), Garry Flood 7 (+1), Peter Nicholas 4 (+1).
BRADFORD - Alan Knapkin 8, Robin Adlington 5 (+1), Alan Bridgett 4, Dave Baugh 2 (+1), Barry Booth* 1, Mick Fairbairn 1, Mick Fielding 0, Sid Sheldrick 0.

Meeting 38 - Tuesday, August 22, 1972 - British League Division II
Barrow Stadium, Holker Street, Barrow-in-Furness
Track Length - 400 yards.

BARROW HAPPY FACES.....44 CREWE KINGS.....33

There were no "happy faces" in the Crewe half of the pits following this surprise defeat. Phil Crump established a new track record of 68.4, and won four of his five rides, falling in Heat 8 while in as a tactical substitute, which left the Kings eight points adrift. Worse was to follow in the next as Garry Flood, also on a tactical ride, fell and was excluded, with John Jackson also retiring. A late revival gave the score some respectability, but the result let Boston, Peterborough and Eastbourne back into the title race.

Heat 01	**Crump**/Sampson/Roynon/**Nicholas** (R)	00.0	3 - 3	03 - 03
Heat 02	K.Evans/**Parry**/Hindle/**Moore** (R)	00.0	4 - 2	07 - 05
Heat 03	Watkins/**Flood**/Owen/**D.Evans**	00.0	4 - 2	11 - 07
Heat 04	**Jackson**/K.Evans/Coles/**Moore** (R)	00.0	3 - 3	14 - 10
Heat 05	**Crump**/Owen/**Moore**/Watkins	00.0	**2 - 4**	16 - 14
Heat 06	Sampson/**Jackson**/Roynon/**Parry**	00.0	4 - 2	20 - 16
Heat 07	Coles/**Flood**/K.Evans/**D.Evans**	00.0	4 - 2	24 - 18
Heat 08	Hindle/**Moore**/Roynon/**Crump** (F)	00.0	4 - 2	28 - 20
Heat 09	Owen/Watkins/**Jackson** (R)/**Flood** (X)	00.0	5 - 0	33 - 20
Heat 10	Sampson/**Flood**/**Jackson**/Roynon	00.0	3 - 3	36 - 23
Heat 11	**Crump**/Coles/**D.Evans**/Hindle	00.0	**2 - 4**	38 - 27
Heat 12	Sampson/**D.Evans**/Owen/**Moore** (F)	00.0	4 - 2	42 - 29
Heat 13	**Crump**/Watkins/**Flood**/Coles (X)	00.0	**2 - 4**	44 - 33

BARROW - Mike Sampson 11, Mike Watkins 7 (+1), Tom Owen 7, Bob Coles 6 (+1), Keith Evans 6, Ian Hindle 4, Chris Roynon 3 (+1).
CREWE - Phil Crump 12, Garry Flood 7, John Jackson 6 (+1), Gary Moore 3, Dai Evans 3, Dave Parry 2, Peter Nicholas 0.

Meeting 39 - Monday, August 28, 1972 - West Midlands Trophy, First Leg
L.M.R. Sports Ground, Earle Street, Crewe
Track Length - 430 yards.

CREWE KINGS.....47 BIRMINGHAM BRUMMIES.....31

Terry Shearer and Mike Lanham became the first visiting riders to defeat John Jackson at Earle Street, since the opening league match of the season. Jackson's proud unbeaten record was ended with a retirement in Heat 11. A respite from the pressures of league and cup speedway saw the Kings establish a sixteen point lead to take to Perry Barr twenty-four hours later. Birmingham put in a vastly improved performance from their 61-17 league drubbing in May, and it kept them in touch for an aggregate victory. Phil Crump rode to his 14th home maximum of the season.

Heat	Result	Time	Score	Total
Heat 01	**Crump**/Shearer/**Hassall**/Lanham	73.4	**4 - 2**	04 - 02
Heat 02	**Moore**/**Parry**/Corradine/Wilson	76.2	**5 - 1**	09 - 03
Heat 03	Major/**Flood**/Hines/**Evans**	75.2	2 - 4	11 - 07
Heat 04	**Jackson**/**Parry**/Wilkinson/Wilson (R)	73.8	**5 - 1**	16 - 08
Heat 05	**Flood**/Shearer/**Evans**/Lanham	74.6	**4 - 2**	20 - 10
Heat 06	**Crump**/**Hassall**/Corradine/Wilkinson	72.6	**5 - 1**	25 - 11
Heat 07	**Parry**/Major/**Moore**/Hines	73.2	**4 - 2**	29 - 13
Heat 08	Shearer/Wilson/**Moore**/**Hassall**	72.4	1 - 5	30 - 18
Heat 09	**Flood**/Major/Hines/**Evans** (R)	74.4	3 - 3	33 - 21
Heat 10	**Crump**/Hines/Major/**Hassall**	72.2	3 - 3	36 - 24
Heat 11	**Moore**/Shearer/Lanham/**Jackson** (R)	76.8	3 - 3	39 - 27
Heat 12	**Crump**/**Flood**/Major/Wilson	72.0	**5 - 1**	44 - 28
Heat 13	Hines/**Evans**/**Jackson**/Shearer (R)	75.8	3 - 3	47 - 31

CREWE - Phil Crump 12, Garry Flood 10 (+1), Gary Moore 8, Dave Parry 7 (+2), John Jackson 4 (+1), Ray Hassall 3 (+1), Dai Evans 3.
BIRMINGHAM - George Major 9 (+1), Terry Shearer 9, Mick Hines 7 (+1), Steve Wilson 2 (+1), Malcolm Corradine 2, Mike Lanham 1 (+1), Archie Wilkinson 1.

Towards the end of August the top of the Division II table still saw Crewe top.

	Matches	Points
1. Crewe	24	34
2. Rayleigh	25	32
3. Boston	25	31
4. Birmingham	27	31
5. Peterborough	21	28

Meeting 40 - Tuesday, August 29, 1972 - West Midlands Trophy, Second Leg
Perry Barr Greyhound Stadium, Regina Drive, Walsall Road, Birmingham
Track Length - 350 yards

BIRMINGHAM BRUMMIES.....40 CREWE KINGS.....38

(Crewe won on aggregate 85 - 71)

The Kings won the West Midlands Trophy after going down by just two points in the return leg. Crewe riders won nine races, but could only turn three into an advantage. During the match, the starting gate failed to operate, and following several unsavoury incidents, John Jackson was excluded from Heat 9, resulting in the Crewe team threatening to pull out of the meeting.

Heat	Result	Time	Score	Total
Heat 01	**Crump**/Browning/Lanham/**Hassall**	**63.2** (=TR)	3 - 3	03 - 03
Heat 02	Wilkinson/**Parry**/Corradine/**Moore** (X)	65.0	4 - 2	07 - 05
Heat 03	Major/Hines/**Flood**/**Evans** (F)	64.4	5 - 1	12 - 06
Heat 04	**Jackson**/Shearer/Wilkinson/**Moore** (F)	64.6	3 - 3	15 - 09
Heat 05	**Crump**/Major/Hines/**Hassall** (F)	64.0	3 - 3	18 - 12
Heat 06	**Jackson**/Browning/Lanham/**Parry**	65.2	3 - 3	21 - 15

Heat 07 .... **Flood**/Shearer/**Evans**/Wilkinson	64.8	**2 - 4**	23 - 19
Heat 08 .... Corradine/**Moore**/Lanham/**Parry**	67.6	4 - 2	27 - 21
Heat 09 .... Major/**Crump**/Hines/**Moore**	64.0	4 - 2	31 - 23
Heat 10 .... **Flood**/**Jackson**/Lanham/Browning (R)	64.2	**1 - 5**	32 - 28
Heat 11 .... **Crump**/Shearer/**Moore**/Corradine	63.6	**2 - 4**	34 - 32
Heat 12 .... **Jackson**/Hines/Browning/**Evans**	65.4	3 - 3	37 - 35
Heat 13 .... **Crump**/Major/Shearer/**Flood**	64.8	3 - 3	40 - 38

BIRMINGHAM - George Major 10, Terry Shearer 7 (+1), Mick Hines 6 (+2), Arthur Browning 5 (+1), Mike Lanham 4 (+2), Archie Wilkinson 4 (+1), Malcolm Corradine 4.
CREWE - Phil Crump 14, John Jackson 11 (+1), Garry Flood 7, Gary Moore 3, Dave Parry 2, Dai Evans 1, Ray Hassall 0.

On August 30, Phil Crump and Garry Flood rode in the Maurice Littlechild Memorial Trophy at King's Lynn, appropriately won by home skipper Terry Betts, who just edged out Ole Olsen to win the inaugural competition. On the same night, the Crewe Princes travelled to Dudley Wood to take on a Cradley Heath training school side. Included in the team were Reg Brassington, Ray Hassall, Peter Nicholas, Robin Peters, Mick Ramsell and Ken Stafford. Meanwhile, junior Barry Booth was released from his contract after putting in a transfer request, with lack of first team opportunities the main reason for his departure. Boston went top of the Division II table with a 50-28 win at Scunthorpe, and a 42-36 home victory over rivals Rayleigh.

Meeting 41 - Monday, September 4, 1972 - Speedway Express Knock Out Cup, Final, First Leg
L.M.R. Sports Ground, Earle Street, Crewe
Track Length - 430 yards.

CREWE KINGS.....51 PETERBOROUGH PANTHERS.....27

In front of Crewe's biggest crowd of the season, Peterborough made a dream start to the first leg of the K.O. Cup final with a 5-1 after Phil Crump had retired - the first time he had failed to win his opening ride in the league and cup at Earle Street all season. Order however, was soon restored, and by the end of Heat 5, the hosts held a ten point advantage. The Panthers, without injured skipper Richard Greer, did manage a share of the points in four heats, but the Kings motored to a twenty-four point lead, which made them hot favourites of landing their first major piece of silverware. John Jackson was unbeatable and twice went within three-fifths of a second of his own track record. The best race of the night was saved until last when Jackson's win was partly eclipsed by a brilliant last lap by Dai Evans, who just managed to overhaul early leader Roy Carter for third place.

Heat 01 .... Carter/Amies/**Nicholas**/**Crump** (R)	73.6	1 - 5	01 - 05
Heat 02 .... **Parry**/**Moore**/Howgego/Clark	73.4	**5 - 1**	06 - 06
Heat 03 .... **Flood**/**Evans**/Ashby/Davis (R)	73.6	**5 - 1**	11 - 07
Heat 04 .... **Jackson**/Carter/**Parry**/Howgego (R)	72.0	**4 - 2**	15 - 09
Heat 05 .... **Evans**/**Flood**/Carter/Amies	74.2	**5 - 1**	20 - 10
Heat 06 .... **Crump**/Davis/Clark/**Nicholas**	73.4	3 - 3	23 - 13
Heat 07 .... **Jackson**/**Parry**/Davis/Ashby	72.2	**5 - 1**	28 - 14
Heat 08 .... Carter/**Moore**/**Parry**/Amies	73.0	3 - 3	31 - 17
Heat 09 .... **Flood**/Clark/Smith/**Evans**	74.2	3 - 3	34 - 20
Heat 10 .... **Crump**/**Nicholas**/Davis/Howgego	74.0	**5 - 1**	39 - 21
Heat 11 .... **Jackson**/Carter/Clark/**Moore**	72.0	3 - 3	42 - 24
Heat 12 .... **Crump**/**Flood**/Amies/Ashby	72.0	**5 - 1**	47 - 25
Heat 13 .... **Jackson**/Clark/**Evans**/Carter	73.0	**4 - 2**	51 - 27

CREWE - John Jackson 12, Garry Flood 10 (+2), Phil Crump 9, Dave Parry 7 (+2), Dai Evans 6 (+1), Gary Moore 4 (+1), Peter Nicholas 3 (+1).
PETERBOROUGH - Roy Carter 11, Brian Clark 6 (+2), John Davis 4, John Amies 3 (+1), Frank Smith 1 (+1), David Ashby 1, Ted Howgego 1. *Richard Greer (R/R).*

Meeting 42 - Sunday, September 10, 1972 - Speedway Express Knock Out Cup Final, Second Leg
East of England Showground, Alwalton, Peterborough
Track Length - 380 yards.

PETERBOROUGH PANTHERS.....40 CREWE KINGS.....38

(Crewe won on aggregate 89 - 67)

It was third time lucky for Crewe when they completed the first part of a possible double, by winning the K.O. Cup. In a magnificent speedway clash, the Kings made sure of the trophy with a 5-1 maximum in Heat 8, which sparked wild scenes in the pits and on the terraces. Phil Crump won four from five and received valuable support from John Jackson, Garry Flood and Gary Moore. Peterborough star Richard Greer returned to top score for the Panthers with eleven points, and was only denied his maximum by Crump in Heat 13.

Heat 01	**Crump**/Carter/Ashby/**Nicholas** (F)	70.2	3 - 3	03 - 03
Heat 02	Clark/**Moore**/Amies/**Parry**	71.8	4 - 2	07 - 05
Heat 03	**Flood**/Davis/Howgego/**Evans**	72.2	3 - 3	10 - 08
Heat 04	Greer/**Jackson**/Clark/**Moore**	70.8	4 - 2	14 - 10
Heat 05	**Crump**/Howgego/Davis/**Nicholas** (F)	70.6	3 - 3	17 - 13
Heat 06	Carter/**Jackson**/Ashby/**Parry**	70.4	4 - 2	21 - 15
Heat 07	Greer/**Flood**/Clark/**Evans**	71.2	4 - 2	25 - 17
Heat 08	**Crump**/**Moore**/Ashby/Amies (F)	71.4	**1 - 5**	26 - 22
Heat 09	**Jackson**/Davis/Howgego/**Parry**	71.2	3 - 3	29 - 25
Heat 10	Carter/**Flood**/**Evans**/Ashby	71.2	3 - 3	32 - 28
Heat 11	Greer/**Moore**/Clark/**Crump** (R)	72.4	4 - 2	36 - 30
Heat 12	**Jackson**/Carter/**Evans**/Howgego	70.4	**2 - 4**	38 - 34
Heat 13	**Crump**/Greer/**Flood**/Davis	71.0	**2 - 4**	40 - 38

PETERBOROUGH - Richard Greer 11, Roy Carter 10, Brian Clark 6, John Davis 5 (+1), Ted Howgego 4 (+2), David Ashby 3 (+1), John Amies 1.
CREWE - Phil Crump 12, John Jackson 10, Garry Flood 8, Gary Moore 6 (+1), Dai Evans 2 (+1), Peter Nicholas 0, Dave Parry 0.

Meeting 43 - Monday, September 11, 1972 - British League Division II
L.M.R. Sports Ground, Earle Street, Crewe
Track Length - 430 yards.

CREWE KINGS.....58 RAYLEIGH ROCKETS.....20

Crewe ended Rayleigh's faint championship hopes by duly hammering the men from Essex. They won every heat, including the sixth, in which Phil Crump pushed his bike home 200 yards to earn a point, after Trevor Barnwell had retired. In all, six of the seven Kings took the chequered flag, with Nantwich youngster Peter Nicholas recording his first league win in Heat 2. Garry Flood and Dave Parry collected paid maximums, but John Jackson missed out when he was headed home by Brian Foote in Heat 13. This was the first time Jackson had been beaten by a visiting rider in league and cup competition since the Peterborough match on April 24.

Heat 01	**Crump**/**Parry**/Foote/Claridge	78.0	**5 - 1**	05 - 01
Heat 02	**Nicholas**/**Moore**/Beech/Barnwell (F)	77.4	**5 - 1**	10 - 02
Heat 03	**Flood**/**Evans**/Ott/Young	76.8	**5 - 1**	15 - 03
Heat 04	**Jackson**/**Nicholas**/Emmett/Beech	74.4	**5 - 1**	20 - 04
Heat 05	**Flood**/Foote/**Evans**/Claridge	74.0	**4 - 2**	24 - 06
Heat 06	**Parry**/Emmett/**Crump**/Barnwell (R)	74.0	**4 - 2**	28 - 08
Heat 07	**Jackson**/Young/**Nicholas**/Ott	73.8	**4 - 2**	32 - 10
Heat 08	**Parry**/Emmett/**Moore**/Foote (R)	74.4	**4 - 2**	36 - 12
Heat 09	**Flood**/Emmett/**Evans**/Barnwell	74.0	**4 - 2**	40 - 14
Heat 10	**Crump**/**Parry**/Young/Ott	74.2	**5 - 1**	45 - 15
Heat 11	**Jackson**/Foote/**Moore**/Barnwell	74.8	**4 - 2**	49 - 17
Heat 12	**Crump**/**Flood**/Emmett/Young	73.4	**5 - 1**	54 - 18
Heat 13	**Evans**/Foote/**Jackson**/Ott	74.4	**4 - 2**	58 - 20

CREWE - Garry Flood 11 (+1), Dave Parry 10 (+2), Phil Crump 10, John Jackson 10, Dai Evans 7 (+1), Peter Nicholas 6 (+1), Gary Moore 4 (+1).
RAYLEIGH - Allan Emmett 8, Brian Foote 7, Bob Young 3, Tiger Beech 1, Les Ott 1, Trevor Barnwell 0, Peter Claridge 0.

During the meeting, a collection was held for Dave Morton, which raised £60. A shake-up in the management department saw Alan Littlechild (Maurice's son) take over as team manager for home meetings, sharing the away duties with Ken Adams. John Jackson meanwhile did his chances of a move into the top flight no harm by winning the Teesside Stadium Silver Helmet Trophy on September 14, after a three-man run-off with home pair Dave Durham and Bruce Forrester.

Meeting 44 - Friday, September 15, 1972 - British League Division II
Derwent Park Stadium, Workington
Track Length - 398 yards.

WORKINGTON COMETS.....48 CREWE KINGS.....30

Workington kept the title race alive by inflicting Crewe's biggest defeat of the season. Phil Crump and John Jackson were given extra rides in the hope of reducing the deficit, and even though they netted twenty-two points, the rest of the Kings were sadly off-form. Dave Parry and Crump provided Crewe's only heat advantage in the eighth.

Heat 01	**Crump**/Stobbart/Owen/**Hassall**	75.0	3 - 3	03 - 03
Heat 02	Graham/Watson/**Moore**/**Parry**	76.6	5 - 1	08 - 04
Heat 03	Sansom/Amundson/**Evans**/**Flood** (R)	77.2	5 - 1	13 - 05
Heat 04	Mackay/Graham/**Jackson**/**Moore**	77.0	5 - 1	18 - 06
Heat 05	Sansom/**Crump**/Amundson/**Hassall**	75.0	4 - 2	22 - 08
Heat 06	**Jackson**/Owen/Stobbart/**Parry**	77.0	3 - 3	25 - 11
Heat 07	Mackay/Graham/**Flood**/**Evans**	77.8	5 - 1	30 - 12
Heat 08	**Parry**/**Crump**/Stobbart/Watson	78.2	**1 - 5**	31 - 17
Heat 09	Sansom/**Jackson**/**Flood**/Amundson	76.2	3 - 3	34 - 20
Heat 10	Graham/Owen/**Flood**/**Evans**	77.2	5 - 1	39 - 21
Heat 11	Mackay/**Crump**/**Jackson**/Watson	75.4	3 - 3	42 - 24
Heat 12	**Jackson**/Owen/Amundson/**Evans**	76.6	3 - 3	45 - 27
Heat 13	**Crump**/Sansom/Mackay/**Hassall**	76.6	3 - 3	48 - 30

WORKINGTON - Lou Sansom 11, Mitch Graham 10 (+2), Malcolm Mackay 10 (+1), Taffy Owen 7 (+2), Kym Amundson 4 (+2), Darrell Stobbart 4 (+1), Steve Watson 2 (+1).
CREWE - Phil Crump 12 (+1), John Jackson 10 (+1), Garry Flood 3 (+1), Dave Parry 3, Dai Evans 1, Gary Moore 1, Ray Hassall 0.

Meeting 45 - Monday, September 18, 1972 - British League Division II
L.M.R. Sports Ground, Earle Street, Crewe
Track Length - 430 yards.

CREWE KINGS.....51 HULL VIKINGS.....27

Phil Crump suffered a rare opening ride defeat, after a groggy motor prevented him from passing Hull's Stan Stevens. Garry Flood then failed to finish in either of his first two races, but after their initial jitters, the Kings got their act together and stormed to a comprehensive victory. John Jackson secured his tenth home league maximum of the season, and Dai Evans chipped in with a paid one. Peter Nicholas impressed the home crowd with seven points and could have scored more but for a retirement in Heat 11, while lying second to Jackson.

Heat 01	Stevens/**Crump**/**Hassall**/Childs	77.0	3 - 3	03 - 03
Heat 02	**Nicholas**/Gavros/**Moore**/Wasden	76.0	**4 - 2**	07 - 05
Heat 03	**Evans**/Loakes/Stevens/**Flood** (R)	75.6	3 - 3	10 - 08
Heat 04	**Jackson**/**Nicholas**/Mills/Wasden	73.6	**5 - 1**	15 - 09
Heat 05	**Evans**/Childs/Stevens/**Flood** (R)	76.0	3 - 3	18 - 12
Heat 06	**Crump**/**Hassall**/Gavros/Mills	73.4	**5 - 1**	23 - 13
Heat 07	**Jackson**/**Moore**/Loakes/Childs	73.8	**5 - 1**	28 - 14
Heat 08	Stevens/**Nicholas**/Loakes/**Hassall**	74.8	2 - 4	30 - 18
Heat 09	**Evans**/**Flood**/Gavros/Mills	74.2	**5 - 1**	35 - 19
Heat 10	**Crump**/Gavros/Loakes/**Hassall**	72.8	3 - 3	38 - 22
Heat 11	**Jackson**/Stevens/Childs/**Nicholas** (R)	74.8	3 - 3	41 - 25
Heat 12	**Crump**/**Flood**/Loakes/Gavros	73.0	**5 - 1**	46 - 26
Heat 13	**Jackson**/**Evans**/Loakes/Childs (R)	73.0	**5 - 1**	51 - 27

CREWE - John Jackson 12, Dai Evans 11 (+1), Phil Crump 11, Peter Nicholas 7 (+1), Garry Flood 4 (+2), Ray Hassall 3 (+2), Gary Moore 3 (+1).

HULL - Stan Stevens 10 (+2), Bryan Loakes 7 (+1), Dennis Gavros 6, Tony Childs 3 (+1), Dave Mills 1, Dennis Wasden 0, *Robin Amundson (R/R).*

Meeting 46 - Tuesday, September 19, 1972 - Four Team Tournament
Ellesmere Port Stadium, Thornton Road, Ellesmere Port
Track Length - 423 yards.

CREWE KINGS.....36 ELLESMERE PORT GUNNERS.....26 BRADFORD NORTHERN.....20 HULL VIKINGS.....14

Dai Evans and Dave Parry provided solid support to Crewe's big guns, making all the difference in the four team event at Thornton Road, which came as a welcome break from the pressures of the title race. The quartet provided a scorer in every race but the last.

			C	E	B	H
Heat 01	**Crump**/Gardner/Loakes/Tattersall	82.0	3	2	0	1
Heat 02	Goad/**Evans**/Baugh/Boston	83.0	2	3	1	0
Heat 03	**Jackson**/Knapkin/Drury/Wasden	84.0	3	1	2	0
Heat 04	Stevens/Bridgett/**Parry**/Francis (R)	84.2	1	0	2	3
Heat 05	**Jackson**/Bridgett/Gardner/Boston	82.8	3	1	2	0
Heat 06	Goad/Knapkin/**Parry**/Loakes	82.2	1	3	2	0
Heat 07	**Crump**/Stevens/Baugh/Drury	81.8	3	0	1	2
Heat 08	**Evans**/Francis/Wasden/Tattersall	83.6	3	2	0	1
Heat 09	Gardner/**Parry**/Baugh/Wasden	81.6	2	3	1	0
Heat 10	**Jackson**/Goad/Stevens/Tattersall	81.8	3	2	0	1
Heat 11	**Evans**/Drury/Loakes/Bridgett	82.8	3	2	0	1
Heat 12	**Crump**/Knapkin/Francis/Boston	81.4	3	1	2	0
Heat 13	Knapkin/Stevens/**Evans**/Hughes (F)	82.8	1	0	3	2
Heat 14	**Crump**/Bridgett/Wasden/Goad (X)	81.8	3	0	2	1
Heat 15	Drury/**Parry**/Boston/Tattersall	82.8	2	3	0	1
Heat 16	Francis/Baugh/Loakes/**Jackson** (R)	84.8	0	3	2	1

CREWE - Phil Crump 12, Dai Evans 9, John Jackson 9, Dave Parry 6.
ELLESMERE PORT - Colin Goad 8, Graham Drury 6, Cyril Francis 6, Robbie Gardner 6, Wayne Hughes (Reserve) 0.
BRADFORD - Alan Knapkin 9, Alan Bridgett 6, Dave Baugh 5, Graham Tattersall 0.
HULL - Stan Stevens 8, Bryan Loakes 3, Dennis Wasden 2, Pete Boston 1.

Meeting 47 - Saturday, September 23, 1972 - British League Division II
Shielfield Park, Tweedmouth, Berwick-upon-Tweed
Track Length - 440 yards.

BERWICK BANDITS.....39 CREWE KINGS.....39

Lowly Berwick led the Kings from Heat 2 until the final race, when a magneto failure sustained by Jimmy Gallacher handed Crewe a valuable point, and possibly the championship. Phil Crump and John Jackson, with the astute use of tactical substitutions, won nine heats between them, but the others failed to deliver. Jackson set the fastest time of the night, equalling the Shielfield track record in Heat 4. Bandits skipper Doug Templeton failed to get his motor to fire before the start of the match and managed just three points on borrowed machinery.

Heat 01	**Crump**/W.Templeton/**Parry**/D.Templeton	76.4	**2 - 4**	02 - 04
Heat 02	Jones/D.Jackson/**Moore**/**Evans** (R)	79.2	5 - 1	07 - 05
Heat 03	Meldrum/Davies/**Nicholas**/**Flood**	77.6	5 - 1	12 - 06
Heat 04	**J.Jackson**/Gallacher/**Moore**/D.Jackson	**75.8** (=TR)	**2 - 4**	14 - 10
Heat 05	**Crump**/Meldrum/Davies/**Parry**	77.8	3 - 3	17 - 13
Heat 06	**J.Jackson**/W.Templeton/D.Templeton/**Evans**	77.6	3 - 3	20 - 16
Heat 07	Gallacher/**Flood**/D.Jackson/**Nicholas**	78.8	4 - 2	24 - 18
Heat 08	**Crump**/W.Templeton/Jones/**Moore**	78.2	3 - 3	27 - 21
Heat 09	Meldrum/**J.Jackson**/**Evans**/Davies	78.8	3 - 3	30 - 24
Heat 10	**J.Jackson**/W.Templeton/**Flood**/D.Templeton	78.6	**2 - 4**	32 - 28
Heat 11	**Crump**/Gallacher/**Parry**/Jones	78.0	**2 - 4**	34 - 32
Heat 12	**J.Jackson**/D.Templeton/Davies/**Moore**	78.4	3 - 3	37 - 35
Heat 13	**Crump**/Meldrum/**Flood**/Gallacher (R)	78.2	**2 - 4**	39 - 39

(ABOVE) Red Cross members, track staff and fellow riders come to the aid of Crewe's Ray Hassall and Canterbury's Ted "Hurricane" Hubbard after their Heat 1 crash at Earle Street on July 24. (BELOW) Junior Ray Hassall.

(ABOVE) Proud Skipper Dai Evans, Ken Adams, John Jackson and Phil Crump clutching the Speedway Express Knock Out Cup at Peterborough.

(ABOVE) The victorious team pose for the camera. Far right is local rider Peter Nicholas, who came into the side in place of the unfortunate Dave Morton.

(ABOVE) The cup shown off to home fans during the match with Rayleigh.
(BELOW) A winners tankard (courtesy of Dai Evans).

BERWICK - Andy Meldrum 10, Willie Templeton 8, Jimmy Gallacher 7, Geoff Davies 4 (+3), Graham Jones 4 (+1), Dennis Jackson 3 (+1), Doug Templeton 3 (+1).
CREWE - Phil Crump 15, John Jackson 14, Garry Flood 4, Gary Moore 2, Dave Parry 2, Dai Evans 1 (+1), Peter Nicholas 1.

The following day, the importance of the Berwick draw was fully realised as the Kings' nearest rivals Boston were beaten 49-28 at Rayleigh. Meanwhile, Crewe's success was being criticised by several teams and promoters, with the Earle Street track once again receiving the brunt. The notes in one Teesside programme, summing up their season and the performance of home rider Bruce Forrester read: *'About as much like the real Bruce Forrester as Crewe is like a speedway track.'*

Meeting 48 - Monday, September 25, 1972 - British League Division II
L.M.R. Sports Ground, Earle Street, Crewe
Track Length - 430 yards.

CREWE KINGS.....50 SUNDERLAND STARS.....28

Jack Millen put in one of his best Earle Street performances to date, collecting thirteen points, but that was as good as it got for the Stars, as the hosts marched a step closer to the championship. The Kiwi however, met his match in Heats 10 and 12 in the form of Phil Crump, who was tuning in a new engine. The victory margin was convincing, but could have been even greater had Dai Evans, John Jackson and Peter Nicholas not dropped points when in scoring positions.

Heat 01	**Crump**/**Parry**/Dent/Hodgson	74.8	**5 - 1**	05 - 01
Heat 02	**Nicholas**/**Moore**/Wrathall/Wells	76.8	**5 - 1**	10 - 02
Heat 03	Millen/**Flood**/Gatenby/**Evans**	75.2	2 - 4	12 - 06
Heat 04	**Nicholas**/Wells/Wrathall/**Jackson** (X)	74.8	3 - 3	15 - 09
Heat 05	**Flood**/**Evans**/Dent/Hodgson	75.0	**5 - 1**	20 - 10
Heat 06	**Crump**/**Parry**/Smith/Wells	75.2	**5 - 1**	25 - 11
Heat 07	Millen/**Jackson**/Gatenby/**Nicholas** (F)	74.8	2 - 4	27 - 15
Heat 08	Millen/**Moore**/**Parry**/Wrathall	75.8	3 - 3	30 - 18
Heat 09	**Flood**/Smith/**Evans**/Wells	75.2	**4 - 2**	34 - 20
Heat 10	**Crump**/Millen/Gatenby/**Parry**	74.2	3 - 3	37 - 23
Heat 11	**Jackson**/Dent/**Moore**/Hodgson	74.2	**4 - 2**	41 - 25
Heat 12	**Crump**/Millen/**Flood**/Smith	74.0	**4 - 2**	45 - 27
Heat 13	**Jackson**/**Evans**/Dent/Gatenby	74.4	**5 - 1**	50 - 28

CREWE - Phil Crump 12, Garry Flood 9, John Jackson 8, Peter Nicholas 6, Dave Parry 5 (+3), Dai Evans 5 (+2), Gary Moore 5 (+1).
SUNDERLAND - Jack Millen 13, Russ Dent 5, Dave Gatenby 3 (+1), Graeme Smith 3, Peter Wrathall 2 (+1), Jim Wells 2, Russ Hodgson 0.

Meeting 49 - Saturday, September 30, 1972 - British League Division II
Canterbury City Football Ground, Kingsmead Road, Canterbury
Track Length - 390 yards.

CANTERBURY CRUSADERS.....36 CREWE KINGS.....40

A magnificent fight back, after trailing by eight points, gave the Kings their seventh away league victory of the season, and this after conceding two heats 5-0! Once again Phil Crump led from the front with a second successive away fifteen point maximum, and yet another track record, with Garry Flood and John Jackson also in good form. The outcome rested on the last heat, with the teams all-square. Crump, with Flood tucked in behind, proved too good for the Canterbury pairing of Banks and Hubbard, giving Crewe the points and one hand on the league trophy.

Heat 01	**Crump**/Gilbertson/**Parry**/Davies	**71.8** (TR)	**2 - 4**	02 - 04
Heat 02	Jones/Rumsey/**Nicholas** (X)/**Moore** (R)	77.2	5 - 0	07 - 04
Heat 03	**Flood**/Hubbard/Kennett/**Evans** (F)	75.2	3 - 3	10 - 07
Heat 04	**Jackson**/Banks/Rumsey/**Moore**	75.0	3 - 3	13 - 10
Heat 05	**Crump**/Kennett/Hubbard/**Parry**	74.2	3 - 3	16 - 13
Heat 06	Davies/Gilbertson/**Jackson** (X)/**Nicholas** (X)	79.0	5 - 0	21 - 13
Heat 07	**Crump**/**Flood**/Banks/Rumsey	75.4	**1 - 5**	22 - 18
Heat 08	**Moore**/**Parry**/Jones/Davies	77.8	**1 - 5**	23 - 23

Heat 09	**Jackson**/Kennett/Hubbard/**Moore** (F)	75.8	3 - 3	26 - 26
Heat 10	**Flood**/Gilbertson/Rumsey/**Evans**	76.2	3 - 3	29 - 29
Heat 11	**Crump**/Banks/Jones/**Parry**	74.8	3 - 3	32 - 32
Heat 12	**Jackson**/Gilbertson/Kennett/**Moore**	75.0	3 - 3	35 - 35
Heat 13	**Crump**/**Flood**/Banks/Hubbard (F)	75.6	**1 - 5**	36 - 40

CANTERBURY - Ross Gilbertson 8 (+1), Barney Kennett 6 (+2), Graham Banks 6, Trevor Jones 5 (+1), Les Rumsey 4 (+3), Ted Hubbard 4 (+2), Steve Davies 3.
CREWE - Phil Crump 15, Garry Flood 10 (+2), John Jackson 9, Dave Parry 3 (+1), Gary Moore 3, Dai Evans 0, Peter Nicholas 0.

Crewe still required two points from their remaining two matches to become champions. They faced a tough trip to Eastbourne, who had yet to be beaten at home in the league, plus a tricky home encounter with bogey side Workington.

Meeting 50 - Sunday, October 1, 1972 - British League Division II
Arlington Raceway, Arlington Road, Hailsham, Eastbourne
Track Length - 342 yards.

EASTBOURNE EAGLES.....41 CREWE KINGS.....37

Reigning champions Eastbourne made sure the title race lasted for at least another day when they won a gripping encounter. Phil Crump and Garry Flood won seven races between them, but crucially for once, a below par John Jackson struggled to find his line around the Arlington Raceway circuit, and twice fell. The rest of the side fared little better, mustering only six points between them.

Heat 01	**Crump**/Ballard/Gachet/**Parry**	65.0	3 - 3	03 - 03
Heat 02	Geer/Dugard/**Moore**/**Nicholas** (F)	68.2	5 - 1	08 - 04
Heat 03	**Flood**/Johns/**Evans**/McNeil (F)	65.8	**2 - 4**	10 - 08
Heat 04	Kennett/Dugard/**Moore**/**Jackson** (F)	66.8	5 - 1	15 - 09
Heat 05	**Crump**/McNeil/**Parry**/Johns	65.4	**2 - 4**	17 - 13
Heat 06	Ballard/**Jackson**/Gachet/**Nicholas**	65.0	4 - 2	21 - 15
Heat 07	Kennett/**Flood**/**Evans**/Dugard	64.8	3 - 3	24 - 18
Heat 08	**Crump**/Gachet/Geer/**Parry**	64.6	3 - 3	27 - 21
Heat 09	**Flood**/Johns/McNeil/**Jackson** (F)	65.0	3 - 3	30 - 24
Heat 10	Ballard/**Flood**/Gachet/**Evans**	64.0	4 - 2	34 - 26
Heat 11	**Crump**/**Jackson**/Geer/Kennett (F)	65.0	**1 - 5**	35 - 31
Heat 12	Johns/Ballard/**Evans**/**Jackson**	64.2	5 - 1	40 - 32
Heat 13	**Flood**/**Crump**/McNeil/Kennett	66.0	**1 - 5**	41 - 37

EASTBOURNE - Malcolm Ballard 10 (+1), Roger Johns 7, Gordon Kennett 6, Paul Gachet 5 (+1), Trevor Geer 5 (+1), Eric Dugard 4 (+2), Bobby McNeil 4 (+1).
CREWE - Phil Crump 14 (+1), Garry Flood 13, John Jackson 4 (+1), Dai Evans 3 (+1), Gary Moore 2, Dave Parry 1, Peter Nicholas 0.

All was set for Crewe's final league match of the season. On October 1, the Division II table read:

	Matches	Points
1. Crewe	31	43
2. Boston	31	41
3. Peterborough	30	40

Meeting 51 - Monday, October 2, 1972 - British League Division II
L.M.R. Sports Ground, Earle Street, Crewe
Track Length - 430 yards.

CREWE KINGS.....49 WORKINGTON COMETS.....29

Crewe made a tentative start to their third match in as many days, and after three heats there was nothing between the teams. It took a 5-1 from Dave Parry and John Jackson in the fourth to settle the nerves, and from then on there was only ever going to be one winner. Finally, the champagne corks began popping as Jackson and Gary Moore crossed the finishing line for a 4-2 in

Heat 11, ensuring victory, with two races to spare, thus completing a memorable league and cup double. Division II Riders Championship favourite Phil Crump fittingly recorded his twenty-first maximum in both competitions, with his contribution from the final five league matches amounting to 68 points from a possible 69.

Heat 01	**Crump**/Owen/Stobbart/**Nicholas** (F)	74.0	3 - 3	03 - 03
Heat 02	Graham/**Parry**/**Moore**/Watson	77.0	3 - 3	06 - 06
Heat 03	Sansom/**Flood**/**Evans**/Amundson	76.8	3 - 3	09 - 09
Heat 04	**Parry**/**Jackson**/Graham/Watson (R)	76.0	**5 - 1**	14 - 10
Heat 05	**Flood**/Owen/**Evans**/Stobbart	75.0	**4 - 2**	18 - 12
Heat 06	**Crump**/Sansom/Graham/**Nicholas** (X)	74.4	3 - 3	21 - 15
Heat 07	**Jackson**/**Parry**/Amundson/Watson	75.2	**5 - 1**	26 - 16
Heat 08	**Moore**/Owen/**Parry**/Sansom	75.8	**4 - 2**	30 - 18
Heat 09	**Flood**/Graham/Owen/**Evans**	75.6	3 - 3	33 - 21
Heat 10	**Crump**/Graham/Sansom/**Nicholas**	74.2	3 - 3	36 - 24
Heat 11	**Jackson**/Owen/**Moore**/Stobbart	74.6	**4 - 2**	40 - 26
Heat 12	**Crump**/**Flood**/Graham/Watson	73.8	**5 - 1**	45 - 27
Heat 13	**Jackson**/Owen/**Evans**/Amundson	75.0	**4 - 2**	49 - 29

CREWE - Phil Crump 12, John Jackson 11 (+1), Garry Flood 10 (+1), Dave Parry 8 (+1), Gary Moore 5 (+1), Dai Evans 3 (+1), Peter Nicholas 0.
WORKINGTON - Taffy Owen 11 (+1), Mitch Graham 10 (+1), Lou Sansom 6 (+1), Darrell Stobbart 1 (+1), Kym Amundson 1, Steve Watson 0, *Malcolm Mackay (R/R)*.

On the same night, Peterborough lost 57-21 at Birmingham, which meant that even if Crewe had lost to the Comets, they would have still been crowned champions. With the echoes of victory still reverberating around Earle Street, the Crewe management filed an application to join Division I. APL also announced they were to spend a considerable sum on further track alterations.

Meeting 52 - Thursday, October 5, 1972 - Four Team Tournament
Long Eaton Stadium, Station Road, Long Eaton
Track Length - 366 yards.

CREWE KINGS.....39 LONG EATON RANGERS.....24
BOSTON BARRACUDAS.....19 PETERBOROUGH PANTHERS.....12

Crewe proved their league and cup success was no fluke by thrashing their two nearest league rivals, plus hosts Long Eaton, in this four team challenge. The Kings quartet recorded at least two race wins apiece, and scored points in all sixteen heats.

			C	L	B	P
Heat 01.....	Bouchard/**Crump**/Featherstone/Howgego	73.4	2	3	1	0
Heat 02.....	Ryman/**Jackson**/Carter/Jarvis (X)	74.2	2	0	3	1
Heat 03.....	Bass/Greer/**Evans**/Bales	74.8	1	3	0	2
Heat 04.....	**Moore**/Hughes/Anderson/Clark	75.4	3	2	1	0
Heat 05.....	Bouchard/Ryman/**Evans**/Clark	74.8	1	3	2	0
Heat 06.....	**Moore**/Greer/Featherstone/Jarvis	75.6	3	0	1	2
Heat 07.....	**Crump**/Carter/Edwards/Anderson (R)	71.6	3	/	0	2
Heat 08.....	**Jackson**/Hughes/Bales/Howgego	75.6	3	2	1	0
Heat 09.....	Bouchard/**Moore**/Bales/Carter	73.8	2	3	1	0
Heat 10.....	**Evans**/Howgego/Edwards/Anderson	76.2	3	/	0	2
Heat 11.....	**Jackson**/Bass/Featherstone/Clark	74.8	3	2	1	0
Heat 12.....	**Crump**/Ryman/Greer/Hughes	73.0	3	0	2	1
Heat 13.....	**Crump**/Bales/Clark/Edwards	72.4	3	0	2	1
Heat 14.....	**Jackson**/Bouchard/Greer/Anderson	73.2	3	2	0	1
Heat 15.....	Ryman/Bass/**Moore**/Howgego	76.0	1	2	3	0
Heat 16.....	**Evans**/Hughes/Featherstone/Carter	75.8	3	2	1	0

CREWE - Phil Crump 11, John Jackson 11, Gary Moore 9, Dai Evans 8.
LONG EATON - Geoff Bouchard 11, Steve Bass 7, Joe Hughes 6, Peter Jarvis 0.
BOSTON - Jim Ryman 10, Ray Bales 4, Tony Featherstone 4, Keith Anderson* 1.
PETERBOROUGH - Richard Greer 6, Roy Carter 3, Ted Howgego 2, Brian Clark 1.
Meeting Reserve: Martin Edwards 2 (These points did not count towards Long Eaton's total).

Meeting 53 - Sunday, October 8, 1972 - Table-Toppers Challenge
Boston Sports Stadium, New Hammond Beck Road, Boston
Track Length - 380 yards.

BOSTON BARRACUDAS.....42 CREWE KINGS.....36

Crewe were now in demand as attractive end of season challenge match opposition, with league runners-up Boston the first to book the champions. The Barracudas kept their unbeaten home record intact in a competitive match, although there could have been a different outcome, but for the mechanical gremlins which plagued John Jackson. Phil Crump and Garry Flood again excelled for the Kings.

Heat 01	Ryman/**Crump**/Featherstone/**Parry**	75.8	4 - 2	04 - 02
Heat 02	Ryman/**Moore**/**Hassall**/Osbourne (R)	73.4	3 - 3	07 - 05
Heat 03	**Flood**/Bales/Laessing/**Evans**	73.4	3 - 3	10 - 08
Heat 04	Ryman/Glover/**Moore**/**Jackson** (R)	74.8	5 - 1	15 - 09
Heat 05	**Crump**/Bales/**Parry**/Laessing	76.5	**2 - 4**	17 - 13
Heat 06	Price/Featherstone/**Hassall**/**Jackson** (R)	73.4	5 - 1	22 - 14
Heat 07	Ryman/**Flood**/Glover/**Evans**	74.5	4 - 2	26 - 16
Heat 08	**Crump**/Featherstone/**Moore**/Osborne	75.4	**2 - 4**	28 - 20
Heat 09	Bales/**Flood**/Laessing/**Jackson** (R)	75.2	4 - 2	32 - 22
Heat 10	**Flood**/**Jackson**/Featherstone/Price (R)	74.7	**1 - 5**	33 - 27
Heat 11	**Crump**/Ryman/Glover/**Moore**	75.6	3 - 3	36 - 30
Heat 12	Price/Laessing/**Evans**/**Jackson**	73.0	5 - 1	41 - 31
Heat 13	**Crump**/**Flood**/Glover/Bales	75.0	**1 - 5**	42 - 36

BOSTON - Jim Ryman 14, Ray Bales 7, Tony Featherstone 6 (+1), Arthur Price 6, Carl Glover 5 (+2), Ted Laessing 4 (+2), Russell Osborne 0.
CREWE - Phil Crump 14, Garry Flood 12 (+1), Gary Moore 4, Ray Hassall 2 (+1), John Jackson 2 (+1), Dai Evans 1, Dave Parry 1.

Meeting 54 - Monday, October 9, 1972 - Challenge
L.M.R. Sports Ground, Earle Street, Crewe
Track Length - 430 yards.

CREWE KINGS.....42 STARS OF THE LEAGUE.....24

Heavy rain, which left the track too dangerous for racing, brought a premature end to the challenge match against a strong Stars of the League side, although the Kings had already secured victory by the time of the call-off after Heat 11.

Heat 01	**Crump**/Owen/Barnwell/**Parry**	72.6	3 - 3	03 - 03
Heat 02	**Moore**/**Hassall**/Gardner/Graham (F)	76.6	**5 - 1**	08 - 04
Heat 03	**Flood**/McNeil/**Evans**/Foote	75.4	**4 - 2**	12 - 06
Heat 04	**Jackson**/**Hassall**/Knapkin/Gardner	74.6	**5 - 1**	17 - 07
Heat 05	**Flood**/Owen/**Evans**/Barnwell	74.8	**4 - 2**	21 - 09
Heat 06	**Crump**/**Parry**/Knapkin/Graham	74.4	**5 - 1**	26 - 10
Heat 07	Foote/**Jackson**/McNeil/**Hassall**	76.0	2 - 4	28 - 14
Heat 08	Owen/Barnwell/**Moore**/**Parry**	75.0	1 - 5	29 - 19
Heat 09	**Evans**/Knapkin/**Flood**/Foote	75.2	**4 - 2**	33 - 21
Heat 10	**Crump**/**Parry**/McNeil/Foote	76.0	**5 - 1**	38 - 22
Heat 11	**Jackson**/Owen/**Moore**/Barnwell (F)	88.0	**4 - 2**	42 - 24

(Abandoned after eleven heats due to rain.)

CREWE - Phil Crump 9, John Jackson 8, Garry Flood 7, Dai Evans 5, Gary Moore 5, Ray Hassall 4 (+2), Dave Parry 4 (+2).
STARS OF THE LEAGUE - Taffy Owen *(Workington)* 9, Alan Knapkin *(Bradford)* 4, Bobby McNeil *(Eastbourne)* 4, Trevor Barnwell *(Rayleigh)* 3 (+2), Brian Foote *(Rayleigh)* 3, Robbie Gardner *(Ellesmere Port)* 1, Mitch Graham *(Workington)* 0.

The bad weather prevented the public presentation of the Division II trophy, so the initial ceremony was performed in the speedway office situated in the pavilion, with the Mayor of Crewe, Councillor Maurice Scholes, doing the honours, handing the trophy over to Violet Littlechild (Maurice's widow) and captain Dai Evans.

Meeting 55 - Tuesday, October 10, 1972 - Cheshire Trophy, First Leg
Ellesmere Port Stadium, Thornton Road, Ellesmere Port
Track Length - 423 yards.

ELLESMERE PORT GUNNERS.....36 CREWE KINGS.....42

Another wet night in Cheshire could not dampen Crewe's enthusiasm to add the Cheshire Trophy to their bulging trophy cabinet. Inspired by a Garry Flood maximum, they ended the night with a handy six-point advantage to take back to Earle Street. Paul Tyrer emerged as the top Gunner, beating both Phil Crump and John Jackson in the process.

Heat 01	Tyrer/**Crump**/Francis/**Parry**	80.4	4 - 2	04 - 02
Heat 02	Blythe/**Brassington**/**Moore**/Pusey (F)	87.0	3 - 3	07 - 05
Heat 03	**Flood**/Drury/Gardner/**Evans**	82.8	3 - 3	10 - 08
Heat 04	**Jackson**/Goad/**Moore**/Pusey (F)	83.0	**2 - 4**	12 - 12
Heat 05	**Crump**/Gardner/Drury/**Parry**	80.8	3 - 3	15 - 15
Heat 06	Tyrer/**Jackson**/Francis/**Brassington**	80.4	4 - 2	19 - 17
Heat 07	**Flood**/Goad/Pusey/**Evans**	81.4	3 - 3	22 - 20
Heat 08	**Moore**/Francis/**Parry**/Blythe	86.2	**2 - 4**	24 - 24
Heat 09	**Jackson**/Drury/Gardner/**Brassington**	82.6	3 - 3	27 - 27
Heat 10	**Flood**/Francis/**Evans**/Blythe (F)	82.2	**2 - 4**	29 - 31
Heat 11	**Crump**/Goad/Blythe/**Parry**	82.4	3 - 3	32 - 34
Heat 12	Tyrer/**Jackson**/**Moore**/Drury	81.4	3 - 3	35 - 37
Heat 13	**Flood**/**Crump**/Goad/Gardner	83.4	**1 - 5**	36 - 42

ELLESMERE PORT - Paul Tyrer 9, Colin Goad 7, Cyril Francis 6, Graham Drury 5 (+1), Robbie Gardner 4 (+2), Chris Blythe 4 (+1), Geoff Pusey 1 (+1).
CREWE - Garry Flood 12, Phil Crump 10 (+1), John Jackson 10, Gary Moore 6 (+2), Reg Brassington 2, Dai Evans 1, Dave Parry 1.

Meeting 56 - Wednesday, October 11, 1972 - Challenge
Boulevard Stadium, Airlie Street, Kingston-upon-Hull
Track Length - 415 yards.

HULL VIKINGS.....38 CREWE KINGS.....40

The Kings avenged their July league defeat at the Boulevard with a narrow victory. There was never more than two points between the teams throughout the meeting even though Crewe riders provided ten of the race winners. Phil Crump warmed up for the Division II Riders Championship with a flawless maximum.

Heat 01	**Crump**/Stevens/Childs/**Parry**	76.2	3 - 3	03 - 03
Heat 02	Gavros/**Hassall**/**Moore**/Boston (X)	78.4	3 - 3	06 - 06
Heat 03	**Flood**/Amundson/**Evans**/Loakes	76.4	**2 - 4**	08 - 10
Heat 04	Mills/Gavros/**Moore**/**Jackson** (R)	76.0	5 - 1	13 - 11
Heat 05	**Crump**/Amundson/Loakes/**Parry**	75.2	3 - 3	16 - 14
Heat 06	**Jackson**/Childs/**Hassall**/Stevens (R)	76.6	**2 - 4**	18 - 18
Heat 07	**Flood**/Gavros/Mills/**Evans**	76.0	3 - 3	21 - 21
Heat 08	Gavros/**Hassall**/Boston/**Moore**	77.0	4 - 2	25 - 23
Heat 09	**Jackson**/Amundson/Loakes/**Hassall**	75.2	3 - 3	28 - 26
Heat 10	**Evans**/Childs/Stevens/**Flood**	77.2	3 - 3	31 - 29
Heat 11	**Crump**/Mills/**Moore**/Boston	75.0	**2 - 4**	33 - 33
Heat 12	**Jackson**/Chiilds/Gavros/**Evans**	75.6	3 - 3	36 - 36
Heat 13	**Crump**/Amundson/**Flood**/Mills	75.6	**2 - 4**	38 - 40

HULL - Dennis Gavros 11 (+2), Robin Amundson 8, Tony Childs 7 (+1), Dave Mills 6 (+1), Stan Stevens 3 (+1), Bryan Loakes 2 (+2), Pete Boston 1.
CREWE - Phil Crump 12, John Jackson 9, Garry Flood 7, Ray Hassall 5, Dai Evans 4, Gary Moore 3 (+1), Dave Parry 0.

Saturday, October 14, 1972 - British League Division II Riders Championship
Wimbledon Stadium, Plough Lane, London
Track Length - 309 yards.

WINNER.....PHIL CRUMP

Phil Crump rounded off a remarkable season by carrying off the Division II Riders Championship. As red-hot favourite, he couldn't have had a worse start, retiring in his first start in Heat 4, due to a broken magneto strap. He won his next race mounted on Garry Flood's machine in the fastest time of the night, before switching back to his own, winning his remaining three rides, with victory in Heat 12 achieved from the back. Veteran Ross Gilberton could have won the event in Heat 17, only needing a second place finish to pip Crump and Arthur Price, who were tied on twelve points. But during the race, he was involved in a pile-up and was excluded from the re-run. This left Crump and Price to compete in a run-off for the title, which was never in doubt when the Crewe ace blasted from the gate to beat the Boston star by 40 yards. Meeting reserve John Jackson finished third in his only ride of the night in Heat 10.

Heat 01	Price/Dent/Owen/Ballard (F)	67.0
Heat 02	Coles/Baugh/Durham/Greer	65.3
Heat 03	Gilbertson/Templeton/Mills/Childs	66.8
Heat 04	Young/Tyrer/Major/**Crump** (R)	66.7
Heat 05	**Crump**/Mills/Baugh/Ballard	63.8
Heat 06	Gilbertson/Greer/Young/Owen	65.5
Heat 07	Coles/Price/Templeton/Major	66.4
Heat 08	Tyrer/Childs/Durham/Dent	67.0
Heat 09	Ballard/Templeton/Greer/Watkins	65.1
Heat 10	Major/Owen/Jackson/Childs	66.5
Heat 11	Price/Mills/Young/Durham	66.5
Heat 12	**Crump**/Gilbertson/Coles/Dent	65.1
Heat 13	Ballard/Young/Coles/Childs	65.6
Heat 14	**Crump**/Templeton/Durham/Owen	64.8
Heat 15	Gilbertson/Price/Baugh/Watkins	65.7
Heat 16	Mills/Major/Dent/Greer	66.1
Heat 17	Ballard/Major/Durham/Gilbertson (X)	65.9
Heat 18	Coles/Mills/Owen/Tyrer	66.5
Heat 19	**Crump**/Price/Greer/Childs	65.4
Heat 20	Baugh/Young/Templeton/Dent	65.8
R/O for 1st	**Crump**/Price	65.3
R/O for 3rd	Coles won by default, as Gilbertson refused to compete.	

Phil Crump *(Crewe)* 12, Arthur Price *(Boston)* 12, Bob Coles *(Barrow)* 11, Ross Gilbertson *(Canterbury)* 11, Roger Mills *(Long Eaton)* 10, Malcolm Ballard *(Eastbourne)* 9, Bob Young *(Rayleigh)* 9, Doug Templeton *(Berwick)* 8, George Major *(Birmingham)* 8, Dave Baugh *(Bradford)* 7, Paul Tyrer *(Ellesmere Port)* 5, Taffy Owen *(Workington)* 4, Dave Durham *(Teesside)* 4, Richard Greer *(Peterborough)* 4, Russ Dent *(Sunderland)* 3, Tony Childs *(Hull)* 2. Meeting Reserves: John Jackson *(Crewe)* 1, Ray Watkins *(Scunthorpe)* 0. *(Dent replaced Graeme Smith.)*

Following the meeting presentation, League President Johnnie Hoskins officially handed over the Division II championship trophy to Dai Evans.

Meeting 57 - Monday, October 16, 1972 - Cheshire Trophy, Second Leg
L.M.R. Sports Ground, Earle Street, Crewe
Track Length - 430 yards.

CREWE KINGS.....43 ELLESMERE PORT GUNNERS.....35

(Crewe won on aggregate 85 - 71)

Ellesmere Port left Earle Street with their heads held high after contesting a fine meeting. Spirited riding by Colin Goad, Graham Drury and Paul Tyrer ensured a close contest, and Ray Hassall replacing Phil Crump, it was left to Garry Flood to steady the Crewe ship with his second Cheshire Trophy maximum. Dave Parry, excluded in Heat 1 for breaking the tapes, won his remaining three rides in some style, and there was a home debut for Reg Brassington, who scored two third places from his three outings.

Heat 01	**Jackson**/Tyrer/**Moore**/Wells	73.4	**4 - 2**	04 - 02
Heat 02	**Moore**/Gills/**Brassington**/Blythe	75.8	**4 - 2**	08 - 04

Heat 03	Drury/**Evans**/**Hassall**/Gardner	76.0	3 - 3	11 - 07
Heat 04	**Flood**/Goad/Blythe/**Brassington**	73.4	3 - 3	14 - 10
Heat 05	Tyrer/Wells/**Hassall**/**Evans** (R)	75.0	1 - 5	15 - 15
Heat 06	**Parry**/Goad/**Jackson**/Gills	73.2	**4 - 2**	19 - 17
Heat 07	**Flood**/Drury/Gardner/**Moore**	73.4	3 - 3	22 - 20
Heat 08	**Parry**/Blythe/**Moore**/Wells (R)	73.2	**4 - 2**	26 - 22
Heat 09	Goad/**Hassall**/Gills/**Evans** (R)	74.2	2 - 4	28 - 26
Heat 10	**Parry**/**Jackson**/Drury/Gardner	73.2	**5 - 1**	33 - 27
Heat 11	**Flood**/Tyrer/Wells/**Moore** (R)	73.2	3 - 3	36 - 30
Heat 12	**Jackson**/Gardner/Goad/**Hassall** (R)	73.4	3 - 3	39 - 33
Heat 13	**Flood**/Drury/**Brassington**/Tyrer (R)	73.8	**4 - 2**	43 - 35

CREWE - Garry Flood 12, John Jackson 9 (+1), Dave Parry 9, Gary Moore 5, Ray Hassall 4 (+1), Reg Brassington 2, Dai Evans 2.
ELLESMERE PORT - Colin Goad 8 (+1), Graham Drury 8, Paul Tyrer 7, Jim Wells* 3 (+2), Chris Blythe 3 (+1), Robbie Gardner 3 (+1), Ian Gills 3.

At the end of the match, riders and supporters finally got the opportunity to celebrate the achievements of the season. The riders received their league medals and cheques and then took a lap of honour on the tractor. Phil Crump, with wrist in plaster following an operation, showed off his League Riders Championship trophy, then received his prize for winning the "Crewe Boot & Shoe Snowball," a second-half tournament run throughout the season for the most points scored in the Rider of the Night final at Earle Street. The final standings were:- 1. Phil Crump 64pts (£30), 2. John Jackson 47pts (£20), 3rd Garry Flood 30pts (£15). Other scorers included Dai Evans 25, Dave Morton 18, Dave Parry 5 and Ray Hassall 1. Unfortunately the night's celebrations were spoiled somewhat when it came to the speeches, after the centre green microphone packed up! Not all was good in the Crewe camp though, as it was reported that Dai Evans was on the verge of quitting over a management fall-out.

Meeting 58 - Tuesday, October 17, 1972 - Challenge
Barrow Stadium, Holker Street, Barrow-in-Furness
Track Length - 415 yards.

BARROW HAPPY FACES.....42 CREWE KINGS.....35

A virtually unrecognisable Crewe team brought the curtain down at Holker Street and provided Barrow with their 13th successive home win. Lou Sansom (Workington), Carl Glover (Boston) and Jim Wells (Sunderland) replaced Phil Crump, Garry Flood and Dave Parry, and the Kings operated rider replacement for John Jackson. Sansom and Glover scored twenty-five points between them, but received poor back-up.

Heat 01	**Sansom**/Sampson/**Wells**/K.Evans	71.8	**2 - 4**	02 - 04
Heat 02	Hindle/Roynon/**Moore**/**Hassall**	74.0	5 - 1	07 - 05
Heat 03	Coles/**D.Evans**/**Glover**/Watkins	72.6	3 - 3	10 - 08
Heat 04	**Sansom**/Owen/Hindle/**Moore**	73.4	3 - 3	13 - 11
Heat 05	Coles/**Sansom**/**Wells**/Watkins	72.2	3 - 3	16 - 14
Heat 06	K.Evans/**Hassall**/Sampson (R)/**D.Evans** (R)	72.0	3 - 2	19 - 16
Heat 07	**Glover**/Hindle/**D.Evans**/Owen (X)	74.0	**2 - 4**	21 - 20
Heat 08	Roynon/K.Evans/**Hassall**/**Moore**	74.6	5 - 1	26 - 21
Heat 09	**Glover**/Coles/Watkins/**Moore**	72.2	3 - 3	29 - 24
Heat 10	Sampson/**Glover**/K.Evans/**D.Evans**	73.4	4 - 2	33 - 26
Heat 11	**Sansom**/Roynon/Owen/**Glover**	73.6	3 - 3	36 - 29
Heat 12	Sampson/**Sansom**/**D.Evans**/Hindle	74.0	3 - 3	39 - 32
Heat 13	Coles/**Sansom**/**Glover**/Owen (X)	73.2	3 - 3	42 - 35

BARROW - Bob Coles 11, Mike Sampson 8, Chris Roynon 7 (+1), Keith Evans 6 (+1), Ian Hindle 6 (+1), Tom Owen 3 (+1), Mike Watkins 1 (+1).
CREWE - Lou Sansom* 15, Carl Glover* 10 (+2), Dai Evans 4 (+1), Ray Hassall 3, Jim Wells* 2 (+1), Gary Moore 1, *John Jackson (R/R)*.

On October 18, Phil Crump and Garry Flood flew back to Australia, with Crump hopeful of being back in action down under within a month.

Meeting 59 - Friday, October 20, 1972 - Challenge
Derwent Park Stadium, Workington
Track Length - 398 yards.

WORKINGTON COMETS.....43 CREWE KINGS.....35

This was Crewe's tenth meeting in twenty days and their final team match of the season. Another makeshift side gave a good account of themselves, especially Derwent Park specialist John Jackson, who thrilled the home crowd on his way to four heat wins and thirteen points.

Heat 01	**Jackson**/Graham/Owen/**Wells**	74.4	3 - 3	03 - 03
Heat 02	Watson/**Moore**/**Hassall**/Stobbart (F)	79.2	3 - 3	06 - 06
Heat 03	Sansom/**Tyrer**/**Evans**/Hornby	76.2	3 - 3	09 - 09
Heat 04	**Jackson**/Watson/Mackay/**Moore** (X)	77.0	3 - 3	12 - 12
Heat 05	Sansom/**Tyrer**/**Wells**/Hornby	76.8	3 - 3	15 - 15
Heat 06	Owen/**Hassall**/**Jackson**/Graham (R)	79.8	3 - 3	18 - 18
Heat 07	Mackay/**Tyrer**/Watson/**Evans**	77.4	4 - 2	22 - 20
Heat 08	Graham/Stobbart/**Wells**/**Moore**	78.0	5 - 1	27 - 21
Heat 09	**Jackson**/Sansom/**Hassall**/Hornby	77.8	**2 - 4**	29 - 25
Heat 10	**Tyrer**/Owen/Graham/**Evans**	78.4	3 - 3	32 - 28
Heat 11	Mackay/**Wells**/Stobbart/**Hassall** (R)	80.4	4 - 2	36 - 30
Heat 12	**Jackson**/Owen/Watson/**Evans**	78.8	3 - 3	39 - 33
Heat 13	Sansom/**Tyrer**/Mackay/**Moore**	78.2	4 - 2	43 - 35

WORKINGTON - Lou Sansom 11, Malcolm Mackay 8 (+1), Taffy Owen 8 (+1), Steve Watson 7 (+1), Mitch Graham 6 (+1), Darrell Stobbart 3 (+1), Bernie Hornby 0.
CREWE - John Jackson 13 (+1), Paul Tyrer* 11, Ray Hassall 4 (+1), Jim Wells* 4 (+1), Gary Moore 2, Dai Evans 1 (+1), *Alan Knapkin (R/R).*

Meeting 60 - Monday, October 23, 1972 - Cheshire Best Pairs
L.M.R. Sports Ground, Earle Street, Crewe
Track Length - 430 yards.

WINNERS.....JOHN JACKSON & GARY MOORE

John Jackson and Gary Moore won the Cheshire Best Pairs on a technicality, after finishing level on points with Dai Evans and Ray Hassall. Following an eventful last heat, in which the points were shared, Jackson and Moore were awarded the trophy because of their five race wins to the four of their opponents. Evans started the night partnering Dave Parry, but when Parry ran into motor problems, first reserve Ray Hassall took over his rides and finished with three second places.

Heat 01	Evans/Blythe/Parry/Pusey	75.6
Heat 02	Coles/Graham/Sampson/Sansom	75.4
Heat 03	Jackson/Moore/Auffret/Forrester	75.6
Heat 04	Evans/Coles/Sampson/Parry	75.6
Heat 05	Jackson/Graham/Moore/Sansom	74.4
Heat 06	Forrester/Pusey/Blythe/Auffret	76.8
Heat 07	Evans/Hassall/Graham/Sansom (R)	76.2
Heat 08	Jackson/Pusey/Moore/Blythe	75.8
Heat 09	Forrester/Sampson/Coles/Auffret	76.2
Heat 10	Graham/Pusey/Blythe/Sansom (R)	75.8
Heat 11	Evans/Hassall/Auffret/Brassington	76.8
Heat 12	Jackson/Coles/Moore/Sampson	75.8
Heat 13	Graham/Auffret/Nicholas/Brassington	76.4
Heat 14	Sampson/Coles/Blythe/Pusey (F)	76.2
Heat 15	Moore/Hassall/Evans/Jackson (R)	76.8

John Jackson 12 & Gary Moore 8 *(Crewe)* 20, Dai Evans 13 & Dave Parry 1 *(Crewe)* 20, Bob Coles 10 & Mike Sampson 7 *(Barrow)* 17, Lou Sansom 0 & Mitch Graham 11 *(Workington)* 12, Geoff Pusey 6 & Chris Blythe 5 *(Ellesmere Port)* 11, Bruce Forrester 6 & Frank Auffret 4 *(Teesside)* 10. Meeting Reserves: Ray Hassall *(Crewe)* 6 for Parry, Peter Nicholas *(Crewe)* 1 for Sansom, Reg Brassington *(Crewe)* 0 for Forrester. *(Pusey and Blythe replaced Graham Drury and Paul Tyrer.)*

On October 27, John Jackson rounded off his own successful season by winning the Cumbria Knock Out Trophy at Workington, in front of over 4,000 fans. Ken Dodd was the star attraction in what was the Comets' final meeting of the season. On the same night, during Wolverhampton's Festival of Speedway, the Crewe juniors once again took on their Wolverhampton counterparts in a five-heat challenge. Dave Morton's younger brother Chris top-scored for Crewe in the fourteen point defeat.

WOLVERHAMPTON WOLF CUBS.....22	**CREWE PRINCES.....8**		
Heat 01 .... Parker/**Morton/Hassall**/Wasley (F)	71.2	3 - 3	03 - 03
Heat 02 .... Freegard/Teale/**Nicholas/Brassington**	69.4	5 - 1	08 - 04
Heat 03 .... Freegard/Teale/**Morton/Hassall**	70.0	5 - 1	13 - 05
Heat 04 .... Parker/**Nicholas**/Wasley/**Brassington**	71.2	4 - 2	17 - 07
Heat 05 .... Wasley/Teale/**Morton/Hassall**	71.6	5 - 1	22 - 08

WOLVERHAMPTON - Tony Freegard 6, Roger Parker 6, Ian Teale 6, Nigel Wasley 4.
CREWE - Chris Morton 4, Peter Nicholas 3, Ray Hassall 1, Reg Brassington 0.

In the final Division II averages, Phil Crump finished top, with John Jackson fourth, although second placed Geoff Maloney and third placed John Harrhy had transferred to Division I tracks during the season.

Meeting 61 - Monday, October 30, 1972 - Chester Vase
L.M.R. Sports Ground, Earle Street, Crewe
Track Length - 430 yards.

WINNER.....DAVE PARRY

In the season finale at Earle Street, it was perhaps fitting that the only surviving member of the original Kings side - Dave Parry - should win the coveted Chester Vase trophy, with an immaculate five ride maximum, winning by two points from British Junior champion Allan Emmett. In his final race, Parry held off three Crewe team-mates, despite a last lap puncture.

Heat 01 .... Knapkin/Moore/D.Templeton/Graham	74.4
Heat 02 .... Parry/Wells/Jackson/Barnwell	73.6
Heat 03 .... Evans/Owen/W.Templeton/McNeil	74.2
Heat 04 .... Emmett/Tyrer/Foote/Hassall	74.4
Heat 05 .... Parry/Emmett/D.Templeton/W.Templeton	74.0
Heat 06 .... Jackson/Owen/Knapkin/Hassall (F)	73.4
Heat 07 .... Evans/Graham/Foote/Barnwell	75.0
Heat 08 .... Wells/Moore/McNeil/Brassington	75.8
Heat 09 .... Jackson/D.Templeton/Evans/Tyrer	73.6
Heat 10 .... Parry/Knapkin/Foote/McNeil	73.4
Heat 11 .... Graham/Wells/W.Templeton/Hassall	75.0
Heat 12 .... Emmett/Owen/Moore/Barnwell	74.6
Heat 13 .... D.Templeton/Barnwell/McNeil/Hassall	74.6
Heat 14 .... Emmett/Knapkin/Wells/Evans	74.8
Heat 15 .... Parry/Graham/Tyrer/Owen	74.0
Heat 16 .... Moore/Foote/Jackson/W.Templeton	74.4
Heat 17 .... D.Templeton/Owen/Wells/Foote (R)	75.0
Heat 18 .... Knapkin/Barnwell/Tyrer/W.Templeton	75.4
Heat 19 .... Jackson/Emmett/Graham/McNeil	74.2
Heat 20 .... Parry/Moore/Evans/Hassall	75.6

Dave Parry 15, Allan Emmett 13, John Jackson 11, Alan Knapkin 11, Doug Templeton 10, Gary Moore 10, Jim Wells 9, Mitch Graham 8, Taffy Owen 8, Dai Evans 8, Brian Foote 5, Paul Tyrer 4, Trevor Barnwell 4, Willie Templeton 2, Bobby McNeil 2, Ray Hassall 0. Meeting Reserve: Reg Brassington 0. *(Graham replaced Jimmy Gallacher, Owen replaced Alan Bridgett and Tyrer replaced Colin Goad.)*

So, Maurice Littlechild's decision to bring speedway to the old railway town, had not been an ill-conceived plan, that some had predicted was "doomed to failure." It had taken just four seasons to become the best team in Division II. Phil Crump and John Jackson quite rightly deserved the plaudits for an outstanding contribution to the success, but it takes a team to win a league title, and the Kings were certainly that in 1972. Garry Flood, competing in British speedway for the first time, started the season at reserve and ended it as third heat leader, finishing with a tremendous 330 points and an average of almost eight and a half. Skipper Dai Evans scored 49 bonus points - more than any other rider in the league, which proved just how good of a team man he really was. In July, he sustained a bad back injury, which affected his riding for the remainder of the campaign. Also in the top ten of the bonus points table was the dependable Dave Parry who amassed 37, as well as 20 heat victories. Ever-present, Gary Moore, put in another steady tail-end performance, scoring in 94 of his 149 starts. Young Dave Morton, was plagued by early season motor troubles, but started to show his true abilities as the season progressed, finishing either first or second in over half of his rides. Sadly, an arm injury robbed him of a cup final appearance and the chance to shine during the run-in for the title. There were also important contributions from juniors Peter Nicholas and Ray Hassall, who were thrown into the pressure cooker atmosphere of a title chase and didn't let the side down. Finding the knack to win on their travels had been the primary reason for the title success, and with seven away league victories (a figure achieved by the champions of Division II for the third consecutive year), plus two in the K.O. Cup, completely destroyed the myth that they could only ride their own "devil's bowl." They in fact had the best away record in the division. At home, Crewe riders won 183 of the 208 races and registered 141 heat advantages, losing just 18. As for Crump, his record and achievements during the season alone could warrant a book, but analysing statistics of Crewe's top two highlights just how good John Jackson was in this remarkable season. Between them they would finish as top scorers in 39 of the 42 league and cup matches. Jackson, Flood and Crump all appeared in Division I racing, but it was Crump who made the biggest impression at King's Lynn. Drafted into the squad after Clive Featherby broke a leg, he rode in 19 league and cup matches for the Stars, finishing with a respectable 7.30 average. Now it was left to the Speedway Control Board to decide on Crewe's application to join Division I; a move that would give the management team a fighting chance of retaining the services of their top three.

- 1972 Season Summary -

				Wins to Crewe	
Date	**Opponents/Meeting**	**Res**	**Score**	**Race**	**Heat**
Fri, March 17	Workington (Ch)	L	35 - 43	8	3
Tue, April 4	Birmingham (BL)	L	35 - 43	4	3
Wed, April 5	Bradford (Ch)	L	36 - 42	7	2
Mon, April 10	**Workington (Ch)**	W	40 - 38	6	6
Mon, April 17	**Long Eaton (Ch)**	W	54 - 24	12	10
Thu, April 20	Long Eaton (Ch)	L	38 - 40	7	3
Mon, April 24	**Peterborough (BL)**	L	37 - 41	7	4
Mon, May 1	**Ellesmere Port (KOC R1)**	W	49 - 29	12	7
Tue, May 2	Ellesmere Port (KOC R1)	W	45 - 33	11	6
Fri, May 12	Peterborough (BL)	L	33 - 45	9	0
Mon, May 15	**Bradford (BL)**	W	49 - 29	10	8
Sat, May 20	Rayleigh (BL)	L	38 - 40	7	5
Sun, May 21	Sunderland (BL)	W	43 - 34	9	5
Mon, May 22	**West Ham (BL)**	W	51 - 27	11	8
Mon, May 29	**Birmingham (BL)**	W	61 - 17	13	13
Sun, June 4	Scunthorpe (KOC R2)	W	59 - 19	13	11
Mon, June 5	**Scunthorpe (KOC R2)**	W	59 - 19	12	12
Mon, June 12	**Ellesmere Port (BL)**	W	44 - 34	9	6
Thu, June 15	Long Eaton (BL)	W	47 - 31	10	7
Mon, June 19	**Eastbourne (BL)**	W	59 - 19	13	10
Wed, June 21	Bradford (BL)	W	40 - 34	9	6
Mon, June 26	**Teesside (BL)**	W	51 - 27	12	8
Mon, July 3	**Sunderland (KOC R3)**	W	53 - 25	11	9
Fri, July 7	Sunderland (KOC R3)	L	36 - 42	6	3
Mon, July 10	**Scunthorpe (BL)**	W	61 - 17	13	12
Wed, July 12	Hull (BL)	L	36 - 41	8	6
Mon, July 17	**Long Eaton (BL)**	W	56 - 22	13	9

Thu, July 20	Teesside (BL)	W	40 - 37	8	4
Mon, July 24	**Canterbury (BL)**	W	58 - 19	13	13
Tue, July 25	Ellesmere Port (BL)	W	40 - 38	11	3
Sun, July 30	Eastbourne (KOC S/F)	L	34 - 44	7	4
Mon, July 31	**Eastbourne (KOC S/F)**	W	47 - 31	11	8
Mon, August 7	**Boston (BL)**	W	54 - 24	12	10
Sun, August 13	Boston (BL)	L	31 - 47	6	1
Mon, August 14	**Berwick (BL)**	W	45 - 33	12	5
Sun, August 20	Scunthorpe (BL)	W	48 - 30	10	7
Mon, August 21	**Bradford (Ch)**	W	57 - 21	12	10
Tue, August 22	Barrow (BL)	L	33 - 44	5	3
Mon, August 28	**Birmingham (Ch)**	W	47 - 31	10	7
Tue, August 29	Birmingham (Ch)	L	38 - 40	9	3
Mon, September 4	**Peterborough (KOC F)**	W	51 - 27	11	8
Sun, September 10	Peterborough (KOC F)	L	38 - 40	7	3
Mon, September 11	**Rayleigh (BL)**	W	58 - 20	13	13
Fri, September 15	Workington (BL)	L	30 - 48	5	1
Mon, September 18	**Hull (BL)**	W	51 - 27	11	7
Tue, September 19	Ell/Hul/Bra (4TT)	W	Crewe 36	9	-
Sat, September 23	Berwick (BL)	D	39 - 39	9	5
Mon, September 25	**Sunderland (BL)**	W	50 - 28	10	8
Sat, September 30	Canterbury (BL)	W	40 - 36	11	4
Sun, October 1	Eastbourne (BL)	L	37 - 41	7	4
Mon, October 2	**Workington (BL)**	W	49 - 29	11	7
Thu, October 5	Lon/Bos/Pet (4TT)	W	Crewe 39	10	-
Sun, October 8	Boston (Ch)	L	36 - 42	6	4
Mon, October 9	**Stars of the League (Ch)**	W	42 - 24	9	8
Tue, October 10	Ellesmere Port (Ch)	W	42 - 36	9	4
Wed, October 11	Hull (Ch)	W	40 - 38	10	4
Mon, October 16	**Ellesmere Port (Ch)**	W	43 - 35	10	6
Tue, October 17	Barrow (Ch)	L	35 - 42	5	2
Fri, October 20	Workington (Ch)	L	35 - 43	5	1
Mon, October 23	**Cheshire Best Pairs (Ind)**	John Jackson & Gary Moore			-
Mon, October 30	**Chester Vase (Ind)**	Dave Parry		-	-

- British League Division II Final Table -

		Home					Away					
	M	W	D	L	F	A	W	D	L	F	A	Pts
1. Crewe	**32**	**15**	**0**	**1**	**834**	**413**	**7**	**1**	**8**	**610**	**628**	**45**
2. Boston	32	16	0	0	785	461	5	1	10	580	666	43
3. Peterborough	32	14	0	2	738	508	7	0	9	574	671	42
4. Rayleigh	32	15	1	0	771	474	2	3	11	562	686	38
5. Eastbourne	32	15	1	0	771	469	3	1	12	552½	691½	38
6. Birmingham	32	15	1	0	782	462	3	0	13	547	695	37
7. Workington	32	15	0	1	777	468	3	0	13	531	715	36
8. Hull	32	12	0	4	673	574	4	0	12	550	695	32
9. Barrow	32	13	0	3	712	532	2	1	13	548	698	31
10. Teesside	32	14	1	1	728	516	0	2	14	490	754	31
11. Bradford	32	13	0	3	710	530	2	0	14	517	729	30
12. Sunderland	32	13	1	2	702	541	0	1	15	478	765	28
13. Canterbury	32	11	0	5	717	526	2	1	13	512	734	27
14. Berwick	32	11	3	2	671	575	1	0	15	485	755	27
15. Ellesmere Port ..	32	11	0	5	667	575	1	0	15	489	754	24
16. Long Eaton	32	10	2	4	655	589	1	0	15	449	796	24
17. Scunthorpe	32	5	1	10	580½	663½	0	0	16	402	841	11

(West Ham moved to Barrow after 12 matches, due to their Custom House Stadium being demolished for re-development.)

- Crewe Rider Averages -

(League and Knock Out Cup only)

	M	R	W	Pts	BP	Tot	F	P	CMA
Phil Crump	41	175	151	481	6	487	21	4	11.131
John Jackson	42	171	124	422	7	429	17	3	10.035
Garry Flood	41	170	74	330	27	357	0	10	8.400
Dai Evans	38	141	16	202	49	251	0	5	7.121
Dave Morton	27	94	12	125	30	155	0	3	6.596
Dave Parry	40	136	20	159	37	196	0	2	5.765
Peter Nicholas	12	32	4	32	8	40	0	1	5.000
Gary Moore	42	149	11	151	19	170	0	0	4.564
Also rode									
Ray Hassall	5	14	0	7	3	10	0	0	2.857
Barry Booth	2	6	0	2	0	2	0	0	1.333
Reg Brassington	2	6	0	2	0	2	0	0	1.333
Substitute									
Nicky Allott	1	3	0	2	0	2	0	0	2.667

- League Heat Scores -

	Home	Away	Total
5 - 1 heat win to Crewe	91	23	114
3 - 0 heat win to Crewe	0	1	1
4 - 2 heat win to Crewe	49	38	87
3 - 2 heat win to Crewe	1	2	3
3 - 3 drawn heat	49	82	131
2 - 4 heat win to Opponents	15	31	46
1 - 5 heat win to Opponents	3	26	29
0 - 5 heat win to Opponents	0	5	5

- Team Honours -

British League Division II Winners.
Speedway Express Knock Out Cup Winners.
Sherwood Trophy Winners.
Top Dogs Trophy Winners.
West Midlands Trophy Winners.
Cheshire Trophy Winners.

- Individual/Pairs Honours -

Northumberland Open Championship (Ashington)
1. Phil Crump 2. Jim Ryman 3. Carl Glover.

Hull Open Championship (Hull)
1. Phil Crump 2. Jim Ryman 3. Arthur Browning.

Teesside Open Championship (Teesside)
1. Phil Crump 2. Arthur Price 3. Russ Dent/Tony Childs.

Cheshire Open Championship (Ellesmere Port)
1. Phil Crump 2. Robin Adlington 3. Robbie Gardner.

The Olympiad (Bradford)
1. Phil Crump 2. Paul Tyrer 3. Andy Meldrum.

Cumberland Open Championship (Workington)
1. John Jackson 2. Dennis Gavros 3. Malcolm Mackay/Lou Sansom.

Handicap Best Pairs (Ellesmere Port)
1. Colin Goad & Ian Gills 2. Phil Crump & Dave Parry 3. Malcolm Mackay & Bernie Hornby.

The Shaytona (Halifax)
1. John Jackson 2. Dave Morton 3. Arthur Browning.

Stadium Silver Helmet (Teesside)
1. John Jackson 2. Dave Durham 3. Bruce Forrester.

Individual Knock-out Trophy (Ellesmere Port)
1. Robbie Gardner 2. Phil Crump 3. Colin Goad.

Supporters Club Trophy (Long Eaton)
1. Geoff Bouchard 2. Garry Flood 3. John Jackson.

British League Division II Riders Championship (Wimbledon)
1. Phil Crump 2. Arthur Price 3. Bob Coles.

Cheshire Best Pairs (Crewe)
1. John Jackson & Gary Moore 2. Dai Evans & Dave Parry 3. Bob Coles & Mike Sampson.

Cumbria Knock Out Trophy (Workington)
1. John Jackson 2. Lou Sansom 3. Tom Owen.

Chester Vase (Crewe)
1. Dave Parry 2. Allan Emmett 3. John Jackson.

(ABOVE) Phil Crump, who swept all before him in 1972.

Eastbourne and Crewe battle it out at Arlington Raceway on Sunday, October 1. (ABOVE) Phil Crump keeps an eye on Gordon Kennett and (BELOW) Trevor Geer tangles with Garry Flood.

(ABOVE) The Mayor of Crewe, Councillor Maurice Scholes, hands over the league championship trophy to Dai Evans after the Stars of the League match. (BELOW) Dai and his wife Trisha holding the trophy, celebrating with members of the Supporters Club.

(ABOVE) Dai Evans receives a tankard from Crewe Speedway Queen Jean Entwistle for scoring the most bonus points. Looking on is Ken Adams.
(BELOW) A league winners medal (courtesy of Dai Evans).

(ABOVE) A disconsolate Phil Crump, with John Jackson and Ken Adams, after his Heat 4 retirement at the Division II Riders Championship.

(ABOVE) "Crumpie" on the podium, with runner-up "Donovan" Price and Bob Coles.

(LEFT) The champion, now all smiles, with the spoils of his victory. (BELOW) The official handing over of the league trophy at Wimbledon.

(ABOVE) Ken Dodd presents John Jackson with the Cumbria Knock Out Trophy, following his victory at Workington on October 27. (BELOW) Dave Parry receives his prize from Jean Entwistle after capturing the Chester Vase at Earle Street three days later.

Where Have All The Aussies Gone?
-1973-

Where Have All The Aussies Gone?

-1973-

During the winter months, the much-criticised Earle Street circuit was once again subject to further modification. The angle of the banking on both bends was reduced, and the drainage system improved. Spectator facilities were also upgraded and viewing areas improved, with the bulk of the work carried out by Sunderland riders Jack Millen and Jim Wells, with the duo taking charge of track maintenance. In early January, the Division I promoters met at Chesford Grange Hotel, near Kenilworth, and delivered the verdict that there would be no teams admitted into the top flight, thus resigning Crewe, Eastbourne and Ellesmere Port (who had made a late bid to purchase the Wembley licence) to another season in Division II. The decision therefore meant that Phil Crump had ridden his last race for the Kings, and it was announced that he was to sign a King's Lynn contract on his return from Australia. The Division II Council were also finalising plans for the new season, with Rochdale and Newtongrange unsuccessful in their bid for league status, but surprised many in the sport when they again turned down Stoke's (Chesterton) application, despite £170,000 being spent on facilities at Loomer Road. The Council were still concerned that attendances at Crewe would be affected if they were granted a place, as many former Sun Street followers regularly attended Earle Street. However, at the end of February, the Crewe management had a change of heart and withdrew their objections for them to enter the league (but only after certain safeguards were put in place*), therefore their application was granted after a narrow 6-5 vote. Promoter Russ Bragg quickly returned the favour, allowing Crewe riders to practice on the new circuit, as work was still on-going at Earle Street. Dave Morton, Dave Parry, Ray Hassall and Peter Nicholas also attended Ivan Mauger's pre-season training school which was held at the venue. So Chesterton Potters became the only new Division II team, and for the first time in the league's short history, no club withdrew from the previous season. Teesside changed their name from "Teessiders" to "Tigers" and the rather comically named Barrow "Happy Faces" were re-christened the "Bombers," much to the relief of their supporters. Following a shake-up at APL, Len Silver relinquished control at Rayleigh to take over the reigns at Crewe, with Tudor Blake brought in as team manager. On the rider side, sixteen-year-old former British Schoolboy scramble and trials champion Keith White (son of former rider Vic), was recruited from Leicester, where his father was team boss. Geoff Ambrose, who was now running a successful business (Speedway Motorcycles) on Earle Street, was coaxed out of retirement, to fill the gap left by Crump. It was hoped that Ambrose, who had ridden for Wolverhampton and Leicester in Division I and had won the Division II Riders Championship while at Crayford in 1969, would still have the appetite to challenge John Jackson, Garry Flood and Dave Morton for the No.1 spot. As for Jackson, he signed for Halifax as their No.8, but this would still allow him to ride for Crewe, and days later, the Yorkshire outfit also confirmed their interest in Morton. On the fixture front, the Kings announced a potential money-spinning Four Team Tournament with local rivals Chesterton, Ellesmere Port and Birmingham and in the K.O. Cup received a first round bye, but a daunting second round clash with much-fancied Boston. Earle Street was one of four lower league venues to be granted a preliminary round of the World Championship, as well as a Division II test match between England and Sweden. The traditional Good Friday opener was switched to Easter Monday, with Workington providing the opposition. Admission prices rose again to 50p for adults and 25p for children, with a programme costing 8p, which was increased to 10p at the end of May. The team would also sport new body colours of red and white halves, featuring a newly designed single crown emblem.

*The stipulations for Chesterton's entry were reported in *The Daily Express* on February 27 by Gordon Burnett. *No.1 'No unfair trading such as meetings above the normal size and type and no unusual number of star names.' No.2 'Chesterton must not open before Crewe's first match on April 9.' No.3 'No weekend racing was to take place at Chesterton.' No.4. 'No racing at Chesterton on Crewe race days.' No.5 'Licence to be granted for Division II racing only - never Division I.' No.6 'No admission prices to be lower than Crewe.'* It was also reported that Crewe had insisted that the name Chesterton be used, and not Stoke.

Meeting 1 - Friday, March 23, 1973 - Cheshire/Cumberland Trophy, First Leg
Derwent Park Stadium, Workington
Track Length - 398 yards.

WORKINGTON COMETS.....49 CREWE KINGS.....29

John Jackson continued his good run of form at Derwent Park, scoring eleven from five rides in the first leg of this challenge match. Geoff Ambrose and Dave Parry provided some support, but the rest of the Kings team contributed little. Garry Flood missed the match as he was yet to arrive back from Australia.

Heat 01	**Jackson**/Sansom/Graham/**Morton**	74.0	3 - 3	03 - 03
Heat 02	**Parry**/Watson/Stobbart/**White**	78.2	3 - 3	06 - 06
Heat 03	Sansom/**Ambrose**/Hornby/**Evans** (R)	75.6	4 - 2	10 - 08
Heat 04	Watson/Mackay/**Moore**/**White**	77.0	5 - 1	15 - 09
Heat 05	**Jackson**/Watson/Hornby/**Morton**	78.6	3 - 3	18 - 12
Heat 06	Graham/Mackay/**Parry**/**Moore**	76.2	5 - 1	23 - 13
Heat 07	Mackay/**Ambrose**/Watson/**Evans**	75.8	4 - 2	27 - 15
Heat 08	**Jackson**/Graham/Stobbart/**White**	76.8	3 - 3	30 - 18
Heat 09	Sansom/**Parry**/Hornby/**Moore**	76.2	4 - 2	34 - 20
Heat 10	Graham/Watson/**Ambrose**/**Evans**	77.0	5 - 1	39 - 21
Heat 11	Mackay/**Morton**/Stobbart/**Jackson** (R)	76.2	4 - 2	43 - 23
Heat 12	Graham/**Ambrose**/**Morton**/Hornby	77.6	3 - 3	46 - 26
Heat 13	Sansom/**Jackson**/**Ambrose**/Mackay (F)	76.0	3 - 3	49 - 29

WORKINGTON - Mitch Graham 12 (+1), Lou Sansom 11, Malcolm Mackay 10 (+2), Steve Watson 10 (+1), Darrell Stobbart 3 (+2), Bernie Hornby 3 (+1), *Taffy Owen (R/R)*.
CREWE - John Jackson 11, Geoff Ambrose 8 (+1), Dave Parry 6, Dave Morton 3 (+1), Gary Moore 1, Dai Evans 0, Keith White 0.

Meeting 2 - Tuesday, March 27, 1973 - Challenge
Barrow Stadium, Holker Street, Barrow-in-Furness
Track Length - 415 yards.

BARROW BOMBERS.....47 CREWE KINGS.....31

A power failure delayed the start of the meeting, which was allowed to continue with flag starts and marshals stationed around the track. When power was restored, Crewe held a slender two point lead, but four home maximums in the final four heats gave the re-christened Bombers a comfortable victory. Barrow No.8 Chris Roynon replaced the absent Dai Evans in the Kings line-up.

Heat 01	Sampson/**Jackson**/Sheldrick/**Morton**	71.4	4 - 2	04 - 02
Heat 02	**White**/Hindle/**Moore**/Evans	72.0	**2 - 4**	06 - 06
Heat 03	**Roynon**/Owen/Kelly/**Ambrose**	72.4	3 - 3	09 - 09
Heat 04	**Flood**/Bailey/**White**/Hindle	73.8	**2 - 4**	11 - 13
Heat 05	**Morton**/Owen/Kelly/**Jackson**	72.8	3 - 3	14 - 16
Heat 06	**Flood**/Sampson/Sheldrick/**White**	73.0	3 - 3	17 - 19
Heat 07	Bailey/**Roynon**/**Ambrose**/Hindle	74.0	3 - 3	20 - 22
Heat 08	**Morton**/Sheldrick/Evans/**Moore**	73.0	3 - 3	23 - 25
Heat 09	Owen/**White**/Kelly/**Flood**	74.0	4 - 2	27 - 27
Heat 10	Sampson/Sheldrick/**Roynon**/**Ambrose**	73.4	5 - 1	32 - 28
Heat 11	Evans/Bailey/**Morton**/**Jackson**	73.4	5 - 1	37 - 29
Heat 12	Sampson/Owen/**White**/**Flood** (R)	72.8	5 - 1	42 - 30
Heat 13	Kelly/Bailey/**Morton**/**Jackson**	73.4	5 - 1	47 - 31

BARROW - Mike Sampson 11, Chris Bailey 9 (+2), Tom Owen 9 (+1), Terry Kelly 6 (+2), Sid Sheldrick 6 (+2), Keith Evans 4 (+1), Ian Hindle 2.
CREWE - Dave Morton 8, Keith White 7, Garry Flood 6, Chris Roynon* 6, John Jackson 2, Geoff Ambrose 1 (+1), Gary Moore 1.

On April 7, Phil Crump's season was brought to a premature end. Returning to his lodgings in Henry Street, Crewe, following a meeting at Leicester, his car developed a puncture, and while attempting to change the wheel, the jack slipped, crushing the right hand that had caused him so many problems the previous season. Within hours of the start of Crewe's opening home meeting, the club was rocked, when Dai Evans announced his shock retirement from the sport. The management immediately handed the captaincy to John Jackson.

Meeting 3 - Monday, April 9, 1973 - Cheshire/Cumberland Trophy, Second Leg
L.M.R. Sports Ground, Earle Street, Crewe
Track Length - 430 yards.

CREWE KINGS.....33 WORKINGTON COMETS.....45

(Workington won on aggregate 94 - 62)

Lack of practice on the newly modified track cost the Kings dear. They struggled to master the new gradual banking on the bends and suffered a rare mauling in front of their own fans. There were spills for Gary Moore, Garry Flood, Geoff Ambrose and John Jackson, with Flood taking no further part after a Heat 3 fall, which resulted in torn ankle ligaments. Dave Morton top scored with thirteen, as the Comets won by thirty-two points on aggregate.

Heat 01	Graham/Owen/**Jackson**/**Moore** (X)	74.8	1 - 5	01 - 05
Heat 02	Stobbart/Watson/**White**/**Parry**	80.4	1 - 5	02 - 10
Heat 03	Sansom/**Morton**/Hornby/**Flood** (X)	76.2	2 - 4	04 - 14
Heat 04	**Ambrose**/**Parry**/Mackay/Stobbart	77.0	**5 - 1**	09 - 15
Heat 05	**Morton**/Graham/**Ambrose**/Owen	76.0	**4 - 2**	13 - 17
Heat 06	**Jackson**/Watson/**Moore**/Mackay (R)	77.8	**4 - 2**	17 - 19
Heat 07	Sansom/Hornby/**Parry**/**Ambrose** (X)	78.6	1 - 5	18 - 24
Heat 08	Graham/**Jackson**/Stobbart/**White**	75.2	2 - 4	20 - 28
Heat 09	**Morton**/Watson/Mackay/**Parry**	77.0	3 - 3	23 - 31
Heat 10	**Morton**/Sansom/Hornby/**Jackson** (R)	77.0	3 - 3	26 - 34
Heat 11	Graham/**Ambrose**/Owen/**White**	75.4	2 - 4	28 - 38
Heat 12	Sansom/**Morton**/Mackay/**Jackson**	77.2	2 - 4	30 - 42
Heat 13	**Ambrose**/Hornby/Owen/**White**	77.8	3 - 3	33 - 45

CREWE - Dave Morton 13, Geoff Ambrose 9, John Jackson 6, Dave Parry 3 (+1), Gary Moore 1, Keith White 1, Garry Flood 0.
WORKINGTON - Mitch Graham 11, Lou Sansom 11, Bernie Hornby 6 (+2), Steve Watson 6 (+1), Taffy Owen 4 (+2), Darrell Stobbart 4, Malcolm Mackay 3 (+1).

Dave Morton gained valuable Division I experience when appearing for Len Silver's Hackney at Belle Vue on April 14, scoring three points. With the departure of Dai Evans leaving the Kings squad threadbare, Silver moved swiftly to sign legendary Australian veteran Chum Taylor and his son Glyn, who had both started the season at Peterborough.

Meeting 4 - Monday, April 16, 1973 - British League Division II
L.M.R. Sports Ground, Earle Street, Crewe
Track Length - 430 yards.

CREWE KINGS.....43 PETERBOROUGH PANTHERS.....35

Dave Morton proved he was fully-recovered from last season's broken arm by recording a brilliant five ride maximum, in the Kings' first league match of the campaign. Crewe operated rider replacement for Garry Flood, with new signing Glyn Taylor stepping in to help his former club, due to the non-arrival of Ted Howgego, who had developed car trouble en-route. The result was decided in the final heat, with the visitors requiring a maximum to snatch a point, but it was the home side which provided the 5-1 to ensure a winning start to the new season.

Heat 01	**Jackson**/Clark/**Ambrose**/Carter	73.4	**4 - 2**	04 - 02
Heat 02	Taylor/**Brassington**/Walker/**White**	77.4	2 - 4	06 - 06
Heat 03	**Morton**/Smith/**Parry**/Davis	76.8	**4 - 2**	10 - 08
Heat 04	**Ambrose**/Walker/**White**/Greer (R)	75.8	**4 - 2**	14 - 10
Heat 05	**Morton**/Clark/Carter/**Parry**	74.8	3 - 3	17 - 13
Heat 06	**Morton**/**Jackson**/Greer/Taylor	75.0	**5 - 1**	22 - 14

Heat 07	Davis/**Ambrose**/Smith/**White**	75.6	2 - 4	24 - 18
Heat 08	Greer/Clark/**Jackson**/**Brassington**	75.2	1 - 5	25 - 23
Heat 09	**Morton**/Greer/**Parry**/Taylor	74.8	**4 - 2**	29 - 25
Heat 10	**Jackson**/Smith/Davis/**Brassington** (F)	75.0	3 - 3	32 - 28
Heat 11	Walker/**Ambrose**/**Brassington**/Clark	76.2	3 - 3	35 - 31
Heat 12	**Jackson**/Greer/Smith/**Parry**	75.0	3 - 3	38 - 34
Heat 13	**Morton**/**Ambrose**/Walker/Davis	75.0	**5 - 1**	43 - 35

CREWE - Dave Morton 15, John Jackson 12 (+1), Geoff Ambrose 10 (+1), Reg Brassington 3 (+1), Dave Parry 2, Keith White 1, *Garry Flood (R/R)*.
PETERBOROUGH - Richard Greer 8, Jack Walker 7, Brian Clark 6 (+1), Frank Smith 6 (+1), John Davis 4 (+1), Glyn Taylor* 3, Roy Carter 1 (+1).

After the match, the Peterborough management, riders and supporters all praised the new Earle Street track layout, adding to the positive comments received from the Workington camp the previous week. During the second-half, Crewe's recent injury jinx struck again when Chum Taylor, riding on his son's bike, crashed and was then struck by Panther Jack Walker, resulting in a suspected fracture of the left shoulder blade.

Meeting 5 - Tuesday, April 17, 1973 - Challenge
Ellesmere Port Stadium, Thornton Road, Ellesmere Port
Track Length - 423 yards.

ELLESMERE PORT GUNNERS.....42 CREWE KINGS.....36

The highlight of this highly competitive challenge match derby was the Heat 9 tussle between Geoff Ambrose and Colin Goad. Ambrose led for two laps, but Goad found an outside line on the pits bend on lap three to squeeze past – an advantage he held to the line, despite the Crewe rider's valiant attempts to re-pass. Ambrose, Dave Morton and John Jackson scored 32 points between them, with the Kings lower order again failing to deliver.

Heat 01	**Ambrose**/Gardner/Gills/**Jackson**	76.8	3 - 3	03 - 03
Heat 02	Anderson/Austin/**White**/**Brassington**	81.8	5 - 1	08 - 04
Heat 03	Goad/**Morton**/Blythe/**Parry**	77.2	**2 - 4**	10 - 08
Heat 04	**Ambrose**/Drury/**Brassington**/Anderson	77.8	4 - 2	14 - 10
Heat 05	Goad/**Jackson**/**Morton**/Blythe	77.8	3 - 3	17 - 13
Heat 06	**Ambrose**/Gardner/Gills/**White**	78.2	3 - 3	20 - 16
Heat 07	**Morton**/Drury/**Parry**/Anderson	77.8	**2 - 4**	22 - 20
Heat 08	**Jackson**/Gills/**Brassington**/Austin	78.2	**2 - 4**	24 - 24
Heat 09	Goad/**Ambrose**/Blythe/**White**	78.8	4 - 2	28 - 26
Heat 10	Gardner/**Morton**/Gills/**Parry**	77.4	4 - 2	32 - 28
Heat 11	**Jackson**/Austin/Drury/**Brassington**	79.0	3 - 3	35 - 31
Heat 12	Gardner/**Morton**/**Ambrose**/Goad	78.0	3 - 3	38 - 34
Heat 13	Drury/**Jackson**/Blythe/**Parry**	79.2	4 - 2	42 - 36

ELLESMERE PORT - Robbie Gardner 10, Colin Goad 9, Graham Drury 8 (+1), Ian Gills 5 (+2), Roger Austin 4 (+1), Cliff Anderson 3, Chris Blythe 3.
CREWE - Geoff Ambrose 12 (+1), Dave Morton 10 (+1), John Jackson 10, Reg Brassington 2, Dave Parry 1, Keith White 1, *Garry Flood (R/R)*.

With just a scribbled note left for his landlady, Garry Flood returned to Australia, still nursing his injured ankle. His departure left his Crewe career in jeopardy and Len Silver would comment: *"If Flood was not keen enough to overcome his injury and the absence of his friend (Phil Crump), to still perform well for the Kings, then in the long run it is better that we lose him now. When Chum Taylor is fit, I hope he will score the points that we expected from Flood, and in any event, I have one or two more riders in view to add power at the bottom end of the team."*

Meeting 6 - Monday, April 23, 1973 - Challenge, First Leg
L.M.R. Sports Ground, Earle Street, Crewe
Track Length - 430 yards.

(ABOVE) The Kings on opening night at Earle Street. (Left to right) Len Silver, Geoff Ambrose, Dave Parry, Keith White, John Jackson, Tudor Blake (team manager), Gary Moore, Garry Flood and Dave Morton. (BELOW) Steve Watson, Keith White, Darrell Stobbart and Dave Parry prepare for Heat 2 of the match.

(ABOVE) New signings Geoff Ambrose and Keith White.
(BELOW) John Jackson and Dave Morton in conversation.

(ABOVE) Crewe versus Peterborough on April 16 with (from left to right) Brian Clark, Dave Parry, Roy Carter and Dave Morton. (BELOW LEFT) Another Aussie to join the ranks was Glyn Taylor, who arrived with father Chum, just prior to the Panthers clash. (BELOW RIGHT) Reg "Brasso" Brassington.

CREWE KINGS.....43 BIRMINGHAM BRUMMIES.....34

Both sets of riders deserved praise for riding a track resembling a skidpan, on a bitterly cold night in South Cheshire. Crewe stormed into an eleven point lead, but could only muster one more heat advantage after Heat 6. Geoff Ambrose showed his class with a first maximum in Kings colours. Brummies Aussie reserve Phil Herne won three races and was the only visitor to taste victory.

Heat 01	**Jackson**/**Taylor**/Moore/Lanham	80.2	**5 - 1**	05 - 01
Heat 02	Herne/**White**/Wilson (F)/**Brassington** (X)	83.8	2 - 3	07 - 04
Heat 03	**Parry**/**Jackson**/Shearer/Corradine	81.2	**5 - 1**	12 - 05
Heat 04	**Ambrose**/Herne/**White**/Major	79.0	**4 - 2**	16 - 07
Heat 05	**Parry**/Lanham/Moore/**Nicholas**	82.6	3 - 3	19 - 10
Heat 06	**Jackson**/Major/**Taylor**/Wilson	82.2	**4 - 2**	23 - 12
Heat 07	**Ambrose**/Corradine/Shearer/**White**	80.0	3 - 3	26 - 15
Heat 08	Herne/**Taylor**/**Brassington**/Lanham	84.0	3 - 3	29 - 18
Heat 09	**Ambrose**/Major/Herne/**Parry**	80.4	3 - 3	32 - 21
Heat 10	Herne/Corradine/**Jackson**/**Brassington**	83.0	1 - 5	33 - 26
Heat 11	**Ambrose**/Major/Lanham/**White**	80.6	3 - 3	36 - 29
Heat 12	**Jackson**/Lanham/**Parry**/Shearer	82.4	**4 - 2**	40 - 31
Heat 13	**Ambrose**/Corradine/Herne/**Nicholas**	80.2	3 - 3	43 - 34

CREWE - Geoff Ambrose 15, John Jackson 12 (+1), Dave Parry 7, Glyn Taylor 5 (+1), Keith White 3, Reg Brassington 1 (+1), Peter Nicholas 0, *Dave Morton (R/R)*.
BIRMINGHAM - Phil Herne 13 (+2), Malcolm Corradine 6 (+1), George Major 6, Mike Lanham 5 (+1), Gary Moore* 2 (+1), Terry Shearer 2 (+1), Steve Wilson 0.

Meeting 7 - Tuesday, April 24, 1973 - Challenge, Second Leg
Perry Barr Greyhound Stadium, Regina Drive, Walsall Road, Birmingham
Track Length - 350 yards.

BIRMINGHAM BRUMMIES.....52 CREWE KINGS.....26

(Birmingham won on aggregate 86 - 69)

It took Birmingham twenty-four hours to avenge their Earle Street defeat, winning the challenge by seventeen points on aggregate. John Jackson won the last three heats and scored all but ten of the Crewe total. Geoff Ambrose fell in Heat 4, and took no further part in the meeting.

Heat 01	**Jackson**/Lanham/**Taylor**/Wilson	65.8	**2 - 4**	02 - 04
Heat 02	Herne/Grahame/**White**/**Brassington** (F)	68.8	5 - 1	07 - 05
Heat 03	Corradine/Shearer/**Parry**/**Hitch**	68.0	5 - 1	12 - 06
Heat 04	Major/Grahame/**White**/**Ambrose** (X)	68.4	5 - 1	17 - 07
Heat 05	Corradine/**Jackson**/Shearer/**Taylor**	66.6	4 - 2	21 - 09
Heat 06	Lanham/**Jackson**/Wilson/**Parry**	66.2	4 - 2	25 - 11
Heat 07	Major/**Parry**/Grahame/**Hitch**	68.2	4 - 2	29 - 13
Heat 08	Lanham/**Taylor**/Herne/**White**	66.2	4 - 2	33 - 15
Heat 09	Corradine/Shearer/**Taylor**/**Brassington**	67.8	5 - 1	38 - 16
Heat 10	Wilson/Lanham/**Parry**/**Hitch**	69.0	5 - 1	43 - 17
Heat 11	**Jackson**/Major/Herne/**Brassington**	66.4	3 - 3	46 - 20
Heat 12	**Jackson**/Wilson/Corradine/**White**	65.8	3 - 3	49 - 23
Heat 13	**Jackson**/Major/Shearer/**Parry**	65.6	3 - 3	52 - 26

BIRMINGHAM - Malcolm Corradine 10 (+1), Mike Lanham 10 (+1), George Major 10, Terry Shearer 6 (+3), Steve Wilson 6, Alan Grahame 5 (+2), Phil Herne 5 (+1).
CREWE - John Jackson 16, Dave Parry 4, Glyn Taylor 4, Keith White 2, Geoff Ambrose 0, Reg Brassington 0, Martin Hitch* 0.

Meeting 8 - Saturday, April 28, 1973 - Challenge
Canterbury City Football Ground, Kingsmead Road, Canterbury
Track Length - 390 yards.

CANTERBURY CRUSADERS.....50 CREWE KINGS.....28

This Kings bore little resemblance to the team of '72, and on this showing, were in for a long and hard season. John Jackson and youngster Keith White won six heats between them, but by the end of Heat 7, the match was as good as over. Teesside's Roger Wright, a late guest replacement for the injured Geoff Ambrose, scored just a point and copped a £2 fine after appealing to the referee over an incident at the tapes. Crewe again operated rider replacement, this time for Chum Taylor, who had yet to make a team appearance, but had been accepted as a heat leader by the Speedway Control Board.

Heat 01	**Jackson**/Gilbertson/**Wright**/Hughes (R)	75.1	**2 - 4**	02 - 04
Heat 02	Rumsey/Kennett/**White**/**Brassington**	76.5	5 - 1	07 - 05
Heat 03	Piddock/**Taylor**/Hubbard/**Parry**	76.6	4 - 2	11 - 07
Heat 04	Banks/Kennett/**Brassington**/**Wright** (R)	77.4	5 - 1	16 - 08
Heat 05	Hubbard/Rumsey/**Jackson**/**Taylor**	76.6	5 - 1	21 - 09
Heat 06	**Jackson**/Gilbertson/Hughes/**Wright** (R)	75.7	3 - 3	24 - 12
Heat 07	Kennett/Banks/**Taylor**/**Parry**	78.2	5 - 1	29 - 13
Heat 08	**Jackson**/Rumsey/Hughes/**Brassington**	77.4	3 - 3	32 - 16
Heat 09	**White**/Hubbard/**Taylor**/Kennett	77.2	**2 - 4**	34 - 20
Heat 10	**White**/Gilbertson/Hughes/**Taylor** (R)	77.8	3 - 3	37 - 23
Heat 11	**Jackson**/Banks/Rumsey/**Parry**	76.4	3 - 3	40 - 26
Heat 12	Gilbertson/Hubbard/**White**/**Taylor** (R)	78.4	5 - 1	45 - 27
Heat 13	Banks/Kennett/**White**/**Jackson** (F)	78.5	5 - 1	50 - 28

CANTERBURY - Graham Banks 10 (+1), Barney Kennett 9 (+3), Ross Gilbertson 9, Les Rumsey 8 (+2), Ted Hubbard 8 (+1), Bob Hughes 3 (+3), Dave Piddock 3.
CREWE - John Jackson 13, Keith White 9, Glyn Taylor 4, Reg Brassington 1, Roger Wright* 1, Dave Parry 0, *Chum Taylor (R/R).*

Dave Morton performed well in the preliminary round of the World Championship at Boston on April 29, despite arriving for the meeting with his neck in a brace. He scored 11 from his five rides to qualify for the next stage. However, on the same day at Eastbourne, John Jackson was not so fortunate, scoring just four points, ending his interest in the competition. The following day, heavy rain washed out the Earle Street round, and on May 3, the same fate befell Crewe's eagerly awaited challenge match at Chesterton.

Meeting 9 - Monday, May 7, 1973 - Sunday Mirror World Championship, Qualifying Round
L.M.R. Sports Ground, Earle Street, Crewe
Track Length - 430 yards.

WINNER.....MITCH GRAHAM

Workington's Mitch Graham beat all before him, recording a faultless maximum. Geoff Ambrose was the highest placed home rider with ten points, achieved despite an opening ride spill on the pits bend. His total left him sweating on a place in the next round, with only the top twenty-four sure to progress from the four Division II stages.

Heat 01	Price/Tyrer/Forrester/Childs	75.6
Heat 02	Auffret/Young/Cameron/Ambrose (F)	79.4
Heat 03	Brown/Moore/Erskine/Templeton	80.0
Heat 04	Graham/Owen/Bouchard/Drury	76.8
Heat 05	Forrester/Erskine/Auffret/Bouchard	76.4
Heat 06	Drury/Childs/Cameron/Moore	78.4
Heat 07	Price/Owen/Young/Brown	75.4
Heat 08	Graham/Ambrose/Templeton/Tyrer (R)	74.8
Heat 09	Graham/Forrester/Brown/Cameron	75.2
Heat 10	Owen/Childs/Auffret/Templeton	78.2
Heat 11	Ambrose/Price/Drury/Erskine	75.2
Heat 12	Young/Bouchard/Moore/Tyrer (R)	77.6
Heat 13	Forrester/Young/Drury/Templeton	76.8
Heat 14	Ambrose/Childs/Brown/Bouchard	77.0
Heat 15	Graham/Price/Auffret/Moore (R)	75.6
Heat 16	Owen/Erskine/Tyrer/Cameron (R)	77.0
Heat 17	Owen/Ambrose/Forrester/Taylor	76.6
Heat 18	Graham/Young/Erskine/Childs	76.0

Heat 19	Price/Templeton/Bouchard/Cameron (R)	77.2
Heat 20	Drury/Tyrer/Auffret/Brown	78.8

Mitch Graham *(Workington)* 15, Arthur Price *(Boston)* 13, Les Owen *(Coventry)* 13, Bruce Forrester *(Teesside)* 10, Bob Young *(Rayleigh)* 10, Geoff Ambrose *(Crewe)* 10, Graham Drury *(Ellesmere Port)* 8, Frank Auffret *(Teesside)* 7, Tony Childs *(Hull)* 6, John Erskine *(Wolverhampton)* 6, Paul Tyrer *(Belle Vue)* 5, Malcolm Brown *(Leicester)* 5, Geoff Bouchard *(Long Eaton)* 4, Peter Moore *(Hackney Wick)* 3, Willie Templeton *(Berwick)* 3, Neil Cameron *(Wimbledon)* 2. Meeting Reserve: Glyn Taylor (*Crewe*) 0. *(Drury replaced Mick Handley, Chesterton and Graham replaced John Dews, Oxford.)*

Len Silver made moves to strengthen the side with the loan signing of teenage Aussie Wayne Forrest from King's Lynn. It was also reported that Chum Taylor was about to resume riding.

Meeting 10 - Friday, May 11, 1973 - British League Division II
East of England Showground, Alwalton, Peterborough
Track Length - 380 yards.

PETERBOROUGH PANTHERS.....41 CREWE KINGS.....37

With Dave Morton and Geoff Ambrose back from injury, and Wayne Forrest making his debut, the Kings came within a whisker of upsetting the hosts. Crewe riders won nine races (including a quartet of wins for Morton), but only managed to turn four into an advantage. Peterborough were more solid throughout and did just enough to secure the league points. Surprisingly, with such a high score, none of the Kings registered a bonus point.

Heat 01	**Jackson**/Howgego/**Taylor**/Clark	69.2	**2 - 4**	02 - 04
Heat 02	**White**/Smith/Walker/**Forrest**	70.0	3 - 3	05 - 07
Heat 03	Davis/**Morton**/Carter/**Parry**	69.2	4 - 2	09 - 09
Heat 04	Greer/Smith/**White**/**Ambrose**	70.2	5 - 1	14 - 10
Heat 05	**Jackson**/Carter/**Taylor**/Davis (R)	70.4	**2 - 4**	16 - 14
Heat 06	Howgego/**Ambrose**/Clark/**Forrest**	70.6	4 - 2	20 - 16
Heat 07	**Morton**/Greer/Smith/**Parry**	70.2	3 - 3	23 - 19
Heat 08	**White**/Walker/Clark/**Taylor**	70.8	3 - 3	26 - 22
Heat 09	Carter/Davis/**Forrest**/**Ambrose**	71.2	5 - 1	31 - 23
Heat 10	**Morton**/Clark/Howgego/**White** (F)	70.8	3 - 3	34 - 26
Heat 11	**Jackson**/Greer/**Taylor**/Walker	70.4	**2 - 4**	36 - 30
Heat 12	**Morton**/Howgego/Carter/**Jackson** (R)	70.8	3 - 3	39 - 33
Heat 13	**Morton**/Davis/**Jackson**/Greer	71.2	**2 - 4**	41 - 37

PETERBOROUGH - Ted Howgego 8 (+1), Roy Carter 7 (+1), John Davis 7 (+1), Richard Greer 7, Frank Smith 5 (+2), Brian Clark 4 (+1), Jack Walker 3 (+1).
CREWE - Dave Morton 14, John Jackson 10, Keith White 7, Glyn Taylor 3, Geoff Ambrose 2, Wayne Forrest 1, Dave Parry 0.

Geoff Ambrose learned his efforts in the Earle Street round of the World Championship had been good enough to see him through to the Division I stages.

Meeting 11 - Monday, May 14, 1973 - British League Division II
L.M.R. Sports Ground, Earle Street, Crewe
Track Length - 430 yards.

CREWE KINGS.....46½ BRADFORD NORTHERN.....31½

John Jackson produced a captain's performance with a fifteen point maximum. In each of his races, he led by the first bend, and his time in Heat 6 was the fastest so far on the modified track. Heat 13 produced a dead heat for second, when Bradford's Dave Baugh just caught Geoff Ambrose in the run to the line. Dave Parry, who had been struggling for form, was relegated to the No.8 spot.

Heat 01	**Jackson**/**Ambrose**/Baugh/Fielding (F)	73.4	**5 - 1**	05 - 01
Heat 02	**Taylor**/Langlois/Freegard/**White** (X)	76.2	3 - 3	08 - 04
Heat 03	**Morton**/Adlington/**Forrest**/Meredith	75.4	**4 - 2**	12 - 06
Heat 04	Knapkin/**White**/**Ambrose**/Freegard	74.2	3 - 3	15 - 09
Heat 05	**Morton**/Baugh/Fielding/**Forrest**	74.2	3 - 3	18 - 12

Heat 06	**Jackson**/Knapkin/**Morton**/Freegard	72.2	**4 - 2**	22 - 14
Heat 07	**Ambrose**/Adlington/**White**/Meredith	74.4	**4 - 2**	26 - 16
Heat 08	**Jackson**/Adlington/**Taylor**/Fielding	73.0	**4 - 2**	30 - 18
Heat 09	**Morton**/Knapkin/**Forrest**/Langlois	73.6	**4 - 2**	34 - 20
Heat 10	**Jackson**/Adlington/Meredith/**White**	73.2	3 - 3	37 - 23
Heat 11	Knapkin/**Ambrose**/Baugh/**Taylor**	73.0	2 - 4	39 - 27
Heat 12	**Jackson**/Adlington/Knapkin/**Forrest**	73.4	3 - 3	42 - 28
Heat 13	**Morton**/**Ambrose** & Baugh/Meredith	74.8	**4½ - 1½**	46½ - 31½

CREWE - John Jackson 15, Dave Morton 13, Geoff Ambrose 9½ (+2), Glyn Taylor 4, Keith White 3, Wayne Forrest 2, *Garry Flood (R/R).*
BRADFORD - Alan Knapkin 11 (+1), Robin Adlington 10, Dave Baugh 5½, Brenton Langlois 2, Mick Fielding 1 (+1), Tony Freegard 1 (+1), Colin Meredith 1 (+1).

On May 16, Dave Morton scored three points in the next stage of the World Championship at Poole and then four at Halifax three nights later. Geoff Ambrose fared no better, recording one point at Wolverhampton on May 18, and two at Belle Vue twenty-four hours later.

Meeting 12 - Sunday, May 20, 1973 - British League Division II
Arlington Raceway, Arlington Road, Hailsham, Eastbourne
Track Length - 342 yards.

EASTBOURNE EAGLES.....48 CREWE KINGS.....29

A weakened Kings side arrived at the Sussex track without Geoff Ambrose, who had been injured the previous night at Belle Vue. John Jackson and Dave Morton provided spirited opposition, but again a lack of experience at the lower end really told. Wayne Forrest won his first race in Crewe colours, heading home seasoned veteran Jimmy Squibb in Heat 9.

Heat 01	**Jackson**/McNeil/Geer/**Taylor**	64.2	3 - 3	03 - 03
Heat 02	Vernam/Dugard/**White**/**A.Johns**	65.4	5 - 1	08 - 04
Heat 03	Gachet/**Morton**/Squibb/**Forrest**	65.0	4 - 2	12 - 06
Heat 04	Dugard/R.Johns/**Jackson**/**A.Johns**	64.6	5 - 1	17 - 07
Heat 05	Gachet/**Jackson**/Squibb/**Taylor**	65.0	4 - 2	21 - 09
Heat 06	**Morton**/Vernam/McNeil/**A.Johns**	64.8	3 - 3	24 - 12
Heat 07	R.Johns/**Morton**/**Forrest**/Dugard	64.0	3 - 3	27 - 15
Heat 08	**Jackson**/Vernam/Geer/**Taylor**	64.6	3 - 3	30 - 18
Heat 09	**Forrest**/Squibb/**White**/Gachet (F)	67.0	**2 - 4**	32 - 22
Heat 10	McNeil/**Morton**/**Forrest**/Dugard (F)	65.2	3 - 3	35 - 25
Heat 11	R.Johns/Vernam/**Jackson**/**Taylor**	64.8	5 - 1	40 - 26
Heat 12	Gachet/**A.Johns**/McNeil (X) (3 riders only)	65.6	3 - 2	43 - 28
Heat 13	R.Johns/Squibb/**Morton**/**Forrest** (X)	65.4	5 - 1	48 - 29

EASTBOURNE - Roger Johns 11 (+1), Mike Vernam 9 (+1), Paul Gachet 9, Bobby McNeil 6 (+1), Jimmy Squibb 6 (+1), Eric Dugard 5 (+1), Trevor Geer 2 (+2).
CREWE - John Jackson 10, Dave Morton 10, Wayne Forrest 5 (+2), Alan Johns* 2, Keith White 2, Glyn Taylor 0, *Geoff Ambrose (R/R).*

There was real concern for Dave Morton when he collapsed after leaving the stadium, following a fall during the second half. He was admitted to Panbury Hospital, where a cracked rib and badly bruised kidneys were diagnosed. It was also discovered that Chum Taylor was not recovering from his shoulder injury and had been advised to return home by his doctor.

Meeting 13 - Monday, May 21, 1973 - British League Division II
L.M.R. Sports Ground, Earle Street, Crewe
Track Length - 430 yards.

CREWE KINGS.....42 BARROW BOMBERS.....36

The injury-hit Kings dug deep into their reserves to record a narrow win over Barrow. John Jackson scored his second successive fifteen point maximum at home, and with the returning Geoff Ambrose also in fine form, it proved just enough to preserve Crewe's unbeaten home record. The most important heat victory for the hosts was in Heat 8, when the Aussie combo of Wayne Forrest and Glyn Taylor scored a crucial 5-1 - the only one of the night. Workington's Mitch Graham, guesting for the Bombers, kept up his impressive run at Earle Street with his eleventh race victory from fourteen rides. Reg Brassington replaced the injured Dave Morton, following a pre-match race to decide the No.5 spot.

Heat 01	**Jackson**/Graham/**Forrest**/Sheldrick (R)	79.0	**4 - 2**	04 - 02
Heat 02	Evans/**White**/Roynon/**Taylor**	83.2	2 - 4	06 - 06
Heat 03	**Jackson**/Owen/Kelly/**Brassington**	78.0	3 - 3	09 - 09
Heat 04	**Ambrose**/Bailey/**White**/Roynon	80.4	**4 - 2**	13 - 11
Heat 05	Graham/**Forrest**/Sheldrick/**White**	80.0	2 - 4	15 - 15
Heat 06	**Jackson**/Bailey/**Forrest**/Evans (R)	78.4	**4 - 2**	19 - 17
Heat 07	**Ambrose**/Owen/Kelly/**White**	80.0	3 - 3	22 - 20
Heat 08	**Forrest**/**Taylor**/Sheldrick/Roynon	83.6	**5 - 1**	27 - 21
Heat 09	Graham/**Ambrose**/**Taylor**/Bailey	80.6	3 - 3	30 - 24
Heat 10	**Jackson**/Owen/**Forrest**/Kelly (R)	78.8	**4 - 2**	34 - 26
Heat 11	**Ambrose**/Graham/Owen/**Taylor**	80.4	3 - 3	37 - 29
Heat 12	**Jackson**/Kelly/Bailey/**Taylor**	78.2	3 - 3	40 - 32
Heat 13	Graham/**Ambrose**/Owen (3 riders only)	79.6	2 - 4	42 - 36

CREWE - John Jackson 15, Geoff Ambrose 13, Wayne Forrest 8, Glyn Taylor 3 (+2), Keith White 3, Reg Brassington 0, *Chum Taylor (R/R)*.
BARROW - Mitch Graham* 13, Tom Owen 8 (+1), Chris Bailey 5 (+1), Terry Kelly 4 (+2), Keith Evans 3, Sid Sheldrick 2, Chris Roynon 1.

Meeting 14 - Friday, May 25, 1973 - British League Division II
Sunderland Greyhound Stadium, Newcastle Road, East Boldon
Track Length - 350 yards.

SUNDERLAND STARS.....53 CREWE KINGS.....25

Sunderland hammered another makeshift Crewe outfit, which failed to win a single race or heat. Without Dave Morton and the non-arrival of new Aussie signing Dave O'Connor, it was youngster Keith White who impressed most with five second places. John Jackson had a night to forget with his throttle jamming open in his first two outings. Heat 5 saw Stars rider George Barclay forced to lay his machine down to avoid hitting Jackson, wrecking the frame in the process. Cliff Anderson, who had been riding with Ellesmere Port, made his Kings bow.

Heat 01	Millen/**White**/Wrathall/**Jackson** (X)	65.0	4 - 2	04 - 02
Heat 02	Wells/**White**/T.Barclay/**Taylor**	66.4	4 - 2	08 - 04
Heat 03	G.Barclay/**Forrest**/**Ambrose**/Dent	66.4	3 - 3	11 - 07
Heat 04	Gatenby/**White**/**Ambrose**/Wells	66.2	3 - 3	14 - 10
Heat 05	Dent/**Taylor**/G.Barclay/**Jackson** (X)	68.0	4 - 2	18 - 12
Heat 06	Millen/Wrathall/**Ambrose**/**Jackson**	66.0	5 - 1	23 - 13
Heat 07	Gatenby/**White**/**Forrest**/Wells	66.4	3 - 3	26 - 16
Heat 08	T.Barclay/**White**/**Ambrose**/Wrathall	68.2	3 - 3	29 - 19
Heat 09	Dent/G.Barclay/**Taylor**/**Ambrose**	67.2	5 - 1	34 - 20
Heat 10	Millen/Wrathall/**Forrest**/**Taylor**	67.2	5 - 1	39 - 21
Heat 11	Gatenby/T.Barclay/**Forrest**/**White**	69.0	5 - 1	44 - 22
Heat 12	Millen/**Anderson**/Dent/**Ambrose** (F)	69.2	4 - 2	48 - 24
Heat 13	Gatenby/Wells/**Forrest**/**Taylor**	68.4	5 - 1	53 - 25

SUNDERLAND - Dave Gatenby 12, Jack Millen 12, Russ Dent 7, George Barclay 6 (+1), Terry Barclay 6 (+1), Peter Wrathall 5 (+2), Jim Wells 5 (+1).
CREWE - Keith White 10, Wayne Forrest 6 (+1), Geoff Ambrose 4 (+3), Glyn Taylor 3, Cliff Anderson 2, John Jackson 0, *Dave Morton (R/R)*.

Meeting 15 - Monday, May 28, 1973 - British League Division II
L.M.R. Sports Ground, Earle Street, Crewe
Track Length - 430 yards.

CREWE KINGS.....39 BIRMINGHAM BRUMMIES.....38

A large Whit Monday crowd witnessed a thriller, which was only decided on the final bend of the final heat. Crewe operated rider replacement for the fifth successive match and gave debuts to Dave O'Connor (signed from Hull) and Halifax junior Ian Cartwright. With John Jackson absent after sustaining leg injuries at Halifax earlier in the day, Geoff Ambrose was the Kings' only remaining heat leader, but it was teenager Wayne Forrest who really came of age with a superb fourteen point return. Birmingham edged ahead after a Heat 11 maximum, but in the last race decider, Ambrose kept his nerve to win, overhauling Mike Lanham on the last lap. O'Connor secured the all-important third place after holding off Malcolm Corradine.

Heat 01	**Forrest**/Browning/**Cartwright**/Lanham (R)	76.0	**4 - 2**	04 - 02
Heat 02	Herne/**Taylor**/Grahame/**White**	75.0	2 - 4	06 - 06
Heat 03	**Forrest**/Corradine/**O'Connor**/Shearer	75.0	**4 - 2**	10 - 08
Heat 04	**Ambrose**/Major/Herne/**White**	75.4	3 - 3	13 - 11
Heat 05	Lanham/**O'Connor**/Browning (F)/**Parry** (F)	75.8	2 - 3	15 - 14
Heat 06	Major/**Forrest**/**Cartwright**/Grahame	75.0	3 - 3	18 - 17
Heat 07	**Ambrose**/Herne/Corradine/**Taylor** (X)	74.6	3 - 3	21 - 20
Heat 08	**Forrest**/Browning/Herne/**White**	76.6	3 - 3	24 - 23
Heat 09	**Ambrose**/Major/**O'Connor**/Herne	74.8	**4 - 2**	28 - 25
Heat 10	**Forrest**/Corradine/Shearer/**Cartwright**	77.4	3 - 3	31 - 28
Heat 11	Lanham/Browning/**Taylor**/**Ambrose**	75.8	1 - 5	32 - 33
Heat 12	Major/**Taylor**/**Cartwright**/Shearer	75.0	3 - 3	35 - 36
Heat 13	**Ambrose**/Lanham/**O'Connor**/Corradine	76.0	**4 - 2**	39 - 38

CREWE - Wayne Forrest 14, Geoff Ambrose 12, Dave O'Connor 5, Glyn Taylor 5, Ian Cartwright 3 (+2), Dave Parry 0, Keith White 0, *Dave Morton (R/R)*.
BIRMINGHAM - George Major 10, Mike Lanham 8, Phil Herne 7 (+2), Arthur Browning 6 (+1), Malcolm Corradine 5 (+1), Terry Shearer 1 (+1), Alan Grahame 1.

Dave Parry, who fell in his only ride of the match, announced he was on the verge of quitting, following a poor run, even though he had invested in new machinery at the start of the season.

Meeting 16 - Tuesday, May 29, 1973 - British League Division II
Perry Barr Greyhound Stadium, Regina Drive, Walsall Road, Birmingham
Track Length - 350 yards.

BIRMINGHAM BRUMMIES.....52 CREWE KINGS.....26

The Kings, lacking their two recognised heat leaders, were well-beaten long before the conclusion of this one-sided contest. Only Geoff Ambrose and Wayne Forrest made any impression on the partisan Perry Barr crowd. Malcolm Corradine missed out on a maximum, after falling in Heat 12.

Heat 01	Lanham/Browning/**Ambrose**/**Taylor**	65.8	5 - 1	05 - 01
Heat 02	Herne/Grahame/**White**/**Brassington**	66.6	5 - 1	10 - 02
Heat 03	Corradine/**Forrest**/Shearer/**O'Connor**	65.2	4 - 2	14 - 04
Heat 04	**Ambrose**/Major/**White**/Grahame	66.6	**2 - 4**	16 - 08
Heat 05	Corradine/Shearer/**Forrest**/**Taylor** (R)	64.0	5 - 1	21 - 09
Heat 06	Browning/**Ambrose**/Lanham/**Brassington**	66.4	4 - 2	25 - 11
Heat 07	Major/**White**/Grahame/**Forrest**	67.2	4 - 2	29 - 13
Heat 08	Herne/Browning/**Taylor**/**White**	66.2	5 - 1	34 - 14
Heat 09	Corradine/**Ambrose**/Shearer/**Brassington**	64.6	4 - 2	38 - 16
Heat 10	Browning/**Forrest**/**O'Connor**/Lanham	65.8	3 - 3	41 - 19
Heat 11	Major/Herne/**White**/**Taylor**	67.0	5 - 1	46 - 20
Heat 12	Lanham/**Ambrose**/**O'Connor**/Corradine (F)	65.8	3 - 3	49 - 23
Heat 13	**Forrest**/Major/Shearer/**Ambrose** (X)	66.4	3 - 3	52 - 26

BIRMINGHAM - Arthur Browning 10 (+2), George Major 10, Malcolm Corradine 9, Phil Herne 8 (+1), Mike Lanham 7, Terry Shearer 5 (+2), Alan Grahame 3 (+1).
CREWE - Geoff Ambrose 10, Wayne Forrest 8, Keith White 5, Dave O'Connor 2 (+2), Glyn Taylor 1, Reg Brassington 0, *Dave Morton (R/R)*.

Meeting 17 - Thursday, May 31, 1973 - Challenge, First Leg
Lyme Valley Sports Stadium, Loomer Road, Chesterton
Track Length - 380 yards.

CHESTERTON POTTERS.....41 CREWE KINGS.....35

The first Potters/Kings derby was well-worth waiting for, and even though Crewe were under-strength, they did enough to stay in touch in the two-legged challenge. Geoff Ambrose was again the most consistent King, recording fourteen points from his six starts. For the Potters, Mike Broadbanks recorded a faultless maximum, but Roger Parker had an altogether different night, when stretchered off with a broken right foot, following a high speed crash in Heat 11.

Heat 01	Broadbanks/Bridgett/**Parry/Forrest**	73.6	5 - 1	05 - 01
Heat 02	**Taylor**/Yeates/**White**/Parker (F)	74.8	**2 - 4**	07 - 05
Heat 03	Handley/**Taylor**/Woodward/**O'Connor**	71.4	4 - 2	11 - 07
Heat 04	**Ambrose**/Pusey/Yeates (R)/**Taylor** (R)	72.0	**2 - 3**	13 - 10
Heat 05	Handley/Woodward/**Forrest/Parry**	71.8	5 - 1	18 - 11
Heat 06	Broadbanks/**Ambrose**/Bridgett/**White**	71.0	4 - 2	22 - 13
Heat 07	**Ambrose/White**/Yeates/Pusey	71.0	**1 - 5**	23 - 18
Heat 08	**Forrest/Taylor**/Bridgett/Parker (F)	74.2	**1 - 5**	24 - 23
Heat 09	Handley/**Ambrose**/Woodward/**White** (R)	71.0	4 - 2	28 - 25
Heat 10	Broadbanks/Bridgett/**Forrest/O'Connor**	73.0	5 - 1	33 - 26
Heat 11	**Taylor/Forrest**/Yeates (R)/Pusey (R)	73.0	**0 - 5**	33 - 31
Heat 12	Broadbanks/Woodward/**Ambrose/O'Connor**	71.2	5 - 1	38 - 32
Heat 13	**Ambrose**/Handley/Pusey/**Taylor** (R)	70.6	3 - 3	41 - 35

CHESTERTON - Mike Broadbanks 12, Mick Handley 11, Alan Bridgett 6 (+2), Bryan Woodward 6 (+2), Geoff Pusey 3 (+1), Martin Yeates 3, Roger Parker 0.
CREWE - Geoff Ambrose 14, Glyn Taylor 10 (+1), Wayne Forrest 7 (+1), Keith White 3 (+1), Dave Parry 1, Dave O'Connor 0, *Dave Morton (R/R).*

Meeting 18 - Sunday, June 3, 1973 - Knock Out Cup, Second Round, First Leg
Boston Sports Stadium, New Hammond Beck Road, Boston
Track Length - 380 yards.

BOSTON BARRACUDAS.....58 CREWE KINGS.....20

Top-of-the-table Boston gave the K.O. Cup holders a right royal thumping in the first leg of their second round tie. Still without the sidelined John Jackson and Dave Morton, Crewe's hopes of an upset were quickly dispelled by a powerful Barracudas display. With Geoff Ambrose restricted to one outing due to bike trouble, and the Kings forced into loaning Boston second-halfer Les Glover due to the non-arrival of Dave O'Connor, they unsurprisingly failed to win a single race, as the home side recorded nine maximums. A pile-up in Heat 11 resulted in David Gagen (strained back) and Kelvin Mullarkey (stitches in a leg wound) taken to hospital.

Heat 01	Price/**White/Forrest**/Featherstone	68.8	3 - 3	03 - 03
Heat 02	Gagen/Bales/**White/Cartwright**	67.2	5 - 1	08 - 04
Heat 03	Osborne/**L.Glover**/Ryman/**Taylor**	68.2	4 - 2	12 - 06
Heat 04	C.Glover/Bales/**Ambrose/Cartwright**	67.2	5 - 1	17 - 07
Heat 05	Ryman/**L.Glover/Forrest**/Osborne	67.4	3 - 3	20 - 10
Heat 06	Price/Featherstone/**L.Glover/Cartwright** (F)	68.0	5 - 1	25 - 11
Heat 07	C.Glover/Bales/**Taylor/L.Glover** (R)	68.2	5 - 1	30 - 12
Heat 08	Featherstone/**Forrest/White**/Gagen (F)	67.4	3 - 3	33 - 15
Heat 09	Osborne/Ryman/**White/Cartwright**	69.8	5 - 1	38 - 16
Heat 10	Featherstone/Price/**L.Glover/Taylor**	68.2	5 - 1	43 - 17
Heat 11	C.Glover/Bales/**Forrest/Mullarkey** (X)	67.6	5 - 1	48 - 18
Heat 12	Price/Osborne/**White/Cartwright**	68.0	5 - 1	53 - 19
Heat 13	C.Glover/Ryman/**Forrest/Taylor**	68.8	5 - 1	58 - 20

BOSTON - Carl Glover 12, Arthur Price 11 (+1), Ray Bales 8 (+4), Jim Ryman 8 (+2), Tony Featherstone 8 (+1), Russell Osborne 8 (+1), David Gagen 3.
CREWE - Wayne Forrest 6 (+2), Keith White 6 (+1), Les Glover* 6, Geoff Ambrose 1, Glyn Taylor 1, Ian Cartwright 0, Kelvin Mullarkey 0, *John Jackson (R/R).*

After just three matches, Dave O'Connor handed in his resignation to Len Silver, deciding to return home, citing a lack of form. The recently married rider came over on the back of a successful season in Australia, where he had beaten the likes of Ivan Mauger and Ole Olsen. Silver commented: *"Don't ask me why. The ink was hardly dry on his contract."*

Meeting 19 - Monday, June 4, 1973 - Knock Out Cup, Second Round, Second Leg
L.M.R. Sports Ground, Earle Street, Crewe
Track Length - 430 yards.

CREWE KINGS.....44 BOSTON BARRACUDAS.....34

(Boston won on aggregate 92 - 64)

The Kings relinquished their hold on the K.O. Cup, but at least kept their home record intact. The return of John Jackson gave Crewe a more experienced look, and there were good returns from Geoff Ambrose and the fast improving Glyn Taylor.

Heat 01	**Jackson**/Price/Featherstone/**Forrest**	72.2	3 - 3	03 - 03
Heat 02	Bales/**Taylor**/**White**/Gagen	75.0	3 - 3	06 - 06
Heat 03	**Jackson**/Ryman/**Cartwright**/Osborne (R)	74.2	**4 - 2**	10 - 08
Heat 04	**Ambrose**/**White**/Glover/Gagen	74.2	**5 - 1**	15 - 09
Heat 05	**Taylor**/Price/Featherstone/**Cartwright**	74.4	3 - 3	18 - 12
Heat 06	**Jackson**/Bales/**Forrest**/Glover	73.6	**4 - 2**	22 - 14
Heat 07	**Ambrose**/Ryman/Osborne/**White**	74.8	3 - 3	25 - 17
Heat 08	Bales/**Taylor**/**Forrest**/Gagen	74.0	3 - 3	28 - 20
Heat 09	Bales/**Ambrose**/**Taylor**/Glover (R)	73.6	3 - 3	31 - 23
Heat 10	Ryman/Osborne/**Jackson**/**Forrest** (R)	75.0	1 - 5	32 - 28
Heat 11	**Ambrose**/**Taylor**/Price/Featherstone	73.6	**5 - 1**	37 - 29
Heat 12	**Jackson**/Ryman/**White**/Bales	73.8	**4 - 2**	41 - 31
Heat 13	Price/**Ambrose**/**Cartwright**/Osborne	74.4	3 - 3	44 - 34

CREWE - Geoff Ambrose 13, John Jackson 13, Glyn Taylor 10 (+2), Keith White 4 (+2), Ian Cartwright 2 (+1), Wayne Forrest 2 (+1), *Dave Morton (R/R)*.
BOSTON - Ray Bales 11, Jim Ryman 9, Arthur Price 8, Russell Osborne 3 (+2), Tony Featherstone 2 (+2), Carl Glover 1, David Gagen 0.

Meeting 20 - Monday, June 11, 1973 - British League Division II
L.M.R. Sports Ground, Earle Street, Crewe
Track Length - 430 yards.

CREWE KINGS.....43 WORKINGTON COMETS.....35

Crewe avenged their challenge defeat in April with a fine display against the high-flying Comets, and it was Glyn Taylor who took the honours with an impressive thirteen point haul. The Kings raced into an eighteen point lead after Heat 8, but Workington battled back with maximums in Heats 9, 10 and 12, after home riders suffered a bout of mechanical trouble. Mitch Graham again showed his liking for the Earle Street track by top-scoring for the Cumbrians.

Heat 01	**Jackson**/Graham/Owen/**Forrest**	73.8	3 - 3	03 - 03
Heat 02	**Taylor**/**White**/Hornby/Watson	76.0	**5 - 1**	08 - 04
Heat 03	**Jackson**/Sansom/**Cartwright**/Amundson	74.4	**4 - 2**	12 - 06
Heat 04	**Ambrose**/**White**/Mackay/Watson	75.0	**5 - 1**	17 - 07
Heat 05	**Taylor**/Graham/Owen/**Ambrose** (R)	74.2	3 - 3	20 - 10
Heat 06	**Jackson**/**Forrest**/Mackay/Hornby	74.6	**5 - 1**	25 - 11
Heat 07	**Taylor**/Sansom/**White**/Amundson	74.6	**4 - 2**	29 - 13
Heat 08	**Taylor**/Graham/**Forrest**/Sansom	75.4	**4 - 2**	33 - 15
Heat 09	Mackay/Graham/**White**/**Cartwright**	75.4	1 - 5	34 - 20
Heat 10	Sansom/Mackay/**Forrest**/**Jackson**	74.2	1 - 5	35 - 25
Heat 11	**Ambrose**/Graham/**Taylor**/Owen	74.4	**4 - 2**	39 - 27
Heat 12	Sansom/Mackay/**Jackson**/**Forrest** (R)	74.8	1 - 5	40 - 32
Heat 13	**Ambrose**/Owen/Amundson/**White**	74.8	3 - 3	43 - 35

CREWE - Glyn Taylor 13, John Jackson 10, Geoff Ambrose 9, Keith White 6 (+2), Wayne Forrest 4 (+1), Ian Cartwright 1, *Dave Morton (R/R)*.
WORKINGTON - Mitch Graham 10 (+1), Lou Sansom 10, Malcolm Mackay 9 (+2), Taffy Owen 4 (+2), Kym Amundson 1 (+1), Bernie Hornby 1, Steve Watson 0.

Twenty-four hours later, Geoff Ambrose emulated Phil Crump's achievement of the previous season, when winning the Cheshire Championship at Ellesmere Port with fifteen points, beating ex-Crewe favourite Paul O'Neil by two points. John Jackson's attempt at the title ended when a motor failure in Heat 5 forced him out of the running. Len Silver announced that a new grandstand was about to be constructed at Earle Street.

Meeting 21 - Thursday, June 14, 1973 - British League Division II
Long Eaton Stadium, Station Road, Long Eaton
Track Length - 366 yards.

LONG EATON RANGERS.....41 CREWE KINGS.....37

Crewe's pointless away run continued despite Geoff Ambrose's magnificent fifteen point haul, as the Kings continued their policy of using rider replacement. Keith White made a dream start winning his first two outings, but from then on Long Eaton won five of the next seven to open up a ten point lead, which Crewe couldn't quite claw back, despite winning the last three heats. The re-run of Heat 3 was delayed for ten minutes when Steve Bass refused to leave the track after being excluded for falling in the original staging.

Heat 01	Bouchard/**Jackson**/Hughes/**Cartwright**	73.6	4 - 2	04 - 02
Heat 02	**White/Taylor**/Molyneux/Witt (F)	73.6	**1 - 5**	05 - 07
Heat 03	**White**/P.Bass/**Forrest**/S.Bass (X)	73.0	**2 - 4**	07 - 11
Heat 04	Mills/**Ambrose/Taylor**/Molyneux	72.8	3 - 3	10 - 14
Heat 05	S.Bass/**Jackson**/P.Bass/**Cartwright**	73.0	4 - 2	14 - 16
Heat 06	Bouchard/**Ambrose**/Hughes/**White** (R)	73.6	4 - 2	18 - 18
Heat 07	Mills/Molyneux/**Jackson/Forrest**	73.8	5 - 1	23 - 19
Heat 08	Witt/Hughes/**White/Taylor**	74.4	5 - 1	28 - 20
Heat 09	**Ambrose**/S.Bass/P.Bass/**White**	72.6	3 - 3	31 - 23
Heat 10	Bouchard/**Ambrose**/Hughes/**Forrest**	73.0	4 - 2	35 - 25
Heat 11	**Ambrose**/Witt/**Jackson**/Mills (R)	72.6	**2 - 4**	37 - 29
Heat 12	**Ambrose**/S.Bass/**Taylor**/Bouchard	73.2	**2 - 4**	39 - 33
Heat 13	**Jackson**/Mills/**Taylor**/P.Bass (R)	73.2	**2 - 4**	41 - 37

LONG EATON - Geoff Bouchard 9, Roger Mills 8, Steve Bass 7, Joe Hughes 5 (+1), Alan Witt 5, Phil Bass 4 (+1), Alan Molyneux 3 (+1).
CREWE - Geoff Ambrose 15, John Jackson 9, Keith White 7, Glyn Taylor 5 (+2), Wayne Forrest 1, Ian Cartwright 0, *Dave Morton (R/R)*.

Following this defeat, Crewe lay 9th in the league table, which was headed by Boston, Peterborough and Workington. On June 16, the Junior Championship of the British Isles took place at Canterbury and was won by favourite Peter Collins. Dave Morton, originally down to ride, was unable to take his place.

Meeting 22 - Monday, June 18, 1973 - Challenge, Second Leg
L.M.R. Sports Ground, Earle Street, Crewe
Track Length - 430 yards.

CREWE KINGS.....46 CHESTERTON POTTERS.....32

(Crewe won on aggregate 81 - 73)

First bragging rights belonged to the Kings, after beating local rivals Chesterton over the two legs. After Heat 5, the Potters were level in the match and six up overall, until a trio of home maximums, and another in Heat 11, eventually saw Crewe home by eight points on aggregate. Geoff Ambrose and reserve Glyn Taylor both recorded paid maximums, with Mick Handley the best Potter on show with a dozen points from five rides. John Jackson won Heat 12 on Glyn Taylor's machine and Reg Brassington blew his engine when crossing the line in Heat 4, after winning his first outing.

Heat 01	Broadbanks/**Jackson/Forrest**/Woodward	73.8	3 - 3	03 - 03
Heat 02	**Brassington/Taylor**/Wasley/Parker	76.4	**5 - 1**	08 - 04
Heat 03	Handley/**Cartwright**/Pusey/**White**	75.4	2 - 4	10 - 08
Heat 04	**Ambrose**/Parker/**Brassington**/Holden	74.8	**4 - 2**	14 - 10
Heat 05	Broadbanks/Woodward/**Cartwright/White**	74.4	1 - 5	15 - 15
Heat 06	**Jackson/Forrest**/Parker/Wasley (R)	75.2	**5 - 1**	20 - 16
Heat 07	**Taylor/Ambrose**/Handley/Pusey	73.8	**5 - 1**	25 - 17
Heat 08	**Forrest/Taylor**/Woodward/Broadbanks	75.4	**5 - 1**	30 - 18

Heat 09	Handley/**White**/**Cartwright**/Parker	75.0	3 - 3	33 - 21
Heat 10	Handley/Pusey/**Forrest**/**Jackson** (R)	75.2	1 - 5	34 - 26
Heat 11	**Ambrose**/**Taylor**/Woodward/Broadbanks	74.4	**5 - 1**	39 - 27
Heat 12	**Jackson**/Handley/**White**/Holden	74.0	**4 - 2**	43 - 29
Heat 13	**Ambrose**/Broadbanks/Pusey/**Cartwright**	74.6	3 - 3	46 - 32

CREWE - Geoff Ambrose 11 (+1), Glyn Taylor 9 (+3), John Jackson 8, Wayne Forrest 7 (+2), Ian Cartwright 4 (+1), Reg Brassington 4, Keith White 3.
CHESTERTON - Mick Handley 12, Mike Broadbanks 8, Geoff Pusey 4 (+2), Bryan Woodward 4 (+1), Roger Parker 3, Nigel Wasley 1, Steve Holden 0.

Meeting 23 - Wednesday, June 20, 1973 - British League Division II
Odsal Stadium, Rooley Avenue, Bradford
Track Length - 375 yards.

BRADFORD NORTHERN.....54 CREWE KINGS.....24

A first heat victory was all that a depleted Crewe side had to show from their trip to West Yorkshire. Still missing the influential Dave Morton, the Kings were further weakened when Geoff Ambrose failed to turn-up. Keith White and Wayne Forrest did their best to make a match of it, but were eventually out-muscled by a solid-scoring Northern team.

Heat 01	**Jackson**/Baugh/**Forrest**/Meredith (F)	73.4	**2 - 4**	02 - 04
Heat 02	Fullerton/Freegard/**Taylor**/**Cartwright**	75.8	5 - 1	07 - 05
Heat 03	**White**/Adlington/Langlois/**Tattersall**	74.4	3 - 3	10 - 08
Heat 04	Knapkin/Fullerton/**Cartwright**/**Taylor**	73.0	5 - 1	15 - 09
Heat 05	Adlington/**Forrest**/Langlois/**Jackson**	75.0	4 - 2	19 - 11
Heat 06	Meredith/Baugh/**Cartwright**/**Taylor** (R)	75.6	5 - 1	24 - 12
Heat 07	Knapkin/Fullerton/**Forrest**/**White**	72.2	5 - 1	29 - 13
Heat 08	Meredith/**White**/Freegard/**Forrest**	73.2	4 - 2	33 - 15
Heat 09	Adlington/Langlois/**Taylor**/**Cartwright**	75.0	5 - 1	38 - 16
Heat 10	Meredith/**White**/**Jackson**/Baugh (R)	73.2	3 - 3	41 - 19
Heat 11	**Forrest**/Freegard/Knapkin/**Jackson**	73.4	3 - 3	44 - 22
Heat 12	Baugh/Langlois/**Taylor**/**White** (F)	74.6	5 - 1	49 - 23
Heat 13	Knapkin/Adlington/**White**/**Jackson**	71.4	5 - 1	54 - 24

BRADFORD - Robin Adlington 10 (+1), Alan Knapkin 10 (+1), Colin Meredith 9, Mike Fullerton 7 (+2), Dave Baugh 7 (+1), Brenton Langlois 6 (+3), Tony Freegard 5 (+1).
CREWE - Keith White 8, Wayne Forrest 7, John Jackson 4 (+1), Glyn Taylor 3, Ian Cartwright 2, Graham Tattersall* 0, *Dave Morton (R/R)*.

Following Geoff Ambrose's no-show, he was fined £3 by the Speedway Control Board and warned of his future conduct. In the weeks following the match at Chesterton, Dave Parry had disappeared from the scene, fuelling rumours that the only surviving member of the original Crewe squad, had followed Dai Evans down the retirement road.

Meeting 24 - Monday, June 25, 1973 - British League Division II
L.M.R. Sports Ground, Earle Street, Crewe
Track Length - 430 yards.

CREWE KINGS.....42 ELLESMERE PORT GUNNERS.....36

There were a few familiar faces in the Ellesmere Port section of the pits for this league clash at Earle Street. Paul O'Neil, now a Crewe landlord at The Stag Inn in Wistaston Road, returned to his old stomping ground for the first time in three years, alongside Barry Booth and Chris Morton, who had been snapped up by Belle Vue and loaned to the Gunners before Crewe could offer him a contract. Dave Morton made a welcome return, winning each of his completed rides. However, he was outscored by his younger brother, who was the top-scoring visitor.

Heat 01	O'Neil/**Jackson**/Gardner/**White**	74.0	2 - 4	02 - 04
Heat 02	C.Morton/**Cartwright**/Hughes/**Taylor** (R)	73.0	2 - 4	04 - 08
Heat 03	**D.Morton**/Goad/**Forrest**/Booth	72.6	**4 - 2**	08 - 10
Heat 04	**Ambrose**/Drury/C.Morton/**Taylor** (R)	72.8	3 - 3	11 - 13
Heat 05	**D.Morton**/**Forrest**/O'Neil/Gardner (R)	72.8	**5 - 1**	16 - 14

Heat 06	Drury/**White**/C.Morton/**Jackson** (R)	75.0	2 - 4	18 - 18
Heat 07	**Ambrose**/Goad/Booth/**Taylor** (R)	73.4	3 - 3	21 - 21
Heat 08	C.Morton/**White**/Hughes/**Cartwright** (F)	74.2	2 - 4	23 - 25
Heat 09	**D.Morton**/**Forrest**/Drury/Hughes	73.6	**5 - 1**	28 - 26
Heat 10	**Jackson**/Goad/Booth/**White**	74.8	3 - 3	31 - 29
Heat 11	**Ambrose**/C.Morton/**Taylor**/O'Neil	73.6	**4 - 2**	35 - 31
Heat 12	**Jackson**/Drury/**Forrest**/Goad	73.0	**4 - 2**	39 - 33
Heat 13	**Ambrose**/C.Morton/O'Neil/**D.Morton** (R)	74.2	3 - 3	42 - 36

CREWE - Geoff Ambrose 12, Dave Morton 9, John Jackson 8, Wayne Forrest 6 (+2), Keith White 4, Ian Cartwright 2, Glyn Taylor 1.
ELLESMERE PORT - Chris Morton 12 (+1), Graham Drury 8, Colin Goad 6, Paul O'Neil 5 (+1), Barry Booth 2 (+2), Wayne Hughes 2, Robbie Gardner 1.

Following Crewe's indifferent start to the season, attendances in the first few meetings were well-down on the previous year, but a gradual upturn saw a healthy crowd turn up for the Cheshire derby match, with many unable to obtain a programme after they were sold-out. The attraction of sidecar racing in the second half added a few hundred to the gate.

Meeting 25 - Sunday, July 1, 1973 - British League Division II
Quibell Park Stadium, Brumby Wood Lane, Scunthorpe
Track Length - 440 yards.

SCUNTHORPE SAINTS.....55 CREWE KINGS.....23

After last season's home and away annihilations, this was rich reward for an improving Saints squad, growing in confidence and climbing the Division II table. Their riders won twelve of the thirteen heats, with only Wayne Forrest breaking the chain. Glyn Taylor hit the safety fence in his second ride and was taken to hospital with a back injury, and Dave Morton suffered a wrist injury. The win was Scunthorpe's best ever league victory.

Heat 01	Bywater/**Jackson**/Garrod/**White**	82.8	4 - 2	04 - 02
Heat 02	Brown/Underwood/**Taylor**/**Cartwright**	83.2	5 - 1	09 - 03
Heat 03	**Forrest**/McKinlay/Haynes/**Morton** (F)	82.0	3 - 3	12 - 06
Heat 04	Hindle/**Ambrose**/Underwood/**Cartwright**	81.0	4 - 2	16 - 08
Heat 05	McKinlay/Haynes/**Jackson**/**White**	81.2	5 - 1	21 - 09
Heat 06	Bywater/Garrod/**Ambrose**/**Taylor** (X)	82.4	5 - 1	26 - 10
Heat 07	Hindle/**Morton**/**Forrest**/Underwood	81.8	3 - 3	29 - 13
Heat 08	Garrod/Brown/**Jackson**/**Morton** (R)	82.0	5 - 1	34 - 14
Heat 09	McKinlay/**Ambrose**/Haynes/**White**	81.8	4 - 2	38 - 16
Heat 10	Garrod/**Forrest**/**Morton**/Bywater	81.8	3 - 3	41 - 19
Heat 11	Brown/Hindle/**Jackson**/**Forrest**	82.2	5 - 1	46 - 20
Heat 12	Haynes/**Ambrose**/Bywater/**Morton**	82.4	4 - 2	50 - 22
Heat 13	Hindle/McKinlay/**Jackson**/**Forrest**	81.6	5 - 1	55 - 23

SCUNTHORPE - Ian Hindle 11 (+1), Ken McKinlay 10 (+1), Rex Garrod 9 (+1), Dingle Brown 8 (+1), Rod Haynes 7 (+2), Jack Bywater 7, Doug Underwood 3 (+1).
CREWE - Geoff Ambrose 7, Wayne Forrest 6 (+1), John Jackson 6, Dave Morton 3 (+1), Glyn Taylor 1, Ian Cartwright 0, Keith White 0.

Meeting 26 - Monday, July 2, 1973 - British League Division II
L.M.R. Sports Ground, Earle Street, Crewe
Track Length - 430 yards.

CREWE KINGS.....42 SCUNTHORPE SAINTS.....36

Further indications of the changing fortunes of the two clubs were highlighted here in this scoreline. The Saints led by six after Heat 6, and at this stage must have harboured thoughts of a first ever away league victory. However, order was partially restored with three home maximums in the next four heats, which put Crewe six points ahead, and a 4-2 in Heat 12 completed the fight back. Ian Cartwright bagged eight points in his best return to date. John Jackson incurred a rare exclusion after hitting the boards first time out, but recovered to win his three remaining rides.

Heat 01	**White**/Bywater/Hindle/**Jackson** (X)	73.2	3 - 3	03 - 03
Heat 02	Haynes/**Cartwright**/Underwood/**Brassington**	73.6	2 - 4	05 - 07
Heat 03	McKinlay/**Forrest**/Brown/**Morton** (R)	74.6	2 - 4	07 - 11
Heat 04	Haynes/**Cartwright**/Garrod/**Ambrose**	73.0	2 - 4	09 - 15
Heat 05	**Morton**/Bywater/Hindle/**Forrest** (R)	73.4	3 - 3	12 - 18
Heat 06	**Jackson**/Garrod/Underwood/**White** (R)	74.0	3 - 3	15 - 21
Heat 07	**Ambrose**/**Morton**/Brown/McKinlay (R)	73.4	**5 - 1**	20 - 22
Heat 08	Bywater/**Cartwright**/**White**/Haynes	74.4	3 - 3	23 - 25
Heat 09	**Morton**/**Forrest**/Underwood/Garrod	73.6	**5 - 1**	28 - 26
Heat 10	**Jackson**/**Cartwright**/Haynes/Brown	74.4	**5 - 1**	33 - 27
Heat 11	**Ambrose**/Bywater/Hindle/**Cartwright**	74.6	3 - 3	36 - 30
Heat 12	**Jackson**/Bywater/**Forrest**/Haynes	74.0	**4 - 2**	40 - 32
Heat 13	Hindle/**Ambrose**/Garrod/**Brassington**	75.0	2 - 4	42 - 36

CREWE - John Jackson 9, Ian Cartwright 8 (+1), Dave Morton 8 (+1), Geoff Ambrose 8, Wayne Forrest 5 (+1), Keith White 4 (+1), Reg Brassington 0.
SCUNTHORPE - Jack Bywater 11, Rod Haynes 7, Ian Hindle 6 (+3), Rex Garrod 4, Doug Underwood 3 (+1), Ken McKinlay 3, Dingle Brown 2.

Track announcer for the night, "Crazy" Jack Millen, who was currently sidelined with a foot injury, had the crowd in stitches with several amusing quips including *"get a good mechanic"* following a string of home retirements. Millen in charge of track maintenance at Earle Street, had recently been spotted stamping down a rough patch on the track with his bare feet! In the Division II averages, Dave Morton was the highest Crewe rider in 15th place.

Meeting 27 - Thursday, July 5, 1973 - British League Division II
Cleveland Park Stadium, Stockton Road, Middlesbrough
Track Length - 335 yards.

TEESSIDE TIGERS.....56 CREWE KINGS.....22

A shambolic ending to the match just about summed up goings-on at Cleveland Park. In past seasons, Crewe's arrival in Middlesbrough had usually meant trouble - and this was no exception. After four heats, with the Kings 18-6 down, a complaint was lodged by the visitors concerning the state of the track. However, the match continued much to the disgust of Crewe officials and riders, and by Heat 10 it was all over as a contest. The final heat had to be started on the green light, and although the Tigers pair jumped the start, all four were called back for the re-run. John Jackson then got a flier and was excluded, to further infuriate the Kings camp.

Heat 01	Swales/**Jackson**/Forrester/**White**	70.4	4 - 2	04 - 02
Heat 02	Auffret/**Cartwright**/Hodgson/**Anderson**	72.0	4 - 2	08 - 04
Heat 03	Reading/Durham/**Jackson**/**Forrest**	71.4	5 - 1	13 - 05
Heat 04	Auffret/Wright/**Cartwright**/**Ambrose**	72.0	5 - 1	18 - 06
Heat 05	**Jackson**/Reading/Durham/**White**	70.2	3 - 3	21 - 09
Heat 06	Swales/Forrester/**Anderson**/**Ambrose**	71.2	5 - 1	26 - 10
Heat 07	Auffret/Wright/**Forrest**/**White**	72.0	5 - 1	31 - 11
Heat 08	Swales/**White**/**Cartwright**/Hodgson	70.0	3 - 3	34 - 14
Heat 09	Durham/**Ambrose**/**Anderson**/Reading (R)	72.6	3 - 3	37 - 17
Heat 10	Swales/Forrester/**Ambrose**/**Forrest**	71.8	5 - 1	42 - 18
Heat 11	Wright/**Jackson**/Hodgson/**White**	71.4	4 - 2	46 - 20
Heat 12	Durham/Forrester/**Ambrose**/**Anderson**	72.0	5 - 1	51 - 21
Heat 13	Auffret/Wright/**Cartwright**/**Forrest**	71.0	5 - 1	56 - 22

TEESSIDE - Frank Auffret 12, Tim Swales 12, Roger Wright 9 (+3), Dave Durham 9 (+2), Bruce Forrester 7 (+3), Pete Reading 5, Russ Hodgson 2.
CREWE - John Jackson 8, Ian Cartwright 5 (+1), Geoff Ambrose 4, Cliff Anderson 2 (+1), Keith White 2, Wayne Forrest 1, *Dave Morton (R/R)*.

On July 7, John Jackson scored one point for England at Peterborough in the fourth test of the Division II series against Poland, won by the tourists 56-52.

Meeting 28 - Monday, July 9, 1973 - British League Division II
L.M.R. Sports Ground, Earle Street, Crewe
Track Length - 430 yards.

CREWE KINGS.....48 EASTBOURNE EAGLES.....30

The Kings maintained their 100% home league record after a comfortable victory over Eastbourne. Bobby McNeil was the only Eagle to cause any concerns after winning on three occasions, although he was slightly fortunate to win Heat 12, following a controversial decision by referee Leo Pendergast. Neil Middleditch fell on the last bend of lap three, leaving his bike in the middle of the track. The leading Kings pair took evasive action, allowing McNeil through for the victory. Crewe operated rider replacement for John Jackson (on international duty), which enabled Geoff Ambrose to record a paid fifteen point maximum. Dave Morton suffered two retirements; the first in Heat 9 and then in the last when his chain snapped while going well.

Heat 01	**Ambrose**/Geer/**White**/Johns	73.2	**4 - 2**	04 - 02
Heat 02	**Taylor**/Middleditch/**Cartwright**/Dugard	74.0	**4 - 2**	08 - 04
Heat 03	**Morton**/Gachet/**Forrest**/Squibb	74.2	**4 - 2**	12 - 06
Heat 04	**Ambrose**/**Taylor**/McNeil/Middleditch	75.0	**5 - 1**	17 - 07
Heat 05	**Forrest**/Johns/**Morton**/Geer	74.6	**4 - 2**	21 - 09
Heat 06	**Morton**/McNeil/Johns/**White** (R)	73.8	3 - 3	24 - 12
Heat 07	**Taylor**/**Ambrose**/Gachet/Squibb (R)	74.8	**5 - 1**	29 - 13
Heat 08	McNeil/**White**/**Cartwright**/Geer (R)	74.8	3 - 3	32 - 16
Heat 09	McNeil/**Forrest**/Dugard/**Morton** (R)	74.0	2 - 4	34 - 20
Heat 10	**Forrest**/Gachet/**White**/Squibb	75.0	**4 - 2**	38 - 22
Heat 11	**Ambrose**/Geer/**Cartwright**/Johns (R)	73.8	**4 - 2**	42 - 24
Heat 12	McNeil/**Forrest**/**Taylor**/Middleditch (F)	74.2	3 - 3	45 - 27
Heat 13	**Ambrose**/Johns/Gachet/**Morton** (R)	74.6	3 - 3	48 - 30

CREWE - Geoff Ambrose 14 (+1), Wayne Forrest 11, Glyn Taylor 9 (+2), Dave Morton 7, Keith White 4, Ian Cartwright 3 (+1), *John Jackson (R/R).*
EASTBOURNE - Bobby McNeil 12, Paul Gachet 6 (+1), Roger Johns 5 (+1), Trevor Geer 4, Neil Middleditch 2, Eric Dugard 1, Jimmy Squibb 0.

After the match, Geoff Ambrose was presented with the Maurice Littlechild Trophy for the top-scoring home rider of the night. The trophy, a silver tray and cash bonus, were handed over by Maurice's widow Violet. Glyn Taylor was judged second (on programmed rides only) and received £5. John Jackson scored a point in England's 64-43 win against Poland in the sixth test at Birmingham.

Meeting 29 - Wednesday, July 11, 1973 - British League Division II
Boulevard Stadium, Airlie Street, Kingston-upon-Hull
Track Length - 415 yards.

HULL VIKINGS.....48 CREWE KINGS.....30

Hull used rider replacement for want away heat leader Robin Amundson, and it paid dividends as Tony Childs, Dave Mills and Dennis Gavros all returned healthy figures. The Kings stayed in contention with an Ambrose/Morton 5-1 in Heat 8, but then fell away as the Vikings registered four successive wins. The 4-2 in Heat 4, ended Crewe's run of 41 away races without a heat advantage.

Heat 01	Childs/Gavros/**Jackson**/**White**	75.6	5 - 1	05 - 01
Heat 02	**Taylor**/Boston/Wasden/**Cartwright**	76.2	3 - 3	08 - 04
Heat 03	Childs/**Morton**/Cowland/**Forrest**	76.2	4 - 2	12 - 06
Heat 04	**Ambrose**/Mills/**Cartwright**/Wasden	75.0	**2 - 4**	14 - 10
Heat 05	Gavros/**Jackson**/Cowland/**White**	76.6	4 - 2	18 - 12
Heat 06	Gavros/Childs/**Taylor**/**Cartwright**	75.4	5 - 1	23 - 13
Heat 07	Mills/**Morton**/**Forrest**/Boston	76.0	3 - 3	26 - 16
Heat 08	**Ambrose**/**Morton**/Gavros/Boston	76.8	**1 - 5**	27 - 21
Heat 09	Mills/**Ambrose**/Cowland/**Taylor**	77.6	4 - 2	31 - 23

Heat 10	Gavros/Childs/**Morton**/**Forrest**	80.2	5 - 1	36 - 24
Heat 11	Mills/**Jackson**/Boston/**White**	80.4	4 - 2	40 - 26
Heat 12	Childs/Cowland/**Ambrose**/**Morton**	80.0	5 - 1	45 - 27
Heat 13	**Jackson**/Cowland/Mills/**Forrest**	79.0	3 - 3	48 - 30

HULL - Tony Childs 13 (+2), Dennis Gavros 12 (+1), Dave Mills 12 (+1), Alan Cowland 7 (+1), Pete Boston 3, Dennis Wasden 1 (+1), *Robin Amundson (R/R).*
CREWE - Geoff Ambrose 9, John Jackson 8, Dave Morton 7 (+1), Glyn Taylor 4, Wayne Forrest 1 (+1), Ian Cartwright 1, Keith White 0.

Meeting 30 - Monday, July 16, 1973 - British League Division II
L.M.R. Sports Ground, Earle Street, Crewe
Track Length - 430 yards.

CREWE KINGS.....53 LONG EATON RANGERS.....25

The Kings topped fifty points for the first time this season, with all bar Keith White in the points. John Jackson recorded a maximum, but it was Dave Morton who stole the show in Heat 5. Plagued by injury and mechanical problems for most of the campaign, he beat Jackson's fifteen month old track record with a time of 71.2, a remarkable feat considering the track was heavy and he wasn't first out of the gate! Glyn Taylor also impressed, equalling the old mark in Heat 7.

Heat 01	**Jackson**/Bouchard/Witt/**White**	72.8	3 - 3	03 - 03
Heat 02	**Taylor**/**Cartwright**/Molyneux/Teale	72.2	**5 - 1**	08 - 04
Heat 03	**Forrest**/**Morton**/P.Bass/S.Bass	73.8	**5 - 1**	13 - 05
Heat 04	**Taylor**/**Ambrose**/Mills/Teale	71.6	**5 - 1**	18 - 06
Heat 05	**Morton**/**Forrest**/Witt/Bouchard	**71.2** (TR)	**5 - 1**	23 - 07
Heat 06	**Jackson**/Mills/Molyneux/**White**	72.6	3 - 3	26 - 10
Heat 07	**Taylor**/**Ambrose**/S.Bass/P.Bass	71.4	**5 - 1**	31 - 11
Heat 08	Bouchard/**Cartwright**/Witt/**White**	72.8	2 - 4	33 - 15
Heat 09	**Morton**/Mills/**Forrest**/Molyneux	73.0	**4 - 2**	37 - 17
Heat 10	**Jackson**/**Taylor**/P.Bass/Molyneux (X)	72.6	**5 - 1**	42 - 18
Heat 11	**Ambrose**/Witt/Bouchard/**Cartwright**	75.6	3 - 3	45 - 21
Heat 12	**Jackson**/Mills/P.Bass/**Forrest**	74.0	3 - 3	48 - 24
Heat 13	**Morton**/**Ambrose**/S.Bass/Bouchard (X)	72.8	**5 - 1**	53 - 25

CREWE - John Jackson 12, Dave Morton 11 (+1), Glyn Taylor 11 (+1), Geoff Ambrose 9 (+3), Wayne Forrest 6 (+1), Ian Cartwright 4 (+1), Keith White 0.
LONG EATON - Roger Mills 7, Geoff Bouchard 6 (+1), Alan Witt 5 (+1), Phil Bass 3 (+1), Alan Molyneux 2 (+1), Steve Bass 2, Ian Teale 0.

Meeting 31 - Monday, July 23, 1973 - British League Division II
L.M.R. Sports Ground, Earle Street, Crewe
Track Length - 430 yards.

CREWE KINGS.....46 TEESSIDE TIGERS.....32

Geoff Ambrose continued his fantastic run at Earle Street with another full house, in a competitive meeting with Teesside. Although the Tigers failed to win a heat, they did share the points on seven occasions, to keep the score within the bounds of respectability. John Jackson (paid maximum), Ian Cartwright, and Dave Morton provided good support to Ambrose, although Morton's score could have been higher but for engine problems in two of his outings.

Heat 01	**Jackson**/Forrester/**White**/Swales	76.6	**4 - 2**	04 - 02
Heat 02	**Cartwright**/Auffret/**Taylor**/Hodgson (F)	76.2	**4 - 2**	08 - 04
Heat 03	Durham/**Morton**/**Forrest**/Reading (F)	76.6	3 - 3	11 - 07
Heat 04	**Ambrose**/Hodgson/**Taylor**/Wright	75.0	**4 - 2**	15 - 09
Heat 05	**Morton**/Forrester/Swales/**Forrest**	75.6	3 - 3	18 - 12
Heat 06	**White**/**Jackson**/Auffret/Wright (F)	75.8	**5 - 1**	23 - 13
Heat 07	**Ambrose**/Durham/Reading/**Taylor**	74.8	3 - 3	26 - 16
Heat 08	**Cartwright**/Forrester/Hodgson/**White**	75.0	3 - 3	29 - 19
Heat 09	**Morton**/Auffret/Durham/**Forrest**	75.0	3 - 3	32 - 22

Heat 10	**Jackson**/Durham/Reading/**White**	75.4	3 - 3	35 - 25
Heat 11	**Ambrose**/Forrester/**Cartwright**/Swales	75.2	**4 - 2**	39 - 27
Heat 12	**Jackson**/Auffret/**Cartwright**/Reading	75.6	**4 - 2**	43 - 29
Heat 13	**Ambrose**/Durham/Forrester/**Morton** (R)	75.8	3 - 3	46 - 32

CREWE - Geoff Ambrose 12, John Jackson 11 (+1), Ian Cartwright 8, Dave Morton 8, Keith White 4, Glyn Taylor 2, Wayne Forrest 1 (+1).
TEESSIDE - Dave Durham 10 (+1), Bruce Forrester 9 (+1), Frank Auffret 7, Russ Hodgson 3 (+1), Pete Reading 2 (+2), Tim Swales 1 (+1), Roger Wright 0.

Len Silver offered Exeter rider Peter Thompson a contract after the Aussie had shown a steady improvement during a series of second-half rides at Earle Street. Also hopeful of putting pen to paper after impressing in a trial was local lad and Cheshire scramble champion Peter Mathia.

Meeting 32 - Thursday, July 26, 1973 - British League Division II
Lyme Valley Sports Stadium, Loomer Road, Chesterton
Track Length - 380 yards.

CHESTERTON POTTERS.....41 CREWE KINGS.....36

Chesterton secured a hard-fought victory in an incident packed meeting, raced in front of a full house. The Potters led from the first heat, and eventually won the points with a maximum in Heat 12 from the reliable pairing of Mike Broadbanks and Geoff Pusey. Both teams started with riders absent. Steve Holden was promoted into the home side for the missing Martin Yeates, despite breaking an ankle only two weeks previous, and Peter Thompson made his Kings bow replacing Keith White who was suffering from tonsillitis. Broadbanks secured his second Loomer Road maximum against Crewe.

Heat 01	Broadbanks/Woodward/**Jackson**/**Taylor**	74.0	5 - 1	05 - 01
Heat 02	Wasley/**Cartwright**/Holden (F)/**Thompson** (R)	74.8	3 - 2	08 - 03
Heat 03	Bridgett/**Morton**/Pusey/**Forrest** (R)	72.0	4 - 2	12 - 05
Heat 04	**Ambrose**/Handley/**Cartwright**/Holden	73.0	**2 - 4**	14 - 09
Heat 05	Pusey/Bridgett/**Jackson**/**Taylor**	73.6	5 - 1	19 - 10
Heat 06	Broadbanks/**Ambrose**/Woodward/**Thompson**	72.0	4 - 2	23 - 12
Heat 07	**Morton**/Handley/Holden/**Forrest**	73.0	3 - 3	26 - 15
Heat 08	**Ambrose**/Woodward/**Cartwright**/Wasley	72.6	**2 - 4**	28 - 19
Heat 09	**Ambrose**/Pusey/**Jackson**/Bridgett	73.0	**2 - 4**	30 - 23
Heat 10	Broadbanks/**Morton**/Woodward/**Forrest**	72.0	4 - 2	34 - 25
Heat 11	**Jackson**/**Taylor**/Wasley/Handley	72.2	**1 - 5**	35 - 30
Heat 12	Broadbanks/Pusey/**Ambrose**/**Morton**	72.0	5 - 1	40 - 31
Heat 13	**Morton**/**Jackson**/Holden/Bridgett	72.4	**1 - 5**	41 - 36

CHESTERTON - Mike Broadbanks 12, Geoff Pusey 8 (+1), Bryan Woodward 6 (+1), Alan Bridgett 5 (+1), Mick Handley 4, Nigel Wasley 4, Steve Holden 2 (+1).
CREWE - Geoff Ambrose 12, Dave Morton 10, John Jackson 8 (+1), Ian Cartwright 4, Glyn Taylor 2 (+1), Wayne Forrest 0, Peter Thompson 0.

Meeting 33 - Monday, July 30, 1973 - British League Division II
L.M.R. Sports Ground, Earle Street, Crewe
Track Length - 430 yards.

CREWE KINGS.....52 CANTERBURY CRUSADERS.....26

Crewe achieved their 26th consecutive league victory at Earle Street, easily overcoming an under-strength Canterbury outfit, after a blitz of early maximums. The visitors arrived minus the services of Barney Kennett (broken collar-bone) and Derek Cook (severe bruising), and gave starts to juniors Dave Gooderham and Gary Cottham. The Kings scored solidly throughout, with only Ian Cartwright failing to win a heat.

Heat 01	**Jackson**/**White**/Murray/Rumsey	72.4	**5 - 1**	05 - 01
Heat 02	**Taylor**/**Cartwright**/Banks/Gooderham	72.6	**5 - 1**	10 - 02
Heat 03	**Forrest**/**Morton**/Jones/Hubbard	72.6	**5 - 1**	15 - 03
Heat 04	**Taylor**/**Ambrose**/Gooderham/Banks	73.4	**5 - 1**	20 - 04

Heat 05	**Forrest**/**Morton**/Rumsey/Murray	73.0	**5 - 1**	25 - 05
Heat 06	**White**/Banks/**Jackson**/Cottham	73.2	**4 - 2**	29 - 07
Heat 07	Hubbard/Jones/**Ambrose**/**Taylor**	73.6	1 - 5	30 - 12
Heat 08	Jones/**Cartwright**/Gooderham/**White** (R)	73.2	2 - 4	32 - 16
Heat 09	**Forrest**/**Morton**/Hubbard/Banks (R)	74.2	**5 - 1**	37 - 17
Heat 10	Hubbard/**Jackson**/Jones/**White** (R)	73.6	2 - 4	39 - 21
Heat 11	**Ambrose**/**Cartwright**/Murray/Rumsey	73.8	**5 - 1**	44 - 22
Heat 12	**Jackson**/Hubbard/**Forrest**/Jones	73.4	**4 - 2**	48 - 24
Heat 13	**Morton**/Jones/**Ambrose**/Hubbard	73.6	**4 - 2**	52 - 26

CREWE - Wayne Forrest 10, Dave Morton 9 (+3), John Jackson 9, Geoff Ambrose 7 (+1), Ian Cartwright 6 (+2), Glyn Taylor 6, Keith White 5 (+1).
CANTERBURY - Trevor Jones 9 (+1), Ted Hubbard 9, Graham Banks 3, Dave Gooderham 2, Peter Murray 2, Les Rumsey 1, Gary Cottham 0, *Barney Kennett (R/R).*

Meeting 34 - Sunday, August 5, 1973 - British League Division II
Boston Sports Stadium, New Hammond Beck Road, Boston
Track Length - 380 yards.

BOSTON BARRACUDAS.....44 CREWE KINGS.....34

Runaway league leaders Boston were given a real fight by a determined Crewe outfit, with racing taking place in atrocious conditions. Kings riders won the first three heats, with Glyn Taylor coming from third on the last bend to win Heat 2. As the rain continued to fall, the 'Cudas eventually took control and confirmed victory in the penultimate heat. Geoff Ambrose was disappointing for the visitors, retiring in his only two rides. The victory put Boston five points clear of Workington in the table with a match in hand.

Heat 01	**Jackson**/Price/Bales/**White**	66.4	3 - 3	03 - 03
Heat 02	**Taylor**/L.Glover/Gagen/**Cartwright** (X)	69.8	3 - 3	06 - 06
Heat 03	**Morton**/Ryman/Osborne/**Forrest**	66.8	3 - 3	09 - 09
Heat 04	C.Glover/Gagen/**Cartwright**/**Ambrose** (R)	67.0	5 - 1	14 - 10
Heat 05	Ryman/Osborne/**White**/**Jackson** (R)	67.8	5 - 1	19 - 11
Heat 06	Price/**Taylor**/Bales/**Ambrose** (R)	68.6	4 - 2	23 - 13
Heat 07	C.Glover/**Morton**/Gagen/**Taylor** (R)	67.6	4 - 2	27 - 15
Heat 08	Bales/**White**/**Cartwright**/L.Glover	72.8	3 - 3	30 - 18
Heat 09	**Jackson**/Ryman/**Taylor**/Osborne	72.4	**2 - 4**	32 - 22
Heat 10	Price/**Taylor**/**Morton**/Bales	74.2	3 - 3	35 - 25
Heat 11	C.Glover/**Jackson**/**White**/Gagen	72.6	3 - 3	38 - 28
Heat 12	**Morton**/Price/Osborne/**Forrest** (R)	75.0	3 - 3	41 - 31
Heat 13	C.Glover/**Jackson**/**White**/Ryman (R)	74.0	3 - 3	44 - 34

BOSTON - Carl Glover 12, Arthur Price 10, Jim Ryman 7, Ray Bales 5 (+1), Russell Osborne 4 (+3), David Gagen 4 (+2), Les Glover 2.
CREWE - John Jackson 10, Dave Morton 9 (+1), Glyn Taylor 8, Keith White 5 (+2), Ian Cartwright 2 (+1), Geoff Ambrose 0, Wayne Forrest 0.

Meeting 35 - Monday, August 6, 1973 - British League Division II
L.M.R. Sports Ground, Earle Street, Crewe.
Track Length - 430 yards

CREWE KINGS.....42 BOSTON BARRACUDAS.....36

The champions faced the champions elect for the second time in twenty-four hours, with the Kings becoming only the fourth side to beat Boston this season. In an explosive affair, Arthur Price equalled Dave Morton's track record in Heat 1, but then lost control entering the home straight during Heat 5, causing Morton to hit the boards before falling 40 yards later. Following this, a number of riders on both sides let their feelings spill over in the pits. There was a further flare-up after Heat 12, when Carl Glover barged past Keith White on the final lap, nearly forcing the youngster into the safety fence. Back in the pits Wayne Forrest accused Glover of unfair riding and the pair came to blows. As for the match, witnessed by a crowd approaching 4,000, Crewe maintained a slender lead until Heat 10, when the Barracudas drew level. A trio of 4-2's however, gave the Kings a record 27th successive home league victory.

Heat 01	Price/**Jackson**/**Taylor**/Gagen	**71.2** (=TR)	3 - 3	03 - 03
Heat 02	Bales/**White**/L.Glover/**Cartwright**	72.6	2 - 4	05 - 07
Heat 03	**Morton**/**Forrest**/Ryman/Osborne	73.0	**5 - 1**	10 - 08
Heat 04	C.Glover/**Ambrose**/**White**/L.Glover	73.4	3 - 3	13 - 11
Heat 05	**Morton**/Gagen/**Forrest**/Price (X)	72.8	**4 - 2**	17 - 13
Heat 06	C.Glover/**Jackson**/Bales/**Taylor** (R)	72.0	2 - 4	19 - 17
Heat 07	**Ambrose**/Ryman/**White**/Osborne	73.0	**4 - 2**	23 - 19
Heat 08	**Taylor**/Gagen/**Cartwright**/Bales (R)	73.8	**4 - 2**	27 - 21
Heat 09	C.Glover/**Morton**/Price/**Forrest**	72.0	2 - 4	29 - 25
Heat 10	Bales/Ryman/**Taylor**/**Jackson**	72.4	1 - 5	30 - 30
Heat 11	**Ambrose**/Price/**White**/Gagen	72.6	**4 - 2**	34 - 32
Heat 12	**Jackson**/C.Glover/**White**/Ryman	73.6	**4 - 2**	38 - 34
Heat 13	**Ambrose**/Price/**Morton**/Bales	73.0	**4 - 2**	42 - 36

CREWE - Geoff Ambrose 11, Dave Morton 9, John Jackson 7, Keith White 6 (+1), Glyn Taylor 5 (+1), Wayne Forrest 3 (+1), Ian Cartwright 1.
BOSTON - Carl Glover 11, Arthur Price 8, Ray Bales 7, Jim Ryman 5 (+1), David Gagen 4, Les Glover 1, Russell Osborne 0.

Meeting 36 - Saturday, August 11, 1973 - British League Division II
Canterbury City Football Ground, Kingsmead Road, Canterbury
Track Length - 390 yards.

CANTERBURY CRUSADERS.....51 CREWE KINGS.....27

Canterbury raced to their biggest win of the season, with reserve Les Rumsey leading the charge by topping the score charts. The Kings, minus Dave Morton (tonsillitis), were again hindered by mechanical failures, but deserved more than their twenty-seven points. Keith White suffered magneto problems and John Jackson lacked power in his final two rides.

Heat 01	**Jackson**/Jones/**Taylor**/Cook	78.4	**2 - 4**	02 - 04
Heat 02	Rumsey/Banks/**White**/**Thompson**	78.8	5 - 1	07 - 05
Heat 03	Jones/Hubbard/**Forrest**/**Cartwright**	81.0	5 - 1	12 - 06
Heat 04	**Ambrose**/Banks/Murray/**Thompson** (F)	75.8	3 - 3	15 - 09
Heat 05	Hubbard/Jones/**Taylor**/**Jackson** (R)	77.6	5 - 1	20 - 10
Heat 06	Rumsey/Cook/**Jackson**/**Ambrose**	77.4	5 - 1	25 - 11
Heat 07	**Forrest**/Banks/Murray/**Cartwright**	78.0	3 - 3	28 - 14
Heat 08	Cook/**Forrest**/**Taylor**/Rumsey	77.0	3 - 3	31 - 17
Heat 09	**White**/**Ambrose**/Hubbard/Jones (R)	77.4	**1 - 5**	32 - 22
Heat 10	Gooderham/Cook/**Cartwright**/**Forrest** (R)	77.0	5 - 1	37 - 23
Heat 11	Rumsey/Murray/**Taylor**/**Jackson** (R)	78.0	5 - 1	42 - 24
Heat 12	Gooderham/**Ambrose**/Jones/**Cartwright**	76.8	4 - 2	46 - 26
Heat 13	Murray/Hubbard/**Forrest**/**Jackson** (R)	77.4	5 - 1	51 - 27

CANTERBURY - Les Rumsey 9, Ted Hubbard 8 (+2), Trevor Jones 8 (+1), Peter Murray 7 (+3), Derek Cook 7 (+2), Graham Banks 6 (+1), Dave Gooderham 6, *Barney Kennett (R/R).*
CREWE - Geoff Ambrose 7 (+1), Wayne Forrest 7, Glyn Taylor 4 (+1), John Jackson 4, Keith White 4, Ian Cartwright 1, Peter Thompson 0.

Meeting 37 - Monday, August 13, 1973 - British League Division II
L.M.R. Sports Ground, Earle Street, Crewe
Track Length - 430 yards.

CREWE KINGS.....48 BERWICK BANDITS.....30

Lowly Berwick performed admirably at Earle Street, with the Templeton brothers responsible for eighteen of the final total. Geoff Ambrose was in imperious form, securing another home full house, and featured in the best race of the night in Heat 13. He and Berwick skipper Doug Templeton fought out a terrific duel, but Templeton's frantic efforts to overhaul the Crewe ace resulted in him bringing down his own team-mate Chris Quigley. Peter Thompson, in for Dave Morton, registered his first points in a Kings race jacket.

Heat 01	D.Templeton/**Taylor**/**Jackson**/Jones	72.2	3 - 3	03 - 03
Heat 02	**White**/Hollingworth/**Thompson**/Morter	72.4	**4 - 2**	07 - 05

(ABOVE) A much-changed Crewe outfit from the start of the campaign. (Left to right) Dave Morton, Glyn Taylor, Wayne Forrest, John Jackson, Keith White, Ian Cartwright, Len Silver and Geoff Ambrose. (BELOW LEFT) Aussie import Wayne Forrest and (BELOW RIGHT) Yorkshireman Ian "Mousetrap" Cartwright.

(ABOVE) Dave Morton tussles with former Crewe rider Barry Booth during Heat 3 of the Crewe versus Ellesmere Port match on June 25. In the background is Wayne Forrest.

(ABOVE) Wayne Forrest holds off Canterbury's Graham Banks and Peter Murray on August 11.

Heat 03	**Forrest**/W.Templeton/Quigley/**Cartwright**	74.2	3 - 3	10 - 08
Heat 04	**Ambrose**/**White**/Meldrum/Morter	71.8	**5 - 1**	15 - 09
Heat 05	D.Templeton/**Thompson**/Jones/**Forrest**	73.4	2 - 4	17 - 13
Heat 06	**Jackson**/Meldrum/**Taylor**/Hollingworth	73.0	**4 - 2**	21 - 15
Heat 07	**Ambrose**/W.Templeton/**White**/Quigley	72.4	**4 - 2**	25 - 17
Heat 08	D.Templeton/**Taylor**/Jones/**Thompson**	73.2	2 - 4	27 - 21
Heat 09	**Forrest**/Meldrum/**Cartwright**/Hollingworth (R)	74.2	**4 - 2**	31 - 23
Heat 10	**Taylor**/W.Templeton/Quigley/**Jackson** (R)	73.0	3 - 3	34 - 26
Heat 11	**Ambrose**/D.Templeton/**White**/Jones	73.2	**4 - 2**	38 - 28
Heat 12	**Jackson**/**Forrest**/W.Templeton/Meldrum	73.2	**5 - 1**	43 - 29
Heat 13	**Ambrose**/**Cartwright**/Quigley/D.Templeton (X)	73.0	**5 - 1**	48 - 30

CREWE - Geoff Ambrose 12, Wayne Forrest 8 (+1), Glyn Taylor 8, John Jackson 7 (+1), Keith White 7 (+1), Ian Cartwright 3 (+1), Peter Thompson 3.
BERWICK - Doug Templeton 11, Willie Templeton 7, Andy Meldrum 5, Chris Quigley 3 (+2), Rob Hollingworth 2, Graham Jones 2, Denny Morter 0.

Meeting 38 - Monday, August 20, 1973 - British League Division II
L.M.R. Sports Ground, Earle Street, Crewe
Track Length - 430 yards.

CREWE KINGS.....53 CHESTERTON POTTERS.....25

Russ Bragg's pre-match prediction that the Potters would end Crewe's long unbeaten home run seemed to have substance when they opened the match with a 5-1. This however, was the only heat advantage gained, as a solid display from the Kings gave them their joint-biggest victory of the season. Potters star Mike Broadbanks did little to endear himself to the home crowd when complaining to referee Bill Daff about the state of the track, after rain started to fall in Heat 11. During the second-half, Geoff Ambrose capped off a great night by snatching the Silver Helmet off Broadbanks.

Heat 01	Bridgett/Broadbanks/**Jackson**/**Taylor**	73.0	1 - 5	01 - 05
Heat 02	Wasley/**Cartwright**/**White**/Yeates	74.4	3 - 3	04 - 08
Heat 03	**Morton**/Woodward/**Forrest**/Handley	72.8	**4 - 2**	08 - 10
Heat 04	**Ambrose**/**White**/Wasley/Pusey	73.0	**5 - 1**	13 - 11
Heat 05	**Forrest**/Broadbanks/Bridgett/**Morton** (R)	73.4	3 - 3	16 - 14
Heat 06	**Jackson**/**Taylor**/Yeates/Pusey	73.2	**5 - 1**	21 - 15
Heat 07	**Ambrose**/Woodward/**White**/Handley (R)	73.4	**4 - 2**	25 - 17
Heat 08	**Taylor**/**Cartwright**/Wasley/Bridgett	73.6	**5 - 1**	30 - 18
Heat 09	**Morton**/Broadbanks/**Forrest**/Pusey	74.0	**4 - 2**	34 - 20
Heat 10	**Jackson**/**Taylor**/Bridgett/Woodward	74.6	**5 - 1**	39 - 21
Heat 11	**Ambrose**/**Cartwright**/Bridgett/Broadbanks	77.8	**5 - 1**	44 - 22
Heat 12	**Jackson**/Wasley/**Forrest**/Pusey	83.0	**4 - 2**	48 - 24
Heat 13	**Ambrose**/**Morton**/Broadbanks/Woodward	83.8	**5 - 1**	53 - 25

CREWE - Geoff Ambrose 12, John Jackson 10, Dave Morton 8 (+1), Glyn Taylor 7 (+2), Ian Cartwright 6 (+2), Wayne Forrest 6, Keith White 4 (+2).
CHESTERTON - Mike Broadbanks 7 (+1), Nigel Wasley 7, Alan Bridgett 6 (+1), Bryan Woodward 4, Martin Yeates 1, Mick Handley 0, Geoff Pusey 0.

Following the meeting, Australian Wayne Forrest left for home, after receiving word that his mother had been taken ill. The news came as a body blow to the club, as he had settled in well as a steady middle order rider. Kiwi Cliff Anderson finally signed a Crewe contract to plug the gap.

Meeting 39 - Saturday, August 25, 1973 - British League Division II
Rayleigh Weir Stadium, Southend Arterial Road, Rayleigh
Track Length - 365 yards.

RAYLEIGH ROCKETS.....39 CREWE KINGS.....39

Rayleigh raced into a twelve-point lead after six heats, only for the Kings to stage an incredible fight back, to snatch their first away point of the season. Reserve Keith White had a tremendous meeting, winning four of his six rides, and with John Jackson and Dave Morton bagging two heat victories apiece, the visitors were full value for the draw. Needing a 5-1 in the last heat, Crewe had some good fortune when Tiger Beech shed a chain on the start line. Peter Moore beat Geoff Ambrose in the Silver Helmet match-up.

Heat 01	Moore/Foote/**Jackson**/**Taylor**	70.4	5 - 1	05 - 01
Heat 02	Cairns/Ott/**Thompson**/**White**	69.6	5 - 1	10 - 02
Heat 03	Barnwell/**Morton**/Young/**Cartwright**	70.2	4 - 2	14 - 04
Heat 04	**White**/Beech/**Ambrose**/Ott	71.2	**2 - 4**	16 - 08
Heat 05	**Jackson**/Barnwell/Young/**Taylor**	70.6	3 - 3	19 - 11
Heat 06	Moore/Foote/**Ambrose**/**Thompson** (F)	71.0	5 - 1	24 - 12
Heat 07	**White**/Beech/**Morton**/Ott	70.8	**2 - 4**	26 - 16
Heat 08	**White**/**Jackson**/Foote/Cairns	71.0	**1 - 5**	27 - 21
Heat 09	**Morton**/Young/**Ambrose**/Barnwell	70.6	**2 - 4**	29 - 25
Heat 10	**Morton**/Moore/Foote/**Cartwright**	70.2	3 - 3	32 - 28
Heat 11	**Jackson**/Beech/Cairns/**White** (X)	71.2	3 - 3	35 - 31
Heat 12	Moore/**Ambrose**/**Morton**/Barnwell	70.4	3 - 3	38 - 34
Heat 13	**White**/**Jackson**/Young/Beech (R)	71.0	**1 - 5**	39 - 39

RAYLEIGH - Peter Moore 11, Brian Foote 6 (+3), Tiger Beech 6, Bob Young 5 (+1), Trevor Barnwell 5, Peter Cairns 4 (+1), Les Ott 2 (+1).
CREWE - Keith White 12, John Jackson 11 (+2), Dave Morton 10 (+1), Geoff Ambrose 5, Peter Thompson 1, Ian Cartwright 0, Glyn Taylor 0.

Meeting 40 - Monday, August 27, 1973 - M6 Trophy, Four Team Tournament, First Leg
L.M.R. Sports Ground, Earle Street, Crewe
Track Length - 430 yards.

CREWE KINGS.....40 CHESTERTON POTTERS.....22
ELLESMERE PORT GUNNERS.....17 BIRMINGHAM BRUMMIES.....17

With a possible forty-eight points at stake, the Kings made a great start to the M6 Trophy, dropping just eight points in the Earle Street leg, witnessed by a bumper Bank Holiday crowd of around 5,000. The only time Crewe failed to score was in Heat 6, when Geoff Ambrose developed motor trouble. Captain John Jackson remained unbeaten, and became the third rider to equal the track record in Heat 1.

			Cr	Ch	E	B
Heat 01....	**Jackson**/Booth/Pusey/Howgego	**71.2** (=TR)	3	1	2	0
Heat 02....	Drury/**Ambrose**/Herne/Broadbanks	73.6	2	0	3	1
Heat 03....	Corradine/**Morton**/Gardner/Woodward	73.0	2	0	1	3
Heat 04....	**Taylor**/Bridgett/Browning/Goad	72.6	3	2	0	1
Heat 05....	**Jackson**/Drury/Browning/Woodward	72.8	3	0	2	1
Heat 06....	Corradine/Bridgett/O'Neil/**Ambrose**	73.8	0	2	1	3
Heat 07....	Pusey/**Morton**/Goad/Herne	73.0	2	3	1	0
Heat 08....	Broadbanks/**Taylor**/Gardner/Howgego	73.0	2	3	1	0
Heat 09....	**Jackson**/Bridgett/Herne/Gardner (R)	73.8	3	2	0	1
Heat 10....	**White**/Goad/Wilson/Woodward	75.0	3	0	2	1
Heat 11....	**Morton**/Broadbanks/O'Neil/Browning	73.2	3	2	1	0
Heat 12....	**Taylor**/Drury/Corradine/Wasley	75.4	3	0	2	1
Heat 13....	Pusey/**White**/Browning/Gardner	74.2	2	3	0	1
Heat 14....	**Jackson**/Broadbanks/Corradine/Goad	73.4	3	2	0	1
Heat 15....	**Morton**/Bridgett/Wilson/Drury (R)	74.0	3	2	0	1
Heat 16....	**White**/Herne/O'Neil/Woodward	75.0	3	0	1	2

CREWE - John Jackson 12, Dave Morton 10, Glyn Taylor 8, Keith White (Reserve) 8, Geoff Ambrose 2.
CHESTERTON - Alan Bridgett 8, Mike Broadbanks 7, Geoff Pusey 7, Nigel Wasley (Reserve) 0, Bryan Woodward 0.
ELLESMERE PORT - Graham Drury 7, Colin Goad 3, Paul O'Neil 3, Barry Booth (Reserve) 2, Robbie Gardner 2.
BIRMINGHAM - Malcolm Corradine 8, Phil Herne 4, Arthur Browning 3, Steve Wilson (Reserve) 2, Ted Howgego 0.

Meeting 41 - Tuesday, August 28, 1973 - M6 Trophy, Four Team Tournament, Second Leg
Perry Barr Greyhound Stadium, Regina Drive, Walsall Road, Birmingham
Track Length - 350 yards.

BIRMINGHAM BRUMMIES.....32 ELLESMERE PORT GUNNERS.....30 CREWE KINGS.....17 CHESTERTON POTTERS.....17

(Scores after two legs - Crewe 57, Birmingham 49, Ellesmere Port 47, Chesterton 39)

John Jackson was the only race winner in a lacklustre Kings performance, as the Brummies and Gunners dominated this second leg at Perry Barr. Keith White was moved up from reserve to replace the absent Geoff Ambrose. Crewe still held an eight point lead overall.

		B	E	Cr	Ch
Heat 01..... **Jackson**/Drury/Broadbanks/Major	66.2	0	2	3	1
Heat 02..... O'Neil/Browning/**Morton**/Handley	66.6	2	3	1	0
Heat 03..... Lanham/Pusey/**White**/Goad	67.2	3	0	1	2
Heat 04..... Gardner/Corradine/Bridgett/**Taylor**	68.0	2	3	0	1
Heat 05..... O'Neil/Major/Bridgett/**White**	67.2	2	3	0	1
Heat 06..... Browning/Drury/**Taylor**/Pusey (F)	67.8	3	2	1	0
Heat 07..... Gardner/Lanham/**Jackson**/Yeates	67.6	2	3	1	0
Heat 08..... Broadbanks/Corradine/**Morton**/Goad (F)	66.6	2	0	1	3
Heat 09..... Major/Booth/Yeates/**Thompson** (R)	67.0	3	2	0	1
Heat 10..... Broadbanks/**White**/Browning/Gardner	66.2	1	0	2	3
Heat 11..... Lanham/**Morton**/Drury/Bridgett	66.8	3	1	2	0
Heat 12..... Corradine/Pusey/O'Neil/**Thompson** (R)	67.4	3	1	0	2
Heat 13..... Gardner/Major/**Morton**/Pusey	66.8	2	3	1	0
Heat 14..... **Jackson**/Booth/Hart/Bridgett	68.2	1	2	3	0
Heat 15..... Broadbanks/O'Neil/Lanham/**Taylor**	66.2	1	2	0	3
Heat 16..... Drury/Corradine/**White**/Handley	67.0	2	3	1	0

BIRMINGHAM - Malcolm Corradine 9, Mike Lanham 9, George Major 7, Arthur Browning 6, John Hart (Reserve) 1.
ELLESMERE PORT - Robbie Gardner 9, Paul O'Neil 9, Graham Drury 8, Barry Booth (Reserve) 4, Colin Goad 0.
CREWE - John Jackson 7, Dave Morton 5, Keith White 4, Glyn Taylor 1, Peter Thompson (Reserve) 0.
CHESTERTON - Mike Broadbanks 10, Geoff Pusey 4, Alan Bridgett 2, Martin Yeates (Reserve) 1, Mick Handley 0.

The M6 Trophy third leg at Ellesmere Port scheduled for the following night, was washed out due to heavy rain.

Meeting 42 - Thursday, August 30, 1973 - M6 Trophy, Four Team Tournament, Third Leg
Lyme Valley Sports Stadium, Loomer Road, Chesterton
Track Length - 380 yards.

ELLESMERE PORT GUNNERS.....34 BIRMINGHAM BRUMMIES.....27 CREWE KINGS.....19 CHESTERTON POTTERS.....16

(Scores after three legs - Ellesmere Port 81, Birmingham 76, Crewe 76, Chesterton 55)

Chesterton suffered a disastrous home leg, but the meeting served up some exhilarating speedway for the large Potteries crowd. Crewe once again struggled, with only John Jackson and Geoff Ambrose winning a race. Ellesmere Port duo Graham Drury and Paul O'Neil top scored to give the Gunners the overall lead, with the final leg at Thornton Road.

		E	B	Cr	Ch
Heat 01..... O'Neil/Broadbanks/Lanham/**D.Morton**	71.0	3	1	0	2
Heat 02..... Drury/Major/**Jackson**/Handley	71.8	3	2	1	0
Heat 03..... **Ambrose**/Corradine/Gardner/Pusey	72.0	1	2	3	0
Heat 04..... Browning/Booth/Bridgett/**Taylor**	71.8	2	3	0	1
Heat 05..... Drury/**Ambrose**/Browning/Broadbanks (R)	70.6	3	1	2	0
Heat 06..... O'Neil/**Taylor**/Handley/Corradine	71.6	3	0	2	1
Heat 07..... Pusey/**D.Morton**/C.Morton/Major	71.5	1	0	2	3
Heat 08..... Gardner/Lanham/Bridgett/**Jackson**	72.4	3	2	0	1

Heat 09..... Woodward/Gardner/Major/**Taylor**	71.6	2	1	0	3
Heat 10..... Lanham/**Ambrose**/Booth/Woodward	71.4	1	3	2	0
Heat 11 ..... Pusey/O'Neil/Browning/**White**	71.4	2	1	0	3
Heat 12..... Drury/**White**/Corradine/Bridgett	72.0	3	1	2	0
Heat 13..... Gardner/Browning/**D.Morton**/Handley	72.6	3	2	1	0
Heat 14..... **Jackson**/Corradine/Woodward/Booth (X)	72.5	0	2	3	1
Heat 15..... Lanham/Drury/Pusey/**White**	71.5	2	3	0	1
Heat 16..... Major/O'Neil/**Ambrose**/Woodward	72.0	2	3	1	0

ELLESMERE PORT - Graham Drury 11, Paul O'Neil 10, Robbie Gardner 9, Barry Booth 3, Chris Morton (Reserve) 1.
BIRMINGHAM - Mike Lanham 9, Arthur Browning 7, George Major 6, Malcolm Corradine 5.
CREWE - Geoff Ambrose 8, John Jackson 4, Dave Morton 3, Glyn Taylor 2, Keith White (Reserve) 2.
CHESTERTON - Geoff Pusey 7, Bryan Woodward (Reserve) 4, Alan Bridgett 2, Mike Broadbanks 2, Mick Handley 1.

Meeting 43 - Monday, September 3, 1973 - British League Division II
L.M.R. Sports Ground, Earle Street, Crewe
Track Length - 430 yards.

CREWE KINGS.....50 SUNDERLAND STARS.....27

With Jack Millen absent due to a gashed foot, and fellow Earle Street track maintenance man Jim Wells retiring early with a sick motor, the decimated Stars failed to provide a single heat advantage. John Jackson was back to his best, winning each time out for a second successive home maximum, and Peter Thompson recorded his first win in Crewe colours when he held off Brian Havelock in Heat 8.

Heat 01 .... **Jackson**/Gatenby/**Taylor** (R)/Wells (R)	74.6	**3 - 2**	03 - 02
Heat 02 .... **White**/**Thompson**/Barclay/Robson	73.6	**5 - 1**	08 - 03
Heat 03 .... Gatenby/**Cartwright**/**Morton**/Dent	75.8	3 - 3	11 - 06
Heat 04 .... **White**/**Ambrose**/Havelock/Barclay (R)	75.4	**5 - 1**	16 - 07
Heat 05 .... **Morton**/**Cartwright**/Robson/Wells	77.0	**5 - 1**	21 - 08
Heat 06 .... **Jackson**/Havelock/**Taylor**/Robson	75.8	**4 - 2**	25 - 10
Heat 07 .... **Ambrose**/Gatenby/Dent/**White** (R)	75.4	3 - 3	28 - 13
Heat 08 .... **Thompson**/Havelock/**Taylor**/Barclay	75.8	**4 - 2**	32 - 15
Heat 09 .... Havelock/**Morton**/**Cartwright**/Robson	75.0	3 - 3	35 - 18
Heat 10 .... **Jackson**/Gatenby/**White**/Barclay	75.0	**4 - 2**	39 - 20
Heat 11 .... Havelock/**Ambrose**/**Thompson** (3 riders only)	75.0	3 - 3	42 - 23
Heat 12 .... **Jackson**/Havelock/Gatenby/**Cartwright**	75.6	3 - 3	45 - 26
Heat 13 .... **Morton**/**Ambrose**/Robson/Pearce	75.6	**5 - 1**	50 - 27

CREWE - John Jackson 12, Geoff Ambrose 9 (+2), Dave Morton 9 (+1), Keith White 7, Peter Thompson 6 (+2), Ian Cartwright 5 (+2), Glyn Taylor 2.
SUNDERLAND - Brian Havelock 13, Dave Gatenby 10 (+1), John Robson 2, Russ Dent 1 (+1), Terry Barclay 1, Steve Pearce 0, Jim Wells 0, *Jack Millen (R/R)*.

Peter Thompson made it into the starting line-up via a pre-match "Vultures Race" against Cliff Anderson. Both riders fell, but Thompson got to his feet and pushed his bike to the line, earning himself the No.7 spot.

Meeting 44 - Tuesday, September 4, 1973 - British League Division II
Barrow Stadium, Holker Street, Barrow-in-Furness
Track Length - 415 yards.

BARROW BOMBERS.....58 CREWE KINGS.....20

Crewe team manager Tudor Blake was not a happy man after seeing his side crash to their joint biggest ever defeat. Due to several days of rainfall, the Holker Street track was not to Crewe's liking and Blake asked referee R. G. Owen to inspect the strip after five races had been concluded. Racing however continued, but only Glyn Taylor had any real success on the deteriorating surface. The Kings cause was not helped after Dave Morton pulled out of the meeting, following a Heat 3 retirement. Barrow's Owen brothers clearly revelled in the conditions, with both scoring maximum points.

Heat 01	Sampson/Sheldrick/**Taylor/Jackson** (R)	74.2	5 - 1	05 - 01
Heat 02	Pendlebury/**Anderson/Thompson**/Roynon (X)	73.8	3 - 3	08 - 04
Heat 03	J.Owen/Kelly/**Cartwright/Morton** (R)	74.4	5 - 1	13 - 05
Heat 04	T.Owen/Roynon/**White/Thompson**	72.2	5 - 1	18 - 06
Heat 05	J.Owen/**Jackson/Taylor**/Kelly (F)	76.0	3 - 3	21 - 09
Heat 06	Sampson/Sheldrick/**Anderson/White** (R)	74.2	5 - 1	26 - 10
Heat 07	T.Owen/Roynon/**Cartwright/Anderson**	72.4	5 - 1	31 - 11
Heat 08	Pendlebury/Sheldrick/**Taylor/Thompson**	75.0	5 - 1	36 - 12
Heat 09	J.Owen/Kelly/**White/Anderson**	74.2	5 - 1	41 - 13
Heat 10	Sheldrick/**Taylor**/Sampson/**Cartwright**	75.0	4 - 2	45 - 15
Heat 11	T.Owen/**Taylor/Jackson**/Pendlebury (R)	73.0	3 - 3	48 - 18
Heat 12	J.Owen/Sampson/**Cartwright/White**	73.2	5 - 1	53 - 19
Heat 13	T.Owen/Kelly/**Cartwright/White**	73.4	5 - 1	58 - 20

BARROW - Joe Owen 12, Tom Owen 12, Sid Sheldrick 9 (+3), Mike Sampson 9 (+1), Terry Kelly 6 (+3), Craig Pendlebury 6, Chris Roynon 4 (+2).
CREWE - Glyn Taylor 7 (+1), Ian Cartwright 4, John Jackson 3 (+1), Cliff Anderson 3, Keith White 2, Peter Thompson 1 (+1), Dave Morton 0.

Crewe's complaints about the Holker Street track had some justification. The lack of shale on the circuit prompted one locally based rider to comment: *"Barrow is like riding around a block of flats."* On September 8, Glyn Taylor rode for Australasia in the first Division II test against England at Canterbury, scoring one point in the 53-55 defeat. Meanwhile, speculation was mounting regarding the Division I licence of fellow APL track Reading being transferred to Earle Street, after their Tilehurst Stadium was to be demolished, ending a six year tenure.

Meeting 45 - Monday, September 10, 1973 - British League Division II
L.M.R. Sports Ground, Earle Street, Crewe
Track Length - 430 yards.

CREWE KINGS.....48 RAYLEIGH ROCKETS.....30

For many, a Crewe walkover was expected considering injury-ravaged Rayleigh arrived in South Cheshire bottom of the league and now minus the services of veteran heat leader Peter Moore (broken leg). This was reflected in the attendance, with one of the poorest ever recorded at Earle Street. However, the Rockets contributed to a highly competitive match, supplying three different race winners, with Brian Foote again showing his liking for the track, winning two. Dave Morton scored his first home maximum since April 16, and earned the right to challenge Trevor Barnwell for the Silver Helmet. All signs pointed to the title returning to Crewe, as the holder had only registered three points from his four rides, but he won the toss, chose gate position two, and shot from the tapes to retain his crown.

Heat 01	**Jackson/Taylor**/Foote/Beech	72.4	**5 - 1**	05 - 01
Heat 02	Ott/Gibbons/**Thompson/White** (R)	76.0	1 - 5	06 - 06
Heat 03	**Morton**/Foote/**Cartwright**/Barnwell	73.4	**4 - 2**	10 - 08
Heat 04	**Ambrose**/Ott/Young/**White**	74.4	3 - 3	13 - 11
Heat 05	**Morton/Cartwright**/Foote/Beech	73.8	**5 - 1**	18 - 12
Heat 06	**Jackson/Taylor**/Young/Gibbons	73.6	**5 - 1**	23 - 13
Heat 07	**Ambrose**/Barnwell/Ott/**White**	73.8	3 - 3	26 - 16
Heat 08	Foote/**White/Thompson**/Ott (F)	75.0	3 - 3	29 - 19
Heat 09	**Morton**/Young/**Cartwright**/Gibbons	74.0	**4 - 2**	33 - 21
Heat 10	Young/**Jackson/Taylor**/Barnwell	74.2	3 - 3	36 - 24
Heat 11	Foote/**Ambrose**/Ott/**Thompson**	74.4	2 - 4	38 - 28
Heat 12	**Jackson/Cartwright**/Barnwell/Young (R)	73.6	**5 - 1**	43 - 29
Heat 13	**Morton/Ambrose**/Ott/Foote (R)	73.6	**5 - 1**	48 - 30

CREWE - Dave Morton 12, John Jackson 11, Geoff Ambrose 10 (+1), Ian Cartwright 6 (+2), Glyn Taylor 5 (+3), Peter Thompson 2 (+1), Keith White 2.
RAYLEIGH - Brian Foote 10, Les Ott 8 (+1), Bob Young 7 (+1), Trevor Barnwell 3, John Gibbons 2 (+1), Tiger Beech 0, *Allan Emmett (R/R)*.

On September 12, Dave Morton scored four points for England at Hull in the Division II test decider with Australasia, won 64-44 by the colonials, who took the series 2-1. Peter Thompson's brief spell with the Kings ended when he returned to Australia after the expiration of his six-month visa.

Meeting 46 - Friday, September 14, 1973 - British League Division II
Derwent Park Stadium, Workington
Track Length - 398 yards.

WORKINGTON COMETS.....50 CREWE KINGS.....28

The Kings were well beaten by a Lou Sansom inspired Workington. Crewe started the match well enough - John Jackson leading home Glyn Taylor in Heat 1, with the pair then reversing their finishing positions to draw level in the fifth. The Comets then stepped up a gear, to record a comfortable victory. Geoff Ambrose again failed to show, and Ian Cartwright withdrew from the meeting following his opening ride, after he blew his motor while warming it up.

Heat 01	**Jackson**/**Taylor**/Owen/Graham	76.2	**1 - 5**	01 - 05
Heat 02	Watson/**White**/**Anderson**/Hornby (F)	78.2	3 - 3	04 - 08
Heat 03	Amundson/Mackay/**Morton**/**Cartwright**	79.0	5 - 1	09 - 09
Heat 04	Sansom/Watson/**White**/**Anderson**	75.4	5 - 1	14 - 10
Heat 05	**Taylor**/**Jackson**/Amundson/Mackay (F)	77.2	**1 - 5**	15 - 15
Heat 06	Owen/Graham/**White**/**Anderson** (X)	79.4	5 - 1	20 - 16
Heat 07	Sansom/Watson/**White**/**Anderson**	76.0	5 - 1	25 - 17
Heat 08	Graham/**Jackson**/**Taylor**/Hornby	77.2	3 - 3	28 - 20
Heat 09	Mackay/Amundson/**Morton**/**Anderson**	78.0	5 - 1	33 - 21
Heat 10	Graham/**Morton**/Owen/**Taylor**	79.2	4 - 2	37 - 23
Heat 11	Sansom/**Jackson**/Hornby/**White**	76.2	4 - 2	41 - 25
Heat 12	Owen/**Anderson**/Amundson/**Morton** (X)	80.8	4 - 2	45 - 27
Heat 13	Sansom/Mackay/**Jackson**/**White**	79.0	5 - 1	50 - 28

WORKINGTON - Lou Sansom 12, Mitch Graham 8 (+1), Taffy Owen 8, Malcolm Mackay 7 (+2), Steve Watson 7 (+2), Kym Amundson 7 (+1), Bernie Hornby 1.
CREWE - John Jackson 10 (+1), Glyn Taylor 6 (+2), Keith White 5, Dave Morton 4, Cliff Anderson 3 (+1), Ian Cartwright 0.

Meeting 47 - Monday, September 17, 1973 - British League Division II
L.M.R. Sports Ground, Earle Street, Crewe
Track Length - 430 yards.

CREWE KINGS.....48 HULL VIKINGS.....30

The final home league meeting saw Crewe stretch their Earle Street league win sequence to thirty-two. Dave Mills top-scored for the Vikings, thanks to the generosity of second-half rider Brian Chaldecott. On hearing that the Hull rider had lost a clutch spring in Heat 1, he came to his rescue by offering him the complete clutch assembly off his own bike, enabling the Aussie to complete his rides. John Jackson re-claimed the track record with a blistering opening ride of 71.0 seconds, and remained unbeaten throughout the evening – his third full-house in the last four home matches. Keith White won his first three races, but was robbed of his first maximum due to a retirement in Heat 11. Glyn Taylor, riding in his final meeting of the season due to his visa expiring, saw his night ruined after a tappet securing screw broke in his first race.

Heat 01	**Jackson**/Mills/**Taylor**/Austin	**71.0** (TR)	**4 - 2**	04 - 02
Heat 02	**White**/**Anderson**/Dawson/Argall	73.2	**5 - 1**	09 - 03
Heat 03	**Morton**/Gavros/**Cartwright**/Cowland	71.8	**4 - 2**	13 - 05
Heat 04	**White**/Cowland/**Ambrose**/Argall	73.8	**4 - 2**	17 - 07
Heat 05	**Morton**/**Cartwright**/Mills/Austin	71.6	**5 - 1**	22 - 08
Heat 06	**Jackson**/Cowland/Dawson/**Taylor** (R)	72.6	3 - 3	25 - 11
Heat 07	**White**/Mills/**Ambrose**/Gavros	73.8	**4 - 2**	29 - 13
Heat 08	Mills/Cowland/**Anderson**/**White**	73.6	1 - 5	30 - 18
Heat 09	**Morton**/**Cartwright**/Dawson/Cowland (R)	73.6	**5 - 1**	35 - 19
Heat 10	**Jackson**/Gavros/**Anderson**/Mullarkey	73.0	**4 - 2**	39 - 21

Heat 11	Mills/**Ambrose**/Mullarkey/**White** (R)	73.4	2 - 4	41 - 25
Heat 12	**Jackson**/Cowland/**Cartwright**/Gavros	73.4	**4 - 2**	45 - 27
Heat 13	Mills/**Morton**/**Ambrose**/Mullarkey	73.4	3 - 3	48 - 30

CREWE - John Jackson 12, Dave Morton 11, Keith White 9, Ian Cartwright 6 (+2), Geoff Ambrose 5 (+1), Cliff Anderson 4 (+1), Glyn Taylor 1.
HULL - Dave Mills 14, Alan Cowland 8 (+1), Dennis Gavros 4, Grahame Dawson 3 (+1), Kelvin Mullarkey 1, Eddie Argall 0, Roger Austin 0, *Tony Childs (R/R).*

The re-arranged leg of the M6 Trophy at Ellesmere Port was again washed out on September 18, and was now unlikely to be staged unless a date could be found in the last few weeks of the season. On September 21, Dave Morton put all his injury and mechanical problems behind him to win the K.R.C. £100 Trophy meeting at Peterborough.

Meeting 48 - Saturday, September 22, 1973 - British League Division II
Shielfield Park, Tweedmouth, Berwick-upon-Tweed
Track Length - 440 yards.

BERWICK BANDITS.....48 CREWE KINGS.....29

A weakened Crewe team made the long trip to Berwick, and were no match for the home side. With Wayne Forrest, Glyn Taylor and Peter Thompson now back in Australia and Geoff Ambrose failing to make the journey, Cliff Anderson was moved up into the main body of the side, with Sunderland junior Lloyd Dobson and Ashington's Robin Dixon completing the Crewe line-up at reserve. Dave Morton won his first race, but retired in his other two due to engine problems, as only John Jackson, with three wins, put up any real resistance. Berwick reserve Graham Jones collected a well-deserved paid maximum.

Heat 01	**Jackson**/Meldrum/**White**/Morter	76.4	**2 - 4**	02 - 04
Heat 02	Jones/**Dixon**/**Dobson**/Olivier (R)	78.6	3 - 3	05 - 07
Heat 03	**Morton**/Templeton/**Cartwright**/Hollingworth	77.8	**2 - 4**	07 - 11
Heat 04	Jones/Meldrum/**Dixon**/**Anderson**	79.0	5 - 1	12 - 12
Heat 05	Templeton/**Jackson**/**White**/Hollingworth (R)	79.8	3 - 3	15 - 15
Heat 06	Meldrum/Morter/**Anderson**/**Dobson**	80.2	5 - 1	20 - 16
Heat 07	Morter/Jones/**Cartwright**/**Morton** (R)	79.8	5 - 1	25 - 17
Heat 08	**Jackson**/Morter/Olivier/**White**	78.4	3 - 3	28 - 20
Heat 09	Templeton/Jones/**Dixon**/**Anderson**	79.6	5 - 1	33 - 21
Heat 10	Meldrum/**Cartwright**/Morter (R)/**Morton** (R)	78.6	3 - 2	36 - 23
Heat 11	**Jackson**/Templeton/Olivier/**White**	78.8	3 - 3	39 - 26
Heat 12	Meldrum/**Cartwright**/Hollingworth/**Anderson**	78.2	4 - 2	43 - 28
Heat 13	Jones/Templeton/**Jackson**/**Cartwright**	77.8	5 - 1	48 - 29

BERWICK - Graham Jones 13 (+2), Andy Meldrum 13 (+1), Willie Templeton 12 (+1), Denny Morter 7 (+1), Ettienne Olivier 2 (+2), Rob Hollingworth 1, *Doug Templeton (R/R).*
CREWE - John Jackson 12, Ian Cartwright 6, Robin Dixon* 4, Dave Morton 3, Keith White 2 (+1), Lloyd Dobson* 1 (+1), Cliff Anderson 1.

Boston took a giant step towards securing the double on September 23, after hammering Workington 58-19 in the first leg of the K.O. Cup final. Meanwhile, Len Silver was already making plans for next season, offering contracts to local juniors Stuart Cope, Charlie Turner and grass tracker Colin Pemberton, who had impressed during a practice session at Earle Street.

Meeting 49 - Monday, September 24, 1973 - Challenge
L.M.R. Sports Ground, Earle Street, Crewe
Track Length - 430 yards.

CREWE KINGS.....44 STARS OF THE LEAGUE.....34

Birthday boy Dave Morton faced younger brother Chris, who lined-up for the Stars of the League side, and it was Dave who came out on top, outscoring him nine to two. The match started with Workington's Lou Sansom clipping a fifth of a second off John Jackson's week old track record, and in the next, Stuart Cope made a dream start to his debut, winning his first race.

Juniors Charlie Turner and Mick Mellor were given a chance in the Stars team after programmed riders, Mitch Graham and Roger Wright failed to arrive.

Heat 01	Sansom/**Jackson/White**/Forrester	**70.8** (TR)	3 - 3	03 - 03
Heat 02	**Cope/Anderson**/Turner/Mellor	74.8	**5 - 1**	08 - 04
Heat 03	**D.Morton**/Pusey/C.Morton/**Cartwright** (R)	71.2	3 - 3	11 - 07
Heat 04	**Ambrose**/Gatenby/**Anderson**/Turner	71.8	**4 - 2**	15 - 09
Heat 05	Sansom/**D.Morton**/Forrester/**Cartwright**	71.6	2 - 4	17 - 13
Heat 06	**White/Jackson**/Gatenby/Mellor	71.6	**5 - 1**	22 - 14
Heat 07	**Ambrose**/Pusey/**Anderson**/C.Morton (R)	71.8	**4 - 2**	26 - 16
Heat 08	Sansom/**White**/Forrester/**Cope**	71.6	2 - 4	28 - 20
Heat 09	Pusey/**D.Morton/Cartwright**/Gatenby	73.0	3 - 3	31 - 23
Heat 10	**Jackson**/Pusey/C.Morton/**White** (R)	72.4	3 - 3	34 - 26
Heat 11	Sansom/**Ambrose**/Forrester/**Cope**	72.0	2 - 4	36 - 30
Heat 12	**Jackson**/Pusey/Gatenby/**Cartwright**	73.2	3 - 3	39 - 33
Heat 13	**Ambrose/D.Morton**/Sansom/Turner	74.8	**5 - 1**	44 - 34

CREWE - Geoff Ambrose 11, John Jackson 10 (+1), Dave Morton 9 (+1), Keith White 6 (+1), Cliff Anderson 4 (+1), Stuart Cope 3, Ian Cartwright 1 (+1).
STARS OF THE LEAGUE - Lou Sansom *(Workington)* 13, Geoff Pusey *(Chesterton)* 11, Dave Gatenby *(Sunderland)* 4 (+1), Bruce Forrester *(Teesside)* 3, Chris Morton *(Ellesmere Port)* 2 (+2), Charlie Turner 1, Mick Mellor 0.

It was announced that Geoff Ambrose had qualified as Crewe's representative for the Division II Riders Championship at Wimbledon, but was withdrawn in favour of Dave Morton by the Kings management for disciplinary reasons, after failing to turn up at several away fixtures due to work commitments.

Meeting 50 - Tuesday, September 25, 1973 - British League Division II
Ellesmere Port Stadium, Thornton Road, Ellesmere Port
Track Length - 423 yards.

ELLESMERE PORT GUNNERS.....41 CREWE KINGS.....37

After six attempts, the Gunners finally achieved a first win in league or cup competition against their Cheshire neighbours, despite Colin Goad having night to forget. Former Crewe second-halfer Gerald Smitherman scored an important five points, which included a win in Heat 2. John Jackson missed out on a maximum, after a first ride defeat. Crewe's final league match however, was not without incident, after the referee changed the result of Heat 3 on no fewer than three occasions, after Chris Morton was originally deemed responsible for bringing down his brother. Following the next race, the meeting was delayed ten minutes for track repairs and to remove a patch of loose shale on the pits bend.

Heat 01	Gardner/**Jackson/White**/Drury	75.0	3 - 3	03 - 03
Heat 02	Smitherman/**Cope/Anderson**/Booth (R)	79.8	3 - 3	06 - 06
Heat 03	C.Morton/**Cartwright**/Smitherman/**D.Morton** (F)	77.4	4 - 2	10 - 08
Heat 04	O'Neil/**Anderson**/Booth/**Ambrose** (F)	80.0	4 - 2	14 - 10
Heat 05	**Jackson/White**/C.Morton/Smitherman	76.0	**1 - 5**	15 - 15
Heat 06	Gardner/Drury/**Ambrose/Cope**	76.4	5 - 1	20 - 16
Heat 07	O'Neil/**D.Morton/Cartwright**/Booth	78.0	3 - 3	23 - 19
Heat 08	Gardner/**White**/Smitherman/**Anderson** (X)	00.0	4 - 2	27 - 21
Heat 09	**Jackson**/C.Morton/**Ambrose**/Goad	75.8	**2 - 4**	29 - 25
Heat 10	Drury/**D.Morton**/Gardner/**Cartwright**	77.4	4 - 2	33 - 27
Heat 11	**Jackson**/O'Neil/**White**/Smitherman	77.0	**2 - 4**	35 - 31
Heat 12	Drury/C.Morton/**Ambrose/D.Morton**	77.8	5 - 1	40 - 32
Heat 13	**Jackson/Cartwright**/O'Neil/Goad	77.0	**1 - 5**	41 - 37

ELLESMERE PORT - Robbie Gardner 10, Paul O'Neil 9, Graham Drury 8 (+1), Chris Morton 8 (+1), Gerald Smitherman 5, Barry Booth 1, Colin Goad 0.
CREWE - John Jackson 14, Keith White 6 (+2), Ian Cartwright 5 (+2), Dave Morton 4, Cliff Anderson 3 (+1), Geoff Ambrose 3, Stuart Cope 2.

On September 26, Workington's 35-42 defeat at Hull confirmed Boston as league champions. Next night, Keith White finished second in the Lunn-Poly Individual Trophy at Long Eaton, and on September 28, Boston repeated Crewe's achievements of the previous season, by completing the double, winning the K.O. Cup, despite losing the second leg 47-31 at Derwent Park. Two nights later, Dave Morton scored a point from his only outing in England's narrow 54-53 win over Sweden in the opening Division II test at Eastbourne.

Meeting 51 - Monday, October 1, 1973 - Division II International, Second Test
L.M.R. Sports Ground, Earle Street, Crewe
Track Length - 430 yards.

ENGLAND.....77 SWEDEN.....31

Skipper Dave Morton, along with Geoff Ambrose and John Jackson, contributed forty points to the Lions total, as the tourist received a thumping. Tommy Nilsson, with two race wins and twelve points, was the only plus in a poor Swedish performance. Peterborough's John Davis topped the score charts with a paid seventeen.

Heat 01	Morton/Jackson/Enecrona/Claesson	72.4	5 - 1	05 - 01
Heat 02	Davis/S.Nilsson/Graham/Smith	72.6	4 - 2	09 - 03
Heat 03	Ambrose/Bales/Selmosson/T.Nilsson (R)	73.8	5 - 1	14 - 04
Heat 04	Davis/Graham/Claesson/Enecrona	73.6	5 - 1	19 - 05
Heat 05	Ambrose/Smith/Bales/S.Nilsson	73.6	4 - 2	23 - 07
Heat 06	Morton/T.Nilsson/Jackson/Selmosson	73.4	4 - 2	27 - 09
Heat 07	Ambrose/Claesson/Enecrona/Bales	73.6	3 - 3	30 - 12
Heat 08	Jackson/Morton/Salomonsson/Smith	73.0	5 - 1	35 - 13
Heat 09	Davis/T.Nilsson/Hellsén/Graham (R)	73.4	3 - 3	38 - 16
Heat 10	Morton/Jackson/Claesson/Enecrona	74.0	5 - 1	43 - 17
Heat 11	Davis/Drury/Hellsén/S.Nilsson	74.0	5 - 1	48 - 18
Heat 12	Bales/T.Nilsson/Ambrose/Selmosson	73.0	4 - 2	52 - 20
Heat 13	Davis/Graham/Enecrona/Claesson	74.0	5 - 1	57 - 21
Heat 14	Bales/Ambrose/Smith/S.Nilsson	72.6	5 - 1	62 - 22
Heat 15	T.Nilsson/Jackson/Morton/Salomonsson	73.0	3 - 3	65 - 25
Heat 16	Bales/Hellsén/Ambrose/Enecrona	73.4	4 - 2	69 - 27
Heat 17	Morton/Jackson/Smith/Salomonsson (F)	74.6	5 - 1	74 - 28
Heat 18	T.Nilsson/Graham/Davis/Selmosson	73.4	3 - 3	77 - 31

ENGLAND - John Davis 16 (+1), Dave Morton 15 (+2), Geoff Ambrose 13 (+1), John Jackson 12 (+3), Ray Bales 12 (+1), Mitch Graham 7 (+2), Graham Drury (Reserve) 2 (+1). Team Manager: Ian Thomas.
SWEDEN - Tommy Nilsson 12, Richard Hellsén (Reserve) 4 (+1), Karl-Eric Claesson 4, Peter Smith 4, Leif Enecrona 3 (+1), Sven Nilsson 2, Stefan Salomonsson (Reserve) 1, Kenneth Selmosson 1. Team Manager: Kim Malmberg.

Saturday, October 6, 1973 - British League Division II Riders Championship
Wimbledon Stadium, Plough Lane, London
Track Length - 309 yards.

WINNER.....ARTHUR PRICE

Boston completed their own treble, when Arthur Price won the title at Wimbledon after a run-off with Bobby McNeil (Eastbourne) and the pre-meeting favourite Lou Sansom (Workington). Dave Morton scored three points from his first two rides, but was excluded after colliding with Rayleigh's Bob Young in his next, and was forced to pull out of the meeting.

Heat 01	Forrester/McNeil/Mills/Drury	63.9
Heat 02	Baugh/**Morton**/Kennett/Owen	65.0
Heat 03	Sansom/Greer/Browning/Bouchard	65.6
Heat 04	Price/Wells/Broadbanks/McKinlay (R)	67.1
Heat 05	McNeil/Baugh/Sansom/Broadbanks	64.7
Heat 06	Drury/Price/Browning/Kennett	65.6
Heat 07	Forrester/Bouchard/**Morton**/Wells	66.7
Heat 08	Greer/McKinlay/Templeton/Owen (X)	66.7
Heat 09	McNeil/McKinlay/Kennett/Bouchard	66.4

Heat 10	Baugh/Drury/Greer/Wells	67.3
Heat 11	Forrester/Sansom/Price/Owen	66.3
Heat 12	Broadbanks/Browning/Young/Morton (X)	66.4
Heat 13	Price/Greer/McNeil/Templeton	66.5
Heat 14	Broadbanks/Drury/Bouchard/Owen (F)	66.6
Heat 15	Baugh/Forrester/Browning/McKinlay	65.8
Heat 16	Sansom/Kennett/Wells/Young (F)	67.9
Heat 17	McNeil/Browning/Owen/Wells	67.0
Heat 18	Sansom/Drury/Templeton (3 riders only)	66.5
Heat 19	Broadbanks/Greer/Kennett/Forrester (F)	66.1
Heat 20	Price/Bouchard/Templeton/Baugh (F)	66.9
R/O for 1st......	Price/McNeil/Sansom	66.3

Arthur Price *(Boston)* 12, Bobby McNeil *(Eastbourne)* 12, Lou Sansom *(Workington)* 12, Bruce Forrester *(Teesside)* 11, Dave Baugh *(Bradford)* 11, Mike Broadbanks *(Chesterton)* 10, Richard Greer *(Peterborough)* 10, Graham Drury *(Ellesmere Port)* 9, Arthur Browning *(Birmingham)* 7, Barney Kennett *(Canterbury)* 5, Geoff Bouchard *(Long Eaton)* 5, Ken McKinlay *(Scunthorpe)* 4, Dave Morton *(Crewe)* 3, Dave Mills *(Hull)* 1, Tom Owen *(Barrow)* 1, Jim Wells *(Sunderland)* 3. Meeting Reserves: Willie Templeton *(Berwick)* 3, Bob Young *(Rayleigh)* 1. *(Morton replaced Geoff Ambrose.)*

Meeting 52 - Monday, October 8, 1973 - Revenge Challenge, First Leg
L.M.R. Sports Ground, Earle Street, Crewe
Track Length - 430 yards.

CREWE KINGS.....41 CHESTERTON POTTERS.....37

Ian Cartwright's first paid maximum of the season, helped Crewe to a narrow first leg lead over Chesterton. In Heat 5, he achieved the fastest time of the night, and his partnership with Dave Morton resulted in three 5-1's. The Potters led by two after nine heats and an upset was on the cards, until a determined fight back saw the Kings edge home in the last team fixture of the season at Earle Street.

Heat 01	**Jackson**/Broadbanks/Woodward/**White**	72.6	3 - 3	03 - 03
Heat 02	Francis/Wasley/**Anderson**/**Cope**	75.0	1 - 5	04 - 08
Heat 03	**Morton**/**Cartwright**/Woodward/Bridgett	72.6	**5 - 1**	09 - 09
Heat 04	Wasley/Pusey/**Ambrose**/**Anderson**	73.8	1 - 5	10 - 14
Heat 05	**Cartwright**/**Morton**/Broadbanks/Woodward (R)	72.0	**5 - 1**	15 - 15
Heat 06	Francis/Pusey/**White**/**Jackson** (R)	74.4	1 - 5	16 - 20
Heat 07	Bridgett/**Ambrose**/Wasley/**Anderson** (F)	74.4	2 - 4	18 - 24
Heat 08	**Morton**/Woodward/Wasley/**White** (R)	73.8	3 - 3	21 - 27
Heat 09	**Morton**/**Cartwright**/Francis/Pusey	73.2	**5 - 1**	26 - 28
Heat 10	**Jackson**/Broadbanks/**White**/Bridgett (R)	73.0	**4 - 2**	30 - 30
Heat 11	Woodward/**Ambrose**/**Cope**/Francis	74.8	3 - 3	33 - 33
Heat 12	**Jackson**/**Cartwright**/Wasley/Pusey	74.0	**5 - 1**	38 - 34
Heat 13	Broadbanks/**Ambrose**/**Morton**/Pusey	72.2	3 - 3	41 - 37

CREWE - Dave Morton 12 (+2), Ian Cartwright 9 (+3), John Jackson 9, Geoff Ambrose 7, Keith White 2, Stuart Cope 1 (+1), Cliff Anderson 1.
CHESTERTON - Nigel Wasley 8 (+2), Mike Broadbanks 8, Bryan Woodward 7 (+1), Cyril Francis 7, Geoff Pusey 4 (+2), Alan Bridgett 3, *Roger Parker (R/R).*

On October 15, Crewe's end-of-season Littlechild £100 trophy meeting was postponed due to thirty-six hours of heavy rain. Len Silver, desperate to re-stage it, decided to extend the season by a week. The prize money had been donated by Littlechild's haulage company.

Meeting 53 - Monday, October 22, 1973 - Littlechild £100 Trophy
L.M.R. Sports Ground, Earle Street, Crewe
Track Length - 430 yards.

WINNER.....JOHN JACKSON

John Jackson ended the season in style, going through the card to win the Littlechild Trophy, which had replaced the traditional Chester Vase meeting. The track, liberally coated with sawdust after continual rain, posed no problems for the Crewe skipper, and his time of 71.2 in Heat 3 was only just outside the track record. In the circumstances, the circuit held up well, but Jack Millen's night ended with a trip to hospital after a fall in Heat 6.

Heat 01	Owen/O'Neil/Cartwright (F)/Beech (R)	72.6
Heat 02	Millen/Baugh/Adlington/Wells	72.0
Heat 03	Jackson/Cowland/Kelly/Ambrose	71.2
Heat 04	White/Morton/Bridgett/Pusey	74.0
Heat 05	Owen/Ambrose/Adlington/Pusey (R)	73.8
Heat 06	Cowland/Cartwright/Bridgett/Millen (F)	75.0
Heat 07	Morton/Wells/Anderson/Kelly	73.6
Heat 08	Jackson/Baugh/O'Neil/White	72.2
Heat 09	Owen/Kelly/White/Cope (F)	74.4
Heat 10	Jackson/Morton/Cartwright/Adlington	71.8
Heat 11	Baugh/Bridgett/Ambrose/Anderson	74.8
Heat 12	Cowland/Pusey/O'Neil/Wells	75.6
Heat 13	Jackson/Owen/Bridgett/Wells	72.2
Heat 14	Cartwright/Baugh/Pusey/Kelly (F)	74.4
Heat 15	Cowland/White/Adlington/Anderson	75.8
Heat 16	Morton/Ambrose/Cope/O'Neil	74.2
Heat 17	Baugh/Owen/Morton/Cowland (R)	74.6
Heat 18	Cartwright/White/Ambrose/Wells	74.2
Heat 19	Jackson/Pusey/Anderson/Cope	73.6
Heat 20	Adlington/Bridgett/O'Neil/Kelly	75.6

John Jackson 15, Tom Owen 13, Dave Baugh 12, Alan Cowland 11, Chris Morton 11, Ian Cartwright 9, Keith White 8, Alan Bridgett 7, Robin Adlington 6, Geoff Ambrose 6, Paul O'Neil 5, Geoff Pusey 5, Jack Millen 3, Terry Kelly 3, Jim Wells 2, Tiger Beech 0. Meeting Reserves: Cliff Anderson 2, Stuart Cope 1. *(Beech replaced Dave Morton and Wells replaced Tony Childs.)*

Following the meeting presentations, the scorers in the season-long second half Boot & Shoe Snowball received their awards. The top three were:- 1. Dave Morton 38 points (£50), 2. Geoff Ambrose 33 points (£20) and 3. John Jackson 23 points (£10). On October 23, a final attempt to stage the Ellesmere Port leg of the M6 Trophy was once again thwarted by rain, so would now be run at the start of next season.

Meeting 54 - Wednesday, October 31, 1973 - Revenge Challenge, Second Leg
Lyme Valley Sports Stadium, Loomer Road, Chesterton
Track Length - 380 yards.

CHESTERTON POTTERS.....41 CREWE KINGS.....34

(Chesterton won on aggregate 78 - 75)

Geoff Ambrose once again failed to honour a fixture, prompting Len Silver to announce that he had ridden his last race for the club. Barney Kennett guested for Dave Morton (broken finger) and Potters junior Andy Cusworth replaced Ambrose. Chesterton wiped out Crewe's slender advantage by Heat 3, but still needed a point in the last race to win on aggregate. Mike Broadbanks secured another Loomer Road maximum against the Kings, and John Jackson finished his season off with thirteen points from five rides, including a win in Heat 11 when he was the only finisher.

Heat 01	Broadbanks/**Jackson**/**White**/Francis	70.4	3 - 3	03 - 03
Heat 02	Holden/**Cope**/Wasley/**Anderson**	71.3	4 - 2	07 - 05
Heat 03	Bridgett/**Kennett**/Woodward/**Cartwright**	71.5	4 - 2	11 - 07
Heat 04	Pusey/Holden/**Anderson**/**Cusworth**	72.0	5 - 1	16 - 08
Heat 05	**Jackson**/Bridgett/**White**/Woodward (F)	71.2	**2 - 4**	18 - 12
Heat 06	Broadbanks/**Jackson**/Francis/**Cope**	70.0	4 - 2	22 - 14
Heat 07	Holden/**Cartwright**/**Kennett**/Pusey (R)	71.5	3 - 3	25 - 17
Heat 08	Francis/**Kennett**/Wasley/**White**	71.5	4 - 2	29 - 19
Heat 09	Bridgett/**Cope**/**Cartwright**/Woodward (F)	71.0	3 - 3	32 - 22
Heat 10	Broadbanks/**Kennett**/**Cartwright**/Francis	70.8	3 - 3	35 - 25
Heat 11	**Jackson**/Pusey (R)/Holden (R)/**Cope** (F)	71.4	**0 - 3**	35 - 28
Heat 12	Broadbanks/**Kennett**/Bridgett/**Cusworth**	71.0	4 - 2	39 - 30
Heat 13	**Jackson**/Pusey/**Cartwright**/Woodward	71.2	**2 - 4**	41 - 34

CHESTERTON - Mike Broadbanks 12, Alan Bridgett 9, Steve Holden 8 (+1), Geoff Pusey 5, Cyril Francis 4, Nigel Wasley 2, Bryan Woodward 1.
CREWE - John Jackson 13, Barney Kennett* 9 (+1), Ian Cartwright 5 (+2), Stuart Cope 4, Keith White 2 (+1), Cliff Anderson 1, Andy Cusworth* 0.

Geoff Ambrose, who missed the match due to a bent valve in his engine, announced his retirement. On signing for the Kings at the start of the season, he had stipulated he would only ride when business commitments allowed; an agreement he had made with Len Silver. With the British speedway season concluded, many of the colonial riders headed home to continue racing in warmer climes. On December 14, former Crewe ace Geoff Curtis crashed during Heat 11 of the New South Wales Championship at the Sydney Showground (Royale), Moore Park. An accidental collision with the machine of Birmingham rider Phil Herne saw him loose control and fall between his bike and the concrete safety fence, receiving fatal head injuries. He passed away in hospital a few hours after the accident. Just a few months previous, he had helped his Reading team to the Division I title.

Looking at season facts, it was hardly surprising that the Kings lost their league title and K.O. Cup too. In the end they finished 8th in the table - their lowest position since formation, and failed to win a single away meeting, picking up their only point at bottom of the table Rayleigh. The team that represented Crewe was hardly recognisable from the double winning squad. Gone was Phil Crump - with Garry Flood, the reliable Dai Evans, and Gary Moore, all retiring in the opening weeks of the campaign - the latter literally disappearing from the face of the earth. Dave Parry announced his retirement mid-term following a downturn in form, and the highly experienced Chum Taylor never had the opportunity to show the Earle Street faithful what he could offer. Dave O'Connor arrived at the end of May, but was back home by early June, and Wayne Forrest left for Australia in August due to a family illness. All this turmoil would have upset even the most organised of teams, but add to the facts that Dave Morton was plagued with injury and mechanical problems throughout, John Jackson's average dropped by a point and a half, and Geoff Ambrose didn't turn-up at five away fixtures, the Kings did extremely well to finish in the top half of the table and remain unbeaten at Earle Street in league and cup competition. Len Silver promised a better team that would again challenge for the league crown in 1974.

- 1973 Season Summary -

				Wins to Crewe	
Date	**Opponents/Meeting**	**Res**	**Score**	**Race**	**Heat**
Fri, March 23	Workington (Ch)	L	29 - 49	4	0
Tue, March 27	Barrow (Ch)	L	31 - 47	6	2
Mon, April 9	**Workington (Ch)**	L	33 - 45	6	3
Mon, April 16	**Peterborough (BL)**	W	43 - 35	9	6
Tue, April 17	Ellesmere Port (Ch)	L	36 - 42	6	3
Mon, April 23	**Birmingham (Ch)**	W	43 - 34	10	5
Tue, April 24	Birmingham (Ch)	L	26 - 52	4	1
Sat, April 28	Canterbury (Ch)	L	28 - 50	6	2
Mon, May 7	**World C'ship QR (Ind)**	Mitch Graham		-	-
Fri, May 11	Peterborough (BL)	L	37 - 41	9	4
Mon, May 14	**Bradford (BL)**	W	46½ - 31½	11	7
Sun, May 20	Eastbourne (BL)	L	29 - 48	4	1
Mon, May 21	**Barrow (BL)**	W	42 - 36	9	5
Fri, May 25	Sunderland (BL)	L	25 - 53	0	0
Mon, May 28	**Birmingham (BL)**	W	39 - 38	8	4
Tue, May 29	Birmingham (BL)	L	26 - 52	2	1
Thu, May 31	Chesterton (Ch)	L	35 - 41	6	5
Sun, June 3	Boston (KOC R2)	L	20 - 58	0	0
Mon, June 4	**Boston (KOC R2)**	W	44 - 34	8	5
Mon, June 11	**Workington (BL)**	W	43 - 35	10	7
Thu, June 14	Long Eaton (BL)	L	37 - 41	6	5

Mon, June 18	**Chesterton (Ch)**	W	46 - 32	8	7
Wed, June 20	Bradford (BL)	L	24 - 54	3	1
Mon, June 25	**Ellesmere Port (BL)**	W	42 - 36	9	5
Sun, July 1	Scunthorpe (BL)	L	23 - 55	1	0
Mon, July 2	**Scunthorpe (BL)**	W	42 - 36	8	4
Thu, July 5	Teesside (BL)	L	22 - 56	1	0
Mon, July 9	**Eastbourne (BL)**	W	48 - 30	10	8
Wed, July 11	Hull (BL)	L	30 - 48	4	2
Mon, July 16	**Long Eaton (BL)**	W	53 - 25	12	8
Mon, July 23	**Teesside (BL)**	W	46 - 32	12	6
Thu, July 26	Chesterton (BL)	L	36 - 41	6	5
Mon, July 30	**Canterbury (BL)**	W	52 - 26	10	10
Sun, August 5	Boston (BL)	L	34 - 44	5	1
Mon, August 6	**Boston (BL)**	W	42 - 36	7	7
Sat, August 11	Canterbury (BL)	L	27 - 51	4	2
Mon, August 13	**Berwick (BL)**	W	48 - 30	10	8
Mon, August 20	**Chesterton (BL)**	W	53 - 25	11	10
Sat, August 25	Rayleigh (BL)	D	39 - 39	8	5
Mon, August 27	**Ell/Che/Bir (4TT)**	W	Crewe 40	10	-
Tue, August 28	Bir/Ell/Che (4TT)	L	Crewe 17	2	-
Thu, August 30	Che/Bir/Ell (4TT)	L	Crewe 19	2	-
Mon, September 3	**Sunderland (BL)**	W	50 - 27	10	8
Tue, September 4	Barrow (BL)	L	20 - 58	0	0
Mon, September 10	**Rayleigh (BL)**	W	48 - 30	9	7
Fri, September 14	Workington (BL)	L	28 - 50	2	2
Mon, September 17	**Hull (BL)**	W	48 - 30	10	9
Sat, September 22	Berwick (BL)	L	29 - 48	4	2
Mon, September 24	**Stars of the League (Ch)**	W	44 - 34	8	5
Tue, September 25	Ellesmere Port (BL)	L	37 - 41	4	4
Mon, October 1	**England v Sweden (Int)**	-	77 - 31	-	-
Mon, October 8	**Chesterton (Ch)**	W	41 - 37	7	5
Mon, October 22	**Littlechild £100 Tr. (Ind)**	John Jackson		-	-
Wed, October 31	Chesterton (Ch)	L	34 - 41	3	3

- British League Division II Final Table -

		Home					Away					
	M	W	D	L	F	A	W	D	L	F	A	Pts
1. Boston	33	17	0	0	853	471	12	0	4	653	590	58
2. Workington	34	16	1	0	841	481	5	1	11	634	690	44
3. Eastbourne	34	17	0	0	791	532	2	2	13	558	762	40
4. Peterborough	34	16	0	1	813	509	3	1	13	592	731	39
5. Birmingham	34	16	0	1	867	456	3	0	14	585	734	38
6. Teesside	34	16	0	1	827	499	3	0	14	562	763	38
7. Bradford	34	16	0	1	805	519	2	0	15	553	770	36
8. Crewe	**34**	**17**	**0**	**0**	**785½**	**538½**	**0**	**1**	**16**	**503**	**820**	**35**
9. Long Eaton	33	14	0	2	743	499	2	1	14	493	831	33
10. Barrow	34	15	0	2	822	499	0	2	15	553	769	32
11. Sunderland	34	15	1	1	777	548	0	1	16	499	824	32
12. Hull	34	10	3	4	707	613	3	2	12	550	775	31
13. Chesterton	34	11	1	5	711	611	3	0	14	540	784	29
14. Ellesmere Port	34	11	0	6	737	586	3	0	14	543	781	28
15. Canterbury	34	11	1	5	718	603	2	1	14	526	797	28
16. Scunthorpe	34	12	1	4	727	598	0	0	17	485	837	25
17. Berwick	34	11	1	5	713	609	0	0	17	435	890	23
18. Rayleigh	34	9	3	5	733½	592½	0	0	17	500	823	21

(The Long Eaton v Boston match finished 39-36, but was eventually declared void following a series of protests and counter-protests by both clubs.)

- Crewe Rider Averages -

(League and Knock Out Cup only)

	M	R	W	Pts	BP	Tot	F	P	CMA
John Jackson	32	145	74	301	9	310	5	1	8.552
Geoff Ambrose	31	133	55	266½	16	282½	4	2	8.496
Dave Morton	24	101	47	202	11	213	2	2	8.436
Wayne Forrest	27	111	19	135	16	151	0	0	5.441
Glyn Taylor	31	121	19	140	20	160	0	1	5.289
Ian Cartwright	29	95	2	95	21	116	0	0	4.884
Keith White	35	146	19	155	16	171	0	0	4.685
Also rode									
Dave O'Connor	2	7	0	7	2	9	0	0	5.143
Stuart Cope	1	2	0	2	0	2	0	0	4.000
Peter Thompson	7	18	1	13	4	17	0	0	3.778
Cliff Anderson	7	27	0	18	4	22	0	0	3.259
Reg Brassington	4	10	0	3	1	4	0	0	1.600
Dave Parry	3	7	0	2	0	2	0	0	1.143
Kelvin Mullarkey	1	1	0	0	0	0	0	0	0.000
Substitutes									
Robin Dixon	1	3	0	4	0	4	0	0	5.333
Les Glover	1	5	0	6	0	6	0	0	4.800
Lloyd Dobson	1	2	0	1	1	2	0	0	4.000
Alan Johns	1	4	0	2	0	2	0	0	2.000
Graham Tattersall	1	1	0	0	0	0	0	0	0.000

- League Heat Scores -

	Home	Away	Total
5 - 1 heat win to Crewe	51	11	62
4½ - 1½ heat win to Crewe	1	0	1
4 - 2 heat win to Crewe	66	24	90
3 - 2 heat win to Crewe	1	0	1
3 - 3 drawn heat	65	59	124
2 - 3 heat win to Opponents	1	3	4
2 - 4 heat win to Opponents	26	45	71
1 - 5 heat win to Opponents	10	79	89

- Individual/Pairs Honours -

Cheshire Open Championship (Ellesmere Port)
1. Geoff Ambrose 2. Paul O'Neil 3. Colin Goad.

K.R.C. £100 Trophy (Peterborough)
1. Dave Morton 2. Carl Glover 3. Bobby McNeil.

Lunn-Poly Trophy (Long Eaton)
1. Arthur Browning 2. Keith White 3. Richard Greer.

Littlechild £100 Trophy (Crewe)
1. John Jackson 2. Tom Owen 3. Dave Baugh.

(ABOVE) Geoff Ambrose clutches the Silver Helmet, after his victory over holder Mike Broadbanks on August 20. He would relinquish the title five days later at Rayleigh. (BELOW) Keith White and Ambrose do a spot of team riding.

(ABOVE) Kings fan Steve Whitehouse of Hungerford Road, pictured with his idols, after an accident on his paperound resulted in a broken thumb and severe bruising. The youngster was resigned to missing his first Earle Street meeting, until Jack Millen stepped in to arrange the special treat, which included a visit to the pits, a seat on the centre green and a spin around the track courtesy of Wayne Forrest.

(ABOVE LEFT) Exeter loanee Peter Thompson and (ABOVE RIGHT) Stalwart Dave Parry, who retired after only a handful of meetings.

The Rainy Season

-1974-

The Rainy Season
-1974-

There were a number of changes to the league structure for the 1974 season. Coatbridge Tigers dropped down from Division I and were surprisingly replaced by Hull, much to the annoyance of Boston and Eastbourne, who were keen on promotion themselves. Rayleigh re-located to nearby training track Rye House, and Weymouth Wizards were successful with their application to return to the league following a six year absence. Chesterton were re-christened Stoke, Bradford became the Barons, Sunderland became the Gladiators and Long Eaton reverted to their old name of the Archers. Crewe's hopes of Division I racing rested on the transfer of the Reading licence, but these were dashed when planning permission was granted for a new stadium in the Smallmead area of the Berkshire town, with the licence put on ice for twelve months, as the facility would not be ready until next season. Dave Parry returned to take up the reigns as general and team manager and boldly predicted that Crewe could challenge for silverware. He commented: *"Speedway is about two riders racing together as a team and that is what I am trying to instil in our riders. I no longer want to see riders going out and racing for themselves. If they work and pull together as a team, then we should be among the honours this season."* A new £4,000 grandstand was ready for use and the pits area received some much-needed improvements. On the rider front, Barry Meeks came out of an eighteen month retirement to try his luck again, after helping out at Charlie Scarbrough's winter training schools. Former Rayleigh, Cradley and Birmingham rider Mike Gardner, who had the distinction of winning the first race at Earle Street in May 1969, was signed along with Paul Wells, younger brother of Sunderland's Jim. The main coup for the Kings though was the re-signing of "Crazy" Jack Millen – the league's most colourful rider and biggest draw. His return would hopefully address the falling attendances at Earle Street. However, they would lose two other colonials from their ranks. Glyn Taylor announced he was to stay in Australia for a year after recently marrying and Peter Thompson went back to Exeter, following a sensational season in Australia. The club received a pre-season boost when the fixture list provided them with one of the five Division II preliminary rounds of the World Championship, and there was further good news when they were chosen to stage a Division II test match between England and Poland. Due to petrol rationing as a result of the economical crisis which was gripping Britain, the draw for the K.O. Cup was regionalised, with the Kings drawn against their old foes from Workington. The Silver Helmet format was changed to a home and away basis, with a nominated rider taking on the holder each month. Admission prices at Earle Street remained at 50p for adults, 25p for children and senior citizens, and programme's stayed at 10p. The season began with a four team tournament at Ellesmere Port.

Meeting 1 - Tuesday, March 26, 1974 - 1973 M6 Trophy, Four Team Tournament, Fourth Leg
Ellesmere Port Stadium, Thornton Road, Ellesmere Port
Track Length - 423 yards.

ELLESMERE PORT GUNNERS.....35 CREWE KINGS.....27
BIRMINGHAM BRUMMIES.....19 STOKE POTTERS.....15

(Final aggregate scores - Ellesmere Port 116, Crewe 103, Birmingham 95, Stoke 70)

The M6 Trophy was finally concluded following the previous season's weather problems, and it was the Gunners who triumphed by a thirteen-point margin. Ex-Ellesmere Port rider Cliff Anderson won on three occasions for the Kings, and there was a double-figure return for John Jackson. Former Division I rider Barry Duke had a Potters debut to forget, scoring just one from three rides.

		E	C	B	S
Heat 01 ..... **Jackson**/Smitherman/Wasley/Askew	78.0	2	3	0	1
Heat 02 ..... **C.Anderson**/Goad/Pusey/Browning (F)	78.2	2	3	0	1
Heat 03 ..... Herne/**Morton**/Meredith/Duke	76.0	1	2	3	0
Heat 04 ..... Drury/Parker/Day/**Forrest**	80.6	3	0	1	2
Heat 05 ..... **C.Anderson**/Day/Duke/Smitherman (R)	78.2	0	3	2	1
Heat 06 ..... Goad/**Jackson**/Herne/Parker	79.0	3	2	1	0
Heat 07 ..... Meredith/**Forrest**/Wasley/Browning (R)	79.0	3	2	0	1

Heat 08 ..... Drury/Askew/Pusey/**Morton** (R)	79.8	3	0	2	1
Heat 09 ..... **Morton**/Hughes/K.Anderson/Cusworth	78.4	2	3	1	0
Heat 10 ..... Goad/Askew/**Forrest**/Duke	79.0	3	1	2	0
Heat 11 ..... Pusey/**Jackson**/Meredith/Day	79.0	1	2	0	3
Heat 12 ..... Drury/Herne/Wasley/**C.Anderson**	78.6	3	0	2	1
Heat 13 ..... Goad/Wasley/Day/**Morton** (F)	00.0	3	0	1	2
Heat 14 ..... Herne/Smitherman/Pusey/**Forrest**	79.4	2	0	3	1
Heat 15 ..... **C.Anderson**/Meredith/Askew/Parker	79.4	2	3	1	0
Heat 16 ..... **Jackson**/Drury/Cusworth (3 riders only)	78.0	2	3	0	1

ELLESMERE PORT - Graham Drury 11, Colin Goad 11, Duncan Meredith 7, Gerald Smitherman 4, Wayne Hughes (Reserve) 2.
CREWE - John Jackson 10, Cliff Anderson 9, Dave Morton 5, Wayne Forrest 3.
BIRMINGHAM - Phil Herne 9, Carl Askew 5, Ricky Day 4, Keith Anderson (Reserve) 1, Arthur Browning 0.
STOKE - Geoff Pusey 6, Nigel Wasley 5, Roger Parker 2, Andy Cusworth (Reserve) 1, Barry Duke 1.

After his first match in charge, Dave Parry had already spelt out his title ambitions. *"I'm only interested in success. The Kings will receive all the management support they need to take them back to the top of the league. In return I shall demand a 100% effort on the part of every rider. Kings for champions is to be our slogan for the new season."*

Meeting 2 - Thursday, March 28, 1974 - Spring Challenge, First Leg
Lyme Valley Sports Stadium, Loomer Road, Chesterton
Track Length - 348 yards.

STOKE POTTERS.....44 CREWE KINGS.....34

On a new shortened Loomer Road circuit, Crewe kept in touch in the first leg of the Spring Challenge thanks to heat wins by Dave Morton, John Jackson and Mike Gardner. Barry Meeks made his return to the Kings line-up and secured two third places.

Heat 01 .... Bridgett/Broadbanks/**Jackson**/**Cartwright**	**69.5** (TR)	5 - 1	05 - 01
Heat 02 .... Woodward/**Gardner**/**Meeks**/Holden	**68.6** (TR)	3 - 3	08 - 04
Heat 03 .... Duke/**White**/Parker/**Forrest**	69.0	4 - 2	12 - 06
Heat 04 .... **Morton**/Pusey/**Meeks**/Holden	69.4	**2 - 4**	14 - 10
Heat 05 .... Duke/**Jackson**/Parker/**Cartwright**	**68.4** (TR)	4 - 2	18 - 12
Heat 06 .... Bridgett/Broadbanks/**Morton**/**Gardner**	69.6	5 - 1	23 - 13
Heat 07 .... **Morton**/Holden/Woodward/**White**	69.4	3 - 3	26 - 16
Heat 08 .... **Gardner**/Woodward/**Cartwright**/Bridgett	69.8	**2 - 4**	28 - 20
Heat 09 .... Parker/**Morton**/Duke/**Gardner**	70.0	4 - 2	32 - 22
Heat 10 .... Bridgett/Broadbanks/**White**/**Forrest**	69.4	5 - 1	37 - 23
Heat 11 .... **Jackson**/**Cartwright**/Pusey/Woodward (R)	69.2	**1 - 5**	38 - 28
Heat 12 .... Broadbanks/**Jackson**/**Morton**/Duke	68.5	3 - 3	41 - 31
Heat 13 .... **Jackson**/Pusey/Parker/**Cartwright** (F)	69.0	3 - 3	44 - 34

STOKE - Mike Broadbanks 9 (+3), Alan Bridgett 9, Barry Duke 7, Roger Parker 6 (+1), Bryan Woodward 6 (+1), Geoff Pusey 5, Steve Holden 2.
CREWE - John Jackson 11, Dave Morton 10 (+1), Mike Gardner 5, Ian Cartwright 3 (+1), Keith White 3, Barry Meeks 2 (+1), Wayne Forrest 0.

On April 2, John Jackson made a good start to his season with a third place finish in the Mayfair Open Championship at Ellesmere Port; won by Gunners skipper Graham Drury.

Meeting 3 - Thursday, April 4, 1974 - British League Division II
Cleveland Park Stadium, Stockton Road, Middlesbrough
Track Length - 335 yards.

TEESSIDE TIGERS.....9 CREWE KINGS.....3

Crewe's opening league fixture of the season was abandoned just two heats into the match, after a thick blanket of fog descended on Cleveland Park.

Heat 01 .... Forrester/**Millen**/Swales/**Cartwright**	71.0	4 - 2	04 - 02

Heat 02	Hodgson/Emerson/**Gardner**/**Anderson**	73.6	5 - 1	09 - 03

(Abandoned after two heats due to fog - result does not stand.)

TEESSIDE - Bruce Forrester 3, Russ Hodgson 3, Alan Emerson 2, Tim Swales 1.
CREWE - Jack Millen 2, Mike Gardner 1, Cliff Anderson 0, Ian Cartwright 0.

Jack Millen just failed to qualify for the Division I stages of the World Championship, scoring 12 points at Workington on April 5. Dave Morton failed to score from his only ride in Heat 4. Millen's fortunes however, improved two days later when he beat Carl Glover 2-0 in the first leg of the Silver Helmet at Boston.

Meeting 4 - Monday, April 8, 1974 - Spring Challenge, Second Leg
L.M.R. Sports Ground, Earle Street, Crewe
Track Length - 430 yards.

CREWE KINGS.....50 STOKE POTTERS.....28

(Crewe won on aggregate 84 - 72)

Dave Parry wielded the axe as promised, dropping Barry Meeks and Wayne Forrest from Crewe's opening home fixture. A crowd in excess of 4,000 witnessed a scintillating performance by John Jackson, who lowered the track record to 70.6 in Heat 4, on his way to a maximum. After Heat 5, Stoke led the match by two, and were twelve ahead on aggregate, but the Kings won all remaining heats to win the Spring Challenge. Jack Millen had earlier beaten Carl Glover 2-1 in the second leg of the Silver Helmet (4-1 on aggregate) to become the first holder under the new format.

Heat 01	**Millen**/Broadbanks/**Cartwright**/Parker (R)	71.6	**4 - 2**	04 - 02
Heat 02	Woodward/**Anderson**/**Gardner**/Wasley	71.4	3 - 3	07 - 05
Heat 03	Bridgett/Holden/**Morton**/**White**	72.0	1 - 5	08 - 10
Heat 04	**Jackson**/Woodward/**Anderson**/Pusey	**70.6** (TR)	**4 - 2**	12 - 12
Heat 05	Broadbanks/**Morton**/Wasley/**White**	71.4	2 - 4	14 - 16
Heat 06	**Millen**/**Cartwright**/Woodward/Wasley	73.8	**5 - 1**	19 - 17
Heat 07	**Jackson**/Bridgett/**Anderson**/Holden (X)	70.8	**4 - 2**	23 - 19
Heat 08	**Gardner**/**Cartwright**/Woodward/Parker	72.4	**5 - 1**	28 - 20
Heat 09	**Morton**/Broadbanks/**White**/Pusey	72.0	**4 - 2**	32 - 22
Heat 10	**Millen**/**Cartwright**/Bridgett/Holden	73.2	**5 - 1**	37 - 23
Heat 11	**Jackson**/Broadbanks/**Gardner**/Woodward	71.8	**4 - 2**	41 - 25
Heat 12	**White**/**Millen**/Bridgett/Pusey	72.0	**5 - 1**	46 - 26
Heat 13	**Jackson**/Broadbanks/**Morton**/Holden (R)	71.2	**4 - 2**	50 - 28

CREWE - John Jackson 12, Jack Millen 11 (+1), Ian Cartwright 7 (+3), Dave Morton 7, Mike Gardner 5 (+1), Cliff Anderson 4, Keith White 4.
STOKE - Mike Broadbanks 11, Alan Bridgett 7, Bryan Woodward 7, Steve Holden 2 (+1), Nigel Wasley 1, Roger Parker 0, Geoff Pusey 0.

Dave Parry was delighted after his first win as Crewe boss. There was bad news however, when Jack Millen aggravated an injury to his right knee in the Silver Helmet at Boston, riding through the pain barrier to win the return leg. The only cure was an operation to remove the cartilage, which would rule the Kiwi out for up to six weeks, and prevent him from defending his title against Eastbourne's Bobby McNeil, scheduled to take place on May 5/6. It was announced his place would be taken by Mal Mackay (Workington), but once fit again, he would become the next challenger. On April 14, John Jackson scored 9 in England's 72-36 Division II second test thrashing of the Young Czechs at Eastbourne.

Meeting 5 - Monday, April 15, 1974 - Easter Challenge, First Leg
L.M.R. Sports Ground, Earle Street, Crewe
Track Length - 430 yards.

CREWE KINGS.....56 BIRMINGHAM BRUMMIES.....22

The first clash of two of the title favourites in the Easter Challenge drew another 4,000 plus crowd to Earle Street, and even without Jack Millen, the Kings were far too strong for their

Midland rivals. The slick Earle Street track was not to Birmingham's liking, and Keith White took full advantage of the fast conditions to break John Jackson's week-old track record in Heat 3. Every Crewe rider, bar Dave Morton, won at least one heat and Jackson's first class gating earned him a paid maximum. Newcomer Mike Gardner also showed his pedigree with a paid eleven against his former club.

Heat 01	**Meeks**/Browning/**Cartwright**/Wilson	73.0	**4 - 2**	04 - 02
Heat 02	**Anderson**/**Gardner**/Askew/Day (R)	71.0	**5 - 1**	09 - 03
Heat 03	**White**/**Morton**/Hart/Major	**70.2** (TR)	**5 - 1**	14 - 04
Heat 04	**Anderson**/**Jackson**/Herne/Askew	71.2	**5 - 1**	19 - 05
Heat 05	**White**/**Morton**/Browning/Wilson	71.2	**5 - 1**	24 - 06
Heat 06	Herne/**Cartwright**/Day/**Meeks**	70.8	2 - 4	26 - 10
Heat 07	**Jackson**/**Anderson**/Major/Hart	70.6	**5 - 1**	31 - 11
Heat 08	**Gardner**/**Cartwright**/Wilson/Askew	72.6	**5 - 1**	36 - 12
Heat 09	**White**/Herne/Day/**Morton**	70.6	3 - 3	39 - 15
Heat 10	**Cartwright**/Hart/**Meeks**/Major (R)	72.6	**4 - 2**	43 - 17
Heat 11	**Jackson**/**Gardner**/Browning/Wilson	71.6	**5 - 1**	48 - 18
Heat 12	Herne/**White**/**Gardner**/Major	72.2	3 - 3	51 - 21
Heat 13	**Jackson**/**Morton**/Hart/Browning	71.6	**5 - 1**	56 - 22

CREWE - John Jackson 11 (+1), Keith White 11, Mike Gardner 8 (+3), Cliff Anderson 8 (+1), Ian Cartwright 8 (+1), Dave Morton 6 (+3), Barry Meeks 4.
BIRMINGHAM - Phil Herne 9, Arthur Browning 4, John Hart 4, Ricky Day 2 (+1), Carl Askew 1, George Major 1, Steve Wilson 1.

Meeting 6 - Tuesday, April 16, 1974 - Easter Challenge, Second Leg
Perry Barr Greyhound Stadium, Regina Drive, Walsall Road, Birmingham
Track Length - 350 yards.

BIRMINGHAM BRUMMIES.....40 CREWE KINGS.....37

(Crewe won on aggregate 93 - 62)

Crewe emerged as easy winners of the Easter Challenge, putting in a first class effort over the two legs. John Jackson scored his fifth successive double figure score, and there was an equally good performance from Keith White, who fought tooth and nail for his dozen points. Aussie Phil Herne completed a fine maximum for the hosts.

Heat 01	Wilson/**Forrest**/Johns/**Cartwright**	67.0	4 - 2	04 - 02
Heat 02	Day/**Anderson**/Askew (F)/**Gardner** (X)	67.0	3 - 2	07 - 04
Heat 03	Major/**White**/**Morton**/Hart	68.0	3 - 3	10 - 07
Heat 04	Herne/**Jackson**/**Anderson**/Day (F)	66.8	3 - 3	13 - 10
Heat 05	Major/Hart/**Cartwright**/**Forrest**	67.6	5 - 1	18 - 11
Heat 06	**Jackson**/Johns/Wilson/**Gardner** (R)	66.8	3 - 3	21 - 14
Heat 07	Herne/**White**/**Morton**/Day	66.8	3 - 3	24 - 17
Heat 08	**Jackson**/Wilson/**White**/Askew	67.6	**2 - 4**	26 - 21
Heat 09	**Jackson**/Major/Hart/**Gardner**	67.4	3 - 3	29 - 24
Heat 10	**White**/Johns/**Morton**/Wilson	67.0	**2 - 4**	31 - 28
Heat 11	Herne/**White**/**Cartwright**/Askew	66.2	3 - 3	34 - 31
Heat 12	**Jackson**/Major/Johns/**Morton** (F)	67.2	3 - 3	37 - 34
Heat 13	Herne/**White**/**Jackson**/Hart	66.4	3 - 3	40 - 37

BIRMINGHAM - Phil Herne 12, George Major 10, Roger Johns* 6 (+1), Steve Wilson 6 (+1), John Hart 3 (+2), Ricky Day 3, Carl Askew 0.
CREWE - John Jackson 15 (+1), Keith White 12, Dave Morton 3 (+2), Cliff Anderson 3 (+1), Ian Cartwright 2 (+1), Wayne Forrest 2, Mike Gardner 0.

During a five day period, John Jackson appeared three times for England in the Division II series with the Czechs. On April 17, he scored 2 in the 58-50 win at Bradford and then four days later at Workington, registered 7 in a narrow 55-53 victory, with Dave Morton scoring 5. Next night at Birmingham, he recorded a second place, before being involved in a Heat 6 crash, which resulted in a badly gashed hand and torn finger nail, forcing his early withdrawal from the meeting. Keith White scored 8 in the Lions 56-52 defeat.

Meeting 7 - Monday, April 22, 1974 - World Championship Qualifying Round
L.M.R. Sports Ground, Earle Street, Crewe
Track Length - 430 yards.

WINNER.....CARL GLOVER

Boston's Carl Glover beat Mike Broadbanks of Stoke in a run-off, to win Crewe's preliminary round of the World Championship, with Richard Greer (Oxford) and Laurie Etheridge (Hackney) also making it through to the next stage. Former King Peter Thompson returned to score eight points and meeting reserve Wayne Forrest replaced Dave Piddock to win Heat 13.

Heat 01	Etheridge/Broadbanks/Jarman/Thompson	71.4
Heat 02	Barnwell/Ryman/Templeton/Hart	72.8
Heat 03	Handley/Mackay/Meeks/Piddock	71.6
Heat 04	Glover/Greer/Kennett/Smith	71.6
Heat 05	Handley/Smith/Templeton/Jarman (R)	71.4
Heat 06	Thompson/Barnwell/Kennett/Meeks	72.0
Heat 07	Glover/Mackay/Ryman/Etheridge (R)	72.2
Heat 08	Broadbanks/Greer/Piddock/Hart	71.0
Heat 09	Greer/Barnwell/Mackay/Jarman (R)	71.2
Heat 10	Glover/Templeton/Thompson/Piddock	72.0
Heat 11	Etheridge/Kennett/Handley/Hart	72.6
Heat 12	Broadbanks/Smith/Meeks/Ryman	72.4
Heat 13	Forrest/Jarman/Ryman/Kennett (R)	73.4
Heat 14	Smith/Thompson/Mackay/Hart	72.8
Heat 15	Etheridge/Greer/Templeton/Meeks	73.0
Heat 16	Broadbanks/Glover/Handley/Barnwell (F)	73.0
Heat 17	Glover/Jarman/Meeks/Hart	73.4
Heat 18	Greer/Thompson/Handley/Ryman	73.2
Heat 19	Smith/Etheridge/Barnwell/Wells	72.8
Heat 20	Broadbanks/Templeton/Forrest/Mackay	73.2
R/O for 1st	Glover/Broadbanks	73.0

Carl Glover *(Boston)* 14, Mike Broadbanks *(Stoke)* 14, Richard Greer *(Oxford)* 12, Laurie Etheridge *(Hackney Wick)* 11, Frank Smith *(Coventry)* 10, Mick Handley *(Swindon)* 9, Peter Thompson *(Exeter)* 8, Trevor Barnwell *(Rye House)* 8, Doug Templeton *(Berwick)* 7, Malcolm Mackay *(Workington)* 6, Peter Jarman *(Unattached)* 5, Jim Ryman *(Boston)* 4, Barney Kennett *(Hackney Wick)* 4, Barry Meeks *(Crewe)* 3, Dave Piddock *(Boston)* 1, John Hart *(Birmingham)* 0. Meeting Reserves: Wayne Forrest (*Crewe)* 4, Paul Wells *(Crewe)* 0. *(Meeks replaced Norman Strachan, Long Eaton and Glover replaced David Gagen, Boston.)*

The meeting announcer was Jack Millen, who once again entertained the crowd with his amusing unorthodox style. On April 23, John Jackson's hand injury prevented him from riding in his World Championship Qualifying Round at Ellesmere Port. Next day, Millen entered Crewe's Leighton Hospital for his cartilage operation, with Jackson agreeing to resume the role of captain, until he was fit. The Kings management reported that they had signed a deal with Phil Crump and former World Champion Ole Olsen (who was based in Holmes Chapel) to ride in three-match races, to be held during the second-half on June 10. Peter Collins had been the original choice to face the Dane.

Meeting 8 - Saturday, April 27, 1974 - British League Division II
Canterbury City Football Ground, Kingsmead Road, Canterbury
Track Length - 390 yards.

CANTERBURY CRUSADERS.....46 CREWE KINGS.....32

The Kings lost their opening league match of the campaign, going down by fourteen points. Minus the services of Jack Millen and John Jackson, Crewe's cause was not helped by a catalogue of mechanical failures which cost them a possible nine points following the retirements of Mike Gardner, Dave Morton and Keith White, when all were in scoring positions. Cliff Anderson and Morton won a total of five heats, but three riders mustered only three points between them. Canterbury boss Johnnie Hoskins praised the Kings' efforts and commented: *"At full strength, few teams are going to beat Crewe this year."*

Heat 01	Kennett/Cook/**Meeks/Cartwright**	75.0	5 - 1	05 - 01
Heat 02	**Anderson**/Gooderham/Mackay/**Gardner** (R)	75.8	3 - 3	08 - 04
Heat 03	Jones/**Morton**/Murray/**White**	75.4	4 - 2	12 - 06
Heat 04	**Anderson**/Johns/**Forrest**/Mackay	76.1	**2 - 4**	14 - 10
Heat 05	Jones/Murray/**Cartwright/Morton** (R)	75.6	5 - 1	19 - 11
Heat 06	Cook/Kennett/**Gardner/Anderson**	76.0	5 - 1	24 - 12
Heat 07	**Morton/White**/Johns/Mackay	75.1	**1 - 5**	25 - 17
Heat 08	**Anderson**/Kennett/**Morton**/Gooderham	76.7	**2 - 4**	27 - 21
Heat 09	Jones/**Gardner**/Murray/**Forrest**	75.9	4 - 2	31 - 23
Heat 10	**White**/Cook/Kennett/**Morton**	75.3	3 - 3	34 - 26
Heat 11	Johns/**Gardner**/Gooderham/**White** (R)	75.3	4 - 2	38 - 28
Heat 12	**Morton**/Cook/Murray/**White**	75.7	3 - 3	41 - 31
Heat 13	Johns/Jones/**Anderson/Meeks**	76.5	5 - 1	46 - 32

CANTERBURY - Trevor Jones 11 (+1), Derek Cook 9 (+1), Roger Johns 9, Barney Kennett 8 (+2), Peter Murray 5 (+2), Dave Gooderham 3, Dave Mackay 1 (+1).
CREWE - Cliff Anderson 10, Dave Morton 9, Keith White 5 (+1), Mike Gardner 5, Ian Cartwright 1, Wayne Forrest 1, Barry Meeks 1, *Jack Millen (R/R)*.

Meeting 9 - Monday, April 29, 1974 - Speedway Mail Knock Out Cup, First Round, First Leg
L.M.R. Sports Ground, Earle Street, Crewe
Track Length - 430 yards.

CREWE KINGS.....43 WORKINGTON COMETS.....35

Another bout of motor troubles left Crewe's progress in the K.O. Cup hanging by a thread, after winning their home leg by just eight points. Dave Morton, riding on a new machine, pulled up in Heat 1 with a magneto fault and two races later he again failed to finish on John Jackson's bike, when the plug lead came adrift. Mike Gardner fared even worse after his second place in Heat 2. He suffered three successive retirements and on the last occasion, hurled his bike down onto the centre green in disgust. As for the match, Mitch Graham lowered the track record in the first heat - the third rider to do so this season, equalling it four races later. Only Dave Morton, in the final heat, prevented the Comet from completing a maximum.

Heat 01	Graham/**Cartwright**/Owen/**Morton** (R)	**70.0** (TR)	2 - 4	02 - 04
Heat 02	**Anderson/Gardner**/Hornby/Stobbart	71.4	**5 - 1**	07 - 05
Heat 03	**White**/Sheldrick/Watson/**Morton** (R)	71.4	3 - 3	10 - 08
Heat 04	Mackay/**Jackson/Anderson**/Hornby	71.6	3 - 3	13 - 11
Heat 05	Graham/**Morton/White**/Owen	**70.0** (=TR)	3 - 3	16 - 14
Heat 06	Mackay/**Cartwright**/Stobbart/**Gardner** (R)	72.2	2 - 4	18 - 18
Heat 07	**Jackson/Anderson**/Sheldrick/Watson	71.4	**5 - 1**	23 - 19
Heat 08	Owen/**Cartwright**/Hornby/**Gardner** (R)	71.6	2 - 4	25 - 23
Heat 09	**Morton**/Mackay/**White**/Stobbart	71.6	**4 - 2**	29 - 25
Heat 10	**White**/Watson/**Cartwright**/Sheldrick	71.0	**4 - 2**	33 - 27
Heat 11	Graham/Owen/**Anderson/Gardner** (R)	70.8	1 - 5	34 - 32
Heat 12	**Jackson/White**/Mackay/Sheldrick	70.6	**5 - 1**	39 - 33
Heat 13	**Morton**/Graham/**Jackson**/Mackay	70.4	**4 - 2**	43 - 35

CREWE - Keith White 10 (+2), John Jackson 9, Dave Morton 8, Cliff Anderson 7 (+2), Ian Cartwright 7, Mike Gardner 2 (+1), *Jack Millen (R/R)*.
WORKINGTON - Mitch Graham 11, Malcolm Mackay 9, Taffy Owen 6 (+1), Steve Watson 3 (+1), Sid Sheldrick* 3, Bernie Hornby 2, Darrell Stobbart 1.

Jack Millen arrived at the track on crutches, just five days after his operation, but still got in on the act, driving the tractor on the team's lap of honour!

Meeting 10 - Friday, May 3, 1974 - Speedway Mail Knock Out Cup, First Round, Second Leg
Derwent Park Stadium, Workington
Track Length - 398 yards.

WORKINGTON COMETS.....46 CREWE KINGS.....32

(Workington won on aggregate 81 - 75)

(ABOVE) New season signings Barry Meeks and Jack Millen, who both returned to the club after a two year absence. (BELOW) Mike Gardner and Paul "Lightning" Wells.

(ABOVE) Dave Parry, next to the partially constructed home straight grandstand.

(ABOVE) The squad of 1974 on press and practice day. (Back row, left to right) Dave Parry, Dave Morton, Charlie Turner, John Jackson, Paul Wells, Colin Farquharson (who signed for Berwick), Jack Millen (on machine), Wayne Forrest, Keith White, Barry Meeks, Ian Cartwright and Len Silver. (Kneeling) Mike Gardner, Cliff Anderson and Stuart Cope.

(ABOVE) Cliff Anderson and Mike Gardner do some close team riding at Canterbury on April 27. (BELOW) Cliff Anderson, Ian Cartwright, Barry Meeks and Wayne Forrest watch the action from the Canterbury pits.

The Kings fell at the first hurdle in the K.O. Cup, but did take the tie to the final heat. John Jackson produced another impressive performance at Derwent Park with 14 points, but it was Mike Gardner who grabbed the headlines, and all for the wrong reasons. Blighted by an epidemic of recent motor troubles, his machine again failed him in his first ride due to a magneto problem. On his return to the pits, he packed up his gear and walked out.

Heat 01	Graham/**Jackson**/Owen/**Cartwright**	74.4	4 - 2	04 - 02
Heat 02	**Anderson**/Stobbart/Lawson/**Gardner** (R)	76.6	3 - 3	07 - 05
Heat 03	**Morton**/Watson/Cowland/**White**	77.0	3 - 3	10 - 08
Heat 04	Mackay/**Jackson**/Stobbart (3 riders only)	76.0	4 - 2	14 - 10
Heat 05	Stobbart/Watson/**White**/**Cartwright** (F)	76.4	5 - 1	19 - 11
Heat 06	Graham/**Jackson**/**Anderson**/Owen	75.2	3 - 3	22 - 14
Heat 07	Mackay/**Morton**/**White**/Stobbart	75.4	3 - 3	25 - 17
Heat 08	Owen/**Jackson**/**Morton**/Stobbart	76.2	3 - 3	28 - 20
Heat 09	**Jackson**/Stobbart/Cowland/**Anderson**	76.8	3 - 3	31 - 23
Heat 10	Graham/Owen/**Morton**/**White**	75.4	5 - 1	36 - 24
Heat 11	Mackay/**White**/**Cartwright**/Lawson	76.8	3 - 3	39 - 27
Heat 12	**Jackson**/Graham/Watson/**Morton**	75.8	3 - 3	42 - 30
Heat 13	Mackay/**Morton**/Cowland/**White**	77.2	4 - 2	46 - 32

WORKINGTON - Malcolm Mackay 12, Mitch Graham 11, Darrell Stobbart 8, Taffy Owen 6 (+1), Steve Watson 5 (+1), Alan Cowland 3 (+2), Steve Lawson 1 (+1).
CREWE - John Jackson 14, Dave Morton 9 (+1), Cliff Anderson 4 (+1), Keith White 4 (+1), Ian Cartwright 1 (+1), Mike Gardner 0, *Jack Millen (R/R).*

Understandably, Dave Parry was not happy following Gardner's walkout, which left Crewe with only one rider in Heat 4. *"I told him an apology was not acceptable. He will be suspended for at least two weeks and may never ride for us again....I know that he has had a lot of problems and he has also lost his job. But there is no excuse for this sort of behaviour. He has let himself down, he has let his team down and he has let the supporters down."* Prior to the start of the match, Parry had told the riders to pool their equipment and not to ride any machinery that failed.

Meeting 11 - Monday, May 6, 1974 - British League Division II
L.M.R. Sports Ground, Earle Street, Crewe
Track Length - 430 yards.

CREWE KINGS.....55 EASTBOURNE EAGLES.....23

A poor Eastbourne performance did little to address falling attendances at Earle Street, which dipped below the 2,000 mark for this first league encounter. The Eagles who had arrived minus the services of heat leader Mike Sampson, then lost Steve Weatherley with a broken collar-bone when he hit the fence on the first lap of Heat 2 and was thrown over his handlebars. Skipper Bobby McNeil became another casualty in the next race, when a fall put him out of the match with a groin injury. For Crewe there were paid maximums for Dave Morton and Keith White and every home rider scored at least one bonus point. Wayne Forrest came back into the side, replacing the suspended Mike Gardner, winning his opening ride.

Heat 01	**Forrest**/**Cartwright**/Jarman/Geer (R)	73.2	**5 - 1**	05 - 01
Heat 02	**Anderson**/Yeates/**Meeks**/Weatherley (X)	72.0	**4 - 2**	09 - 03
Heat 03	**Morton**/**White**/Gachet/McNeil (R)	71.2	**5 - 1**	14 - 04
Heat 04	Yeates/**Jackson**/**Anderson**/Middleditch	71.8	3 - 3	17 - 07
Heat 05	**Morton**/**White**/Jarman/Geer	71.6	**5 - 1**	22 - 08
Heat 06	Middleditch/Yeates/**Forrest**/**Cartwright** (R)	73.0	1 - 5	23 - 13
Heat 07	**Jackson**/**Anderson**/Gachet/Jarman	71.6	**5 - 1**	28 - 14
Heat 08	**Cartwright**/**Meeks**/Yeates/Gachet	72.0	**5 - 1**	33 - 15
Heat 09	**White**/**Morton**/Yeates/Middleditch	71.4	**5 - 1**	38 - 16
Heat 10	**Cartwright**/**Forrest**/Gachet (3 riders only)	72.0	**5 - 1**	43 - 17
Heat 11	**Jackson**/Yeates/Jarman/**Meeks**	71.2	3 - 3	46 - 20
Heat 12	**White**/Gachet/**Forrest**/Middleditch	73.2	**4 - 2**	50 - 22
Heat 13	**Morton**/**Jackson**/Middleditch (3 riders only)	71.2	**5 - 1**	55 - 23

CREWE - Dave Morton 11 (+1), Keith White 10 (+2), John Jackson 10 (+1), Ian Cartwright 8 (+1), Wayne Forrest 7 (+1), Cliff Anderson 6 (+2), Barry Meeks 3 (+1).
EASTBOURNE - Martin Yeates 11 (+1), Paul Gachet 5, Neil Middleditch 4, Peter Jarman 3 (+1), Trevor Geer 0, Bobby McNeil 0, Steve Weatherley 0.

Meeting 12 - Thursday, May 9, 1974 - British League Division II
Lyme Valley Stadium, Loomer Road, Chesterton
Track Length - 348 yards.

STOKE POTTERS.....41 CREWE KINGS.....37

The Kings recovered from some early mishaps to more than play their part in an enthralling derby clash, which ended in a last heat decider. Cliff Anderson fell in Heat 2 and was excluded from the re-run, Dave Morton broke the tapes in the next, and John Jackson was ruled out of Heat 4 after exceeding the two minute time allowance, due to his engine refusing to start. Rain fell throughout the meeting and many of the races were decided from the gate. Crewe operated rider replacement for Jack Millen, but Stoke brought in Birmingham's Phil Herne as a guest for Mike Broadbanks, and his eleven points proved crucial to the eventual outcome.

Heat 01	**Jackson**/Pusey/**Cartwright**/Holden (F)	67.5	**2 - 4**	02 - 04
Heat 02	**White**/Cusworth/Wasley/**Anderson** (X)	70.2	3 - 3	05 - 07
Heat 03	Herne/**White**/Bridgett/**Forrest**	70.2	4 - 2	09 - 09
Heat 04	Woodward/**White**/Wasley/**Anderson**	70.2	4 - 2	13 - 11
Heat 05	Herne/**Cartwright**/Bridgett/**Morton**	70.8	4 - 2	17 - 13
Heat 06	**Jackson**/Pusey/Cusworth/**Anderson**	71.8	3 - 3	20 - 16
Heat 07	**Morton**/**Forrest**/Woodward/Wasley	71.0	**1 - 5**	21 - 21
Heat 08	**White**/**Cartwright**/Wasley/Cusworth (X)	71.4	**1 - 5**	22 - 26
Heat 09	Herne/Bridgett/**Jackson**/**White**	70.6	5 - 1	27 - 27
Heat 10	**Morton**/Pusey/Cusworth/**Forrest**	72.4	3 - 3	30 - 30
Heat 11	Woodward/**Anderson**/Cusworth/**Cartwright** (F)	71.0	4 - 2	34 - 32
Heat 12	**Jackson**/Herne/**Morton**/Wasley	68.4	**2 - 4**	36 - 36
Heat 13	Bridgett/Woodward/**Cartwright**/**Anderson**	70.0	5 - 1	41 - 37

STOKE - Phil Herne* 11, Bryan Woodward 9 (+1), Alan Bridgett 7 (+1), Geoff Pusey 6, Andy Cusworth 5 (+2), Nigel Wasley 3 (+1), Steve Holden 0.
CREWE - John Jackson 10, Keith White 10, Dave Morton 7, Ian Cartwright 6 (+1), Wayne Forrest 2 (+1), Cliff Anderson 2, *Jack Millen (R/R).*

Dave Jessup (15pts) and John Jackson (5pts) finished third in the Halifax Pairs Championship held on May 11. Dave Morton also took part, replacing the injured Graham Plant, scoring 11 points alongside Mick Newton. Ian Cartwright partnered Reg Wilson and scored 3 points.

Meeting 13 - Sunday, May 12, 1974 - British League Division II
Boston Sports Stadium, New Hammond Beck Road, Boston
Track Length - 380 yards.

BOSTON BARRACUDAS.....50 CREWE KINGS.....28

Heat 1 set the tone for the Kings, when both riders took a spill. Keith White, promoted to No.1, was the first to fall after a bad start and Ian Cartwright soon followed suit, but remounted to claim a point. The under-strength visitors were denied use of rider replacement much to the annoyance of the management, so Paul Wells was given his debut, and although Crewe riders won Heats 2, 3, 4 and 8, the Barracudas dominated the remainder of the match.

Heat 01	Glover/Hollingworth/**Cartwright**/**White** (F)	67.8	5 - 1	05 - 01
Heat 02	**Anderson**/Mouncer/Burton/**Wells**	68.8	3 - 3	08 - 04
Heat 03	**Morton**/Ryman/Gagen/**Forrest**	67.6	3 - 3	11 - 07
Heat 04	**Jackson**/Mouncer/Burton/**Wells**	67.2	3 - 3	14 - 10
Heat 05	Gagen/Ryman/**White**/**Cartwright** (R)	67.0	5 - 1	19 - 11
Heat 06	Hollingworth/Glover/**Anderson**/**Jackson** (F)	67.0	5 - 1	24 - 12
Heat 07	Osborne/**Jackson**/**Morton**/Burton	67.8	3 - 3	27 - 15
Heat 08	**Morton**/Hollingworth/**Cartwright**/Mouncer	67.2	**2 - 4**	29 - 19
Heat 09	Ryman/**Jackson**/Gagen/**Anderson** (F)	67.4	4 - 2	33 - 21

Heat 10	Glover/**Morton/Forrest**/Hollingworth	66.8	3 - 3	36 - 24
Heat 11	Osborne/**White**/Mouncer/**Cartwright**	67.6	4 - 2	40 - 26
Heat 12	Glover/Ryman/**Morton/Jackson**	65.8	5 - 1	45 - 27
Heat 13	Osborne/Gagen/**White/Forrest**	67.2	5 - 1	50 - 28

BOSTON - Carl Glover 11 (+1), Jim Ryman 9 (+2), Russell Osborne 9, David Gagen 7 (+2), Rob Hollingworth 7 (+1), Rob Mouncer 5, Billy Burton 2 (+2).
CREWE - Dave Morton 10 (+1), John Jackson 7, Cliff Anderson 4, Keith White 4, Ian Cartwright 2, Wayne Forrest 1 (+1), Paul Wells 0.

A few days after the meeting, Dave Parry lodged an appeal over the referee's refusal to allow rider replacement for Jack Millen and demanded the match be re-run. The appeal however, was rejected as it was not submitted within the statutory three days, even though the Speedway Control Board agreed that Crewe had been harshly treated, and could indeed have used the ruling. This prompted Parry to send another letter to the ACU official in charge of referees, suggesting that two referees should be present at every meeting, with the second stationed on the centre green, and also stated: *'The Kings have recently been on the wrong end of some diabolical refereeing decisions.'* Jack Millen meanwhile, was raring to get back into action just three weeks after his operation, and to prove his fitness, completed 60 laps of the Earle Street track on a pushbike! His return however, was delayed for a further seven days.

Meeting 14 - Monday, May 13, 1974 - British League Division II
L.M.R. Sports Ground, Earle Street, Crewe
Track Length - 430 yards.

CREWE KINGS.....49 LONG EATON ARCHERS.....29

Paid maximums for John Jackson and Keith White, as well as a twelve point return for Dave Morton, saw the Kings earn a comfortable two league points, and with Jack Millen set to return, all signals pointed to a strong Crewe assault on the title. Morton looked set for a full-house, until a motor failure forced him out of Heat 9.

Heat 01	**White**/Bouchard/Bond/**Meeks**	72.4	3 - 3	03 - 03
Heat 02	**White/Anderson**/Witt/Austin	72.4	**5 - 1**	08 - 04
Heat 03	**Morton**/Bass/**Forrest**/Harvey	72.4	**4 - 2**	12 - 06
Heat 04	**Jackson**/Molyneux/**Anderson**/Austin	72.2	**4 - 2**	16 - 08
Heat 05	**Morton/Forrest**/Bond/Bouchard	73.8	**5 - 1**	21 - 09
Heat 06	Bass/Witt/**Meeks/Cartwright**	72.6	1 - 5	22 - 14
Heat 07	**Jackson**/Bass/**Anderson**/Molyneux	72.0	**4 - 2**	26 - 16
Heat 08	**Morton/White**/Bond/Harvey	72.8	**5 - 1**	31 - 17
Heat 09	Witt/Molyneux/**Forrest/Morton** (R)	73.2	1 - 5	32 - 22
Heat 10	**Jackson**/Bass/**Cartwright**/Bouchard	71.6	**4 - 2**	36 - 24
Heat 11	**Jackson/White**/Bouchard/Witt	72.0	**5 - 1**	41 - 25
Heat 12	**Cartwright**/Bass/Molyneux/**Forrest**	73.2	3 - 3	44 - 28
Heat 13	**Morton/Jackson**/Bouchard/Harvey	71.0	**5 - 1**	49 - 29

CREWE - John Jackson 14 (+1), Dave Morton 12, Keith White 10 (+2), Cliff Anderson 4 (+1), Wayne Forrest 4 (+1), Ian Cartwright 4, Barry Meeks 1, *Jack Millen (R/R).*
LONG EATON - Phil Bass 11, Alan Witt 6 (+1), Alan Molyneux 5 (+2), Geoff Bouchard 4, James Bond 3 (+1), Pip Austin 0, Dave Harvey 0.

The worst kept secret in speedway was announced after Dave Morton signed for Len Silver's Division I club Hackney, despite interest from Halifax. He would continue to ride on loan at Earle Street until a suitable replacement was found.

Meeting 15 - Monday, May 20, 1974 - British League Division II
L.M.R. Sports Ground, Earle Street, Crewe
Track Length - 430 yards.

CREWE KINGS.....61 BERWICK BANDITS.....17

Jack Millen made a winning return to the saddle in Heat 1, as the Kings, back to full-strength, hammered top-of-the-table Berwick - inflicting upon them their biggest ever defeat. Dave Morton netted a maximum and there were paid ones for John Jackson, Millen and Ian Cartwright. Only Denny Morter won a race for the Bandits, as Crewe reeled off successive 5-1's in the final eight heats of the night. Crewe based New Zealander, "Cowboy" Colin Farquharson, who worked part-time on the Earle Street track, scored just one point for the visitors.

Heat 01	**Millen/Cartwright**/D.Templeton/Jones	75.2	**5 - 1**	05 - 01
Heat 02	Morter/**White/Anderson**/Wilson	75.0	3 - 3	08 - 04
Heat 03	**Morton**/W.Templeton/**Forrest**/Dixon	71.4	**4 - 2**	12 - 06
Heat 04	**Jackson/Anderson**/Farquharson/Morter	72.4	**5 - 1**	17 - 07
Heat 05	**Morton**/D.Templeton/**Forrest**/Jones	70.8	**4 - 2**	21 - 09
Heat 06	**Cartwright/Millen**/Wilson/Farquharson (R)	72.4	**5 - 1**	26 - 10
Heat 07	**Jackson/Anderson**/W.Templeton/Dixon	72.2	**5 - 1**	31 - 11
Heat 08	**White/Millen**/D.Templeton/Morter	73.6	**5 - 1**	36 - 12
Heat 09	**Morton/Forrest**/W.Templeton/Wilson	73.0	**5 - 1**	41 - 13
Heat 10	**Millen/Cartwright**/W.Templeton/Morter	73.2	**5 - 1**	46 - 14
Heat 11	**Jackson/White**/D.Templeton/Jones	72.6	**5 - 1**	51 - 15
Heat 12	**Cartwright/Forrest**/W.Templeton/Morter (R)	73.4	**5 - 1**	56 - 16
Heat 13	**Morton/Jackson**/D.Templeton/Wilson	72.4	**5 - 1**	61 - 17

CREWE - Dave Morton 12, John Jackson 11 (+1), Ian Cartwright 10 (+2), Jack Millen 10 (+2), Keith White 7 (+1), Wayne Forrest 6 (+2), Cliff Anderson 5 (+3).
BERWICK - Doug Templeton 6, Willie Templeton 6, Denny Morter 3, Colin Farquharson 1, Ian Wilson 1, Robin Dixon 0, Graham Jones 0.

Crewe rejected an approach from Scunthorpe to sign Wayne Forrest, and in a bid to break into the Crewe side, junior Charlie Turner enrolled in a Belle Vue training school.

Meeting 16 - Monday, May 27, 1974 - British League Division II
L.M.R. Sports Ground, Earle Street, Crewe
Track Length - 430 yards.

CREWE KINGS.....40 BIRMINGHAM BRUMMIES.....37

A real blood and guts affair was only decided in the last heat with a John Jackson and Dave Morton 5-1, despite Jackson losing power on the final home straight. The tension overflowed in Heat 10, when Jack Millen was excluded for dangerous riding, after bringing down Carl Askew, who then earned himself an exclusion in the re-run, after putting Ian Cartwright into the boards. The impact resulted in a female spectator being taken to hospital with a lacerated leg after being struck by a dislodged fence panel. The second re-run saw Keith White just pip Ricky Day to the finish line by half a wheel, but referee E. W. Roe awarded the victory to the Birmingham rider. He then reversed his decision after consulting with start marshal Alan Pedley. Tempers frayed between both sets of riders in the pits, during and after the heat, including an altercation between Cartwright and Askew.

Heat 01	**Millen**/Browning/**Cartwright**/Hart	72.0	**4 - 2**	04 - 02
Heat 02	**C.Anderson**/Day/**White**/Askew	72.4	**4 - 2**	08 - 04
Heat 03	**Forrest/Morton**/Major/K.Anderson	71.2	**5 - 1**	13 - 05
Heat 04	Herne/**Jackson**/Askew/**C.Anderson**	70.4	2 - 4	15 - 09
Heat 05	Browning/**Forrest**/Hart/**Morton** (R)	72.0	2 - 4	17 - 13
Heat 06	Herne/Day/**Millen/Cartwright**	70.4	1 - 5	18 - 18
Heat 07	**Jackson**/Day/**C.Anderson**/Major	70.4	**4 - 2**	22 - 20
Heat 08	Hart/Askew/**Cartwright/White**	72.0	1 - 5	23 - 25
Heat 09	**Morton**/Herne/**White**/Day	70.4	**4 - 2**	27 - 27
Heat 10	**White**/Day/**Millen** (X)/Askew (X)	72.8	**3 - 2**	30 - 29
Heat 11	**Jackson**/Browning/Hart/**White**	71.8	3 - 3	33 - 32
Heat 12	Herne/**Millen**/Askew/**Forrest**	72.0	2 - 4	35 - 36
Heat 13	**Morton/Jackson**/Browning/K.Anderson	72.0	**5 - 1**	40 - 37

CREWE - John Jackson 10 (+1), Dave Morton 8 (+1), Jack Millen 6, Wayne Forrest 5, Keith White 5, Cliff Anderson 4, Ian Cartwright 2.
BIRMINGHAM - Phil Herne 11, Ricky Day 8 (+1), Arthur Browning 8, John Hart 5 (+1), Carl Askew 4 (+1), George Major 1, Keith Anderson 0.

With the forthcoming appearance of Phil Crump and Ole Olsen approaching, Dave Parry offered the supporters a vote on the option of including Crump as a guest in the Kings line-up for the Inter-League Four Team Tournament at Earle Street on August 19. He was also reported to be interested in signing nineteen-year-old Yorkshireman Max Clift, who had impressed him in a recent second-half.

Meeting 17 - Tuesday, May 28, 1974 - British League Division II
Perry Barr Greyhound Stadium, Regina Drive, Walsall Road, Birmingham
Track Length - 350 yards.

BIRMINGHAM BRUMMIES.....49 CREWE KINGS.....29

Jack Millen received his second exclusion for dangerous riding in the space of twenty-four hours, when he put Arthur Browning into the fence in the first heat. Millen bent the frame of his bike in the incident, and took a further ride on borrowed machinery, before withdrawing from the meeting. Keith White was the only visitor to win a heat and contributed eleven to the Kings total on a machine sporting an engine loaned by Leicester and England star Ray Wilson. Ian Cartwright and Carl Askew continued their spat from the previous night with another pits flare-up, which resulted in Cartwright being fined £2 by the referee for a gesture made towards the Birmingham rider. Arthur Browning and Phil Herne both scored maximums for the hosts.

Heat 01	Browning/Hart/**Cartwright**/**Millen** (X)	66.2	5 - 1	05 - 01
Heat 02	**White**/Day/Askew/**C.Anderson**	65.2	3 - 3	08 - 04
Heat 03	Major/**Morton**/K.Anderson/**Forrest**	66.2	4 - 2	12 - 06
Heat 04	Herne/**Jackson**/Day/**C.Anderson**	65.8	4 - 2	16 - 08
Heat 05	Major/**Cartwright**/K.Anderson/**Millen**	66.6	4 - 2	20 - 10
Heat 06	Browning/**White**/**Jackson**/Hart	65.8	3 - 3	23 - 13
Heat 07	Herne/**Morton**/Day/**Forrest**	65.2	4 - 2	27 - 15
Heat 08	Hart/**White**/**Cartwright**/Askew	66.8	3 - 3	30 - 18
Heat 09	Major/**Jackson**/**White**/K.Anderson	66.0	3 - 3	33 - 21
Heat 10	Browning/Hart/**Jackson**/**Morton**	65.8	5 - 1	38 - 22
Heat 11	Herne/**White**/**Cartwright**/Askew	65.4	3 - 3	41 - 25
Heat 12	Browning/**Jackson**/**Morton**/K.Anderson	65.8	3 - 3	44 - 28
Heat 13	Herne/Major/**White**/**Morton**	66.0	5 - 1	49 - 29

BIRMINGHAM - Arthur Browning 12, Phil Herne 12, George Major 11 (+1), John Hart 7 (+2), Ricky Day 4, Keith Anderson 2, Carl Askew 1 (+1).
CREWE - Keith White 11 (+1), John Jackson 8 (+1), Ian Cartwright 5 (+2), Dave Morton 5 (+1), Cliff Anderson 0, Wayne Forrest 0, Jack Millen 0.

Crewe signed Dave Morton's mechanic Andy Reid, following the youngster's recent impressive second-half performances. Dave Parry was also hoping to bring Kings old boy Peter Nicholas back after offering him a trial, as well as trying to tempt Rye House rider Allan Emmett to Earle Street in a rider exchange deal (believed to be Wayne Forrest). Emmett had missed virtually the whole of the previous season after breaking a thigh while riding for Hackney at Waterden Road.

Meeting 18 - Monday, June 3, 1974 - British League Division II
L.M.R. Sports Ground, Earle Street, Crewe
Track Length - 430 yards.

CREWE KINGS.....52 TEESSIDE TIGERS.....26

John Jackson and Jack Millen both recorded maximums in an easy Kings win over a disappointing Teesside outfit. Millen came from the back to win Heat 6, a feat that was replicated by Jackson in the next. The Tigers suffered a number of mechanical failures, but didn't help themselves by not employing a tactical substitute until Heat 12.

Heat 01	**Millen**/Forrester/Hodgson/**Cartwright**	71.4	3 - 3	03 - 03
Heat 02	**White**/**Anderson**/Emerson/Swales (R)	71.4	**5 - 1**	08 - 04
Heat 03	**Forrest**/**Morton**/Wright/Durham	72.0	**5 - 1**	13 - 05
Heat 04	**Jackson**/**Anderson**/Emerson/Reading	70.2	**5 - 1**	18 - 06
Heat 05	Forrester/**Forrest**/Hodgson/**Morton** (R)	71.4	2 - 4	20 - 10

Heat 06	**Millen**/Reading/**Cartwright**/Emerson (F)	71.8	**4 - 2**	24 - 12
Heat 07	**Jackson**/Durham/Wright/**Anderson**	71.8	3 - 3	27 - 15
Heat 08	**Millen**/**White**/Hodgson/Swales	71.6	**5 - 1**	32 - 16
Heat 09	**Morton**/**Forrest**/Reading/Emerson	71.4	**5 - 1**	37 - 17
Heat 10	**Millen**/Durham/**Cartwright**/Wright (R)	72.2	**4 - 2**	41 - 19
Heat 11	**Jackson**/Forrester/**White**/Hodgson (R)	71.0	**4 - 2**	45 - 21
Heat 12	Durham/**Cartwright**/Reading/**Forrest**	71.4	2 - 4	47 - 25
Heat 13	**Jackson**/**Morton**/Forrester/Durham	70.4	**5 - 1**	52 - 26

CREWE - John Jackson 12, Jack Millen 12, Dave Morton 7 (+2), Wayne Forrest 7 (+1), Keith White 6 (+1), Cliff Anderson 4 (+2), Ian Cartwright 4.
TEESSIDE - Bruce Forrester 8, Dave Durham 7, Pete Reading 4, Russ Hodgson 3 (+1), Roger Wright 2 (+1), Alan Emerson 2, Tony Swales 0.

John Jackson's good form continued on June 4 at Ellesmere Port, when he became the third Crewe rider in successive years to win the Cheshire Open Championship, after scoring a five ride maximum. Home riders Colin Goad (13) and Graham Drury (13) finished second and third. Rain washed out Crewe's match with Rye House on June 10, denying the Earle Street public the opportunity of witnessing (as billed in the programme) *'The Match Race of the Century'* between Phil Crump and Ole Olsen. Fifty tons of shale had been laid on the track to provide conditions as near as perfect for a possible track record, and a crowd in excess of 5,000 had been anticipated. The match-up was quickly re-arranged for July 15.

Meeting 19 - Tuesday, June 11, 1974 - British League Division II
Barrow Stadium, Holker Street, Barrow-in-Furness
Track Length - 370 yards.

BARROW BOMBERS.....48 CREWE KINGS.....30

Paul O'Neil led Barrow to a comprehensive victory over his former employers with three wins and a second. There was a nasty crash in the first running of Heat 5 involving Graham Tattersall and Jack Millen. Tattersall fell while leading and was run into by Millen, who was unable to avoid the prone rider, with both stretchered off and neither taking any further part in the meeting. Millen sustained a badly sprained ankle and a £70 repair bill for his damaged bike. Crewe failed to gain a single heat advantage despite Dave Morton's three wins and Ian Cartwright's five second places. Wayne Forrest endured another wretched away day, with a second successive blank score.

Heat 01	**Millen**/T.Owen/Kelly/**White**	69.0	3 - 3	03 - 03
Heat 02	Sheldrick/**Cartwright**/Tattersall/**Forrest**	70.0	4 - 2	07 - 05
Heat 03	**Anderson**/Roynon/J.Owen/**Morton** (X)	68.4	3 - 3	10 - 08
Heat 04	O'Neil/**Cartwright**/Sheldrick/**Jackson**	69.8	4 - 2	14 - 10
Heat 05	J.Owen/**Cartwright**/**White**/Tattersall (X)	69.2	3 - 3	17 - 13
Heat 06	T.Owen/Kelly/**Jackson**/**Forrest**	70.8	5 - 1	22 - 14
Heat 07	**Morton**/O'Neil/Sheldrick/**Anderson**	70.8	3 - 3	25 - 17
Heat 08	Sheldrick/**Cartwright**/Kelly/**White**	70.4	4 - 2	29 - 19
Heat 09	J.Owen/Roynon/**Jackson**/**Morton**	70.0	5 - 1	34 - 20
Heat 10	**Morton**/Kelly/T.Owen/**Anderson**	70.0	3 - 3	37 - 23
Heat 11	O'Neil/**Cartwright**/**White** (3 riders only)	71.0	3 - 3	40 - 26
Heat 12	**Morton**/T.Owen/J.Owen/**Forrest** (R)	69.0	3 - 3	43 - 29
Heat 13	O'Neil/Roynon/**Cartwright**/**Anderson** (X)	71.2	5 - 1	48 - 30

BARROW - Paul O'Neil 11, Joe Owen 8 (+2), Tom Owen 8 (+1), Sid Sheldrick 8 (+1), Terry Kelly 6 (+2), Chris Roynon 6 (+2), Graham Tattersall 1.
CREWE - Ian Cartwright 11, Dave Morton 9, Cliff Anderson 3, Jack Millen 3, Keith White 2 (+2), John Jackson 2, Wayne Forrest 0.

Dave Parry was again upset at his team's performance with only Ian Cartwright escaping his criticism. On June 16, Jack Millen was beaten 2-0 by holder Bobby McNeil in the first leg of the Silver Helmet at Eastbourne. Next day, Crewe's attractive clash with Workington became the second consecutive home meeting to be rained off, further adding to their fixture backlog.

A thunderstorm forty minutes prior to the scheduled start time, made an already saturated track waterlogged.

Meeting 20 - Friday, June 21, 1974 - British League Division II
Sunderland Greyhound Stadium, Newcastle Road, East Boldon
Track Length - 310 yards.

SUNDERLAND GLADIATORS.....32 CREWE KINGS.....46

Crewe's winless away run of 24 league matches was finally ended on Wearside, with a fourteen point victory - Sunderland's seventh defeat in a row. The Kings' heat leader trio all scored heavily, with Jack Millen returning to Boldon and helping himself to a paid maximum. John Jackson, due to be married the next day, celebrated his last few hours of bachelorhood with a maximum as Crewe chalked up eight heat advantages and ten individual heat wins. Reserve Brian Johnson top-scored for the home side after winning a pre-match race for the No.7 spot, but Andy Reid, in for the out-of-sorts Wayne Forrest, failed to score on his Crewe debut. Ex-King Gary Moore scored three for the Gladiators in a rare team start.

Heat 01	**Millen**/Wells/**Anderson**/Moore (F)	**64.4** (=TR)	**2 - 4**	02 - 04
Heat 02	Johnson/Harding/**Cartwright**/**Reid** (X)	65.0	5 - 1	07 - 05
Heat 03	Havelock/**Morton**/Meldrum/**White**	66.0	4 - 2	11 - 07
Heat 04	**Jackson**/Dent/**Cartwright**/Harding	65.6	**2 - 4**	13 - 11
Heat 05	**Millen**/Havelock/Meldrum/**Anderson**	65.4	3 - 3	16 - 14
Heat 06	**Jackson**/Moore/Wells/**Reid**	66.4	3 - 3	19 - 17
Heat 07	**Morton**/Dent/**White**/Harding	65.8	**2 - 4**	21 - 21
Heat 08	Johnson/**Anderson**/Moore/**Cartwright** (R)	65.4	4 - 2	25 - 23
Heat 09	**Jackson**/Meldrum/**Cartwright**/Havelock	65.2	**2 - 4**	27 - 27
Heat 10	**White**/**Morton**/Johnson/Wells	65.4	**1 - 5**	28 - 32
Heat 11	**Anderson**/**Millen**/Johnson/Dent	66.6	**1 - 5**	29 - 37
Heat 12	**Jackson**/**Morton**/Meldrum/Havelock (R)	65.6	**1 - 5**	30 - 42
Heat 13	**Millen**/Havelock/**White**/Dent	66.0	**2 - 4**	32 - 46

SUNDERLAND - Brian Johnson 8, Brian Havelock 7, Andy Meldrum 5 (+1), Russ Dent 4, Jim Wells 3 (+1), Gary Moore 3, Vic Harding 2 (+1).
CREWE - John Jackson 12, Jack Millen 11 (+1), Dave Morton 9 (+2), Cliff Anderson 6, Keith White 5, Ian Cartwright 3, Andy Reid 0.

Following Wayne Forrest's demotion, he was put on the transfer list, and replaced in the squad by Mike Gardner, who was given a reprieve by Dave Parry, after the Crewe boss discussed the situation with Jack Millen.

Meeting 21 - Saturday, June 22, 1974 - British League Division II
Shielfield Park Stadium, Tweedmouth, Berwick-upon-Tweed
Track Length - 440 yards.

BERWICK BANDITS.....49 CREWE KINGS.....28

The match took over two hours to complete after a series of delays. In the absence of John Jackson (who was getting married), Crewe finally agreed to move Ian Cartwright to the No.3 spot after Berwick protested to Keith White filling the position. A pile-up in Heat 5 involving Jack Millen and Cartwright, saw a long delay when Millen and Dave Parry complained to the referee, Mr Miller, that a home rider was responsible and should have been excluded for the incident that saw the Kiwi taken to Berwick Infirmary with severe hand and finger injuries. Eventually, the re-run was allowed to take place, with Mike Gardner replacing the Crewe skipper. Later in the meeting, Millen returned and grabbed the track microphone to inform the crowd what he thought of the referee, who had earlier fined him £5 fine for pushing away a St. John Ambulance man who had offered assistance following his fall. Willie Templeton scored his third successive home maximum to help win the points for the Bandits.

Heat 01	**Millen**/Jones/**Anderson**/Morter	75.8	**2 - 4**	02 - 04
Heat 02	Trownson/Morter/**Gardner** (R)/**Reid** (X)	78.4	5 - 0	07 - 04
Heat 03	W.Templeton/Dixon/**Gardner**/**White**	75.4	5 - 1	12 - 05

Heat 04	Farquharson/**Cartwright**/Trownson/**Reid**	76.2	4 - 2	16 - 07
Heat 05	W.Templeton/**Gardner**/**Anderson**/Morter	76.0	3 - 3	19 - 10
Heat 06	D.Templeton/Jones/**Cartwright**/**Gardner** (R)	75.6	5 - 1	24 - 11
Heat 07	**Morton**/Farquharson/Trownson/**White**	76.2	3 - 3	27 - 14
Heat 08	Jones/**Morton**/Morter/**Anderson** (R)	75.4	4 - 2	31 - 16
Heat 09	W.Templeton/**Cartwright**/**Gardner**/Dixon	76.4	3 - 3	34 - 19
Heat 10	D.Templeton/Jones/**Morton**/**White**	75.2	5 - 1	39 - 20
Heat 11	Farquharson/Morter/**Anderson**/**Cartwright** (F)	76.0	5 - 1	44 - 21
Heat 12	**Morton**/Dixon/**Cartwright**/D.Templeton (R)	76.6	**2 - 4**	46 - 25
Heat 13	W.Templeton/**Gardner**/**White**/Farquharson (F)	76.2	3 - 3	49 - 28

BERWICK - Willie Templeton 12, Graham Jones 9 (+2), Colin Farquharson 8, Doug Templeton 6, Denny Morter 5 (+2), Dave Trownson 5 (+1), Robin Dixon 4 (+1).
CREWE - Dave Morton 9, Mike Gardner 6 (+1), Ian Cartwright 6, Cliff Anderson 3 (+1), Jack Millen 3, Keith White 1 (+1), Andy Reid 0.

After the match, Dave Parry commented: *"It was not to be our night as the Kings came across some of the poorest standard of refereeing we have known. I know I have spoken about referee decisions before, but in this case both teams complained. The result of one race was the loss of a Crewe machine and Jack Millen needing hospital treatment after the blatant foul riding of a Berwick rider, but the referee decided that all four riders should contest a re-run."*

Meeting 22 - Monday, June 24, 1974 - British League Division II
L.M.R. Sports Ground, Earle Street, Crewe
Track Length - 430 yards.

CREWE KINGS.....52 BOSTON BARRACUDAS.....26

Speedway returned to Earle Street after a three week rain-imposed break, and started with Bobby McNeil defeating Jack Millen 2-0 (4-0 on aggregate) to retain the Silver Helmet. He lowered the track record to 69.6 in the first heat, then equalled it in the next. Millen rode with a special rubber guard to protect his injured hand. The track record however, didn't last long. John Jackson, interrupting his honeymoon and riding at No.1 to give Millen some respite after his Silver Helmet rides, clipped 0.6 seconds off it, in the first heat of the match, and clearly enjoyed the track conditions which had been specially prepared for the rained-off Crump/Olsen clash. Dave Piddock failed to show for the 'Cudas as only Carl Glover, recent winner of Crewe's World Championship preliminary round, showed any real fight on an evening dominated by the hosts.

Heat 01	**Jackson**/C.Glover/**Anderson**/Hollingworth	**69.0** (TR)	**4 - 2**	04 - 02
Heat 02	**Cartwright**/L.Glover/Burton/**Gardner** (R)	71.4	3 - 3	07 - 05
Heat 03	**Morton**/**White**/Gagen/L.Glover	69.8	**5 - 1**	12 - 06
Heat 04	**Millen**/**Cartwright**/Osborne/Burton	71.4	**5 - 1**	17 - 07
Heat 05	**Morton**/C.Glover/Hollingworth/**White**	70.2	3 - 3	20 - 10
Heat 06	**Jackson**/**Anderson**/Osborne/L.Glover	71.4	**5 - 1**	25 - 11
Heat 07	**Millen**/C.Glover/**Cartwright**/Gagen	71.2	**4 - 2**	29 - 13
Heat 08	**Anderson**/Osborne/**Gardner**/Hollingworth	72.0	**4 - 2**	33 - 15
Heat 09	**Morton**/Osborne/L.Glover/**White**	71.0	3 - 3	36 - 18
Heat 10	**Anderson**/**Jackson**/Hollingworth/Gagen	72.4	**5 - 1**	41 - 19
Heat 11	C.Glover/**Millen**/**Cartwright**/Hollingworth	71.0	3 - 3	44 - 22
Heat 12	**Jackson**/**Cartwright**/Osborne/Gagen (F)	71.6	**5 - 1**	49 - 23
Heat 13	C.Glover/**Morton**/**Millen**/Burton	71.0	3 - 3	52 - 26

CREWE - John Jackson 11 (+1), Dave Morton 11, Ian Cartwright 9 (+3), Cliff Anderson 9 (+1), Jack Millen 9 (+1), Keith White 2 (+1), Mike Gardner 1.
BOSTON - Carl Glover 12, Russell Osborne 7, Les Glover 3 (+1), Rob Hollingworth 2 (+1), Billy Burton 1 (+1), David Gagen 1.

On June 29, Keith White finished joint fourth with 10 points in the Junior Championship of the British Isles at Canterbury, won by favourite Chris Morton. Ian Cartwright also put in a good performance, finishing with one point less than his Crewe team-mate. Meanwhile, transfer listed Wayne Forrest turned down a move to Berwick, due to the travelling involved from his

Leicester base. At Earle Street, a rift was developing between the club and their cricketing landlords over the theft of a few bars of soap! Allegations that Jack Millen had painted some abusive words on the shower wall proved unfounded, although the Kings skipper did state that he fully endorsed the message. The L.M.R. cricket secretary commented: *"Our players took exception to being referred to as Pommie bastards."*

Meeting 23 - Sunday, June 30, 1974 - British League Division II
Quibell Park Stadium, Brumby Wood Lane, Scunthorpe
Track Length - 440 yards.

SCUNTHORPE SAINTS.....35 CREWE KINGS.....43

Scunthorpe's recent revival was halted by an impressive Kings outfit, who provided ten race wins and turned six of these into an advantage. Jack Millen was again in the wars, falling on the final bend of the last lap in Heat 13, while disputing second place with Andy Sims.

Heat 01	McKinlay/**Millen**/Underwood/**Anderson**	79.4	4 - 2	04 - 02
Heat 02	**Cartwright**/Sims/**Gardner**/Hines	81.2	**2 - 4**	06 - 06
Heat 03	**Morton**/**White**/Brown/Evans (F)	80.0	**1 - 5**	07 - 11
Heat 04	**Jackson**/Bywater/Sims/**Cartwright**	80.0	3 - 3	10 - 14
Heat 05	**Millen**/Brown/**Anderson**/Hines	81.0	**2 - 4**	12 - 18
Heat 06	McKinlay/**Jackson**/Underwood/**Gardner** (R)	80.8	4 - 2	16 - 20
Heat 07	**Morton**/**White**/Bywater/Hines	80.2	**1 - 5**	17 - 25
Heat 08	Sims/Underwood/**Anderson**/**Cartwright**	80.4	5 - 1	22 - 26
Heat 09	**Jackson**/Sims/Brown/**Cartwright**	79.6	3 - 3	25 - 29
Heat 10	**Morton**/McKinlay/**White**/Underwood	80.8	**2 - 4**	27 - 33
Heat 11	**Millen**/Brown/**Anderson**/Bywater	81.8	**2 - 4**	29 - 37
Heat 12	**Jackson**/McKinlay/Brown/**Morton** (F)	81.0	3 - 3	32 - 40
Heat 13	**White**/Sims/Bywater/**Millen** (F)	81.2	3 - 3	35 - 43

SCUNTHORPE - Andy Sims 10 (+1), Ken McKinlay 10, Dingle Brown 7 (+2), Jack Bywater 4 (+1), Doug Underwood 4 (+1), Keith Evans 0, Andy Hines 0.
CREWE - John Jackson 11, Dave Morton 9, Keith White 8 (+2), Jack Millen 8, Cliff Anderson 3, Ian Cartwright 3, Mike Gardner 1.

The second away win of the season had Dave Parry believing his team could still force their way into the title race, and he targeted a further five more away victories. He commented: *"I can't see any team picking up points at Crewe, and we are beginning to show some form on opponents' tracks. We have had victories at Sunderland and Scunthorpe and we have quite a few away matches coming up which I expect us to be capable of winning. Among the tracks we still have to visit are Bradford, Weymouth, Long Eaton, Ellesmere Port and Rye House and these matches could conceivably supply us with another five away victories."* Parry rated Eastbourne and Boston as the main rivals, with Birmingham as dangerous outsiders. The boss however, was unhappy that, apart from the Crewe test, his riders had been overlooked for the other six matches in the Division II series with Poland.

Meeting 24 - Monday, July 1, 1974 - British League Division II
L.M.R. Sports Ground, Earle Street, Crewe
Track Length - 430 yards.

CREWE KINGS.....46 SCUNTHORPE SAINTS.....32

The unfancied Saints put up quite a performance at Earle Street, and after a shrewd tactical substitute move in Heat 8, they trailed by only two points. Doug Underwood, Dingle Brown and Andy Sims all scored well, with home junior Andy Reid loaned to the visitors for the night, contributing three points. For the Kings, John Jackson scored his customary full house and there were double figure returns for Dave Morton and Ian Cartwright, who had been elevated to No.1 in the absence of Jack Millen. Paul Wells made his home league debut, but Mike Gardner's mechanical woes continued. After putting his own machine out of action at Scunthorpe the previous day, he loaned Colin Farquharson's, only to blow it up in Heat 4!

Heat 01	Sims/**Cartwright**/McKinlay/**Anderson**	72.8	2 - 4	02 - 04
Heat 02	**Gardner**/Reid/**Wells**/Hines	73.0	**4 - 2**	06 - 06
Heat 03	Underwood/**Morton**/**White**/Bywater	71.0	3 - 3	09 - 09
Heat 04	**Jackson**/Brown/Reid/**Gardner** (R)	69.6	3 - 3	12 - 12
Heat 05	**Morton**/**White**/Sims/McKinlay (R)	70.6	**5 - 1**	17 - 13
Heat 06	Brown/**Cartwright**/**Anderson**/Hines	72.2	3 - 3	20 - 16
Heat 07	**Jackson**/Underwood/**Gardner**/Bywater	70.6	**4 - 2**	24 - 18
Heat 08	Underwood/Sims/**Anderson**/**Wells**	72.0	1 - 5	25 - 23
Heat 09	**Morton**/Brown/**White**/Hines	71.0	**4 - 2**	29 - 25
Heat 10	**Cartwright**/Underwood/**Anderson**/Bywater (R)	71.8	**4 - 2**	33 - 27
Heat 11	**Jackson**/McKinlay/Sims/**Wells**	71.0	3 - 3	36 - 30
Heat 12	**Cartwright**/**White**/Brown/Sims	72.2	**5 - 1**	41 - 31
Heat 13	**Jackson**/**Morton**/Underwood/Hines	71.0	**5 - 1**	46 - 32

CREWE - John Jackson 12, Dave Morton 10 (+1), Ian Cartwright 10, Keith White 6 (+3), Mike Gardner 4, Cliff Anderson 3 (+1), Paul Wells 1.
SCUNTHORPE - Doug Underwood 11, Dingle Brown 8, Andy Sims 7 (+2), Andy Reid* 3 (+1), Ken McKinlay 3, Jack Bywater 0, Andy Hines 0.

Dave Morton proved he was more than capable of competing in Division I racing, when scoring his first senior maximum for Hackney in their 49-29 home win over Wolverhampton on July 5. Among his victims was Ole Olsen, whom he beat twice.

Meeting 25 - Sunday, July 7, 1974 - British League Division II
Arlington Raceway, Arlington Road, Hailsham, Eastbourne
Track Length - 342 yards.

EASTBOURNE EAGLES.....54 CREWE KINGS.....24

The Kings made the long journey south to ride in Eastbourne's first evening meeting for three seasons. With Bobby McNeil on international duty, Crewe held hopes of a possible upset, but these soon disappeared as the Eagles banged in four maximums to lead by eighteen points after six heats. The scoreline suggested a walkover, but there was some close crowd-pleasing racing.

Heat 01	Geer/Jarman/**Cartwright**/**Anderson**	62.8	5 - 1	05 - 01
Heat 02	Yeates/Weatherley/**Wells**/**Bessent**	62.4	5 - 1	10 - 02
Heat 03	Gachet/**Morton**/**White**/Middleditch	63.2	3 - 3	13 - 05
Heat 04	Weatherley/**Jackson**/Sampson/**Wells**	63.6	4 - 2	17 - 07
Heat 05	Gachet/Middleditch/**Anderson**/**Cartwright**	64.2	5 - 1	22 - 08
Heat 06	Geer/Jarman/**Jackson**/**Bessent** (F)	63.2	5 - 1	27 - 09
Heat 07	Sampson/**Morton**/Weatherley/**Wells**	64.4	4 - 2	31 - 11
Heat 08	Jarman/**White**/Yeates/**Cartwright**	63.0	4 - 2	35 - 13
Heat 09	Gachet/**Morton**/Middleditch/**Jackson**	64.0	4 - 2	39 - 15
Heat 10	Jarman/**White**/**Morton**/Geer (R)	63.2	3 - 3	42 - 18
Heat 11	Yeates/**Cartwright**/**Anderson**/Sampson (X)	63.2	3 - 3	45 - 21
Heat 12	Geer/**Morton**/Middleditch/**Jackson**	63.8	4 - 2	49 - 23
Heat 13	Yeates/Gachet/**Anderson**/**White**	63.6	5 - 1	54 - 24

EASTBOURNE - Paul Gachet 11 (+1), Peter Jarman 10 (+2), Martin Yeates 10, Trevor Geer 9, Steve Weatherley 6 (+1), Neil Middleditch 4 (+1), Mike Sampson 4.
CREWE - Dave Morton 9 (+1), Keith White 5 (+1), Cliff Anderson 3 (+1), Ian Cartwright 3, John Jackson 3, Paul Wells 1, Mike Bessent* 0.

Meeting 26 - Monday, July 8, 1974 - Division II International, Third Test
L.M.R. Sports Ground, Earle Street, Crewe
Track Length - 430 yards.

ENGLAND.....74 POLAND.....34

With Poland 2-0 up in the series, England finally broke their duck with a forty point victory at Earle Street. Crewe trio Jackson, Morton and White scored as many points as the combined total of the tourists, and with Graham Drury, Carl Glover and Mitch Graham also scoring double figures, it was hardly surprising that the match result was decided with four heats still to race.

Heat 01	Cieslak/Glover/Drury/Wozniak (F)	70.4	3 - 3	03 - 03
Heat 02	Nowak/Forrester/Rembas/Graham	71.4	2 - 4	05 - 07
Heat 03	Jackson/Morton/Goerlitz/Stach (F)	70.2	5 - 1	10 - 08
Heat 04	Graham/Cieslak/Wozniak/Forrester	71.0	3 - 3	13 - 11
Heat 05	Morton/Jackson/Nowak/Rembas	71.2	5 - 1	18 - 12
Heat 06	Glover/Drury/Stach/Goerlitz	70.6	5 - 1	23 - 13
Heat 07	White/Cieslak/Pusey/Wozniak	70.8	4 - 2	27 - 15
Heat 08	Drury/Rembas/Glover/Nowak (X)	71.4	4 - 2	31 - 17
Heat 09	White/Stach/Forrester/Goerlitz	72.0	4 - 2	35 - 19
Heat 10	Glover/Drury/Cieslak/Wozniak	71.4	5 - 1	40 - 20
Heat 11	Nowak/Graham/Forrester/Rembas	71.6	3 - 3	43 - 23
Heat 12	Morton/Jackson/Stach/Goerlitz	70.6	5 - 1	48 - 24
Heat 13	Graham/White/Cieslak/Wozniak	71.2	5 - 1	53 - 25
Heat 14	Jackson/Morton/Nowak/Rembas	70.4	5 - 1	58 - 26
Heat 15	Drury/Stach/Glover/Goerlitz	71.4	4 - 2	62 - 28
Heat 16	Morton/Cieslak/Jackson/Wozniak	71.6	4 - 2	66 - 30
Heat 17	Nowak/Glover/Drury/Rembas	72.0	3 - 3	69 - 33
Heat 18	Graham/White/Stach/Goerlitz	71.4	5 - 1	74 - 34

ENGLAND - Dave Morton 13 (+2), Graham Drury 12 (+4), Carl Glover 12, John Jackson 11 (+2), Mitch Graham 11, Keith White (Reserve) 10 (+2), Bruce Forrester 4 (+1), Geoff Pusey (Reserve) 1. Team Manager: Joe Thurley.
POLAND - Marek Cieslak 11, Boguslaw Nowak 11, Franciszek Stach 7, Jerzy Rembas 3, Mieczyslaw Wozniak 1 (+1), Jacek Goerlitz 1. Team Manager: Josef Olejeczak. *(Wozniak replaced Andrzej Jurczynski and Nowak replaced Ryszard Fabiszewski.)*

Meeting 27 - Friday, July 12, 1974 - British League Division II
Derwent Park Stadium, Workington
Track Length - 398 yards.

WORKINGTON COMETS.....42 CREWE KINGS.....36

A depleted Kings outfit almost pulled off a surprise win. John Jackson continued his good run of form at Derwent Park with five race wins, and there was a first race victory for Comets' sixteen-year-old schoolboy Steve Lawson, loaned to Crewe in place of Mike Gardner. Paul Wells came in for Cliff Anderson, who was missing due to a scheduled trip to Denmark. Jackson ended a good evening's work by winning the Rider of the Night final.

Heat 01	Graham/**Jackson**/Owen/**Cartwright**	74.2	4 - 2	04 - 02
Heat 02	**Lawson**/Hornby/Stobbart/**Wells** (F)	75.2	3 - 3	07 - 05
Heat 03	Watson/**White**/Cowland/**Lawson** (F)	78.0	4 - 2	11 - 07
Heat 04	**Jackson**/Mackay/Stobbart/**Wells**	75.0	3 - 3	14 - 10
Heat 05	**Morton**/**Cartwright**/Watson/Cowland (R)	76.0	**1 - 5**	15 - 15
Heat 06	**Jackson**/Graham/Owen/**Lawson**	74.4	3 - 3	18 - 18
Heat 07	**Morton**/Mackay/**White**/Stobbart	75.2	**2 - 4**	20 - 22
Heat 08	Hornby/Owen/**Cartwright**/**Wells**	77.6	5 - 1	25 - 23
Heat 09	**Jackson**/Cowland/Watson/**Lawson**	76.6	3 - 3	28 - 26
Heat 10	Graham/**Morton**/Owen/**White**	77.2	4 - 2	32 - 28
Heat 11	Hornby/Mackay/**Cartwright**/**White**	77.8	5 - 1	37 - 29
Heat 12	**Jackson**/Graham/**Morton**/Watson	76.0	**2 - 4**	39 - 33
Heat 13	**Jackson**/Cowland/Mackay/**Morton** (F)	76.8	3 - 3	42 - 36

WORKINGTON - Mitch Graham 10, Bernie Hornby 8, Malcolm Mackay 7 (+2), Taffy Owen 5 (+2), Steve Watson 5 (+1), Alan Cowland 5, Darrell Stobbart 2 (+2).
CREWE - John Jackson 17, Dave Morton 9, Ian Cartwright 4 (+1), Steve Lawson* 3, Keith White 3, Paul Wells 0, *Jack Millen (R/R).*

Meeting 28 - Monday, July 15, 1974 - British League Division II
L.M.R. Sports Ground, Earle Street, Crewe
Track Length - 430 yards.

CREWE KINGS.....49 SUNDERLAND GLADIATORS.....29

The Kings won their 40th successive home league match and completed their second double of the season. The visitors made the perfect start when Andy Meldrum and Jim Wells raced to a

5-1 win, but that was as good as it got for the Gladiators. For the Kings, Paul Wells won his first league race in Heat 2, and John Jackson chalked up yet another Earle Street maximum. Dave Morton had an expensive ride in Heat 9, when he blew an engine, and Andy Reid avoided a near disaster when his front wheel came loose during one of his outings.

Heat 01	Meldrum/J.Wells/**Anderson/Cartwright**	71.0	1 - 5	01 - 05
Heat 02	**P.Wells/Reid**/Harding/Johnson	73.4	**5 - 1**	06 - 06
Heat 03	**White/Morton**/Havelock/Barclay	71.8	**5 - 1**	11 - 07
Heat 04	**Jackson**/Swales/**P.Wells**/Johnson	70.0	**4 - 2**	15 - 09
Heat 05	**White/Morton**/J.Wells/Meldrum	70.2	**5 - 1**	20 - 10
Heat 06	**Anderson/Cartwright**/Swales/Havelock (R)	72.2	**5 - 1**	25 - 11
Heat 07	**Jackson**/Havelock/Barclay/**P.Wells**	70.6	3 - 3	28 - 14
Heat 08	**Cartwright**/Meldrum/J.Wells/**Reid** (R)	72.8	3 - 3	31 - 17
Heat 09	**White**/Swales/Harding/**Morton** (R)	72.0	3 - 3	34 - 20
Heat 10	**Anderson**/Havelock/**Cartwright**/Barclay	72.6	**4 - 2**	38 - 22
Heat 11	**Jackson**/J.Wells/Meldrum/**Reid**	71.0	3 - 3	41 - 25
Heat 12	Havelock/**White/Anderson**/Swales	71.4	3 - 3	44 - 28
Heat 13	**Jackson/Morton**/Meldrum/J.Wells	72.2	**5 - 1**	49 - 29

CREWE - John Jackson 12, Keith White 11, Cliff Anderson 8 (+1), Dave Morton 6 (+3), Ian Cartwright 6 (+1), Paul Wells 4, Andy Reid 2 (+1).
SUNDERLAND - Brian Havelock 8, Andy Meldrum 7 (+1), Jim Wells 6 (+2), Tim Swales 5, Vic Harding 2 (+1), George Barclay 1 (+1), Brian Johnson 0.

On a normal evening, following the conclusion of the main event, a number of supporters would make an early exit, but on this occasion nobody left the stadium, as the second-half contained the three race international match-up between ex-Crewe hero Phil Crump and the two-times World Champion Ole Olsen. The Earle Street faithful were hoping for a classic encounter and they were not to be disappointed. Olsen won the first by a tyre width in a time of 70.6, but Crump, roared on by the majority of the crowd, took the next, then swept round the boards on the last bend to pip Olsen on the line to win 2-1. Olsen though, would have the final say when winning the Oliver Rix Garages sponsored Rider of the Night final, beating Crump, John Jackson and Dave Morton. Dave Parry meanwhile, made a move for Hackney's Les Ott, who was currently on loan at Rye House and recovering from a broken collar-bone. To ensure that Crewe did not break the maximum three loan rider rule (Jackson - Halifax, White - Leicester and Morton - Hackney), Ott ended his association with Hackney, to become a club asset.

Meeting 29 - Monday, July 22, 1974 - British League Division II
L.M.R. Sports Ground, Earle Street, Crewe
Track Length - 430 yards.

CREWE KINGS.....55 PETERBOROUGH PANTHERS.....23

The injury-decimated Panthers were loaned new signing Les Ott, who showed up well with two second places after initially out-gating Dave Morton in Heat 9 and John Jackson two races later. The Kings' big win was achieved on a wet evening and on an already heavily watered track. Jackson again went through the card and there was a paid maximum for Morton. Jack Millen's return to action however, didn't last long, as he withdrew from the meeting after retiring in the opening heat. Conditions in the latter stages of the match had deteriorated so much, the second-half was cancelled.

Heat 01	Carter/**Cartwright**/Clark/**Millen** (R)	72.0	2 - 4	02 - 04
Heat 02	**Anderson/Gardner**/Cornwell/Drewett (F)	73.0	**5 - 1**	07 - 05
Heat 03	**Morton/White**/Carter/Osborn	71.4	**5 - 1**	12 - 06
Heat 04	**Jackson/Gardner**/Cornwell/Cairns (R)	73.2	**5 - 1**	17 - 07
Heat 05	**Morton/White**/Clark/Osborn	71.0	**5 - 1**	22 - 08
Heat 06	**Anderson/Cartwright**/Drewett/Cairns (R)	73.2	**5 - 1**	27 - 09
Heat 07	**Jackson**/Clark/**Gardner**/Carter (R)	72.8	**4 - 2**	31 - 11
Heat 08	Clark/**Cartwright/Anderson**/Cornwell	75.8	3 - 3	34 - 14
Heat 09	**Morton**/Ott/**White**/Drewett	75.2	**4 - 2**	38 - 16

Heat 10	**Cartwright**/**Gardner**/Osborn/Carter (R)	81.0	**5 - 1**	43 - 17
Heat 11	**Jackson**/Ott/Clark/**Anderson**	77.0	3 - 3	46 - 20
Heat 12	**White**/Osborn/**Gardner**/Cornwell	80.2	**4 - 2**	50 - 22
Heat 13	**Jackson**/**Morton**/Clark/Osborn	76.0	**5 - 1**	55 - 23

CREWE - John Jackson 12, Dave Morton 11 (+1), Ian Cartwright 9 (+1), Mike Gardner 8 (+3), Keith White 8 (+2), Cliff Anderson 7 (+1), Jack Millen 0.
PETERBOROUGH - Brian Clark 9 (+1), Roy Carter 4, Les Ott* 4, Steve Osborn 3, Phil Cornwell 2, Chris Drewett 1, Peter Cairns 0, *Ken Matthews (R/R).*

On July 25, Keith White confirmed his reputation as one of England's most promising young riders, when he won the Lunn-Poly Trophy at Long Eaton.

Meeting 30 - Monday, July 29, 1974 - British League Division II
L.M.R. Sports Ground, Earle Street, Crewe
Track Length - 430 yards.

CREWE KINGS.....54 STOKE POTTERS.....24

A second home meeting in a row was affected by pouring rain, but despite treacherous conditions, the meeting passed off with only a few minor mishaps. John Jackson again remained unbeaten, stretching his sequence of Earle Street successive league wins to 18 (29 races unbeaten by an opponent). Les Ott's debut in Crewe colours ended with a second place, but a fall in the first attempt to run Heat 4, put him out of the match with a badly sprained wrist and a broken bone in his index finger. As a contest, Crewe riders provided all but one race winner, and had secured the league points by the end of Heat 9. Cliff Anderson had his best meeting of the season so far, winning two races on the way to collecting a paid eleven points.

Heat 01	**Morton**/Broadbanks/Bridgett/**Cartwright**	73.6	3 - 3	03 - 03
Heat 02	**Anderson**/**Ott**/Cusworth/Newton	75.4	**5 - 1**	08 - 04
Heat 03	**White**/**Morton**/Pusey/Holden (R)	72.4	**5 - 1**	13 - 05
Heat 04	**Jackson**/**Anderson**/Newton/Bastable	72.8	**5 - 1**	18 - 06
Heat 05	**Morton**/Broadbanks/**White**/Bridgett	73.0	**4 - 2**	22 - 08
Heat 06	**Jackson**/**Cartwright**/Bastable/Cusworth	73.4	**5 - 1**	27 - 09
Heat 07	**Jackson**/Broadbanks/**Anderson**/Pusey	71.6	**4 - 2**	31 - 11
Heat 08	**Anderson**/**Cartwright**/Bridgett/Newton	73.8	**5 - 1**	36 - 12
Heat 09	**White**/**Morton**/Cusworth/Bastable	74.0	**5 - 1**	41 - 13
Heat 10	Bridgett/**White**/**Cartwright**/Pusey	76.8	3 - 3	44 - 16
Heat 11	**Jackson**/Broadbanks/**Anderson**/Bridgett	75.2	**4 - 2**	48 - 18
Heat 12	**White**/Cusworth/Pusey/**Cartwright**	77.0	3 - 3	51 - 21
Heat 13	**Jackson**/Broadbanks/Cusworth/**Morton** (R)	73.0	3 - 3	54 - 24

CREWE - John Jackson 15, Keith White 12, Dave Morton 10 (+2), Cliff Anderson 10 (+1), Ian Cartwright 5 (+3), Les Ott 2 (+1), *Jack Millen (R/R).*
STOKE - Mike Broadbanks 10, Alan Bridgett 5 (+1), Andy Cusworth 5 (+1), Geoff Pusey 2 (+1), Steve Bastable 1, Mick Newton 1, Steve Holden 0.

Jack Millen's future was in doubt after his withdrawal from the match the previous week. His knee had again failed to hold-up, and the specialist who had operated on his troublesome joint stated that the problem was serious enough to end the Kiwi's career. Millen though, not content to rest at his Church Lane home in Wistaston, was in the pits for the Potters clash, and performed an admirable welding job on the frame of Keith White's bike, when a crack appeared after the youngster's Heat 3 win.

Meeting 31 - Tuesday, July 30, 1974 - British League Division II
Wessex Stadium, Radipole Lane, Weymouth
Track Length - 380 yards.

WEYMOUTH WIZARDS.....41 CREWE KINGS.....37

Crewe's faint title hopes faded on the south coast, in front of a healthy 2,256 holiday crowd, when they narrowly lost to bottom club Weymouth. A combination of falls and retirements didn't help the away cause, but the Wizards, missing their two strongest heat leaders, fought like tigers for every point and fully-deserved victory. Transfer-listed Wayne Forrest was recalled to the Crewe line-up in place of Les Ott, scoring six points, including a victory in Heat 2.

Heat 01	**Morton**/Mullarkey/Foot/**Cartwright**	73.3	3 - 3	03 - 03
Heat 02	**Forrest**/**Wells**/Lomas/Paddington (F)	76.8	**1 - 5**	04 - 08
Heat 03	**White**/Couzens/Swindells/**Anderson**	73.2	3 - 3	07 - 11
Heat 04	Mullarkey/**Forrest**/Paddington/**Jackson** (R)	75.0	4 - 2	11 - 13
Heat 05	Couzens/Swindells/**Cartwright**/**Morton** (F)	72.8	5 - 1	16 - 14
Heat 06	**Jackson**/Foot/Lomas/**Wells** (F)	73.0	3 - 3	19 - 17
Heat 07	**White**/Mullarkey/Paddington/**Anderson**	72.5	3 - 3	22 - 20
Heat 08	Lomas/**Cartwright**/**Forrest**/Foot (F)	75.0	3 - 3	25 - 23
Heat 09	Couzens/Swindells/**Jackson**/**Wells**	73.0	5 - 1	30 - 24
Heat 10	**White**/**Morton**/Couzens/Foot (R)	72.4	**1 - 5**	31 - 29
Heat 11	Mullarkey/**Morton**/Lomas/**Cartwright**	72.7	4 - 2	35 - 31
Heat 12	Foot/**White**/**Jackson**/Swindells	73.5	3 - 3	38 - 34
Heat 13	**Morton**/Couzens/Mullarkey/**Anderson** (R)	72.9	3 - 3	41 - 37

WEYMOUTH - Kelvin Mullarkey 11 (+1), Nigel Couzens 11, Steve Lomas 6 (+1), Russell Foot 6, Geoff Swindells 5 (+3), Brian Paddington 2 (+1), *Clark Facey (R/R)*.
CREWE - Keith White 11, Dave Morton 10 (+1), Wayne Forrest 6 (+1), John Jackson 5 (+1), Ian Cartwright 3, Paul Wells 2 (+1), Cliff Anderson 0.

Dave Parry was full of praise for the Weymouth riders following their gritty performance. Mike Gardner missed the trip and the previous night's home match, to try and solve his mechanical problems, following a catalogue of engine failures. Jack Millen, keen to get back into action, turned to the Crewe Alexandra physio Mick Gill, in an attempt to improve the strength in his right knee.

Meeting 32 - Monday, August 5, 1974 - British League Division II
L.M.R. Sports Ground, Earle Street, Crewe
Track Length - 430 yards.

CREWE KINGS.....51 COATBRIDGE TIGERS.....27

Dave Morton stole the limelight from maximum man John Jackson with his own full house and a string of fast times. The Partington youngster, clearly benefiting from his rides with Hackney, equalled Jackson's six week-old track record in Heat 12, and recorded two more sub 70 second times. Coatbridge gated well and led briefly early on, but were swept aside by eight home heat advantages from Heat 6 onwards. Every Crewe rider, except Mike Gardner, enjoyed another bumper pay night.

Heat 01	**Morton**/Gifford/Adlington/**Cartwright** (R)	71.4	3 - 3	03 - 03
Heat 02	Wilson/Ferreira/**Anderson**/**Gardner** (R)	74.0	1 - 5	04 - 08
Heat 03	**White**/Dawson/**Ott**/Gallacher	70.4	**4 - 2**	08 - 10
Heat 04	**Jackson**/**Anderson**/Ferreira/Quigley	70.0	**5 - 1**	13 - 11
Heat 05	Gifford/**White**/**Ott**/Adlington (F)	71.6	3 - 3	16 - 14
Heat 06	**Morton**/**Cartwright**/Wilson/Quigley	69.4	**5 - 1**	21 - 15
Heat 07	**Jackson**/Gallacher/**Anderson**/Dawson	70.0	**4 - 2**	25 - 17
Heat 08	**Cartwright**/Adlington/**Anderson**/Ferreira	71.2	**4 - 2**	29 - 19
Heat 09	**White**/Gifford/**Ott**/Wilson	70.2	**4 - 2**	33 - 21
Heat 10	**Morton**/Gallacher/**Cartwright**/Dawson (R)	69.2	**4 - 2**	37 - 23
Heat 11	**Jackson**/Gifford/**Anderson**/Wilson	70.0	**4 - 2**	41 - 25
Heat 12	**Morton**/**Ott**/Quigley/Gallacher	**69.0** (=TR)	**5 - 1**	46 - 26
Heat 13	**Jackson**/**White**/Ferreira/Wilson (R)	70.2	**5 - 1**	51 - 27

CREWE - John Jackson 12, Dave Morton 12, Keith White 10 (+1), Cliff Anderson 6 (+1), Ian Cartwright 6 (+1), Les Ott 5 (+2), Mike Gardner 0.
COATBRIDGE - Dave Gifford 9, Mike Ferreira 4 (+1), Jimmy Gallacher 4, John Wilson 4, Robin Adlington 3 (+1), Grahame Dawson 2, Chris Quigley 1.

Mike Gardner's spell at Crewe ended after completing just half a lap of his opening ride in Heat 2. On returning to the pits, he collected his equipment and stormed out of the meeting, leaving

Dave Parry little alternative but to sack him. On August 8, the challenge match at Stoke became another victim of the inclement weather. In the published Division II averages, John Jackson lay in 5th place, with a mark of just under 10.00.

Meeting 33 - Friday, August 9, 1974 - British League Division II
East of England Showground, Alwalton, Peterborough
Track Length - 380 yards.

PETERBOROUGH PANTHERS.....37 CREWE KINGS.....41

For once it was the opposition who suffered crucial mechanical failures, as the Kings pulled off a surprise victory in the first part of this double header with Stoke, inflicting the Panthers first home reversal of the season. The visitors started with a 4-2 in Heat 1, and they led throughout, with Dave Morton claiming a second successive maximum, ably backed by John Jackson and Les Ott, who won his first race in Crewe colours.

Heat 01	**Morton**/Clark/**Cartwright**/Drewett (F)	70.4	**2 - 4**	02 - 04
Heat 02	Dugard/**Ott**/**Forrest**/Cairns	73.4	3 - 3	05 - 07
Heat 03	**White**/Osborn/**Anderson**/Carter (R)	71.6	**2 - 4**	07 - 11
Heat 04	**Jackson**/Lanham/**Ott**/Dugard	70.0	**2 - 4**	09 - 15
Heat 05	**Morton**/Clark/Osborn/**Cartwright**	69.6	3 - 3	12 - 18
Heat 06	Clark/Lanham/**Jackson**/**Forrest** (R)	69.8	5 - 1	17 - 19
Heat 07	Lanham/**Ott**/**White**/Dugard	70.4	3 - 3	20 - 22
Heat 08	**Ott**/Drewett/**Cartwright**/Cairns	72.8	**2 - 4**	22 - 26
Heat 09	**Jackson**/Carter/Osborn/**Forrest** (R)	71.0	3 - 3	25 - 29
Heat 10	Clark/**White**/Drewett/**Anderson**	70.0	4 - 2	29 - 31
Heat 11	**Morton**/Dugard/**Cartwright**/Lanham (R)	69.6	**2 - 4**	31 - 35
Heat 12	**Jackson**/Clark/Osborn/**White** (F)	70.0	3 - 3	34 - 38
Heat 13	**Morton**/Lanham/Carter/**Ott**	70.4	3 - 3	37 - 41

PETERBOROUGH - Brian Clark 12, Mike Lanham 9 (+1), Steve Osborn 5 (+3), Eric Dugard 5, Roy Carter 3 (+1), Chris Drewett 3, Peter Cairns 0.
CREWE - Dave Morton 12, John Jackson 10, Les Ott 8, Keith White 6 (+1), Ian Cartwright 3, Wayne Forrest 1 (+1), Cliff Anderson 1.

Meeting 34 - Monday, August 12, 1974 - British League Division II
L.M.R. Sports Ground, Earle Street, Crewe
Track Length - 430 yards.

CREWE KINGS.....61 BARROW BOMBERS.....17

Crewe well and truly grounded the sorry looking Bombers, with ten maximum heat scores, and at one stage, looked set to challenge Belle Vue Colts' record 63-15 league win. Needing another 5-1 in the final heat to equal the 1968 score, John Jackson won the race, to complete a sixth consecutive home maximum, but Keith White retired when the earth wire worked loose on his magneto. Les Ott showed what a valuable acquisition he could turn out to be with a paid twelve, but it was Dave Morton who again stole the show, knocking a full second off the old track record, clocking a breathtaking time of 68.0. Stuart Cope scored four points in a rare team appearance and Andy Reid was loaned to Barrow as a replacement for the injured Sid Sheldrick.

Heat 01	**Morton**/**Cartwright**/T.Owen/Roynon	**68.0** (TR)	**5 - 1**	05 - 01
Heat 02	**Anderson**/**Cope**/Sheldrick/Tattersall	70.4	**5 - 1**	10 - 02
Heat 03	**White**/**Ott**/Kelly/J.Owen	70.0	**5 - 1**	15 - 03
Heat 04	**Jackson**/**Anderson**/Reid/Tattersall	70.2	**5 - 1**	20 - 04
Heat 05	**White**/**Ott**/T.Owen/Roynon (R)	70.2	**5 - 1**	25 - 05
Heat 06	**Morton**/**Cartwright**/Sheldrick/Reid (R)	69.6	**5 - 1**	30 - 06
Heat 07	**Jackson**/**Anderson**/Kelly/J.Owen	71.6	**5 - 1**	35 - 07
Heat 08	**Cartwright**/T.Owen/**Cope**/Tattersall	69.8	**4 - 2**	39 - 09
Heat 09	**White**/**Ott**/Reid/Sheldrick	70.4	**5 - 1**	44 - 10
Heat 10	**Morton**/**Cartwright**/J.Owen/Kelly (R)	69.8	**5 - 1**	49 - 11
Heat 11	**Jackson**/T.Owen/**Cope**/Reid (R)	69.8	**4 - 2**	53 - 13
Heat 12	**Morton**/**Ott**/Sheldrick/Reid	72.4	**5 - 1**	58 - 14
Heat 13	**Jackson**/T.Owen/J.Owen/**White** (R)	70.4	3 - 3	61 - 17

CREWE - John Jackson 12, Dave Morton 12, Ian Cartwright 9 (+3), Keith White 9, Les Ott 8 (+4), Cliff Anderson 7 (+2), Stuart Cope 4 (+1).
BARROW - Tom Owen 8, Mick Sheldrick 3, Joe Owen 2 (+1), Terry Kelly 2, Andy Reid* 2, Chris Roynon 0, Graham Tattersall 0.

Dave Morton's Heat 1 time was later recognised by the *Guinness Book Of Records* and he joined Barry Meeks in the *Lap Speed* section (see page 288).

Meeting 35 - Thursday, August 15, 1974 - British League Division II
Long Eaton Stadium, Station Road, Long Eaton
Track Length - 366 yards.

LONG EATON ARCHERS.....41 CREWE KINGS.....37

The two teams had a history of postponed meetings, and at 3.00pm it looked as though the weather hoodoo had struck again, after referee Bill Daff originally declared the track unfit for racing following three days of heavy rain. However, with a drying wind and the exhaustive efforts of the track crew plus a number of hardy helpers, he changed his mind at 5.00pm, allowing the match to go ahead. In fact, conditions improved so much, by the time racing commenced, parts of the track had to be watered after the first heat! John Jackson topped the score charts with 16 points and cropped a fifth of a second off Barry Duke's 1969 track record in Heat 7. The contest seemed to be heading for an easy home win, until the Kings staged a comeback in the second half of the match to take it to a last heat decider.

Heat 01	Bouchard/**Morton**/Rackett/**Cartwright**	71.2	4 - 2	04 - 02
Heat 02	Brown/**Ott**/Finch/**Cope**	74.8	4 - 2	08 - 04
Heat 03	Bass/**White**/Witt/**Anderson**	72.2	4 - 2	12 - 06
Heat 04	Molyneux/**Jackson**/Brown/**Ott**	71.2	4 - 2	16 - 08
Heat 05	Bass/Witt/**White**/**Morton**	72.4	5 - 1	21 - 09
Heat 06	**Jackson**/Bouchard/Rackett/**Cope**	69.6	3 - 3	24 - 12
Heat 07	**Jackson**/Molyneux/Brown/**White** (R)	**69.2** (TR)	3 - 3	27 - 15
Heat 08	**Morton**/**Ott**/Finch/Rackett	71.6	**1 - 5**	28 - 20
Heat 09	**Jackson**/Witt/Bass/**Cartwright**	70.6	3 - 3	31 - 23
Heat 10	**Morton**/**White**/Bouchard/Rackett	70.4	**1 - 5**	32 - 28
Heat 11	Molyneux/**Ott**/Finch/**Morton** (F)	70.6	4 - 2	36 - 30
Heat 12	**Jackson**/Bouchard/**White**/Witt	70.2	**2 - 4**	38 - 34
Heat 13	Molyneux/**Jackson**/**Morton**/Bass	70.0	3 - 3	41 - 37

LONG EATON - Alan Molyneux 11, Geoff Bouchard 8, Phil Bass 7 (+1), Max Brown 5 (+1), Alan Witt 5 (+1), Steve Finch 3, Nigel Rackett 2 (+1).
CREWE - John Jackson 16, Dave Morton 9 (+1), Les Ott 6 (+1), Keith White 6 (+1), Cliff Anderson 0, Ian Cartwright 0, Stuart Cope 0, *Jack Millen (R/R)*.

Crewe's glamour four team tournament featuring Division I sides Belle Vue, Cradley and Wolverhampton hit a snag over appearance money demanded by Ole Olsen, reputed to be £150. Len Silver quickly resolved matters by replacing Wolves with his own Hackney team. The Kings received a further set-back for the money-spinner, when the speedway authorities refused them permission to use Phil Crump in their line-up. Admission was raised for the meeting to 60p for adults, 30p for children and senior citizens, with an extra 10p charge for a grandstand seat. On Saturday, August 17, the Crewe management and Supporters Club entered a float in the Crewe Carnival in the hope of drumming up some extra support. On board were Dave Parry, Stuart Cope and Mick Mellor.

Meeting 36 - Monday, August 19, 1974 - Inter-League Four Team Tournament
L.M.R. Sports Ground, Earle Street, Crewe
Track Length - 430 yards.

BELLE VUE ACES.....33 CRADLEY UNITED.....25
CREWE KINGS.....22 HACKNEY HAWKS.....16

Crewe failed to bridge the Division I class barrier, but did beat Hackney and gave Cradley a run for their money. A season's best crowd approaching 5,000 turned up to witness a Belle Vue victory, but the majority of the crowd had to wait until Heat 12 before they were cheering a home win, when John Jackson headed Hackney's Barry Thomas. Dave Morton and Ian Cartwright added to the wins, as only Cradley's John Boulger managed to remain unbeaten. Jack Millen returned after a seven week absence and escaped unhurt after falling in Heat 13.

		B	CU	CK	H
Heat 01..... Price/Pusey/**D.Morton**/Maloney	70.2	2	3	1	0
Heat 02..... Lovaas/Tyrer/**Millen**/Cribb	69.8	2	0	1	3
Heat 03..... Boulger/Sjösten/**White**/Thomas	69.4	2	3	1	0
Heat 04..... C.Morton/Saunders/Cole/**Jackson** (R)	70.6	3	1	0	2
Heat 05..... Boulger/**D.Morton**/Tyrer/Saunders	69.4	1	3	2	0
Heat 06..... Pusey/**Millen**/Thomas/Cole	70.2	3	0	2	1
Heat 07..... Lovaas/Price/C.Morton/**White**	70.4	1	2	0	3
Heat 08..... Sjösten/**Jackson**/Cribb/Maloney	69.6	3	1	2	0
Heat 09..... Sjösten/**D.Morton**/Lovaas/Cole	69.6	3	0	2	1
Heat 10..... Boulger/C.Morton/**Cartwright**/Maloney	69.8	2	3	1	0
Heat 11..... Pusey/Cribb/Saunders/**White**	70.8	3	2	0	1
Heat 12..... **Jackson**/Thomas/Tyrer/Price	70.4	1	0	3	2
Heat 13..... Sjösten/Price/Saunders/**Millen** (F)	71.0	3	2	0	1
Heat 14..... **D.Morton**/Thomas/Cribb/C.Morton	70.4	0	1	3	2
Heat 15..... **Cartwright**/Tyrer/Cole/Maloney	71.2	2	1	3	0
Heat 16..... Boulger/Pusey/**Jackson**/Lovaas	70.0	2	3	1	0

BELLE VUE - Sören Sjösten 11, Chris Pusey 10, Chris Morton 6, Paul Tyrer 6.
CRADLEY - John Boulger 12, Arthur Price 7, Bruce Cribb 4, Howard Cole 2.
CREWE - Dave Morton 8, John Jackson 6, Ian Cartwright (Reserve) 4, Jack Millen 3, Keith White 1.
HACKNEY - Dag Lovaas 7, Barry Thomas 5, Hugh Saunders 4, Geoff Maloney 0.

Dave Parry was quick to praise the new concept and was hopeful that a new knockout cup could be set-up involving all first and second division teams. He commented: *"Considering that it is the Second Division which is producing all the stars and then being robbed of them, something ought to be done to bring the top riders to Division II tracks in genuine competition, and there are Division II teams capable of defeating senior grade opponents. I think Crewe could hold most Division I teams at Earle Street, although I wouldn't expect us to defeat the likes of Belle Vue."*

Meeting 37 - Monday, August 26, 1974 - M6 Trophy, Four Team Tournament, First Leg
L.M.R. Sports Ground, Earle Street, Crewe
Track Length - 430 yards.

CREWE KINGS.....32 BIRMINGHAM BRUMMIES.....27
ELLESMERE PORT GUNNERS.....20 STOKE POTTERS.....17

Rain marred the opening leg of the M6 Trophy at Earle Street, but proved a great leveller, with the Kings only winning by a slender five point margin. Title-chasing Birmingham turned up with only three riders, so drafted in Crewe junior Paul Wells, as a replacement for Phil Herne.

		C	B	E	S
Heat 01.... Pusey/Browning/**Cartwright**/Drury	73.8	1	2	0	3
Heat 02.... **White**/Goad/Wells/Bastable	72.2	3	1	2	0
Heat 03.... **Ott**/Broadbanks/Wasley/Day	72.6	3	0	1	2
Heat 04.... **Jackson**/Taylor/Cusworth/Askew	72.4	3	0	2	1
Heat 05.... Askew/Broadbanks/**Cartwright**/Goad	76.2	1	3	0	2
Heat 06.... **White**/Day/Cusworth/Drury	72.2	3	2	0	1
Heat 07.... Taylor/Wells/Pusey/**Ott** (R)	75.4	0	2	3	1
Heat 08.... Browning/**Jackson**/Wasley/Bastable	76.0	2	3	1	0
Heat 09.... Wasley/Cusworth/**Cartwright**/Wells (R)	75.4	1	0	3	2
Heat 10.... Browning/Taylor/Broadbanks/**White**	76.0	0	3	2	1
Heat 11.... **Ott**/Bridgett/Hughes/Askew (R)	76.6	3	0	1	2
Heat 12.... **Jackson**/Day/Goad/Pusey (R)	74.0	3	2	1	0
Heat 13.... **White**/Askew/Wasley/Pusey (R)	75.2	3	2	1	0

Heat 14 .... Day/**Cartwright**/Taylor/Bridgett	75.0	2	3	1	0
Heat 15 .... Browning/Cusworth/**Ott**/Goad	76.8	1	3	0	2
Heat 16 .... **Jackson**/Hughes/Wells/Broadbanks (R)	75.0	3	1	2	0

CREWE - John Jackson 11, Keith White 9, Les Ott 7, Ian Cartwright 5.
BIRMINGHAM - Arthur Browning 11, Ricky Day 7, Carl Askew 5, Paul Wells* 4
ELLESMERE PORT - Steve Taylor 8, Nigel Wasley 6, Colin Goad 3, Wayne Hughes (Reserve) 3, Graham Drury 0.
STOKE - Andy Cusworth 6, Mike Broadbanks 5, Geoff Pusey 4, Alan Bridgett (Reserve) 2, Steve Bastable 0.

Outspoken Crewe boss Dave Parry reacted furiously to the news that no Crewe rider had been chosen for the Divison II test series with Australasia, and ordered his riders to boycott any international calls if they were requested to fill-in as replacements.

Meeting 38 - Tuesday, August 27, 1974 - M6 Trophy, Four Team Tournament, Second Leg
Perry Barr Greyhound Stadium, Regina Drive, Walsall Road, Birmingham
Track Length - 350 yards.

BIRMINGHAM BRUMMIES.....34 STOKE POTTERS.....27
ELLESMERE PORT GUNNERS.....18 CREWE KINGS.....17

(Scores after two legs – Birmingham 61, Crewe 49, Stoke 44, Ellesmere Port 38)

Only John Jackson won a heat for the Kings as Birmingham took control of the M6 Trophy. A George Major maximum helped secure a seven point victory over Stoke.

		B	S	E	C
Heat 01 ..... Broadbanks/Drury/**Jackson**/Day	65.8	0	3	2	1
Heat 02 ..... Browning/**White**/Pusey/Goad	66.0	3	1	0	2
Heat 03 ..... Hart/Newton/Allott/**Morton** (F)	64.8	3	2	1	0
Heat 04 ..... Major/Bastable/Meredith/**Ott**	65.4	3	2	1	0
Heat 05 ..... Day/**Morton**/Bastable/Goad	65.6	3	1	0	2
Heat 06 ..... Browning/Drury/Newton/**Ott**	65.8	3	1	2	0
Heat 07 ..... Hart/Meredith/**Jackson**/Pusey	65.0	3	0	2	1
Heat 08 ..... Major/Broadbanks/**White**/Taylor	64.8	3	2	0	1
Heat 09 ..... Pusey/Taylor/**Ott**/Day	66.2	0	3	2	1
Heat 10 ..... Broadbanks/Meredith/**Morton**/Browning (F)	68.0	0	3	2	1
Heat 11 ..... Bastable/Hart/**White**/Drury	65.2	2	3	0	1
Heat 12 ..... Major/**Jackson**/Newton/Allott	65.6	3	1	0	2
Heat 13 ..... Meredith/**White**/Day/Bridgett (R)	65.6	1	0	3	2
Heat 14 ..... **Jackson**/Browning/Bastable/Taylor (R)	65.8	2	1	0	3
Heat 15 ..... Broadbanks/Hart/Goad/**Ott**	65.4	2	3	1	0
Heat 16 ..... Major/Drury/Pusey/**Morton**	66.0	3	1	2	0

BIRMINGHAM - George Major 12, John Hart 10, Arthur Browning 8, Ricky Day 4.
STOKE - Mike Broadbanks 11, Steve Bastable 7, Geoff Pusey 5, Mick Newton 4, Alan Bridgett (Reserve) 0.
ELLESMERE PORT - Duncan Meredith 8, Graham Drury 6, Steve Taylor 2, Nicky Allott (Reserve) 1, Colin Goad 1.
CREWE - John Jackson 7, Keith White 6, Dave Morton 3, Les Ott 1.

Meeting 39 - Wednesday, August 28, 1974 - M6 Trophy, Four Team Tournament, Third Leg
Ellesmere Port Stadium, Thornton Road, Ellesmere Port
Track Length - 423 yards.

CREWE KINGS.....32 ELLESMERE PORT GUNNERS.....25
BIRMINGHAM BRUMMIES.....21 STOKE POTTERS.....16

(Scores after three legs – Birmingham 82, Crewe 81, Ellesmere Port 63, Stoke 60)

Dave Morton and John Jackson were both unbeaten, as the Kings pulled eleven points back on Birmingham, to trail by just a single point going into the deciding leg. Morton achieved his maximum the hard way, by coming from the back on two occasions.

		C	E	B	S
Heat 01 .... **Morton**/Day/Goad (R)/Woodward (R)	77.0	3	0	2	0
Heat 02 .... **Jackson**/Browning/Drury/Broadbanks	75.2	3	1	2	0
Heat 03 .... Wasley/Pusey/Askew/**White**	76.2	0	3	1	2

Heat 04	Taylor/**Ott**/Major/Bridgett	76.8	2	3	1	0
Heat 05	**Morton**/Pusey/Drury/Major	75.8	3	1	0	2
Heat 06	**Jackson**/Hughes/Askew (F)/Bridgett (R)	76.8	3	2	0	0
Heat 07	Browning/Taylor/**White**/Woodward	77.0	1	2	3	0
Heat 08	Broadbanks/Wasley/Day/**Ott**	75.8	0	2	1	3
Heat 09	**Morton**/Browning/Wasley/Cusworth	76.4	3	1	2	0
Heat 10	**Jackson**/Taylor/Pusey/Day (F)	75.8	3	2	0	1
Heat 11	Broadbanks/Major/**White**/Hughes	77.0	1	0	2	3
Heat 12	Drury/Askew/Woodward/**Ott**	76.8	0	3	2	1
Heat 13	**Jackson**/Major/Wasley/Woodward	76.6	3	1	2	0
Heat 14	**Morton**/Taylor/Askew/Broadbanks (X)	76.4	3	2	1	0
Heat 15	**White**/Drury/Cusworth/Day	77.4	3	2	0	1
Heat 16	Pusey/Browning/**Ott**/Goad (R)	76.4	1	0	2	3

CREWE - John Jackson 12, Dave Morton 12, Keith White 5, Les Ott 3.
ELLESMERE PORT - Steve Taylor 9, Graham Drury 7, Nigel Wasley 7, Wayne Hughes (Reserve) 2, Colin Goad 0.
BIRMINGHAM - Arthur Browning 9, George Major 5, Carl Askew 4, Ricky Day 3.
STOKE - Geoff Pusey 8, Mike Broadbanks 6, Andy Cusworth (Reserve) 1, Bryan Woodward 1, Alan Bridgett 0.

John Jackson was confirmed as the Crewe representative for the Division II Riders Championship at Wimbledon on September 28.

Meeting 40 - Thursday, August 29, 1974 - M6 Trophy, Four Team Tournament, Fourth Leg
Lyme Valley Sports Stadium, Loomer Road, Chesterton
Track Length - 348 yards.

STOKE POTTERS.....30 BIRMINGHAM BRUMMIES.....28
CREWE KINGS.....25 ELLESMERE PORT GUNNERS.....13

(Final aggregate scores - Birmingham 110, Crewe 106, Stoke 90, Ellesmere Port 76)

The Brummies secured the M6 Trophy by a four point margin from Crewe, who finished runners-up for the second season in a row. The meeting was delayed due to crowd congestion outside the stadium and by the eventual start, Loomer Road was bursting at the seams. Potters star Mike Broadbanks was unbeaten, with Keith White top of the Kings quartet.

			S	B	C	E
Heat 01	Broadbanks/Major/**White**/Meredith	65.6	3	2	1	0
Heat 02	**Jackson**/Browning/Pusey/Allott	65.4	1	2	3	0
Heat 03	Askew/Drury/**Morton**/Woodward (X)	67.3	0	3	1	2
Heat 04	Bastable/**Ott**/Taylor/Day (X)	68.7	3	0	2	1
Heat 05	Broadbanks/Askew/**Jackson**/Taylor	66.7	3	2	1	0
Heat 06	Drury/**White**/Grahame/Bridgett (R)	67.9	0	1	2	3
Heat 07	Major/**Ott**/Hughes/Woodward (R)	67.0	0	3	2	1
Heat 08	Browning/Bastable/**Morton**/Meredith	67.7	2	3	1	0
Heat 09	Broadbanks/**Morton**/Allott/Day	66.8	3	0	2	1
Heat 10	Pusey/Meredith/**Ott**/Askew	67.9	3	0	1	2
Heat 11	Browning/**White**/Bridgett/Taylor	67.6	1	3	2	0
Heat 12	Bastable/Major/Drury/**Jackson**	68.0	3	2	0	1
Heat 13	Major/Pusey/**Morton**/Taylor (R)	67.8	2	3	1	0
Heat 14	Broadbanks/Browning/Drury/**Ott**	66.9	3	2	0	1
Heat 15	**Jackson**/Bridgett/Meredith/Day	67.1	2	0	3	1
Heat 16	**White**/Askew/Bastable/Hughes (F)	67.5	1	2	3	0

STOKE - Mike Broadbanks 12, Steve Bastable 9, Geoff Pusey 6, Alan Bridgett (Reserve) 3, Bryan Woodward 0.
BIRMINGHAM - Arthur Browning 10, George Major 10, Carl Askew 7, Alan Grahame (Reserve) 1, Ricky Day 0.
CREWE - Keith White 8, John Jackson 7, Dave Morton 5, Les Ott 5.
ELLESMERE PORT - Graham Drury 7, Duncan Meredith 3, Nicky Allott 1, Wayne Hughes (Reserve) 1, Steve Taylor 1.

On September 2, Crewe's home match with Canterbury was postponed following heavy morning rain. Jack Millen also announced his retirement for the season, unless called upon in an emergency. He was hoping a complete rest would help him regain fitness for next season. On September 9, another home fixture was rained off, this time against Weymouth, prompting the

Crewe management to extend the season to October 21.

Meeting 41 - Tuesday, September 10, 1974 - British League Division II
Ellesmere Port Stadium, Thornton Road, Ellesmere Port
Track Length - 423 yards.

ELLESMERE PORT GUNNERS.....37 CREWE KINGS.....41

With Gunner Colin Goad on international duty at Barrow, the Kings took full advantage by winning a thriller at Thornton Road. The home side led by four after Heat 10, but a late Crewe surge saw them win the remaining heats to see them home by four points. John Jackson and Dave Morton dropped a single point apiece.

Heat 01	Drury/**Morton**/Meredith/**Ott**	75.8	4 - 2	04 - 02
Heat 02	Allott/**Cope/Forrest**/Stafford (F)	80.4	3 - 3	07 - 05
Heat 03	Hughes/**White/Cartwright**/Wasley (X)	75.4	3 - 3	10 - 08
Heat 04	**Jackson**/Pusey/**Forrest**/Allott	77.8	**2 - 4**	12 - 12
Heat 05	**Morton**/Hughes/**Ott**/Wasley	76.2	**2 - 4**	14 - 16
Heat 06	Drury/**Jackson**/Meredith/**Cope**	76.0	4 - 2	18 - 18
Heat 07	Allott/**Cartwright/White**/Pusey	78.0	3 - 3	21 - 21
Heat 08	Meredith/**Ott/Forrest**/Stafford	79.6	3 - 3	24 - 24
Heat 09	**Jackson**/Hughes/Wasley/**Cope** (F)	77.8	3 - 3	27 - 27
Heat 10	Drury/Meredith/**Cartwright/White**	78.4	5 - 1	32 - 28
Heat 11	**Morton/Ott**/Stafford/Allott	78.2	**1 - 5**	33 - 33
Heat 12	**Jackson**/Drury/**White**/Hughes	77.8	**2 - 4**	35 - 37
Heat 13	**Morton**/Pusey/**Cartwright**/Wasley	78.8	**2 - 4**	37 - 41

ELLESMERE PORT - Graham Drury 11, Duncan Meredith 7 (+1), Wayne Hughes 7, Nicky Allott 6, Geoff Pusey* 4, Nigel Wasley 1 (+1), Ken Stafford 1.
CREWE - John Jackson 11, Dave Morton 11, Ian Cartwright 5 (+1), Les Ott 5 (+1), Keith White 4 (+1), Wayne Forrest 3 (+2), Stuart Cope 2.

On the same night, Birmingham won 58-20 at Weymouth to consolidate their lead at the top. Jack Millen gave up his track maintenance duties at Earle Street to take up a welding contract in Germany, with Dave Parry and Cliff Anderson taking over.

Meeting 42 - Friday, September 13, 1974 - British League Division II
Albion Rovers Stadium, Cliftonhill Park, Main Street, Coatbridge
Track Length - 409 yards.

COATBRIDGE TIGERS.....57 CREWE KINGS.....20

Only Ian Cartwright mastered the Cliftonhill Park track for the visitors, as they were duly hammered in a one-sided league encounter. Heavy lunchtime rain didn't help matters, and during the match, rain again fell to make track conditions even worse. Brian Collins maintained his fine run of form for the Tigers with another maximum.

Heat 01	Dawson/Gifford/**Cartwright/Ott**	74.6	5 - 1	05 - 01
Heat 02	**Cartwright**/Wilson/Beresford/**Forrest**	72.4	3 - 3	08 - 04
Heat 03	Adlington/Gallacher/**Cartwright/White**	72.0	5 - 1	13 - 05
Heat 04	Collins/Wilson/**Jackson/Forrest**	74.0	5 - 1	18 - 06
Heat 05	Adlington/**Ott**/Gallacher (F)/**Morton** (F)	72.4	3 - 2	21 - 08
Heat 06	Gifford/**Cartwright**/Dawson/**Jackson**	73.2	4 - 2	25 - 10
Heat 07	Collins/Wilson/**White/Morton** (R)	74.6	5 - 1	30 - 11
Heat 08	**Cartwright**/Dawson/**Ott**/Beresford	73.6	**2 - 4**	32 - 15
Heat 09	Gallacher/Adlington/**Cartwright/Jackson** (R)	72.6	5 - 1	37 - 16
Heat 10	Dawson/Gifford/**Ott/White**	74.2	5 - 1	42 - 17
Heat 11	Collins/Beresford/**Ott/Morton**	76.4	5 - 1	47 - 18
Heat 12	Gallacher/Gifford/**Jackson/White**	75.0	5 - 1	52 - 19
Heat 13	Collins/Adlington/**Cope/Morton** (R)	76.4	5 - 1	57 - 20

COATBRIDGE - Brian Collins 12, Robin Adlington 10 (+2), Dave Gifford 9 (+3), Grahame Dawson 9, Jimmy Gallacher 8 (+1), John Wilson 6 (+2), Jim Beresford 3 (+2).

CREWE - Ian Cartwright 11, Les Ott 5, John Jackson 2, Stuart Cope 1, Keith White 1, Wayne Forrest 0, Dave Morton 0, *Jack Millen (R/R).*

Meeting 43 - Monday, September 16, 1974 - British League Division II
L.M.R. Sports Ground, Earle Street, Crewe
Track Length - 430 yards.

CREWE KINGS.....54 ELLESMERE PORT GUNNERS.....24

Crewe completed another double over the Gunners with a convincing win. Dave Morton and John Jackson were both unbeaten, although Jackson almost suffered his first defeat to a visiting rider since May 27. The Crewe skipper was rather fortunate to win Heat 7, as Nigel Wasley led until a puncture on the last lap allowed him to pass. Keith White and Ian Cartwright proved a formidable winning partnership, both recording paid maximums. For Ellesmere Port, Graham Drury hit the boards in Heat 1 and was stretchered off with arm and ankle injuries. Colin Goad, Ken Stafford and Duncan Meredith all lost the use of their machines during the match, and Wayne Hughes was their only starter in Heat 13.

Heat 01	**Morton**/Hughes/**Ott**/Drury (X)	71.6	**4 - 2**	04 - 02
Heat 02	**Cope**/Stafford/Allott/**Forrest**	72.6	3 - 3	07 - 05
Heat 03	**White**/**Cartwright**/Wasley/Meredith	70.8	**5 - 1**	12 - 06
Heat 04	**Jackson**/Stafford/Allott/**Cope**	71.2	3 - 3	15 - 09
Heat 05	**White**/**Cartwright**/Wasley/Hughes	71.6	**5 - 1**	20 - 10
Heat 06	**Morton**/Allott/**Ott**/Goad	72.6	**4 - 2**	24 - 12
Heat 07	**Jackson**/Wasley/**Cope**/Meredith	72.0	**4 - 2**	28 - 14
Heat 08	**Ott**/**Forrest**/Hughes/Stafford (R)	73.0	**5 - 1**	33 - 15
Heat 09	**Cartwright**/**White**/Allott/Goad	71.6	**5 - 1**	38 - 16
Heat 10	**Morton**/Allott/Wasley/**Ott** (R)	71.4	3 - 3	41 - 19
Heat 11	**Jackson**/Allott/Hughes/**Forrest**	71.6	3 - 3	44 - 22
Heat 12	**Morton**/**Cartwright**/Wasley/Meredith	71.6	**5 - 1**	49 - 23
Heat 13	**Jackson**/**White**/Hughes (3 riders only)	71.2	**5 - 1**	54 - 24

CREWE - John Jackson 12, Dave Morton 12, Keith White 10 (+2), Ian Cartwright 9 (+3), Les Ott 5, Stuart Cope 4, Wayne Forrest 2 (+1).
ELLESMERE PORT - Nicky Allott 9 (+2), Nigel Wasley 6 (+1), Wayne Hughes 5 (+1), Ken Stafford 4, Graham Drury 0, Colin Goad 0, Duncan Meredith 0.

During the second-half, a mini-match between Crewe and Belle Vue, ended all-square. The Kings management were later reported for staging the match as it breached league rules regarding Division I riders appearing at Division II tracks more than a set number of times.

CREWE.....9 BELLE VUE.....9

Heat 01	**D.Morton**/Sjösten/C.Morton/**Jackson** (R)	70.8	3 - 3	03 - 03
Heat 02	Sjösten/**Cartwright**/**D.Morton**/C.Morton	71.4	3 - 3	06 - 06
Heat 03	Sjösten/**Jackson**/**D.Morton**/C.Morton	71.2	3 - 3	09 - 09

CREWE - Dave Morton 5, Ian Cartwright 2, John Jackson 2.
BELLE VUE - Sören Sjösten 8, Chris Morton 1.

Meeting 44 - Wednesday, September 18, 1974 - British League Division II
Odsal Stadium, Rooley Avenue, Bradford
Track Length - 375 yards.

BRADFORD BARONS.....42 CREWE KINGS.....36

In Bradford's final league match of the season, Crewe led by four going into Heat 8, but three successive 5-1's gave the Barons the impetus to hold on. John Jackson and Dave Morton scored twenty-five of the away total, but apart from Keith White's Heat 3 victory, the rest struggled around the Odsal bowl.

Heat 01	**Morton**/Featherstone/Argall/**Ott**	72.2	3 - 3	03 - 03
Heat 02	Fielding/**Forrest**/**Cartwright**/Parkin	75.0	3 - 3	06 - 06

Heat 03	**White**/**Morton**/Wilcock/Fairbairn (X)	72.6	**1 - 5**	07 - 11
Heat 04	Meredith/**Jackson**/Fielding/**Forrest**	74.0	4 - 2	11 - 13
Heat 05	**Morton**/Wilcock/Fairbairn/**Ott**	72.4	3 - 3	14 - 16
Heat 06	**Jackson**/Argall/**Cartwright**/Featherstone	71.4	**2 - 4**	16 - 20
Heat 07	Meredith/**Jackson**/**White**/Parkin	73.2	3 - 3	19 - 23
Heat 08	Fielding/Argall/**Cartwright**/**Forrest**	72.8	5 - 1	24 - 24
Heat 09	Wilcock/Fairbairn/**Jackson**/**Cartwright**	72.2	5 - 1	29 - 25
Heat 10	Featherstone/Argall/**Ott**/**White**	73.4	5 - 1	34 - 26
Heat 11	**Jackson**/Meredith/**Morton**/Parkin	71.6	**2 - 4**	36 - 30
Heat 12	Featherstone/**Jackson**/**White**/Wilcock	72.2	3 - 3	39 - 33
Heat 13	**Morton**/Meredith/Fairbairn/**Cope**	72.2	3 - 3	42 - 36

BRADFORD - Colin Meredith 10, Tony Feathersone 8, Eddie Argall 7 (+3), Mick Fielding 7, Steve Wilcock 6, Mick Fairbairn 4 (+3), Dave Parkin 0.
CREWE - John Jackson 13, Dave Morton 12 (+1), Keith White 5 (+2), Ian Cartwright 3 (+1), Wayne Forrest 2, Les Ott 1, Stuart Cope 0, *Jack Millen (R/R).*

Dave Parry was seething following the defeat and lambasted his team for losing a match they should have won. *"We have thrown the league championship away this season and this was typical of the sort of lazy slapdash performance which has prevented us walking away with the title.....I really laid into my riders and it didn't cool my anger when Keith White went out and won the Rider of the Night final. The Division II Championship has never been as easy to win as it has this year. There isn't a team in the division of the outstanding quality of previous campaigns. We had the riders capable of lifting the title, but we have tossed the opportunity away."*

Meeting 45 - Monday, September 23, 1974 - Cheshire Triangle, Three Team Tournament, First Leg
L.M.R. Sports Ground, Earle Street, Crewe
Track Length - 430 yards.

CREWE KINGS.....46 STOKE POTTERS.....33 ELLESMERE PORT GUNNERS.....29

John Jackson and Dave Morton again went through the card undefeated, and for the second week in succession, the pairing of Keith White and Ian Cartwright caught the eye, dropping only a single point to Nigel Wasley in Heat 4. Crewe took a healthy thirteen lead into the next leg.

			C	S	E
Heat 01	**Morton**/**Ott**/Hughes/Stafford	69.6	**5**	/	**1**
Heat 02	Goad/Pusey/Bastable/Meredith	71.6	/	3	3
Heat 03	**Jackson**/Bouchard/Woodward/**Forrest**	69.6	3	3	/
Heat 04	**Cartwright**/Wasley/**White**/Allott	71.8	**4**	/	**2**
Heat 05	Bridgett/Hughes/Cusworth/Stafford	73.2	/	4	2
Heat 06	**Morton**/Bouchard/Woodward/**Ott**	70.4	3	3	/
Heat 07	**White**/**Cartwright**/Goad/Meredith	71.6	**5**	/	**1**
Heat 08	Allott/Wasley/Cusworth/Bridgett	73.4	/	1	5
Heat 09	**Jackson**/Bastable/Pusey/**Forrest**	73.4	3	3	/
Heat 10	**Morton**/Allott/Wasley/**Ott**	71.8	3	/	3
Heat 11	Bouchard/Hughes/Stafford/Woodward (R)	73.6	/	3	3
Heat 12	**White**/**Cartwright**/Bridgett/Cusworth	73.2	**5**	**1**	/
Heat 13	**Jackson**/Goad/Meredith/**Cope**	73.8	3	/	3
Heat 14	Bastable/Allott/Pusey/Wasley	75.4	/	4	2
Heat 15	**Morton**/Bridgett/**Ott**/Cusworth	74.0	**4**	**2**	/
Heat 16	**Jackson**/Hughes/Stafford/**Cope**	72.8	3	/	3
Heat 17	Woodward/Bouchard/Goad/Meredith	75.4	/	5	1
Heat 18	**White**/**Cartwright**/Pusey/Bastable	73.2	**5**	**1**	/

CREWE - John Jackson 12, Dave Morton 12, Keith White 10, Ian Cartwright 9 (+3), Les Ott 3 (+1), Stuart Cope (Reserve) 0, Wayne Forrest 0.
STOKE - Geoff Bouchard* 9 (+1), Steve Bastable 6 (+1), Alan Bridgett 6, Bryan Woodward 5 (+2), Geoff Pusey 5 (+1), Andy Cusworth 2.
ELLESMERE PORT - Nicky Allott 7, Colin Goad 7, Wayne Hughes 7, Nigel Wasley 5 (+2), Ken Stafford 2 (+2), Duncan Meredith 1 (+1).

It was reported in the *Crewe Chronicle* that the Earle Street track length of 430 yards was in fact incorrect, confirmed by Dave Parry: *"We measured the track last week and found the inner circumference came to 436 yards."* The figure was amended in the match programme on September 30.

Meeting 46 - Tuesday, September 24, 1974 - Cheshire Triangle, Three Team Tournament, Second Leg
Ellesmere Port Stadium, Thornton Road, Ellesmere Port
Track Length - 423 yards.

CREWE KINGS.....43 STOKE POTTERS.....35 ELLESMERE PORT GUNNERS.....29

(Scores after two legs – Crewe 89, Stoke 68, Ellesmere Port 58)

This was Crewe's third win of the season at Thornton Road, which virtually assured them the Cheshire Triangle trophy, with one leg still to complete. John Jackson continued his rich vein of form remaining unbeaten on the night, and there were two heat wins apiece for Keith White and Les Ott, plus a paid ten for Ian Cartwright. Dave Morton celebrated his 21st birthday by cutting his nose and bending the forks of his bike, in a Heat 11 spill.

Heat	Riders	Time	C	S	E
Heat 01	Hughes/**Ott**/**Morton**/Stafford (R)	78.0	3	/	3
Heat 02	**Jackson**/**Anderson**/Bastable/Pusey	79.6	**5**	**1**	/
Heat 03	Woodward/Bouchard/Goad/Meredith	79.8	/	5	1
Heat 04	**White**/**Cartwright**/Wasley/Allott	79.8	**5**	/	**1**
Heat 05	**Ott**/**Morton**/Cusworth/Bridgett	79.0	**5**	**1**	/
Heat 06	Hughes/Bouchard/Woodward/Cusworth	78.8	/	3	3
Heat 07	**Jackson**/Wasley/Allott/**Anderson**	79.8	3	/	3
Heat 08	Cusworth/**White**/**Cartwright**/Bridgett	78.6	3	3	/
Heat 09	Pusey/Meredith/Goad/Bastable	80.8	/	3	3
Heat 10	Hughes/**White**/**Cartwright**/Casey	78.0	3	/	3
Heat 11	**Ott**/Woodward/Bouchard/**Morton** (X)	79.0	3	3	/
Heat 12	Cusworth/Wasley/Allott/Bridgett	78.8	/	3	3
Heat 13	**Jackson**/Meredith/Goad/**Forrest**	80.6	3	/	3
Heat 14	**White**/**Cartwright**/Bastable/Pusey	79.8	**5**	**1**	/
Heat 15	Cusworth/Bridgett/Stafford/Casey	80.2	/	5	1
Heat 16	Meredith/**Forrest**/Casey (F)/**Ott** (X)	83.4	2	/	3
Heat 17	**Jackson**/Bouchard/Woodward/**Forrest**	81.6	3	3	/
Heat 18	Pusey/Wasley/Bastable/Allott	87.2	/	4	2

CREWE - John Jackson 12, Keith White 10, Les Ott 8, Ian Cartwright 6 (+4), Dave Morton 3 (+2), Cliff Anderson 2 (+1), Wayne Forrest (Reserve) 2.
STOKE - Andy Cusworth 10, Geoff Bouchard* 7 (+2), Bryan Woodward 7 (+2), Geoff Pusey 6, Steve Bastable 3, Alan Bridgett 2 (+1).
ELLESMERE PORT - Wayne Hughes 9, Duncan Meredith 7, Nigel Wasley 7, Colin Goad 3 (+2), Nicky Allott 2 (+2), Ken Stafford 1, Steve Casey (Reserve) 0.

Two days later, John Jackson finished runner-up in the Stadium Silver Helmet at Teesside, which was won by home rider Dave Durham.

Saturday, September 28, 1974 - British League Division II Riders Championship
Wimbledon Stadium, Plough Lane, London
Track Length - 309 yards.

WINNER.....CARL GLOVER

John Jackson made his full debut in the Division II Riders Championship, where he finished a credible joint-fourth with 10 points. He started on Cliff Anderson's bike fitted with a new engine, but the high revving unit produced poor grip on the wet Wimbledon track, so reverted back to his own bike for his final three rides, winning Heats 10 and 18. Boston's Carl Glover was the eventual winner after a run-off with Canterbury's Ted Hubbard.

Heat	Riders	Time
Heat 01	Herne/Gifford/**Jackson**/Graham	64.1
Heat 02	Hubbard/Glover/Bouchard/McKinlay	66.0
Heat 03	Forrester/Broadbanks/Owen/Foote	66.4

Heat 04	Lanham/Meredith/McNeil/Drury	65.2
Heat 05	McNeil/Bouchard/Foote/Graham (X)	65.7
Heat 06	McKinlay/Meredith/Owen/**Jackson**	66.4
Heat 07	Glover/Broadbanks/Gifford/Drury	66.4
Heat 08	Hubbard/Lanham/Herne/Forrester	66.8
Heat 09	Broadbanks/Lanham/McKinlay/Templeton	66.6
Heat 10	**Jackson**/Bouchard/Drury/Forrester (F)	65.8
Heat 11	Hubbard/Meredith/Foote/Gifford	67.4
Heat 12	Glover/Herne/Owen (F)/McNeil (X)	65.8
Heat 13	Glover/Meredith/Hughes/Forrester (X)	66.8
Heat 14	**Jackson**/Hubbard/Havelock/Broadbanks (X)	65.6
Heat 15	Bouchard/Lanham/Owen/Gifford	67.5
Heat 16	Herne/Drury/Foote/McKinlay (X)	67.7
Heat 17	Drury/Hubbard/Templeton/Owen (R)	71.1
Heat 18	**Jackson**/Glover/Lanham/Foote	64.9
Heat 19	Havelock/Gifford/Hughes/Forrester (X)	68.4
Heat 20	Herne/Bouchard/Meredith/Templeton (X)	69.5
R/O for 1st......	Glover/Hubbard	66.6

Carl Glover *(Boston)* 13, Ted Hubbard *(Canterbury)* 13, Phil Herne *(Birmingham)* 12, John Jackson *(Crewe)* 10, Geoff Bouchard *(Long Eaton)* 10, Mike Lanham *(Peterborough)* 10, Colin Meredith *(Bradford)* 9, Mike Broadbanks *(Stoke)* 7, Graham Drury *(Ellesmere Port)* 6, Dave Gifford *(Coatbridge)* 5, Ken McKinlay *(Scunthorpe)* 4, Bobby McNeil *(Eastbourne)* 4, Tom Owen *(Barrow)* 3, Bruce Forrester *(Teesside)* 3, Brian Foote *(Rye House)* 3, Mitch Graham *(Workington)* 0. Meeting Reserves: Brian Havelock *(Sunderland)* 4, Bob Hughes *(Weymouth)* 2, Willie Templeton *(Berwick)* 1.

Meetings 47 & 48 - Monday, September 30, 1974 - British League Division II (Double Header)
L.M.R. Sports Ground, Earle Street, Crewe
Track Length - 436 yards.

CREWE KINGS.....52 BRADFORD BARONS.....26

Followed by

CREWE KINGS.....48 RYE HOUSE ROCKETS.....30

The first double header of the season produced two comfortable wins for the Kings. In the Bradford match, John Jackson's run of 30 successive home league and cup victories finally came to an end when Ian Cartwright beat him to the line in Heat 4. Dave Morton, enjoying a fabulous end to the season, recorded his fourth Earle Street maximum in a row, and there were paid ones for Jackson and Cartwright, as the Kings gained a handsome revenge over the Yorkshiremen following their Odsal defeat twelve days previous. Top scorer for the Barons was Tony Featherstone who missed his first scheduled ride after breaking down en-route. In the second match, normal service was resumed with a John Jackson maximum, with double figure returns from Cartwright and Morton. Brian Foote had an outstanding meeting for the Rockets, taking three heat victories on his way to scoring half the visiting total.

Heat 01	**Morton**/**Ott**/Argall/Parkin	73.2	**5 - 1**	05 - 01
Heat 02	**Cartwright**/Fielding/Parkin/**Anderson** (R)	75.4	3 - 3	08 - 04
Heat 03	**White**/Fairbairn/Wilcock/**Forrest**	74.2	3 - 3	11 - 07
Heat 04	**Cartwright**/**Jackson**/Meredith/Fielding	72.4	**5 - 1**	16 - 08
Heat 05	**White**/Featherstone/**Forrest**/Argall	72.8	**4 - 2**	20 - 10
Heat 06	**Morton**/Meredith/**Ott**/Parkin	71.0	**4 - 2**	24 - 12
Heat 07	**Jackson**/**Cartwright**/Wilcock/Fairbairn (R)	72.8	**5 - 1**	29 - 13
Heat 08	Featherstone/**Ott**/Wilcock/**Anderson**	71.8	2 - 4	31 - 17
Heat 09	**Cartwright**/**White**/Meredith/Fielding	72.2	**5 - 1**	36 - 18
Heat 10	**Morton**/Wilcock/**Ott**/Fairbairn	72.2	**4 - 2**	40 - 20
Heat 11	**Jackson**/Featherstone/Argall/**Anderson**	73.0	3 - 3	43 - 23
Heat 12	**Morton**/**White**/Meredith/Fairbairn	71.6	**5 - 1**	48 - 24
Heat 13	**Jackson**/Featherstone/**White**/Wilcock	71.4	**4 - 2**	52 - 26

CREWE - Dave Morton 12, Keith White 11 (+2), Ian Cartwright 11 (+1), John Jackson 11 (+1), Les Ott 6 (+1), Wayne Forrest 1, Cliff Anderson 0, *Jack Millen R/R.*
BRADFORD - Tony Featherstone 9, Steve Wilcock 5 (+1), Colin Meredith 5, Eddie Argall 2 (+1), Mick Fairbairn 2, Mick Fielding 2, Dave Parkin 1 (+1).

Heat 01	Foote/**Morton**/**Ott**/Barclay	74.4	3 - 3	03 - 03
Heat 02	**Forrest**/Cooper/Young/**Cope**	75.8	3 - 3	06 - 06
Heat 03	**Cartwright**/**White**/Wigley/Gibbons (R)	73.0	**5 - 1**	11 - 07
Heat 04	**Jackson**/Barclay/**Forrest**/Cooper	72.0	**4 - 2**	15 - 09
Heat 05	Foote/**Cartwright**/Stevens/**White**	74.4	2 - 4	17 - 13
Heat 06	**Ott**/**Morton**/Barclay/Young	73.8	**5 - 1**	22 - 14
Heat 07	**Jackson**/**Forrest**/Wigley/Gibbons	73.6	**5 - 1**	27 - 15
Heat 08	Foote/Cooper/**Cope**/**Forrest**	75.0	1 - 5	28 - 20
Heat 09	**Cartwright**/**White**/Young/Barclay	75.2	**5 - 1**	33 - 21
Heat 10	**Morton**/Foote/**Ott**/Wigley	73.0	**4 - 2**	37 - 23
Heat 11	**Jackson**/Foote/Stevens/**Forrest**	73.0	3 - 3	40 - 26
Heat 12	**Morton**/**Cartwright**/Gibbons/Barclay	74.8	**5 - 1**	45 - 27
Heat 13	**Jackson**/Foote/Cooper/**White** (R)	73.2	3 - 3	48 - 30

CREWE - John Jackson 12, Ian Cartwright 10 (+1), Dave Morton 10 (+1), Wayne Forrest 6 (+1), Les Ott 5 (+1), Keith White 4 (+2), Stuart Cope 1.
RYE HOUSE - Brian Foote 15, Bob Cooper 5 (+2), George Barclay 3, Stan Stevens 2 (+1), Bob Young 2 (+1), Pete Wigley 2, John Gibbons 1, *Steve Clarke (R/R).*

Meeting 49 - Thursday, October 3, 1974 - Cheshire Triangle, Three Team Tournament, Third Leg
Lyme Valley Sports Stadium, Loomer Road, Chesterton
Track Length - 348 yards.

STOKE POTTERS.....40 CREWE KINGS.....39
ELLESMERE PORT GUNNERS.....27

(Final aggregate scores - Crewe 128, Stoke 108, Ellesmere Port 85)

The Potters prevented a Kings clean sweep, but could not stop them from winning the Cheshire Triangle. Crewe lost Dave Morton after he piled into the safety fence in Heat 1, bending the frame of his machine in the process. John Jackson was replaced by Wayne Forrest in the next, after his mechanic accidentally filled his fuel tank with water! Keith White (maximum) and Les Ott steered the Kings to an emphatic victory margin.

			S	C	E
Heat 01	Woodward/**Ott**/**Morton** (F) (3 riders only)	66.9	3	2	/
Heat 02	**Anderson**/Goad/Meredith (F)/**Forrest** (X)	69.0	/	3	2
Heat 03	Owen/Bastable/Pusey/Hughes (X)	66.5	3	/	3
Heat 04	**White**/Bridgett/Holden/**Cartwright**	68.9	3	3	/
Heat 05	**Ott**/Wasley/**Forrest**/Allott (X)	69.1	/	**4**	**2**
Heat 06	Owen/Woodward/Broadbanks/Stafford (F)	67.4	3	/	3
Heat 07	Holden/**Anderson**/**Jackson**/Bridgett	70.0	3	3	/
Heat 08	**White**/**Cartwright**/Wasley/Allott (R)	69.2	/	**5**	**1**
Heat 09	Bastable/Meredith/Pusey/Goad	68.8	4	/	2
Heat 10	**White**/Woodward/Broadbanks/**Cartwright**	68.8	3	3	/
Heat 11	Owen/**Ott**/Stafford/**Forrest**	69.0	/	2	4
Heat 12	Bridgett/Holden/Wasley/Allott	70.0	5	/	1
Heat 13	**Jackson**/Bastable/Pusey/**Anderson**	68.8	3	3	/
Heat 14	**White**/**Cartwright**/Meredith/Goad	70.2	/	**5**	**1**
Heat 15	Woodward/Broadbanks/Wasley/Allott (R)	69.9	5	/	1
Heat 16	Bastable/**Ott**/**Forrest**/Pusey	70.0	3	3	/
Heat 17	Owen/**Jackson**/**Anderson**/Stafford	69.0	/	3	3
Heat 18	Goad/Bridgett/Meredith/Holden	69.4	2	/	4

STOKE - Steve Bastable 10, Bryan Woodward 10, Alan Bridgett 7, Steve Holden 6 (+2), Mike Broadbanks 4 (+3), Geoff Pusey 3 (+2).
CREWE - Keith White 12, Les Ott 9, Cliff Anderson 6 (+1), John Jackson 6 (+1), Ian Cartwright 4 (+2), Wayne Forrest (Reserve) 2 (+1), Dave Morton 0.
ELLESMERE PORT - Joe Owen* 12, Colin Goad 5, Nigel Wasley 5, Duncan Meredith 4, Ken Stafford (Reserve) 1, Nicky Allott 0, Wayne Hughes 0.

Meeting 50 - Sunday, October 6, 1974 - British League Division II
Rye House Stadium, Rye Road, Hoddesdon
Track Length - 284 yards.

RYE HOUSE ROCKETS.....37 CREWE KINGS.....40

Canterbury were beaten 44-33 in the first match of this double header by Rye House, but found Crewe a much tougher test. The Kings made a dream start with a first heat 5-0, after Dave Morton was twice brought down. The Rockets fought back to lead by one going into Heat 12, but a White/Jackson 5-1 gave Crewe a three point advantage going into the last, where Dave Morton kept his nerve to grab the three points necessary for victory.

Heat 01	**Morton**/**Ott**/Foote (X)/Stevens (X)	73.6	**0 - 5**	00 - 05
Heat 02	Young/Cooper/**Anderson**/**Forrest**	72.0	5 - 1	05 - 06
Heat 03	**White**/Wigley/Gibbons/**Cartwright**	70.4	3 - 3	08 - 09
Heat 04	**Jackson**/Barclay/Young/**Forrest**	68.0	3 - 3	11 - 12
Heat 05	Gibbons/Wigley/**Anderson**/**Ott** (F)	71.0	5 - 1	16 - 13
Heat 06	**Jackson**/Stevens/Foote/**Anderson**	68.0	3 - 3	19 - 16
Heat 07	**White**/Young/**Cartwright**/Barclay	71.4	**2 - 4**	21 - 20
Heat 08	Foote/**Ott**/Cooper/**Anderson**	71.0	4 - 2	25 - 22
Heat 09	**Jackson**/Gibbons/**Forrest**/Wigley (F)	68.2	**2 - 4**	27 - 26
Heat 10	Foote/**White**/Stevens/**Cartwright**	70.0	4 - 2	31 - 28
Heat 11	**Morton**/Barclay/**Ott**/Cooper	71.6	**2 - 4**	33 - 32
Heat 12	**White**/**Jackson**/Foote/Young	68.6	**1 - 5**	34 - 37
Heat 13	**Morton**/Barclay/Gibbons/**Cartwright**	71.4	3 - 3	37 - 40

RYE HOUSE - Brian Foote 8 (+1), John Gibbons 7 (+2), Bob Young 6 (+1), George Barclay 6, Pete Wigley 4 (+1), Bob Cooper 3 (+1), Stan Stevens 3, *Steve Clarke (R/R)*.
CREWE - John Jackson 11 (+1), Keith White 11, Dave Morton 9, Les Ott 5 (+1), Cliff Anderson 2, Ian Cartwright 1, Wayne Forrest 1.

The following night, the home meeting with Workington was called off for a second time, after the Comets refused to ride on the heavy Earle Street track. Dave Parry was adamant that the match should go ahead, but referee Leo Pendergast sided with the visitors. Following the postponement, Parry ordered a re-grading of the track and cancelled a midweek training session. The wet weather was playing havoc with teams trying to complete fixtures, and on October 10, this disruption continued with Teesside's double header, featuring the Kings and Weymouth, rained-off. Two days later, Birmingham were confirmed as league champions following a 46-32 victory at Berwick.

Meetings 51 & 52 - Monday, October 14, 1974 - British League Division II (Double Header)
L.M.R. Sports Ground, Earle Street, Crewe
Track Length - 436 yards.

CREWE KINGS.....52 CANTERBURY CRUSADERS.....26

Followed by

CREWE KINGS.....38 WORKINGTON COMETS.....40

Canterbury were well-beaten in the first match of another double header, but the score did not reflect their efforts, and although only Les Rumsey won a heat, the majority of races were closely contested affairs. John Jackson registered a twelfth successive home maximum (full or paid) and Dave Morton dropped just a single point to team-mate Ian Cartwright in Heat 12. In the second match, two long standing records fell, when the Kings took on bogey side Workington. John Jackson's 56 race unbeaten home run against a visiting rider was ended when he pulled-up in Heat 11. Although Crewe stormed into an early ten point lead, they started to tire in the latter stages, with the extra races taking their toll on man and machinery. A series of tactical substitutions by Comets manager Ian Thomas saw the Cumbrians draw level going into the last, where Mitch Graham and Steve Watson got the better of Jackson and Keith White, to finally end Crewe's winning home league run of 48 matches.

Heat 01	**Morton**/**Ott**/Gooderham/Kennett	72.2	**5 - 1**	05 - 01
Heat 02	Rumsey/**Cartwright**/**Anderson**/Clifton	74.8	3 - 3	08 - 04
Heat 03	**White**/Jones/Cook/**Forrest**	72.4	3 - 3	11 - 07
Heat 04	**Cartwright**/**Jackson**/Hubbard/Clifton	73.0	**5 - 1**	16 - 08
Heat 05	**White**/Gooderham/Kennett/**Forrest**	72.8	3 - 3	19 - 11
Heat 06	**Morton**/Hubbard/**Ott**/Rumsey	72.6	**4 - 2**	23 - 13

Heat 07	**Jackson**/**Cartwright**/Jones/Cook	72.6	**5 - 1**	28 - 14
Heat 08	**Ott**/Kennett/Hubbard/**Anderson**	74.0	3 - 3	31 - 17
Heat 09	**White**/**Jackson**/Hubbard/Rumsey	72.8	**5 - 1**	36 - 18
Heat 10	**Morton**/Jones/**Ott**/Kennett	72.4	**4 - 2**	40 - 20
Heat 11	**Jackson**/Gooderham/Kennett/**Anderson**	72.4	3 - 3	43 - 23
Heat 12	**Cartwright**/**Morton**/Hubbard/Jones	73.8	**5 - 1**	48 - 24
Heat 13	**Jackson**/Gooderham/**White**/Jones	73.0	**4 - 2**	52 - 26

CREWE - John Jackson 13 (+2), Dave Morton 11 (+1), Ian Cartwright 10 (+1), Keith White 10, Les Ott 7 (+1), Cliff Anderson 1 (+1), Wayne Forrest 0, *Jack Millen R/R.*
CANTERBURY - Dave Gooderham 7, Ted Hubbard 6 (+1), Trevor Jones 5, Barney Kennett 4 (+2), Les Rumsey 3, Derek Cook 1 (+1), Graham Clifton 0.

Heat 01	**Morton**/Graham/Stobbart/**Ott** (R)	72.8	3 - 3	03 - 03
Heat 02	**Anderson**/**Forrest**/Hornby/Lawson (R)	76.8	**5 - 1**	08 - 04
Heat 03	**White**/Owen/**Cartwright**/Watson	74.2	**4 - 2**	12 - 06
Heat 04	**Jackson**/Cowland/**Anderson**/Hornby (F)	73.6	**4 - 2**	16 - 08
Heat 05	Graham/**White**/**Cartwright**/Stobbart	71.6	3 - 3	19 - 11
Heat 06	**Morton**/Cowland/**Ott**/Lawson	73.2	**4 - 2**	23 - 13
Heat 07	**Jackson**/Owen/Watson/**Anderson**	73.0	3 - 3	26 - 16
Heat 08	Owen/Cowland/**Ott**/**Forrest**	73.8	1 - 5	27 - 21
Heat 09	Graham/**White**/Cowland/**Cartwright**	72.2	2 - 4	29 - 25
Heat 10	**Morton**/Owen/**Ott**/Hornby	73.6	**4 - 2**	33 - 27
Heat 11	Graham/Hornby/**Forrest**/**Jackson** (R)	72.2	1 - 5	34 - 32
Heat 12	Owen/**Cartwright**/Cowland/**Morton**	73.8	2 - 4	36 - 36
Heat 13	Graham/**Jackson**/Watson/**White**	72.8	2 - 4	38 - 40

CREWE - Dave Morton 9, John Jackson 8, Keith White 7, Ian Cartwright 4 (+1), Cliff Anderson 4, Wayne Forrest 3 (+1), Les Ott 3.
WORKINGTON - Mitch Graham 14, Taffy Owen 12, Alan Cowland 8 (+1), Bernie Hornby 3 (+1), Steve Watson 2 (+1), Darrell Stobbart 1 (+1), Steve Lawson 0.

Dave Parry was gracious in defeat, after seeing the Kings' proud home record ended. *"I have no moans. Workington put up a good show and I would rather see a team come here and do that than have us romping away to a succession of easy wins. They rode hard and they rode well and it was great speedway."* On October 20, Eastbourne beat Birmingham 47-31 in the first leg of the K.O. Cup Final.

Meeting 53 - Monday, October 21, 1974 - British League Division II
L.M.R. Sports Ground, Earle Street, Crewe
Track Length - 436 yards.

CREWE KINGS.....50½ WEYMOUTH WIZARDS.....26½

The season drew to a close at Earle Street with Dave Morton bidding farewell to the Crewe faithful, with a dead-heat for second place in his final race. He won his first two outings, then borrowed John Jackson's bike in Heat 10, after encountering problems with his own machine, only to splutter to a halt on the second lap whilst leading. Jackson secured his ninth full home maximum to win the Supporters Trophy, with Keith White collecting a paid one.

Heat 01	**Morton**/**Ott**/Swindells/Hughes	71.8	**5 - 1**	05 - 01
Heat 02	**Forrest**/Paddington/**Cope**/Foote (R)	73.2	**4 - 2**	09 - 03
Heat 03	**White**/Lomas/**Anderson**/Couzens	72.4	**4 - 2**	13 - 05
Heat 04	**Jackson**/Paddington/Mullarkey/**Cope**	70.4	3 - 3	16 - 08
Heat 05	**White**/**Anderson**/Swindells/Hughes	71.6	**5 - 1**	21 - 09
Heat 06	**Morton**/**Ott**/Mullarkey/Paddington	71.6	**5 - 1**	26 - 10
Heat 07	**Jackson**/Couzens/Lomas/**Cope** (F)	70.8	3 - 3	29 - 13
Heat 08	Swindells/**Ott**/**Forrest**/Foote (R)	73.8	3 - 3	32 - 16
Heat 09	**White**/**Anderson**/Paddington/Mullarkey (R)	73.0	**5 - 1**	37 - 17
Heat 10	Lomas/Couzens/**Ott** (X)/**Morton** (R)	73.4	0 - 5	37 - 22
Heat 11	**Jackson**/Swindells/**Forrest**/Paddington	71.8	**4 - 2**	41 - 24
Heat 12	**Anderson**/**Morton** & Lomas/Couzens	74.2	**4½ - 1½**	45½ - 25½
Heat 13	**Jackson**/**White**/Lomas/Swindells	72.0	**5 - 1**	50½ - 26½

CREWE - John Jackson 12, Keith White 11 (+1), Cliff Anderson 8 (+2), Dave Morton 7½, Les Ott 6 (+2), Wayne Forrest 5 (+1), Stuart Cope 1.
WEYMOUTH - Steve Lomas 8½ (+1), Geoff Swindells 7, Brian Paddington 5, Nigel Couzens 4 (+1), Kelvin Mullarkey 2 (+1), Russell Foot 0, Bob Hughes 0.

In between the fun and games of the second-half, John Jackson won the combined Littlechild Trophy and Geoff Curtis Cup, and there were races between Len Silver and Vic White and Dave Parry and ex-King Pete Saunders. Dave Morton was presented with the Harry W. Dodd Ltd. sponsored Mazda Snowball Trophy, which had been contested in the second half throughout the season. He won the competition with 37 points, with Jackson runner-up (28), and Keith White third (13). On the same night, Birmingham became the third team in successive seasons to achieve the coveted double, when they added the K.O. Cup to their trophy cabinet after beating Eastbourne 50-27 at Perry Barr, to win 81-74 on aggregate.

Meeting 54 - Thursday, October 31, 1974 - British League Division II
Cleveland Park Stadium, Stockton Road, Middlesbrough
Track Length - 335 yards.

TEESSIDE TIGERS.....46 CREWE KINGS.....31

It was third time lucky for the staging of this meeting, which was the first half of a double header. The Kings, minus the services of Dave Morton and Ian Cartwright, who were preparing themselves for a racing stint in New Zealand, turned up with only five riders, so loaned Weymouth's Brian Paddington, who was due to ride in the second match. John Jackson ended the season the way he had started it, when topping the score chart for Crewe. Teesside also beat the Wizards (52-26) in the second meeting.

Heat	Result	Time	Score	Total
Heat 01	Forrester/**Anderson**/**Jackson**/Hodgson	70.2	3 - 3	03 - 03
Heat 02	**Paddington**/Swales/Emerson (R)/**Cope** (F)	73.2	**2 - 3**	05 - 06
Heat 03	**Jackson**/Wright/Reading/**Ott**	69.0	3 - 3	08 - 09
Heat 04	Durham/**Cope**/**White**/Emerson (R)	70.8	3 - 3	11 - 12
Heat 05	Wright/**Jackson**/Reading/**Anderson** (R)	71.2	4 - 2	15 - 14
Heat 06	Forrester/Hodgson/**Paddington**/**White** (R)	70.4	5 - 1	20 - 15
Heat 07	Durham/**Ott**/**Paddington**/Emerson	71.0	3 - 3	23 - 18
Heat 08	Hodgson/**Anderson**/Swales/**Cope**	72.4	4 - 2	27 - 20
Heat 09	Reading/**Jackson**/Wright/**White**	70.4	4 - 2	31 - 22
Heat 10	Forrester/Hodgson/**White**/**Ott**	71.4	5 - 1	36 - 23
Heat 11	**Jackson**/Durham/**Anderson**/Swales	71.2	**2 - 4**	38 - 27
Heat 12	Forrester/Wright/**White**/**Ott**	72.4	5 - 1	43 - 28
Heat 13	**Jackson**/Reading/Durham/**Anderson**	70.2	3 - 3	46 - 31

TEESSIDE - Bruce Forrester 12, Dave Durham 9 (+1), Roger Wright 8 (+1), Russ Hodgson 7 (+2), Pete Reading 7 (+1), Tony Swales 3, Alan Emerson 0.
CREWE - John Jackson 14 (+1), Brian Paddington* 5 (+1), Cliff Anderson 5, Keith White 3 (+1), Stuart Cope 2, Les Ott 2, *Dave Morton (R/R).*

The final league table had a somewhat "unfinished look" about it as Peterborough had given up on staging their double header against champions Birmingham and Ellesmere Port, due to the poor weather. The final standings of the Division II averages saw John Jackson finish 5th and Dave Morton 15th.

In November, Charlie Scarbrough recommenced the training schools in the hope that his riders could compete in matches against fellow training schools around the country. Among the early instructors were John Jackson, Peter Collins, Chris Pusey and Reg Wilson, who passed on their wealth of knowledge and experience to riders from as far afield as Glasgow. On December 22, the Crewe Trainees made their debut in the new "Training Track League" losing 56-18 to the Fen Tigers at the new Mildenhall track. Jack Millen meanwhile, was now employed at neighbours Stoke, supervising further alterations to the Loomer Road circuit, as well as operating his own training school, fuelling rumours that he was about to make the switch to the Potters for the '75 season. Towards the end of the year, Len Silver departed the Crewe scene, and took over at Rye House, after APL relinquished control of all their tracks, bar Reading, which left Violet Littlechild as the only Kings promoter. It was also announced that Division II was to be re-named the New National League, with a number of additional clubs expected to join.

Apart from the 1972 double winning season, the Kings' 1974 campaign was viewed as reasonably successful. True, they had fallen at the first hurdle in the K.O. Cup, and had lost their long unbeaten run at Earle Street, but had certain circumstances been different, the team would have made a far more serious challenge for the title. One of the main reasons for their failure was the lengthy absence of skipper Jack Millen, whose presence on their travels fully fit, would have turned several narrow defeats into victories. Would this have been enough for the Kings to have won back their title? The answer to this lies in the performance of the one outstanding team in the division - Birmingham. They remained unbeaten at home and the fact that they won on nine occasions on the road, indicates that even with Millen, Crewe would still have struggled to overcome the powerful Midlands outfit. Looking at the facts, John Jackson again emerged as the top King, adding 1.4 to his '73 average. His record at Earle Street was actually even more impressive than his 1972 figures. In the league and cup he boasted 65 wins from 79 rides, registering ten full maximums and five paid. Dave Morton too showed why Hackney were so keen for him to race full time for them in the '75 season. His six full and three paid maximums for Crewe didn't really tell the story of his true abilities, but his 6.34 average from 26 matches for the Hawks, more than proved he was ready for first grade speedway. No more could have been asked of Ian Cartwright, Keith White and Cliff Anderson, who all upped their averages considerably. The biggest disappointment was Mike Gardner, signed by Dave Parry to strengthen the middle order, who was finally dismissed after walking out during a meeting for a second time. The one major concern for the club however, was the financial implications brought on by a series of rained-off meetings at Earle Street. Five matches in all fell victim, and of those that survived, many were affected by bad weather that seriously affected attendances. Double header meetings relieved a congested fixture backlog, but didn't produce double the gate receipts. For Crewe to sustain a speedway team in the town, attendances had to significantly improve. The decline could not continue.

- 1974 Season Summary -

				Wins to Crewe	
Date	**Opponents/Meeting**	**Res**	**Score**	**Race**	**Heat**
Tue, March 26	Ell/Sto/Bir (4TT)	L	Crewe 27	6	-
Thu, March 28	Stoke (Ch)	L	34 - 44	5	3
Thu, April 4	Teesside (BL)	A	03 - 09	-	-
Mon, April 8	**Stoke (Ch)**	W	50 - 28	10	10
Mon, April 15	**Birmingham (Ch)**	W	56 - 22	11	10
Tue, April 16	Birmingham (Ch)	L	37 - 40	5	2
Mon, April 22	**World C'ship QR (Ind)**	Carl Glover		-	-
Sat, April 27	Canterbury (BL)	L	32 - 46	6	3
Mon, April 29	**Workington (KOC R1)**	W	43 - 35	7	6
Fri, May 3	Workington (KOC R1)	L	32 - 46	4	0
Mon, May 6	**Eastbourne (BL)**	W	55 - 23	11	10
Thu, May 9	Stoke (BL)	L	37 - 41	7	4
Sun, May 12	Boston (BL)	L	28 - 50	4	1
Mon, May 13	**Long Eaton (BL)**	W	49 - 29	11	9
Mon, May 20	**Berwick (BL)**	W	61 - 17	12	12
Mon, May 27	**Birmingham (BL)**	W	40 - 37	8	7
Tue, May 28	Birmingham (BL)	L	29 - 49	1	0
Mon, June 3	**Teesside (BL)**	W	52 - 26	11	9
Tue, June 11	Barrow (BL)	L	30 - 48	5	0
Fri, June 21	Sunderland (BL)	W	46 - 32	10	8
Sat, June 22	Berwick (BL)	L	28 - 49	3	2
Mon, June 24	**Boston (BL)**	W	52 - 26	11	8

Sun, June 30	Scunthorpe (BL)	W	43 - 35	10	6
Mon, July 1	**Scunthorpe (BL)**	W	46 - 32	9	7
Sun, July 7	Eastbourne (BL)	L	24 - 54	0	0
Mon, July 8	**England v Poland (Int)**	-	74 - 34	-	-
Fri, July 12	Workington (BL)	L	36 - 42	8	3
Mon, July 15	**Sunderland (BL)**	W	49 - 29	11	7
Mon, July 22	**Peterborough (BL)**	W	55 - 23	11	10
Mon, July 29	**Stoke (BL)**	W	54 - 24	12	9
Tue, July 30	Weymouth (BL)	L	37 - 41	7	2
Mon, August 5	**Coatbridge (BL)**	W	51 - 27	11	10
Fri, August 9	Peterborough (BL)	W	41 - 37	9	5
Mon, August 12	**Barrow (BL)**	W	61 - 17	13	12
Thu, August 15	Long Eaton (BL)	L	37 - 41	6	3
Mon, August 19	**Bel/Cra/Hac (IL 4TT)**	L	Crewe 22	3	-
Mon, August 26	**Ell/Sto/Bir (4TT)**	W	Crewe 32	8	-
Tue, August 27	Bir/Ell/Sto (4TT)	L	Crewe 17	1	-
Wed, August 28	Ell/Sto/Bir (4TT)	W	Crewe 32	9	-
Thu, August 29	Sto/Bir/Ell (4TT)	L	Crewe 25	3	-
Tue, September 10	Ellesmere Port (BL)	W	41 - 37	6	5
Fri, September 13	Coatbridge (BL)	L	20 - 57	2	1
Mon, September 16	**Ellesmere Port (BL)**	W	54 - 24	13	9
Wed, September 18	Bradford (BL)	L	36 - 42	6	3
Mon, September 23	**Ellesmere P./Stoke (3TT)**	W	Crewe 46	12	6
Tue, September 24	Ellesmere P./Stoke (3TT)	W	Crewe 43	8	4
Mon, September 30	**Bradford (BL)**	W	52 - 26	12	9
Mon, September 30	**Rye House (BL)**	W	48 - 30	10	7
Thu, October 3	Stoke/Ellesmere P. (3TT)	W	Crewe 39	7	3
Sun, October 6	Rye House (BL)	W	40 - 37	9	5
Mon, October 14	**Canterbury (BL)**	W	52 - 26	12	8
Mon, October 14	**Workington (BL)**	L	38 - 40	7	5
Mon, October 21	**Weymouth (BL)**	W	50½ - 26½	11	9
Thu, October 31	Teesside (BL)	L	31 - 46	4	2

- British League Division II Final Table -

		Home					Away					
	M	W	D	L	F	A	W	D	L	F	A	Pts
1. Birmingham	35	17	1	0	917	485	9	2	6	711	611	55
2. Eastbourne	36	17	0	1	927½	474½	7	3	8	709	692	51
3. Boston	36	18	0	0	841	560	5	2	11	667½	734½	48
4. Workington	36	17	1	0	856	546	5	2	11	626	778	47
5. Crewe	**36**	**17**	**0**	**1**	**919½**	**482½**	**5**	**0**	**13**	**616**	**784**	**44**
6. Teesside	36	15	1	2	834	568	4	0	14	614	788	39
7. Bradford	36	17	0	1	787	614	2	1	15	552	849	39
8. Peterborough	34	14	0	2	740	507	4	1	13	579	822	37
9. Coatbridge	36	17	0	1	879	521	1	0	17	559	814	36
10. Canterbury	36	14	0	4	796	578	4	0	14	606	794	36
11. Berwick	36	14	1	3	762	640	2	0	16	522	879	33
12. Barrow	36	12	2	4	810	589	3	0	15	592½	807½	32
13. Stoke	36	15	0	3	815	588	1	0	17	574	830	32
14. Ellesmere Port ..	35	13	2	3	784	616	1	1	15	547	778	31
15. Long Eaton	36	14	2	2	772	630	0	0	18	530	872	30
16. Rye House	36	12	0	6	745	651	1	0	17	484	915	26
17. Scunthorpe	36	9	2	7	760	640	1	0	17	573	827	22
18. Sunderland	36	10	0	8	755	647	1	0	17	476	923	22
19. Weymouth	36	10	0	8	711½	687½	0	0	18	486½	913½	20

(The Peterborough v Birmingham and Peterborough v Ellesmere Port matches were not raced.)

- Crewe Rider Averages -

(League and Knock Out Cup only)

	M	R	W	Pts	BP	Tot	F	P	CMA
John Jackson	36	160	102	386	12	398	11	6	9.950
Jack Millen	10	29	16	62	4	66	1	2	9.103
Dave Morton	37	167	87	348½	22	370½	6	3	8.874
Keith White	**38**	**162**	**46**	**264**	**37**	**301**	**0**	**4**	**7.432**
Ian Cartwright	36	145	23	204	29	233	0	4	6.428
Les Ott	16	62	4	79	15	94	0	1	6.065
Cliff Anderson	32	114	21	139	24	163	0	0	5.719
Wayne Forrest	22	68	6	63	15	78	0	0	4.588
Also rode									
Mike Gardner	9	28	1	27	5	32	0	0	4.571
Barry Meeks	3	7	0	5	1	6	0	0	3.429
Stuart Cope	9	22	1	15	1	16	0	0	2.909
Paul Wells	6	17	1	8	1	9	0	0	2.118
Andy Reid	3	7	0	2	1	3	0	0	1.714
Substitutes									
Brian Paddington	1	3	1	5	1	6	0	0	8.000
Steve Lawson	1	4	1	3	0	3	0	0	3.000
Mike Bessent	1	2	0	0	0	0	0	0	0.000

-League Heat Scores-

	Home	Away	Total
5 - 0 heat win to Crewe	0	1	1
5 - 1 heat win to Crewe	98	16	114
4½ - 1½ heat win to Crewe	1	0	1
4 - 2 heat win to Crewe	57	35	92
3 - 2 heat win to Crewe	1	1	2
3 - 3 drawn heat	53	80	133
2 - 3 heat win to Opponents	0	1	1
2 - 4 heat win to Opponents	12	47	59
1 - 5 heat win to Opponents	11	52	63
0 - 5 heat win to Opponents	1	1	2

- Team Honours -

Cheshire Triangle Winners.

- Individual/Pairs Honours -

Mayfair Open Championship (Ellesmere Port)
1. Graham Drury 2. Phil Herne 3. John Jackson.

K.R.C. £100 Trophy (Peterborough)
1. Brian Clark 2. Phil Herne 3. Jack Millen.

Cheshire Open Championship (Ellesmere Port)
1. John Jackson 2. Colin Goad 3. Graham Drury.

Lunn-Poly Trophy (Long Eaton)
1. Keith White 2. Alan Molyneux 3. Ricky Day.

Stadium Silver Helmet (Teesside)
1. Dave Durham 2. John Jackson 3. Roger Wright.

Littlechild/Geoff Curtis Memorial Trophies (Crewe)
1. John Jackson 2. Cliff Anderson 3. Keith White.

John Jackson, who topped the Kings averages for the second season in a row.

(TOP) Ian Cartwright in the Crewe pits, with Vic White nearest the camera, and to his left, John Jackson's father. (BELOW) Dave Morton, who smashed the Earle Street track record on August 12 and his entry in the Guinness Book Of Records.

Lap speed

The fastest recorded speed on a British speedway track is 54.62 m.p.h. *87,90 km/h* on the 470 yd *429 m* 2nd Division track at Crewe by Barry Meeks. This track was shortened by 40 yd *36 m* in 1970 and the current fastest track record on a British circuit is an average of 52.46 m.p.h. *84,42 km/h* on the re-shaped Crewe track by Dave Morton on 12 Aug. 1974.

(ABOVE) The enemy come to town, as Crewe and Stoke riders line-up on parade on April 8. (BELOW) Les "Red" Ott.

(ABOVE LEFT) "Young Ole" Cliff Anderson and (RIGHT) "Chalky" White, who was Crewe's only ever-present. (BELOW) Dave Parry talking tactics with Les Ott (left) and Keith White.

A Nightmare At Earle Street -1975-

A Nightmare At Earle Street
-1975-

The inaugural season of the New National League saw several changes from the previous campaign, which included the introduction of an experimental Inter-League Knock Out competition, consisting of the top eight finishers in the 1974 Division II table pitted against eight selected Gulf British League outfits, with the first round ties all taking place on the lower league tracks. Crayford and Newcastle returned to league racing following a break of five years and were joined by newcomers Mildenhall and Paisley. Barrow, Long Eaton and Sunderland were non-starters. At one stage, it looked likely that Crewe would lose league status too, after Violet Littlechild relinquished control. Charlie Scarbrough was one of the first to show an interest in buying the licence, but in mid-February, Midlands businessman John Adams and team boss Dave Parry stepped in with the required £10,000 bond, to purchase the licence, fund the stadium rental and make the necessary renovations to facilities. On February 21, they appeared in front of the New National League Management Committee in Hull to forward their case. A few days later a majority vote granted them permission to take over the licence, although this was not officially ratified by the B.S.P.A. until March 25. The only problem for the new regime was they didn't yet have a team to compete, with only Cliff Anderson remaining from the previous campaign. The newly-crowned New Zealand champion Dave Morton, had now departed to Hackney, and Ian Cartwright, who had finished fourth in New Zealand, transferred to Halifax. Crewe's all-time top points scorer John Jackson, an original target for Birmingham and Bradford, signed for Ellesmere Port, after being offered a lucrative sponsorship deal too good to turn down, and Keith White rejected initial advances from Len Silver to join Rye House, and opted for a spot at Birmingham. Les Ott moved to Crayford, which was nearer to his London home, and Jack Millen made the expected short journey to join arch rivals Stoke, after being offered the General Manager's job. So with only a month to go before the start of the season, the new promoters had to act fast to assemble a team. Their first task was to coax former favourite Geoff Ambrose out of retirement to captain the side and fill one of the heat leader berths, and this signing was closely followed by Graham Drury and Nigel Wasley arriving from Ellesmere Port. The £900 paid to Halifax for Drury became Crewe's first ever transfer fee. Sixteen-year-old Les Collins (younger brother of Peter), who had been attending Charlie Scarbrough's training schools, signed on loan from Belle Vue, and Stuart Cope was handed a regular team spot. In the K.O. Cup, the Kings drew Bradford in the first round and in the Inter-League Cup, they drew a plum tie against Phil Crump's Newport and were hopeful of a bumper crowd. The banking on the Earle Street bends were subject to further reduction, with the stadium itself receiving a much-needed spring clean. Admission was increased to 60p for adults, but remained at 25p for children and senior citizens. This figure however, would rise to 70p and 40p after six meetings, due to spiralling costs. The price of the programme started at 10p, but rose to 15p after the third meeting, as the poor quality was improved. With little time to practice, the new-look Kings opened their make or break season on March 31, with a home league encounter against Crayford.

Meeting 1 - Monday, March 31, 1975 - New National League
L.M.R. Sports Ground, Earle Street, Crewe
Track Length - 436 yards.

CREWE KINGS.....37 CRAYFORD KESTRELS.....41

It was hardly surprising that Crewe lost their opening league match of the season. The team were short of match practice and fitness, and were virtual strangers to their own track. New skipper Geoff Ambrose was clearly one to suffer after his long lay-off, and it was evident on this performance that they lacked another heat leader of genuine quality. However, there were positives, with Cliff Anderson scoring well, and a promising debut by eighteen year-old Londoner Graham Crook, who had only previously featured in second-half rides at Wimbledon, Hackney and Rye House. Ex-King Les Ott made a quick return to top score for Crayford with 11 points.

Heat 01	**Anderson**/Etheridge/**Drury**/Barclay	70.0	**4 - 2**	04 - 02
Heat 02	Wigley/**Crook**/**Collins**/Howard	73.0	3 - 3	07 - 05
Heat 03	Ott/**Ambrose**/**Cope**/Barnwell (R)	72.6	3 - 3	10 - 08
Heat 04	Sage/**Wasley**/**Crook**/Howard	72.2	3 - 3	13 - 11
Heat 05	Etheridge/**Ambrose**/**Cope**/Barclay	71.6	3 - 3	16 - 14
Heat 06	**Drury**/Sage/Wigley/**Collins**	72.6	3 - 3	19 - 17
Heat 07	Ott/Barnwell/**Crook**/**Wasley**	72.0	1 - 5	20 - 22
Heat 08	**Anderson**/Wigley/**Collins**/Barclay (R)	72.8	**4 - 2**	24 - 24
Heat 09	**Cope**/Sage/Wigley/**Collins**	72.6	3 - 3	27 - 27
Heat 10	**Anderson**/Ott/**Drury**/Barnwell (R)	72.0	**4 - 2**	31 - 29
Heat 11	**Wasley**/Etheridge/Wigley/**Collins**	71.8	3 - 3	34 - 32
Heat 12	Ott/Sage/**Drury**/**Cope** (F)	71.8	1 - 5	35 - 37
Heat 13	Etheridge/**Ambrose**/Barnwell/**Wasley**	73.0	2 - 4	37 - 41

CREWE - Cliff Anderson 9, Geoff Ambrose 6, Graham Drury 6, Stuart Cope 5 (+2), Nigel Wasley 5, Graham Crook 4 (+1), Les Collins 2 (+1).
CRAYFORD - Les Ott 11, Laurie Etheridge 10, Alan Sage 9 (+1), Pete Wigley 8 (+3), Trevor Barnwell 3 (+1), George Barclay 0, Dave Howard 0.

On April 1, Geoff Ambrose, Graham Drury and Cliff Anderson rode in a Stars of the League team, who were defeated 40-38 at Ellesmere Port. John Jackson made his debut for the Gunners scoring a maximum, breaking Lou Sansom's track record in his very first outing, with a time of 74.2.

Meeting 2 - Thursday, April 3, 1975 - New National League
Lyme Valley Sports Stadium, Loomer Road, Chesterton
Track Length - 395 yards.

STOKE POTTERS.....54 CREWE KINGS.....24

Jack Millen scored a maximum in Stoke's league romp over their neighbours. Former Potter Nigel Wasley scored more than half of Crewe's total, as the visitors failed to record a single heat advantage in a dismal performance.

Heat 01	Millen/**Drury**/Wells/**Anderson**	72.0	4 - 2	04 - 02
Heat 02	Bastable/Cusworth/**Collins**/**Crook**	70.8	5 - 1	09 - 03
Heat 03	**Wasley**/Molyneux/Bass/**Cope**	71.1	3 - 3	12 - 06
Heat 04	Bastable/Handley/**Ambrose**/**Collins**	70.4	5 - 1	17 - 07
Heat 05	Bass/Molyneux/**Drury**/**Anderson** (R)	71.9	5 - 1	22 - 08
Heat 06	Millen/Wells/**Ambrose**/**Crook**	71.8	5 - 1	27 - 09
Heat 07	**Wasley**/Bastable/Handley/**Cope** (R)	70.6	3 - 3	30 - 12
Heat 08	**Wasley**/Wells/Cusworth/**Anderson**	71.0	3 - 3	33 - 15
Heat 09	Bass/Molyneux/**Drury**/**Ambrose**	72.5	5 - 1	38 - 16
Heat 10	Millen/**Wasley**/**Collins**/Wells	71.1	3 - 3	41 - 19
Heat 11	Cusworth/Handley/**Anderson**/**Drury** (X)	72.0	5 - 1	46 - 20
Heat 12	Millen/**Wasley**/Bass/**Ambrose**	71.8	4 - 2	50 - 22
Heat 13	Handley/**Collins**/Molyneux/**Cope** (F)	00.0	4 - 2	54 - 24

STOKE - Jack Millen 12, Mick Handley 8 (+3), Phil Bass 8 (+1), Steve Bastable 8, Alan Molyneux 7 (+2), Andy Cusworth 6 (+2), Jim Wells 5 (+1).
CREWE - Nigel Wasley 13, Les Collins 4 (+1), Graham Drury 4, Geoff Ambrose 2, Cliff Anderson 1, Stuart Cope 0, Graham Crook 0.

Jack Millen was allowed to ride following a £500 transfer fee paid to Crewe. The Kings management finally reached an agreement to sign Nigel Wasley on loan from Wolverhampton, after paying a small fee to Ellesmere Port to release him. Dave Parry was also hopeful of adding Tom Leadbitter from Wolves and Alan Bridgett from Stoke, to boost his inexperienced squad.

Meeting 3 - Monday, April 7, 1975 - New National League
L.M.R. Sports Ground, Earle Street, Crewe
Track Length - 436 yards.

(ABOVE) The hastily assembled team that started the season. (Back row, left to right) Stuart Cope, Graham Drury, Geoff Ambrose (on machine), Nigel Wasley, Cliff Anderson and Dave Parry. (Kneeling) Graham Crook and Les Collins. (BELOW) Cliff Anderson, the only surviving first team member from the previous season.

CREWE KINGS.....51 COATBRIDGE TIGERS.....26

On a bitterly cold evening, the Kings registered their first league points, with an emphatic twenty-five point victory over a poor Coatbridge outfit. Stuart Cope was star of the meeting with his first maximum, and clocked the fastest time of the night with 71.0 seconds in Heat 6. Les Collins and Nigel Wasley also recorded healthy scores as Graham Drury picked up a bonus point in each of his rides. Not all went well for the hosts however, after Cliff Anderson and Mitch Shirra touched on the first lap of Heat 4, resulting in Graham Crook crashing into the boards and breaking a collar-bone.

Heat	Riders	Time	Score	Total
Heat 01	**Cope**/**Drury**/Wilson/B.Collins	71.2	**5 - 1**	05 - 01
Heat 02	Heller/**L.Collins**/**Crook**/Rae	75.2	3 - 3	08 - 04
Heat 03	**Wasley**/Dawson/**Ambrose**/Gallacher	73.8	**4 - 2**	12 - 06
Heat 04	Heller/**L.Collins**/Shirra (R)/**Anderson** (X)	74.6	2 - 3	14 - 09
Heat 05	**Wasley**/Wilson/**Ambrose**/B.Collins (R)	71.6	**4 - 2**	18 - 11
Heat 06	**Cope**/**Drury**/Heller/Shirra (R)	71.0	**5 - 1**	23 - 12
Heat 07	**Anderson**/Dawson/**L.Collins**/Gallacher	73.8	**4 - 2**	27 - 14
Heat 08	**Cope**/**L.Collins**/Wilson/Rae	72.0	**5 - 1**	32 - 15
Heat 09	**Wasley**/Heller/Shirra/**Ambrose** (R)	73.4	3 - 3	35 - 18
Heat 10	**Cope**/**Drury**/Gallacher/Dawson	72.8	**5 - 1**	40 - 19
Heat 11	Wilson/**L.Collins**/**Anderson**/Heller	75.0	3 - 3	43 - 22
Heat 12	Shirra/**Wasley**/**Drury**/Dawson	73.2	3 - 3	46 - 25
Heat 13	**Ambrose**/**Anderson**/B.Collins/Gallacher	73.6	**5 - 1**	51 - 26

CREWE - Stuart Cope 12, Nigel Wasley 11, Les Collins 9 (+1), Graham Drury 7 (+4), Cliff Anderson 6 (+2), Geoff Ambrose 5, Graham Crook 1 (+1).
COATBRIDGE - Paul Heller 9, John Wilson 7, Mitch Shirra 4 (+1), Grahame Dawson 4, Brian Collins 1, Jimmy Gallacher 1, Billy Rae 0.

Meeting 4 - Monday, April 14, 1975 - New National League
L.M.R. Sports Ground, Earle Street, Crewe
Track Length - 436 yards.

CREWE KINGS.....42 WORKINGTON COMETS.....36

The injury-hit Comets put in another excellent Earle Street performance, but just ran out of options at the crucial time. Already operating rider replacement for Mal Mackay, they were further reduced after Taffy Owen walked out without explanation after his second ride in Heat 5. Having played their tactical cards early on, they had to go into the final heat with only one rider, as reserves Graham Tattersall and Andy Walker had already used up their permitted number of rides, and a failure to finish by the home pair was their only hope of victory. Lou Sansom scored a fifteen point maximum for the visitors and Ray Hassall made a return to the Kings line-up for the first time in three years, winning Heat 2. Geoff Ambrose played a captain's role with a bonus point from each of his four rides.

Heat	Riders	Time	Score	Total
Heat 01	Sansom/**Drury**/Owen/**Anderson**	71.6	2 - 4	02 - 04
Heat 02	**Hassall**/Tattersall/Walker/**Collins** (R)	75.8	3 - 3	05 - 07
Heat 03	Kelly/**Cope**/**Ambrose**/Watson	73.6	3 - 3	08 - 10
Heat 04	Sansom/**Wasley**/**Hassall**/Walker	72.0	3 - 3	11 - 13
Heat 05	Kelly/**Cope**/**Ambrose**/Owen	73.4	3 - 3	14 - 16
Heat 06	Sansom/**Anderson**/**Drury**/Tattersall	73.8	3 - 3	17 - 19
Heat 07	**Wasley**/Watson/Kelly/**Hassall**	72.0	3 - 3	20 - 22
Heat 08	**Anderson**/**Collins**/Walker/Tattersall	74.2	**5 - 1**	25 - 23
Heat 09	Sansom/**Cope**/**Ambrose**/Tattersall (F)	72.8	3 - 3	28 - 26
Heat 10	**Drury**/Kelly/Watson/**Anderson**	73.0	3 - 3	31 - 29
Heat 11	**Wasley**/Watson/**Collins**/Walker	71.8	**4 - 2**	35 - 31
Heat 12	Sansom/**Drury**/Kelly/**Cope**	73.6	2 - 4	37 - 35
Heat 13	**Wasley**/**Ambrose**/Watson (3 riders only)	72.6	**5 - 1**	42 - 36

CREWE - Nigel Wasley 11, Graham Drury 8 (+1), Stuart Cope 6, Geoff Ambrose 5 (+4), Cliff Anderson 5, Ray Hassall 4 (+1), Les Collins 3 (+1).
WORKINGTON - Lou Sansom 15, Terry Kelly 10 (+1), Steve Watson 6 (+1), Andy Walker 2 (+1), Graham Tattersall 2, Taffy Owen 1, *Malcolm Mackay (R/R).*

On April 19, Nigel Wasley progressed to the next stage of the World Championship with a third place finish at Canterbury, scoring 13 points. Graham Drury also competed, but failed to qualify with 8 points.

Meeting 5 - Monday, April 21, 1975 - New National League
Brough Park Stadium, The Fossway, Byker, Newcastle-upon-Tyne
Track Length - 340 yards.

NEWCASTLE DIAMONDS..... 50 CREWE KINGS.....28

A crowd of 6,200 turned up for Newcastle's re-opening league encounter, and witnessed a fine home performance. Only Nigel Wasley won a race for the Kings, as brothers Tom and Joe Owen dominated affairs with maximums. The only black spot of the night concerned Diamonds Robbie Blackadder, who lost half a finger during a nasty fall, in the first attempt to run Heat 8.

Heat 01	T.Owen/**Drury**/Henderson/**Anderson**	70.0	4 - 2	04 - 02
Heat 02	Blackadder/Henderson/**Collins**/**Hassall** (F)	72.2	5 - 1	09 - 03
Heat 03	J.Owen/**Cope**/Swales/**Ambrose**	71.2	4 - 2	13 - 05
Heat 04	Havelock/**Wasley**/Henderson/**Collins**	73.6	4 - 2	17 - 07
Heat 05	J.Owen/**Drury**/Swales/**Anderson**	71.0	4 - 2	21 - 09
Heat 06	T.Owen/Micheledies/**Wasley**/**Hassall**	72.6	5 - 1	26 - 10
Heat 07	Blackadder/**Drury**/Henderson/**Cope**	71.8	4 - 2	30 - 12
Heat 08	**Wasley**/Henderson/**Anderson**/Micheledies	71.8	**2 - 4**	32 - 16
Heat 09	J.Owen/**Collins**/Swales/**Wasley**	71.4	4 - 2	36 - 18
Heat 10	T.Owen/Micheledies/**Anderson**/**Cope**	73.8	5 - 1	41 - 19
Heat 11	Havelock/**Drury**/**Anderson** (3 riders only)	74.2	3 - 3	44 - 22
Heat 12	T.Owen/**Wasley**/**Collins**/Swales	73.0	3 - 3	47 - 25
Heat 13	J.Owen/**Cope**/**Drury**/Havelock	72.0	3 - 3	50 - 28

NEWCASTLE - Joe Owen 12, Tom Owen 12, Ron Henderson 7 (+1), Robbie Blackadder 6, Brian Havelock 6, Phil Micheledies 4 (+2), Tim Swales 3.
CREWE - Graham Drury 9 (+1), Nigel Wasley 8, Les Collins 4 (+1), Stuart Cope 4, Cliff Anderson 3 (+1), Geoff Ambrose 0, Ray Hassall 0.

To add a competitive edge to the squad, Dave Parry signed talented Warmingham grass-tracker Chris Turner on loan from Belle Vue, although he was still on the hunt for an experienced heat leader. Sixteen-year-old Turner had been recommended by ex-King Barry Meeks. On April 22, Graham Drury returned to Ellesmere Port to take part in the Michael Nesbitt Memorial Trophy, where he finished runner-up to Brummie Arthur Browning. The following evening, Crewe staged their first ever Wednesday meeting. As a new promotion, the Kings had lost their seniority of staging fixtures against fellow Monday night tracks.

Meeting 6 - Wednesday, April 23, 1975 - New National League
L.M.R. Sports Ground, Earle Street, Crewe
Track Length - 436 yards.

CREWE KINGS.....38 NEWCASTLE DIAMONDS.....39

Crewe suffered their second home defeat of the season - the first time in their history they had lost more than one league match at Earle Street in a single campaign. Behind by seven after five heats, they stormed back to lead by seven with only three races remaining, but still somehow contrived to lose the points. Chris Turner won his first race during a commendable debut, as the Owen brothers again scored heavily for the Diamonds. The match was delayed after a Heat 8 smash involving Tony Boyle and Les Collins, after part of the safety fence was demolished. Boyle took a trip to hospital for treatment to a cut eye, while Collins took no further part in the meeting.

Heat 01	T.Owen/Micheledies/**Drury** (F)/**Cope** (F)	74.8	0 - 5	00 - 05
Heat 02	**Turner**/Henderson/**Collins**/Boyle	75.2	**4 - 2**	04 - 07
Heat 03	J.Owen/**Anderson**/Swales/**Ambrose**	75.2	2 - 4	06 - 11
Heat 04	Havelock/**Wasley**/**Turner**/Henderson (R)	74.8	3 - 3	09 - 14
Heat 05	T.Owen/**Ambrose**/Micheledies/**Anderson**	72.6	2 - 4	11 - 18

Heat 06	**Drury**/**Wasley**/Havelock/Henderson (R)	73.6	**5 - 1**	16 - 19
Heat 07	J.Owen/**Wasley**/**Turner**/Swales	73.0	3 - 3	19 - 22
Heat 08	**Cope**/**Turner**/Micheledies/Boyle (X)	73.4	**5 - 1**	24 - 23
Heat 09	**Ambrose**/**Anderson**/Henderson/Havelock (R)	76.0	**5 - 1**	29 - 24
Heat 10	**Drury**/J.Owen/**Cope**/Swales	73.6	**4 - 2**	33 - 26
Heat 11	J.Owen/T.Owen/**Wasley**/**Turner**	73.0	1 - 5	34 - 31
Heat 12	J.Owen/**Drury**/Havelock/**Anderson**	73.4	2 - 4	36 - 35
Heat 13	T.Owen/**Ambrose**/Swales/**Wasley** (X)	73.4	2 - 4	38 - 39

CREWE - Graham Drury 8, Chris Turner 7 (+3), Nigel Wasley 7 (+1), Geoff Ambrose 7, Cliff Anderson 4 (+1), Stuart Cope 4, Les Collins 1.
NEWCASTLE - Joe Owen 14, Tom Owen 11 (+1), Brian Havelock 5, Phil Micheledies 4 (+1), Ron Henderson 3, Tim Swales 2, Tony Boyle 0.

Crewe co-promoter Dave Parry was under no illusions about the forthcoming Inter-League Cup tie with Newport: *"We will lose"* forecast Parry. *"I don't think even the most partisan of our supporters can expect us to win. All we can do is to try as hard as we can and make sure that we contribute to a fantastic night's racing. It is the biggest crowd-puller we have ever had at Crewe and I am sure it is going to be a memorable meeting."*

Meeting 7 - Monday, April 28, 1975 - Inter-League Knock Out Cup, First Round
L.M.R. Sports Ground, Earle Street, Crewe
Track Length - 436 yards.

CREWE KINGS.....20 NEWPORT.....58

Dave Parry's prediction came true, but not even he could have envisaged such a big losing margin. Graham Drury won Heat 1, but that was as good as it got for the Earle Street faithful. Phil Crump won his four rides with ease on his new Street four-valve Jawa, recording the fastest time of the night in Heat 3. Crewe managed a share of the points in two heats, but lost the rest, as the difference in class showed, especially from the tapes.

Heat 01	**Drury**/Street/Tebby/**Cope**	73.8	3 - 3	03 - 03
Heat 02	Herne/Woodward/**Collins**/**Turner**	72.2	1 - 5	04 - 08
Heat 03	Crump/Gresham/**Ambrose**/**Anderson**	70.6	1 - 5	05 - 13
Heat 04	Eide/Herne/**Wasley**/**Turner** (R)	74.2	1 - 5	06 - 18
Heat 05	Street/**Ambrose**/Tebby/**Anderson**	74.0	2 - 4	08 - 22
Heat 06	Eide/Woodward/**Cope**/**Drury**	73.2	1 - 5	09 - 27
Heat 07	Crump/**Turner**/Gresham/**Wasley**	71.0	2 - 4	11 - 31
Heat 08	Herne/**Cope**/Tebby/**Collins**	72.8	2 - 4	13 - 35
Heat 09	Eide/Woodward/**Ambrose**/**Drury**	73.8	1 - 5	14 - 40
Heat 10	Crump/Gresham/**Drury**/**Cope**	72.0	1 - 5	15 - 45
Heat 11	Street/**Wasley**/**Collins**/Tebby	74.8	3 - 3	18 - 48
Heat 12	Crump/Eide/**Drury**/**Anderson**	73.2	1 - 5	19 - 53
Heat 13	Street/Woodward/**Ambrose**/**Wasley**	74.8	1 - 5	20 - 58

CREWE - Geoff Ambrose 5, Graham Drury 5, Stuart Cope 3, Nigel Wasley 3, Les Collins 2 (+1), Chris Turner 2, Cliff Anderson 0.
NEWPORT - Phil Crump 12, Reidar Eide 11 (+1), Neil Street 11, Bryan Woodward 8 (+4), Phil Herne 8 (+1), Steve Gresham 5 (+2), Jim Tebby 3 (+1).

A price increase for the match (80p for adults) didn't go down well with supporters, and only around 2,000 turned up for a fixture that was hoped would attract at least double that figure. Crewe were not the only lower league casualties in the opening round of the Inter-League competition. Of the eight ties, only Boston caused an upset, beating Hackney 40-38. Birmingham and Workington lost narrowly to Belle Vue (38-40) and Swindon (38-39) respectively, and Bradford lost by ten points (34-44) to Oxford. The rest suffered heavy defeats; Eastbourne losing 28-50 to Halifax, Peterborough going down 28-49 to Ipswich and Teesside were on the wrong end of a 26-52 hammering by Cradley. New Zealander Max Brown signed for the Kings from defunct Long Eaton after several promising second-half rides. He went straight into the side, replacing the out-of-sorts Cliff Anderson.

Meeting 8 - Monday, May 5, 1975 - Knock Out Cup, First Round, First Leg
L.M.R. Sports Ground, Earle Street, Crewe
Track Length - 436 yards.

CREWE KINGS.....38 BRADFORD BARONS.....40

Crewe lost their third home meeting on the bounce after leading by six points going into the last three heats, with the Barons snatching the win in Heat 13. Stuart Cope and Graham Drury secured paid maximums, but it was a disappointing debut for Max Brown, who scored just three from his four outings. The result left the Kings facing an early exit from the K.O. Cup.

Heat 01	**Drury**/**Cope**/Featherstone/Argall	73.8	**5 - 1**	05 - 01
Heat 02	Wilcock/Fielding/**Turner**/**Collins**	74.6	1 - 5	06 - 06
Heat 03	Baugh/Langlois/**Brown**/**Ambrose** (X)	74.8	1 - 5	07 - 11
Heat 04	**Wasley**/Fielding/**Turner**/Meredith (R)	73.0	**4 - 2**	11 - 13
Heat 05	Featherstone/**Ambrose**/**Brown**/Argall	75.0	3 - 3	14 - 16
Heat 06	**Cope**/**Drury**/Wilcock/Meredith (X)	72.8	**5 - 1**	19 - 17
Heat 07	**Wasley**/Baugh/**Turner**/Langlois (R)	73.0	**4 - 2**	23 - 19
Heat 08	**Cope**/Fielding/**Collins**/Argall	73.6	**4 - 2**	27 - 21
Heat 09	Wilcock/Featherstone/**Brown**/**Ambrose**	74.8	1 - 5	28 - 26
Heat 10	**Cope**/**Drury**/Baugh/Langlois	73.8	**5 - 1**	33 - 27
Heat 11	Featherstone/Fielding/**Collins**/**Wasley** (R)	75.4	1 - 5	34 - 32
Heat 12	**Drury**/Wilcock/Langlois/**Brown** (F)	74.2	3 - 3	37 - 35
Heat 13	Featherstone/Baugh/**Wasley**/**Ambrose** (R)	75.4	1 - 5	38 - 40

CREWE - Stuart Cope 11 (+1), Graham Drury 10 (+2), Nigel Wasley 7, Max Brown 3 (+1), Chris Turner 3, Geoff Ambrose 2, Les Collins 2.
BRADFORD - Tony Featherstone 12 (+1), Steve Wilcock 9, Mick Fielding 8 (+2), Dave Baugh 8 (+1), Brenton Langlois 3 (+2), Eddie Argall 0, Colin Meredith 0.

Understandably Dave Parry was left fuming following another home reversal: *"I am sick of the way some of the riders simply are not pulling their weight. They will find themselves out of the team if they don't put in more effort. We are not getting the crowds, but I don't blame the public for not supporting this team."* On May 8, the management were rocked when Geoff Ambrose announced that he had retired again, following a somewhat disappointing comeback.

Meeting 9 - Monday, May 12, 1975 - New National League
L.M.R. Sports Ground, Earle Street, Crewe
Track Length - 436 yards.

CREWE KINGS.....47 ELLESMERE PORT GUNNERS.....31

John Jackson unsurprisingly helped himself to a faultless five-ride maximum on his return to his former home, but his efforts were never going to be enough, as he received no support. Crewe got back to winning ways thanks to Graham Drury, Nigel Wasley, Chris Turner and Stuart Cope, who was occupying a heat-leader berth for the first time. Gunner Steve Taylor was taken to hospital with concussion after bringing down Cliff Anderson and hitting the boards in Heat 3. The Kiwi was then involved in a coming together with Wayne Hughes in Heat 9, escaping unhurt, but damaging his bike. Hughes was badly shaken and spent the rest of the meeting in the First Aid room.

Heat 01	Jackson/**Drury**/**Brown**/Hughes	70.8	3 - 3	03 - 03
Heat 02	**Turner**/Meredith/**Collins**/Booth	74.0	**4 - 2**	07 - 05
Heat 03	**Wasley**/**Anderson**/Smitherman/Taylor (X)	72.4	**5 - 1**	12 - 06
Heat 04	**Cope**/**Turner**/Goad/Booth	74.6	**5 - 1**	17 - 07
Heat 05	Jackson/**Wasley**/Hughes/**Anderson**	71.8	2 - 4	19 - 11
Heat 06	**Drury**/Booth/Goad/**Brown**	74.4	3 - 3	22 - 14
Heat 07	Jackson/**Cope**/**Turner**/Smitherman	72.0	3 - 3	25 - 17
Heat 08	Hughes/**Collins**/**Brown**/Booth	74.2	3 - 3	28 - 20
Heat 09	**Turner**/**Wasley**/Booth/Meredith	73.8	**5 - 1**	33 - 21
Heat 10	**Drury**/Meredith/**Brown**/Smitherman	74.2	**4 - 2**	37 - 23
Heat 11	Jackson/**Cope**/**Collins**/Meredith	72.4	3 - 3	40 - 26
Heat 12	**Wasley**/**Drury**/Goad/Meredith	73.4	**5 - 1**	45 - 27
Heat 13	Jackson/**Cope**/Smitherman/**Anderson**	72.6	2 - 4	47 - 31

CREWE - Graham Drury 10 (+1), Nigel Wasley 10 (+1), Chris Turner 9 (+2), Stuart Cope 9, Les Collins 4 (+1), Max Brown 3 (+2), Cliff Anderson 2 (+1).
ELLESMERE PORT - John Jackson 15, Wayne Hughes 4, Duncan Meredith 4, Colin Goad 3 (+1), Barry Booth 3, Gerald Smitherman 2, Steve Taylor 0.

In the programme notes, *Crewe Chronicle* reporter Roy Greer predicted big problems for speedway in Crewe due to poor attendance figures. He would comment: *"Unless there is some improvement, there won't be a Crewe Kings next season."* Cliff Anderson returned to the Crewe side following the retirement of Geoff Ambrose, with Graham Drury taking over the captaincy for the Ellesmere Port match. Meanwhile, another face was to leave the scene, when co-promoter John Adams withdrew his interest due to "ill-health," with Violet Littlechild and family returning to take over the licence. Dave Parry reverted back to his previous role as general manager, as well as continuing as team boss.

Meeting 10 - Wednesday, May 14, 1975 - Knock Out Cup, First Round, Second Leg
Odsal Stadium, Rooley Avenue, Bradford
Track Length - 375 yards.

BRADFORD BARONS.....48 CREWE KINGS.....30

(Bradford won on aggregate 88 - 68)

A depleted Kings, without the services of the injured Graham Drury and Cliff Anderson, were predictably dumped out of the K.O. Cup. Andy Reid came into the team, and they loaned Bradford's Eddie Argall for the night. Max Brown and Chris Turner both returned eight points and would have added to their totals but for falls in Heats 2 and 5. Argall registered a win in Heat 5, but Nigel Wasley had a night to forget. In his first outing he was leading until a broken magneto strap resulted in a last lap retirement, and then went on to score just a single point on borrowed machinery.

Heat 01	**Brown**/Featherstone/**Argall**/Wilcock	71.0	**2 - 4**	02 - 04
Heat 02	Fielding/Parkin/**Collins**/**Turner** (F)	72.4	5 - 1	07 - 05
Heat 03	Langlois/Baugh/**Cope**/**Reid**	74.0	5 - 1	12 - 06
Heat 04	Meredith/**Collins**/Fielding/**Wasley** (R)	71.8	4 - 2	16 - 08
Heat 05	**Argall**/Baugh/Langlois/**Brown** (F)	71.6	3 - 3	19 - 11
Heat 06	Wilcock/**Turner**/Featherstone/**Wasley**	72.0	4 - 2	23 - 13
Heat 07	Meredith/**Cope**/**Argall**/Fielding (R)	72.2	3 - 3	26 - 16
Heat 08	**Brown**/Wilcock/Parkin/**Collins**	72.6	3 - 3	29 - 19
Heat 09	**Turner**/Langlois/Baugh/**Wasley**	71.0	3 - 3	32 - 22
Heat 10	Featherstone/**Turner**/**Brown**/Wilcock	71.8	3 - 3	35 - 25
Heat 11	Meredith/**Argall**/**Brown**/Parkin	71.2	3 - 3	38 - 28
Heat 12	Featherstone/Langlois/**Wasley**/**Cope**	71.4	5 - 1	43 - 29
Heat 13	Meredith/Baugh/**Turner**/**Argall**	72.2	5 - 1	48 - 30

BRADFORD - Colin Meredith 12, Tony Featherstone 9, Brenton Langlois 8 (+2), Dave Baugh 7 (+3), Steve Wilcock 5, Mick Fielding 4, Dave Parkin 3 (+2).
CREWE - Max Brown 8 (+2), Chris Turner 8, Eddie Argall* 7 (+1), Les Collins 3, Stuart Cope 3, Nigel Wasley 1, Andy Reid 0.

On May 16, Nigel Wasley's hopes of progress in the World Championship were thwarted somewhat when he only scored 2 points at Newport. Crewe meanwhile, were giving extended trials to Aussies Andy Cowan, John Howell and Barry Weaver.

Saturday, May 17, 1975 - New National League Pairs Championship
Zoological Gardens, Hyde Road, West Gorton, Manchester
Track Length - 418 yards.

WINNERS.....NEWCASTLE DIAMONDS

Graham Drury and Nigel Wasley failed in their attempt to win the inaugural New National League Pairs. The Crewe duo were drawn in Group D of the competition, but finished runners-up to Newcastle's Brian Havelock and Tom Owen, who went on to win the championship, defeating John Jackson and Colin Goad of Ellesmere Port in the final.

Group A: Eastbourne 14, Scunthorpe 10, Workington, Paisley 4.
Group B: Crayford 14, Birmingham 10, Bradford 9, Rye House 3.
Group C: Ellesmere Port 12, Peterborough 11, Coatbridge 7, Stoke 6.

Group D:		N	C	T	B
Heat 01..... **Drury**/Reading/Durham/**Wasley** (F)	75.4	/	3	3	/
Heat 02..... Havelock/Owen/Gifford/Templeton	76.2	5	/	/	1
Heat 03..... Owen/Havelock/Reading/Durham	75.4	5	/	1	/
Heat 04..... **Drury**/Gifford/**Wasley**/Templeton	77.8	/	**4**	/	**2**
Heat 05..... Durham/Reading/Gifford/Templeton	77.0	/	/	5	1
Heat 06..... Havelock/**Drury**/**Wasley**/Owen (R)	76.4	3	3	/	/

NEWCASTLE 13 - Brian Havelock 8 & Tom Owen 5.
CREWE 10 - Graham Drury 8 & Nigel Wasley 2. *(Wasley replaced Geoff Ambrose.)*
TEESSIDE 9 - Pete Reading 5 & Dave Durham 4. *(Reading replaced Bruce Forrester.)*
BERWICK 4 - Dave Gifford 4 & Willie Templeton 0.

S/F 1 .... Jackson/Goad/Gachet/Middleditch	76.4	Ellesmere Port 5 - Eastbourne 1.
S/F 2 .... Havelock/Etheridge/Sage/Owen	76.8	Newcastle 3 - Crayford 3.
Final .... Havelock/Jackson/Owen/Goad	76.0	Newcastle 4 - Ellesmere Port 2.

Meeting 11 - Monday, May 19, 1975 - New National League
L.M.R. Sports Ground, Earle Street, Crewe
Track Length - 436 yards.

CREWE KINGS.....42 PAISLEY LIONS.....36

Sid Sheldrick's fourteen point haul kept Paisley in the hunt right up to the final heat, but he could not prevent the league newcomers from falling short at the death. Graham Drury and Nigel Wasley both recorded double figure scores, and there was another impressive performance from Chris Turner who won Heats 2 and 9.

Heat 01 .... **Drury**/S.Sheldrick/**Brown**/Davie	73.0	**4 - 2**	04 - 02
Heat 02 .... **Turner**/Foot/M.Sheldrick/**Collins**	70.8	3 - 3	07 - 05
Heat 03 .... S.Sheldrick/**Cope**/**Anderson**/Fullerton (X)	72.2	3 - 3	10 - 08
Heat 04 .... **Wasley**/Bridgett/Foot/**Turner** (F)	72.4	3 - 3	13 - 11
Heat 05 .... S.Sheldrick/**Cope**/Davie/**Anderson**	72.0	2 - 4	15 - 15
Heat 06 .... **Drury**/**Brown**/Bridgett/M.Sheldrick	73.4	**5 - 1**	20 - 16
Heat 07 .... **Wasley**/**Turner**/M.Sheldrick/Davie	72.6	**5 - 1**	25 - 17
Heat 08 .... Davie/S.Sheldrick/**Brown**/**Collins**	72.4	1 - 5	26 - 22
Heat 09 .... **Turner**/Bridgett/Foot/**Cope** (F)	72.0	3 - 3	29 - 25
Heat 10 .... **Drury**/**Brown**/Bridgett/Fullerton	74.2	**5 - 1**	34 - 26
Heat 11 .... Davie/S.Sheldrick/**Wasley**/**Collins** (R)	72.4	1 - 5	35 - 31
Heat 12 .... Fullerton/**Drury**/**Turner**/Bridgett (R)	73.4	3 - 3	38 - 34
Heat 13 .... **Wasley**/S.Sheldrick/**Cope**/Fullerton	72.0	**4 - 2**	42 - 36

CREWE - Graham Drury 11, Nigel Wasley 10, Chris Turner 9 (+2), Max Brown 6 (+2), Stuart Cope 5, Cliff Anderson 1 (+1), Les Collins 0.
PAISLEY - Sid Sheldrick 14 (+2), Tom Davie 7, Alan Bridgett 6, Bernie Foot 4 (+2), Mike Fullerton 3, Mick Sheldrick 2 (+1), *(R/R at No.4).*

Nigel Wasley failed in his attempt to advance to the next stage of the World Championship. In his second round on May 20, he failed to score at Leicester, and in his final round four days later, scored three at King's Lynn.

Meeting 12 - Sunday, May 25, 1975 - New National League
Mildenhall Stadium, West Row, Mildenhall
Track Length - 307 yards.

MILDENHALL FEN TIGERS.....36 CREWE KINGS.....41

The Kings pulled off their first away win of the season in an entertaining encounter at West Row, despite only having four riders for the first half of the meeting! The supporters coach, with riders Stuart Cope, Cliff Anderson, Max Brown and Graham Crook aboard, did not arrive until after Heat 6 after losing their way en-route. Mildenhall junior John McNeil was loaned to the short-handed visitors until the absentees arrived, which meant, for the first time in league competition, Crewe tracked eight riders throughout the match.

Heat 01	Coles/**McNeil**/**Drury**/Austin (X)	60.0	3 - 3	03 - 03
Heat 02	**McNeil**/**Turner**/Jolly/Kerry	60.3	**1 - 5**	04 - 08
Heat 03	**Turner**/**McNeil**/Witt/Mills	60.6	**1 - 5**	05 - 13
Heat 04	Kerry/**Wasley**/Stevens (3 riders only)	61.4	4 - 2	09 - 15
Heat 05	**Drury**/Mills/Witt (F) (3 riders only)	61.3	2 - 3	11 - 18
Heat 06	Coles/**Wasley**/**Turner** (3 riders only)	60.5	3 - 3	14 - 21
Heat 07	Stevens/**Turner**/**Cope**/Kerry	61.7	3 - 3	17 - 24
Heat 08	Austin/Jolly/**Brown**/**Crook**	62.8	5 - 1	22 - 25
Heat 09	**Wasley**/Jolly/**Turner**/Mills	61.8	**2 - 4**	24 - 29
Heat 10	Coles/Austin/**Anderson**/**Cope**	61.8	5 - 1	29 - 30
Heat 11	**Drury**/Stevens/**Brown**/Jolly	62.2	**2 - 4**	31 - 34
Heat 12	Coles/**Cope**/**Wasley**/Kerry (X)	61.7	3 - 3	34 - 37
Heat 13	**Drury**/Jolly/**Anderson**/Stevens	62.6	**2 - 4**	36 - 41

MILDENHALL - Bob Coles 12, Kevin Jolly 7 (+1), Stan Stevens 6, Roger Austin 5 (+1), Graham Kerry 3, Fred Mills 2, Alan Witt 1.
CREWE - Graham Drury 10 (+1), Chris Turner 9 (+2), Nigel Wasley 8 (+1), John McNeil* 7 (+1), Stuart Cope 3 (+1), Cliff Anderson 2, Max Brown 2, Graham Crook 0.

Meeting 13 - Monday, May 26, 1975 - Spring Holiday Challenge
L.M.R. Sports Ground, Earle Street, Crewe
Track Length - 436 yards.

CREWE KINGS.....39 STARS OF THE LEAGUE.....38

Trailing by four points going into the final heat, the Kings somehow snatched victory from the jaws of defeat. John Jackson had to face the home pair without a partner as Ricky Day was a non-starter after dropping a valve in his machine, and reserves Andy Reid and John McNeil had taken their permitted number of rides. He was then excluded for breaking the tapes, which resulted in the Crewe duo completing four laps unopposed to take the victory. Chris Turner continued his fine progress, top-scoring with thirteen.

Heat 01	Jackson/**Drury**/**Brown**/Weaver	71.6	3 - 3	03 - 03
Heat 02	**Turner**/McNeil/Reid/**Collins**	72.2	3 - 3	06 - 06
Heat 03	Day/Kelly/**Anderson**/**Cope** (X)	73.2	1 - 5	07 - 11
Heat 04	Sansom/**Turner**/**Wasley**/McNeil	71.4	3 - 3	10 - 14
Heat 05	Jackson/**Cope**/Weaver/**Anderson**	71.4	2 - 4	12 - 18
Heat 06	Sansom/**Drury**/**Brown**/Reid	71.6	3 - 3	15 - 21
Heat 07	**Turner**/Kelly/Day/**Wasley**	72.4	3 - 3	18 - 24
Heat 08	**Drury**/**Brown**/McNeil/Reid	74.6	**5 - 1**	23 - 25
Heat 09	**Turner**/**Cope**/McNeil/Reid	73.2	**5 - 1**	28 - 26
Heat 10	**Drury**/McNeil/Kelly/**Brown**	73.6	3 - 3	31 - 29
Heat 11	Jackson/Reid/**Wasley**/**Collins**	71.4	1 - 5	32 - 34
Heat 12	Sansom/**Turner**/Kelly/**Drury**	72.2	2 - 4	34 - 38
Heat 13	**Wasley**/**Cope**/Jackson (X) (3 riders only)	73.2	**5 - 0**	39 - 38

CREWE - Chris Turner 13, Graham Drury 10, Stuart Cope 6 (+2), Nigel Wasley 5 (+1), Max Brown 4 (+3), Cliff Anderson 1, Les Collins 0.
STARS OF THE LEAGUE - John Jackson *(Ellesmere Port)* 9, Lou Sansom *(Workington)* 9, Terry Kelly *(Workington)* 6 (+2), John McNeil *(Mildenhall)* 6, Ricky Day *(Birmingham)* 4 (+1), Andy Reid *(Crewe)* 3 (+2), Barry Weaver 1.

Concerns over dwindling attendances at Earle Street prompted the management to propose several schemes, including block bookings at reduced rates for factory and school parties, and improved advertising and sponsorship campaigns. There were also discussions regarding changing the traditional Monday race night. Dave Parry commented: *"We have to get people in who perhaps haven't sampled speedway, in the hope that they will like what they see and come again. People like to go around in groups, so the block booking scheme at cheaper rates could be the answer. We are especially eager to try out this idea with schoolchildren and would welcome*

(ABOVE) Jim Tebby and Stuart Cope prepare for Heat 1 of the Kings versus Newport Inter League Knock Out clash. (BELOW) Local youngster Chris Turner, warming his machine.

(ABOVE) Crewe v Paisley. Cliff Anderson and Sid Sheldrick battle for the lead, as Mike Fullerton hits the deck. (BELOW) Graham Drury and Nigel Wasley, who were Crewe's representatives in the New National League Pairsat Belle Vue on May 17.

enquiries." The concerns were hardly helped when Stoke promoter Russ Bragg reported crowds at Loomer Road were 300% up on the previous season.

Meeting 14 - Tuesday, May 27, 1975 - New National League
Ellesmere Port Stadium, Thornton Road, Ellesmere Port
Track Length - 423 yards.

ELLESMERE PORT GUNNERS.....44 CREWE KINGS.....33

Chris Turner's fourteen points from his six outings could not prevent a John Jackson inspired Ellesmere Port side from collecting the league points. Graham Drury won three races on his league return to Thornton Road, but the rest of the visiting riders failed to impress. Dave Parry gave home grown youngster Mick Mellor a first senior team start.

Heat 01	Jackson/**Drury**/Hughes/**Brown**	75.4	4 - 2	04 - 02
Heat 02	**Turner**/Booth/**Mellor** (F)/Meredith (R)	76.8	**2 - 3**	06 - 05
Heat 03	Goad/Smitherman/**Anderson**/**Cope**	76.6	5 - 1	11 - 06
Heat 04	Hughes/Meredith/**Wasley**/**Mellor**	77.2	5 - 1	16 - 07
Heat 05	**Drury**/Goad/**Brown**/Smitherman (F)	77.0	**2 - 4**	18 - 11
Heat 06	Jackson/Hughes/**Turner**/**Wasley**	76.2	5 - 1	23 - 12
Heat 07	**Drury**/Meredith/**Anderson**/Allott	77.6	**2 - 4**	25 - 16
Heat 08	**Turner**/Hughes/**Wasley**/Booth	77.8	**2 - 4**	27 - 20
Heat 09	**Turner**/Goad/Smitherman/**Wasley**	77.2	3 - 3	30 - 23
Heat 10	Jackson/**Anderson**/Hughes/**Cope**	78.0	4 - 2	34 - 25
Heat 11	**Drury**/**Turner**/Meredith/Booth	78.2	**1 - 5**	35 - 30
Heat 12	Jackson/**Turner**/Smitherman/**Wasley**	77.0	4 - 2	39 - 32
Heat 13	Goad/Jackson/**Drury**/**Anderson**	77.4	5 - 1	44 - 33

ELLESMERE PORT - John Jackson 14 (+1), Colin Goad 10, Wayne Hughes 9 (+1), Duncan Meredith 5 (+1), Gerald Smitherman 4 (+2), Barry Booth 2, Nicky Allott 0, *Steve Taylor (R/R)*.
CREWE - Chris Turner 14 (+1), Graham Drury 12, Cliff Anderson 4, Nigel Wasley 2, Max Brown 1, Stuart Cope 0, Mick Mellor 0.

Meeting 15 - Thursday May 29, 1975 - New National League
Cleveland Park Stadium, Stockton Road, Middlesbrough
Track Length - 335 yards.

TEESSIDE TIGERS.....52 CREWE KINGS.....26

The toothless Kings were savaged by the Tigers in a one-sided affair, with only Chris Turner emerging from the defeat with any real praise, winning two heats on his way to scoring paid twelve, with the rest mustering a disappointing sixteen points between them. In the final heat, Roger Wright and Graham Drury tangled, with the Crewe captain hitting the deck. The pair then had to be separated back in the pits. Teesside had earlier beaten Bradford 49-29.

Heat 01	Leadbitter/Reading/**Drury**/**Brown**	72.2	5 - 1	05 - 01
Heat 02	Emerson/**Turner**/**Collins**/Pestell (R)	72.8	3 - 3	08 - 04
Heat 03	Durham/Wright/**Cope**/**Anderson**	70.6	5 - 1	13 - 05
Heat 04	Emerson/Underwood/**Wasley**/**Collins**	71.8	5 - 1	18 - 06
Heat 05	Wright/Durham/**Drury**/**Brown** (F)	71.6	5 - 1	23 - 07
Heat 06	**Turner**/Reading/Leadbitter/**Wasley**	70.8	3 - 3	26 - 10
Heat 07	Emerson/Underwood/**Anderson**/**Cope** (F)	71.2	5 - 1	31 - 11
Heat 08	Emerson/**Brown**/**Turner**/Reading	70.8	3 - 3	34 - 14
Heat 09	Durham/**Wasley**/**Turner**/Wright	71.0	3 - 3	37 - 17
Heat 10	Leadbitter/**Drury**/Reading/**Turner**	71.4	4 - 2	41 - 19
Heat 11	Underwood/**Drury**/**Brown**/Pestell (R)	71.2	3 - 3	44 - 22
Heat 12	Leadbitter/Durham/**Cope**/**Wasley**	72.0	5 - 1	49 - 23
Heat 13	**Turner**/Wright/Underwood/**Drury** (F)	71.8	3 - 3	52 - 26

TEESSIDE - Alan Emerson 12, Dave Durham 10 (+2), Tom Leadbitter 10 (+1), Doug Underwood 8 (+3), Roger Wright 7 (+1), Pete Reading 5 (+1), Colin Pestell 0.
CREWE - Chris Turner 10 (+2), Graham Drury 6, Max Brown 3 (+1), Nigel Wasley 3, Stuart Cope 2, Les Collins 1 (+1), Cliff Anderson 1.

Meeting 16 - Sunday, June 1, 1975 - New National League
Rye House Stadium, Rye Road, Hoddesdon
Track Length - 284 yards.

RYE HOUSE ROCKETS.....53 CREWE KINGS.....25

Len Silver's lowly Rockets inflicted another heavy defeat on a tired-looking Kings outfit. Graham Drury battled hard for his dozen points, but to no avail, as Rye House bagged the league points in Heat 10, thanks to maximums from Brian Foote (full) and Bob Cooper (paid).

Heat 01	Foote/**Drury**/D.Brown/**M.Brown**	65.6	4 - 2	04 - 02
Heat 02	Cooper/Young/**Turner**/**Collins**	66.2	5 - 1	09 - 03
Heat 03	D.Brown/Gibbons/**Anderson**/**Cope**	67.4	5 - 1	14 - 04
Heat 04	Cooper/Beech/**Collins**/**Wasley**	66.4	5 - 1	19 - 05
Heat 05	**Drury**/Gibbons/D.Brown/**M.Brown**	66.4	3 - 3	22 - 08
Heat 06	Foote/Cooper/**Wasley**/**Turner**	66.2	5 - 1	27 - 09
Heat 07	Cooper/**Drury**/Beech/**Anderson**	66.4	4 - 2	31 - 11
Heat 08	Young/**M.Brown**/Fiala/**Collins**	67.2	4 - 2	35 - 13
Heat 09	**Turner**/Gibbons/D.Brown/**Wasley**	67.6	3 - 3	38 - 16
Heat 10	Foote/Fiala/**Anderson**/**Turner** (F)	66.6	5 - 1	43 - 17
Heat 11	Young/**Drury**/Beech/**M.Brown**	64.8	4 - 2	47 - 19
Heat 12	Foote/**Wasley**/Gibbons/**Cope**	66.8	4 - 2	51 - 21
Heat 13	**Drury**/D.Brown/**Turner**/Beech (R)	66.6	**2 - 4**	53 - 25

RYE HOUSE - Brian Foote 12, Bob Cooper 11 (+1), Dingle Brown 8 (+2), Bob Young 8 (+1), John Gibbons 7 (+1), Tiger Beech 4 (+1), Karl Fiala 3 (+1), *Kelvin Mullarkey (R/R)*.
CREWE - Graham Drury 12, Chris Turner 5, Nigel Wasley 3, Cliff Anderson 2, Max Brown 2, Les Collins 1, Stuart Cope 0.

Meeting 17 - Monday, June 2, 1975 - New National League
L.M.R. Sports Ground, Earle Street, Crewe
Track Length - 436 yards.

CREWE KINGS.....47 MILDENHALL FEN TIGERS.....31

Crewe, competing in their sixth meeting in nine days, completed their first league double of the season, after easily overcoming bottom-of-the-table Mildenhall, on a bitterley cold night at an almost deserted Earle Street. Five home maximums in the first seven heats saw the Kings heading for a big victory, but a one man show from visiting skipper Bob Coles ensured the score remained at a respectable margin.

Heat 01	Coles/**Drury**/**Collins**/Clipstone	71.6	3 - 3	03 - 03
Heat 02	**Brown**/**Turner**/Jolly/Kerry	73.2	**5 - 1**	08 - 04
Heat 03	**Cope**/**Anderson**/McNeil/Harvey	73.6	**5 - 1**	13 - 05
Heat 04	**Turner**/**Wasley**/Stevens/Jolly	72.0	**5 - 1**	18 - 06
Heat 05	Coles/**Anderson**/**Cope**/Clipstone	72.0	3 - 3	21 - 09
Heat 06	**Drury**/**Collins**/Stevens/Kerry	73.8	**5 - 1**	26 - 10
Heat 07	**Turner**/**Brown**/Harvey/McNeil	72.6	**5 - 1**	31 - 11
Heat 08	Coles/**Collins**/**Brown**/Jolly	71.4	3 - 3	34 - 14
Heat 09	**Anderson**/**Cope**/Stevens/Kerry	75.0	**5 - 1**	39 - 15
Heat 10	McNeil/**Drury**/**Collins**/Harvey	72.6	3 - 3	42 - 18
Heat 11	Coles/Clipstone/**Turner**/**Brown**	72.6	1 - 5	43 - 23
Heat 12	Stevens/**Drury**/McNeil/**Anderson**	74.4	2 - 4	45 - 27
Heat 13	Coles/**Cope**/Clipstone/**Wasley**	73.2	2 - 4	47 - 31

CREWE - Chris Turner 9 (+1), Graham Drury 9, Stuart Cope 8 (+2), Cliff Anderson 7 (+1), Les Collins 6 (+3), Max Brown 6 (+2), Nigel Wasley 2 (+1).
MILDENHALL - Bob Coles 15, Stan Stevens 6, John McNeil 5, Paul Clipstone 3 (+1), Trevor Harvey 1, Kevin Jolly 1, Graham Kerry 0.

Crewe strengthened their squad with the signing of Birmingham's Australian Ricky Day, initially on a 28 day loan. He was unable to ride in the Peterborough match on June 9 due to being on international duty.

(ABOVE) Rye House and Crewe do battle on June 1, with Brian Foote leading Graham Drury and Max Brown.

(ABOVE) Ouch! Chris Turner in trouble at Rye House.

Meeting 18 - Monday, June 9, 1975 - New National League
L.M.R. Sports Ground, Earle Street, Crewe
Track Length - 436 yards.

CREWE KINGS.....46 PETERBOROUGH PANTHERS.....32

Old foes Peterborough became Crewe's 100th home league victim, after the Panthers could only register a single heat advantage all evening. The match was evenly poised going into Heat 9, but successive home 5-1's took the match away from the visitors. Nigel Wasley and Chris Turner were joint top-scorers with eleven points.

Heat 01	**Drury**/Clark/Walker/**Cope**	72.6	3 - 3	03 - 03
Heat 02	**Turner**/Taylor/**Brown**/Matthews (R)	72.4	**4 - 2**	07 - 05
Heat 03	Carter/**Anderson**/**Collins**/Sizmore	71.8	3 - 3	10 - 08
Heat 04	Matthews/**Wasley**/**Turner**/Cake	71.4	3 - 3	13 - 11
Heat 05	Clark/**Collins**/Walker/**Anderson**	73.0	2 - 4	15 - 15
Heat 06	Cake/**Drury**/**Cope**/Taylor	72.6	3 - 3	18 - 18
Heat 07	**Wasley**/**Turner**/Carter/Sizmore	71.4	**5 - 1**	23 - 19
Heat 08	Matthews/**Cope**/**Brown**/Walker (R)	72.0	3 - 3	26 - 22
Heat 09	**Turner**/**Collins**/Cake/Taylor	72.4	**5 - 1**	31 - 23
Heat 10	**Cope**/**Turner**/Matthews/Carter	72.2	**5 - 1**	36 - 24
Heat 11	**Wasley**/Clark/Matthews/**Brown**	71.6	3 - 3	39 - 27
Heat 12	**Drury**/Cake/Carter/**Anderson**	73.0	3 - 3	42 - 30
Heat 13	**Wasley**/Clark/**Collins**/Walker	72.4	**4 - 2**	46 - 32

CREWE - Chris Turner 11 (+3), Nigel Wasley 11, Graham Drury 8, Les Collins 6 (+2), Stuart Cope 6 (+1), Max Brown 2 (+1), Cliff Anderson 2.
PETERBOROUGH - Brian Clark 9, Ken Matthews 8 (+1), Mike Cake 6, Roy Carter 5 (+1), Jack Walker 2 (+1), Steve Taylor 2, Roy Sizmore 0.

Before the match even started, there was a disagreement over Crewe's attempts to use rider replacement for Ricky Day. Peterborough were eventually successful in their objections. Added to the second-half events was a four heat mini-match between the juniors of Crewe and King's Lynn, which produced a comfortable win for the home side.

CREWE.....18 KING'S LYNN.....6

Heat 01	**Argall**/Smith/**Crook**/Ellis	74.8	**4 - 2**	04 - 02
Heat 02	**Roberts**/Davey/**Mellor**/Worthington	75.6	**4 - 2**	08 - 04
Heat 03	**Argall**/**Crook**/Davey/Worthington	75.0	**5 - 1**	13 - 05
Heat 04	**Mellor**/**Roberts**/Ellis/Smith	75.2	**5 - 1**	18 - 06

CREWE - Eddie Argall 6, Stuart Roberts 5, Mick Mellor 4, Graham Crook 3.
KING'S LYNN - Richard Davey 3, Pete Smith 2, Gerard Ellis 1, Neil Worthington 0.

Violet Littlechild, concerned at falling gate receipts, applied to the Crewe and Nantwich Borough Council for permission to switch, for a trial period, to Sunday afternoon racing. The idea, however, immediately attracted stern opposition from several church organisations in the vicinity, and in the space of a few days, two petitions containing 130 and 59 signatures had been handed in to the council. On June 10, Crewe took the long trek to Weymouth, but without Aussie trialist Andy Cowan, who had been set to make his debut, but joined Leicester on the eve of the match.

Meeting 19 - Tuesday June 10, 1975 - New National League
Wessex Stadium, Radipole Lane, Weymouth
Track Length - 380 yards.

WEYMOUTH WIZARDS.....43 CREWE KINGS.....35

The Wizards conjured up their first home league win of the season thanks to a Vic Harding paid maximum and healthy returns from Bryan Woodward and Martin Yeates. Crewe had their moments, including three 5-1 wins, with Nigel Wasley continuing his good form from the previous night, scoring thirteen points.

Heat 01	Woodward/**Drury**/Robins/**Cope**	73.8	4 - 2	04 - 02
Heat 02	**Turner**/**Brown**/Soffe/Owen (F)	76.1	**1 - 5**	05 - 07
Heat 03	Couzens/Yeates/**Collins**/**Day**	74.8	5 - 1	10 - 08
Heat 04	Harding/**Wasley**/Soffe/**Brown**	76.1	4 - 2	14 - 10
Heat 05	Couzens/Yeates/**Drury**/**Cope**	75.2	5 - 1	19 - 11
Heat 06	Woodward/**Wasley**/Robins/**Turner**	74.7	4 - 2	23 - 13
Heat 07	Harding/**Day**/Soffe/**Collins**	75.5	4 - 2	27 - 15
Heat 08	**Wasley**/**Turner**/Robins/Owen	74.3	**1 - 5**	28 - 20
Heat 09	**Wasley**/Yeates/Couzens/**Turner**	74.8	3 - 3	31 - 23
Heat 10	Woodward/**Drury**/**Day**/Robins	75.0	3 - 3	34 - 26
Heat 11	Harding/**Drury**/**Turner**/Owen	75.8	3 - 3	37 - 29
Heat 12	**Wasley**/**Day**/Woodward/Couzens	75.5	**1 - 5**	38 - 34
Heat 13	Yeates/Harding/**Drury**/**Turner**	75.5	5 - 1	43 - 35

WEYMOUTH - Vic Harding 11 (+1), Bryan Woodward 10, Martin Yeates 9 (+2), Nigel Couzens 7 (+1), Chris Robins 3, Melvin Soffe 3, Ricky Owen 0.
CREWE - Nigel Wasley 13, Graham Drury 8, Chris Turner 6 (+2), Ricky Day 5 (+2), Max Brown 2 (+1), Les Collins 1, Stuart Cope 0.

Meeting 20 - Monday, June 16, 1975 - New National League
L.M.R. Sports Ground, Earle Street, Crewe
Track Length - 436 yards.

CREWE KINGS.....50 CANTERBURY CRUSADERS.....28

Nigel Wasley, Ricky Day and Chris Turner provided the foundations for a big Kings win, with Day particulary impressive on his home debut. Crewe led by eighteen after just seven heats, and although Les Rumsey and Graham Clifton fought hard for their nineteen points, it was never going to be enough to halt a determined Kings outfit, which was at last showing potential following five successive home victories. Graham Drury was hurt in a spill after Terry Casserly fell in his path, in the first attempt at running Heat 6, but picked himself up to contest the re-run.

Heat 01	**Drury**/Clifton/Kennett/**Cope** (F)	74.6	3 - 3	03 - 03
Heat 02	**Turner**/**Brown**/Spelta/Casserly	73.0	**5 - 1**	08 - 04
Heat 03	**Day**/Rumsey/**Collins**/Purkiss	73.2	**4 - 2**	12 - 06
Heat 04	**Wasley**/**Turner**/Gooderham/Spelta	71.4	**5 - 1**	17 - 07
Heat 05	**Day**/Clifton/**Collins**/Kennett	73.0	**4 - 2**	21 - 09
Heat 06	**Cope**/Gooderham/**Drury**/Casserly (X)	71.8	**4 - 2**	25 - 11
Heat 07	**Wasley**/**Turner**/Rumsey/Purkiss	71.4	**5 - 1**	30 - 12
Heat 08	**Cope**/Rumsey/Clifton/**Brown**	71.8	3 - 3	33 - 15
Heat 09	**Day**/Casserly/**Collins**/Gooderham	73.4	**4 - 2**	37 - 17
Heat 10	Rumsey/Clifton/**Cope**/**Drury**	73.8	1 - 5	38 - 22
Heat 11	**Wasley**/Clifton/**Brown**/Kennett	72.8	**4 - 2**	42 - 24
Heat 12	**Turner**/Rumsey/Gooderham/**Collins**	73.4	3 - 3	45 - 27
Heat 13	**Wasley**/**Day**/Casserly/Gooderham	72.2	**5 - 1**	50 - 28

CREWE - Nigel Wasley 12, Ricky Day 11 (+1), Chris Turner 10 (+2), Stuart Cope 7, Graham Drury 4, Max Brown 3 (+1), Les Collins 3.
CANTERBURY - Les Rumsey 10, Graham Clifton 9 (+2), Dave Gooderham 4 (+1), Terry Casserly 3, Barney Kennett 1 (+1), Bob Spelta 1, Jaffa Purkiss 0.

Meeting 21 - Wednesday, June 18, 1975 - New National League
Odsal Stadium, Rooley Avenue, Bradford
Track Length - 375 yards.

BRADFORD BARONS.....48 CREWE KINGS.....30

Bradford completed their third win of the season over the Kings with relative ease. Nigel Wasley was again the pick of the Crewe team, but it was Barons reserve Steve Wilcock who stole the headlines, with four heat wins and a paid maximum.

Heat 01	**Drury**/Featherstone/**Collins**/Fielding (R)	72.8	**2 - 4**	02 - 04
Heat 02	Wilcock/**Turner**/**Brown**/Parkin	73.0	3 - 3	05 - 07
Heat 03	Langlois/Baugh/**Day**/**Cope**	74.6	5 - 1	10 - 08

Heat 04	**Wasley**/Meredith/Wilcock/**Brown**	72.0	3 - 3	13 - 11
Heat 05	Baugh/**Drury**/**Collins**/Langlois (F)	73.0	3 - 3	16 - 14
Heat 06	Wilcock/Featherstone/**Wasley**/**Turner**	72.2	5 - 1	21 - 15
Heat 07	Wilcock/Meredith/**Wasley**/**Day**	72.0	5 - 1	26 - 16
Heat 08	**Brown**/Fielding/**Collins**/Parkin	73.2	**2 - 4**	28 - 20
Heat 09	Baugh/**Wasley**/**Turner**/Langlois	72.2	3 - 3	31 - 23
Heat 10	Featherstone/**Cope**/Fielding/**Day**	73.0	4 - 2	35 - 25
Heat 11	Wilcock/Meredith/**Turner**/**Brown**	73.2	5 - 1	40 - 26
Heat 12	Featherstone/**Wasley**/**Day**/Langlois	72.8	3 - 3	43 - 29
Heat 13	Baugh/Meredith/**Cope**/**Collins**	74.0	5 - 1	48 - 30

BRADFORD - Steve Wilcock 13 (+1), Dave Baugh 11 (+1), Tony Featherstone 10 (+1), Colin Meredith 8 (+3), Mick Fielding 3, Brenton Langlois 3, Dave Parkin 0.
CREWE - Nigel Wasley 9, Graham Drury 5, Max Brown 4 (+1), Chris Turner 4 (+1), Les Collins 3 (+1), Stuart Cope 3, Ricky Day 2 (+1).

In the league table, Crewe lay 8th, with Stoke top, after losing just one of their opening sixteen matches.

Meeting 22 - Saturday, June 21, 1975 - New National League
St. Mirren Football Stadium, Love Street, Paisley
Track Length - 427 yards.

PAISLEY LIONS.....46 CREWE KINGS.....32

For the third away meeting in a row, the Kings managed to top thirty points, but again returned home empty handed. Chris Turner and Graham Drury contributed eighteen towards the Crewe total, but apart from Stuart Cope's win in the last heat, the rest of the squad failed to cope with the tricky Paisley circuit. Home rider Bryan Townsend stood in for the visitors, after Max Brown failed to turn up.

Heat 01	S.Sheldrick/**Drury**/**Collins**/Mountford (F)	78.8	3 - 3	03 - 03
Heat 02	**Turner**/M.Sheldrick/Foot/**Townsend** (F)	79.8	3 - 3	06 - 06
Heat 03	Bridgett/Roynon/**Cope**/**Day**	78.0	5 - 1	11 - 07
Heat 04	Fullerton/**Townsend**/**Wasley**/M.Sheldrick (R)	78.4	3 - 3	14 - 10
Heat 05	Roynon/Bridgett/**Drury**/**Collins**	79.0	5 - 1	19 - 11
Heat 06	**Turner**/S.Sheldrick/**Wasley**/Mountford (R)	79.4	**2 - 4**	21 - 15
Heat 07	Fullerton/**Day**/M.Sheldrick/**Cope**	78.8	4 - 2	25 - 17
Heat 08	**Drury**/Foot/**Collins**/Mountford	80.0	**2 - 4**	27 - 21
Heat 09	Bridgett/**Turner**/Roynon/**Wasley**	78.6	4 - 2	31 - 23
Heat 10	S.Sheldrick/Bridgett/**Day**/**Turner**	80.4	5 - 1	36 - 24
Heat 11	Fullerton/**Drury**/**Collins**/Foot (R)	79.6	3 - 3	39 - 27
Heat 12	S.Sheldrick/**Turner**/Roynon/**Day**	78.4	4 - 2	43 - 29
Heat 13	**Cope**/Fullerton/Bridgett/**Drury**	80.0	3 - 3	46 - 32

PAISLEY - Alan Bridgett 11 (+3), Mick Fullerton 11, Sid Sheldrick 11, Chris Roynon 7 (+1), Bernie Foot 3 (+1), Mick Sheldrick 3, Stuart Mountford 0, *Tom Davie (R/R).*
CREWE - Chris Turner 10, Graham Drury 8, Stuart Cope 4, Les Collins 3 (+2), Ricky Day 3, Nigel Wasley 2 (+1), Bryan Townsend* 2.

Travelling companions Dave Parry and Max Brown arrived late for the meeting, following a 40 mile taxi dash, after their car had broken down en-route.

Meeting 23 - Monday, June 23, 1975 - New National League
L.M.R. Sports Ground, Earle Street, Crewe
Track Length - 436 yards.

CREWE KINGS.....54 BRADFORD BARONS.....24

The Barons arrived in confident mood following their recent run of results against the Kings, but were firmly put in their place by a team finally emerging from the doldrums. Home riders won all thirteen heats, with Ricky Day securing his second successive home paid maximum. Nigel Wasley stretched his run at Earle Street without defeat to a visiting rider to eleven races.

Heat 01	**Drury**/Featherstone/**Cope**/Fielding	72.2	**4 - 2**	04 - 02
Heat 02	**Turner**/Wilcock/**Brown**/Weaver (F)	72.8	**4 - 2**	08 - 04
Heat 03	**Day**/Langlois/**Collins**/Baugh (R)	72.6	**4 - 2**	12 - 06
Heat 04	**Wasley**/**Turner**/Meredith/Weaver	70.8	**5 - 1**	17 - 07
Heat 05	**Day**/Fielding/Featherstone/**Collins**	72.0	3 - 3	20 - 10
Heat 06	**Cope**/Meredith/**Drury**/Wilcock	72.8	**4 - 2**	24 - 12
Heat 07	**Turner**/**Wasley**/Langlois/Baugh (R)	72.0	**5 - 1**	29 - 13
Heat 08	**Cope**/Featherstone/Fielding/**Brown**	72.4	3 - 3	32 - 16
Heat 09	**Day**/**Collins**/Meredith/Wilcock (R)	72.4	**5 - 1**	37 - 17
Heat 10	**Drury**/Langlois/**Cope**/Baugh	72.8	**4 - 2**	41 - 19
Heat 11	**Wasley**/Featherstone/**Brown**/Fielding	71.8	**4 - 2**	45 - 21
Heat 12	**Drury**/Baugh/**Collins**/Meredith	73.4	**4 - 2**	49 - 23
Heat 13	**Wasley**/**Day**/Langlois/Fielding	72.4	**5 - 1**	54 - 24

CREWE - Ricky Day 11 (+1), Nigel Wasley 11 (+1), Graham Drury 10, Chris Turner 8 (+1), Stuart Cope 8, Les Collins 4 (+1), Max Brown 2.
BRADFORD - Tony Featherstone 7 (+1), Brenton Langlois 6, Colin Meredith 4, Mick Fielding 3 (+1), Dave Baugh 2, Steve Wilcock 2, Barry Weaver 0.

Max Brown ended the night £5 richer, after winning a match race challenge against his boss Dave Parry during the second half.

Meeting 24 - Tuesday, June 24, 1975 - New National League
Crayford and Bexley Heath Stadium, London Road, Crayford
Track Length - 265 yards.

CRAYFORD KESTRELS.....48 CREWE KINGS.....30

Second-in-the-table Crayford rode to a comfortable victory over gutsy opposition, with Trevor Barnwell, Alan Sage and Laurie Etheridge going through the programme unbeaten by an opponent. Graham Drury and Chris Turner spearheaded the Kings challenge with sixteen points between them.

Heat 01	Barclay/Etheridge/**Drury**/**Collins**	62.2	5 - 1	05 - 01
Heat 02	**Turner**/**Brown**/Archer/Johns (R)	64.4	**1 - 5**	06 - 06
Heat 03	Barnwell/Wigley/**Day**/**Cope** (X)	61.2	5 - 1	11 - 07
Heat 04	Sage/**Wasley**/**Brown**/Johns	60.2	3 - 3	14 - 10
Heat 05	Barnwell/**Drury**/Wigley/**Collins**	62.0	4 - 2	18 - 12
Heat 06	Etheridge/**Wasley**/Barclay/**Turner**	61.2	4 - 2	22 - 14
Heat 07	Sage/Johns/**Day**/**Brown**	61.0	5 - 1	27 - 15
Heat 08	**Turner**/**Drury**/Barclay/Archer	62.8	**1 - 5**	28 - 20
Heat 09	Barnwell/Wigley/**Wasley**/**Turner**	61.8	5 - 1	33 - 21
Heat 10	Etheridge/**Day**/**Cope**/Barclay (F)	61.6	3 - 3	36 - 24
Heat 11	Sage/**Drury**/Archer/**Day**	60.8	4 - 2	40 - 26
Heat 12	Barnwell/Etheridge/**Brown**/**Wasley**	62.6	5 - 1	45 - 27
Heat 13	Sage/**Drury**/**Turner**/Wigley	60.6	3 - 3	48 - 30

CRAYFORD - Trevor Barnwell 12, Alan Sage 12, Laurie Etheridge 10 (+2), Pete Wigley 5 (+2), George Barclay 5, Alan Johns 2 (+1), Bill Archer 2.
CREWE - Graham Drury 9 (+1), Chris Turner 7 (+1), Nigel Wasley 5, Max Brown 4 (+2), Ricky Day 4, Stuart Cope 1 (+1), Les Collins 0.

Meeting 25 - Monday, June 30, 1975 - New National League
Quibell Park Stadium, Brumby Wood Lane, Scunthorpe
Track Length - 440 yards.

SCUNTHORPE SAINTS.....41 CREWE KINGS.....37

Successful use of the tactical substitute rule together with a lively performance by Nigel Wasley, almost brought a second away win of the season. Graham Drury and Stuart Cope provided good back-up, but the visitors just didn't have enough left in the tank. Saints reserve Ray Watkins suffered a severe thumb injury following a fall in Heat 4 and took no further part in the match. Cliff Anderson returned to the Kings line-up for the struggling Les Collins, but failed to impress in his two rides.

Heat 01	Childs/**Drury**/**Cope**/Hines (F)	80.8	3 - 3	03 - 03
Heat 02	Sims/Watkins/**Brown** (3 riders only)	79.8	5 - 1	08 - 04
Heat 03	Evans/Emery/**Day**/**Anderson**	79.2	5 - 1	13 - 05
Heat 04	McKinlay/**Wasley**/**Brown**/Watkins (F)	80.4	3 - 3	16 - 08
Heat 05	**Cope**/**Drury**/Evans/Emery	80.8	**1 - 5**	17 - 13
Heat 06	**Wasley**/Childs/Hines/**Turner**	78.8	3 - 3	20 - 16
Heat 07	McKinlay/**Day**/Sims/**Anderson**	80.6	4 - 2	24 - 18
Heat 08	**Drury**/Hines/**Cope**/Sims	80.2	**2 - 4**	26 - 22
Heat 09	Emery/**Wasley**/Evans/**Turner**	79.4	4 - 2	30 - 24
Heat 10	**Wasley**/**Day**/Childs/Hines	79.2	**1 - 5**	31 - 29
Heat 11	McKinlay/Sims/**Drury**/**Cope** (F)	80.0	5 - 1	36 - 30
Heat 12	**Wasley**/Childs/Emery/**Day**	79.2	3 - 3	39 - 33
Heat 13	**Cope**/Evans/**Drury**/Sims	80.2	**2 - 4**	41 - 37

SCUNTHORPE - Ken McKinlay 9, Tony Childs 8, Keith Evans 7, Chris Emery 6 (+2), Andy Sims 6 (+1), Andy Hines 3 (+1), Ray Watkins 2 (+1).
CREWE - Nigel Wasley 13, Graham Drury 9 (+1), Stuart Cope 8 (+1), Ricky Day 5 (+1), Max Brown 2 (+1), Cliff Anderson 0, Chris Turner 0.

Meeting 26 - Wednesday, July 2, 1975 - Challenge
L.M.R. Sports Ground, Earle Street, Crewe
Track Length - 436 yards.

CREWE KINGS.....48 BIRMINGHAM BRUMMIES.....30

Improving Crewe gained a satisfying win over the current league and cup holders in a cracking challenge match. They raced into an early six-point lead, but by the sixth heat, the Brummies had drawn level. The match remained in the balance until a Wasley/Anderson maximum in Heat 11 effectively won the match for the hosts.

Heat 01	**Cope**/White/**Drury**/Hart	71.8	**4 - 2**	04 - 02
Heat 02	**Turner**/**C.Anderson**/Major/Grahame	72.8	**5 - 1**	09 - 03
Heat 03	**Day**/Browning/Askew/**Collins**	72.4	3 - 3	12 - 06
Heat 04	K.Anderson/**Wasley**/**Turner**/Grahame	72.0	3 - 3	15 - 09
Heat 05	White/**Day**/Hart/**Collins**	72.2	2 - 4	17 - 13
Heat 06	K.Anderson/Major/**Drury**/**Cope**	72.0	1 - 5	18 - 18
Heat 07	**Wasley**/**Turner**/Browning/Askew	71.2	**5 - 1**	23 - 19
Heat 08	**Cope**/White/**C.Anderson**/Grahame	72.4	**4 - 2**	27 - 21
Heat 09	K.Anderson/**Day**/Major/**Turner**	72.4	2 - 4	29 - 25
Heat 10	**Drury**/Browning/**Cope**/Askew	72.2	**4 - 2**	33 - 27
Heat 11	**Wasley**/**C.Anderson**/White/Hart	71.2	**5 - 1**	38 - 28
Heat 12	**Drury**/**Collins**/K.Anderson/Major	72.0	**5 - 1**	43 - 29
Heat 13	**Wasley**/**Day**/Askew/Hart (F)	72.0	**5 - 1**	48 - 30

CREWE - Nigel Wasley 11, Ricky Day 9 (+1), Graham Drury 8, Stuart Cope 7, Chris Turner 6 (+2), Cliff Anderson 5 (+2), Les Collins 2 (+1).
BIRMINGHAM - Keith Anderson 10, Keith White 8, Arthur Browning 5, George Major 4 (+1), Carl Askew 2 (+1), John Hart 1, Alan Grahame 0.

On July 4, Crewe refused to take part in the league match against Peterborough. Dave Parry was unhappy about the home side's insistence on using rider replacement for the absent Russell Osborne, who they had signed on a 7.50 assessed average, making him third heat leader. This information however, did not appear on the current green sheet averages. The Crewe boss was concerned that the Panthers couldn't prove the rider had in fact signed and commented: *"We were perfectly willing to ride if Peterborough had not insisted on using rider replacement for Osborne, which I am convinced they were not entitled to do. He wasn't injured or ill. He simply didn't turn up and there was no satisfactory explanation. He didn't even have a National League average, so he couldn't be classified as a heat leader and therefore the regulation couldn't be applied."* Referee Geoff Dalby, after consulting with Harry Louis of the Speedway Control Board, fined Parry £10 for refusing to allow his team to ride. The Panthers had earlier beaten Bradford (who had ridden under protest) in the first match of the proposed double-header. Ironically, Peterborough had successfully objected to Crewe using rider replacement for Ricky Day in the match Earle Street on June 9.

Meeting 27 - Saturday, July 5, 1975 - New National League
Shielfield Park, Tweedmouth, Berwick-upon-Tweed
Track Length - 440 yards.

BERWICK BANDITS.....43 CREWE KINGS.....35

Another encouraging away performance, this time against title chasers Berwick, saw Crewe provide four different race winners and the match go down to the final heat. A Kings maximum was needed for a share of the points, but Chris Turner and Graham Drury were easily beaten by the Bandits pairing of Dave Gifford and Willie Templeton.

Heat 01	Farquharson/**Drury**/Finch/**Cope**	74.6	4 - 2	04 - 02
Heat 02	**Turner**/**Brown**/Farquharson/Trownson (X)	76.8	**1 - 5**	05 - 07
Heat 03	Hornby/Gifford/**Day**/**Collins**	78.2	5 - 1	10 - 08
Heat 04	**Wasley**/Trownson/**Brown**/Templeton	77.2	**2 - 4**	12 - 12
Heat 05	Hornby/**Drury**/Gifford/**Cope** (F)	77.0	4 - 2	16 - 14
Heat 06	**Turner**/Jones/Finch/**Wasley**	76.8	3 - 3	19 - 17
Heat 07	**Collins**/Trownson/Templeton/**Day**	76.8	3 - 3	22 - 20
Heat 08	Trownson/**Turner**/Finch/**Brown**	77.0	4 - 2	26 - 22
Heat 09	Hornby/**Turner**/**Wasley**/Gifford	78.4	3 - 3	29 - 25
Heat 10	Jones/Finch/**Day**/**Collins**	77.6	5 - 1	34 - 26
Heat 11	**Drury**/**Turner**/Templeton/Trownson	78.2	**1 - 5**	35 - 31
Heat 12	Jones/**Wasley**/**Brown**/Hornby (F)	77.4	3 - 3	38 - 34
Heat 13	Gifford/Templeton/**Drury**/**Turner**	78.2	5 - 1	43 - 35

BERWICK - Bernie Hornby 9, Graham Jones 8, Dave Trownson 7, Dave Gifford 6 (+1), Steve Finch 5 (+2), Willie Templeton 4 (+2), Colin Farquharson 4.
CREWE - Chris Turner 12 (+1), Graham Drury 8, Nigel Wasley 6 (+1), Max Brown 4 (+2), Les Collins 3, Ricky Day 2, Stuart Cope 0.

Meeting 28 - Monday, July 7, 1975 - New National League
L.M.R. Sports Ground, Earle Street, Crewe
Track Length - 436 yards.

CREWE KINGS.....37 STOKE POTTERS.....41

This was one of the best meetings witnessed at Earle Street for some time, with no more than six points separating the two sides throughout the match. Any hopes of the Kings inflicting Stoke's third league defeat of the season evaporated during the latter stages, when firstly Graham Drury was excluded from Heat 10 for breaking the tapes. Les Collins then lost ground after lifting at the start of the next and Chris Turner contested the penultimate race with a machine that was not on full power. A 4-2 from Alan Molyneux and Phil Bass sealed victory for the Potters which put them ten points clear at the top of the table, sending the large visiting contingent home happy.

Heat 01	Molyneux/Wells/**Drury**/**Cope**	72.6	1 - 5	01 - 05
Heat 02	Bass/**Collins**/**Brown**/Handley	73.8	3 - 3	04 - 08
Heat 03	**Turner**/**Day**/Cusworth/Millen	72.2	**5 - 1**	09 - 09
Heat 04	**Wasley**/**Collins**/Bastable/Handley (R)	72.6	**5 - 1**	14 - 10
Heat 05	**Turner**/Molyneux/Wells/**Day**	72.0	3 - 3	17 - 13
Heat 06	**Cope**/Bastable/Bass/**Drury** (R)	73.0	3 - 3	20 - 16
Heat 07	Millen/**Wasley**/**Collins**/Cusworth	73.0	3 - 3	23 - 19
Heat 08	**Cope**/Wells/Bass/**Brown**	72.8	3 - 3	26 - 22
Heat 09	**Turner**/Bastable/**Day**/Bass	73.0	**4 - 2**	30 - 24
Heat 10	Molyneux/**Collins**/Millen/**Cope**	72.8	2 - 4	32 - 28
Heat 11	Molyneux/**Wasley**/Wells/**Collins**	73.0	2 - 4	34 - 32
Heat 12	Millen/Bastable/**Drury**/**Turner**	73.2	1 - 5	35 - 37
Heat 13	Molyneux/**Wasley**/Bass/**Day**	72.4	2 - 4	37 - 41

CREWE - Chris Turner 9, Nigel Wasley 9, Les Collins 7 (+2), Stuart Cope 6, Ricky Day 3 (+1), Graham Drury 2, Max Brown 1 (+1).

STOKE - Alan Molyneux 14, Steve Bastable 7 (+1), Jack Millen 7, Phil Bass 6 (+2), Jim Wells 6 (+2), Andy Cusworth 1, Mick Handley 0.

Due to an injury sustained by Birmingham's Keith Anderson, Ricky Day was re-called to assist in their title bid, although Crewe were still expecting to sign the popular Australian on a permanent basis on his return, after agreeing a fee with the Brummies. Dave Parry moved quickly to try and fill the temporary gap by approaching ex-King's Lynn, Canterbury and Wimbledon rider Barry Crowson, hoping to tempt him out of retirement, but his request was politely turned down, due to travelling problems. Cliff Anderson was another rider whose future at the club was in doubt following a lean spell of form. He was put on the transfer list after travelling to Berwick against the advice of Parry. Max Brown was offered the job of track maintenance.

Meeting 29 - Monday, July 14, 1975 - Inter-League Four Team Tournament
L.M.R. Sports Ground, Earle Street, Crewe
Track Length - 436 yards.

CREWE KINGS.....39 BELLE VUE ACES.....24
KING'S LYNN STARS.....16 CRADLEY UNITED.....14

The Kings, with guest John Jackson replacing Ricky Day, caused a major upset by comprehensively beating their Gulf British League opposition. Chris Turner upstaged his Aces team-mates with a brilliant maximum, which included heat wins over both Chris Morton and Sören Sjösten. Nigel Wasley and Graham Drury also showed they could hack it with the big boys with polished performances. Ian Cartwright returned as a guest for Cradley, but failed to score in his two outings. Cliff Anderson and Graham Crook also rode for King's Lynn and Cradley respectively.

		CK	B	K	CU
Heat 01 ..... Sjösten/**Jackson** (R)/Cartwright (R)/Anderson (R)	73.8	0	3	0	0
Heat 02 ..... **C.Turner**/Tyrer/Betts/Levai	71.4	3	2	1	0
Heat 03 ..... **Wasley**/Persson/Middleton/Pusey (F)	72.0	3	0	1	2
Heat 04 ..... Morton/**Drury**/I.Turner/Price	71.2	2	3	1	0
Heat 05 ..... Persson/**Jackson**/I.Turner/Tyrer	72.2	2	0	1	3
Heat 06 ..... **C.Turner**/Sjösten/Middleton/Price (R)	72.0	3	2	1	0
Heat 07 ..... Morton/**Wasley**/Betts/Cartwright	72.0	2	3	1	0
Heat 08 ..... Levai/**Drury**/Anderson/Pusey	73.4	2	0	1	3
Heat 09 ..... **Jackson**/Betts/Price/Pusey	72.0	3	0	2	1
Heat 10 ..... **C.Turner**/Morton/Anderson/Persson (R)	72.8	3	2	1	0
Heat 11 ..... **Wasley**/I.Turner/Levai/Sjösten	72.4	3	0	2	1
Heat 12 ..... **Drury**/Tyrer/Middleton/Crook	72.8	3	2	1	0
Heat 13 ..... **C.Turner**/I.Turner/Pusey/Crook	72.6	3	1	2	0
Heat 14 ..... Morton/**Jackson**/Levai/Middleton	72.4	2	3	0	1
Heat 15 ..... **Wasley**/Price/Anderson/Tyrer (R)	73.0	3	0	1	2
Heat 16 ..... Sjösten/**Drury**/Persson/Betts	72.0	2	3	0	1

CREWE - Chris Turner 12, Nigel Wasley 11, Graham Drury 9, John Jackson* 7.
BELLE VUE - Chris Morton 11, Sören Sjösten 8, Paul Tyrer 4, Chris Pusey 1.
KING'S LYNN - Ian Turner 6, Terry Betts 4, Cliff Anderson* 3, Garry Middleton 3.
CRADLEY - Bernt Persson 6, Sandor Levai 5, Arthur Price 3, Ian Cartwright* 0, Graham Crook* (Reserve) 0.

Just as it appeared that Crewe had turned the corner, news came that Chris Turner was in King's Lynn Hospital after undergoing an emergency appendix operation. He had collapsed at Saddlebow Road on July 19, after travelling there for a second-half ride. He would be sidelined for four weeks. Dave Parry commented: *"The pity is that we have hit problems just when we seemed to be getting everything sorted out. We could have done with Ricky Day now, for he is a fairly impressive performer around Earle Street, and the loss of Chris is a real body blow. But this is typical of our luck this season. We seldom seem to get the breaks."*

Meeting 30 - Monday, July 21, 1975 - New National League
L.M.R. Sports Ground, Earle Street, Crewe
Track Length - 436 yards.

CREWE KINGS.....39 BOSTON BARRACUDAS.....39

Even though Crewe were below strength, they were still guilty of throwing away the match. After leading from Heat 1, they needed just a second place in the last race for victory, and with their strongest pair facing a Boston duo who had collected only seven points between them, everything pointed to a home win. Young Barracudas Michael Lee and Billy Burton obviously hadn't read the script, as they shot from the tapes to record the 5-1 required for the unlikeliest of draws. Cliff Anderson was given a reprieve in the absence of Chris Turner.

Heat 01	**Drury**/**Cope**/Burton/Forrester	72.2	**5 - 1**	05 - 01
Heat 02	Glover/**Anderson**/**Collins**/Mouncer (F)	72.8	3 - 3	08 - 04
Heat 03	Hollingworth/**Cope**/Lee/**Brown**	72.2	2 - 4	10 - 08
Heat 04	**Wasley**/Glover/**Collins**/Gagen (F)	72.4	**4 - 2**	14 - 10
Heat 05	**Anderson**/**Brown**/Forrester/Burton	73.2	**5 - 1**	19 - 11
Heat 06	Hollingworth/**Drury**/**Cope**/Gagen (R)	72.6	3 - 3	22 - 14
Heat 07	**Wasley**/Hollingworth/Lee/**Collins**	72.0	3 - 3	25 - 17
Heat 08	Glover/Forrester/**Cope**/**Anderson**	72.6	1 - 5	26 - 22
Heat 09	Glover/**Wasley**/**Brown**/Mouncer	73.0	3 - 3	29 - 25
Heat 10	Lee/**Drury**/**Cope**/Hollingworth (R)	72.2	3 - 3	32 - 28
Heat 11	**Wasley**/Forrester/Burton/**Anderson**	73.2	3 - 3	35 - 31
Heat 12	Hollingworth/**Drury**/**Brown**/Glover	73.0	3 - 3	38 - 34
Heat 13	Lee/Burton/**Drury**/**Wasley**	72.2	1 - 5	39 - 39

CREWE - Nigel Wasley 11, Graham Drury 10, Stuart Cope 7 (+3), Cliff Anderson 5, Max Brown 4 (+3), Les Collins 2 (+1), *Chris Turner (R/R).*
BOSTON - Les Glover 11, Rob Hollingworth 11, Michael Lee 8 (+1), Bruce Forrester 5 (+1), Billy Burton 4 (+2), David Gagen 0, Rob Mouncer 0.

Another junior mini-match took place in the second half, with the Crewe youngsters taking on and beating Bradford.

CREWE.....15 BRADFORD.....9

Heat 01	**Crook**/**Robertson**/Weaver/Cusworth	77.8	**5 - 1**	05 - 01
Heat 02	Cowen/**Mellor**/**Roberts**/Wilkins	76.0	3 - 3	08 - 04
Heat 03	**Robertson**/Cowen/Wilkins/**Crook** (R)	76.0	3 - 3	11 - 07
Heat 04	**Roberts**/Cusworth/**Mellor**/Weaver	76.0	**4 - 2**	15 - 09

CREWE - Ian Robertson 5, Stuart Roberts 4, Graham Crook 3, Mick Mellor 3.
BRADFORD - Andy Cowen 5, Martin Cusworth 2, Barry Weaver 1, John Wilkins 1.

Meeting 31 - Friday, July 25, 1975 - New National League
Derwent Park Stadium, Workington
Track Length - 398 yards.

WORKINGTON COMETS.....44 CREWE KINGS.....34

Although the Cumbrians had effectively won by the end of Heat 11, the Kings gave a good account of themselves, and won a few friends among the home contingent. Comets reserve Mick Newton was the main reason why Workington collected the points, with three wins from five rides. Ian Robertson, signed on loan from Ellesmere Port, made his Crewe first team debut, but failed to score in either of his two outings.

Heat 01	Owen/**Drury**/**Collins**/Kelly	74.0	3 - 3	03 - 03
Heat 02	Newton/**Anderson**/Lawson/**Robertson**	75.0	4 - 2	07 - 05
Heat 03	Wright/**Cope**/Gardner/**Brown**	76.8	4 - 2	11 - 07
Heat 04	Newton/**Wasley**/Sansom/**Robertson**	74.8	4 - 2	15 - 09
Heat 05	Gardner/Wright/**Drury**/**Collins**	75.4	5 - 1	20 - 10
Heat 06	**Anderson**/Owen/**Wasley**/Kelly	76.0	**2 - 4**	22 - 14
Heat 07	Newton/**Brown**/Sansom/**Cope**	75.0	4 - 2	26 - 16
Heat 08	**Drury**/Newton/**Collins**/Lawson	73.8	**2 - 4**	28 - 20
Heat 09	**Wasley**/Wright/Gardner/**Anderson**	75.8	3 - 3	31 - 23
Heat 10	Owen/**Brown**/Kelly/**Cope**	77.0	4 - 2	35 - 25

Heat 11 .... Sansom/**Drury**/Newton/**Wasley**	74.6	4 - 2	39 - 27
Heat 12 .... Owen/**Wasley**/**Brown**/Gardner	77.0	3 - 3	42 - 30
Heat 13 .... **Drury**/Sansom/**Cope**/Wright	75.0	**2 - 4**	44 - 34

WORKINGTON - Mick Newton 12, Taffy Owen 11, Roger Wright 7 (+1), Lou Sansom 7, Robbie Gardner 5 (+1), Terry Kelly 1, Steve Lawson 1.
CREWE - Graham Drury 11, Nigel Wasley 8, Max Brown 5 (+1), Cliff Anderson 5, Stuart Cope 3, Les Collins 2 (+1), Ian Robertson 0.

Meeting 32 - Monday, July 28, 1975 - Geoff Curtis Memorial Trophy
L.M.R. Sports Ground, Earle Street, Crewe
Track Length - 436 yards.

WINNER.....ALAN MOLYNEUX

Stoke's Alan Molyneux continued his rich vein of form at Earle Street, winning the Geoff Curtis Memorial Trophy by a single point, despite a fighting performance by Stuart Cope, who was the surprise package, winning all but his duel with the eventual victor in Heat 19.

Heat 01 .... Cope/Gifford/Wasley/Shirra (R)	71.8
Heat 02 .... Drury/Jackson/Featherstone/Anderson	71.8
Heat 03 .... Molyneux/Bridgett/Sheldrick/Hornby	71.4
Heat 04 .... Jarman/Collins/Farquharson/Crook	72.4
Heat 05 .... Jackson/Jarman/Hornby/Wasley (F)	71.6
Heat 06 .... Shirra/Farquharson/Drury/Bridgett	71.4
Heat 07 .... Cope/Sheldrick/Collins/Featherstone	71.8
Heat 08 .... Molyneux/Gifford/Anderson/Robertson	71.6
Heat 09 .... Drury/Sheldrick/Crook/Robertson	72.2
Heat 10 .... Molyneux/Jackson/Shirra/Collins	71.0
Heat 11 .... Cope/Farquharson/Roberts/Hornby (F)	71.8
Heat 12 .... Gifford/Jarman/Featherstone/Bridgett	73.0
Heat 13 .... Molyneux/Farquharson/Featherstone/Crook	71.6
Heat 14 .... Shirra/Jarman/Sheldrick/Anderson	71.8
Heat 15 .... Cope/Jackson/Bridgett/Robertson	72.6
Heat 16 .... Drury/Gifford/Collins/Hornby	73.2
Heat 17 .... Collins/Roberts/Bridgett/Anderson (R)	73.2
Heat 18 .... Shirra/Featherstone/Crook/Hornby (F)	72.6
Heat 19 .... Molyneux/Cope/Drury/Jarman	72.2
Heat 20 .... Jackson/Gifford/Farquharson/Sheldrick	72.0

Alan Molyneux 15, Stuart Cope 14, John Jackson 12, Graham Drury 11, Dave Gifford 11, Mitch Shirra 10, Peter Jarman 9, Colin Farquharson 8, Les Collins 7, Sid Sheldrick 6, Tony Featherstone 5, Alan Bridgett 4, Nigel Wasley 1, Cliff Anderson 1, Bernie Hornby 1. Meeting Reserves: Stuart Roberts 3, Graham Crook 2, Ian Robertson 0. *(Gifford replaced Bob Coles.)*

Crewe received more bad news when it was confirmed that Nigel Wasley had broken a bone just above his wrist during a fall in Heat 5. A collection was held during the interval for the sidelined Warmingham youngster Chris Turner which raised £57.

Meeting 33 - Monday, August 4, 1975 - New National League
L.M.R. Sports Ground, Earle Street, Crewe
Track Length - 436 yards.

CREWE KINGS.....36 SCUNTHORPE SAINTS.....40

Scunthorpe took full advantage of Crewe's recent problems with a shock win at Earle Street. Graham Drury registered a maximum, but with Nigel Wasley and Chris Turner confined to spectating roles, and Cliff Anderson missing due to mechanical problems, a lot of pressure was heaped on the inexperienced shoulders of Mick Mellor, Ian Robertson and Graham Crook. With the squad already stretched to breaking point, things got even worse when Stuart Cope was added to the injury list after looping at the gate in a Heat 4 re-run, and was taken to hospital with a fractured right ankle. Mellor and Robertson didn't let the management down, performing well under the circumstances, although Crook saw his scoring hampered by machine problems, snapping a chain on his own, then seizing the track spare.

Heat 01	**Drury**/Childs/Sims/**Mellor**	72.4	3 - 3	03 - 03
Heat 02	Gillias/**Robertson**/**Crook**/Cook	72.8	3 - 3	06 - 06
Heat 03	Hines/**Collins**/Watkins/**Brown** (R)	73.2	2 - 4	08 - 10
Heat 04	Emery/Cook/**Crook**/**Robertson** (X)	72.6	1 - 5	09 - 15
Heat 05	**Collins**/Childs/**Brown**/Sims	73.2	**4 - 2**	13 - 17
Heat 06	**Drury**/**Mellor**/Emery (F)/Gillias (R)	73.4	**5 - 0**	18 - 17
Heat 07	Hines/Watkins/**Crook** (R)/**Robertson** (X)	74.2	0 - 5	18 - 22
Heat 08	Sims/**Robertson**/**Mellor**/Gillias	74.8	3 - 3	21 - 25
Heat 09	**Brown**/Gillias/Emery/**Collins**	74.8	3 - 3	24 - 28
Heat 10	**Drury**/**Mellor**/Gillias/Watkins	75.2	**5 - 1**	29 - 29
Heat 11	Childs/Sims/**Robertson**/**Crook**	74.2	1 - 5	30 - 34
Heat 12	**Drury**/Emery/Hines/**Brown**	72.0	3 - 3	33 - 37
Heat 13	**Collins**/Watkins/Childs/**Crook**	73.4	3 - 3	36 - 40

CREWE - Graham Drury 12, Les Collins 8, Mick Mellor 5 (+3), Ian Robertson 5, Max Brown 4, Graham Crook 2 (+1), Stuart Cope 0.
SCUNTHORPE - Tony Childs 8 (+1), Mick Hines 7 (+1), Andy Sims 6 (+2), Chris Emery 6 (+1), Tony Gillias 6, Ray Watkins 5 (+1), Colin Cook 2 (+1).

Dave Parry missed the meeting following a disagreement with Alan and Violet Littlechild. However, things were soon resolved and he resumed his role for the trip to Canterbury on August 9. It was also reported that Crewe's application for a six-match trial of Sunday racing had been turned down by the Crewe and Nantwich Borough Council Development Committee. The main reasons for the rejection were nuisance to local residents through noise, traffic congestion, parking, and interference with a number of church services in the immediate area. A petition in favour of Sunday racing hardly helped matters as it contained just 246 signatures.

Meeting 34 - Saturday, August 9, 1975 - New National League
Canterbury City Football Ground, Kingsmead Road, Canterbury
Track Length - 390 yards.

CANTERBURY CRUSADERS.....42 CREWE KINGS.....36

Another admirable Crewe away performance once again counted for nothing, despite three heat wins for Graham Drury and two for loaned Crusader Jaffa Purkiss. The Kings stayed in contention, until a home maximum in the penultimate heat.

Heat 01	**Drury**/Rumsey/Clifton/**Hughes**	73.4	3 - 3	03 - 03
Heat 02	Mittell/Casserly/**Robertson**/**Roberts**	75.9	5 - 1	08 - 04
Heat 03	**Collins**/Spelta/**Brown**/Mittell	75.3	**2 - 4**	10 - 08
Heat 04	**Purkiss**/Gooderham/**Roberts**/Mittell	73.9	**2 - 4**	12 - 12
Heat 05	Spelta/**Drury**/Casserly/**Hughes** (F)	75.4	4 - 2	16 - 14
Heat 06	Clifton/**Robertson**/**Purkiss**/Rumsey (X)	73.4	3 - 3	19 - 17
Heat 07	Gooderham/Mittell/**Collins**/**Brown**	75.1	5 - 1	24 - 18
Heat 08	**Drury**/Clifton/**Roberts**/Casserly (X)	75.1	**2 - 4**	26 - 22
Heat 09	**Purkiss**/Spelta/Casserly/**Robertson**	75.6	3 - 3	29 - 25
Heat 10	Rumsey/**Brown**/**Collins**/Clifton	74.5	3 - 3	32 - 28
Heat 11	**Drury**/Gooderham/**Purkiss**/Casserly (F)	74.2	**2 - 4**	34 - 32
Heat 12	Spelta/Rumsey/**Purkiss**/**Brown** (F)	75.8	5 - 1	39 - 33
Heat 13	Gooderham/**Drury**/**Collins**/Mittell	74.5	3 - 3	42 - 36

CANTERBURY - Dave Gooderham 10, Bob Spelta 10, Les Rumsey 7 (+1), Graham Clifton 6 (+1), Peter Mittell 5 (+1), Terry Casserly 4 (+2).
CREWE - Graham Drury 13, Jaffa Purkiss* 9 (+1), Les Collins 6 (+2), Max Brown 3, Ian Robertson 3, Stuart Roberts 2, Dave Hughes* 0, *Chris Turner (R/R)*.

Graham Crook failed to appear for the match, resulting in him being suspended for an indefinite period. Dave Parry moved to sign Chris Emery on loan from Scunthorpe, following an impressive display in the previous home meeting, when he won heat and final in the second half Rider of the Night. Coatbridge meanwhile, came in for Cliff Anderson, but with Crewe's injury predicament, the transfer request was turned down.

Meeting 35 - Sunday, August 10, 1975 - New National League
Arlington Raceway, Arlington Road, Hailsham, Eastbourne
Track Length - 342 yards.

EASTBOURNE EAGLES.....55 CREWE KINGS.....23

Crewe riders failed to win a single race during an expected mauling in Sussex. Even though they contributed little to the match, Chris Emery, Max Brown and Stuart Roberts earned praise from the terraces for their efforts. On loan Cradley junior Roberts was involved in the race of the match in Heat 6, after he battled for three laps with Paul Gachet and Steve Weatherley, until his efforts were curtailed by a spill on the pits bend. The Eagles had beaten Peterborough 59-19 earlier in the afternoon.

Heat 01	Gachet/Middleditch/**Drury**/**Emery**	62.6	5 - 1	05 - 01
Heat 02	Dugard/Richardson/**Robertson**/**Roberts**	64.2	5 - 1	10 - 02
Heat 03	Jarman/Sampson/**Brown**/**Collins**	64.6	5 - 1	15 - 03
Heat 04	Middleditch/**Emery**/**Robertson**/Richardson (X)	63.0	3 - 3	18 - 06
Heat 05	Jarman/**Drury**/Sampson/**Brown** (F)	64.2	4 - 2	22 - 08
Heat 06	Weatherley/Gachet/**Emery**/**Roberts** (F)	62.4	5 - 1	27 - 09
Heat 07	Middleditch/**Brown**/Richardson/**Collins**	63.2	4 - 2	31 - 11
Heat 08	Weatherley/**Emery**/**Drury**/Dugard	62.0	3 - 3	34 - 14
Heat 09	Jarman/**Emery**/Sampson/**Drury**	64.4	4 - 2	38 - 16
Heat 10	Weatherley/Gachet/**Brown**/**Collins** (R)	62.2	5 - 1	43 - 17
Heat 11	Middleditch/**Brown**/Dugard/**Robertson**	63.2	4 - 2	47 - 19
Heat 12	Gachet/**Brown**/**Emery**/Jarman (X)	64.2	3 - 3	50 - 22
Heat 13	Middleditch/Sampson/**Robertson**/**Collins**	63.6	5 - 1	55 - 23

EASTBOURNE - Neil Middleditch 14 (+1), Paul Gachet 10 (+2), Peter Jarman 9, Steve Weatherley 9, Mike Sampson 6 (+2), Eric Dugard 4, Colin Richardson 3 (+1).
CREWE - Chris Emery 8 (+1), Max Brown 8, Graham Drury 4 (+1), Ian Robertson 3 (+1), Les Collins 0, Stuart Roberts 0, *Chris Turner (R/R)*.

Meeting 36 - Monday, August 11, 1975 - New National League
L.M.R. Sports Ground, Earle Street, Crewe
Track Length - 436 yards.

CREWE KINGS.....31 EASTBOURNE EAGLES.....46

Despite the heroics of skipper Graham Drury and home debutant Chris Emery, the injury-decimated Kings suffered their worst ever home league reversal, as Eastbourne recorded their first ever win at Earle Street, to complete a quick-fire double. Ten of the thirteen heats were won by the visitors and there was a full house for Eagles starlet Paul Gachet.

Heat 01	Gachet/**Drury**/**Collins**/Weatherley	71.6	3 - 3	03 - 03
Heat 02	**Emery**/Dugard/**Robertson**/Richardson	73.2	**4 - 2**	07 - 05
Heat 03	Jarman/**Brown**/Sampson/**Collins**	73.0	2 - 4	09 - 09
Heat 04	Middleditch/**Anderson**/**Emery**/Richardson	73.2	3 - 3	12 - 12
Heat 05	Gachet/Weatherley/**Collins**/**Brown** (F)	72.8	1 - 5	13 - 17
Heat 06	**Drury**/Middleditch/**Emery**/Dugard	72.4	**4 - 2**	17 - 19
Heat 07	Sampson/**Emery**/Jarman/**Anderson**	72.0	2 - 4	19 - 23
Heat 08	Weatherley/**Drury**/Richardson/**Robertson**	71.6	2 - 4	21 - 27
Heat 09	Middleditch/**Drury**/Dugard (X)/**Brown** (X)	73.4	2 - 3	23 - 30
Heat 10	Sampson/**Drury**/**Emery**/Jarman	72.6	3 - 3	26 - 33
Heat 11	Gachet/Weatherley/**Emery**/**Anderson**	72.2	1 - 5	27 - 38
Heat 12	**Drury**/Sampson/Middleditch/**Collins** (R)	72.8	3 - 3	30 - 41
Heat 13	Gachet/Jarman/**Brown**/**Roberts**	73.6	1 - 5	31 - 46

CREWE - Graham Drury 14, Chris Emery 9 (+2), Max Brown 3, Les Collins 2 (+1), Cliff Anderson 2, Ian Robertson 1, Stuart Roberts 0, *Chris Turner (R/R)*.
EASTBOURNE - Paul Gachet 12, Neil Middleditch 9 (+1), Mike Sampson 9, Steve Weatherley 7 (+2), Peter Jarman 6 (+1), Eric Dugard 2, Colin Richardson 1.

The Crewe injury jinx struck again when local junior Mick Mellor broke his right ankle after crashing into the boards during a second-half ride. In his programme notes, Dave Parry was very disappointed with the Crewe and Nantwich Borough Council's decision to turn down the application for Sunday racing. His comments aimed directly at the council included: *"....should Crewe speedway close at the end of the season, you may take delight in the fact that you did not help in our hour of need."* On August 12, the Crewe boss appeared before a B.S.P.A. tribunal in London, to answer allegations that he had wrongly withdrawn his team from their match at Peterborough. He was also accused of ungentlemanly conduct towards referee Geoff Dalby and fined £50 plus costs. Further bad news reached the camp, when they were informed by Birmingham, that Keith Anderson had been ruled out for the rest of the season, meaning that Ricky Day would not be returning to Earle Street.

Meeting 37 - Monday, August 18, 1975 - New National League
L.M.R. Sports Ground, Earle Street, Crewe
Track Length - 436 yards.

CREWE KINGS.....41 TEESSIDE TIGERS.....37

Following a run of ten successive league matches without a win, the Kings faced a Teesside outfit yet to taste victory on the road. After five heats, the scores were level, but a run of four heat advantages in the next five races saw Crewe lead by ten. However, the Tigers then staged a spirited fightback. In Heat 11, Chris Turner, back in action following a five week absence, pulled up while in front, then in the next, Graham Drury couldn't get his bike started and was excluded under the two minute time allowance.Thankfully for the home faithful, Turner kept his nerve in the last to outgate Tom Leadbitter and Harry MacLean to hold on for a much-needed victory. Bradford loanee Mick Fielding made his Kings debut and contributed four points from his four rides, which included a win in Heat 5.

Heat 01	**Drury**/Reading/Leadbitter/**Brown**	71.8	3 - 3	03 - 03
Heat 02	**Anderson**/Levings/**Emery**/Pestell	72.0	**4 - 2**	07 - 05
Heat 03	Emerson/**Collins**/MacLean/**Fielding**	72.6	2 - 4	09 - 09
Heat 04	Underwood/**Emery**/**Turner**/Levings	71.6	3 - 3	12 - 12
Heat 05	**Fielding**/Reading/Leadbitter/**Collins**	72.8	3 - 3	15 - 15
Heat 06	**Drury**/Underwood/**Brown**/Levings	71.4	**4 - 2**	19 - 17
Heat 07	**Turner**/**Emery**/MacLean/Emerson	72.2	**5 - 1**	24 - 18
Heat 08	Underwood/**Anderson**/Reading/**Brown**	71.4	2 - 4	26 - 22
Heat 09	**Collins**/Underwood/**Fielding**/Pestell	72.2	**4 - 2**	30 - 24
Heat 10	**Emery**/**Drury**/MacLean/Emerson	71.2	**5 - 1**	35 - 25
Heat 11	Leadbitter/**Anderson**/Reading/**Turner** (R)	73.8	2 - 4	37 - 29
Heat 12	Emerson/Underwood/**Anderson**/**Fielding**	72.4	1 - 5	38 - 34
Heat 13	**Turner**/Leadbitter/MacLean/**Collins**	72.4	3 - 3	41 - 37

CREWE - Graham Drury 8 (+1), Chris Emery 8 (+1), Cliff Anderson 8, Chris Turner 7 (+1), Les Collins 5, Mick Fielding 4, Max Brown 1.
TEESSIDE - Doug Underwood 12 (+1), Tom Leadbitter 7 (+2), Alan Emerson 6, Pete Reading 6, Harry MacLean 4 (+1), David Levings 2, Colin Pestell 0.

Meeting 38 - Monday, August 25, 1975 - New National League
L.M.R. Sports Ground, Earle Street, Crewe
Track Length - 436 yards.

CREWE KINGS.....32 BIRMINGHAM BRUMMIES.....46

The Brummies, closing in on the faltering Stoke Potters at the top of the league, made a positive step towards retaining their title with an impressive Earle Street win, which condemned the Kings to their sixth home league defeat of the season. Graham Drury did his utmost to keep the score respectable with a battling fifteen points, but apart from Chris Turner's win in Heat 4, and another by Les Collins in the last, the rest of the side struggled against the powerful Birmingham outfit. Turner hit the boards in Heat 7 and withdrew from the remainder of his rides. Former Kings Keith White and Ricky Day both scored well on their return.

Heat 01	**Drury**/Hart/Major/**Brown** (F)	72.0	3 - 3	03 - 03
Heat 02	Day/**Anderson**/Askew/**Emery**	72.0	2 - 4	05 - 07
Heat 03	**Drury**/White/**Collins**/Grahame (R)	71.8	**4 - 2**	09 - 09

Heat 04 .... **Turner**/Day/Browning/**Emery**	71.2	3 - 3	12 - 12
Heat 05 .... Hart/**Turner**/**Collins**/Major	71.8	3 - 3	15 - 15
Heat 06 .... **Drury**/Browning/Askew/**Brown**	72.0	3 - 3	18 - 18
Heat 07 .... Grahame/White/**Emery**/**Turner** (F)	71.6	1 - 5	19 - 23
Heat 08 .... Day/Major/**Brown**/**Anderson**	71.6	1 - 5	20 - 28
Heat 09 .... **Drury**/**Emery**/Browning/Askew	72.2	**5 - 1**	25 - 29
Heat 10 .... White/Grahame/**Drury**/**Emery** (R)	71.6	1 - 5	26 - 34
Heat 11 .... Major/Hart/**Brown**/**Anderson**	72.0	1 - 5	27 - 39
Heat 12 .... White/**Drury**/Browning/**Fielding**	71.8	2 - 4	29 - 43
Heat 13 .... **Collins**/Grahame/Hart/**Emery**	72.0	3 - 3	32 - 46

CREWE - Graham Drury 15, Les Collins 5 (+1), Chris Turner 5, Chris Emery 3 (+1), Cliff Anderson 2, Max Brown 2, Mick Fielding 0, *Nigel Wasley (R/R)*.
BIRMINGHAM - Keith White 10 (+1), John Hart 8 (+2), Ricky Day 8, Alan Grahame 7 (+1), George Major 6 (+2), Arthur Browning 5 (+1), Carl Askew 2 (+1).

Meeting 39 - Tuesday, August 26, 1975 - New National League
Perry Bar Greyhound Stadium, Regina Drive, Walsall Road, Birmingham
Track Length - 350 yards.

BIRMINGHAM BRUMMIES.....55 CREWE KINGS.....23

Birmingham hammered the Kings for a second time in twenty-four hours, with Graham Drury the sole Crewe rider to emerge with pride intact. Les Collins was the only other visitor to win a race. Chris Turner's bad luck against the Midlanders continued, when he looped at the gate first time out, injuring his back, forcing his withdrawal from the meeting. Alan Grahame top-scored for the Brummies with maximum points.

Heat 01 .... **Drury**/Major/Hart/**Collins**	64.8	3 - 3	03 - 03
Heat 02 .... Askew/Day/**Emery**/**Anderson**	65.2	5 - 1	08 - 04
Heat 03 .... Grahame/White/**Brown**/**Fielding**	64.0	5 - 1	13 - 05
Heat 04 .... Askew/Browning/**Anderson**/**Turner** (F)	65.8	5 - 1	18 - 06
Heat 05 .... Grahame/White/**Drury**/**Collins**	63.8	5 - 1	23 - 07
Heat 06 .... Major/Hart/**Emery**/**Brown** (F)	66.2	5 - 1	28 - 08
Heat 07 .... **Drury**/Askew/**Brown**/Day	65.0	**2 - 4**	30 - 12
Heat 08 .... Day/**Drury**/Major/**Collins**	64.8	4 - 2	34 - 14
Heat 09 .... Grahame/White/**Emery**/**Anderson**	64.2	5 - 1	39 - 15
Heat 10 .... Hart/Major/**Brown**/**Collins**	66.0	5 - 1	44 - 16
Heat 11 .... **Collins**/Browning/**Drury**/Askew	65.2	**2 - 4**	46 - 20
Heat 12 .... Grahame/Hart/**Brown**/**Collins**	64.6	5 - 1	51 - 21
Heat 13 .... Browning/**Drury**/White/**Brown**	65.4	4 - 2	55 - 23

BIRMINGHAM - Alan Grahame 12, John Hart 8 (+3), George Major 8 (+1), Carl Askew 8, Keith White 7 (+3), Arthur Browning 7 (+1), Ricky Day 5 (+1).
CREWE - Graham Drury 12, Max Brown 4, Les Collins 3, Chris Emery 3, Cliff Anderson 1, Mick Fielding 0, Chris Turner 0, *Nigel Wasley (R/R)*.

Meeting 40 - Friday, August 29, 1975 - New National League
L.M.R. Sports Ground, Earle Street, Crewe
Track Length - 436 yards.

CREWE KINGS.....59 WEYMOUTH WIZARDS.....19

Crewe took out all of their frustrations on a poor Weymouth side, with full maximums from Graham Drury, Chris Turner plus a paid one for Max Brown. The Kings racked up nine 5-1's and provided every race winner. However, there was a cool reception for the first trial Friday night meeting, which was reflected by an attendance of just 700.

Heat 01 .... **Drury**/**Brown**/Robins/Harding (F)	71.0	**5 - 1**	05 - 01
Heat 02 .... **Emery**/**Robertson**/Stratten/Soffe	72.0	**5 - 1**	10 - 02
Heat 03 .... **Collins**/**Anderson**/Freegard/Couzens	71.8	**5 - 1**	15 - 03
Heat 04 .... **Turner**/**Emery**/Yeates/Stratten	72.4	**5 - 1**	20 - 04
Heat 05 .... **Anderson**/Robins/**Collins**/Harding	73.8	**4 - 2**	24 - 06
Heat 06 .... **Drury**/**Brown**/Yeates/Soffe	72.2	**5 - 1**	29 - 07

Heat 07	**Turner**/**Emery**/Freegard/Couzens	72.4	**5 - 1**	34 - 08
Heat 08	**Brown**/Robins/Stratten/**Robertson** (R)	73.6	3 - 3	37 - 11
Heat 09	**Anderson**/**Collins**/Robins/Yeates	74.4	**5 - 1**	42 - 12
Heat 10	**Drury**/**Brown**/Couzens/Freegard	73.0	**5 - 1**	47 - 13
Heat 11	**Turner**/Harding/Robins/**Robertson**	72.2	3 - 3	50 - 16
Heat 12	**Drury**/Yeates/**Anderson**/Couzens	72.6	**4 - 2**	54 - 18
Heat 13	**Turner**/**Collins**/Harding/Freegard	73.0	**5 - 1**	59 - 19

CREWE - Graham Drury 12, Chris Turner 12, Max Brown 9 (+3), Cliff Anderson 9 (+1), Les Collins 8 (+2), Chris Emery 7 (+2), Ian Robertson 2 (+1).
WEYMOUTH - Chris Robins 7 (+1), Martin Yeates 4, Vic Harding 3, Roger Stratten 2 (+1), Tony Freegard 2, Nigel Couzens 1, Melvin Soffe 0.

Rumours continued to circulate that this was to be the last season of speedway at Earle Street, especially when news was leaked that British Rail were considering selling the land for development for around £250,000. It had already been announced that the L.M.R. cricket team were to move to Willaston, following their amalgamation with the Crewe Vagrants. On September 1, Supporters Club members met in the Kings Arms to discuss the setting up of a Crewe Speedway Development Fund, and the construction of a clubhouse at the stadium.

Meeting 41 - Friday, September 5, 1975 - Littlechild Trophy
L.M.R. Sports Ground, Earle Street, Crewe
Track Length - 436 yards.

WINNER.....PAUL GACHET

Eastbourne's Paul Gachet followed up his recent Earle Street maximum by lifting the Littlechild Trophy and the £50 first prize. Chris Turner was the highest placed home rider, followed closely by Max Brown and Graham Drury. Favourite for the title John Jackson suffered two retirements due to blown engines, and finished well down the field, although his time of 69.6 in Heat 2 was the first under 70 seconds recorded on the track this season.

Heat 01	Sage/Brown/Hughes/Drury	70.8
Heat 02	Jackson/Day/Collins/Bastable	69.6
Heat 03	Sampson/Bass/Glover/Turner (F)	71.8
Heat 04	Gachet/White/Hollingworth/Emery	71.2
Heat 05	Sampson/Hollingworth/Sage/Jackson (R)	71.4
Heat 06	Gachet/Bastable/Hughes/Bass	71.6
Heat 07	Brown/Emery/Collins/Turner	71.8
Heat 08	Day/Drury/White/Glover	71.4
Heat 09	White/Turner/Sage/Bastable	71.2
Heat 10	Jackson/Emery/Hughes/Glover	71.8
Heat 11	Day/Gachet/Sampson/Brown	71.4
Heat 12	Hollingworth/Collins/Bass/Drury (R)	72.2
Heat 13	Gachet/Collins/Sage/Anderson	72.4
Heat 14	Turner/Hollingworth/Day/Hughes	72.4
Heat 15	White/Bass/Brown (R)/Jackson (R)	71.8
Heat 16	Drury/Emery/Sampson (R)/Bastable (R)	73.0
Heat 17	Sage/Day/Bass/Emery	72.6
Heat 18	White/Sampson/Hughes/Collins	71.8
Heat 19	Hollingworth/Brown/Anderson/Roberts (X)	72.4
Heat 20	Turner/Gachet/Drury/Roberts	71.8
R/O for 3rd	Hollingworth/Day	00.0

Paul Gachet 13, Keith White 12, Rob Hollingworth 11, Ricky Day 11, Alan Sage 9, Mike Sampson 9, Chris Turner 8, Max Brown 7, Graham Drury 6, John Jackson 6, Les Collins 6, Phil Bass 6, Chris Emery 6, Wayne Hughes 4, Steve Bastable 2, Les Glover 1, Meeting Reserves: Cliff Anderson 1, Stuart Roberts 0. *(Brown replaced Nigel Wasley.)*

There was more disappointing news regarding the forthcoming League Riders Championship at Wimbledon, when it was announced that Crewe representative Graham Drury would only be third reserve.

Meeting 42 - Monday, September 15, 1975 - New National League
L.M.R. Sports Ground, Earle Street, Crewe
Track Length - 436 yards.

CREWE KINGS.....58 RYE HOUSE ROCKETS.....20

Nigel Wasley returned after a seven week absence to inspire the Kings to their second biggest win of the season. No fewer than four home riders recorded paid maximums, including Chris Emery with four bonus points, as all thirteen heats were won by a Crewe rider for the second successive home match. Following a drawn first heat, the Kings rattled up six 5-1's in a row. Rye House were without the services of Tiger Beech and Kelvin Mullarkey.

Heat 01	**Drury**/Foote/D.Brown/**M.Brown**	72.6	3 - 3	03 - 03
Heat 02	**Anderson**/**Emery**/Waldrab/Clarke	72.6	**5 - 1**	08 - 04
Heat 03	**Wasley**/**Collins**/Saunders/Cooper	71.0	**5 - 1**	13 - 05
Heat 04	**Turner**/**Emery**/Waldrab/Fiala	72.6	**5 - 1**	18 - 06
Heat 05	**Wasley**/**Collins**/Foote/D.Brown	71.6	**5 - 1**	23 - 07
Heat 06	**Drury**/**M.Brown**/Fiala/Clarke	72.4	**5 - 1**	28 - 08
Heat 07	**Turner**/**Emery**/Saunders/Cooper	72.4	**5 - 1**	33 - 09
Heat 08	**M.Brown**/Foote/Waldrab/**Anderson**	72.8	3 - 3	36 - 12
Heat 09	**Collins**/**Emery**/Saunders/Fiala	71.6	**5 - 1**	41 - 13
Heat 10	**Drury**/Waldrab/Saunders/**M.Brown**	73.0	3 - 3	44 - 16
Heat 11	**Turner**/Foote/**Anderson**/D.Brown	72.6	**4 - 2**	48 - 18
Heat 12	**Wasley**/**Drury**/Saunders/Waldrab (X)	72.0	**5 - 1**	53 - 19
Heat 13	**Collins**/**Turner**/Cooper/Foote (R)	72.4	**5 - 1**	58 - 20

CREWE - Graham Drury 11 (+1), Chris Turner 11 (+1), Les Collins 10 (+2), Nigel Wasley 9, Chris Emery 8 (+4), Max Brown 5 (+1), Cliff Anderson 4.
RYE HOUSE - Brian Foote 7, Hugh Saunders 5 (+1), John Waldrab 5 (+1), Dingle Brown 1 (+1), Bob Cooper 1, Karl Fiala 1, Steve Clarke 0.

Meeting 43 - Monday, September 22, 1975 - Challenge
L.M.R. Sports Ground, Earle Street, Crewe
Track Length - 436 yards.

CREWE KINGS.....42 WORKINGTON COMETS.....35

An incident-packed challenge match with old rivals Workington went to the final heat, with Crewe taking the honours thanks to a maximum from Nigel Wasley and Chris Turner. The under-strength Comets, who went into the match without Robbie Gardner and Roger Wright, contested the crucial final heat with only one rider, after referee Reg Owen sent Mick Newton back to the pits, once it was realised he had already taken his maximum permitted rides. To add to Workington's woes, Taffy Owen had already walked out of the match following an exclusion in Heat 8, after bringing down Max Brown.

Heat 01	Owen/**Brown**/**Drury**/Sansom	71.4	3 - 3	03 - 03
Heat 02	Kelly/**Anderson**/**Emery**/Newton	72.6	3 - 3	06 - 06
Heat 03	**Wasley**/**Collins**/Lawson/Robertson (R)	70.2	**5 - 1**	11 - 07
Heat 04	Sansom/**Emery**/Newton/**Turner** (R)	72.0	2 - 4	13 - 11
Heat 05	**Wasley**/Owen/**Collins**/Lawson	70.8	**4 - 2**	17 - 13
Heat 06	Sansom/**Drury**/**Brown**/Newton	70.6	3 - 3	20 - 16
Heat 07	**Turner**/Kelly/**Emery**/Lawson	72.0	**4 - 2**	24 - 18
Heat 08	Sansom/**Anderson**/**Brown**/Owen (X)	75.0	3 - 3	27 - 21
Heat 09	**Wasley**/Sansom/Kelly (R)/**Collins** (X)	71.8	**3 - 2**	30 - 23
Heat 10	**Drury**/Newton/**Brown**/Robertson	72.6	**4 - 2**	34 - 25
Heat 11	Newton/**Turner**/Kelly/**Anderson**	72.6	2 - 4	36 - 29
Heat 12	Sansom/Robertson/**Drury**/**Collins**	71.4	1 - 5	37 - 34
Heat 13	**Wasley**/**Turner**/Kelly (3 riders only)	71.6	**5 - 1**	42 - 35

CREWE - Nigel Wasley 12, Graham Drury 7 (+1), Chris Turner 7 (+1), Max Brown 5 (+2), Chris Emery 4 (+1), Cliff Anderson 4, Les Collins 3 (+1).
WORKINGTON - Lou Sansom 14, Terry Kelly 7, Mick Newton 6, Taffy Owen 5, Ian Robertson* 2 (+1), Steve Lawson 1, *Malcolm Mackay (R/R)*.

Meeting 44 - Thursday, September 25, 1975 - Potters/Kings Trophy, First Leg
Lyme Valley Sports Stadium, Loomer Road, Chesterton
Track Length - 395 yards.

STOKE POTTERS.....49 CREWE KINGS.....29

Alan Molyneux and Steve Bastable were in irresistible form for the Potters. Only Nigel Wasley and Chris Turner won races for Crewe, although Graham Drury did feature in some highly-contested races. Stoke brought in Steve Wilcock (Bradford) and Peter Jarman (Eastbourne), due to injuries.

Heat 01	Molyneux/**Drury**/Jarman/**Brown**	75.6	4 - 2	04 - 02
Heat 02	Wilcock/Canning/**Emery**/**Anderson**	79.8	5 - 1	09 - 03
Heat 03	Bastable/**Wasley**/Handley/**Collins**	75.2	4 - 2	13 - 05
Heat 04	**Turner**/Jarman/Wilcock/**Anderson**	78.0	3 - 3	16 - 08
Heat 05	Bastable/**Drury**/Handley/**Brown**	75.8	4 - 2	20 - 10
Heat 06	Molyneux/Bastable/**Turner**/**Emery**	76.4	5 - 1	25 - 11
Heat 07	**Wasley**/Wilcock/**Drury**/Jarman	79.8	**2 - 4**	27 - 15
Heat 08	Molyneux/**Collins**/Canning/**Turner**	79.0	4 - 2	31 - 17
Heat 09	Bastable/**Turner**/Handley/**Emery**	77.2	4 - 2	35 - 19
Heat 10	Molyneux/Wilcock/**Wasley**/**Collins**	77.8	5 - 1	40 - 20
Heat 11	Jarman/**Drury**/**Wasley**/Canning	78.6	3 - 3	43 - 23
Heat 12	Molyneux/**Turner**/**Wasley**/Handley	77.6	3 - 3	46 - 26
Heat 13	Bastable/**Drury**/**Collins**/Jarman	77.8	3 - 3	49 - 29

STOKE - Alan Molyneux 15, Steve Bastable 14 (+1), Steve Wilcock* 8 (+2), Peter Jarman* 6, Len Canning 3 (+1), Mick Handley 3, *Steve Holden (R/R)*.
CREWE - Graham Drury 9, Nigel Wasley 8 (+2), Chris Turner 8, Les Collins 3 (+1), Chris Emery 1, Cliff Anderson 0, Max Brown 0.

Meeting 45 - Friday, September 26, 1975 - New National League
Albion Rovers Stadium, Cliftonhill Park, Main Street, Coatbridge
Track Length - 380 yards.

COATBRIDGE TIGERS.....41 CREWE KINGS.....37

Although they were never ahead, the Kings had the opportunity of stealing the points in the last heat. Mitch Shirra however, had other ideas, and streaked from the gate to finish ahead of Graham Drury. Brian Collins equalled his own six week old track record in Heat 1. Coatbridge had earlier beaten Paisley 45-33 in the first leg of the BSM Trophy.

Heat 01	B.Collins/**Drury**/Templeton/**L.Collins**	**68.2** (=TR)	4 - 2	04 - 02
Heat 02	**Emery**/Richardson/Argall/**Anderson**	71.2	3 - 3	07 - 05
Heat 03	B.Collins/Dawson/**Wasley**/**Brown**	69.8	5 - 1	12 - 06
Heat 04	**Turner**/**Anderson**/Richardson/Shirra (R)	71.2	**1 - 5**	13 - 11
Heat 05	Dawson/**Drury**/**L.Collins**/Argall	71.0	3 - 3	16 - 14
Heat 06	**Turner**/B.Collins/**Emery**/Templeton	70.8	**2 - 4**	18 - 18
Heat 07	Shirra/**Wasley**/**Brown**/Richardson	70.0	3 - 3	21 - 21
Heat 08	**L.Collins**/Argall/Templeton/**Emery**	71.0	3 - 3	24 - 24
Heat 09	Dawson/Shirra/**Turner**/**Anderson**	71.4	5 - 1	29 - 25
Heat 10	B.Collins/**Wasley**/Templeton/**Brown**	71.0	4 - 2	33 - 27
Heat 11	**Drury**/**L.Collins**/Argall/Shirra (R)	71.4	**1 - 5**	34 - 32
Heat 12	B.Collins/**Turner**/**Brown**/Richardson	71.2	3 - 3	37 - 35
Heat 13	Shirra/**Drury**/Dawson/**Wasley**	71.6	4 - 2	41 - 37

COATBRIDGE - Brian Collins 14, Grahame Dawson 9 (+1), Mitch Shirra 8 (+1), Eddie Argall 4 (+1), Doug Templeton 3 (+1), Derek Richardson 3, *Jimmy Gallacher (R/R)*.
CREWE - Graham Drury 9, Chris Turner 9, Les Collins 6 (+2), Nigel Wasley 5, Chris Emery 4, Max Brown 2 (+2), Cliff Anderson 2 (+1).

Saturday, September 27, 1975 - Gauloises New National League Riders Championship
Wimbledon Stadium, Plough Lane, London
Track Length - 309 yards.

WINNER.....LAURIE ETHERIDGE

Crayford's Laurie Etheridge emerged as the New National League Riders champion, after he defeated Brian Collins of Coatbridge in a dramatic run-off. Arthur Browning was third, following a three man run-off. Crewe representative Graham Drury was third reserve and was not called upon to ride.

Heat 01	Jackson/Browning/Meredith/Clark	62.7
Heat 02	Etheridge/Owen/Lee/Leadbitter	62.3
Heat 03	Gachet/Rumsey/Childs/Sansom	63.1
Heat 04	Collins/Coles/Molyneux/Foote	62.9
Heat 05	Gachet/Browning/Molyneux/Owen	62.9
Heat 06	Collins/Leadbitter/Jackson/Childs	63.4
Heat 07	Rumsey/Coles/Lee/Meredith	64.0
Heat 08	Sansom/Etheridge/Clark/Foote	62.8
Heat 09	Browning/Leadbitter/Foote/Rumsey	63.0
Heat 10	Jackson/Coles/Owen/Sansom	63.4
Heat 11	Collins/Etheridge/Meredith/Gachet (X)	63.6
Heat 12	Lee/Clark/Molyneux/Childs	63.7
Heat 13	Collins/Lee/Browning/Sansom	63.0
Heat 14	Etheridge/Rumsey/Jackson/Molyneux	63.0
Heat 15	Owen/Foote/Meredith/Childs	63.4
Heat 16	Clark/Gachet/Leadbitter/Coles	64.3
Heat 17	Etheridge/Browning/Coles/Childs	63.8
Heat 18	Lee/Foote/Jackson/Gachet	63.4
Heat 19	Leadbitter/Molyneux/Meredith/Sansom	64.6
Heat 20	Rumsey/Owen/Collins/Clark	64.5
R/O for 1st	Etheridge/Collins	64.1
R/O for 3rd	Browning/Rumsey/Lee	64.4

Laurie Etheridge *(Crayford)* 13, Brian Collins *(Coatbridge)* 13, Arthur Browning *(Birmingham)* 10, Les Rumsey *(Canterbury)* 10, Michael Lee *(Boston)* 10, John Jackson *(Ellesmere Port)* 9, Paul Gachet *(Eastbourne)* 8, Joe Owen *(Newcastle)* 8, Tom Leadbitter *(Teesside)* 8, Bob Coles *(Mildenhall)* 7, Brian Clark *(Peterborough)* 6, Brian Foote *(Rye House)* 5, Alan Molyneux *(Stoke)* 5, Colin Meredith *(Bradford)* 4, Lou Sansom *(Workington)* 3, Tony Childs *(Scunthorpe)* 1. Meeting Reserves: Sid Sheldrick *(Paisley)*, Dave Gifford *(Berwick)*, Graham Drury *(Crewe)*, Martin Yeates *(Weymouth)*.

Meeting 46 - Monday, September 29, 1975 - Potters/Kings Trophy, Second Leg
L.M.R. Sports Ground, Earle Street, Crewe
Track Length - 436 yards.

CREWE KINGS.....36 STOKE POTTERS.....41

(Stoke won on aggregate 90 - 65)

The Stoke pairing of Steve Bastable and Alan Molyneux who did the damage in the first leg of the Potters/Kings Trophy, repeated it on a saturated Earle Street circuit. Molyneux again looked at home on the big Crewe bowl, as did Bastable, who recorded a paid maximum. The home side managed just three race wins, with Les Collins mounted on brother Peter's Westlake machine, taking two of these.

Heat 01	Molyneux/Bastable/**Drury**/**Brown**	71.2	1 - 5	01 - 05
Heat 02	Young/**Anderson**/**Emery**/Handley (X)	74.6	3 - 3	04 - 08
Heat 03	Bastable/**Wasley**/**Collins**/Cusworth	70.6	3 - 3	07 - 11
Heat 04	Jarman/**Turner**/**Emery**/Young	73.6	3 - 3	10 - 14
Heat 05	**Collins**/Molyneux/Cusworth/**Wasley**	70.8	3 - 3	13 - 17
Heat 06	**Brown**/**Drury**/Handley (R)/Jarman (R)	74.6	**5 - 0**	18 - 17
Heat 07	Bastable/**Turner**/Cusworth/**Emery**	72.0	2 - 4	20 - 21
Heat 08	Molyneux/**Brown**/Young/**Anderson**	73.0	2 - 4	22 - 25
Heat 09	**Collins**/Jarman/**Wasley**/Handley	73.4	**4 - 2**	26 - 27
Heat 10	Bastable/**Drury**/**Brown**/Young	73.0	3 - 3	29 - 30
Heat 11	Molyneux/**Turner**/**Emery**/Young	73.6	3 - 3	32 - 33
Heat 12	Bastable/**Collins**/**Drury**/Jarman	72.8	3 - 3	35 - 36
Heat 13	Molyneux/Cusworth/**Turner**/**Wasley**	72.6	1 - 5	36 - 41

CREWE - Les Collins 9 (+1), Chris Turner 7, Graham Drury 6 (+2), Max Brown 6 (+1), Chris Emery 3 (+3), Nigel Wasley 3, Cliff Anderson 2.
STOKE - Steve Bastable 14 (+1), Alan Molyneux 14, Peter Jarman* 5, Andy Cusworth 4 (+2), Kevin Young 4, Mick Handley 0, *Steve Holden (R/R)*.

With no re-staging date for the outstanding Peterborough away fixture agreed, Dave Parry wrote to the B.S.P.A. informing them that unless the Panthers management offered a new date for the match, Crewe were to claim the points.

Meeting 47 - Monday, October 6, 1975 - New National League
L.M.R. Sports Ground, Earle Street, Crewe
Track Length - 436 yards.

CREWE KINGS.....50 BERWICK BANDITS.....28

Crewe completed their home league programme on a high, with a comfortable victory over Berwick. The visitors shared the points on five occasions, with Steve Finch the sole away winner in Heat 8, as only he and Dave Gifford adapted to the track. The Kings put on a solid all round display, with Nigel Wasley going through the card unbeaten by an opponent.

Heat 01	**Drury**/Finch/Jones/**Emery**	72.8	3 - 3	03 - 03
Heat 02	**Brown**/Trownson/Hornby/**Robertson**	72.2	3 - 3	06 - 06
Heat 03	**Wasley**/**Collins**/Gifford/Farquharson	70.2	**5 - 1**	11 - 07
Heat 04	**Brown**/Hornby/**Turner**/Templeton	72.0	**4 - 2**	15 - 09
Heat 05	**Collins**/**Wasley**/Finch/Jones	70.4	**5 - 1**	20 - 10
Heat 06	**Drury**/Templeton/Trownson/**Emery** (R)	71.6	3 - 3	23 - 13
Heat 07	**Turner**/Gifford/**Brown**/Finch	71.0	**4 - 2**	27 - 15
Heat 08	Finch/**Robertson**/**Emery**/Hornby (R)	72.8	3 - 3	30 - 18
Heat 09	**Wasley**/Templeton/**Collins**/Trownson	71.2	**4 - 2**	34 - 20
Heat 10	**Emery**/**Drury**/Gifford/Farquharson	72.2	**5 - 1**	39 - 21
Heat 11	**Turner**/Finch/Jones/**Robertson**	71.4	3 - 3	42 - 24
Heat 12	**Wasley**/Gifford/**Drury**/Templeton	71.0	**4 - 2**	46 - 26
Heat 13	**Turner**/Gifford/**Collins**/Templeton	70.8	**4 - 2**	50 - 28

CREWE - Nigel Wasley 11 (+1), Chris Turner 10, Graham Drury 9 (+1), Les Collins 7 (+1), Max Brown 7, Chris Emery 4 (+1), Ian Robertson 2.
BERWICK - Steve Finch 8, Dave Gifford 8, Willie Templeton 4, Bernie Hornby 3 (+1), Dave Trownson 3 (+1), Graham Jones 2 (+2), Colin Farquharson 0.

Recent sparse attendances at Earle Street forced the promoters to postpone the final meeting of the season originally scheduled for October 20. Phil Crump had been booked to appear, but it was feared that not even his appearance could guarantee a break-even crowd figure. Crewe executive Tommy Rumble, indicated that the Kings were still hopeful of coming to the tapes in 1976 as long as there was no marked increase in stadium rental. On October 10, Graham Drury finished third in the Scottish Open Championship at Coatbridge, won by home skipper Brian Collins.

Meeting 48 - Monday, October 13, 1975 - Whitbread Cheshire Trophy, First Leg
L.M.R. Sports Ground, Earle Street, Crewe
Track Length - 436 yards.

CREWE KINGS.....45 ELLESMERE PORT GUNNERS.....33

In the final meeting of the season at Earle Street, Ellesmere Port rallied to hold the home side to a twelve point lead in this first leg encounter, after the Kings had threatened to run away with the tie, scoring three successive 5-1's in the middle stage of the match. John Jackson top-scored for the Gunners, with Chris Turner top of the Kings chart with three wins, dropping his only point to the former skipper in Heat 13.

Heat 01	Jackson/**Drury**/**Emery**/Hughes	70.8	3 - 3	03 - 03
Heat 02	**Brown**/Smitherman/Meredith/**Robertson**	72.8	3 - 3	06 - 06
Heat 03	**Wasley**/Goad/**Collins**/Allott	72.0	**4 - 2**	10 - 08

Heat 04	**Turner**/Goad/**Brown**/Smitherman	72.0	**4 - 2**	14 - 10
Heat 05	Jackson/**Wasley**/**Collins**/Hughes	70.8	3 - 3	17 - 13
Heat 06	**Drury**/Jackson/Meredith/**Emery**	72.0	3 - 3	20 - 16
Heat 07	**Turner**/**Brown**/Allott/Goad	72.0	**5 - 1**	25 - 17
Heat 08	**Brown**/**Emery**/Smitherman/Jackson (R)	73.6	**5 - 1**	30 - 18
Heat 09	**Collins**/**Wasley**/Goad/Meredith	71.6	**5 - 1**	35 - 19
Heat 10	Allott/**Emery**/**Drury**/Goad	71.8	3 - 3	38 - 22
Heat 11	**Turner**/Jackson/Hughes/**Robertson**	71.6	3 - 3	41 - 25
Heat 12	Allott/**Drury**/Goad/**Wasley**	72.0	2 - 4	43 - 29
Heat 13	Jackson/**Turner**/Allott/**Collins**	71.6	2 - 4	45 - 33

CREWE - Chris Turner 11, Max Brown 9 (+1), Graham Drury 8 (+1), Nigel Wasley 7 (+1), Chris Emery 5 (+2), Les Collins 5 (+1), Ian Robertson 0.
ELLESMERE PORT - John Jackson 13, Nicky Allott 8, Colin Goad 6, Gerald Smitherman 3, Duncan Meredith 2 (+2), Wayne Hughes 1 (+1), *Steve Taylor (R/R).*

During the second-half, there were two races between former Kings Dave Parry, Barry Meeks and Dai Evans. *"Race of the Century" (Pension holders only)* and the *"Old Timers' Second Chance" (Breath Permitting)* were how they were listed in the programme, with both won by Meeks in times of 76.0 and 75.6. There was also a special ladies race with Anne Collins (sister of Les and Peter) beating local girl Susan Hind. The Rider of the Night Final was won by Chris Turner, who beat Graham Drury, John Jackson and Nicky Allott. The significance of this race was the fact that, if Crewe were to fold before next season, then this would be the final race held at Earle Street. In Dave Parry's programme notes, his final message had an air of resignation about the future of Crewe speedway: *'Well now is the time I must say goodbye. What the future holds I don't know. I only hope speedway will remain at the track I have known so well. The memory of the riders and times we have had at Earle Street will remain forever. My last thank you is for the team. Thanks lads for the season, it has been a pleasure to work with you. Until we meet again, take care and enjoy your speedway.'* On the same night Birmingham retained their league crown after a hard fought home victory over Boston.

Meeting 49 - Tuesday, October 14, 1975 - Whitbread Cheshire Trophy, Second Leg
Ellesmere Port Stadium, Thornton Road, Ellesmere Port
Track Length - 423 yards.

ELLESMERE PORT GUNNERS.....53 CREWE KINGS.....24

(Ellesmere Port won on aggregate 86 - 69)

Crewe's last chance of silverware evaporated long before the end of the second leg of the Cheshire Trophy. The match was not without incident, with numerous falls, exclusions and retirements, causing it to overrun. The Kings were thirty-one points adrift after nine heats, but a John Jackson exclusion in Heat 10 and a Colin Goad flat tyre in the next, allowed the visitors to restore some pride with a brace of 4-2 wins.

Heat 01	Jackson/Hughes/**Drury**/**Emery** (R)	78.2	5 - 1	05 - 01
Heat 02	Smitherman/Meredith/**Brown** (X)/**Robertson** (X)	78.8	5 - 0	10 - 01
Heat 03	Allott/Goad/**Wasley**/**Collins**	79.4	5 - 1	15 - 02
Heat 04	Hughes/Meredith/**Robertson**/**Turner**	79.2	5 - 1	20 - 03
Heat 05	Allott/**Drury**/Goad/**Emery** (R)	79.0	4 - 2	24 - 05
Heat 06	Jackson/Hughes/**Turner**/**Brown**	78.4	5 - 1	29 - 06
Heat 07	Allott/Meredith/**Collins**/**Wasley**	79.8	5 - 1	34 - 07
Heat 08	Hughes/**Emery**/**Robertson**/Smitherman	79.4	3 - 3	37 - 10
Heat 09	Allott/Goad/**Turner**/**Brown**	78.8	5 - 1	42 - 11
Heat 10	**Wasley**/Meredith/**Collins**/Jackson (X)	79.0	**2 - 4**	44 - 15
Heat 11	**Drury**/Smitherman/**Emery**/Goad (R)	80.0	**2 - 4**	46 - 19
Heat 12	Jackson/**Collins**/Allott/**Turner**	78.4	4 - 2	50 - 21
Heat 13	**Drury**/Jackson/Smitherman/**Wasley**	79.4	3 - 3	53 - 24

ELLESMERE PORT - Nicky Allott 13, John Jackson 11, Wayne Hughes 10 (+2), Duncan Meredith 8 (+3), Gerald Smitherman 6 (+1), Colin Goad 5 (+2), *Steve Taylor (R/R).*
CREWE - Graham Drury 9, Les Collins 4, Nigel Wasley 4, Chris Emery 3, Ian Robertson 2 (+1), Chris Turner 2, Max Brown 0.

After the match, Dave Parry was critical of the Ellesmere Port track and complained about the lack of shale, which made the circuit "like riding on ice." On October 17, Workington beat Eastbourne 47-31 at Derwent Park, in the first leg of the K.O. Cup Final. Two days later, a young Crewe quartet lost heavily to a junior Stars side at Saddlebow Road, during the second half of the Anglian Cup first leg against Ipswich.

KING'S LYNN.....24 CREWE.....6

Heat 01	Bales/**Robertson**/Spiers/**Roberts**	72.4	4 - 2	04 - 02
Heat 02	Davey/Smith/**Owen**/**Fryer**	72.6	5 - 1	09 - 03
Heat 03	Sims/Spiers/**Roberts**/**Robertson** (F)	72.6	5 - 1	14 - 04
Heat 04	Bales/Davey/**Owen**/**Fryer** (F)	72.0	5 - 1	19 - 05
Heat 05	Sims/Smith/**Robertson**/**Owen** (F)	70.8	5 - 1	24 - 06

KING'S LYNN - Andrew Bales 6, Andy Sims 6, Richard Davey 5, Pete Smith 4, Billy Spiers 3.
CREWE - Ian Robertson 3, Terry Owen 2, Stuart Roberts 1, Jim Fryer 0.

Meeting 50 - Sunday, October 19, 1975 - New National League
Boston Sports Stadium, New Hammond Beck Road, Boston
Track Length - 380 yards.

BOSTON BARRACUDAS.....49 CREWE KINGS.....29

Hot teenage prospect Michael Lee was at his brilliant best with four easy victories. Graham Drury won on three occasions, but only Chris Turner with eight, and Les Collins with five, offered any support. Midland grass-tracker Terry Owen made his Kings debut after earlier appearing for the junior team at King's Lynn. Nigel Wasley blew his engine approaching the tapes for his first ride and withdrew from the meeting.

Heat 01	Lee/**Drury**/Glover/**Emery**	67.7	4 - 2	04 - 02
Heat 02	Hollingworth/Cooper/**Owen**/**Brown**	69.8	5 - 1	09 - 03
Heat 03	Burton/Forrester/**Brown**/**Collins**	70.6	5 - 1	14 - 04
Heat 04	**Turner**/Gagen/Hollingworth/**Owen** (R)	69.6	3 - 3	17 - 07
Heat 05	**Drury**/Forrester/Burton/**Brown**	69.2	3 - 3	20 - 10
Heat 06	Lee/Glover/**Turner**/**Collins**	67.0	5 - 1	25 - 11
Heat 07	**Drury**/**Collins**/Hollingworth/Gagen	67.8	**1 - 5**	26 - 16
Heat 08	Glover/**Turner**/**Emery**/Cooper	69.0	3 - 3	29 - 19
Heat 09	Burton/Forrester/**Owen**/**Turner** (X)	68.8	5 - 1	34 - 20
Heat 10	Lee/**Collins**/Glover/**Emery**	66.2	4 - 2	38 - 22
Heat 11	**Drury**/Gagen/Cooper/**Owen**	68.0	3 - 3	41 - 25
Heat 12	Lee/**Turner**/**Collins**/Burton	66.8	3 - 3	44 - 28
Heat 13	Forrester/Gagen/**Drury**/**Owen**	68.2	5 - 1	49 - 29

BOSTON - Michael Lee 12, Bruce Forrester 9 (+2), Billy Burton 7 (+1), Les Glover 7 (+1), David Gagen 6 (+1), Rob Hollingworth 5 (+1), Ron Cooper 3 (+2).
CREWE - Graham Drury 12, Chris Turner 8, Les Collins 5 (+2), Terry Owen 2, Chris Emery 1 (+1), Max Brown 1, Nigel Wasley 0.

On the same day, Eastbourne overturned their first leg deficit, to claim the K.O. Cup, with a 52-25 victory and an 83-72 win on aggregate.

If season analysis was based purely on final league position, then Crewe's 1975 campaign can only be viewed as one of disappointment. However, when circumstances surrounding their fortunes are properly scrutinised, then Dave Parry and his team produced a minor miracle in performing as well as they did. With just a month to go before the start of the season, Crewe didn't even have a team to represent them. Halfway through the campaign, and with a young squad showing signs of some potential, a series of injuries and bad fortune left them decimated, leaving Parry with little option but to fill the side with loanees and largely inexperienced juniors. A lowly league position therefore resulted in a continuing fall in attendances. Ever since Stoke's return, crowd figures had plummeted in South Cheshire, and in 1975 these fell further as the Potters started with a long unbeaten run ensuring the floating local support went to Loomer Road instead of Earle Street. The prospects of the Kings starting in 1976 therefore were bleak indeed.

Just a month after the end of the season, and with nearly all the doom and gloom merchants predicting the end of racing at Earle Street, Norfolk Speedways - the same organisation who now controlled events at King's Lynn - announced an unexpected takeover. Violet Littlechild was delighted with the news and announced: *"I'm glad we shall be continuing. We could never neglect King's Lynn, but the family have an equally soft spot for Crewe. Both tracks can benefit. King's Lynn have a further outlet for fostering junior talent and Crewe gain the benefit of the administration which I like to feel has made King's Lynn one of the foremost circuits in British speedway."* Alan Littlechild was also pleased with the announcement. *"The public in Crewe have given an indication of the sort of support they are ready to give if we put on a good show. I don't see any reason why we should not bring back the crowds and give the town a team and a level of entertainment to match the best."* The takeover however, would mean little or no future for Dave Parry. The Supporters Club met on December 8 at the Kings Arms in Earle Street to discuss fund raising ideas, which included a weekly lottery draw and race sponsorship for next season. As Christmas approached, Graham Drury reported that his Saturday afternoon training schools were progressing well, with an average of eighteen youngsters turning up every week. All now looked promising for the future of speedway in Crewe.

- 1975 Season Summary -

Date	Opponents/Meeting	Res	Score	Wins to Crewe Race	Wins to Crewe Heat
Mon, March 31	**Crayford (NNL)**	L	37 - 41	6	3
Thu, April 3	Stoke (NNL)	L	24 - 54	3	0
Mon, April 7	**Coatbridge (NNL)**	W	51 - 26	9	8
Mon, April 14	**Workington (NNL)**	W	42 - 36	6	3
Mon, April 21	Newcastle (NNL)	L	28 - 50	1	1
Wed, April 23	**Newcastle (NNL)**	L	38 - 39	5	5
Mon, April 28	**Newport (IL KOC R1)**	L	20 - 58	1	0
Mon, May 5	**Bradford (KOC R1)**	L	38 - 40	7	6
Mon, May 12	**Ellesmere Port (NNL)**	W	47 - 31	7	6
Wed, May 14	Bradford (KOC R1)	L	30 - 48	4	1
Mon, May 19	**Paisley (NNL)**	W	42 - 36	8	5
Sun, May 25	Mildenhall (NNL)	W	41 - 36	6	5
Mon, May 26	**Stars of the League (Ch)**	W	39 - 38	6	3
Tue, May 27	Ellesmere Port (NNL)	L	33 - 44	6	5
Thu, May 29	Teesside (NNL)	L	26 - 52	2	0
Sun, June 1	Rye House (NNL)	L	25 - 53	3	1
Mon, June 2	**Mildenhall (NNL)**	W	47 - 31	6	6
Mon, June 9	**Peterborough (NNL)**	W	46 - 32	8	5
Tue, June 10	Weymouth (NNL)	L	35 - 43	4	3
Mon, June 16	**Canterbury (NNL)**	W	50 - 28	12	9
Wed, June 18	Bradford (NNL)	L	30 - 48	3	2
Sat, June 21	Paisley (NNL)	L	32 - 46	4	2
Mon, June 23	**Bradford (NNL)**	W	54 - 24	13	11
Tue, June 24	Crayford (NNL)	L	30 - 48	2	2
Mon, June 30	Scunthorpe (NNL)	L	37 - 41	6	4
Wed, July 2	**Birmingham (Ch)**	W	48 - 30	9	8
Sat, July 5	Berwick (NNL)	L	35 - 43	5	3
Mon, July 7	**Stoke (NNL)**	L	37 - 41	6	3
Mon, July 14	**Bel/Cra/Kin (IL 4TT)**	W	Crewe 39	9	-
Mon, July 21	**Boston (NNL)**	D	39 - 39	5	3
Fri, July 25	Workington (NNL)	L	34 - 44	4	3
Mon, July 28	**Geoff Curtis Mem (Ind)**	Alan Molyneux		-	-
Mon, August 4	**Scunthorpe (NNL)**	L	36 - 40	7	3
Sat, August 9	Canterbury (NNL)	L	36 - 42	6	4
Sun, August 10	Eastbourne (NNL)	L	23 - 55	0	0
Mon, August 11	**Eastbourne (NNL)**	L	31 - 46	3	2
Mon, August 18	**Teesside (NNL)**	W	41 - 37	8	5

Mon, August 25	**Birmingham (NNL)**	L	32 - 46	6	2
Tue, August 26	Birmingham (NNL)	L	23 - 55	3	2
Fri, August 29	**Weymouth (NNL)**	W	59 - 19	13	11
Fri, September 5	**Littlechild Trophy (Ind)**	Paul Gachet		-	-
Mon, September 15	**Rye House (NNL)**	W	58 - 20	13	10
Mon, September 22	**Workington (Ch)**	W	42 - 35	6	6
Thu, September 25	Stoke (Ch)	L	29 - 49	2	1
Fri, September 26	Coatbridge (NNL)	L	37 - 41	5	3
Mon, September 29	**Stoke (Ch)**	L	36 - 41	3	2
Mon, October 6	**Berwick (NNL)**	W	50 - 28	12	8
Mon, October 13	**Ellesmere Port (Ch)**	W	45 - 33	8	5
Tue, October 14	Ellesmere Port (Ch)	L	24 - 53	3	2
Sun, October 19	Boston (NNL)	L	29 - 49	4	1

- New National League Final Table -

		Home					Away					
	M	W	D	L	F	A	W	D	L	F	A	Pts
1. Birmingham	38	19	0	0	963	515	10	1	8	738	737	59
2. Newcastle	38	18	0	1	915	565	9	0	10	720	758	54
3. Stoke	38	18	0	1	936	545	8	0	11	714½	764½	52
4. Eastbourne	38	18	0	1	982	497	7	0	12	694	783	50
5. Boston	38	17	0	2	932	549	7	2	10	699	776	50
6. Workington	38	17	1	1	881½	598½	6	1	12	682	798	48
7. Berwick	38	18	1	0	890	586	3	2	14	596	886	45
8. Crayford	38	17	0	2	930	546	3	2	14	619	860	42
9. Ellesmere Port	38	17	1	1	868	612	2	0	17	587	889	39
10. Canterbury	38	17	0	2	917	560	2	0	17	616	862	38
11. Bradford	38	16	2	1	883	597	1	0	18	523	955	36
12. Coatbridge	38	15	0	4	861	615	2	1	16	594	883	35
13. Scunthorpe	38	14	0	5	801	680	3	0	16	572½	904½	34
14. Rye House	38	13	1	5	813	659	0	1	18	574	904	28
15. Paisley	38	14	0	5	809	666	0	0	19	504	973	28
16. Crewe	**37**	**12**	**1**	**6**	**837**	**640**	**1**	**0**	**17**	**558**	**844**	**27**
17. Teesside	38	13	0	6	841	637	0	0	19	590	889	26
18. Peterborough	37	12	0	6	735	665	1	0	18	540	940	26
19. Mildenhall	38	11	1	7	758½	718½	0	0	19	515	963	23
20. Weymouth	38	8	2	9	756	723	0	0	19	538	940	18

(The Peterborough v Crewe match was not raced. Crewe refused to ride at the original staging due to Peterborough's planned use of rider replacement for Russell Osborne.)

- Crewe Rider Averages -

(League and Knock Out Cup only)

	M	R	W	Pts	BP	Tot	F	P	CMA
Graham Drury	38	166	63	345	16	361	2	2	8.699
Chris Turner	28	122	47	222	26	248	1	2	8.131
Nigel Wasley	30	126	48	236	8	244	1	2	7.746
Chris Emery	10	43	5	55	13	68	0	1	6.326
Stuart Cope	28	94	21	125	12	137	1	1	5.830
Les Collins	36	131	12	139	33	172	0	1	5.252
Max Brown	32	117	9	116	30	146	0	1	4.991
Cliff Anderson	24	80	12	87	9	96	0	0	4.800
Also rode									
Ricky Day	9	35	6	46	7	53	0	2	6.057
Mick Mellor	2	6	0	5	3	8	0	0	5.333
Geoff Ambrose	7	25	2	27	4	31	0	0	4.960
Ray Hassall	2	5	1	4	1	5	0	0	4.000
Graham Crook	5	12	0	7	3	10	0	0	3.333

Ian Robertson	7	22	0	16	2	18	0	0	3.273
Mick Fielding	3	7	1	4	0	4	0	0	2.286
Terry Owen	1	5	0	2	0	2	0	0	1.600
Stuart Roberts	3	6	0	2	0	2	0	0	1.333
Andy Reid	1	1	0	0	0	0	0	0	0.000
Substitutes									
John McNeil	1	3	1	7	1	8	0	0	10.666
Jaffa Purkiss	1	5	2	9	1	10	0	0	8.000
Eddie Argall	1	5	1	7	1	8	0	0	6.400
Bryan Townsend	1	2	0	2	0	2	0	0	4.000
Dave Hughes	1	2	0	0	0	0	0	0	0.000

- League Heat Scores -

	Home	Away	Total
5 - 0 heat win to Crewe	1	0	1
5 - 1 heat win to Crewe	63	15	78
4 - 2 heat win to Crewe	44	25	69
3 - 2 heat win to Crewe	0	2	2
3 - 3 drawn heat	88	66	154
2 - 3 heat win to Opponents	2	0	2
2 - 4 heat win to Opponents	26	53	79
1 - 5 heat win to Opponents	21	73	94
0 - 5 heat win to Opponents	2	0	2

- Individual/Pairs Honours -

Michael Nesbitt Memorial Trophy (Ellesmere Port)
1. Arthur Browning 2. Graham Drury 3. Lou Sansom.

Geoff Curtis Memorial Trophy (Crewe)
1. Alan Molyneux 2. Stuart Cope 3. John Jackson.

Scotianapolis (Coatbridge)
1. Jimmy Gallacher 2. Brian Collins 3. Grahame Dawson/Graham Drury.

Scottish Open Championship (Coatbridge)
1. Brian Collins 2. Mitch Shirra 3. Graham Drury.

(ABOVE) Graham Drury, who topped the Crewe averages.

(ABOVE) The Kings mid-season. (Left to right standing) Graham Crook, Max Brown, Cliff Anderson, Nigel Wasley, Graham Drury, Chris Turner and Ricky Day. (Kneeling) Stuart Cope and Les Collins. (BELOW) Max Brown, Les Collins and Chris Emery, working on a machine.

(ABOVE) Nigel Wasley receives a stretcher ride as Cliff Anderson looks on.

(ABOVE) First bend action as Nigel Wasley and Chris Turner lead the Bradford pairing of Colin Meredith and Barry Weaver (partially hidden).

(ABOVE) Alan Pedley brings the riders under starter's orders. (BELOW) Heat 1 of the Geoff Curtis Memorial Trophy, featuring from the inside - Nigel Wasley, Mitch Shirra, Stuart Cope and Dave Gifford.

(ABOVE) Nigel Wasley (far right) entertains Cliff Anderson, Graham Drury, Les Collins, Graham Crook and Stuart Cope in the Crewe pits. (BELOW LEFT) Bradford loanee Mick Fielding and (BELOW RIGHT) Australian Ricky Day.

On February 5, with Crewe supporters looking forward to the start of the new season, Violet Littlechild dropped the bombshell that the Kings would not be running after all in 1976, unless a different promotion came in with a last minute reprieve. Originally Norfolk Speedways were to install directors from King's Lynn to run affairs, but the deal fell through when several problems arose. The B.S.P.A. had set a February 4 deadline for Littlechild to put forward a satisfactory agreement, but when the date passed, the decision was made to freeze the licence for a twelve month period. Cyril Crane, co-director at King's Lynn explained the reasons why Norfolk Speedways had pulled out of the deal. *"We began to learn about the many problems attached to keeping the sport going at Crewe. What with the economic situation, this is not the time to undertake the sort of stadium improvements which we feel necessary, and there was another blow when several thousand pounds worth of damage was caused by a recent storm. Reluctantly it was decided that we would not after all be able to run Crewe as we had hoped."* Martin Rogers, originally earmarked for the general manager's job, was also disappointed with the news: *"Obviously it is a bitter blow to the fans, especially those who have supported Crewe through thick and thin. In different circumstances, I believe that there is still good potential at Crewe. The interest and build up of support even over the last few weeks underlines that."* Dave Parry was another to have his say over the closure. *"I got together a young team which could have done really well this season. Now that team has been disbanded, and what narks me is that the promoters have made a profit out of my riders I signed out of my own pocket. And they haven't even had the courtesy to consult me......Mrs Littlechild made an unsuccessful attempt to transfer the licence from Crewe a year ago and it is my guess that ultimately, the Crewe licence will be transferred to a new venture at Norwich under the Norfolk Speedways banner."*

After seven seasons of racing, the Crewe speedway story was all but over.

Of the 1975 team, Graham Drury signed for Hull and Nigel Wasley went to Cradley. Cliff Anderson ended up at Swindon, with Chris Turner and Les Collins returning to Belle Vue and loaned out to Ellesmere Port and Stoke respectively, to gain further experience. Stuart Cope and Chris Emery were snapped up by Boston and Max Brown went to Coatbridge. Geoff Ambrose remained in retirement, concentrating on running his "Speedway Motorcycles" business in Earle Street. As for boss Dave Parry, he returned to his native Wolverhampton as team manager. Almost as soon as the closure was announced, Charlie Scarbrough held talks with the British Rail landlords in the hope that speedway could continue in the form of training schools. Meanwhile, Mick Smith of Midlands based Trackstar Promotions Ltd. also opened negotiations to hold stock car racing at Earle Street, which culminated in the first meeting on Monday, May 31. In June, Scarbrough put in an application for an open licence, and at the start of July it was announced that speedway was to return with a series of challenge matches against other training school teams, plus an individual meeting sponsored by Frodsham businessman and motor sports enthusiast Jim Rowlinson. The training school graduates were soon kitted out in new blue and yellow body colours and were christened the Crewe Locos. At the start of October, the Crewe Speedway Supporters Club handed in a petition to the local council containing 1,195 signatures for the return of league speedway to the town. A year had now passed since the demise of the Kings, but already the track had been battered by the stock cars, and the stadium had suffered from a spate of vandalism. A return to league speedway therefore, would only ever be achieved by a massive cash injection. Training school activities continued throughout 1977, but after that, the Crewe speedway story ended for good. Stock cars continued until December 1993, when the land was sold and the stadium demolished to make way for the Grand Junction Retail Park.

Sadly, some of the riders who proudly donned the Kings race-jacket, are no longer with us, namely Geoff Curtis, who as already mentioned, tragically lost his life following an accident at the Sydney Showground in 1973, and two others were to die as a result of unfortunate accidents. On April 29, 1978, the sport lost one of its most colourful characters when Jack Millen was killed on the A1 at Grantshouse, after colliding with an articulated lorry, on a return journey from Edinburgh to Berwick. Then in the following year, Nigel Wasley died on September 14 from a blood clot, after breaking a leg in a fall whilst riding for Nottingham Outlaws against Ellesmere

Port at Long Eaton Stadium on August 29. As the years pass, more have left us with only memories of past achievements, including Ian Robertson, Peter Thompson and more recently Charlie Scarbrough, who passed away in the Minshull Court Nursing Home in Crewe, following a long illness on August 2, 2008.

On a final note, it has now been over thirty years since Crewe reverberated to the sounds of speedway. Those halcyon days, we doubt, will ever return. Let those who attended and took part in the Crewe speedway story never forget the efforts and sacrifices of the few who entertained us for seven seasons – **When They Were KINGS**.

(ABOVE) Banger racing on the old speedway circuit during the rolling lap.
(BELOW) The aftermath of a race, with the old pits on the far right.

Training School and Junior Results

-Training School and Junior Results-

(Every effort has been made to ensure that all details listed below are correct, but due to lack of authenticated information, not all facts and dates can be guaranteed as completely accurate.)

Sunday, December 22, 1974 - Training Track League
Mildenhall Stadium, West Row, Mildenhall
Track Length - 307 yards.

MILDENHALL FEN TIGERS.....56 CREWE TRAINEES.....18

Heat	Riders	Time	Score	Total
Heat 01	Gilbert/Jolly/**Fryer**/**Mellor**	68.0	5 - 1	05 - 01
Heat 02	Kerry/Mills/**Race**/**Oats**	69.1	5 - 1	10 - 02
Heat 03	Clipstone/Taylor/**Share**/**Lawley**	68.3	5 - 1	15 - 03
Heat 04	Lee/Kerry/**Race** (F)/**Brett** (X)	72.0	5 - 0	20 - 03
Heat 05	Clipstone/**Mellor**/Taylor (X)/**Fryer** (X)	65.8	3 - 2	23 - 05
Heat 06	Jolly/**Brett**/Gilbert/**Oats**	67.5	4 - 2	27 - 07
Heat 07	Lee/Kerry/**Lawley**/**Share** (F)	67.0	5 - 1	32 - 08
Heat 08	Jolly/Mills/**Fryer**/**Race**	66.7	5 - 1	37 - 09
Heat 09	Taylor/**Oats**/**Robertson** (X)/Clipstone (X)	69.2	3 - 2	40 - 11
Heat 10	Jolly/**Share**/**Lawley**/Gilbert (F)	67.2	3 - 3	43 - 14
Heat 11	Mills/**Mellor**/**Fryer** (F)/Lee (R)	71.1	3 - 2	46 - 16
Heat 12	Clipstone/Gilbert/**Brett**/**Share**	67.1	5 - 1	51 - 17
Heat 13	Taylor/Lee/**Mellor**/**Lawley**	69.7	5 - 1	56 - 18

MILDENHALL - Kevin Jolly 11, Paul Clipstone 9, Michael Lee 8, Steve Taylor 8, Graham Kerry 7, Fred Mills 7, Paul Gilbert 6.
CREWE - Mick Mellor 5, Jim Brett 3, Paul Share 3, Jim Fryer 2, K. Lawley 2, J. Oats 2, Les Race 1, Ian Robertson 0.

Saturday, January 18, 1975 - Training Track League
L.M.R. Sports Ground, Earle Street, Crewe
Track Length - 436 yards.

CREWE TRAINEES.....37 MILDENHALL FEN TIGERS.....39

Heat	Riders	Time	Score	Total
Heat 01	Jolly/**Fryer**/Gilbert/**Mellor** (F)	00.0	2 - 4	02 - 04
Heat 02	**Robertson**/Kerry/**Race**/Mills (F)	00.0	**4 - 2**	06 - 06
Heat 03	**Share**/**Rogers**/Taylor (F)/Clipstone (X)	00.0	**5 - 0**	11 - 06
Heat 04	Lee/Mills/**Brett**/**Robertson**	00.0	1 - 5	12 - 11
Heat 05	Gilbert/**Rogers**/Jolly/**Share** (F)	00.0	2 - 4	14 - 15
Heat 06	Lee/**Mellor**/Kerry/**Fryer**	00.0	2 - 4	16 - 19
Heat 07	**Brett**/Kerry/**Robertson**/Taylor (F)	00.0	**4 - 2**	20 - 21
Heat 08	**Fryer**/Jolly/**Race**/Mills	00.0	**4 - 2**	24 - 23
Heat 09	Lee/**Rogers**/Kerry/**Share**	00.0	2 - 4	26 - 27
Heat 10	Clipstone/**Fryer**/**Brett** (F)/Taylor (X)	00.0	2 - 3	28 - 30
Heat 11	Gilbert/Jolly/**Brett**/**Race**	00.0	1 - 5	29 - 35
Heat 12	Lee/**Mellor**/**Rogers**/Taylor	00.0	3 - 3	32 - 38
Heat 13	**Brett**/**Share**/Clipstone/Gilbert (R)	00.0	**5 - 1**	37 - 39

CREWE - Jim Brett 8, Jim Fryer 7, Geoff Rogers 7, Paul Share 5, Mick Mellor 4, Ian Robertson 4, Les Race 2.
MILDENHALL - Michael Lee 12, Kevin Jolly 8, Paul Gilbert 7, Graham Kerry 6, Paul Clipstone 4, Fred Mills 2, Steve Taylor 0.

Sunday, January 25, 1976 - Training School Challenge - Mildenhall
Mildenhall Fen Tigers v Crewe Trainees
(Cancelled, due to the inactivity of the Crewe training school.)

Saturday, July 17, 1976 - Motorsport Cavalcade
Crewe Stadium, Earle Street, Crewe
Track Length - 436 yards.

Training School Match

BLUES.....43 REDS.....35

Individual Mini-Tournament

WINNER.....BRIAN BAGSHAW

(No other details available.)

Sunday, July 25, 1976 - Training School Challenge
Iwade Training Track, Old Ferry Road, Iwade
Track Length - 315 yards.

IWADE COLTS.....53 CREWE LOCOS.....24

IWADE - Steve Davey 12, Dave Ross 12, Kevin Garcia 8, Duane Kent 8, Dave Hughes 6, Fred Stubberfield 4, Bob Pittock 3.
CREWE - Dougie Poole 6, Tim Cash 5, Keith Williamson 5, Billy Fieldhouse 4, Brian Adshead 2, Ray Hassall 2.
(No other details available.)

Saturday, July 31, 1976 - Training School Challenge
Crewe Stadium, Earle Street, Crewe
Track Length - 436 yards.

CREWE LOCOS.....41 IWADE COLTS.....37

Heat	Riders	Time	Heat score	Score
Heat 01	**Adshead**/Ross/**Cash**/Pittock (F)	78.2	**4 - 2**	04 - 02
Heat 02	Kent/**K.Eastwood**/**Williamson**/Hughes	79.0	3 - 3	07 - 05
Heat 03	Davey/**P.Eastwood**/Stubberfield/**Fieldhouse**	78.1	2 - 4	09 - 09
Heat 04	Ross/**Poole**/**Williamson**/Kent	**78.0** (TR)	3 - 3	12 - 12
Heat 05	**P.Eastwood**/Ross/Pittock/**Fieldhouse**	79.0	3 - 3	15 - 15
Heat 06	**Adshead**/Davey/**Cash**/Kent (R)	79.1	**4 - 2**	19 - 17
Heat 07	Davey/**Williamson**/**Poole**/Stubberfield	79.5	3 - 3	22 - 20
Heat 08	**K.Eastwood**/Pittock/**Cash**/Kent (R)	80.0	**4 - 2**	26 - 22
Heat 09	**P.Eastwood**/Stubberfield/**K.Eastwood**/Kent	81.0	**4 - 2**	30 - 24
Heat 10	Ross/**Adshead**/Davey/**Cash**	79.5	2 - 4	32 - 28
Heat 11	Ross/**K.Eastwood**/**Poole**/Pittock (F)	79.0	3 - 3	35 - 31
Heat 12	Davey/**Adshead**/**Fieldhouse**/Pittock	79.0	3 - 3	38 - 34
Heat 13	Ross/**P.Eastwood**/**Poole**/Stubberfield	77.6	3 - 3	41 - 37

CREWE - Brian Adshead 10, Paul Eastwood 10, Keith Eastwood 8, Dougie Poole 5, Keith Williamson 4, Tim Cash 3, Billy Fieldhouse 1.
IWADE - Dave Ross 16, Steve Davey 12, Duane Kent 3, Bob Pittock 3, Fred Stubberfield 3, Dave Hughes 0, *Kevin Garcia (R/R)*.

Saturday, August 14, 1976 - Individual Trophy
Crewe Stadium, Earle Street, Crewe
Track Length - 436 yards.

WINNER.....PAUL EASTWOOD

Heat	Riders	Time
Heat 01	Cook/Slade/Edgerton/Westwell	00.0
Heat 02	Fieldhouse/Haysall/Adshead (R)/Williamson (F)	00.0
Heat 03	P.Eastwood/Woodcock/Williams/Scott	00.0
Heat 04	Messer/K.Eastwood/Flavell/Poole (R)	00.0
Heat 05	Fieldhouse/Poole/Scott/Cook (R)	00.0
Heat 06	P.Eastwood/Edgerton/Messer/Kelly (R)	00.0
Heat 07	Messer/Slade/Haysall/Williams (R)	00.0
Heat 08	Flavell/Woodcock/Williamson/Westwell	00.0
Heat 09	Flavell/Williams/Kelly/Cook (R)	00.0
Heat 10	K.Eastwood/Fieldhouse/Woodcock/Edgerton (F)	00.0
Heat 11	Scott/Slade/Williamson/Kelly	00.0
Heat 12	P.Eastwood/Poole/Haysall/Westwell	00.0
Heat 13	K.Eastwood/Woodcock/Haysall/Cook (X)	00.0
Heat 14	Poole/Edgerton/Williamson/Williams (F)	00.0
Heat 15	P.Eastwood/Flavell/Fieldhouse/Slade	00.0
Heat 16	Adshead/Messer/Westwell/Kelly	00.0
Heat 17	P.Eastwood/Williamson/Messer/Cook (R)	00.0
Heat 18	Scott/Flavell/Haysall/Edgerton	00.0
Heat 19	Poole/Woodcock/Slade/Kelly	00.0
Heat 20	K.Eastwood/Westwell/Fieldhouse/Kelly	00.0
R/O for 2nd	K.Eastwood/Flavell	00.0

Paul Eastwood 15, Keith Eastwood 11, Jim Flavell 11, Dougie Poole 10, Billy Fieldhouse 10, Shaun Messer 10, Geoff Woodcock 9, Tony Slade 7, Mel Scott 7, Paul Haysall 6, Colin Edgerton 5, Keith Williamson 5, Ian Westwell 3, Rod Williams 3, Brian Adshead 3, Steve Cook 3. Meeting Reserve: M. Kelly 1.

Saturday, September 25, 1976 - Best Pairs Trophy
Crewe Stadium, Earle Street, Crewe
Track Length - 436 yards.

WINNERS.....BRIAN BAGSHAW & DOUGIE POOLE

Heat	Result	Time
Heat 01	P.Eastwood/Westwell/Grey/Edgerton	00.0
Heat 02	Bagshaw/Poole/K.Eastwood/Messer	00.0
Heat 03	Flavell/Fieldhouse/Cook (R)/Cash (X)	00.0
Heat 04	P.Eastwood/Messer/K.Eastwood/Edgerton (F)	00.0
Heat 05	Bagshaw/Poole/Cash/Cook (R)	00.0
Heat 06	Fieldhouse/Flavell/Westwell/Grey	00.0
Heat 07	P.Eastwood/Poole/Bagshaw (F)/Edgerton (X)	00.0
Heat 08	Cook/Cash/Grey/Westwell	00.0
Heat 09	Messer/K.Eastwood/Flavell/Fieldhouse (R)	00.0
Heat 10	Bagshaw/Poole/Murray/Grey	00.0
Heat 11	P.Eastwood/Flavell/Edgerton (F)/Fieldhouse (X)	00.0
Heat 12	Messer/K.Eastwood/Cash/Cook (F)	00.0
Heat 13	Bagshaw/Poole/Flavell/Fieldhouse (R)	00.0
Heat 14	Messer/K.Eastwood/Grey/Westwell	00.0
Heat 15	P.Eastwood/Cash/Murray/Cook	00.0

Brian Bagshaw (12) & Dougie Poole (10) 22, Shaun Messer (11) & Keith Eastwood (8) 19, Paul Eastwood (15) & Colin Edgerton (0) 15, Billy Fieldhouse (5) & Jim Flavell (9) 14, Steve Cook (3) & Tim Cash (6) 9, Ian Westwell (3) & Colin Grey (3) 6. Meeting Reserve: Tony Murray 2.

Friday, October 15, 1976 - Anglo-Scots Junior Three Team Tournament
Albion Rovers Stadium, Cliftonhill Park, Main Street, Coatbridge
Track Length - 380 yards.

COATBRIDGE TIGER CUBS.....51 SASSENACHS.....32 CREWE LOCOS.....23

Heat	Result	Time	Co	S	Cr
Heat 01	Jarvie/Hall/Poole/Adshead	79.6	5	/	1
Heat 02	Cash/Messer/K.Eastwood/Williamson (F)	82.6	/	3	3
Heat 03	McLean/Cook/Dow/Fieldhouse	60.8	4	2	/
Heat 04	Allan/McGuiness/P.Eastwood/Bagshaw (R)	62.2	5	/	1
Heat 05	Priest/Adshead/Slade/Poole (X)	60.0	/	4	2
Heat 06	Hall/Jarvie/Fieldhouse/Cook	57.4	5	1	/
Heat 07	K.Eastwood/Messer/Allan/McGuiness	58.4	1	/	5
Heat 08	Priest/Bagshaw/Flavell/Slade	60.2	/	3	3
Heat 09	Dow/Cash/McLean/Williamson	61.6	4	2	/
Heat 10	Hall/Jarvie/Bagshaw (F)/Flavell (X)	65.2	5	/	0
Heat 11	Cook/Poole/Fieldhouse/Adshead	61.8	/	4	2
Heat 12	Allan/McGuiness/Slade/Priest	61.2	5	1	/
Heat 13	McLean/Dow/K.Eastwood (F)/Messer (R)	72.8	5	/	0
Heat 14	Cash/Bagshaw/Williamson/Flavell (F)	65.2	/	4	2
Heat 15	Hall/Priest/Slade/Jarvis (R)	61.0	3	3	/
Heat 16	Dow/McLean/Adshead/Poole (F)	67.2	5	/	1
Heat 17	Messer/Cook/Fieldhouse/K.Eastwood (X)	63.4	/	3	3
Heat 18	Allan/Williamson/McGuiness/Cash	61.8	4	2	/

(Races were run over three laps after two heats due to heavy rain.)

COATBRIDGE - Frankie Hall 11, Norrie Allan 10, Ross Dow 9, Aly McLean 9, Kenny Jarvie 7, Jim McGuiness 5.
SASSENACHS - Tim Cash 8, John Priest 8, Steve Cook 7, Billy Fieldhouse 3, Tony Slade 3, Keith Williamson 3.
CREWE - Shaun Messer 7, Brian Bagshaw 4, Keith Eastwood 4, Brian Adshead 3, Dougie Poole 3, Paul Eastwood 1, Jim Flavell 1.

Saturday, October 23, 1976 - Anglo-Scots Junior Three Team Tournament
Crewe Stadium, Earle Street, Crewe
Track Length - 436 yards.

COATBRIDGE TIGER CUBS.....41 CREWE LOCOS.....36 INTER-CITY.....29

			Co	Cr	I
Heat 01	Hack/Richardson/Jarvie/Adshead	00.0	3	3	/
Heat 02	Messer/Eastwood/Cash/Williamson	00.0	/	5	1
Heat 03	Hall/Slade/Dow (F)/Cook (R)	00.0	3	/	2
Heat 04	Fieldhouse/Poole/Allan/McGuinness	00.0	1	5	/
Heat 05	Slade/Woodcock/Adshead (R)/Hack (R)	00.0	/	0	5
Heat 06	Jarvie/Cook/Richardson/Stamford	00.0	4	/	2
Heat 07	Eastwood/Messer/Allan/King	00.0	1	5	/
Heat 08	Woodcock/Slade/Fieldhouse/Westwell	00.0	/	1	5
Heat 09	Hall/Cash/Williamson/Dow	00.0	3	/	3
Heat 10	Jarvie/Richardson/Poole/Fieldhouse	00.0	5	1	/
Heat 11	Hack/Cook/Slade/Adshead (R)	00.0	/	3	3
Heat 12	McGuinness/Allan/Woodcock/Stamford	00.0	5	/	1
Heat 13	Hall/Eastwood/Messer/Dow	00.0	3	3	/
Heat 14	Fieldhouse/Cash/Westwell/Williamson	00.0	/	4	2
Heat 15	Jarvie/Slade/Richardson/Woodcock	00.0	4	/	2
Heat 16	Hall/Hack/Dow/Westwell	00.0	4	2	/
Heat 17	Messer/Slade/Eastwood/Cook (R)	00.0	/	4	2
Heat 18	McGuinness/Allan/Cash/Willamson	00.0	5	/	1

COATBRIDGE - Frankie Hall 12, Kenny Jarvie 10, Norrie Allan 6, Jim McGuiness 6, Paul Richardson 6, Ross Dow 1, Tam King 0.
CREWE - Shaun Messer 9, Paul Eastwood 8, John Hack 8, Billy Fieldhouse 7, Dougie Poole 3, Ian Westwell 1, Brian Adshead 0.
INTER-CITY - Tony Slade 12, Tim Cash 6, Geoff Woodcock 6, Steve Cook 4, Keith Williamson 1, Steve Stamford 0.

Saturday, November 20, 1976 - Junior Three Team Tournament - Crewe
Crewe Locos v Inter-City v Peterborough Panther Cubs
(Cancelled, due to a ban on training school matches by the Speedway authorities.)

Saturday, November 27, 1976 - Rider of the Night Trophy
Crewe Stadium, Earle Street, Crewe
Track Length - 436 yards.

WINNER.....JOHN HACK

Heat 01	Cash/Fieldhouse/Williamson/Adshead	87.8
Heat 02	Jarvie/Cook/Slade/Woodcock	82.6
Heat 03	Hack/Allan/Jack/Westwell (R)	83.2
Heat 04	Hack/Allan/Woodcock/Adshead (F)	82.8
Heat 05	Fieldhouse/Westwell/Slade/Cook (F)	87.5
Heat 06	Jarvie/Cash/Williamson/Jack	85.0
Heat 07	Westwell/Woodcock/Williamson/Adshead (X)	88.6
Heat 08	Hack/Cash/Slade/Cook (R)	82.0
Heat 09	Jarvie/Fieldhouse/Allan/Jack	83.4
Heat 10	Woodcock/Cash/Fieldhouse/Hack (R)	84.6
Heat 11	Allan/Williamson/Jack/Slade (R)	89.0
Heat 12	Jarvie/Westwell/Cook (F) (3 Riders only)	89.4
S/F 1	Fieldhouse/Westwell/Woodcock/Jarvie (X)	86.0
S/F 2	Hack/Allan/Cash/Williamson (F)	81.8
Final	Hack/Allan/Westwell/Fieldhouse (X)	81.4

Kenny Jarvie 12, Tim Cash 9, John Hack 9, Billy Fieldhouse 8, Norrie Allan 8, Ian Westwell 7, Geoff Woodcock 6, Keith Williamson 5, Tony Slade 3, Steve Jack 2, Steve Cook 2, Brian Adshead 0.

Date Unknown, 1976 - Training School Match - Crewe
Crewe Locos v Inter-City
(No other details available.)

Saturday, March 19, 1977 - Training School Match
Crewe Stadium, Earle Street, Crewe
Track Length - 436 yards.

CREWE LOCOS.....39 MANCHESTER REBELS.....37

CREWE - Alan Williams 9, Geoff Woodcock 9, Kevin Groos 8, John Hough 7, Trevor Oldham 3, Bob Tonks 3, Brian Adshead 0.
MANCHESTER - Steve Crowe 8, Tony Slade 8, Jim Sudall 8, Peter Wallace 7, Mark Litherland 3, Terry Cooper 2, Alan Smith 1.

(No other details available.)

Saturday, March 26, 1977 - Training School Mini-Match
Crewe Stadium, Earle Street, Crewe
Track Length - 436 yards.

CREWE LOCOS.....18 ALL STARS.....12

CREWE - Tony Slade 8, Tony Murray 6, Colin Newton 2, Sid Smith 2.
ALL STARS - Peter Wilson 6, Ian Peel 3, Willie York 2, Jim Lupton 1.

(No other details available.)

Saturday, April 16, 1977 - L.M.R. Progress Trophy
Crewe Stadium, Earle Street, Crewe
Track Length - 436 yards.

WINNER.....PAUL SHARE

Riders programmed to compete were: Steve Cook, Tony Slade, Bob Tonks, Tim Cash, Brian Charlton, Geoff Woodcock, John Hough, M. Jones, Lance Bates, Terry Cooper, Paul Share, Brian Adshead, Jim Sudall, Billy Fieldhouse, G. Wade, Tony Murray. Meeting Reserve: Malc Roe.

(No other details available.)

Friday, April 29, 1977 - L.M.R. Spring Classic
Crewe Stadium, Earle Street, Crewe
Track Length - 436 yards.

WINNER.....TREVOR OLDHAM

Riders programmed to compete were included: Brian Adshead, Geoff Woodcock, Billy Fieldhouse, Peter Wilson, Paul Share, Steve Cook, Terry Freeman, Trevor Oldham, Colin Grey, Shaun Messer, Tony Slade, Tim Cash, John Hough, Jeff Shirley, Ian Wilson, Graham Tattersall. Meeting Reserves: K. Norris, Keith Williamson.

(No other details available.)

Friday, June 3, 1977 - Best Pairs Trophy - Crewe
(No other details available.)

Saturday, July 23, 1977 - Training School Match
Crewe Stadium, Earle Street, Crewe
Track Length - 436 yards.

NORTH.....37 SOUTH.....40

NORTH - Robbie Hammond 12, Kevin Garcia 10.
SOUTH - Peter Wallace 8, Brian Charlton 7.

(No other details available.)

Saturday, August 20, 1977 - Training School Challenge
Iwade Colts v Crewe Locos
(No other details available.)

Saturday, September 10, 1977 - Training School Match
Crewe Stadium, Earle Street, Crewe
Track Length - 436 yards.

NORTH.....34 SOUTH.....42

Heat 01	Adshead/Clarke/Sparks/Johnston (R)	00.0	5 - 1	05 - 01
Heat 02	Streets/Garnett (2 riders only)	64.0	2 - 3	07 - 04
Heat 03	Wallace/Etherington/Hancock (R) (3 riders only)	57.0	2 - 3	09 - 07
Heat 04	Robson/Dawson/Garnett/Streets	63.0	3 - 3	12 - 10

Heat 05	Etherington/Sparks/Johnston/Williamson	57.0	3 - 3	15 - 13
Heat 06	Robson/Adshead/Clarke/Streets	62.0	3 - 3	18 - 16
Heat 07	Wallace/Hancock/Dawson/Garnett	57.0	1 - 5	19 - 21
Heat 08	Sparks/Clarke/Streets/Baugh (R)	63.0	2 - 4	21 - 25
Heat 09	Robson/Williamson/Etherington/Streets	58.0	3 - 3	24 - 28
Heat 10	Wallace/Adshead/Clarke/Hancock (R)	58.0	3 - 3	27 - 31
Heat 11	Sparks/Johnston/Dawson/Garnett (R)	64.0	1 - 5	28 - 36
Heat 12	Adshead/Robson/Williamson/Hancock	57.0	4 - 2	32 - 38
Heat 13	Wallace/Etherington/Johnston/Dawson	56.0	2 - 4	34 - 42

(Races were run over three laps.)

NORTH - Brian Adshead 10, Barry Etherington 8, Rob Clarke 6, L. Dawson 4, David Garnett 3, Keith Williamson 3, Dave Baugh 0.
SOUTH - Pete Wallace 12, Guy Robson 11, Andy Sparks 9, D. Johnston 4, Dave Streets 4, Lee Hancock 2.

Sunday, August 10, 2003 - Junior Challenge
Buxton Speedway Stadium, Dale Head Lane, Axe Edge, Buxton
Track Length - 240 metres.

BUXTON SELECT.....20 CREWE KINGS.....16

Heat 01	**Derbyshire**/Sharples/Brown/**G.Walsh**	57.5	3 - 3	03 - 03
Heat 02	**Jackson**/McDermott/**R.Walsh**/Blackburn (R)	62.2	**2 - 4**	05 - 07
Heat 03	**Derbyshire**/Brown/McDermott/**R.Walsh**	58.8	3 - 3	08 - 10
Heat 04	Sharples/**Jackson**/Blackburn/**G.Walsh**	61.7	4 - 2	12 - 12
Heat 05	Sharples/Brown/**R.Walsh**/**Jackson** (F)	62.0	5 - 1	17 - 13
Heat 06	**Derbyshire**/McDermott/Blackburn/**G.Walsh**	59.5	3 - 3	20 - 16

BUXTON - Paul Sharples 8, Alan Brown 5, Martin McDermott 5, Andrew Blackburn 2.
CREWE - Lee Derbyshire 9, Drew Jackson 5, Richard Walsh 2, Greg Walsh 0.

Sunday, September 7, 2003 - Junior Challenge
Buxton Speedway Stadium, Dale Head Lane, Axe Edge, Buxton
Track Length - 240 metres.

BUXTON SELECT.....15 CREWE KINGS.....21

Heat 01	**Edwards**/**Downes**/Matlak/Hendriksen	64.8	**1 - 5**	01 - 05
Heat 02	McDermott/**Hill**/R.Walsh/**G.Walsh**	60.8	4 - 2	05 - 07
Heat 03	**Hill**/**Edwards**/R.Walsh/Matlak (F)	64.8	**1 - 5**	06 - 12
Heat 04	McDermott/**Downes**/Hendriksen/**G.Walsh**	61.8	4 - 2	10 - 14
Heat 05	**Hill**/Matlak/**G.Walsh**/Hendriksen	64.2	**2 - 4**	12 - 18
Heat 06	McDermott/**Downes**/**Edwards**/R.Walsh	60.2	3 - 3	15 - 21

BUXTON - Martin McDermott 9, Tom Matlak 3, Richard Walsh 2, Gary Hendriksen 1.
CREWE - Tom Hill 8, Phil Downes 6, Glyn Edwards 6, Greg Walsh 1.

Sunday, September 21, 2003 - Junior Challenge
Buxton Speedway Stadium, Dale Head Lane, Axe Edge, Buxton
Track Length - 240 metres.

BUXTON SELECT.....19 CREWE KINGS.....17

Heat 01	Bethell/**Roynon**/McDermott/**Edwards**	59.1	4 - 2	04 - 02
Heat 02	**Jackson**/R.Walsh/Hendriksen/**G.Walsh**	61.1	3 - 3	07 - 05
Heat 03	**Roynon**/McDermott/Hendriksen/**G.Walsh** (X)	60.0	3 - 3	10 - 08
Heat 04	Bethell/**Jackson**/**Edwards**/R.Walsh	59.9	3 - 3	13 - 11
Heat 05	Bethell/McDermott/**Jackson**/**G.Walsh**	59.7	5 - 1	18 - 12
Heat 06	**Roynon**/**Edwards**/R.Walsh/Hendriksen	58.1	**1 - 5**	19 - 17

BUXTON - Jonathon Bethell 9, Martin McDermott 5, Richard Walsh 3, Gary Hendriksen 2.
CREWE - Adam Roynon 8, Drew Jackson 6, Glyn Edwards 3, Greg Walsh 0.

Sunday, April 25, 2004 - Junior Challenge
Buxton Speedway Stadium, Dale Head Lane, Axe Edge, Buxton
Track Length - 240 metres.

BUXTON SELECT.....25 CREWE KINGS.....10

Heat 01	Wright/Downes/**R.Walsh**/**Jackson** (R)	63.0	5 - 1	05 - 01
Heat 02	Hill/Morrison/**G.Walsh** (3 Riders only)	61.0	5 - 1	10 - 02
Heat 03	Morrison/Downes/**Doherty**/**R.Walsh**	62.0	5 - 1	15 - 03
Heat 04	Wright/Hill/**Jackson**/**G.Walsh**	61.0	5 - 1	20 - 04
Heat 05	Wright/**G.Walsh**/Downes (R)/**Doherty** (X)	00.0	3 - 2	23 - 06
Heat 06	**Jackson**/Morrison/**R.Walsh**/Hill (X)	00.0	**2 - 4**	25 - 10

BUXTON - Charles Wright 9, John Morrison 7, Tom Hill 5, Phil Downes 4.
CREWE - Drew Jackson 4, Greg Walsh 3, Richard Walsh 2, John Doherty 1.

Thursday, May 20, 2004 - Junior Challenge
Owlerton Sports Stadium, Penistone Road, Sheffield
Track Length - 361 metres.

SHEFFIELD PROWLERS.....21 CREWE KINGS.....9

Heat 01	Compton/Speight/**Downes**/**Jackson** (R)	65.7	5 - 1	05 - 01
Heat 02	Compton/**Roynon**/Mitchell/**Hill**	65.8	4 - 2	09 - 03
Heat 03	Speight/Mitchell/**Jackson**/**Downes**	66.3	5 - 1	14 - 04
Heat 04	Compton/Speight/**Roynon**/**Hill**	67.2	5 - 1	19 - 05
Heat 05	**Roynon**/Compton/**Jackson**/Mitchell (R)	65.8	**2 - 4**	21 - 09

SHEFFIELD - Benji Compton 11, David Speight 7, Michael Mitchell 3.
CREWE - Adam Roynon 6, Drew Jackson 2, Phil Downes 1, Tom Hill 0.

Sunday, May 30, 2004 - Junior Challenge
Buxton Speedway Stadium, Dale Head Lane, Axe Edge, Buxton
Track Length - 240 metres.

CREWE KINGS.....19 BELLE VUE COLTS.....17

Heat 01	**Bethell**/Burnett/Naylor/**Parker**	00.0	3 - 3	03 - 03
Heat 02	Hill/**Jackson**/**Blackburn**/Roynon (R)	59.0	3 - 3	06 - 06
Heat 03	**Bethell**/Roynon/Burnett/**Blackburn** (F)	59.2	3 - 3	09 - 09
Heat 04	**Jackson**/Hill/**Parker**/Naylor (X)	00.0	**4 - 2**	13 - 11
Heat 05	**Bethell**/Hill/Roynon/**Parker**	61.0	3 - 3	16 - 14
Heat 06	Burnett/**Jackson**/**Blackburn**/Naylor	00.0	3 - 3	19 - 17

CREWE - Jonathon Bethell 9, Drew Jackson 7, Andrew Blackburn 2, Ross Parker 1.
BELLE VUE - Tom Hill 7, Paul Burnett 6, Adam Roynon 3, Phil Naylor 1.

Wednesday, June 9, 2004 - Junior Challenge
New Craven Park Stadium, Kingston-upon-Hull
Track Length - 346 metres.

MIDDLESBROUGH BEARS.....19 CREWE KINGS.....17

Heat 01	**Pickering**/Burnett/**Wright**/Nettleship	71.4	**2 - 4**	02 - 04
Heat 02	Bethell/**Belfield**/**Hill**/Downes (F)	73.5	3 - 3	05 - 07
Heat 03	Bethell/**Pickering**/**Belfield**/Nettleship	71.2	3 - 3	08 - 10
Heat 04	Burnett/**Wright**/Downes/**Hill**	72.3	4 - 2	12 - 12
Heat 05	**Belfield**/Burnett/Nettleship/**Hill**	72.5	3 - 3	15 - 15
Heat 06	Bethell/**Pickering**/Downes/**Wright**	71.6	4 - 2	19 - 17

MIDDLESBROUGH - Jonathon Bethell 9, Paul Burnett 7, Phil Downes 2, Scott Nettleship 1.
CREWE - Mike Pickering 7, Carl Belfield 6, Charles Wright 3, Tom Hill 1.

Sunday, July 18, 2004 - Junior Challenge
Abbey Stadium, Blunsdon, Swindon
Track Length - 359.6 metres.

SWINDON SPROCKETS.....30 CREWE KINGS.....6

Heat 01	Purchase/Downs/**Jackson**/**R.Walsh**	73.08	5 - 1	05 - 01
Heat 02	Irwin/Harding/**Downes**/**G.Walsh**	72.93	5 - 1	10 - 02
Heat 03	Irwin/Downs/**Downes**/**R.Walsh**	72.34	5 - 1	15 - 03

Heat 04 .... Purchase/Harding/**Jackson**/**G.Walsh**	73.86	5 - 1	20 - 04
Heat 05 .... Purchase/Downs/**Downes**/**G.Walsh**	73.02	5 - 1	25 - 05
Heat 06 .... Irwin/Harding/**Jackson**/**R.Walsh**	73.49	5 - 1	30 - 06

SWINDON - Nathan Irwin 9, James Purchase 9, Carl Downs 6, Daniel Harding 6.
CREWE - Phil Downes 3, Drew Jackson 3, Greg Walsh 0, Richard Walsh 0.

Sunday, July 25, 2004 - Junior Challenge
Brough Park Stadium, The Fossway, Byker, Newcastle-upon-Tyne
Track Length - 300 metres.

NEWCASTLE GEMS.....19 CREWE KINGS.....17

Heat 01 .... Branney/Haigh/**Downs**/**Baker**	71.6	5 - 1	05 - 01
Heat 02 .... Nettleship/**Hough**/Hodgeson/**Downes** (X)	00.0	4 - 2	09 - 03
Heat 03 .... **Downs**/**Baker**/Haigh/Nettleship	69.9	**1 - 5**	10 - 08
Heat 04 .... **Downs**/Branney/**Hough**/Hodgeson	68.9	**2 - 4**	12 - 12
Heat 05 .... Branney/**Baker**/Haigh/**Hough**	69.8	4 - 2	16 - 14
Heat 06 .... **Downs**/Branney/Nettleship/**Baker** (R)	69.0	3 - 3	19 - 17

NEWCASTLE - John Branney 10, David Haigh 4, Scott Nettleship 4, Liam Hodgeson 1.
CREWE - Carl Downs 10, Dave Baker 4, John Hough 3, Phil Downes 0.

Saturday, July 31, 2004 - Junior Challenge
New Craven Park Stadium, Kingston-upon-Hull
Track Length - 346 metres.

HULL ANGELS.....15 CREWE KINGS.....21

Heat 01 .... **Compton**/Norton/**Burnett**/Downes	69.6	**2 - 4**	02 - 04
Heat 02 .... **Downs**/**Belfield**/Pickering/Martin	71.1	**1 - 5**	03 - 09
Heat 03 .... **Compton**/Martin/**Belfield**/Downes	69.5	**2 - 4**	05 - 13
Heat 04 .... Pickering/**Downs**/**Burnett**/Norton	70.8	3 - 3	08 - 16
Heat 05 .... Norton/**Belfield**/Downes/**Downs** (R)	78.2	4 - 2	12 - 18
Heat 06 .... Pickering/**Compton**/**Burnett**/Martin	71.2	3 - 3	15 - 21

HULL - Mike Pickering 7, Danny Norton 5, Neil Martin 2, Phil Downes 1.
CREWE - Benji Compton 8, Carl Belfield 5, Carl Downs 5, Paul Burnett 3.

Sunday, August 8, 2004 - Junior Challenge
Buxton Speedway Stadium, Dale Head Lane, Axe Edge, Buxton
Track Length - 240 metres.

CREWE KINGS.....17 MIDDLESBROUGH BEARS.....19

Heat 01 .... Irwin/**Burnett**/**Baker**/Blackburn	58.4	3 - 3	03 - 03
Heat 02 .... Belfield/**Hill**/**Hough**/Downes (X)	00.0	3 - 3	06 - 06
Heat 03 .... Downes/**Baker**/**Hill**/Blackburn	60.2	3 - 3	09 - 09
Heat 04 .... **Burnett**/Irwin/Belfield/**Hough**	59.0	3 - 3	12 - 12
Heat 05 .... Belfield/**Burnett**/Downes/**Baker** (R)	60.3	2 - 4	14 - 16
Heat 06 .... Irwin/**Hill**/**Hough**/Blackburn	59.5	3 - 3	17 - 19

CREWE - Paul Burnett 7, Tom Hill 5, Dave Baker 3, John Hough 2.
MIDDLESBROUGH - Nathan Irwin 8, Carl Belfield 7, Phil Downes 4, Andrew Blackburn 0.

Sunday, September 12, 2004 - Junior Challenge
Buxton Speedway Stadium, Dale Head Lane, Axe Edge, Buxton
Track Length - 240 metres.

CREWE KINGS.....25 KING'S LYNN STARLETS.....11

Heat 01 .... **Derbyshire**/**Hill**/Parker/Davies	61.0	**5 - 1**	05 - 01
Heat 02 .... **Belfield**/Branney/Chester/**Downes**	59.8	3 - 3	08 - 04
Heat 03 .... **Belfield**/**Hill**/Chester/Davies	60.0	**5 - 1**	13 - 05
Heat 04 .... **Derbyshire**/Branney/Parker/**Downes**	59.1	3 - 3	16 - 08
Heat 05 .... **Derbyshire**/**Hill**/Chester/Branney	59.5	**5 - 1**	21 - 09
Heat 06 .... **Belfield**/Parker/**Downes**/Davies	61.0	**4 - 2**	25 - 11

CREWE - Carl Belfield 9, Lee Derbyshire 9, Tom Hill 6, Phil Downes 1.
KING'S LYNN - John Branney 4, Ross Parker 4, Scott Chester 3, Wayne Davies 0.

Thursday, September 16, 2004 - Junior Challenge
Owlerton Sports Stadium, Penistone Road, Sheffield
Track Length - 361 metres.

SHEFFIELD PROWLERS.....18 CREWE KINGS.....18

Heat 01	Speight/Richardson/**Sharples**/**Belfield**	65.4	5 - 1	05 - 01
Heat 02	**Derbyshire**/Mitchell/**Parker**/Quinn	67.0	**2 - 4**	07 - 05
Heat 03	Speight/**Belfield**/**Derbyshire**/Mitchell (F)	65.7	3 - 3	10 - 08
Heat 04	Richardson/**Parker**/**Sharples**/Quinn	66.0	3 - 3	13 - 11
Heat 05	Richardson/**Derbyshire**/Speight/**Parker**	65.6	4 - 2	17 - 13
Heat 06	**Belfield**/**Sharples**/Mitchell/Richardson (X)	67.0	**1 - 5**	18 - 18

SHEFFIELD - Mark Richardson 8, David Speight 7, Michael Mitchell 3, Craig Quinn 0.
CREWE - Lee Derbyshire 6, Carl Belfield 5, Paul Sharples 4, Ross Parker 3.

Sunday, September 26, 2004 - Junior Challenge
Buxton Speedway Stadium, Dale Head Lane, Axe Edge, Buxton
Track Length - 240 metres.

CREWE KINGS.....25 WEYMOUTH WILDCATS.....11

Heat 01	**Belfield**/Ferguson/**Chester**/Hill (F)	59.0	**4 - 2**	04 - 02
Heat 02	**Derbyshire**/**Parker**/Lidgett/Blackburn	58.4	**5 - 1**	09 - 03
Heat 03	**Derbyshire**/Hill/**Chester**/Lidgett (F)	58.0	**4 - 2**	13 - 05
Heat 04	**Belfield**/Ferguson/**Parker**/Blackburn	57.0	**4 - 2**	17 - 07
Heat 05	**Belfield**/Lidgett/**Chester**/Blackburn	57.4	**4 - 2**	21 - 09
Heat 06	**Parker**/Hill/**Derbyshire**/Ferguson (R)	60.0	**4 - 2**	25 - 11

CREWE - Carl Belfield 9, Lee Derbyshire 7, Ross Parker 6, Scott Chester 3.
WEYMOUTH - Chris Ferguson 4, Tom Hill 4, Dave Lidgett 3, Andrew Blackburn 0.

(ABOVE) The Crewe Locos in the pits at Earle Street.

Crewe Locos v Iwade Colts on July 31, 1976.

(ABOVE) Instructor Charlie Scarbrough (far left) with a group of his trainees.

(ABOVE) Stock car promoter Mick Farley, assisted by Charlie Scarbrough, making presentations to the riders.

(ABOVE) Mick Mellor, one of the training school riders who graduated to the full Kings side. He made two league appearances during 1975 season. Attending to Mick's machine is former Earle Street machine examiner Mike Smith.

(ABOVE) The Kings re-born at Buxton in 2003. (Left to right) Richard Walsh, Lee Derbyshire, Drew Jackson, Kev Tew (team manager) and Greg Walsh. (BELOW) The team twelve months later. (Back row) Phil Downes, Kev Tew, Tom Hill and (kneeling) Carl Belfield and Lee Derbyshire.

(ABOVE) Action from the narrow 17-19 defeat to Newcastle Gems at Brough Park Stadium on July 25, 2004, as John Hough evades the falling Liam Hodgeson.

(ABOVE) The Crewe pairing of Lee Derbyshire and Tom Hill on a 5-1 against the King's Lynn Starlets at Buxton on September 12, during the same season.

Kings Facts & Figures

- Kings Facts & Figures -

- League Sequences -

Home wins in succession: **48** (May 15, 1972 - October 14, 1974)
Away wins in succession: **3** (May 21, 1972 - June 21, 1972)
Combined wins in succession: **9** (May 21, 1972 - July 10, 1972)
Biggest home win: **62 - 16** (Reading, September 1, 1969 & Birmingham, August 30, 1971)
Biggest away win: **48 - 29** (King's Lynn II, August 3, 1969)
Home defeats in succession: **2** (August 4, 1975 - August 11, 1975)
Away defeats in succession: **24** (May 24, 1970 - August 13, 1971)
Combined defeats in succession: **6** (September 2, 1970 - September 20, 1970)
Biggest home defeat: **31 - 46** (Eastbourne, August 11, 1975)
Biggest away defeat: **20 - 58** (Eastbourne, May 24, 1970 & Barrow, September 4, 1973)

- Final League Positions -

		Home					Away					
Year/Position	**M**	**W**	**D**	**L**	**F**	**A**	**W**	**D**	**L**	**F**	**A**	**Pts**
1969 - Seventh	30	14	0	1	754	377	1	0	14	503	662	30
1970 - Seventh	32	16	0	0	800	445	1	1	14	505	741	35
1971 - Seventh	32	15	1	0	826	418	1	0	15	475	766	33
1972 - First	32	15	0	1	834	413	7	1	8	610	628	45
1973 - Eighth	34	17	0	0	785½	538½	0	1	16	503	820	35
1974 - Fifth	36	17	0	1	919½	482½	5	0	13	616	784	44
1975 - Sixteenth	37	12	1	6	837	640	1	0	17	558	844	27

- Crewe League Record - Club by Club -

		Home					Away					
	M	**W**	**D**	**L**	**F**	**A**	**W**	**D**	**L**	**F**	**A**	**Pts**
Barrow	5	2	0	0	103	53	0	0	3	83	150	4
Belle Vue II	2	0	0	1	34	44	0	0	1	21	57	0
Berwick	14	7	0	0	359	186	0	1	6	222	321	15
Birmingham	10	4	0	1	234	154	0	0	5	141	249	8
Boston	10	4	1	0	237	153	0	0	5	147	243	9
Bradford	12	6	0	0	287½	180½	1	0	5	177½	287½	14
Canterbury	14	7	0	0	362	183	1	0	6	226	318	16
Coatbridge	4	2	0	0	102	53	0	0	2	57	98	4
Crayford	6	2	0	1	144	89	0	0	3	95	139	4
Doncaster	4	2	0	0	105	51	0	0	2	66	89	4
Eastbourne	14	6	0	1	357	188	0	0	7	190	353	12
Ellesmere Port	8	4	0	0	187	125	2	0	2	151	160	12
Hull	6	3	0	0	145	89	0	0	3	97	136	6
Ipswich	6	3	0	0	150	84	0	0	3	98	135	6
King's Lynn II	4	2	0	0	109	46	1	0	1	79	76	6
Long Eaton	12	6	0	0	297	131	1	0	5	214	253	14
Mildenhall	2	1	0	0	47	31	1	0	0	41	36	4
Nelson	2	1	0	0	54	24	0	0	1	37	41	2
Newcastle	2	0	0	1	38	39	0	0	1	28	50	0
Paisley	2	1	0	0	42	36	0	0	1	32	46	2
Peterborough	11	5	0	1	295	173	1	0	4	177	212	12
Plymouth	2	1	0	0	61	17	0	0	1	28	49	2
Rayleigh	10	5	0	0	247	141	1	2	2	186	203	14
Reading	4	2	0	0	109	47	0	0	2	65	89	4
Rochdale	4	2	0	0	102	54	0	0	2	74	82	4
Romford	6	3	0	0	160	73	0	0	3	98	136	6
Rye House	4	2	0	0	106	50	1	0	1	65	90	6
Scunthorpe	8	3	0	1	185	125	2	0	2	151	161	10

Stoke	6	2	0	1	144	90	0	0	3	97	136	4
Sunderland	8	4	0	0	210	101	2	0	2	152	159	12
Teesside	14	7	0	0	331	215	2	0	5	223	319	18
West Ham	1	1	0	0	51	27	0	0	0	0	0	2
Weymouth	4	2	0	0	109½	45½	0	0	2	72	84	4
Workington	12	4	1	1	252	216	0	0	6	180	288	9

(Stoke were known as Chesterton in 1973 and Teesside were known as Middlesbrough in 1969.)

- League Heat Details 1969 - 1975 -

	Home	Away	Total
5 - 0 heat win to Crewe	1	1	2
5 - 1 heat win to Crewe	563	101	664
4½ - 1½ heat win to Crewe	2	0	2
4 - 2 heat win to Crewe	349	189	538
3 - 0 heat win to Crewe	1	1	2
3 - 2 heat win to Crewe	6	9	15
3 - 3 drawn heat	399	476	875
2 - 3 heat win to Opponents	5	11	16
2 - 4 heat win to Opponents	119	313	432
1 - 5 heat win to Opponents	65	398	463
0 - 5 heat win to Opponents	5	9	14

- All Time Crewe Rider Statistics -

(League and Knock Out Cup)

	M	R	W	Pts	BP	Tot	F	P	CMA
1. John Jackson	179	764	404	1653	70	1723	37	14	9.021
2. Phil Crump	79	339	236	830	25	855	27	10	10.088
3. Dai Evans	107	436	83	667	107	774	2	10	7.101
4. Dave Morton	90	368	146	678½	65	743½	8	8	8.082
5. Dave Parry	129	450	73	553	103	656	0	7	5.831
6. Barry Meeks	99	371	79	538	78	616	3	6	6.642
7. Paul O'Neil*	59	241	140	540	19	559	12	4	9.278
8. Keith White	73	308	65	419	53	472	0	4	6.130
9. Graham Drury	38	166	63	345	16	361	2	2	8.699
10. Gary Moore	81	292	29	311	49	360	0	0	4.932
11. Garry Flood	41	170	74	330	27	357	0	10	8.400
12. Ian Bottomley	62	218	59	311	43	354	3	3	6.495
13. Ian Cartwright	65	240	25	299	50	349	0	4	5.817
14. Geoff Curtis	33	135	88½	329½	11½	341	6	3	10.104
15. Geoff Ambrose	38	158	57	293½	20	313½	4	2	7.937
16. Cliff Anderson	63	221	33	244	37	281	0	0	5.086
17. Chris Turner	28	122	47	222	26	248	1	2	8.131
18. Jack Millen	41	138	39	217	29	246	2	4	7.130
19. Nigel Wasley	30	126	48	236	8	244	1	2	7.746
20. Wayne Forrest	49	179	25	198	31	229	0	0	5.117
21. Colin Tucker	37	134	31½	197½	24½	222	0	1	6.627
22. Pete Saunders	34	119	14	146	30	176	0	2	5.916
23. Les Collins	36	131	12	139	33	172	0	1	5.252
24. Glyn Taylor	31	121	19	140	20	160	0	1	5.289
25. Stuart Cope	38	118	22	142	13	155	1	1	5.254
26. Max Brown	32	117	9	116	30	146	0	1	4.991
27. Warren Hawkins	23	78	12	103	16	119	0	0	6.103
28. Les Ott	16	62	4	79	15	94	0	1	6.065
29. Glyn Blackburn	24	75	6	73	18	91	0	0	4.853
30. Chris Emery	10	43	5	55	13	68	0	1	6.326
31. Ricky Day	9	35	6	46	7	53	0	2	6.057

		M	R	W	Pts	BP	Tot	F	P	CMA
32.	Peter Seaton*	8	30	6	45	5	50	0	0	6.667
33.	Peter Nicholas	12	32	4	32	8	40	0	1	5.000
34.	Mike Gardner	9	28	1	27	5	32	0	0	4.571
35.	Rob Jackson	10	27	3	26	5	31	0	0	4.593
36.	Ray Hassall	8	23	1	17	6	23	0	0	4.000
37.	Ian Robertson	7	22	0	16	2	18	0	0	3.273
38.	Peter Thompson ..	7	18	1	13	4	17	0	0	3.778
39.	Dave Jessup	1	6	4	12	0	12	0	0	8.000
40.	Ross Gilbertson ...	1	5	2	12	0	12	0	0	9.600
41.	Jaffa Purkiss	1	5	2	9	1	10	0	0	8.000
42.	Graham Crook	5	12	0	7	3	10	0	0	3.333
43.	Paul Wells	6	17	1	8	1	9	0	0	2.118
44.	Dave O'Connor ...	2	7	0	7	2	9	0	0	5.143
45.	John McNeil	1	3	1	7	1	8	0	0	10.666
46.	Eddie Argall	1	5	1	7	1	8	0	0	6.400
47.	Mick Mellor	2	6	0	5	3	8	0	0	5.333
48.	Bob Jameson	1	5	0	6	1	7	0	0	5.600
49.	Les Glover	1	5	0	6	0	6	0	0	4.800
50.	Brian Paddington..	1	3	1	5	1	6	0	0	8.000
51.	Reg Brassington ...	6	16	0	5	1	6	0	0	1.500
52.	Allan Emmett	1	4	0	4	1	5	0	0	5.000
=	John Harrhy	1	4	0	4	1	5	0	0	5.000
54.	Robin Dixon	1	3	0	4	0	4	0	0	5.333
55.	Mick Fielding	3	7	1	4	0	4	0	0	2.286
56.	Steve Lawson	1	4	1	3	0	3	0	0	3.000
57.	Ray Cousins	2	7	0	2	1	3	0	0	1.714
58.	Andy Reid	4	8	0	2	1	3	0	0	1.500
59.	Bryan Townsend..	1	2	0	2	0	2	0	0	4.000
60.	Nicky Allott	1	3	0	2	0	2	0	0	2.667
61.	Alan Johns	1	4	0	2	0	2	0	0	2.000
=	Stuart Wallace	1	4	0	2	0	2	0	0	2.000
63.	Terry Owen	1	5	0	2	0	2	0	0	1.600
64.	Stuart Riley	2	5	0	2	0	2	0	0	1.600
65.	Barry Booth	2	6	0	2	0	2	0	0	1.333
66.	Stuart Roberts	3	6	0	2	0	2	0	0	1.333
67.	John Mulligan	5	13	0	2	0	2	0	0	0.615
68.	Lloyd Dobson	1	2	0	1	1	2	0	0	4.000
69.	Mick Beaton	1	2	0	1	0	1	0	0	2.000
=	Malcolm Bruce	1	2	0	1	0	1	0	0	2.000
=	Brian Osborn	1	2	0	1	0	1	0	0	2.000
=	Charlie Scarbrough.	1	2	0	1	0	1	0	0	2.000
73.	Kelvin Mullarkey..	1	1	0	0	0	0	0	0	0.000
=	Dave Percy	1	1	0	0	0	0	0	0	0.000
=	Graham Tattersall..	1	1	0	0	0	0	0	0	0.000
76.	Mike Bessent	1	2	0	0	0	0	0	0	0.000
=	Dave Hughes	1	2	0	0	0	0	0	0	0.000
=	Barrie Smitherman.	1	2	0	0	0	0	0	0	0.000
79.	Freddie Sweet	1	3	0	0	0	0	0	0	0.000
80.	Don Beecroft	3	6	0	0	0	0	0	0	0.000

(*Includes guest appearance(s) either before or after riding for the club.)

- All Time Crewe Rider Statistics -

(Challenge, Inter-League Knock Out Cup, Three and Four Team Tournaments)

		M	R	W	Pts	BP	Tot	F	P	CMA
1.	John Jackson*	80	331	150	653	36	689	7	3	7.891
2.	Barry Meeks	38	145	38	245	18	263	0	3	6.759

3.	Dai Evans	48	176	32	232	28	260	2	0	5.273
4.	Phil Crump	25	101	71	241	5	246	9	0	9.743
5.	Dave Parry	42	143	23	174	20	194	0	0	4.867
6.	Paul O'Neil	21	90	42	179	8	187	1	0	7.956
7.	Dave Morton	26	98	26	160	14	174	2	0	6.531
8.	Ian Bottomley	26	100	22	138	20	158	0	0	5.520
9.	Gary Moore*	34	123	17	140½	15	155½	0	0	4.569
10.	Keith White	27	105	25	144	3	147	1	0	5.486
11.	Garry Flood	14	53	23	105	9	114	2	0	7.925
12.	Geoff Ambrose	13	52	20	103	4	107	1	1	7.923
13.	Ian Cartwright	14	51	4	67	22	89	0	2	5.255
14.	Jack Millen	12	45	17	76	6	82	1	1	6.756
15.	Graham Drury	9	39	10	71	4	75	0	0	7.282
16.	Warren Hawkins	14	52	5	59	15	74	0	0	4.538
17.	Chris Turner	9	37	13	68	3	71	1	0	7.351
18.	Nigel Wasley	9	37	14	64	4	68	1	0	6.919
19.	Cliff Anderson	15	41	6	50	7	57	0	0	4.878
20.	Glyn Taylor	8	32	5	43	5	48	0	1	5.375
21.	Colin Tucker	11	36	5	36	4	40	0	0	4.000
22.	Les Ott	7	28	5	36	1	37	0	0	5.143
23.	Les Collins	8	28	3	28	6	34	0	0	4.000
24.	Ray Hassall	10	32	0	25	6	31	0	0	3.125
25.	Max Brown	6	21	3	24	7	31	0	0	4.571
26.	Peter Seaton	5	23	1	28	2	30	0	0	4.870
27.	Stuart Cope	7	23	3	24	3	27	0	0	4.174
28.	Wayne Forrest	8	26	2	23	4	27	0	0	3.538
29.	Mike Gardner	4	14	3	18	4	22	0	0	5.143
30.	Chris Emery	5	18	0	16	6	22	0	0	3.556
31.	Pete Saunders	4	16	2	18	2	20	0	0	4.500
32.	Geoff Curtis	3	10	5	18	1	19	1	0	7.200
33.	Don Beecroft	4	11	1	14	3	17	0	0	5.091
34.	Lou Sansom	1	6	3	15	0	15	0	0	10.000
35.	Glyn Blackburn	5	19	1	14	0	14	0	0	2.947
36.	Reg Brassington	7	21	1	12	1	13	0	0	2.286
37.	Carl Glover	1	6	2	10	2	12	0	0	6.667
38.	Paul Tyrer	1	5	1	11	0	11	0	0	8.800
39.	Jim Ryman	1	4	3	10	0	10	0	0	10.000
40.	Tony Childs	1	5	2	10	0	10	0	0	8.000
41.	Ricky Day	1	4	1	9	1	10	0	0	9.000
42.	Barney Kennett	1	5	0	9	1	10	0	0	7.200
43.	Graham Edmonds	1	5	1	8	1	9	0	0	6.400
44.	Barrie Smitherman	3	6	0	7	2	9	0	0	4.667
45.	Terry Lee	1	4	0	7	1	8	0	0	7.000
46.	Ian Champion	1	4	0	6	2	8	0	0	6.000
47.	Jim Wells	2	6	0	6	2	8	0	0	4.000
48.	Dene Davies	1	4	1	6	1	7	0	0	6.000
49.	Chris Roynon	1	3	1	6	0	6	0	0	8.000
50.	Reg Wilson	1	3	1	5	1	6	0	0	6.667
51.	Peter Nicholas	2	6	0	4	1	5	0	0	2.667
52.	John Mulligan	3	7	0	4	1	5	0	0	2.286
53.	Rob Jackson	7	15	0	4	1	5	0	0	1.067
54.	Stuart Jay	1	4	0	3	1	4	0	0	3.000
55.	Bob Jameson	1	4	0	3	0	3	0	0	3.000
56.	Roger Mills	1	3	0	2	1	3	0	0	2.667
57.	Charlie Scarbrough	1	3	0	2	1	3	0	0	2.667

58.	Ian Robertson	2	5	0	2	1	3	0	0	1.600
59.	Gil Farmer	1	3	0	1	1	2	0	0	1.333
60.	Vince Mann	1	2	0	1	0	1	0	0	2.000
61.	Roger Wright	1	3	0	1	0	1	0	0	1.333
62.	Andy Cusworth	1	2	0	0	0	0	0	0	0.000
=	Chris Moore	1	2	0	0	0	0	0	0	0.000
=	Stuart Riley	1	2	0	0	0	0	0	0	0.000
=	Peter Thompson	1	2	0	0	0	0	0	0	0.000
66.	Martin Hitch	1	3	0	0	0	0	0	0	0.000
=	Brian Morris	1	3	0	0	0	0	0	0	0.000
=	Dave O'Connor	1	3	0	0	0	0	0	0	0.000

(*Includes guest appearance(s) either before or after riding for the club. The CMA's do not include bonus points in this listing. Chris Fell rode as Chris Moore and Vince Smitherman rode as Vince Mann.)

- Silver Helmet Match Races -

1970

Holder Malcolm Shakespeare forfeited the title to Paul O'Neil on June 8, due to injury.

Monday, June 15 - Crewe .... Paul O'Neil defeated Andy Ross.
Monday, June 22 - Crewe .... Paul O'Neil defeated Alan Paynter.
Monday, June 29 - Crewe .... Paul O'Neil defeated Graeme Smith.
Monday, July 13 - Crewe .... Paul O'Neil defeated Taffy Owen.
Sunday, July 19 - Doncaster .... George Major defeated Paul O'Neil.

1971

Thursday, September 30 - Ipswich ...... John Louis (Holder) defeated Phil Crump.
Monday, October 11 - Crewe .... Phil Crump defeated John Louis (Holder).
Thursday, October 14 - Ipswich .... Phil Crump defeated John Louis.

1972

Tuesday, April 4 - Birmingham .... Phil Crump (Holder) defeated Pete Bailey.
Monday, April 24 - Crewe .... Richard Greer defeated Phil Crump.

1973

Monday, August 20 - Crewe .... Geoff Ambrose defeated Mike Broadbanks (Holder).
Saturday, August 25 - Rayleigh .... Peter Moore defeated Geoff Ambrose.
Monday, September 10 - Crewe .... Trevor Barnwell (Holder) defeated Dave Morton.

1974

The title was changed to a monthly competition on a home and away basis, with a deciding leg on a neutral track if needed.

Sunday, April 7 - Boston .... Heat 1 Millen/Glover.
Heat 2 Millen/Glover.
Monday, April 8 - Crewe .... Heat 1 Glover/Millen.
Heat 2 Millen/Glover.
Heat 3 Millen/Glover.
Jack Millen defeated Carl Glover 4-1.
Jack Millen forfeited the title in May due to injury.
Sunday, June 16 - Eastbourne .... Heat 1 McNeil/Millen.
Heat 2 McNeil/Millen.
Monday, June 24 - Crewe .... Heat 1 McNeil/Millen.
Heat 2 McNeil/Millen.
Bobby McNeil (Holder) defeated Jack Millen 4-0.

No Crewe rider was involved in the competition during 1975.

- Earle Street Track Records -

(Track Length 470 yards)

1969

Date	Heat	Rider	Time
Monday, May 19	Heat 1	Mike Gardner (Rayleigh)	77.0
	Heat 3	Dingle Brown (Rayleigh)	76.8
	Heat 4	Geoff Curtis (Crewe)	74.2
	Heat 6	Geoff Curtis (Crewe)	73.2
Monday, June 16	Heat 7	Geoff Curtis (Crewe)	72.8
Monday, June 30	Heat 4	Geoff Curtis (Crewe)	71.8

1970

Date	Heat	Rider	Time
Friday, March 27	Heat 1	Paul O'Neil (Crewe)	71.0
	Heat 5	Barry Meeks (Crewe)	70.4

(Track Length reduced to 436 yards)

1971

Date	Heat	Rider	Time
Friday, April 9	Heat 1	Barry Meeks (Crewe)	78.0
	Heat 3	Dave Parry (Crewe)	77.4
	Heat 9	Alan Knapkin (Bradford)	77.0
Monday, April 19	Heat 7	John Jackson (Crewe)	77.0
Monday, April 26	Heat 4	Paul Tyrer (Rochdale)	76.8
	Heat 5	Alan Wilkinson (Rochdale)	76.6
	Heat 7	John Jackson (Crewe)	76.2
Monday, May 17	Heat 10	Hugh Saunders (Rayleigh)	76.2
	Heat 13	Dave Parry (Crewe)	76.2
Monday, June 7	Heat 4	John Jackson (Crewe)	75.8
	Heat 7	John Jackson (Crewe)	75.8
Monday, June 14	Heat 2	Barry Meeks (Crewe)	75.8
	Heat 5	Dai Evans (Crewe)	75.6
	Heat 6	Phil Crump (Crewe)	75.6
	Heat 7	Reg Wilson (Hull)	75.2
	Heat 11	Barry Meeks (Crewe)	75.0
	Heat 12	Dai Evans (Crewe)	75.0
Monday, July 5	Heat 1	John Jackson (Crewe)	74.2
	Heat 5	Peter Collins (Rochdale)	74.0
	Heat 7	Phil Crump (Crewe)	74.0
	Heat 10	Peter Collins (Rochdale)	74.0
Monday, July 12	Heat 10	Phil Crump (Crewe)	73.8
	Heat 12	Phil Crump (Crewe)	72.8
Monday, August 2	Heat 9	Dai Evans (Crewe)	72.6
	Heat 13	Dai Evans (Crewe)	72.6

1972

Date	Heat	Rider	Time
Monday, April 17	Heat 4	John Jackson (Crewe)	71.4

1973

Date	Heat	Rider	Time
Monday, July 16	Heat 5	Dave Morton (Crewe)	71.2
Monday, August 6	Heat 1	Arthur Price (Boston)	71.2
Monday, August 27	Heat 1	John Jackson (Crewe)	71.2
Monday, September 17	Heat 1	John Jackson (Crewe)	71.0
Monday, September 24	Heat 1	Lou Sansom (Workington)	70.8

1974

Date	Heat	Rider	Time
Monday, April 8	Heat 4	John Jackson (Crewe)	70.6
Monday, April 15	Heat 3	Keith White (Crewe)	70.2
Monday, April 29	Heat 1	Mitch Graham (Workington)	70.0
	Heat 5	Mitch Graham (Workington)	70.0
Monday, June 24	S/H	Bobby McNeil (Eastbourne)	69.6
	Heat 1	John Jackson (Crewe)	69.0
Monday, August 5	Heat 12	Dave Morton (Crewe)	69.0
Monday, August 12	Heat 1	Dave Morton (Crewe)	68.0

Interviews & Memories

- Interviews & Memories -

Colin Tucker.

Full Name? - "*Leonard Allen Colin Tucker, but have always been called Colin after my Uncle who was killed near the end of World War Two.*"

When and where were you born? - *"January 8, 1946 in Auckland, New Zealand. To start racing in NZ you had to be 16 and I was only 15, so changed my date of birth to 1945. I knew Mum would not sign it, so got someone else to do that."*

What jobs did you do before entering into speedway? - *"At the time I was an apprentice Master Carpenter & Builder and am still involved with building today."*

How did you get into speedway? - *"By accident really. At a very young age I remember going to speedway in Auckland. Then we moved from Davenport to West Auckland and I went more regularly with the Ward family. NZ Speedway was not just bikes but midget cars as well. Then as a teenager, Norm Ward got me a job of helping out Maury Dunn, a New Zealander, who had also ridden for Harringay in England. Then after one practice evening, Maury put me on a bike and sent me out on the track."*

Did you base your style of riding on anyone in particular? - *"No not really."*

Who first approached you to come to Crewe and what was the pay? - *"It was December 1968 and I was working in Germany, selling 'English Bone China and Crystal Ware' to the American Forces. Just before Christmas I phoned Colin Pratt, whose parents I lodged with in Harlow Oldtown, just up from the Greyhound Pub (I love the way the English give their directions to somewhere, always via the pubs). Anyway I decided to come back for Christmas (my first Christmas in England, but that's another story). After my arrival back from Germany, Pratty said Maury Littlechild wanted to see me, so a few days after Christmas off we went to Maury's at Waltham Abbey not far from Harlow. It was then that I learned about the Crewe plans. So a week later we went north so I could have a look, after picking up Ken Adams from Winterley Pool. It was cold, damp, miserable weather with snow on the ground. My initial reaction was it looked very possible, and the time frame did not seem a problem to me, if the weather permitted (understand this was my first winter in England and I did not understand at that time how bad it could get). Maury offered me £10 a week."*

You had approximately four months to transform the L.M.R. Sports Ground into a speedway stadium and track. What turned out to be the most difficult task during construction? - *"Just about everything was done by hand, from digging out the centre grass strip between the running and cycle track, digging post holes, drainage lines for the track drainage, toilet drainage and foundations and hand mixing all the concrete, the list goes on and on, including unloading the sleepers off the carriages onto the truck for milling, then hand unloading the truck from the mill. The most difficult task was working in the damp English winter weather. Some days I just could not get warm, no matter how hard I worked, and my hands were like ice, even with gloves on, and my nose just dripped continually."*

How many helped you during the project and any names? - *"On arrival to start the project, the caretaker of the L.M.R. Sports ground was most welcoming, his name was Gerry (I have forgotten his surname). He looked after the cricket and bowling greens. He had a little smoko shed and became our 'brew up king' a real salt of the earth person. Then in the first week a big lad called in while I was setting everything out, to see if there was any labouring jobs. Looking at his size, I reckoned I could use his strength, so Roy (I have forgotten his surname too) started, and was with me until we finished. The only days he had off, was when the local constabulary came looking for him. I never really got to the bottom of those visits from the law, but he did like his ale, so maybe it was something to do with that. Two thirds into the work, I had a visit from a person who arrived in a flash Volvo, looking for part time work for some of his mates. That person was 'Blaster Bates.' The name meant nothing to me at that time, but I was soon having plenty of laughs, especially his stories re the naming of 'Nicker Brook' at Oulton Park and 'The Shower of Shit' over in Shropshire, plus many more. Anyway, his assistance with part time labour came in handy in the last two weeks before opening with the painting. Apparently 'Blaster'* *was also a special constable at the time, and the labour he was providing were off duty policemen. Roy was not a 'Happy Chappie' to see these policemen working on his patch."*

Can you explain the science behind why the track was so incredibly fast? - *"There was no special science behind the track shape or size etc. We had an existing running track and banked cycle track with a post and top rail barrier at the top of the cycle track to work with. Maury Littlechild wanted as little as possible spent, so the dividing grassed area was dug out, the banking left and just 6 inches taken off the top of to fill in the middle area slightly. Then in with the shale top surface from Arbury Shale Quarries, near Coventry. As we did not have a tractor and grader blade until the week before opening, I found a local agricultural contractor with an old tow behind tractor grader, who got the levels of the shale surface just as I required. Then came the compaction, using the watering truck, which had just arrived with a few days to opening. I could not get the compaction right for our first meeting, but the next 10 days with continual watering, compacting and levelling, managed to get it perfect. If I did not get it right, the top surface would have washed down off the banking in heavy rain and would have been one hell of a job to put right again. During the season we did get flooded (drainage blocked), but it did no real damage. At the time of laying the track, everybody was giving me advice of what to do, all conflicting, so in the end I did what I had logically worked out, considering what the existing base was. The speed of the track came from three things; the five foot banking and overall width of track, a consistent track surface and the rider being game enough to race high going into the corner no more than 6 feet from the fence, at the apex this would allow you to race down off the banking into the straight. That's what made it fast."*

Why didn't you ride in Crewe's first league match at Reading on May 12? - *"Ten days out from opening, it was obvious with the amount of work still to do, it was best I stay at Crewe and work. The Reading meeting was only one week out from our opening."*

I suppose it was a proud moment for you on opening night v Rayleigh, especially when 6,000 turned up? - *"Opening night I had worked right up to 5.30pm to get everything finished. I was so mentally and physically buggered it meant nothing to me at that time. I was stuffed, all I wanted to do was sleep for a week. It really did not hit home what I had achieved until about the third meeting, and with the good attendances continuing it did make you feel proud."*

On that night, was it true that, apart from you and Geoff Curtis, no other Crewe rider had ridden on the track? - *"If I remember correctly, but I am not completely sure, understanding I was still trying to get the track completed and painting done and wanting nobody on the track, it is more than likely that no other rider other than myself doing 4 laps of the track for the Press (that photo shows that the fence was still not painted at that time) then Geoff doing 4 laps a day or two before opening to advise on bike gear ratios. I remember Geoff coming in and saying once we get the gear ratios sorted, it's going to be a quick one and bike tyres might be a problem flexing too much."*

What was Geoff Curtis like as a person and rider? - *"Geoff was a hell of a nice guy, with a good sense of humour. That first season we shared the same workshop area I had built and I learnt a lot more mechanically from him. He loved those 'clip on' handle bars of his, and as a rider he would have been at least as good as his Aussie mate Jim Airey, if not better. It was a shame, a real shame, his life was cut short. Someone I will always fondly remember."*

You were regarded as a rider who would stand no trouble, but what was it with you and your trips to Long Eaton in 1969, when you clash with two different home riders? - *"The first incident as I recall, originated at the start. Long Eaton riders trying to cheat, and holding the start up. Anyway the race eventually got underway, after a bad start from me. I got past a couple of riders and fell, the race stopped, I am excluded, when I felt that Roy Carter should have been excluded for holding up the start of the race. Seeing the referee was not going to do anything about the starts, I reckoned he was leaving it up to me to sort things. So I did. The second incident involved Gil Farmer, I think he was trying to pay me back for the Carter incident as he knocked me off. He got excluded, so when I got back to the pits, I had to remind him of his pedigree."*

Crewe had a very good first season, but what do you remember about the K.O. Cup Final with the Belle Vue Colts? - *"After the first leg at Crewe, which we won by only a few points, Geoff Curtis and I reckoned we could at least finish equal with Belle Vue at Hyde Road. We had plenty of motivation to try, but what we did not realise, was that it was the Colts' last meeting at Belle Vue, as the next season they were relocating to Rochdale. Dent Oliver was determined to leave the track on a high, and they thrashed us, but we did well to make the final."*

During that season you continue to work on the stadium. What other jobs did you do, and did you have anything to do with the floodlights? - *"During the season my job was mainly maintaining the stadium and track, something I took great pride in. I wanted the track to be constantly perfect with the grounds and facilities looking good. Instead of having a beer at the end of the meeting, I would get straight on to grading the track and with great help from Mick Smith, Geoff Adams and Alan Corbett, they would do a quick clean up and general check everywhere and lock the place up, then we would all sit down and have a cup of tea. By starting on the track straight after the meeting whilst still damp, it gave me a flying start to complete it the next day, ready for final raking and watering starting the night before our next meeting. My dedication to good track maintenance came about in 1968 when I remember visiting Sheffield with Bob Andrews and I was impressed with how Frank Varey looked after the track. Little did I know then, that my opportunity would come at Crewe to do the same as Frank and then try harder to do it better. The lights were done on the cheap (promoters don't like spending money). The track electrician at the time, Alan Corbett, was mainly responsible for the installation with myself putting in the poles and assisting generally."*

At the end of the season, you start construction of covered accommodation, but why didn't you take your planned holiday to New Zealand? - *"My intention was to return to NZ for a break in the sunshine, but a sequence of events unfolded just before the end of the season and the final decision was made, to stay for another winter. Firstly a blown motor that cost £65 to repair, then Maury was talking about the start of some cheap covered areas on part of the turn, Manchester rail line end, plus A.P.L. were looking at re-opening Newcastle and would require new safety fence, track drainage, reshaping of track, plus new track surface and rewiring for exclusion lights, red lights and starting gate. Then out of the blue, Geoff Curtis said he could not get enough money together for his fare home and asked if I could loan him the required amount. I had a return boat passage ticket to NZ, but I wanted to cash that in and put the extra money in and fly home, as four weeks on a boat trip home seemed a waste of time as flying took 3 days, but because of the engine blow ups I did not have enough, so I helped Geoff out instead to get home. I stayed on and started the covered area. It was a cheap job as they wanted. Maury supplied second hand scaffold tubing and iron sheeting. At the same time Ken Adams was running a training school, which I assisted in, looking after the track. Then on February 17, 1970, I went north to Newcastle to do the track redevelopment."*

After a good start to the 1970 season by yourself, an incident occurs against Ipswich concerning Paul O'Neil. What really happened that night, and was it just an isolated incident, or was it that you just didn't get on? - *"The 1970 season started okay, but from the back end of the '69 season Paul was borrowing a lot of bits and pieces, plus I was loaning him my bike on numerous occasions, which seemed to carry over into the beginning of the 1970 season. As Captain I felt obliged to assist. We did have a track spare, but it was not a good one. Also, during that time, I observed how Paul would spend his pay cheques on crates of beer, instead of his equipment, thus leaving it wanting at times, along with his constant pissing around at the starts, trying to cheat with 'flyers' it came to a head in the Rider of the Night Final. After that race I asked Paul for everything back from his bike that I had loaned him. He told me where to go, so I started to take my bits back and a scrap erupted. This had been brewing for a while as I, like Barry Briggs, deplored any cheating at the starts and had had enough of O'Neil's antics."*

What happened after the bust-up? - *"Maury spoke to me on the phone the next morning, giving me his decision. I was gutted. Besides being out of the team, I had to find new accommodation (bye bye caravan), plus he said that as I was contracted to him, he would not release me to sign for another team, but might in time loan me out. I also had to find a job plus my Mother and Aunt were due over in the middle of the year for a stay of two months. It really felt that his knife had been put in my back and twisted several times. I realised then that I was of no further use to Maury. I had completed Crewe and rebuilt Newcastle's track, plus I was only an average rider. Paul O'Neil no doubt was a better prospect for points and with me out, that would allow Maury to bring in a better rider to replace me. I was very lucky in other respects. Mick and Flo Smith, in due course, found me a flat above the chemist in Hightown. I got a job with Northern Ideal Homes, doing second fix building work near Chester. I got my bits and pieces back from O'Neil and I did not have to loan him my bike again. Between Mick and Flo, Geoff and Marion Adams, and Alan and May Corbett, they all made sure I did not starve, and my Mother and Aunt had a good stay in England."*

Before this, how had you got on with Maury? - *"Up until the O'Neil incident, I always felt Maury and I had a good understanding of one another, but on reflection cracks had started to occur after getting back from doing Newcastle, as I remember him saying, he wanted a real strong Crewe team for 1970 and 'I had better pull finger.'"*

You sign for Long Eaton soon after. What was it like to return to Earle Street as an away rider? - *"After the O'Neil incident, Maury left me on the sideline, but eventually loaned me out to the non-league team, Newtongrange in Scotland, run by Mrs Taylor from Berwick. Then ironically, he loaned me out to Long Eaton, which meant that I would now return to Crewe as an away rider. This did not bother me in any way, but I was saddened to see that the upkeep of the track was not good, that was the really sad part, but they are my values, not somebody else's."*

In 1971, you ride for Hull, then become team manager the following year. What satisfaction did you get from the league victory over Crewe in 1972? - *"The end of the 1970 season saw me return home, but before I left, Ian Thomas contacted me for my NZ phone numbers. During your winter, Ian had managed to get my full release from Maury, which left me free to sign for him. In March 1971, I arrived at Hull to complete the building of their track, fence and pit area, drainage etc. Aussie, Pete Baldock had started the job, but it took Tucker to get it finished on time, and I always like reminding the Aussies of that. Then in 1972, Ian offered me the job of manager. Leading up to the Crewe visit, they had won 9 straight league matches as I recall, but I figured they were beatable with a bit of luck, plus Maury had been crowing a bit loud for me, about how they would beat us. So I sat down 'with a cup of English tea' and devised a plan to create 3 drivey areas in the track, which only our riders knew about, thereby giving us an advantage for at least the first 4-6 heats before the Crewe riders sorted themselves out as to where these areas were. It worked and we won 41-36, which was very satisfying. That meeting only put a 'dent' in Crewe's championship bid, but proved they could be beaten."*

What happened during the rest of your speedway days in England? You helped build other tracks didn't you? - *"I really enjoyed the rest of my speedway days there and I met a lot of really nice helpful and genuine people. It was certainly a good time to be in England for speedway and I will always be thankful to Ian Thomas, a very fair man. The one thing I could never get used to, was your winters. I suppose if I'd had a nice warm inside job, then it would have been okay. But mine were spent outside doing speedway tracks, six in total (Crewe, Newcastle, Hull, Ellesmere Port, Barrow and Workington) with varying degrees of my input, from complete building, rebuilding and upgrading."*

At the end of 1973, you leave England to return to New Zealand. We believe a surprise farewell party was held for you in Crewe? - *"The surprise farewell parties in Crewe, yes there were two, one in 1970, which was held in the Hightown flat. I did not suspect a thing, the culprits for setting it up, the Smith, Adams and Corbett families with the assistance 'I think' of Geoff Ambrose and Alan Bridgett - a great night. Then in 1973, again I did not suspect a thing, but can't remember much about that one, except I had a sore head the next day. Others, no doubt, will be able to tell a few stories, that's for sure! Good people, good parties, good times and plenty of good memories, and I will leave it to you to work out if some of the stories of others are believable, I say that with a smile on my face!"*

What were your proudest achievements in speedway? - *"There were many, but the first was winning the 1968 'Stars of Tomorrow' championship at King's Lynn. Russell Osborne was the favourite and my mechanic and advisors for the day were Colin Pratt and Terry Betts, who travelled up along with Martin Rodgers, the journalist, all of which lived locally in Essex. Martin travelled back to Harlow with me, in my ex 'Tesco's' Morris 1000 van, a trip, he said, would never be forgotten, as I was racing Pratty and Bettsy back, in their Corsair. Martin's comments about that win 'it was a modest enough sort of win, but you would have thought it was the world championship.' At that time of my life, it was. Then there was the building and maintaining of Crewe, then Hull to that consistently high standard that I witnessed Frank Varey achieve in 1968. The next was managing the Young Australasian team to a series win against Young England, who had the strongest team on paper. During my speedway career, I have had plenty of great moments and achievements which I consider all equal because of the circumstances of how they came about."*

What were your favourite and worst tracks? - *"Crewe and Hull were the favourites, because I looked after them, with the worst ones being any wet, deep heavy tracks."*

Worst crash? - *"There were a few of them along the way, but the Crewe one, when Jack Millen speared me going into the last bend. I really highsided it, nothing was broken, but the body felt it for weeks and the bike was a right off."*
Best friend in speedway while you were riding at Crewe? - *"Not one, but several, especially the three families mentioned earlier."*
Which Crewe rider did you admire the most? - *"Geoff Curtis."*
Biggest influence on your speedway career? - *"When I started in NZ, it was Norm Ward and Maury Dunn before he was killed. Early days in England – Bob Andrews and Colin Pratt. After moving to North England – Guy Allott and Ivan Mauger. And managing – Ian Thomas."*
Who was your speedway idol? - *"Never really had one."*
Apart from the travelling, what was the worst thing about being a speedway rider? - *"The travel in England was never a problem. Remember NZ is a very young country, England has all the history and for a young colonial it was great to go and visit and see all those different places. There was no 'worse things' about being a rider, one chose to be in the sport, for the love of it, for better or worse. I was just an average rider, who had a few good meetings along the way. I knew I could do better, but the wet, deep and inconsistent tracks really turned me off."*
Did you have any fierce rivals on the track while at Crewe and afterwards? - *"No fierce rivals on the track, just riders who pissed me off big time, with frustrating cheating antics at the start line, trying to get rollers or flyers and delaying the start."*
In your opinion, who was the best rider you ever rode against? - *"Ivan Mauger on NZ tracks in the 70's."*
Do you still attend speedway or watch is on TV? - *"Very, very little."*
What do you do now and what hobbies do you have? - *"I run my own business, 'Building and Property Management Services Ltd' specialising in Project Management and Clerk of Works, and hobbies – developing my farm, photography and life member of Lopdell Gallery. Community service – and have been a Justice of the Peace for 28 years, a Marriage Celebrant and Patron of the Celebrants Guild, all of which keeps one somewhat busy."*
Finally, can you sum up in a few words your time at Crewe? - *"Generally a great time. Crewe and a lot of the Crewe people will always hold a special place in my thoughts. Having some nice mementoes about, as a reminder, including a Rolls Royce Silver Lady and Bentley badge, given to me after a factory visit in 1969. It was a real special time in a young colonial's life and I will always be grateful to the people of Crewe who welcomed my Uncle Harry (in 1969) and my Mother and Aunty Nel (in 1970) when they came over. You really made their stay, helping to give them such a wonderful time. Everybody was so friendly, even stopping them in the street and market to say hello. Thank you again.....but this time from an 'ageing colonial!'"*

(Colin Tucker.)

'When a friend suggested I go to Crewe Speedway in 1970, my initial reaction was no way, as I had already conjured up in my mind, motorbikes equal Hells Angels and Hells Angels equals trouble! Fortunately he persuaded me to give it a try and I was hooked from that moment on. "The Cats Choir" was formed in the heady days of the 1972 season and consisted of, in no particular order, myself, Dave Whalley, Linda Whalley, Sandra Whalley, Nick Hatton, Danny Brotherton, Karl Griffin, Brian Lofkin, Laury Allcock, Dave Smith, Bill and George Bennett (with the bells), not forgetting the one and only Alan "Fluff" Bebbington, and a special mention to the late members Mark McCormick and Kevin Hancock. If I've missed anybody out, or mis-spelt any names, I can only apologise, as it's been a while you can appreciate. We would always try to go everywhere in 1972 to support the Kings and highlights were many. I recall we took loads of coaches to Scunthorpe for the K.O. Cup match, winning there 59-19 and repeating the dose at home the next day was unbelievable. The weekend trip to Canterbury and Eastbourne was great and as I recall at Canterbury I asked a local fan before Heat 1 "What's the track record mate?" to which he replied "Don't you mean what is the track record?" "No" I said, "Phil Crump is going to break it in Heat 1" and sure enough so he did. Oh happy days! In 1974 local rivals Stoke came a visiting to Earle Street, so to give them a good welcome I had handed the announcer some records to play at certain times of the evening. Firstly for Mike Broadbanks he played "Grandad" by Clive Dunn, "What's New Pussycat" for Geoff Pusey and for the first Stoke rider to have an engine failure "Chitty Chitty Bang Bang." Those times I had supporting

Crewe Kings were the best and it broke my heart in 1975 when it all came to an end. Nowadays I go to Stoke when I can and always cheer on the away side. I could never support any other speedway team like I supported the Kings.'

(Alan Critchley.)

'One of the strangest memories I have of Crewe Speedway happened outside the stadium. It was one night towards the end, of what turned out to be the final season of racing at Earle Street. I was walking towards the turnstiles, and as I approached, there were two small queues forming and it was after start time. What happened next was quite embarrassing. A chap I was walking with pulled at my sleeve and said: "This way will be quicker." We entered into what must have been Rainbow Street, which was made up mainly of builder's yards, and we entered the first premises. Here was a nice caravan, in front of which was a lady sitting at a card table. She requested an amount of money, which was about 50% of the going rate, and when it was paid, a young lad pulled at one of the corrugated iron sheets that made up the fence. The sheet was held only by a large nail at the top centre and he held open the sheet until we climbed through. How long the "additional turnstile" had been in operation I have no idea. I was quite amazed at such an enterprise and at the end of the season I informed promoter Violet Littlechild of the scam, as I was very concerned about the future of the sport in Crewe. However, it didn't matter as Crewe Speedway had ridden their last race, and the enterprising lady at the card table had found herself on the dole!'

(Brian Edge.)

'My first memory of attending the speedway at Crewe was as a nine-year-old one cold and rainy evening in 1970. I went along with my brother and a neighbour, and when I arrived at the stadium I looked for the best place to stand. "Why don't you stand on the first corner?" my brother said: "You'll see just how fast the riders are going if you stand there." So about a minute before the first heat I took up my position, half wondering why I was the only one standing in what I thought was the prime position. I soon found out why, when the riders sped past me and I was showered from head to foot in wet sticky red shale. I spent all next day at school picking the stuff out of my hair! My other outstanding memory of Earle Street was making the mistake one meeting of catching the coin thrown into the crowd following the toss for gate positions. Seconds after making the catch, I disappeared under a pile of eager young lads also keen to claim the 50p prize. I emerged from the scrummage with a split lip, a torn shirt, but with the prized coin tucked safely in my back pocket.'

(Mark Potts.)

Dai Evans.

Full name? – *"David Evans. When I signed for Wolves there were so many Dave's at the club, they re-christened me Dai."*
Where were you born? – *"Morville, Shropshire."*
What jobs did you do before entering into speedway? – *"I had a lot to do with cattle, before entering the Army."*
How did you get into the world of speedway? – *"I used to pushbike to Wolverhampton to watch the Wasps and also Perry Barr to see Birmingham and thought I wouldn't mind having a go at that."*
Did you base your style of riding on anyone in particular? – *"Yes, the Aussie Graham Warren."*
Who did you ride for before arriving at Earle Street? – *"Wolves (twice), Cradley, West Ham, Newport, Crayford and Nelson."*
Is it true that if you had known that Nelson were moving to Bradford, you wouldn't have come to Crewe? – *"Yes that's true, as I used to love riding at Odsal and did well there during my visits to the track."*
Can you remember signing for Crewe? – *"I didn't actually sign a contract. I just shook hands with Maury Littlechild. I knew Maury quite well and that was good enough for me."*
Why did Crewe have such a poor away record during your first two years at the club? – *"No excuses really, but the standard of the tracks we rode on in 1970 and 1971 were very poor, apart from Peterborough and Ipswich. Also many of the Crewe riders rode away as though they were riding at Earle Street, so didn't adapt to the away circuits."*

In 1972 you were made skipper. What was your main role as captain? – *"Motivating the team and looking after the younger members, second-halfers and juniors."*

At the start of 1972, the Kings lose three out of their first four league matches. At this time did you still think that the team was good enough for honours? – *"Yes definitely. With Crumpie and Jacko in the team you were always going to go close."*

When Maury dies half way through the season, did this inspire the team to go on and win the double? – *"No, not really. We had already jelled as a team before Maury passed away."*

Did you attend Maury's funeral? – *"No. I received a bad injury a few days before and couldn't travel. To be honest all the lads wanted to go and act as bearers, but they had to ride at Hull on the same day."*

During 1972, you score the most bonus points in the league and cup, but did you consciously go out to team ride? – *"Always team rode. My job was to protect my team man."*

How did the team celebrate after winning the league? – *"With a good drink and a Chinese!"*

Which Crewe rider did you most admire? – *"Had to be Crumpie. He should have been World Champion."*

What was your relationship like with Jack Millen? – *"He was a great showman and crowd-puller, and on the track was quite fearless. I got on fine with Jack."*

Apart from travelling, what was the worst part of being a speedway rider? – *"Bad refereeing decisions."*

Talking about long away trips. Which one stands out as the worst for you while at Crewe? – *"Coming home from Ipswich after the second leg of the K.O. Cup final. We were on a train with the supporters, but I was gutted because we had been well-beaten."*

Who was the biggest influence in your career? – *"My brother-in-law Les Moore, who for a time was team manager at Crewe."*

Did you have a nickname? – *"Yes it was 'Never Say Dai,' which I attained during my time at Crayford."*

Who were your best friends in speedway while you were riding? – *"Ivor Hughes, Ken McKinlay and Sverre Harrfeldt."*

Did have any lucky charms while riding? – *"I wore a St. Christopher on a silk scarf which my wife Trish gave me. I was mortified one time when I was taken to hospital after a spill, to find the doctor cutting off my scarf!"*

Who were the best riders you rode against? – *"Ivan Mauger and Barry Briggs."*

Favourite and worst tracks? – *"I liked Edinburgh, Berwick, Peterborough and of course Bradford. The worst was my old home track at West Ham."*

Best moment in speedway? – *"In 1971 I travelled with Crumpie to the star-studded Bradford Open at Odsal, acting as his mechanic. When I arrived they were a rider down, so I agreed to fill in – and won it!"*

Strengths and weaknesses? – *"I was a fair team rider and a good motivator. Gating was one of my weaknesses."*

Before the first home match of 1973 you retired. Why? – *"I was disillusioned with the sport and I didn't like the way Crewe were heading."*

Any speedway regrets? – *"Yes, I suppose retiring maybe a season or two too early."*

You didn't start a family until you retired from speedway. Why was that? – *"One of my best friends, Ivor Hughes, was killed while racing in 1966, so I vowed not to have children until I retired. We later had two, Gaynor and Dan."*

What hobbies do you have now? – *"I love gardening, travelling and reading."*

Do you still watch speedway? – *"Only on the television now. I've been to Cardiff to watch the British Grand Prix for the last few years, but it's now all too expensive, especially the hotel prices."*

What do you think of modern-day speedway? – *"I'm glad to see a Third Division has been put into practice. Much needed for the younger riders."*

Finally Dai, what are your memories of your time at Crewe? – *"Great days, loved every minute. Enjoyed racing the Crewe bowl, and got on well with nearly everybody involved in the Kings, especially those marvellous supporters."*

(Dai Evans.)

'As a Sunderland Speedway supporter, it has been well documented that I consider the "Stars" skipper Russ Dent to be "Mr Sunderland Speedway," for all he achieved over the four seasons in the early 1970's. However, the rider who had the most impact for Sunderland was without doubt Jack Millen. Jack started his speedway career in Britain in 1971, by briefly riding for the newly reformed Sunderland Stars, in their first two away fixtures, scoring an unremarkable zero and five points. Jack Millen swiftly moved on to ride for the Crewe Kings, and there the legend began to take shape. 1972 saw Jack return to ride for Sunderland, teaming up with fellow Kiwi Graeme Smith. They bolstered the hard pressed and over worked Russ Dent and George Barclay, who between them had kept the Stars outfit afloat in 71, without them the Stars would have been sunk without trace! Jack had instant impact, no longer were Sunderland the whipping boys of speedway. With Jack in the team we feared nobody, we always had hope, he provided the wow factor……and boy did he wow the home fans. If he stayed on board his machine, he was capable of scoring a maximum at home or away. The trouble with Jack was that he took risks, and they didn't always pay off, hence his performances were punctuated with injuries. Not that injuries kept him out of the saddle for very long, he was frequently seen with his arm or leg in plaster, ribs strapped up, you name it, he had broken it. It was at Sunderland that "Crazy Jack" had his best seasons, topping the averages in 1972 and 1973. And it was at Sunderland that the legend of "Crazy Jack," or "Millen the Villain" really took off. When he was on the rampage...look out... as the sparks would fly, the atmosphere was electric everywhere he rode. Jeers didn't bother him, "give the fans something to remember" Jack would say, "they'll come back next time I'm in town." Ron Wilson the promoter of North East rivals the Teesside Tigers, used to say that Jack Millen put a good 500 on the gate each time he rode there. He would book him for any possible open meetings (helped by the bitter feud between Jack and Teesside's Frankie Auffrett), that always added spice to the proceedings. Jack Millen was a showman, an entertainer, a hellraiser and above all a real character, sadly missing in speedway today. It was tragic to have him taken away from us in 1978, killed in a blazing car crash ……so sad, so very sad. But Jack left us with so many memories, and the fans still remember him, and still say "Ah, Jack Millen, now there was a character."'

(Bob Ferry.)

'My memory of my time at Crewe Kings involved a match at the end of the 1969 season against Long Eaton. The match started with good weather, when suddenly a thick mist started to drift across the stadium from the town end. After some discussion, the referee decided to send one rider around the track, and decided that if he could see him on the back straight and on the third bend, then the match could carry on. The rider in question was Ian Bottomley, and it was quite strange, as you could quite clearly hear him as he roared round the track, but only saw him when he appeared out of the mist. The referee had no other choice but to abandon the meeting, as it was too dangerous to continue.'

(Tom Jones.)

'I was fortunate to be involved in the speedway at Earle Street from the very beginning. I was a train driver, but during my time off I helped Colin Tucker with the construction of the track and stadium, employed mainly as a painter. After about three or four meetings I was offered a part-time role on the tractor, grading the track between heats. Maurice Littlechild paid me the princely sum of £2 a week for my efforts! In 1970, Maury asked me if I was interested in becoming an ACU official, so I took up the post of machine examiner, which involved inspecting every machine at the meeting. I had to check the bike all over, which included the condition of the foot rest, operation of the throttle, inspection of the ball end on the clutch handle and for some reason make sure that the rider's name was on the rear mudguard. I also used to take the readings off the turnstiles and give the figures to Colin Tucker, who would then telephone the figure to the Evening Sentinel, after Maury (like most promoters of the day) had knocked a few hundred off the figure! During the early days, the Kings regularly rode in front of 5,000 plus crowds, which were around three times the number at Gresty Road to watch the football. In 1974, I took somewhat of a backstep, after my stepson Mick Mellor became interested in the

sport and was attending Charlie Scarbrough's training school. He had originally bought Gary Moore's bike after being offered Phil Crump's old machine. "Don't buy that" some of the Crewe lads told him: "It's been run on nitro and had the flywheels blown apart!" During this time I became involved in making speedway mudguards with a talented chap called Terry Lowe. We made them for all the stars including Ole Olsen, Ivan Mauger and Peter Collins. My one funny memory that springs to mind was when we all went to Wembley to watch the 1969 World Final. All the lads and riders met in a multi-storey car park in London for a few tinnies and then we went into the stadium. I remember looking through my binoculars at the dignitaries on the hallowed Wembley turf - and spotted a certain Mr. Tucker, who had got on the centre green courtesy of a pass, two years out of date! After the meeting, Crewe were in action at Doncaster the next day, so we travelled through the night to reach the stadium, where we grabbed about four hours sleep on the car park. Unfortunately the match was rained off, so after a few more beers in the Doncaster bar, we headed home - convoy style - which was a good job, as Tucker's Morris van's brakes failed (again!) and the only way he could stop was by barging up the back end of Barry Meeks' Hillman!!!'

(Mike Smith.)

'I had a great time at Crewe. The town is always on my mind and the people there were fantastic. I could never thank them enough for the reception they gave me. I had many funny times while there, but as you could imagine, most of them would be unprintable, because at the time, my cohorts were Ian Bottomley and Dave Parry - enough said! I always loved the big track at Crewe. I liked the higher speeds, and you could ride the fence if you wanted (same as Sydney Showground) and was a real buzz. One time we got a few looks was when I was out with a broken ankle and Parry was out after a shoulder operation. We went to a meeting in my van and stopped at a transport cafe beside a tourist bus. We got a few funny looks with myself driving with a leg in plaster and Dave's arm in a sling. During the trip, Dave had been operating the clutch for me! Too many memories of the Borough Arms and the Kings Arms. Like I said, it was a great time.'

(Warren Hawkins.)

'I had just left school and lived in Gresty Terrace just over the bridge from the Earle Street Sports Ground. I had always watched the cricket on the ground as a small boy. My mum had taken me to watch speedway at Belle Vue for many years prior to starting at Crewe, so I knew what to expect when Maury Littlechild first arrived on the scene. I first met Colin Tucker in the local chip shop and we got talking about what was going to happen. He asked me if I would like to work with him, no money, just hard work, loads of booze and fags as well as some extras! The first load of sleepers arrived and under Colin's instruction his team of labourers began work. At the end of each day we would retire to his caravan and smoke and drink. At this time Colin would tell so many stories of his exploits, the vast majority of these are un-printable. Then one night about midnight Dermot challenged Colin to a race around the track. So Colin and Dermot lined up against me and John with Angie as Starting Marshal. She dropped something, I am not sure what, but it was no flag and the race began. Four push bikes lurched forward, Colin barged me off on bend two with his right elbow, he then knocked Dermot off half way down the back straight with his foot, John fell off by himself laughing after Dermot was bitten by a dog owned by Colin I think, and Colin finished the race alone very cream crackered. Great fun! In the first season I was a track raker and rode occasionally on Col's bike after the meeting had finished. I travelled to many of the meetings with Colin and on occasions with the late Geoff Curtis. Worst first season moment was losing by two points at Romford, when the meeting was there to be won; best was winning at King's Lynn and the night out in Spalding afterwards. Strangest was the fog against Long Eaton, it was impossible to see the back straight. I also remember when Phil Crump first arrived at Earle Street. He was so small he could not jump over the safety fence. So he placed his helmet on the track and stood on it to climb over. Shame though he could not reach far enough over to retrieve it and had to walk around to get it back, much to the great amusement of all watching. He will kill me for that one.'

(Jeff Lukomiak.)

Phil Crump.

Full Name? – *"Philip John Crump."*
When and where were you born? – *"I was born on February 9, 1952, at Red Cliffs, which is about ten miles south of Mildura."*
First job? – *"I was a welding apprentice in Red Cliffs."*
How did you get into speedway? – *"I used to ride around the bush on an old motorbike. Then after I bought a motocross bike, I decided to also have a go on the speedway track at Mildura. Funnily enough, Phil Sedgman, who borrowed me a bike that day, still has it, and it now looks as though his two grandsons, Ryan and Justin, will be riding at Swindon in 2009."*
Did you style your riding on anyone in particular during those early days? – *"No not really. I remember when the English test team arrived at Mildura and watching Nigel Boocock, but I didn't base my riding style on anyone in particular."*
Had you ridden any other tracks in Australia before coming to England? – *"No, nowhere else. Mildura was tiny compared to Earle Street."*
So how did you come about riding for the Kings? – *"I'd only been riding speedway for about four months and I didn't even know about speedway in England. Then out of the blue Neil Street rang me up on the Tuesday night and asked if I wanted to go to England to ride. Before I knew it my parents had bought me a ticket and I was on a plane to England with just a bag and a set of handlebars. I arrived in England on the Sunday. Maury Littlechild and his wife picked me up at the airport and I stayed the night with them. Next day we went to the track at Crewe and I rode the track spare in a race before the match with Long Eaton in the hope of winning a place in the team. I lost that one, but won the one during the second half, which gained me a place in the team at Hull on the Wednesday. Dai took me to Briggo's at Southampton to pick up my bike which had been bought for me by Maury."*
Any recollections of your first ride at Hull. You won your first race didn't you? – *"Did I? Can't remember much about that night, but I do remember riding at Long Eaton on the Thursday because I hit the bloody fence and hurt myself. I nearly knocked myself out after I'd tangled with Steve Bass."*
Where did you lodge that first season? – *"I lodged with Dai and his wife Trisha. Dai took me everywhere that season. Dai and Trish were like my parents and really looked after me. It had all happened so quick coming to England and at first it was a bit of a culture shock."*
How long does it take you to tame the Crewe track and how did you ride it? – *"Crewe was massive compared to Mildura, but to most Aussies, Crewe was a similar track to those back in Australia. It was exactly opposite to what I was used to riding. It took me a little while to learn how to ride the track as it was such a different place to Mildura, which was a bit like Wimbledon really. As for riding at Earle Street, I tried to get ahead for the first bend, then clip the first corner before going up to the fence and then come back down the banking to clip the inside of the next bend, which was very similar to how Jacko rode the track. The only time you had to change your riding style was when you had Jack Millen riding against you!"*
Talking of Jack Millen, how did you get on with him? – *"I had no problems with Jack. He was certainly a different sort of character though."*
You are now established after your first season, but was there any track you disliked more than any other? – *"No, I liked all the tracks to be honest. When I went into the First Division with Newport and Exeter people used to hate those places, but I never disliked anywhere really. Streety always said to me 'You're not riding the track you're riding a bike. If you ride the bike properly you'll go fast so don't worry about the track.'"*
When riding for Crewe, did you receive any stick from away fans? – *"No not that I can remember. When we were winning away all the time in 1972, I'm sure we would have been given a hard time sometimes, but there wasn't an incident that sticks out while we rode away."*
Strength and weaknesses during your time at Crewe? – *"I'm sure when I first started I had plenty of weaknesses, but my strength was I could adapt to any track fairly quickly. That's where the Australians even now struggle a bit because the track sizes and conditions are so different to the ones back in Australia. But to be honest, I didn't have a problem with the different tracks. The only places I really struggled during my career were the tracks that were really slick."*

Did you have a nickname? – *"I suppose it was just 'Crumpie.'"*
During your spell at Crewe, was there one rider you admired most at Earle Street and one you wanted to be as good as? – *"Probably Jacko really at Crewe and everybody wanted to be as good as Ivan Mauger. Since I've finished riding, I have a house on the Gold Coast and have become very good friends with Ivan as we live only a few miles apart."*
At the start of 1972 you recommend Garry Flood to Maurice Littlechild. How did you know him? – *"Garry was a Melbourne lad and his father and Neil Street grew up together and I got to know Garry through Neil. He was a very good motorbike rider. In 1971 he was over in England riding motocross for Bultaco and when he came back in 1972 he decided he wanted a go at speedway."*
When Garry comes over you both lodge in Crewe. Can you remember where? – *"We stayed in Henry Street, but I can't remember the number, although I do know it was with Bill and Shirley Warrender."*
Where did you go socialising in the town? – *"I very rarely ever went out. I was riding that many meetings during the 1972 season, I had little time to go out and socialise. I could count on one hand I reckon the times when we went out around the town."*
Following your success in 1972, did you realise that Division I was the place to be, especially as you had ridden well for King's Lynn in the same season? – *"Coming back again to Neil Street. He told me to have two seasons riding in Division II to gain experience and see how things turned out. A lot of people thought I was going to go to the first division in '72, but it was always my intentions to stay in Division II for two years."*
What was your relationship like with Maury Littlechild and was it a shock when he passed away? – *"Maury was a fine man. I didn't know he was as sick as he really was as he always did things at a million miles an hour."*
You and John Jackson were Crewe's two big guns in 1972. Was there any rivalry between the pair of you? – *"Not on my part no. I know John wanted to be No.1 and his performances certainly kept me from easing up."*
Were you aware of the resentment about the track at Earle Street among other team managers and promoters? – *"Dave Lanning was one bloke I never got on with and he was constantly having a go about the Earle Street track. I remember one story when we went to Eastbourne on a bus and Jack Millen grabbed Lanning around the throat after he had been moaning about something. I don't think Dave Lanning ever wrote anything about me, good or bad, in the Speedway Star in all the time I rode, so I always put it down to when Jack grabbed him."*
In 1972 you help win the league, the cup and you win the Division II Riders Championship. Which one meant the most to you? – *"None really. I just liked to ride my motorbike and win as many races as possible. I never thought much about winning cups or titles really. That, you could say, was one of my downfalls, as I went through my career and never really prioritised my races, especially when I was riding in the World Championships. To me it was just another ride."*
Who were your fiercest rivals while in Division II? – *"Doug Wyer and Reg Wilson. Even though Peter Collins and John Louis were big rivals on the track, it was Doug Wyer for some bloody reason, who always had a real go at me."*
Who were your friends during your time at Earle Street? – *"Obviously Garry Flood and Dai. Dai was like a father-figure to me and if it hadn't have been for Dai during the first few months I was here, it would have been so much harder and I might have gone home, as I was fairly homesick at first."*
If the Kings had gained Division I status for the 1973 season, would you have stayed, or was your heart set on a move to King's Lynn? – *"No, I would have stayed. I liked the place, so would have stayed at Crewe. All of a sudden Crewe felt like home to me."*
At the start of the1973 season you go home after being ruled out due to your wrist injury. Did Garry Flood come home with you? – *"No. I didn't know for a long time that Garry had left Crewe. He was a bloody good speedway rider, but only rode for a year and then returned to Australia and that was it. He never rode in it again. He came back to England as he was good with engines, especially two-strokes. Garry prepared a bike for some bloke that won at Brands Hatch, who ended up beating the likes of Sheen and Kenny Roberts. Bob Graves, who owned the Ford Cosworth factory, offered him a job after that and Garry built a twin-cylinder road racing*

motorbike and they went to Daytona in America where they used to have the 'Battle of the Twins.' And they won this race with Garry's bike. Agostini, who was running this Yamaha road race team, wanted Garry to do all the engine stuff for him, but Garry wasn't that bothered about anything like that and just went back to Australia working in his father's motorbike shop. He now helps run an ultra lights shop, importing them. I speak to him a couple of times a year, but I haven't seen him for two or three years. He was bloody good with engines and could have maybe been boss of a Ferrari team or something as big. He just didn't push himself."

You return to Crewe with Newport in 1975. How did you feel to be back? – *"It was very special. I was probably more wound up for that meeting than any other as I didn't want to come back and not ride well."*

Which title give you the most satisfaction during your career? – *"Winning the Australian Championship at Mildura in 1979. As you can imagine, there was a lot of pressure for me to do well on my old track. My first Australian Championship at Sydney in 1975 was also special as this was the first time I had ridden my new 4-valve bike."*

Who were the best riders you ever rode against? – *"Ivan Mauger was the best I ever rode against. He was a real professional. He was a bit ahead of his time. Peter Collins, Malcolm Simmons and John Boulger were also fantastic riders."*

In your prime Phil, who would have won between you and your son Jason? – *"He's a better rider than I ever was, but I have to say that I've only raced him twice and beat him on both occasions, although he had only just started in speedway. It was in a long track meeting at Mildura."*

What do you do now? – *"I have a workshop where I service speedway engines in Milton Keynes. I do Jason's engines, as well as many other riders, including those at Lakeside. Grand Prix weeks are just crazy and I'm so busy."*

Do you still have your old Kings race jackets? – *"Yes I do. They're in the house on the Gold Coast. After I left Crewe, I sometimes used to ride in them while in Australia."*

In a few words, can you sum up your time at Crewe? – *"It gave me the best footing possible to start my speedway career and there were so many good and helpful people. It was a great grounding for me. I could have gone somewhere else, but it wouldn't have been as good as it was at Crewe. That's why Neil wanted me to go to Crewe with Maury, as he knew I would be well looked after."*

(Phil Crump.)

'I have racked my brains to come up with some memories of my time as colour marshal at Crewe Speedway - so here I go. First and foremost I remain a speedway fan, and I still hanker for the smell, noise and atmosphere that Monday night at Crewe Speedway produced. Who could not be excited by the "Kings" in full flight. When I watch Sky Sports and the wonderful camera work that gives you an "almost there" view, how I wish this could have been captured at Earle Street. So many riders gave us cause to cheer and gasp at their courage and skills; the likes of John Jackson hugging the inside line and Barry Meeks setting the world speed record for speedway. I dont know if this is still a record, never the less we have had the pleasure to witness some of the most exciting speedway racing ever at Crewe. I got to know most of the riders through being colour marshal and would socialise with them after the race meeting. At times being colour marshal was not an easy job. What I had to do was to ensure that riders wore the correct helmet colour for each race. I would have to know any changes, rider replacements, tactical changes, and any other reason to issue the right colour, as we physically only had two of each. I had to run around after each race and ask the riders for the helmet colour back; not so bad if they won, but you were not welcome if they had not. The last thing they wanted is you making a request for the helmet colour back when they were in the middle of trying to work out why they could not keep up with Phil Crump. As you can imagine, I retrieved these with less than helpful requests as to where I should stick them! I shake my head in wonder when I watch the modern riders with their array of four different coloured helmets; no colour marshal to harass them. In addition to issuing helmet colours, I was in charge of the "device" that gave the riders their gate positions. In the individual event after the main meeting the "device" consisted of four ping pong balls with a number painted on each one; 1,2,3,4 (I did these myself), and a large blue cloth bag once used to hold small bags of money for the bank. Once the balls were placed in the bag I gave it a shake and the riders would pick one out giving them their gate number. Sounds simple enough, until the

riders, one at a time, would whisper to me their preferred gate position. I remember once Taffy Owen complaining that this method always seemed to benefit the Crewe riders. I dont know what he meant! One of my endearing and lasting memories at Crewe was not a racing one, but one involving my best friend Derek Riches, who at one stage had Warren Hawkins staying with him. Derek was on the pit gate and car park, and once the meeting started, he would come in and watch the racing. He would stand on the bank by the side of the pits and track gate at the railway end. As used to happen after each race and before the track announcer gave information for the next race, music would blare out at high volume. Often people would join in, singing out loud. Well this particular time, Gary Glitter's "Do You Want To Be In My Gang" was being played. The chorus went something like "Come on come on, Come on come on." Derek was well into the chorus, when all of a sudden the music stopped with ear shattering silence, leaving him on his own singing at the top of his voice and still doing the actions, which was to thrust your fist in the air at each "Come on." He was completely isolated and on his own. If only I had recorded that.'

(Pete Muirhead.)

'My first impressions were of a big, fast, almost circular bowl, quite different to any other track I had visited. It had to be that shape as it was built around a cricket field. The floodlighting was not too good so riders on the opposite straight could seem like silhouettes on a dark night. There were usually good, solid teams with often one rider who could dominate the opposition. John Jackson at full speed round the boards was a sight to be seen, Phil Crump developed rapidly from an unknown Australian junior to a world class star. Dave Morton also came up from the second half to be an international class rider. Graham Drury went well for the Kings after his exchange for Jacko and there were lots of other memorable names. A good night's entertainment was often rounded off with a pint and a quick game of dominoes in the nearby pub, also named the Kings, where spectators and even the occasional riders gathered to chat over the evening's events. In the early seventies I had a contract to make tape recorded commentaries of the racing which were then sold in the track shop. The well respected promoter, Len Silver, believed that if you were visible to the public you were part of the show, so behind the track staff and the Red Cross team, the reporters from local radio and papers and me with my tape recorder had to march smartly out of the pits and wheel off to our positions on the centre green. As I was constantly turning to follow the racing it was easy to forget just where I was on a dark night. One night I slowly realised that angry shouts from the crowd were aimed at me as I had committed the dreadful sin of standing on the cricket club's carefully prepared wicket. If I had not quickly moved away I think some irate spectators would have climbed the fence and lynched me on the spot! The track was once visited by the Czech speedway rider and then current ice racing World Champion Milan Spinka. I tried to get an interview with him but found he spoke no English nor I any Czech so the whole conversation was done in German with me translating as we went along. I'm not sure if that bit of tape was ever published! Out of curiosity, I once went to one of the unlicensed meetings run by Charlie Scarbrough. About eighty spectators were present, mostly, I think, related to the riders. The PA system broke down so the tractor carried round a board with the result of each race chalked on it. No doctor or first aider was on hand so when one rider fell heavily there was a slight panic. He slid into the fence and dislodged a board which fell onto the poor man as he lay there. The track looked rough and a comment from a rider was "bloody great boulders coming up at you!" A sad end to a great place of entertainment. Earle Street stadium was never luxurious for riders or spectators but I fondly remember a good atmosphere, attractive teams, junior hopefuls developing from second half to stardom and lots of spectacular racing on an unusual but always exciting track.'

(Phil Hagerty.)

'Here are a few memories from my days at Crewe Speedway. It all began in 1975 when Graham Drury came to one of our practice days after the season had finished and saw myself and Brian Bagshaw riding and wanted to sign us up for next season's second halfs. Unfortunately next season never came. Hence came Charlie Scarborough to the rescue, to run the Locos Training Schools. Charlie was a character and always had ideas to attract people to come. We got on like a house on fire and he became a dear friend. I remember he got the famous wrestler

Count Bartelli to present the trophies one meeting. We ran an evening meeting once only for fog to descend over the stadium. You couldn't see from one bend to the other, so Charlie's idea was to build a fire on the centre green to clear the fog. Only thing it did though was fill the stadium with thick black smoke! Then there was the time an all girl motorcycle stunt team were performing in the town and Charlie got them to perform at the stadium with the local press and media there. We took them round on the back of our bikes, and let them have a go themselves. Then we did some demo races - anything to attract publicity. We had a meeting at Coatbridge one evening and it rained all day and night. We rode in atrocious conditions but the Scottish fans loved it. Whilst we were getting changed, they sent us a crate of beer, and as the track operated at a football stadium, they had big communal baths into which some of us dived still in our leathers, just to get the mud off. Not hard to forget the rematch a week later, as it was my wedding day. True to form, I arrived at the registry office with bike on the back of the car, did the deed, had some photos taken then made my apologies and left for the meeting, leaving the guests to make their way to the reception. Needless to say that marriage didn't last. Another day Eric Boocock came looking for two riders for second halfs at Belle Vue's Hyde Road, and picked me and a guy called Pete Wilson. I, after a coming together off the start line with Roger Lambert, ended up being throw off the bike and dragged to the first bend, ending my night. As for Pete, he made the final finished third and won ten quid which was a lot in those days. The SCB blacklisted the Earle Street track as it wasn't licensed and threatened to ban riders if they rode there, but to my knowledge no one ever was. Finally, the Crewe Stock Car promoter called me into his office and told me he was going to build a new speedway team and enter the league, and wanted me as captain. When I asked him where Charlie fitted in he said he didn't, so my reply was then neither do I. As it was it never happened anyway.'

(Steve Cook.)

'One of the memories I have of speedway at Crewe happened when I was doing odd jobs there during the school holidays. One day out of the blue, two people turned up with a bike in the back of a van. The elder of the pair I was told was a former rider, and I believe his name was Brian Brett. The young lad with him was a novice rider and they asked if the lad could have a few laps around the track. Nobody seemed to have a problem with this, so the young lad set off. He seemed to be doing alright, but on his return to the pits, his mentor told him that the only way to ride Earle Street was flat out and around the boards. So the youngster went out again, but failed to impress Mr. Brett, who then decided to show him how it should be done. He borrowed a helmet, gloves and boots, but did not see any need for leathers, and set off in his shirt and trousers that he had arrived in. He certainly knew his way around the vast Crewe bowl, and with lots of throttle, he sped past with shirt and trousers flapping away. I suppose he was tempting fate, and on his third lap, the bike slid from under him on the pits bend and he went down with a mighty crash. Everybody present rushed up to him, but he was already on his feet. His trousers on the left side were nearly non-existent and there was no elbow in his shirt. It was the worst case of gravel rash I had ever seen and his leg and arms were streaked with blood. I do not know what hurt more, his cuts and bruises or his pride, but the informal practice session ended and the bike was quickly packed away.'

(Danny Brotherton.)

'I came to Crewe for the 1969 season on loan from Oxford. I was living near Watford at the time and used to stop off at Dave Parry's house at Cheslyn Hay to have a cup of tea, before we would set out in convoy to Crewe, with me in my Mk.III Zephyr and Dave in his Mk.III Zodiac. I remember the first meeting at Crewe against Rayleigh on May 19, 1969. The crowd was reported as 6,000, but I know for a fact that they could not handle the number of people at the turnstiles, so the riders' wives helped out by taking the money and throwing it in plastic buckets. On July 10, we rode at Romford and Ian Bottomley was flying that night. He had won his first three rides and was coming out for his last, when he decided to do a practice start along the back straight. He ended up flipping his bike, so we had to get it back to the pits to straighten the handlebars etc. We got him out before the two minutes time allowance and he won to complete his maximum, but unknown to us at the time, he had broken his wrist in the fall! At Nelson on August 23, I was on the brand new ESO track spare having broken the footrest on my JAP, and put it straight through the fence! Another moment I recall was at

Doncaster later in the season. Dave and his wife Gail stayed at my place on the Saturday and we set off Sunday morning, as Doncaster raced in the afternoon. When we got there the meeting had been rained off, and as we were at Crewe on the Monday, we thought we would travel to Crewe and get a hotel. We arrived early evening, but couldn't find any accommodation, so ended up going back to the M6 junction to the Saxon Cross. We booked two rooms, had a meal and decided to have a drink before calling it a day. The four of us were the only guests at the bar, and we got the bartender completely bladdered. He left us there to help ourselves, which we did, although it was not a good way to prepare for the Berwick match. During the meeting in Heat 3, I was leading Pete Kelly of the Bandits after a couple of laps, when I thought my handlebars were coming loose as I entered the pits bend. The next thing I realised was that I had the clutch side in my hand, but not attached to the bike! Kelly came past me, but I held on for second place and we won the contest 51-26. My last league match for Crewe was on October 20, against Long Eaton, but it ended prematurely when the fog came down. Two weeks later my family and Dave's went on holiday to Majorca, where everybody we bumped into had something to do with speedway.'

(Pete Saunders.)

John Jackson.

Full name? – *"John Jackson."*
When and where were you born? – *"I was born on June 26, 1952 at Dolly Peg in Waverton."*
What job did you do before entering speedway? – *"I was a panel beater at Christleton."*
How did you get into speedway? – *"Through my brother Fred who did grass-tracking. I tried it myself and did okay. Then a bloke named George Crewe recommended me to try speedway."*
Is that how you come to sign for the Kings? – *"Yes. I did some second-halfs at the back end of the 1969 season, then attended Crewe's winter training school run by Ken Adams. I must have done alright as they offered me a contract for the 1970 season."*
What were your feelings when you first rode the Earle Street track? – *"It didn't scare me as it was the first track I had ridden on so didn't know any different."*
Did you style yourself on anybody in particular? – *"Yes, I suppose on my favourite riders Ole Olsen and Ivan Mauger."*
During your five seasons at Crewe you were virtually unbeatable at home. So how did you ride the track and set the bike up for it? – *"Nowhere in the country was as fast as Crewe, and I mean nowhere. I rode the track a lot different than other riders. I used to turn early and come into the corner on the inside, just clipping the corner, head for the fence, then come back down again and clip the next corner. Ken Adams used to tell the juniors and new riders 'Don't ride the track like John Jackson as you won't be able to do it.' As for the bike, you had to put on the highest gear which was a 19 engine sprocket with a 58 on the back. Most you rode at away was a 17 or an 18 maximum."*
What were your favourite and worst tracks? – *"Obviously Crewe, as well as Workington, Ellesmere Port and Teesside. I didn't like Bradford (Odsal) and could never master Exeter and Glasgow."*
Did you get jeered at any venues? – *"Workington fans used to give me plenty of stick, especially as I did quite well there nearly every time I raced at Derwent Park. Teesside and Stoke fans were the same too. Jack Millen used to give me stick as I was so thin. When in the showers he used to tell me to run around so I'd get wet!"*
Who was the biggest influence on your speedway career? – *"My father and brother."*
What was the best atmosphere at a meeting you rode in? – *"It has to be the 1974 League Riders Championship at Wimbledon. There must have been 15,000 there, and walking out on the parade was something really special."*
You won many titles during your illustrious career. What do you consider as being your best? – *"Winning the National League Pairs at Belle Vue in 1976 sticks out as one of my best moments. I won it with Chris Turner, who rode for the Kings in 1975. In 1978 I was fortunate enough to win it again at Halifax."*

Did you have a nickname at Crewe? – *" 'Jacko' or 'J.J.' were the main ones."*
Apart from 1972 and 1974, the Kings really struggle to win away from home. Any ideas why? – *"As Earle Street was so different and was so much faster than anywhere else, we struggled to adapt to the slower smaller tracks. It was the same when the away teams came to us. Many were scared stiff of the Crewe track."*
Did you have any fierce rivals? – *"Tom Owen was one that comes to mind. He put me through the fence once at Newcastle and we were always at it when we rode against each other."*
Who was the best rider you ever rode against? – *"Peter Collins."*
You introduced Peter to speedway didn't you? – *"Yes, me and my brother. He had a few second halfs at Crewe, using my bike."*
Did you have any bad crashes? – *"I remember one time while riding at Halifax, I took a spill and my foot was caught between the wheel and mud guard. Eric Boocock had to help me prise my foot from the wheel. I missed a few Crewe meetings because of that fall."*
Did you have a job as well as riding? – *"No. I was a full-time rider. There was no way I could have worked as well."*
Who was your best friend in speedway while you were riding? – *"Dai Evans was a good friend to me, especially when I first came to Crewe. He was like a father and really looked after me. Jack Millen was another and Ray Hassall was a good mate."*
What were your strengths and weaknesses? – *"I was a fair gater, but I didn't like riding in the rain, especially when the track was heavy."*
Apart from the travelling, what was the worst part about being a speedway rider? – *"Motorway cafes and eating all that rubbish food!"*
After you left Crewe you sign for Ellesmere Port. Did you still follow events at Crewe? – *"No not really. I concentrated on what I was doing at my new club."*
When you returned to Earle Street with Ellesmere Port, what reception did you get from the Kings fans? – *"Very good. I had left on fairly good terms, so had no problem."*
Where did you end your career? – *"After I left Ellesmere Port in 1982, I signed for Stoke. I rode for them a few times and then after a meeting at Boston I decided I'd had enough so retired."*
In the 1970's you were regarded as one of the best Division II/National League riders of that decade. But why didn't it quite happen for you in Division I? - *"I felt comfortable in Division II and could make a reasonable living without having to move up."*
Finally John, can you sum up your time at Crewe? – *"Probably the best time of my life. I used to really look forward to riding on a Monday night. Crewe speedway track used to give you the biggest buzz you could ever imagine. It was so incredibly fast. My time at Crewe was brilliant."*

(John Jackson.)

'I first caught the speedway bug as a young lad in the late forties, early fifties when I was taken by my parents every Saturday evening to the Birchfield Harriers Stadium, Perry Barr, Birmingham to watch the Brummies. These were the glory days of Stan Dell and Arthur Payne and later the exciting, Aussie blonde bombshell, Graham Warren. Later, with my friend, we used to go to the Dudley Wood Stadium to watch Cradley. Their big star was Alan Hunt, who later went on to ride for the Brummies. In 1959 I left the Black Country for Liverpool University and where I pretty well forgot all about speedway with the typical distractions of a medical student. Ten years later, and married to a nurse with two very young children and a third on the way, I found myself looking for a job at the Hungerford Road Surgery, Crewe. During the interview, the then senior partner, Dr Tony Hartley, who lived near the pool at Winterley said, "I don't suppose you like speedway do you?" "Yes, yes indeed I do," I replied as I told him and the other doctors present of my passion for the cinders, the noise, the smell and of course the sheer excitement of it all. "Marvellous" he said, "because I can't stand being the track doctor at Crewe and have only been doing it for three or four months to help out a friend of mine, Ken Adams, who has a garage near me and is managing the team." I'm sure it was the combination of his dislike for the sport and my enthusiasm that got me the job, rather than any medical skills I may have possessed! My first day in practice was August 1, and within a week I attended my first meeting as track

doctor and where I remained throughout the life of the Crewe Kings. I admired the skill and enthusiasm of the riders; only a serious injury would stop them from competing in their next race. I remember well the likes of Colin Tucker, Jack Millen, Phil Crump and the plucky Charlie Scarbrough. Considering how dangerous the sport was, particularly in those days of hard, unforgiving safety fences, I was surprised how infrequent there were any serious injuries. Lacerations, needing two or three stitches I would sort out in the first aid department, at the rear end of the workshop! Head injuries, involving a loss of consciousness and any fracture would clearly need immediate admission to hospital but, as stated, this fortunately only occurred two or three times a season. I liked to stand on the centre green, especially near the starting gate, where I very much appreciated the company of the Starting Marshall, Alan Pedley, the Flag Marshal, Barrie Lunt and the "sparky," Alan Corbett. After the meeting, we frequently used to continue our chat over a pint or two with many others, either in the Kings Arms or the Belle Vue. In 1973, speedway started at Loomer Road, Chesterton, the home of Stoke Potters and I didn't need to be asked twice to act as the MO there as well, although, I have to say, I found it nowhere near as fascinating or homely as at Earle Street. I did have the pleasure of meeting there, however, at one meeting, my great hero, Ivan Mauger. I consider myself very fortunate to have been the MO at Crewe Speedway since not only did I meet a great bunch of people and found the whole experience most enjoyable but, you know, they also paid me. I didn't say so at the time, but I might well have done it for nothing!'

(Doctor Mike Wilson.)

'It is hard to believe that it is forty years since Alan Pedley and I first arrived at Earle Street stadium as Starting Marshals along with Colin Tyrell and Dr. Mike Wilson. Colin at first looked after the riders' entrance at the rear of the stadium, but such was his enthusiasm for the sport, became a trainee referee, and ended up as a qualified one. Mike Wilson as you all probably know was the track doctor. Alan and I upon arrival, at about 5.00pm would check that all the equipment necessary under the rules of speedway in the starting area were in place and in correct order i.e. flags, exclusion discs, fire extinguisher, telephone to the referee's box. We also had to mark out the start line and four boxes and check that the tapes were working properly and that the spare tape was available. After talking with Ken Adams about any changes to the programme and a briefing from the referee, it was all systems go! During the meeting, it was our responsibility to bring the riders to the tapes in their correct boxes and ensure a sensible distance between them. When the starting marshal was happy, he would walk away and allow the referee to start the heat. Remember in those days, there was no rule against touching the tapes and no green light to inform the starter that the ref was happy with the start line. Consequently there was a lot of too-ing and fro-ing by the riders of both teams, hoping that one of the opposition would break the tapes and be excluded. Before each heat, the gate had to be raked and holes filled in, much to the annoyance of some riders, who liked them left for a better grip when starting. There were of course unofficial duties that had to be carried out on occasions, like protecting the trackside telephone when some riders disagreed with a referee's decision, or having to separate the riders who often clashed, especially in the days of Paul O'Neil and "Mad Jack" Millen. Jack of course doubted the parentage of all referees and many of the riders too! I was asked about happy memories and I can truthfully say that all my memories of our time at Crewe were happy, in particular when Alan and I officiated at the international between England and Poland and also when my wife and I attended Colin Tucker's wedding and we met Ivan Mauger and his wife Raye. I also enjoyed the after meeting pint or two in the Belle Vue with Alan and Mike. There were sad times as well, especially when we received the terrible news that Geoff Curtis had died following a crash at the Sydney Showground and when the Kings missed out on the first division licence in 1970 in favour of Newcastle (thanks very much L.M.R.). Sadly Alan Pedley passed away on June 3, 2008 and Colin Tyrell on April 1, 1985. Both were great friends and speedway fans and are greatly missed. It is pleasing to see in print a history of Crewe Kings and I congratulate all who have worked so hard to produce it, and hope one day we shall see the Kings ride again.'

(Barrie Lunt.)

'My parents were the licensees of The Borough Arms public house on Earle Street, from 1968 until 1972 and consequently were there during the golden era of the Crewe Kings speedway team. In fact, at its peak, the Kings had a huge fan base and the pub would be so full, that spectators would spill out onto the streets on a Monday night; such was the popularity of the team. This popularity was due in part to the fact that several members of the Crewe team lived at the pub and so the fans came to the pub after meetings in the hope of spending some valuable time with their favourites. During their heyday, the Kings were one of the best around, and as far as I was concerned were only second to the Belle Vue Aces. Many of the riders came from far and wide, some as far afield as Australia and New Zealand, and these were the ones that lived with us at the pub. They were young men, far away from home, so they lived as part of our family and my mother and father would become replacement parents for them. Their own parents would write to my parents from Australia etc. just to make sure that their young sons were being looked after and not being led astray by any young British women who might be taking advantage of them! The riders that actually lived with us were Geoff Curtis and Warren Hawkins, both of whom were Australian. Colin Tucker was also a regular visitor and spent a lot of time at the pub, but actually lived in a caravan at the track. Several of the riders kept their bikes in the cellar of the pub and were there for hours on end tending to their much loved machines, in order that they could attain the best possible performance on a Monday night! My father, Ted Morgan, actually sponsored Geoff Curtis, who was a real gentleman. The other riders who were always around included Barry Meeks, Gary Moore and Charlie Scarbrough. Crewe speedway did a power of good for the town and brought in people from far and wide, and really did set Crewe on the sporting calendar. It is a great pity that there is nothing to compare with it these days. Myself and my family have some wonderful memories that we shall always treasure.'

(Sandra Link, nee Morgan.)

Dave Morton.

Full Name? – *"David James Morton."*
When and where were you born? – *"I was born on September 24, 1953 in Eccles."*
How did you get into speedway? – *"My interest first started as a lad, when myself, brother Chris and Peter Collins used to race an old motorbike in the fields on Peter Collins' Dad's farm. We then all got into grass-tracking and then progressed into speedway."*
So how did a Manchester lad end up at Crewe? – *"I had done some second-halfs at Belle Vue, but there were so many riders there, my rides were limited, so someone suggested why didn't I try at Crewe, where I would get regular rides."*
You had just started work when you come to Earle Street hadn't you? – *"Yes, I was an apprentice at Shell Chemicals at Carrington."*
What were your feelings first time you rode at Crewe? – *"I thought wow this is great. All the grass-trackers loved a big track and Crewe was huge. The faster I could go, the more I enjoyed it."*
Being so young when you signed for the club, who took you under their wing? – *"Dai and his wife Trisha always kept an eye on me, but it was Jack Millen who took to me for some reason, helping me set up my bike properly etc."*
At first were you a bit in awe of Crewe's big two – Phil Crump and John Jackson? – *"I was at first as they were both so quick around Earle Street, but after a while I wanted to beat them, especially when I got used to riding the track and setting my bike up properly."*
After a slow start in 1972, you start to hit form, when you break your arm against Berwick. How did it happen? – *"I was leading Heat 8, when I came into the corner and spun right round. I hit the deck and was missed by the first two riders, but the back marker didn't know how to lay down his bike. I put up my arm to protect my head and his crankcase cover hit my raised arm. The bone in my arm ended up poking through my leathers. I had it plated twice and it still gives me trouble today."*
That incident put you out for the year. You must have been disappointed to miss the climax of the season? – *"Yes I was really fed up as we had done so well. Missing the cup final and the run-in to the league was really disappointing as that season we felt we could win where ever we went and also felt invincible at home."*

When Crewe win the league, were you old enough to celebrate with a few glasses of champagne? – *"Yes – just!"*

In 1973 you are now a heat leader and also appearing in Division I with Hackney. Was it your goal at this stage to move up? – *"I wanted to stay at Crewe another season to gain further experience, but ultimately my aim was to ride in the top league."*

In this season you first ride against your brother Chris. Any sibling rivalry? – *"Oh yes. We always wanted to beat each other, all the way throughout our careers."*

At the start of 1974, now as an established Division II international, you surprise many by staying at Crewe and not going full-time at Hackney. Why? – *"I realised I was not quite ready for Division I. I was doubling up with Hackney, so I was getting my Division I experience and earning a few quid with all my rides."*

Mid-season you sign for Hackney full-time, but Belle Vue were interested in you as well weren't they? – *"Jack Millen had a big say in me going to Hackney. I liked the track at Hackney, but would have preferred a northern track like Halifax, Belle Vue or Sheffield. With Hackney being an APL track like Crewe and with Len Silver already at Crewe, I was sort of pressured into signing for them."*

How did you get on with Len Silver? – *"Okay, but the relationship soured somewhat when I tried to leave. I was No.1 at Hackney with a ten-point average, so they wanted somebody similar before letting me go. I ended up at Wolverhampton, which wasn't my sort of track really."*

On July 5, 1974 you score your first Division I maximum, and beat Ole Olsen twice in the process. A defining moment in your career? – *"Yes it was. I passed him twice from the back and he didn't like it very much. After the match he didn't shake hands or acknowledge me at all. Len Silver was over the moon I had done Ole twice."*

On August 12, you smash the Earle Street track record. Is it true this had something to do with track electrician Alan Corbett? – *"Alan had noticed that in many of my races that I had won, I was shutting down and coasting over the line, especially when I was about a quarter of a lap up. He told me to keep the power on until I crossed the line, so that's what I did. I remember that night that the track was very grippy."*

Your last appearance for Crewe against Weymouth must have been quite emotional for you? – *"Yes it was. I had really enjoyed my stay at Crewe, but realised if I wanted to progress, then I would have to move on to ride full-time in Division I."*

In 1975, you are crowned New Zealand champion. How highly does this rate during your speedway career? – *"To me this was really special. Barry Briggs and Ivan Mauger had won it, so to have my name on the trophy as well made it even more special. I had a really good four months out there. Jack Millen organised for me to stay at Jim Wells' mum and dad's in Auckland and while there I struck up a good relationship with ex-Crewe captain Colin Tucker, who did a great job for me setting up my bike."*

What was it like to ride in the United Arab Emirates? – *"The Arabs were absolutely fanatical. The first time we raced, there were about 30,000 in the stadium and they kept throwing things on the track, which was nothing more than an old running track. So we couldn't really race properly on it, so we basically went through the motions, but the crowd still went crazy."*

What was the proudest moment in your career? – *"Probably winning the Ashes series of 75/76 in Australia with the British Lions. We won 6-1 and would have whitewashed them, but they doctored the track at Sydney. Only Phil Crump performed anything like for the Aussies that series."*

Favourite and worst tracks? – *"Crewe obviously and Sheffield, Halifax, Peterborough and Poole. All the big tracks really. The only one I didn't look forward to was Newport as it was a bit rough and bumpy. Everybody tried to duck out of riding there and many mysteriously broke down en-route!"*

Worst crash or injury? – *"I did break my leg at Hackney, but the scariest time was while still in Division II. It happened at Eastbourne in 1973. I fell during the second half and hit my back on the carburettor cover. On the way home in my mate's car, we stopped for some petrol as I was dying to go to the toilet. I passed a lot of blood when I had a pee, so we went to hospital where I stayed for two weeks with badly bruised kidneys. When I returned home, an X-Ray revealed I had an enlarged kidney, as one wasn't functioning correctly, so was booked in to have an operation to whip out the faulty kidney, but as it was mid-season, I put it off – even though the doctor told* *me another fall could prove fatal! I had it removed at the end of the season, but I was lucky really that the fall at Eastbourne had highlighted the problem. If I hadn't had the spill, then in later life I would have had serious kidney problems."*

Best friends during your career? – *"Jack Millen and Dai at Crewe, and our kid and Peter Collins. I always roomed with Peter while on international duty."*

Strengths and weaknesses? – *"I was always a fair gater. I could usually anticipate when the tapes were going to go up, especially at Crewe. From the pits for the first few races we would work out how long after the green light went on the tapes would go up. This would usually depend on the referee, but normally I would count to three after the green light had come on, then drop the clutch and away I went. My one weakness was probably that I wasn't aggressive enough when racing on the smaller tracks. In 1972, we had riders who could ride on any track, especially Crumpie."*

As a lad when you were attending Belle Vue matches, who was your idol? – *"Cyril Maidment. At Crewe I wanted to be as good as Chris Pusey as we had come through grass-tracking together. He had so much talent as a speedway rider."*

Did you have any rivals? – *"None really while at Crewe, but afterwards I had a few clashes with Alan Grahame of Cradley. I know while I was at Earle Street, Jack Millen had a few scrapes with Arthur Browning. He didn't like him at all."*

Best rider you ever rode against? – *"Had to be Ivan Mauger. He was just so professional."*

Any superstitions when riding? – *"I would never have any green on my leathers."*

Did you have a nickname while at Crewe? – *"'Wee Dave' and for some reason Jack Millen always used to call me 'Buttons.'"*

Do you still attend speedway matches and do you watch it on the television? – *"Not so much now. The tracks are far too slick and there isn't much passing anymore. You could never have ridden today's bikes on the tracks of the 70's, as you wouldn't have been able to turn. We used to play with the throttle and try and find that extra bit of grip to help us pass. The riders of today seem a bit aloof. We used to enjoy mixing with the supporters after the match, but I shouldn't imagine that goes on today."*

What do you do now Dave and what are your hobbies? – *"I'm a ground support technician at Manchester Airport, working with all the motorised equipment used to tow the aeroplanes around the place. I enjoy music and play the banjo. I like to go to concerts, but I'm a bit stuck in the 70's really. I enjoy listening to AC/DC, Status Quo, Deep Purple and Rory Gallagher, but do like more up to date bands like Kings of Leon."*

Finally Dave can you sum up your time at Earle Street? – *"Really enjoyed it. It was a great place to learn your apprenticeship. The track suited me down to the ground. I used to really look forward to Monday night's for my weekly adrenalin rush. As for that track, there was nothing as big, fast or wide as Crewe. Exeter and Halifax were a bit similar but they weren't as fast as Crewe - no way. You either loved Crewe or hated it, there was no in between. Mitch Graham was one of the better away riders to ride at Earle Street."*

(Dave Morton.)

'I have many wonderful recollections of the Kings at Earle Street, like queuing at the turnstiles by 6.30pm in order to get my favourite spot standing on the wooden benches in front of the tearoom, and the hot dog vans that used to be waiting in the side streets around the stadium after the meetings. I also remember sitting at school on Wednesday afternoons in nearby Brierley Street listening to the sound of the weekly practice session; it was torture not being there! However, my most vivid memories are of the many away meetings I travelled to with my fellow Kings fans. My first ever away meeting was to watch the Kings take on Bradford Northern at Odsal stadium in 1971. I'll never forget going through the turnstiles on the main road and seeing the track way below in the bottom of a huge bowl! The away trip that will always stick out in my mind was the K.O. Cup Final at Ipswich in 1971, when the Supporters Club chartered, not the usual coach to transport both the team and the supporters to Foxhall Heath, but a train! What a journey; leaving Crewe at around 1.30pm; arriving at Ipswich five hours later; to be met by a double decker bus to complete the journey. It was a bit like being royalty! I seem to remember a couple of riders missing the train, was it Phil Crump and Gary Moore? For me, the most exciting and enjoyable meeting away from Earle Street, had to be the K.O. Cup Final and the League Riders Final both in the 1972 season. At least four coaches ferried the Kings fans to the Peterborough venue at Alwalton on a sunny Sunday afternoon, to see us walk away with the trophy, making up

for our disappointment the previous year. The excitement of that glorious season continued to build towards the League Riders Final. What tension and excitement awaited us at Wimbledon! Everyone who watched that meeting will remember the nerves that we felt building up as we watched Crumpie suffer from engine failure in his first ride, being replaced with feelings of elation as we watched him reel off four straight wins to go into a run-off for the title with Boston's Arthur Price. The tension continued to build throughout the four fantastic laps, and I'll always remember the Kings fans, packed around the last bend, erupting as Phil crossed the line, a clear winner to take the title. What a season! Whoever said you should always be early for a meeting was clearly not at the Kings first ever visit to Mildenhall in 1975. Most of the team, plus bikes, plus 50 odd (very odd) supporters travelled together on one of Dave Parry's coaches. We set off late Sunday morning, already a bit tight on time. Cambridge was found relatively easily, but Mildenhall proved more elusive, as in fact none of us knew where to find it! Mildenhall was eventually discovered, but no speedway here! Time was pressing now and the tension was mounting. After a stop at a phone box to call the track, it became clear that the stadium (aka as a field) was a further 2 miles away at West Row. We finally arrived about Heat 6, and found, to the disbelief of the team members on the coach, that the Kings had a 7 point lead with a make shift team! A quick turn around saw our travelling companions into leathers and onto their bikes to help Chris Turner maintain their lead, eventually winning 41-36. On a more personal note, it could be said that speedway shaped my life having met my wife Debbie on the terraces at Ellesmere Port (sorry Kings fans!) 30 years ago. As a Kings fan I had two great ambitions; to have a go at racing myself and to fill a programme in without any mistakes. The first I achieved on an old J.A.P at Charlie Scarbrough's training school, and later at Ellesmere Port (without any success!). The second... well you can't win 'em all!'

(Nick Hatton.)

'I came about signing for the Kings in 1972, after impressing Maury Littlechild one particular second half at Belle Vue. My riding had improved under the guidance of Jim Rowlinson and Guy Allott, who had shown me how to turn the bike correctly and how to ride the Hyde Road track. As I was also doing second halfs at Crewe as well, Maury knew all about me, and had tried to sign me on several occasions. After my exploits at Belle Vue, I left the stadium with Aces manager Dent Oliver's words still ringing in my ears: "What ever you do, don't sign for anybody else." A few days later I turned up at Earle Street, but noticed I was not down to ride in the second half at all, and had been replaced by "A. N. Other." I went to see Maury and he informed me that I wouldn't be allowed to ride again at Earle Street unless I signed. So I put pen to paper and was somewhat shocked to learn that I was in the team to face Canterbury. I did okay on my debut, but only realised I had scored a paid maximum when the other riders gave me the "bumps." Shortly afterwards I rang up Dent to inform him that I'd signed for Crewe. He went berserk and called me all the names under the sun and told me that if I ever returned to Belle Vue, he would "kick me all the way back to Nantwich!" One abiding memory I have of the 1972 season occurred at Ellesmere Port. During one race, I hit the safety fence, but instead of falling off, I rode it like "the wall of death," with both wheels on the fence. I ended up going all the way round on the bottom turn before putting it down on the straight. One supporter who witnessed the event said I was "bloody crackers!" I did alright that season and ended up with a five average, despite my machinery not being the best. I remember Dave Morton once borrowing my bike, but he never asked again, commenting: "How the hell you win on this bloody thing, I'll never know!"'

(Peter Nicholas.)

'I went to my first meeting at Earle Street due to my love of motorbike racing. I had heard that Maurie Littlechild was looking for a standby electrician, and when I put myself forward, so began seven years of happy times. I started going to the track on a regular basis, learning from the electrician who had done the original installation. I was asked if I would help him with the new floodlighting, which consisted of 52 x 1,000 Watt bulbs and something like 5,000 yards of cable. Colin Tucker was busy erecting the lighting poles, and during this time I started to get to know the likeable Kiwi, and we became very good friends, as well as striking up a friendship with the Aussie Geoff Curtis. I can honestly say that Geoff was one of the nicest people I have ever met. He appeared to be a very quiet person, until you got to know him properly, and then you learned of

his razor sharp wit and wicked sense of humour. I was deeply saddened to hear that he had died in a speedway crash in Sydney. I started helping Colin with his bike and going with him to away meetings, along with another good mate, Mick Smith, who became the pit marshal at Earle Street. This is where I have to mention Colin's van. It was a Morris 1000 which we nicknamed "The Flying Flea." It was black and rust, with a white roof, with Champion spark plug stickers covering the rust holes and stopping the front wings from flapping about. It didn't look much, but it could certainly shift, and to use the words of Ivan Mauger, who once borrowed the van: "It didn't know how to go slow." Somehow the three of us used to travel in this van, with me usually in the back, perched on a deckchair. Colin used to get great pleasure in speeding around corners and watching me slide from one side of the van to the other, and this with a Jawa in the back as well! One time Colin and Geoff Curtis were returning from Newcastle, when Colin asked Geoff to take over the driving. All went well until Geoff came to pull up in Sandbach and screamed out "We've got no brakes!" to which Colin replied: "I could have told you that when we left Newcastle!!!" When you were with Colin, Geoff and Mick, you had to have your wits about you, as we were always playing tricks on one and other. I remember one time we were in Tuck's caravan drinking coffee after one particular meeting and there had been a number of tape breaking incidents. I mentioned that I could come up with an idea of a beam across the front of the tapes, so if a rider broke the beam with his front wheel, the tapes would not go up. In those days riders didn't get excluded unless they actually broke the tapes, but it was common for riders to push the tapes to make the other riders in the heat think they were about to go up, and for them then to drop the clutch and break the tapes. The following week in The Speedway Star was an article about a Cheshire electronics expert working on an experimental starting system! Needless to say, it was another Tuck wind-up, but I also had my moments. One night we were on our way to Belle Vue as Colin was riding at No.8 for Cradley. During the journey, I said to Tuck: "Well, at least we won't have to clean your bike afterwards" to which he replied: "Why, do you think I'll be winning?" to which I replied: "No, by the time you cross the line, the dust would have settled." One time he was spraying his foot and ankle with pain relieving spray, which numbed the area. I asked him politely when he had sprayed his head! Many years later, I was delighted to hear from Bob Andrews that Tuck was a Justice of the Peace and a Registrar of Marriages and had acquired the nickname in the New Zealand speedway community of "The Vicar of Dibley." During my time at Crewe I stood in one night as stadium announcer, after Bill Carman's train was delayed. I didn't really want to do it, but I didn't get much choice in the matter as Maurie told me I had to do it until Bill arrived. I even stood in as temporary team manager on a number of occasions and even got my wrist slapped by a report in The Speedway Star over a meeting at Long Eaton. It was the second leg of a pre-season friendly and we had won the first leg easily. To say the track was bad was an understatement, and a ploughed field springs to mind as the best way to describe it. It was Phil Crump's second outing as a Crewe rider and he crashed out while leading in Heat 8 and bent his bike frame. Throughout the meeting our riders pulled up with mechanical faults or refused to ride, so in the last heat I had one fit rider (Dai Evans), so as the match over the two legs had been easily won, I asked the Long Eaton manager if we could use our No.8 Don Beecroft as the result had already been decided. However, when the report appeared in The Speedway Star, it read that the Crewe team manager had showed total disregard for the Speedway Control Board rules and regulations for using a No.8 rider when rider replacement was not being used. Had it been a league match, I wouldn't have done it, but I just wanted to give the fans value for money. Dave Parry used to work for British Rail on the dining cars, and on some Monday nights, his train didn't arrive in Crewe until about 7.00pm. So sometimes I had to go to the station to meet him and it used to be quite amusing to see Dave come flying up the steps from Platform 2 in full racing leathers. Other memories spring to mind, and one includes being instrumental in helping Dave Morton smash the track record. I was talking to him in the pits and advised him to "keep it screwed on until you cross the line" as Mort had a habit of closing the throttle early and coasting over the line, especially when he was so far in front of his rivals. Sure enough, his times improved and after equalling the old one, he eventually set a new time. Rather funnily, when I met Dave nearly 25 years later at our first reunion, the first thing he said to me was: "Keep it screwed on until you cross the line." Looking back and remembering things (some I daren't put down!) I can say that Crewe Kings was a good thing to be involved with, and I met and made some good friends, many of which I am still in contact with today. Not only Crewe riders, but riders from other teams and track staff and supporters. It was a very happy part of my life, but occasionally tinged with sadness when learning about friends who had lost their lives through racing.'

(Alan Corbett.)

Chris Turner.

Full name? – *"Christopher Turner."*
When were you born and where? – *"I was born on May 28, 1958 at the Cliffe Maternity Hospital, Wybunbury."*
As a lad, you attended Earle Street with your father. Did you go every week? – *"I think I only ever missed two or three matches throughout the seven seasons at Crewe – and one of them was when I was in hospital in King's Lynn after an appendix operation. The other two were when we were on holiday in Abersoch. We wanted to drive back to Crewe then drive back to Wales, but Mother put her foot down! My Dad used to go to Sun Street originally, to watch Stoke."*
How did you get into speedway? – *"Barry Meeks used to do some grass-tracking on my Dad's farm. I had a go and liked it, and after winning a few trophies, Barry suggested I have a go at speedway. So at the back end of 1974, I attended the Belle Vue and Stoke training schools, and at Stoke I was tutored by Jack Millen, who taught me a great deal – including how to lay down my bike. He used to jump out in front of you on the track, so you had to know what to do, or else you would have killed him! Off the track, Jack was a real gentleman, but when he had his leathers on, he could be a really dirty rider, although to be fair, he never roughed me up the few times I rode against him."*
How did you come to sign for the Kings? – *"I had signed for Belle Vue, but was about to sign for Stoke on loan, after riding for the Potters training school in a number of matches, but I wanted to go to Crewe as I knew every inch of the track after watching all those seasons. I think Meeksy had a lot to do with me signing at Crewe."*
Did you style yourself on anybody in particular? – *"I'd like to have styled myself on Ole Olsen, who had a lovely speedway style. He would just sit on his bike and hardly moved throughout his race. When Jack Millen taught me how to ride a speedway bike he showed me how to hold the twist grip the same way as Olsen and Mauger, so your right elbow would be up in the air. Of course I wasn't the calibre of Olsen, but I would have liked to have been."*
Being so young when you came to Earle Street, were you still at school or working? – *"I didn't like school, so didn't go much in my final year. I first worked on my Dad's farm, and then I worked for Terry Lowe, the fibre glass man, making speedway mudguards for all the big riders, which later became Star Canoes. After that I went to Alan Walker's in Sandbach, making ERF and Fodens cabs. That was great, as he was a big speedway fan and would give me as much time off as I wanted. I used to go in on a Sunday and make up my hours."*
On April 23, 1975 you make your league debut for the Kings against Newcastle. What were your memories of the night and did any of your family attend? – *"I can't remember much about it really. My Mum came, but she didn't like it until it was all over. My young sister came as well, but didn't like it either, but my Dad and brother enjoyed the match."*
You have a great start to your speedway career. Even at this early stage, were you dreaming of riding in Division One? – *"Yes, I was, but only after riding at Crewe for a second season. I was very ambitious, and like all young speedway riders, I wanted to be World Champion."*
As a massive Crewe Kings fan, what was it like to ride against Phil Crump, when Newport come to Earle Street? – *"Fantastic. They were a very good team at the time and gave us a good hiding. I think I retired in one heat and fell off in another, but in Heat 7 gave Crumpie one hell of a race. I remember next day after the match, Graham Drury told me I had to get a better bike, so my Dad borrowed me the money to buy Nicky Allott's bike, which was much faster than my old one."*
How did you ride Earle Street Chris? – *"I used to keep my wheels in line as much as I could. You didn't turn left coming out of the gate; instead you headed for the fence, keeping it flat out basically. The less turns you made, the faster you went. I had worked all this out while I was a supporter. The only rider to go round Crewe on the inside was John Jackson. Jacko rode Earle*

Street like the modern riders would have ridden it today."

On Monday, July 14, you score a brilliant maximum in the Inter-League Four Team event. Was this the highlight of your Crewe career? – *"Definitely. I was very nervous that night. I remember Terry Lowe had put up a prize to the highest scoring rider of a set of specially made mud guards. He made a set of Belle Vue, Cradley and King's Lynn mud guards, but didn't bother making a Crewe set, as we were expected to get heavily beaten. So I was really proud that night, especially when Terry had to make me a set for top-scoring during Crewe's shock win. A week later somebody showed me a photo from the meeting and I noticed on the picture that my front springs had broken on my first ride and remained detached from my forks all match!"*

Just as Crewe are looking something like a half-decent team, everything falls apart mid-season. You yourself also have some bad luck? – *"Yes, I was on the way to King's Lynn with Stuart Cope for a second-half ride, but had stomach pains during the journey. The track doctor checked me out on arrival and told me to go straight to hospital. By this time my knees were forced into my chest as I was in so much pain from an appendix on the verge of bursting. I was operated on almost immediately and spent two days in King's Lynn hospital, before spending a week in a convalescent home. My parents came to take me home, but when I arrived back I was sweating a lot and didn't feel well at all. I was very very tired as well, so went to bed, and next morning a doctor had to be called and I was diagnosed with pleurisy. I don't think I was ever really fit after this."*

In what turned out to be Crewe's last ever home fixture, it seems only fitting that John Jackson wins the last heat of the match, but I believe a certain local rider won the last ever race? – *"Yes that's correct. I won the Rider of the Night final, which at the time, we didn't know was to be the last ever race at Earle Street. I am very proud of that fact, although I remember Nicky Allott was winning until he broke down. Whether I'd have beaten him I don't know, but I suppose it was fate that I won that evening, being a local lad."*

What were your best moments as a speedway rider? – *"One was getting the maximum in the 4TT at Crewe. A proud moment for me was when Edinburgh won the Four Team Championship at Peterborough in 1981, after coming from behind to beat Newcastle and Middlesbrough. I was also a member of the Edinburgh team that won the K.O. Cup, but another moment that comes to mind was again while I was at Ellesmere Port and we were riding at Newcastle and I beat Joe Owen – the only visiting rider to beat him all season. I remember winning the National League Pairs title with Jacko, although to be fair, I had a bad meeting that night and Jacko won it virtually on his own."*

What were your best and worst tracks? – *"Obviously Crewe was my first favourite, with the old Belle Vue track second and also Edinburgh. There weren't really any tracks I hated, although I didn't really like Exeter, but always did quite well there. The old Bristol track was bad, but I only rode there once and Odsal was also another that was not one of my favourites. I hit the concrete fence at Paisley once, but they didn't last that long."*

Did you have any bad falls or injuries in your career? – *"During the Junior Championship at Canterbury, I remember I was a bit worked up, as the track was wet and heavy and I hated conditions like that when racing. But I really wanted to win it as I was one of the favourites. In my first ride I hit the fence and received a bad blow to the chest, which resulted in me coughing up a lot of blood. I had also damaged my kidneys, so ended up in hospital for a week. The most pain I ever encountered however, was at Workington. It was rainy again and I fell off going into the corner. I was lying on the floor waiting for Andy Hines to go past me, as he was nearly half a lap behind me, when he struck my left arm. The pain was unbelievable. The muscle on my left arm was black for about three weeks and I couldn't lift my arm in that period. I was very fortunate that I never broke a single bone in my ten years as a speedway rider."*

While at Crewe, who were your best friends? – *"Stuart Cope, Les Collins and my mechanic Dave Blackburn."*

During your time as a supporter and rider, which Crewe rider did you admire the most? – *"A toss up between Paul O'Neil and Dave Morton. I would probably just plump for Dave."*

Strengths and weaknesses? – *"My strengths were my determination to win every race, especially in the early part of my career. But later on, if I wasn't up for it, then nobody could snap me out of it. Eric Boocock and Vic White always used to ask me why I hadn't scored in the meeting, but always reached the Rider of the Night final. In my latter years, if I didn't like the look of the track,*

or the conditions weren't to my liking, then nobody could talk me round to riding well."
Did you have any fierce rivals? – *"I wanted to beat them all, but probably Tom and Joe Owen as they always gated in front of me."*
Who was the best rider you ever rode against? – *"Sorry to repeat myself, but it had to be Ole Olsen really."*
While riding did you have any superstitions or lucky charms? – *"Never ever had any green on my leathers, or on any part of my clothing while I was riding. My wife Jennifer, who was my girlfriend then, came to a meeting one night in a green coat and I made her take it off and take it back to the car. I had to have orange somewhere on my leathers. I was convinced if I had orange on my leathers I wouldn't get hurt."*
Did you have a nickname while you were at Crewe? – *"Yes – 'Shirley.' The grass-track lads first gave me this nickname and it was picked up by the riders at Crewe. It came about when my long hair used to go blonde in the summer, so it looked like Shirley Temple's."*
Who was the biggest influence on your speedway career? – *"Jack Millen and Barry Meeks."*
As a big speedway fan, who would you regard as your speedway idol? – *"Again I have to go for Ole Olsen. He was my favourite for a long long time, although Peter Collins and Chris Morton also gave me a lot of enjoyment as well."*
When did you decide to call it a day? – *"It was in 1983. I came off the track after finishing my race at Edinburgh and said to my mechanic Dave Slight that I wasn't enjoying it anymore so was packing it in. I collected my tools and clothes, chucked my helmet in the back with my bike, and drove home still in leathers. I've never been on a bike since."*
Do you still watch speedway? – *"Yes, I always go to Cardiff every year for the Grand Prix and usually go to Wolverhampton two or three times a season. I like Wolves as it's one of the few tracks left that's not all about horse-power. If they had a World Championship at Monmore Green then it would be something else, because the passing would be unbelievable. I've been back to Belle Vue a few times, but I don't like the new track, as there is hardly ever any passing."*
What do you do now and what hobbies do you have? – *"I own two trucks and operate in the concrete industry from Winsford. My son now works with me as well. My hobbies - I enjoy Ceroc dancing, and go once a week, which keeps me fit and also DIY. I'm currently building a garage and workshop at home."*
Finally Chris, can you sum up your time at Crewe? – *"As a speedway rider it was the best time of my life. I achieved my ambition of riding for the team I used to support. It was a crying shame when it shut in 1976. I was absolutely gutted when I heard the news that the Kings had gone under. I'm sure we could have had a fair team if we had stuck together for another season. I went to Ellesmere Port and teamed up with Jacko and I think I had a near ten average and Les Collins had a brilliant season at Stoke topping the averages. But even though Crewe had gone, I was still so very grateful that I'd got to ride for them."*

(Chris Turner.)

*'I first fell for speedway one Saturday afternoon. I was in Crewe town centre with my brother, who drove the grader at Earle Street. I heard a bike being ridden around the track, so we went to the stadium and saw Colin Tucker in action. I was blown away with it all, so on the Monday night I went to my first match. As my brother was on the grader, I found a nice open space to stand on the last bend. The first heat started and when the riders passed me, I was covered from head to toe in shale. As you can imagine, I didn't stand there again! After a few meetings, I made friends with a few fans and we used to go to the Kings Arms for a beer after the meetings. Here we came up with the idea of forming the "Cats Choir." We all bought red and white coats with our names and numbers on them, and I was voted to become the No.1 cheer leader. We used to go to all the away meetings either by coach or in our own cars and would also meet once a week to write an article for the programme. I never missed a meeting until I emigrated to Australia. When in Perth, England came over for a test match, and I had the honour of meeting some ex-Kings riders, including Dave and Chris Morton, Glyn Taylor, Phil Crump plus Peter Collins. After the match, I was invited into the riders lounge for a few drinks. It had been some experience to see them ride again, something I will never forget. So on that note, all I can say is..... **GIVE US A K!!!**'*

(Allan "Fluff" Bebbington.)

- Kings Scrapbook -

(1) "Gentleman" Geoff Curtis. (2) Kings of 1970. (3) Dave Parry at the tapes.

(3)

(4)

(5)

(4) Ian Bottomley. (5) Phil Crump signing autographs. (6) "Jacko" and Jack.
(7) Presentation time in 1972.

(8)

(9)

(10)

(8) Gary "Bones" Moore. (9) John Jackson, with nephews Gary and Alan.
(10) Chesterton v Crewe in 1973. (11) Len Silver giving instructions to Glyn Taylor.

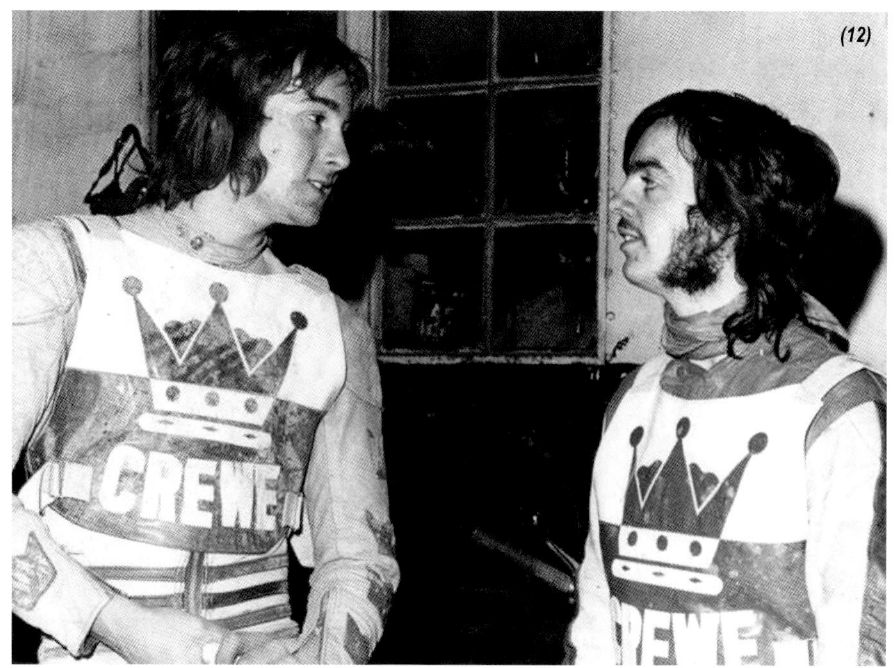

(12) "Chalky" and "Mort." (13) Ian Cartwright at Sunderland. (14) Doctor Mike Wilson, Crewe and Stoke medical officer, inspects Ivan Mauger's gold bike. (15) A young female supporter injured at Earle Street.

(14)

(15)

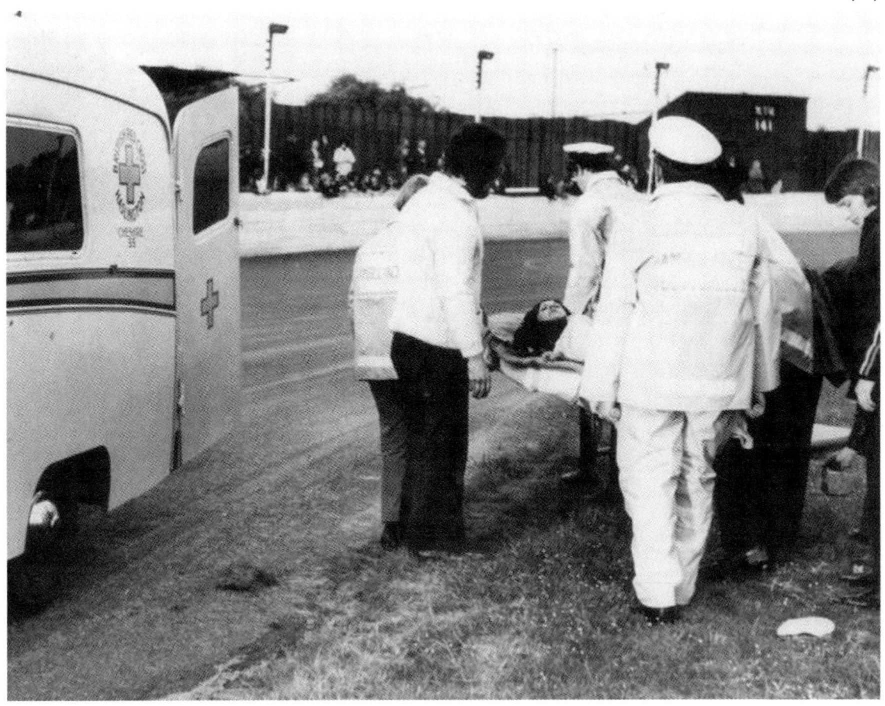

(16)

(17)

(16) Assistant Start Marshal Barrie Lunt. (17) Les Collins and Chris Turner. (18) Cliff Anderson gives Turner a lift, after a heavy fall at Rye House. (19) Stuart Cope and Graham Drury on parade against Birmingham.

- In Memorium -

Geoffrey Curtis
1943 - 1973

Robert Jack Millen
1942 - 1978

Nigel Brian Wasley
1955 - 1979

Ian Jackson Robertson
1957 - 1987

Peter Thompson
1950 - 2004

Charles Henry Scarbrough
1937 - 2008

- Team Index -

- Supporters Roll of Honour -

Ashton, Steve
Austin, Liz
Bates, Kevin
Bebbington, Alan ("Fluff")
Bebbington, John
Bebbington, Peter
Berisford, Chris
Billington, Alan
Blackburn, Dave
Blackburn, Ron
Blakemore, Phil
Bloor, Duncan
Blount, John
Boulton, Peter
Bourne, Martin
Brehaut, David
Brereton, Bill
Brereton, Malc
Brereton, Phil
Briggs, Andrew
Brotherton, Danny
Buckley, Geoffrey
Buckley, Terry
Butters, Eric
Campbell, Terry
Cann, Roy
Cann, Steve
Capewell, Richard
Carless, D. ("Diddy")
Chatwin, Michael
Clayton, Neil
Cook, Steve
Cornes, Trevor
Crawford, Malcolm
Critchley, Alan
Davies, Allan
Davies, Andy
Davies, Chris
Dean, John
Dean, Kathleen
Dry, Johnny
Dunn, George
Earp, Colin
Edge, Brian
Edge, Diane
Edwards, John
Ellis, Bob
Ellis, Gordon
Ellis, Susan
Evans, Mark
Farrington, Wayne
Fitch, Colin
Fleet, Derek
Foster, David
Fox, Martyn
Garnett, Terry
George, Gerard
Glover, Nigel
Gordon, Ray
Grant, Jim
Grant, Tess
Greatbanks, Christine
Greatbanks, Darren
Greatbanks, Michael
Griffin, Terry
Halliwell, Keith
Hassall, Steve
Hatton, Nick
Heath, Peter
Horton, Alice
Hughes, A. D.
Hughes, Dai
Jones, Dave
Jones, Tom
Kelly, Andrew
Kelly, Bernard
Langford, Peter
Lea, Gordon
Lewis, Robert
Lloyd, Paul
Lockett, Keith
Lockett, Sue
Louth, Cyril
Louth, Val
Lowe, Peter
Madeley, R. J.
Malam, Graeme
Marriott, Alan
Martin, Tommy
Massey, Clive
Massey, John
McKay, Charles
McVety, Clive
McVety, Derek
Mitchell, John
Montague, Barry
Morgan, Ted
Morris, Ian
Mottram, Barbara
Mottram, Paul
Mottram, Terry
Mould, Clifton ("Cheese")
Newton, Jeff
Ogden, Neil ("Stan")
Oliver, Peter
Ollier, David
Ollier, F. H.
O'Malley, Mick
Parker, Andy
Parry, Jean
Parry, Leslie
Parton, Kenneth
Parton, Susan
Peake, Brian
Pedley, Derek
Pedley, Mark
Pedley, Martin
Peters, Mark
Peters, Pauline
Peters, Philip
Piggott, Stephen
Pitchford, Roy
Preston, Ian ("Ernie")
Price, George
Pye, Craig
Pye, Dennis
Pye, Glyn
Richardson, John
Richardson, Tim
Ridgway, John
Roberts, Llew
Roberts, Stephen
Robinson, Peter
Russell, Norman
Salmon, Tony
Scoffin, Brian
Scoffin, Diane
Sexton, Greg
Shephard, Dave
Shephard, John
Sherratt, Andy
Simm, Mark
Smith, Nigel
Steadman, Ron
Stubbs, Graham
Sutton, G. H.
Sutton, J. E.
Talbot, Adrian Lee
Talbot, Jeffrey
Tew, Betty
Tew, Norman
Tibbs, Desmond
Tibbs, Judith
Tomkinson, Ken
Tweats, Anthony
Vaughan, Mike
Vickerman, Jim
Walker, Ian
Walker, Jill
Walker, Thelma
Walker, Tony
Walker, Walter
Walley, Sandra
Walton, Keith
Warren, Alan
Warren, Graham
Warren, Julie
Wells, Jim
Wells, Pat
Whalley, Eve
Whalley, George
Whitby, Stuart
Whittaker, J.
Whittingham, John
Williams, Linda
Wilson, Barry
Wilson, Dave
Wycherley, John
Yeomans, Janet
Yeomans, Nick
Yeomans, Reg